Treatment
of Complicated
Mourning

Treatment of Complicated Mourning

Therese A. Rando

Research Press
2612 North Mattis Avenue
Champaign, Illinois 61822
www.researchpress.com

Advisory Editor, Frederick H. Kanfer

Cover design by Candis Kelly
Composition by Wadley Graphix Corporation
Printed by BookCrafters
ISBN 0-87822-329-0
Library of Congress Catalog No. 90-64044

This book is lovingly dedicated:

In celebration of Elizabeth-Ann

With deepest gratitude to my aunt,
Dorothy G. Morris, who was there when
it was so good and after it got so bad,
and to my uncle, Joseph D. Morris,
who was with her all the way

With fondest recollection, to my dear friend,
Esther M. D'Orsi, who lived living and dying
her own unique way

In joyful commemoration of the remarkable life
and exceptional spirit of
Father Frederick W. Kelly, S. J.

In solemn observance of the little one
who never came to be

and

In memory of Clara

CONTENTS

FIGURES AND TABLES

ACKNOWLEDGMENTS

When I proposed this book in 1989, I and my world were quite different than they are today. The interim 3 years—2 more than I expected it would take to complete this book—have been without question the most painful, stressful, and loss-filled of my entire life. Although significant losses and stresses certainly had been a part of my life in the past, they were never as preventable, unnecessary, intentional, and violating of my assumptive world as some of the many recent ones. In this regard, it is difficult to discern how much these personal experiences informed the writing of many aspects of this book and how much my concurrent writing of this book provided me with the concepts and words to comprehend my personal experiences. Indeed, the personal losses—both physical and psychosocial—ranged figuratively, and in a number of cases literally, across all four of the major categories of death: natural, accidental, suicide, and homicide. As well, six of the seven high-risk variables for complicated mourning were present among the most serious of the losses: suddenness and lack of anticipation, overly lengthy duration of demise, loss of a child, preventability, existence of concurrent losses and stresses, and elements of disenfranchised grief. All of these losses and stresses severely affected the production as well as the content of *Treatment of Complicated Mourning.*

The majority of those who must be individually acknowledged in this book, therefore, are those who have helped me contend with the losses and stresses experienced coincidentally with it. Without such support, this book never would have been finished. I owe these persons public recognition here for all they have given to me and, through me, to this book.

Interestingly, the largest number of these individuals are my long-time colleagues in the Association for Death Education and Counseling. Although these persons undeniably contributed to this book through their education of me in various ways over the years, they also provided the assistance and nurturance that contributed to my being able to withstand such a period of personal trauma and bring this work to fruition. Some of these individuals may not even remember what they said or did that made such a difference to me; others may be more aware of the invaluable nature of their contributions. My deep gratitude and permanent friendship go to Thomas Attig, Sandra Bertman, Dana Cable, Charles Corr, Lynn DeSpelder, Kenneth Doka, Richard Ellis, Sally Featherstone, Earl and Netta Grollman, E. Neil Heflin-Wells, Jeffrey Kauffman, J. Eugene Knott, Terry Martin, David Meagher, Jane Nichols, Lula Redmond, Catherine Sanders, Victor Scalise, Shirley Scott, Edie Stark, John Stephenson, Judith Stillion, and Ellen Zinner.

Research Press went well above and beyond the call of professional duty in understanding, tolerating, and supporting me throughout the constant delays, frustrations, and crises of the past 3 years. My inability to deliver this book when promised caused them numerous times of awkwardness, embarrassment, and discomfort. Yet the company's president, Ann Wendel, was never anything but understanding. There was never any blame, hostility, or frustration conveyed to me. I do not know how she had the room to be as compassionate as she was. Her responses to me during this most difficult period were especially meaningful. As I have repeatedly said in the past, I cannot ascertain whether I am prouder to call her my publisher or my friend. I guess that when pride is of such intensity it does not have to be prioritized.

There are others at Research Press who merit particular mention. I refer specifically to Russ Pence, Gail Salyards, and Dennis Wiziecki, who constantly have been of enormous assistance to me in my work with this most special publishing house. Most importantly, I could not legitimately offer any acknowledgments without mentioning the particular debt I owe my editor, Karen Steiner. Although others at Research Press had worked with me before and had a history of knowing that I could meet deadlines, engage in a conversation without having to report a new trauma that interfered with my ability to do my work, and have a life that was more or less normal, Karen lacked such data. I have often wondered whether, or indeed how, she could believe me when I would tell her that the me she was dealing with was not the real me and that what she was experiencing working with me was not my typical modus operandi. Without a doubt, this book owes an incalculable amount to her organizational skills, her keen intelligence and clarity of thought, her dogged persistence, her patience, and, above all, her great sense of humor. I cannot thank her enough.

My colleagues and staff at Therese A. Rando Associates, Ltd., sustained and assisted me in myriad personal and professional fashions during the writing of this book. Their empathy, compassion, patience, and support helped me bear some particularly difficult times. I wish to publicly acknowledge my deep gratitude to Lena DeQuattro, Marta Dietrich, Peggy Gale, Mark Solomon, and Christie Toth. Throughout the first 2 years, Felicia Lambros was a member of this group as well, and deserves special mention for her dedicated help as a research assistant.

I would be seriously remiss not to state my extreme debt to those individuals to whom I have provided psychotherapy, consultation, and training. My work with these persons has exposed me to complicated mourning in unparalleled dimensions, educating and sensitizing me in profound ways. The content of this book reflects much of what they have taught me. I thank them for the privilege of working with them.

Lawrence C. Grebstein continues to serve in the roles of mentor, confidant, and advisor. His presence during the last 3 years has been crucial, and I offer him my heartfelt gratitude. As well, I must convey deepest appreciation to my siblings, Mary E. Mancini and Thomas A. Rando, Jr., for being there in the unique ways that only a sister and brother with such intimate knowledge, long-term bonds, and shared cohistory can. My aunt, Rita E. Rando, as always, has been an unfailing support and a model of family love. My esteem and respect for her knows no bounds. My dear friend, Marion A. Humphrey, reached into the depths of my grief and grounded me in innumerable therapeutic ways. She was always available to me, and her wise counsel, loving nurturance, and gentle confrontation was pivotal during times of stress. Devon and Berkeley provided affection, diversion, and reminders about normalcy.

During the very most difficult times, one person made all the difference in my ability to keep on going. In attempting to articulate what he has done or how he did it, I find words woefully inadequate. They simply are too trite or contribute to too much understatement. He knows precisely what he means and what he has given to me. He is well aware that without him there would be no book—and indeed few vestiges of me after the last 3 ravaging years. The brevity of my acknowledgment of him reflects the incapacity of words to capture the extent of his impact on me, as well as my refusal to suffer vain attempts to convey the depth of my feelings. Along with my deceased parents, Thomas A. and Letitia G. Rando, he has been the most profound influence in my life and, with them, has contributed to enabling me to survive this most difficult time in my life. To my best friend, Anthony, I acknowledge that "for every tomorrow" has been preserved—and even enhanced—because of his love and dedication.

PART I

Fundamentals

CHAPTER 1

Introduction

For the third time at a particular conference, yet another participant wondered what resources would help her intervene with someone whose mourning had been resistant to typical grief facilitation techniques. As I had for the previous two participants who had inquired, I suggested a few works I deemed helpful for her particular problem but told her that the literature was widespread and that she would have to synthesize it for herself. For the third time, I wondered why no comprehensive clinical resource on the topic was available. For the first time, I decided to try to create one. *Treatment of Complicated Mourning* is the culmination of that attempt. It has been written for all clinicians and caregivers who work with individuals whose grief and mourning does not respond to mere therapeutic facilitation.

Because uncomplicated bereavement has been documented to precipitate a host of negative psychological, behavioral, social, physical, and economic sequelae (Osterweis, Solomon, & Green, 1984), bereavement that exceeds the norm can be expected to create additional problems. For whatever reasons, individuals experiencing such complications require more extensive, more intensive, or different interventions. In these situations, primary prevention and secondary level intervention (Caplan, 1964) have failed, and tertiary intervention is mandated. This book is directed toward this level of intervention.

GROWING INTEREST IN THE TOPIC

In recent years, there has been a plethora of writings and investigations pertaining to loss and the reactions stimulated by it. Loss, grief, and mourning—relating to both death and nondeath situations—have been examined throughout the entire life cycle, and the field has burgeoned exponentially. For example, in Simpson's (1979) first critical bibliography in the field of thanatology, a total of 763 titles were listed as being available

3

up to that year. His subsequent bibliography (Simpson, 1987) noted that well over 1,700 books had been published to that point, most in the interim 8 years.

Working with the inherently oxymoronic aspects of uncomplicated grief and mourning (i.e., its "normal abnormality") is sufficient for many caregivers. However, others are extremely interested in the prediction, development, description, assessment, diagnosis, classification, and treatment of the more complicated varieties of these processes. As I have noted previously (Rando, 1986d), such interest has shifted gradually from bereavement in general to different types of losses and how they are experienced. Much early research centered on the loss experience in the first year of white, middle-class widows whose husbands had died of cancer, in accidents, or from heart attacks. An understanding of three points has helped clinicians and researchers move beyond description of such "typical" reactions to death: First, because of the complex interaction of factors known to influence response to loss, no two bereavements are exactly alike. Second, different types of bereavement experiences will require different types of treatment interventions. And third, although it is always dangerous to compare different losses (e.g., "My loss is worse than yours"), it is equally dangerous *not* to look at the unique dilemmas posed by specific types of losses and to ignore the distinct needs of mourners experiencing different types of bereavement (Rando, 1986d).

As a result of these new understandings, research now generates better data about uncomplicated grief and mourning. Thanks to the work of such researchers as John Bowlby, Colin Murray Parkes, Beverley Raphael, Sidney Zisook, and others, a more accurate comprehension of the variations in loss response is being achieved. Investigations now continually yield information that extends the limits of so-called normal responses to loss.

It must be noted that previous literature has not omitted complicated mourning entirely; however, the topic has been severely neglected. Usually, discussion is relegated to a few paragraphs at the end of a given article or book. Despite this relative lack of consideration, it does not appear that authors are uninterested in complicated mourning. On the contrary, many are quite interested but simply do not know what to say on the topic. Most describe the phenomenon as a variation of uncomplicated grief and mourning, pick a particular term to label it, cite some predisposing characteristics, offer a few classic references, and leave it at that.

With relatively few exceptions, when complicated mourning has been addressed, the literature has not been synthesized. If the work focuses on complicated mourning, discussion generally centers on its characteristics but not its treatment. If the discussion is about both complicated mourning and its treatment, focus may be directed toward only some of the grief aspects or certain of the treatments. In view of this, it seems that the time has arrived for an in-depth examination of the theoretical, practical, and clinical aspects of complicated mourning. The purpose of the present book is to provide just that, then to identify the specific caregiver perspectives, clinical strategies, assessments, treatment approaches, and interventions known to promote healthy accommodation of loss.

PREVALENCE AND COSTS OF COMPLICATED MOURNING

A significant proportion of the bereaved experience complications. There are approximately 2 million deaths per year in the United States, with each individual death affecting from 8 to 10 family members (Hocker, 1989; Redmond, 1989), for a total of 16 to 20 million new mourners each year. After exhaustively studying the literature, Raphael (1983) estimates that as many as one in three bereavements result in "morbid outcome or pathological patterns of grief" (p. 64). If Raphael's statistic is applied, the potential exists for 5 to 6 million new cases of complicated mourning each year.

In fact, these figures may be misleadingly low because they fail to account for other individuals affected by the death, such as neighbors, friends, coworkers, students, former in-laws, or others outside of the family system who are vulnerable to complications. Although the number of individuals experiencing complicated mourning cannot be ascertained precisely, one can presume that these other affected persons certainly increase the ranks.

The costs of complicated mourning not only relate to personal suffering, they also extend economically, socially, politically, and philosophically into the family, social network, workplace, community, and society as a whole. Persons who believe that the losses suffered by others do not concern them should probably not examine too closely the realities of increased health insurance premiums; the financial and social costs of worker drug abuse, absenteeism, accidents, and lowered productivity and product quality; the effects of escalating social violence; and so forth— all of which are among the many sequelae of complicated mourning.

FACTORS CONTRIBUTING TO INCREASED COMPLICATED MOURNING

Seven high-risk factors, falling generally into two categories, predispose any individual to complicated mourning. The first category includes factors associated with the specific death: sudden, unexpected death (especially when traumatic, violent, mutilating, or random); death from an overly lengthy illness; loss of a child; and the mourner's perception of the death as preventable. The second category includes antecedent and subsequent variables: a premorbid relationship with the deceased that was markedly angry or ambivalent, or markedly dependent; prior or concurrent mourner liabilities—specifically, unaccommodated losses and/or stresses and mental health problems; and the mourner's perceived lack of social support. All of these factors appear to be on the rise, resulting in greater numbers of people experiencing complicated mourning.

Sociocultural and Technological Trends

A number of sociocultural and technological trends in Western society have complicated healthy grief and mourning. First, the phenomenon of social change, occurring at an increasingly rapid rate, has exerted a significant impact. A number of processes have been especially influential in this regard. These include urbanization; industrialization; technicalization; secularization and deritualization; increasing social mobility; social reorganization (specifically, breakdown of the nuclear family, increases in single parent and blended families, and the relative exclusion of the aged and dying); rising societal, interpersonal, and institutional violence (physical, sexual, and psychological); and unemployment, poverty, and economic problems. Relevant social consequences include increases in social alienation, personal helplessness and hopelessness, parental absence and neglect of children, discrepancy between the "haves" and "have-nots," drug and alcohol abuse, physical and sexual abuse of children and others without power (e.g., women, the elderly, minorities), and availability of guns. These sequelae all have tended to sever or weaken the link between children and adults, increase violence, and expose individuals to more traumatic and unnatural deaths. Second, medical advances have resulted in an increased lifespan, altered mortality rates, lengthier chronic illnesses, and intensified bioethical dilemmas. Finally, these trends are accompanied by the realities of increasing political terrorism, assassination, torture, and genocide, played out against the ever-present possibility of ecological disaster, nuclear holocaust, and megadeath. All of these factors have a dramatic and undeniable impact on today's mourner (see Feifel, 1971; Krupp, 1972; Rando, 1984, 1987a; Volkart, 1957).

Unfortunately, contemporary trends have resulted in death's being a way of life. Previously, thanatologists observed that urbanization, resulting in less contact with nature and the extended family, caused a lack of exposure to death in a natural context. They pointed out that this lack of exposure contributed to an array of problematic responses, particularly increased death anxiety and denial of death. Today, as a result of current sociocultural and technological trends, many persons are exposed to death all the time. But the deaths they are exposed to are often unnatural, violent, and frequent. Such exposure—often sensationalized and exploitative, if not personally traumatizing—fosters desensitization and repression. To these trends must be added problems caused either by the still significant lack of open communication about loss, dying, and death or by inappropriate romanticization of these phenomena. These problems impede mental health, foster pathology, and further compromise the individual's ability to cope with death when it does occur (Rando, 1987a).

In particular, violence in contemporary society contributes significantly to the increasing prevalence of complicated mourning. As reported by the Federal Bureau of Investigation (1990), one crime index offense occurs every 2 seconds in the United States, with one violent crime occurring every 19 seconds (a murder every 24 minutes, a forcible rape every 6 minutes, a robbery every 55 seconds, and an aggravated assault every 33 seconds).

Three social trends are often associated with this increase in violent crime: breakdown of the family, availability of weapons, and increased alcohol and drug abuse. Violent crime in this country increased by 10 percent in 1990, according to the FBI, such that Attorney General Dick Thornburgh stated that "a citizen of this country is today more likely to be the victim of a violent crime than of an automobile accident ("FBI Reports," 1991). The United States Department of Justice estimates that five out of six of today's 12-year-olds will become victims of violent crime during their lifetimes (National Victim Center, 1991), with estimates for the lifetime chance of becoming a victim of homicide ranging from 1 in 133 to 1 in 153, depending upon the source of the statistics (U. S. Department of Justice, 1985). Frighteningly impressive statistics document significant increases in murder by juveniles, wife beating, abuse of senior citizens, hate-motivated crimes, sexual assault, and child abuse and neglect. The reader is referred to Rando (in press-b) for delineation of the statistics and discussion of media violence believed to perpetuate such crimes.

Type of Death

Today, deaths are more frequently of a type known to contribute to complicated mourning. In particular, these include sudden, unexpected death, especially when traumatic, violent, mutilating, or random; death resulting from an overly lengthy illness; death of a child; and death the mourner perceives as preventable.

Sudden, unexpected death associated with traumatic circumstances

Technological advances have decreased the proportion of natural death and increased the proportion of sudden, unexpected deaths associated with trauma. The decrease in natural death hinges upon the substantial improvements in biomedical technology. Very simply, people are capable now of surviving illnesses that previously would have killed them. This leaves them alive longer to be susceptible to unnatural death. In addition, the increase in unnatural death results from greater exposure to machinery, motor vehicles, airplanes, chemicals, firearms, and other potentially dangerous technology. To all of this must be added increased risks of unnatural death consequent to the development of new weapons and weapons systems, capable of killing ever greater numbers. These types of deaths frequently are traumatic in nature and incorporate one or more of the following factors: suddenness and lack of anticipation; violence, mutilation, and destruction; randomness and/or preventability; multiple death; or the mourner's personal encounter with death (Rando, in press-a). Generally associated with accidents, homicides, and suicides, deaths of this sort translate into higher probabilities of complicated mourning.

Frequently associated with trauma, accidents are the single most common type of sudden, unexpected death for persons of any age. Including most deaths involving motor vehicles, falls, poisoning, drowning, fire, suffocation, and firearms, accidents are the leading cause of death among all persons ages 1 to 37 and represent the fourth leading cause of death among persons of all ages (National Safety Council, 1991). On the average, there are 11 accidental deaths and about 1,030 disabling injuries every hour during the year (National Safety Council, 1991). Close to 100,000 accident fatalities occur each year in the United States, with death by accident ranking first in terms of lives lost prematurely (Dixon & Clearwater, 1991).

Homicide is the second scenario in which sudden, unexpected deaths associated with trauma commonly occur. The increase in the incidence of homicide, the rising number of serial killers, and the nature of the violence perpetrated before, during, and after the final homicidal act suggest that, today, sicker individuals are doing sicker things. More than ever before, homicide may take the form of cult or ritual killing, thrill killing, random killing, or drive-by shooting. More than ever before, it may be accompanied by predeath torture and postdeath defilement. The increasing pathology of those who commit murder may be seen as a result of decreasing social prohibitions, increasing social violence, escalating social disconnection and sense of personal powerlessness, and, perhaps most important, increasing impairment of psychological development, often characterized by an absent conscience, low frustration tolerance, poor impulse control, inability to delay gratification or modulate aggression, a sense of deprivation and entitlement, and notably poor attachment bonds and pathological patterns of relating. Once again, these deficits have been hypothesized at various times as due to a number of social phenomena, all of which enable violence. Among these phenomena are decline of the nuclear family; increased parental absence or neglect; increased physical and sexual abuse of children (who, once victimized, can go on to become victimizers themselves); exposure to violence on television and in the environment; the availability of guns, drugs, and alcohol; and poverty, unemployment, and other recession-era realities.

The third scenario in which sudden, unexpected deaths occur is suicide. Higher suicide rates currently found in Western society appear to derive from the same sociocultural trends that generally contribute to complicated mourning.

Death associated with an overly lengthy illness

Another increasingly frequent type of death results from long-term chronic illness. Because of biomedical and technological advances, today many illnesses are longer than ever before. Depending on the circumstances, deaths associated with long-term chronic illness can bring a host of unique stresses, including previously unheard of bioethical dilemmas. These stresses generate the types of experiences that can come back to haunt the survivor and interfere with healthy adaptation to loss (see Rando, 1986a, 1986e, 1986h for a complete discussion of these experiences).

It has been well documented that survivors are at risk for significant problems in mourning when a loved one's terminal illness persists for too long (e.g., Rando, 1983; Sanders, 1982–1983). AIDS and other illnesses associated with the Human Immunodeficiency Virus, or HIV, pose perhaps the most striking contemporary example of this situation. In the case of HIV infection, the multidimensional stresses that accompany other long-term illnesses are compounded by anger, ambivalence, guilt, stigmatization, social disenfranchisement, problems obtaining health care, and parental bereavement. Indeed, the fact that an individual may test positive for the HIV virus long before developing any clinical manifestation of illness—coupled with a particularly unpredictable and difficult disease course—gives new meaning to the notion of stress in both the individual with the infection and in survivors.

Death of a child

In the past, parents commonly predeceased their adult children. However, advances in medical technology and resulting increases in the lifespan have permitted parents to survive long enough to witness the deaths of their adult children. The problems associated with death of any child are extreme; frequently, death of an adult child poses additional complications (Rando, 1986b).

Death the mourner perceives as preventable

When a death is perceived as having been preventable, the individual experiences additional complications in mourning. This was a death that did not have to happen—it could have been avoided. Carelessness, negligence, or maliciousness perceived to have caused the death brings anger, feelings of victimization and unfairness, the need to assign blame and responsibility and mete out punishment, obsession and rumination, attempts to regain control, lack of closure, significant violations of the assumptive world, and the search for reasons and meaning. All of these sequelae complicate mourning and interfere with coping.

Antecedent and Subsequent Factors Associated With the Individual Mourner

Complicating factors associated with the individual include a markedly angry or ambivalent, or markedly dependent, premorbid relationship with the deceased; mourner liabilities associated with prior or concurrent (a) unaccommodated losses and/or stresses or (b) mental health problems; and the mourner's perceived lack of social support. Each of these factors is on the rise in our society.

As a consequence of the aforementioned social trends, there has been an increase in conflicted (i.e., markedly angry or ambivalent) and dependent relationships in our society. Specifically, these have escalated secondary to the exclusivity and limited range of interaction within the American family (Volkart, 1957); the overall increase in physical and sexual abuse and victimization of children and adults; and the developmental consequences of being raised in families headed by parents who are psychologically impaired, substance abusing, absent, or neglectful.

A growing liability for today's mourner is the existence of increased prior or concurrent unaccommodated losses or stresses. There is no question that current sociocultural trends bring additional losses and stresses into an individual's life, both prior to a given death (e.g., parental divorce) and concomitant with it (e.g., unemployment). Because such losses and stresses may contribute to complicated mourning, the contemporary mourner is relatively more disadvantaged.

The mourner's personality and mental health also critically influence the ability to mourn a loss successfully. The sociocultural trends previously outlined may negatively affect psychosocial development, resulting in increases in both individual deficiency and conflicted or dependent relationships with others. In particular, clinical observation suggests that impairments subsequent to poor attachment bonds with one's parents can be transmitted intergenerationally and result in psychosocial deficits in one's own offspring. In addition, it appears appropriate to have increased concern about the long-term impact of family destabilization (e.g., divorce, multiple caretakers for children, decreased quality and quantity of family time) on ability to cope with loss and stress. Difficulties related to the types of early developmental defects and poor psychosocial experiences known to ensue from such situations are reflected in rising rates of anxiety disorders, as well as in the dramatically increased frequency of borderline, narcissistic, and antisocial personality disorders and the notable escalation of impaired superego development and poor impulse control. The increased incidence of such disorders implies that a greater proportion of individuals will experience complicated mourning, given that such diagnoses predispose toward negative outcomes.

Another reason for increased complications in mourning concerns the compromise of the mourner's resources and the mourner's subsequent perception of a lack of social support. It is quite clear that conditions in society today promote disenfranchisement in the three areas in which it may occur (i.e., invalidation of the loss, the relationship, or the mourner; Doka, 1989). Examples of invalidated losses that are on the increase include abortions, adoption placements, the death of pets, and losses associated with Alzheimer's disease. Invalidations of the lost relationship include scenarios in which the mourner does not share a kin tie, a socially sanctioned relationship (e.g., gay or lesbian relationship, extramarital affair), or a current relationship with the deceased (e.g., former spouse or in-laws). Situations where the mourner is invalidated occur frequently when the mourner is an elder or a child, or has a mental disability.

PROBLEMS IN THE FIELD

Two main problems in the field exist with regard to complicated mourning. The first concerns difficulty defining the phenomenon. The second relates to failures on the part of the mental health profession to recognize and/or understand the phenomenon.

Difficulty Defining Complicated Mourning

An adequate definition of complicated mourning has been elusive, mainly because imprecise and inconsistent terminology is used and because objective criteria to determine when mourning becomes complicated are lacking. At various times and by various authors the phenomenon of complicated mourning has been described as *morbid, atypical, pathological, neurotic, unresolved, complicated, distorted, abnormal, deviant,* or *dysfunctional.* All of these terms and more have been employed to indicate that a mourner's response to loss is somehow failing to progress as the person evaluating it thinks it should. Each of these terms has its own qualifications and implications, yet with little or no definition their usefulness is limited. The fact that the terminology used to denote complicated mourning is vague and inconsistent impedes consensus on what the phenomenon entails and interferes with communication between mourners and caregivers, as well as among caregivers.

In addition to imprecise and inconsistent terminology, objective criteria to determine just when grief and mourning become complicated are absent, primarily because what may constitute pathology in one set of circumstances may not in another. Several physicians will likely agree that a bone is broken. However, mourning phenomena tend not to be so inarguable. For instance, a woman's hearing her deceased husband's voice in some circumstances is quite appropriate but in others reflects gross pathology.

In brief, the demarcation between uncomplicated and complicated mourning is hazy at best and constantly changing. Such change is due not only to advancements in data collection in this area but also to the fact that no determination of abnormality can be made without taking into consideration the various sets of factors known to influence any response to loss (Rando, 1984). Reactions to loss can only be interpreted within the context of those factors that circumscribe the *particular* loss for the *particular* mourner in the *particular* circumstances in which the loss took place.

The idiopathic perspective required by such a situation prohibits a rigid definition of complicated mourning. Unfortunately, the lack of specific and objective criteria interferes with the development of a valid, reliable, and precise definition, which in turn impairs operationalization of the phenomenon and ultimately the generalizability of findings about it. For all these reasons, it is more useful to look at complications in mourning *processes* than to focus on particular symptoms of complicated mourning. Although these processes—identified in the present volume as the six "R" processes of mourning—certainly are influenced by idiosyncratic factors, they do provide an objective bench mark against which to evaluate mourning. Because subjective pain cannot be compared among mourners, these processes also serve as the areas in which to compare and contrast impediments and complications. Therefore, as defined in this book, *complicated mourning* is a generic term indicating that, given the amount of time since the death, there is some compromise, distortion, or failure of one or more of the "R" processes of mourning.

Issues in the Mental Health Profession

The mental health profession sustains three specific problems when it comes to bereavement. (For the purpose of discussion, the mental health profession is construed as including all those who provide care to the bereaved, whether or not they are formally considered mental health workers.) These problems are lack of a diagnostic category for complicated mourning, insufficient understanding of bereavement, and limitations on treatment.

Lack of a diagnostic category for complicated mourning

First among the problems in the mental health profession is the lack of a diagnostic category for anything but the most basic uncomplicated grief. At present, the *Diagnostic and Statistical Manual of Mental Disorders* (DSM-III-R; American Psychiatric Association, 1987) contains only the diagnostic category for uncomplicated bereavement (V62.82). The criteria for this diagnosis typically are seen as quite unrealistic in light of contemporary information about uncomplicated mourning. Thus, caregivers are forced to assign other diagnoses that have clinical implications unacceptable to many bereaved individuals. Common diagnoses include one of the depressive, anxiety, or adjustment disorders; brief reactive psychosis; or one of the other V-code diagnoses.

A number of authors argue persuasively for delineating diagnostic criteria for bereavement reactions and including these in subsequent revisions of the *Diagnostic and Statistical Manual*. Several proposals for new diagnostic criteria for mourning have been offered in recent years. After examining adult grief and its interface with mood disorder, Hartz (1986) proposes preliminary diagnostic criteria for the syndromes of complicated bereavement and uncomplicated bereavement. He finds the diagnostic criteria for the latter especially unsatisfactory in the DSM-III-R because a time frame for determining when bereavement becomes complicated is lacking. Noting that there is little doubt that symptoms other than depression are present in mourning but that no evidence exists that any of these symptoms point clearly to abnormality, Hartz suggests using symptoms of depression and a period of a year as beginning criteria. However, he recognizes the limitations of using symptoms of depression exclusively and recommends further research in order to determine which symptoms should be used to formulate diagnoses. In addition, he urges more research to develop the most appropriate criteria for different populations of bereaved individuals (e.g., bereaved parents; adults losing parents, siblings, and close friends).

Parkes and Weiss (1983) agree that more emphasis must be placed on grief as a condition that stands by itself. They note that a number of detailed studies of bereaved psychiatric patients reveal that most suffer from atypical forms of grief and that the symptoms bringing them into psychiatric care are part of an overall clinical picture having the form of distorted or abnormally persistent and severe forms of grief. Yet because grief is not, and has not been, a recognized clinical diagnosis, such individuals tend to be diagnosed as suffering from reactive depression or a similar condition, depending upon the symptoms predominating at the initial request for help. Parkes and Weiss propose a method they feel is better than diagnosing grieving psychiatric patients as having some form of depression—advocating the recognition of pathological forms of grief as separate conditions in their own right, each having a distinct etiology, psychopathology, symptomatology, and prognosis.

In articulating the problem of fitting grief and mourning into traditional medical diagnostic categories, Parkes (1987) observes that most clinicians classify a bereavement reaction as a reactive depression and overlook the fact that, although depression is a prominent feature, separation anxiety is more characteristic of the pang of grief. However, because separation anxiety is not always the symptom causing a bereaved individual to seek help, Parkes does not see putting mourning under a subgroup of anxiety states as the answer. Parkes and Weiss (1983) suggest a tripartite classification of unanticipated, conflicted, and chronic grief, each of which has the two features evident in all forms of atypical grief: intense separation anxiety and strong but only partially successful attempts to avoid grieving. Parkes (1987) concludes as follows:

> I know of only one functional psychiatric disorder whose cause is known, whose features are distinctive, and whose course is usually predictable, and this is grief, the reaction to loss. Yet this condition has been so neglected by psychiatrists that until recently it was not even mentioned in the indexes of most of the best-known general textbooks of psychiatry. (p. 26)

Also sensitive to problems in diagnosis, Beverley Raphael and her colleagues in Australia have reviewed the scientific and clinical literature and surveyed the opinions of experts in the field in an effort to devise Research Diagnostic Criteria for normal and pathological grief. These have been developed and now are being proposed for adoption by researchers and clinicians in order that reliability and validity can be further established (Raphael, Middleton, Dunne, Martinek, & Smith, 1990).

It appears from the literature, as well as from general complaint among clinicians, that the near future must bring improved diagnostic categories for uncomplicated and complicated bereavement in the psychiatric nomenclature and subsequent revisions of the *Diagnostic and Statistical Manual*. Inclusion of these diagnoses will indicate an appropriate awareness of the need to focus research and intervention on grief and mourning, now that its serious consequences have been impressively documented (e.g., Osterweis et al., 1984). In addition, such recognition will represent yet another step in the continued evolution of the conceptualization of the mourning experience as complex, wide-ranging, and deeply influential.

Insufficient understanding of bereavement

The second problem in the mental health profession is that most practitioners have an insufficient understanding of bereavement. Like the general public, they tend to have inappropriate expectations and unrealistic attitudes about grief and mourning, and to believe in and promote the stereotypes pervasive in society at large (see Rando, 1988). Caregiver misinformation is probably the major cause of iatrogenesis in the treatment of grief and mourning.

In particular, insufficient understanding of the concurrence of bereavement with psychiatric complications causes much difficulty. Jacobs and Kim (1990) have made it clear that, in the past 20 years, attention to the psychiatric complications of bereavement has diminished. The result has been two serious conceptual problems that contribute to the prevailing professional uncertainty regarding the nature and clinical significance of the "psychopathologic syndromes observed during acute bereavement" (Jacobs & Kim, 1990, p. 314). The first conceptual problem concerns the question of whether pathological syndromes occur and how to distinguish them, given that no DSM-III-R category for them exists. Along with many others, Jacobs and Kim are frustrated by the DSM-III-R's lack of an appropriate formal category for complicated mourning. They note that a number of DSM-III-R symptoms of major depression (e.g., morbid preoccupation with worthlessness, prolonged or marked functional impairment, marked psychomotor retardation, and suicidal gestures) are absent for many of the unremitting depressions of bereavement. If such symptoms are required criteria for diagnosing major depression among the bereaved, the result will be a significant underestimation of the rate of depression as a complication of bereavement (Jacobs & Lieberman, 1987). In addition, anxiety disorders have been found to complicate bereavement (Jacobs, Hanson, Kasl, Ostfeld, Berkman, & Kim, 1990) but are not included as potential complications in the DSM-III-R. Consequently, they too may go unrecognized, increasing both their underestimation and the likelihood that they will go untreated.

The second conceptual problem identified by Jacobs and Kim (1990) concerns the problem of understanding the psychiatric complications of bereavement, given the two competing models and nosologies in psychiatry. On the one hand, in psychoanalytic psychiatry, complications are characterized as symptoms of pathological mourning. On the other, in the current nosology of American psychiatry (i.e., the atheoretical model underlying the DSM-III-R), pathological mourning is not considered to be a psychiatric syndrome despite clinical evidence to the contrary. Jacobs and Kim find that depression and anxiety have significant overlap in uncomplicated and complicated mourning and report on statistics for the prevalence, duration, comorbidity, and isomorphy of these two responses. Arguing that this information must become common knowledge for all mental health professionals, they conclude as follows:

> If the causative nature of the loss were ignored, clinical understanding of the psychopathologic syndrome as a maladaptation and implications for psychotherapeutic intervention would be missed. On the other hand, if the relationship between pathologic grief and anxiety or depressive disorders were ignored there would be an underestimation of psychiatric complications, as well as the possibility that psychopharmacologic interventions would be withheld.
>
> An integrated concept combines an etiologic perspective with standardized criteria and aids in understanding the

nature of the psychopathologic process and the objectives of treatment. Neither approach to treatment is sufficient, and an integrated model holds more promise for both the diagnosis and the treatment of the patient. (Jacobs & Kim, 1990, pp. 316–317)

Limitations on treatment

The third problem inherent in the profession concerns decisions by third-party payers to decrease funds and increase restrictions on mental health services. Unfortunately, these changes do not take into account the findings that uncomplicated grief and mourning are more significantly associated with psychiatric distress (e.g., Jacobs & Kim, 1990) and persist for a longer duration (e.g., Zisook & Shuchter, 1985) than previously believed. Such policies also coincide with the reality that the incidence of complicated mourning is increasing and that higher proportions of the bereaved will require more extensive treatment. In other words, at the exact point when the mental health community will have more bereaved individuals, with more complicated mourning, requiring treatment for longer periods of time, mental health services will be subjected to limitations, preapprovals, third-party reviews (often by persons ignorant about the area), the application of short-term models, and inappropriate diagnosis (forced by an inadequate classification system). Plainly, the current system will be unable to respond to the coming onslaught of individuals experiencing complications in mourning. As caregivers, we must find models, approaches, and treatments appropriate to these grim realities.

CONTENT AND ORGANIZATION OF THIS BOOK

This book focuses on adult bereavement. The interventions described are primarily pertinent to individual treatment, although certainly most information can be readily extrapolated to fit other treatment modalities. Part I provides an overview of the fundamentals required to place complicated mourning in the proper context. Specifically, chapter 2 offers a perspective on loss, grief, and mourning, reviewing the information about uncomplicated grief and mourning that underpins the remainder of the discussion. This chapter briefly identifies the six "R" processes of mourning, or the processes whereby the mourner moves from an initial recognition of the loss through eventual reinvestment in other sources of gratification. As noted, it is the compromise, distortion, or failure of one or more of these processes that by definition constitutes complicated mourning. This review is relatively brief; the presumption is that the reader is well acquainted with the literature in this area. If this is not the case, the reader is urged to consult *Grief, Dying, and Death: Clinical Interventions for Caregivers* (Rando, 1984) for the necessary background.

Chapter 3 reviews the work of 19 individuals whom I feel have made the most significant contributions to the literature on complicated mourning. The work of many fine contributors to other areas of thanatology has been omitted solely because of a strict focus on complicated grief and mourning. The chapter is exceptionally long for a review of this sort because, unfortunately, too many professionals are unfamiliar with the classic literature in the field. An understanding of the precise development of this literature is essential to comprehension of much of the subsequent discussion in the book. In addition, important information about treatment can be extrapolated from these sources. This is not a critical review but a summary of available writings: When reporting the work of a particular author, I have used his or her own terminology and have assumed that the underlying philosophy and treatment approaches are valid. The reader is urged to be open-minded when considering the work of an author whose language, philosophical approach, theoretical bias, or empirical data might be personally unacceptable.

Chapters 4 and 5 detail four complicated outcomes that may result from loss: (a) complicated grief and mourning symptoms—psychological, behavioral, social, or physical manifestations that are of insufficient number, intensity, or duration to qualify as a complicated mourning syndrome or a diagnosable mental or physical disorder; (b) one of seven complicated mourning syndromes; (c) a diagnosable mental or physical disorder; or (d) death. Specifically, chapter 4 synthesizes information on the symptoms of complicated mourning and the clinical syndromes of complicated mourning into which they may coalesce. Treatment issues are described for each syndrome. Chapter 5 follows the classification system of the DSM-III-R in examining the associations between complicated mourning and recognized mental and physical disorders. The discussion also briefly examines the potential for death in extreme cases, noting that this outcome may result from suicide, acute consequences of complicated mourning symptoms (e.g., fast driving), or the long-term sequelae of complicated mourning (e.g., cardiac problems secondary to increased smoking and drinking).

Part II addresses concerns relating to assessment and treatment of complicated mourning. In particular, chapter 6 outlines issues in assessment and describes the proper use of a new clinical tool, the Grief and Mourning Status Interview and Inventory (GAMSII). (The GAMSII itself is presented in an appendix to this volume.) Chapter 7 discusses seven specific treatment approaches to complicated mourning, offering an extensive review of primary sources. Chapter 8 gives a brief overview of research concerning the efficacy of intervention in mourning and discusses philosophical perspectives on treatment and generic treatment guidelines pertinent to all work with complicated mourning. Finally, chapter 9 identifies specific interventions for working through the six "R" processes of mourning, which by definition are incomplete if mourning has become complicated.

Specific clinical problems are the topic of Part III. The first three chapters in this section deal with risks and therapeutic implications associated with various factors implicit in the loss. Chapter 10 focuses on individual, relationship, and system factors such as mourner liabilities, anger, ambivalence, guilt, dependency and codependency, and social support. Chapter 11 concerns potential problems associated with the various modes of death (i.e., natural death; accidental death, including disaster and war death; suicide; and homicide). The high-risk factor of the mourner's perception of the death as preventable is discussed under the topic of homicide. Issues relating to sudden, unexpected death; multiple death; and traumatic death are the topic of chapter 12, and concerns associated with death of a child and AIDS-related death are the focus of chapter 13. Chapter 14 identifies various caregiver concerns in the treatment of complicated mourning, specifically discussing common therapeutic errors, countertransference, and stress-related issues.

Except where the work of a particular theorist is discussed, the generic term *caregiver* has been chosen in order to help readers from all professions identify with the person attempting to intervene therapeutically. Likewise, the term *complicated mourning* has been chosen over other variants unless another term is characteristic of a particular author's work. Finally, throughout the book, masculine and feminine pronouns have been used alternately to designate the mourner.

CHAPTER 2

A Perspective on Loss, Grief, and Mourning

In order to be able to understand and treat complicated mourning, one must comprehend the uncomplicated mourning processes from which it departs. This chapter offers an overview of uncomplicated grief and mourning. First, the terms *loss, grief,* and *mourning* are defined as used throughout this book. The inevitability of loss and myths and realities of mourning are next discussed, followed by an outline of factors influencing individual response to loss. Next described are three phases of grief and mourning and the six "R" processes of mourning that take place within these three phases. Finally, perspectives on the duration and course of mourning are presented, and the phenomenon of subsequent temporary upsurges of grief—STUG reactions—is discussed.

As will be noted repeatedly in subsequent chapters, the treatment of complicated mourning involves its conversion to uncomplicated mourning. Therefore, it is imperative that the caregiver be totally familiar and comfortable with the content of this chapter. For more detailed discussion of uncomplicated mourning, the reader is referred to Rando (1984, 1988). Other recommended resources for further analysis of these topics include Bowlby (1980); Freud (1917/1957c); Glick, Weiss, and Parkes (1974); Lindemann (1944); Osterweis et al. (1984); Parkes (1987); Parkes and Weiss (1983); and Raphael (1983).

DEFINITIONS

Definitions of loss, grief, and mourning are important because the caregiver's inability to appreciate the implications of their differences may contribute to the devolution of loss reactions into complicated mourning.

Loss

Two general categories of loss exist: physical loss and psychosocial loss. A *physical loss* is the loss of something tangible. Examples include a car that is stolen, a house that burns down, a breast that is surgically removed, or a memento that is misplaced. Often, others recognize physical losses as such; usually, there is at least minimal awareness that the individual will have feelings about the loss and may have to deal with them. In contrast, a *psychosocial loss*—sometimes called a *symbolic loss*—is the loss of something intangible, psychosocial in nature. Examples include getting a divorce, retiring, developing a chronic illness, or having a dream shattered. Such events are seldom recognized by others as losses generating feelings that require processing.

A related term is *bereavement,* or the state of having suffered a loss. It is interesting to note that the words *bereave* and *rob* derive from the same root, which implies an unwilling deprivation by force, having something withheld unjustly and injuriously, a stealing away of something valuable—all of which leave the individual victimized.

Any type of change necessarily involves loss. At the very least, loss of the status quo is involved. Unpleasant changes or deprivations (e.g., the theft of valued jewelry, the development of a serious illness) are usually clearly recognized by both the mourner and her social group. However, change that is not unpleasant also brings loss, and this usually goes unrecognized by the mourner's social group and often by the mourner herself. Three types of change that automatically constitute loss (whether defined as such or not) are developmental loss, loss resulting from normal change and growth, and competency-based loss. Developmental loss occurs as a natural consequence of the human development and aging process (e.g., eyesight deteriorates, strength diminishes, thinking processes slow). Loss resulting from normal change and growth follows from usual development and maturation in life (e.g., a couple goes from being a dyad to a triad with the birth of their first child, an adolescent relinquishes dependency on his parents). Finally, competency-based loss stems from the attainment of certain abilities, capacities, or functioning (e.g., graduation from college, a child's leaving home, even the achievement of a desired goal).

A *secondary loss* is a physical or psychosocial loss that coincides with or develops as a consequence of the initial loss. For example, with the death of a loved one, the mourner experiences the secondary physical loss of the loved one's presence. If the mourner has to relocate due to economic hardship after the death, this creates another secondary physical loss.

The mourner typically sustains much more than physical loss after a death. Loved ones play many roles in an individual's life. For instance, a spouse may be one's lover, best friend, helpmate, confidant, coparent, social partner, housemate, traveling companion, business associate, career supporter, auto repair person, housekeeper, and "other half," among myriad other roles. With the death, the mourner loses someone to fill these roles and to gratify the needs and sustain the feelings associated with them in the particular way the deceased did. In addition, the mourner loses a view of the world and the countless feelings, thoughts, behavior and interaction patterns, hopes, wishes, fantasies, dreams, assumptions, expectations, and beliefs that required the loved one's presence. The deprivation of the gratification the loved one once provided, the unfulfilled needs, the unreinforced behavior patterns, the unmet expectations, the emotional privation, the violated views of the world, the dashed hopes, the frustrated wishes, and the role relationships left empty are all examples of secondary psychosocial losses associated with the death.

Each of these secondary losses initiates its own grief and mourning reactions, which ultimately may be greater or lesser in intensity and scope than those following the precipitating loss. At the proper time, each of these secondary losses must be identified and mourned just as the actual death precipitating it must be mourned. The following case example illustrates this point.

> John was 20 when his father died. He was in college studying engineering at the time. After the death John was forced to abandon his dream of becoming an engineer in order to take over the family grocery store his father had owned and operated. Without this there would have been insufficient income for John's mother and three siblings.
>
> John not only lost his father; he also lost his vocation, his independence (he had to move back home), his girlfriend (after John's withdrawal from the university she found someone else who was near enough to spend more time with her), and his role as a happy-go-lucky young adult (he now assumed his father's role in the family as eldest male and chief provider). Until John could identify and grieve over these secondary losses, his grief could not be resolved. Ironically, he could cope better with the loss of his father, which he had been gradually preparing for, than with the other losses that his father's death brought about. (Rando, 1984, pp. 53–54)

A mourner may sustain a psychosocial loss without an accompanying or consequent physical loss. It is impossible, however, to experience a physical loss without an accompanying or consequent psychosocial loss. At the very least, the significance the mourner assigned to the tangible object is lost when the object is lost. Therefore, every physical loss will engender psychosocial loss.

In summary, in mourning the death of any loved one, a mixture of both physical and psychosocial losses, as well as a number of secondary losses, accrues. These secondary losses can be physical or psychosocial in nature and generate their own grief and mourning reactions. Because the death of a loved one brings many losses, what one perceives as a given individual's grief and mourning for a specific death is actually the sum total of all the grief and mourning for each of the losses experienced in connection with this death.

Grief

As used in this book, *grief* refers to the process of experiencing the psychological, behavioral, social, and physical reactions to the perception of loss. Five important clinical implications derive from this definition.

1. Grief is experienced in four major ways: psychologically (through affects, cognitions, perceptions, attitudes, and philosophy/spirituality), behaviorally (through personal action, conduct, or demeanor), socially (through reactions to and interactions with others), and physically (through bodily symptoms and physical health).

2. Grief is a continuing development. It is not a static state; rather, it involves many changes over time.

3. Grief is a natural, expectable reaction. The absence of it, when warranted by the factors circumscribing the loss, is abnormal and indicative of pathology.

4. Grief is a reaction to all types of loss, not just death. Death is but one example of loss, albeit the most dramatic one.

5. Grief is dependent upon the individual's unique perception of loss. It is not necessary for the loss to be socially recognized or validated by others for the individual to grieve, although it is most helpful when this can occur.

Any particular grief response expresses one or a combination of four things: (a) the mourner's feelings about the loss and the deprivation it causes (e.g., sorrow, depression, guilt); (b) the mourner's protest at the loss and wish to undo it and have it not be true (e.g., anger, searching, preoccupation with the deceased); (c) the effects caused by the assault on the mourner as a result of the loss (e.g., disorganization and confusion, fear and anxiety, physical symptoms); and (d) the mourner's personal actions stimulated by these first three (e.g., crying, social withdrawal, increased use of medication and/or psychoactive substances).

Any specific grief response is a reaction to the loss. However, the ultimate goal of grief and mourning is to take the mourner beyond these reactions to the loss. Mourning requires more than the passive reactions of grief; it demands working actively to adapt to the loss. Failure to accommodate or respond appropriately to the changes following a major loss (i.e., not adapting but persisting as if the world is the same when it is not) constitutes an unhealthy response to a new reality. For this reason, more than grief is required. Mere expression of reaction to the loss is too passive. There must be active movement and change if a major loss is to be processed, worked through, reconciled, and integrated into a mourner's life, and if that individual is to be able to continue on in a healthy fashion in the new life without the loved one. Thus, grief is a necessary but not sufficient condition to come to successful accommodation of loss. The active processes of mourning are required as well.

Mourning

Traditionally, *mourning* has been defined as the cultural and/or public display of grief through one's behaviors. This definition focuses on mourning as a vehicle for social communication. However, as defined in this book, the term follows the psychoanalytic tradition of focusing on intrapsychic work, expanding on it by including adaptive behaviors necessitated by the loss of the loved one (or whatever has been lost physically or psychosocially). For purposes of clarity, the following discussion focuses exclusively on the loss of a loved one.

Specifically, then, mourning refers to the conscious and unconscious processes and courses of action that promote three operations, each with its own particular focus. The first operation promoted by mourning is the undoing of the psychosocial ties binding the mourner to the loved one, with the eventual facilitation of the development of new ties. In this operation, an internal focus on the deceased helps stimulate the acute grief resulting from the separation, the recollection and reexperience of the deceased and the relationship, and the ultimate changing of emotional investment in the deceased and development of a new relationship. In the second operation, mourning processes help the survivor adapt to the loss. Here there is an internal focus on the mourner as he undertakes the necessary revision of the assumptive world; adoption or modification of roles, skills, and behaviors; and development of a new identity. The third and final operation promoted by mourning helps the mourner learn how to live in a healthy way in the new world without the deceased. There is an external focus as the mourner attempts to move adaptively into the new world without the presence of the loved one through the adoption of new ways of being in that world and reinvestment in people, objects, roles, hopes, beliefs, causes, ideals, goals, or pursuits.

Therefore, mourning involves processes related to the deceased, the self, and the external world. Basically, after the death of a loved one the mourner must reorient himself in relation to the deceased, the self, and the external world. These processes all occur within the larger context of the six "R" processes of mourning, to be discussed later in the chapter. Specifically, mourning processes related to the deceased include the following.

1. Coming to grips with the reality of the loss by gradually acknowledging and understanding the death and its implications and ultimately relinquishing hope that the loss can be reversed

2. Reacting to separation from the loved one (i.e., acute grief) and finding ways to experience, express, and channel all the pain and other psychological reactions

3. Reviewing and reexperiencing psychosocial ties with the deceased (e.g., memories, thoughts, feelings, hopes, needs), modifying them, and reacting to changes in them

4. Doing something with the unfinished business with the deceased that presses for completion

5. Transforming the attachment to the deceased from one anchored in physical presence to one of symbolic interaction; changing the relationship to recognize the death and develop appropriate new ways to relate to the deceased

Mourning processes related to the self involve the following phenomena.

1. Altering the needs, feelings, thoughts, behavior and interaction patterns, hopes, wishes, fantasies, dreams, assumptions, expectations, and beliefs that had been predicated on the presence of the loved one

2. Coping with the defenses and behaviors used to mitigate the pain of the loss, minimizing and ultimately relinquishing those that interfere with the necessary completion of the six "R" processes of mourning

3. Finding ways to incorporate the loss into the philosophical framework of one's life and integrate the loss with other meanings and systems of belief in the assumptive world; finding ways to eliminate, reduce, or accommodate cognitive dissonance

4. Sustaining meaning in the face of major loss—which can destabilize meaning—and creating some sense out of the "non-sense" of the loss

5. Developing a new sense of identity to reflect and incorporate the many changes and readjustments that occur as a consequence of the death

6. Deciding what can and cannot be controlled in terms of the loss; making choices about what can be controlled

7. Deciding whether the loss will be survived and, if the decision is to survive, choosing how to do so

Mourning processes related to the external world include the following.

1. Readjusting to the loss by taking on healthy new ways of being in the new world without the loved one (i.e., adopting or modifying specific roles, skills, and behaviors in response to the losses sustained and to compensate for the absence of the loved one)

2. Accommodating the loss by integrating its psychosocial and physical realities, demands, and implications into ongoing life

3. Finding new people, objects, roles, hopes, beliefs, causes, ideals, goals, or pursuits in which to put the emotional investment that formerly had been placed in the relationship with the deceased

In order to offer appropriate interventions, caregivers must understand the relationship of grief to mourning. The purpose of the active work of grief and mourning is to assist the mourner in recognizing that the loved one truly is gone and then in making the necessary internal (psychological) and external (behavioral and social) changes to accommodate this reality. Grief helps the individual recognize the loss and prepare for the processes of mourning. Without the experiences and learning provided by acute grief, mourning cannot take place. (For more on this issue, see the subsequent discussion of the Confrontation Phase of mourning.)

Grief is actually the beginning part of mourning. Uncomplicated reactions of acute grief may last a number of months and, in some specific cases, even longer. In contrast, uncomplicated mourning can last for a number of years if not forever under some circumstances. This does not mean that the individual is in acute grief all of this time. One can mourn but not be in acute grief (i.e., not manifesting psychological, behavioral, social, or physical reactions to the perception of loss). Even though grief reactions may be spent, the mourner still may have to achieve much adaptation and integration before the loss is successfully accommodated in ongoing and future life. Also, there will be times when the mourner experiences subsequent temporary upsurges of grief, as discussed later in this chapter. Hence, just as infancy is a part of childhood but childhood is composed of more than that one phase (e.g., toddlerhood, latency stage, early adolescence), grief is a part of mourning but mourning is not necessarily a part of grief. By definition, mourning encompasses much more than grief.

In his classic article "Symptomatology and Management of Acute Grief," Lindemann (1944) coined the term *grief work*. It is an apt expression, explicitly recognizing the labor required in coming to grips with and adapting to the loss of a loved one. However, the phrase more appropriately might be *grief and mourning work* because the tasks Lindemann delineates (i.e., emancipation from the bondage to the deceased, readjustment to the environment in which the deceased is missing, and the formation of new relationships) do not reside exclusively within the domain of grief, but are also a part of mourning.

The distinction between grief and mourning is crucial to treatment. Many caregivers assist the bereaved with the beginning process (i.e., expressing their reactions to the loss) but not with the important latter processes (i.e., reorienting in relation to the deceased, the self, and the external world). As a result, mourners are frequently left on their own to reshape self and world after the loss of a loved one.

INEVITABILITY OF LOSS

Repeatedly, human beings are mourners in life. There is no escaping the inevitability of continued confrontation with loss, whether that loss is associated with death of a pet, rejection by a particular college, divorce, development of a chronic illness, or some other event. The reactions seen after these experiences (e.g., loneliness after the loss of the pet, depression after being rejected by the college, dysfunction during the divorce, social withdrawal after contracting the chronic illness) are part and parcel of mourning associated with loss. They may never reach the same intensity as reactions after the death of a beloved person, but they are variations on the same theme—psychological, behavioral, social, or physical reactions to the perception of loss.

The most difficult experiences in life always involve some measure of loss—physical, psychosocial, or a mixture of these two. Caregivers must help individuals undergoing these experiences to comprehend them as losses and to perceive their reactions as grief and mourning responses. This affords them better understanding, increased meaning, reduced helplessness, and a greater sense of control—all of which improve coping ability. Merely having a label or a cognitive framework for distress (e.g., "In reacting to this divorce you are mourning the death of your marriage and the loss of your dreams for the future with this person") allows human beings to manage more effectively.

In the field of mental health intervention today, a number of treatment areas are receiving well-deserved attention. These areas include, among others, physical and sexual abuse, rape, problems experienced by adult children of alcoholics and by members of other dysfunctional families, divorce, suicide, sexual dysfunction, fear of intimacy, and post-traumatic stress. Although the literature may address these areas in the isolation of special focus, loss, grief, and mourning are major, inherent aspects of each. These currently visible areas of concern have their own jargon; nevertheless, all are loss experiences. Such categorization in no way diminishes their importance; rather, it highlights their shared dynamics. Although the caregiver must of course be aware of the unique content, demands, strategies, techniques, and issues specific to treatment of these particular problems, placing them on a continuum of loss can provide insight into their commonality and offer a new perspective on intervention. Indeed, to the extent that a caregiver can identify the aspects of loss in human experience and respond to and facilitate grief and mourning, that individual possesses knowledge and skill fundamental to intervention in every human condition.

MYTHS AND REALITIES OF MOURNING

Work associated with grief and mourning demands energy. Unfortunately, this need is sadly misperceived by society, which maintains a host of unrealistic assumptions about and inappropriate expectations for such work and those who undertake it (Rando, 1988). Some notable myths include the following.

1. Grief and mourning decline in a steadily decreasing fashion over time.

2. All losses prompt the same type of mourning.

3. Bereaved individuals need only express their feelings in order to resolve their mourning.

4. To be healthy after the death of a loved one, the mourner must put that person out of mind.

5. Grief will affect the mourner psychologically but will not interfere in other ways.

6. Intensity and length of mourning are a testimony to love for the deceased.

7. When one mourns a death, one mourns only the loss of that person and nothing else.

8. Losing someone to a sudden, unexpected death is the same as losing someone to an anticipated death.

9. Mourning is over in a year.

One particularly egregious myth concerns the presumed role of time as healer, as in the familiar phrases "Time heals all wounds," "Just give it time," and "Time will ease the pain." However, time does not heal in and of itself, nor does it necessarily affect mourning, although it does have an influence on the amount of support available to the mourner and thus can be construed to affect mourning indirectly. Rather, what is done during that time makes the difference. Time can lend perspective, and this can be quite helpful. However, it is the mourner who must develop this perspective and use it. What time alone can do is serve as an objective marker indicating that the person left behind has continued to survive for an extended period. In cases of major loss, in which the mourner might have questioned her ability to endure without the deceased, the passage of time can be most validating.

Myths about grief and mourning not only fail to help mourners, they actually make the experience worse than it necessarily has to be. This is because mourners evaluate themselves by the myth's incorrect information; caregivers treat mourners according to it; and family, friends, and society determine the type and extent of support offered based upon it. Consequently, proper knowledge about grief and mourning is essential for all involved to minimize such potentially deleterious consequences as mourners' personal assumption of failure and caregivers' insufficient provision of support or inappropriate diagnosis of pathology.

In addition to the negative impact of society's erroneous information and expectations about mourning in general and its course and duration in particular, several other often unrecognized issues bear brief mention. A major issue, already discussed, pertains to the need to mourn not only the loss of the person but the secondary physical and psychosocial losses that accrue to that loss.

Another issue concerns the fact that a loss reaction sometimes entails grief and mourning not only for what one had that now is lost but also for what one never had and now never will have. This situation would exist, for example, when the death of an individual's mother calls forth mourning for the fact that there had never been a positive relationship with that parent and now, with her death, all hope is lost of ever establishing one. Another example would concern the individual mourning the experience of traumatization by child abuse. Although that person may never have had an appropriate childhood, the lack of it is still deeply mourned. Mourners and those who seek to assist them often fail to recognize that the loss of potential (both for what still could have been up until the death or for what once could have been in the past) is a loss like any other. Because of misunderstanding about this issue, mourners can be left without necessary legitimization and support. This only serves to victimize them further.

A final important point is that major loss tends to resurrect old issues and unresolved conflicts (e.g., early childhood experiences of anxiety and helplessness; old conflicts about separation, dependency, ambivalence, or insecurity). Also, the experience of a major loss not uncommonly tugs at the roots of old, incompletely mourned losses; losses that are not so old but are still partially unmourned; or even losses that although mourned remain quite sensitive. In other words, the destabilization occasioned by major loss often puts one in touch with past pain and previous times of chaos, stress, and transition, and can summon unfinished business from the past—all of which can add to the distress of the current experience. Bowlby (1980) offers the additional notion that when one loses a person to whom he currently is attached it is natural for him to turn for comfort to an earlier attachment figure; if this person is also deceased, the pain of the earlier loss may be felt afresh—perhaps even for the first time.

This phenomenon, the resurrection of previous losses, explains why mourners can be surprised to find themselves at the time of a current loss reflecting on earlier losses and feeling additionally burdened and bereaved (e.g., "I wonder why I keep thinking about my divorce as I'm trying to deal with my best friend's death"). It illustrates why caregivers must be thorough in their assessment of a mourner and not assume that all currently experienced reactions pertain to the death at hand. Quite frequently, and often unfortunately, the mourner has to struggle not only with the contemporary loss but also with the vestiges of previous losses as well. Sometimes this is the sole condition under which delayed or inhibited mourning for a previous loss is expressed (see chapter 4). I once interviewed a woman who ostensibly sought treatment for the death of her husband 2 months prior. However, during the interview it became clear that, notwithstanding genuine grief over her husband's loss, the more dynamic catalyst for her acute grief was the fact that the recent death forced her to contend with the death of her only child 20 years earlier. What appeared on the surface as acute grief for a recent death was actually more reflective of delayed mourning for a loss decades before.

FACTORS INFLUENCING GRIEF AND MOURNING

No person's grief or mourning response occurs in a vacuum. Rather, it is influenced, shaped, and determined by a constellation of factors that combine to render a mourner's response unique—as individual as a fingerprint. In order to correctly diagnose and treat, caregivers must possess complete knowledge of the factors circumscribing the particular loss of a particular mourner at a particular point in time. A response perfectly appropriate and healthy for one person under one set of circumstances may be pathological for another in different circumstances. This is why an accurate assessment for each mourner is so important and why each assessment must consider the various sets of factors that can influence individual response.

Three broad categories of factors influence grief and mourning: psychological factors, social factors, and physiological factors. These are listed in Table 2.1, along with pertinent subcategories. For a more comprehensive discussion of most of these sets of factors and the different impact of variables within each set, the reader is referred to Rando (1984).

THREE PHASES OF GRIEF AND MOURNING

Professionals have been bombarded by stage theories of dying and bereavement in the last several decades. However, most have been cautioned about the dangers of rigidly applying such theories and warned against pigeonholing mourners by inappropriately employing models to "explain" persons instead of ascertaining their particular needs, experiences, or realities. Without question, commonalities exist within the human experience; equally without question, idiosyncratic variations occur. The astute caregiver identifies and responds to both, recognizing that even universals are experienced distinctly and individually. Thus, data gathering and intervention must occur at both general and specific levels.

To say that grief and mourning follow a progression is not to imply an invariable sequence, for human beings are not so uniform or predictable that individuality is precluded in any response. However, the schema described in the following pages elucidates common responses to major loss over time. This schema, condensed from a variety of sources and discussed in greater depth in Rando (1984), divides responses into three time periods or phases, each characterized by a major response set toward the loss: Avoidance, Confrontation, and Accommodation. These three phases house all of the different loss reactions, regardless of number, type, or source (e.g., conceptualizations describing dying patients, divorcing individuals, persons coping with chronic illness, survivors of disasters). Although various theories may have different names and examine diverse populations, they all acknowledge these same basic reactions.

It is important to keep in mind that these three phases are not discrete. The mourner probably will move back and forth among them depending upon (a) the precise issue at hand (some issues are easier to cope with than others), (b) how that issue stands with regard to other pertinent issues with which the mourner must contend, (c) where the individual is in the mourning process, and (d) the interaction of factors circumscribing this particular loss for this specific mourner. Not all mourners will experience all of the reactions described. Which ones are experienced depends on the specific factors associated with the mourner's loss.

For the purpose of illustration, the following discussion will describe the three phases as they would apply to a sudden, unexpected death. To the extent that circumstances differ, responses will differ. For example, in the situation of an anticipated death from a terminal illness, the

Table 2.1 Factors Influencing Grief and Mourning

PSYCHOLOGICAL FACTORS

Characteristics Pertaining to the Nature and Meaning of the Specific Loss

The unique nature and meaning of the loss sustained or relationship severed

Qualities of the relationship lost (psychological character, strength, and security of the attachment)

Roles the deceased occupied in the mourner's family or social system (number of roles, functions served, their centrality and importance)

Characteristics of the deceased

Amount of unfinished business between the mourner and the deceased

Mourner's perception of the deceased's fulfillment in life

Number, type, and quality of secondary losses

Nature of any ongoing relationship with the deceased

Characteristics of the Mourner

Coping behaviors, personality, and mental health

Level of maturity and intelligence

Assumptive world

Previous life experiences, especially past experiences with loss and death

Expectations about grief and mourning

Social, cultural, ethnic, generational, and religious/philosophical/spiritual background

Sex-role conditioning

Age

Developmental stage of life, life-style, and sense of meaning and fulfillment

Presence of concurrent stresses or crises

Table 2.1 (cont'd)

Characteristics of the Death

The death surround (location, type of death, reasons for it, mourner's presence at it, degree of confirmation of it, mourner's degree of preparation and participation)

Timeliness

Psychosocial context within which the death occurs

Amount of mourner's anticipation of the death

Degree of suddenness

Mourner's perception of preventability

Length of illness prior to the death

Amount, type, and quality of anticipatory grief and involvement with the dying person

SOCIAL FACTORS

Mourner's social support system and the recognition, validation, acceptance, and assistance provided by its members

Mourner's social, cultural, ethnic, generational, and religious/philosophical/spiritual background

Mourner's educational, economic, and occupational status

Funerary or memorial rites

Involvement in the legal system

Amount of time since the death

PHYSIOLOGICAL FACTORS

Drugs (including alcohol, caffeine, and nicotine)

Nutrition

Rest and sleep

Exercise

Physical health

Avoidance Phase may not be as dramatic as portrayed here. Many of the reactions witnessed in the Avoidance Phase after a sudden, unexpected death are present at the time of diagnosis in cases of terminal illness because, for mourners dealing with such situations, this is the time when they initially contend with the loss and therefore try to avoid it. (See Rando, 1986e for a full discussion of losses inherent in terminal illness.) It is important to qualify this statement by saying, however, that anticipating and actually encountering a death are two different things, and avoidance of the reality of the death certainly may be evident in those who lose loved ones to terminal illness.

Avoidance Phase

The Avoidance Phase covers the time period in which the news of the death is initially received and briefly thereafter. It is marked by the understandable desire to avoid the terrible acknowledgment that the loved one is lost. The world is shaken, and the mourner may be overwhelmed. Like the physical shock that occurs with trauma to the body, the human psyche goes into shock with the traumatic assault of the death of the loved one. Emotionally, the mourner may become numb. It is not uncommon for the individual to feel confused, dazed, bewildered, and unable to comprehend what has happened. There may be disorganization of thought, emotion, and/or behavior. In brief, the mourner is reeling from the news.

As recognition of what has happened starts to seep in and shock and numbness slowly start to wear off, denial immediately takes its place. Denial is natural and therapeutic at this juncture. It functions as a buffer, allowing the mourner to absorb the reality of the loss gradually over time and serving as emotional anesthesia while the mourner begins to experience the painful awareness of the loss. Possible reactions that may be manifested at this point are disbelief and a need to know why. From some, there may be outbursts of emotion—anger, intense sorrow and sadness, hysteria, tears, rageful protest, screaming. From others, there may be quiet withdrawal or mechanical action without feeling. Some report feeling depersonalized, as if they were witnessing the experience happening to someone else.

Some survivors appear initially to accept the death and begin immediately to comfort others and make arrangements. They recognize the loss but consciously put aside their emotions as they try to be strong or carry out particular roles. This tendency is especially prevalent in our society with males, with those expected to care for others (e.g., adult children of older parents), and sometimes with parents when younger surviving children are present. This temporary delay of mourning need not be harmful if it is reversed relatively soon. In other cases, mourners may respond this way in an attempt to deny the fact of death, its implications, or feelings about it. When this denial continues for too long, it is quite pathological.

Confrontation Phase

The Confrontation Phase is a time when grief is experienced most intensely and reactions to the loss are most acute. Separation from the loved one generates alarm in the mourner, which results in heightened autonomic arousal, anger, and protest, and calls forth biologically based searching behavior. The mourner reacts to the strong urge to find, recover, and reunite with the lost one (see Bowlby, 1980, and Parkes, 1987). Pining or yearning (i.e., the persistent and obtrusive wishing and longing for the deceased) is the subjective and emotional component of the biological urge to search. This pining or yearning constitutes separation anxiety and is the characteristic feature of the pang of grief indicative of this time (Parkes, 1987).

This phase is a painful interval when the mourner confronts the reality of the loss and gradually absorbs what it means. It is a time in which a most excruciating learning process takes place—one that is necessary for the mourner ultimately to come to see that changes must be made. However, even though this critical function moves the mourner ever closer to healthy accommodation of the loss, it does not take away the pain.

Each time the mourner is frustrated in his desire to be with the deceased, he "learns" again that the loved one is dead. Each pang of grief, each stab of pain whenever the mourner's expectation, desire, or need for the loved one is unfulfilled "teaches" the mourner that the loved one is no longer there. When the mourner hears a hilarious joke and reaches for the phone to pass it on to his brother, only to remember that his brother is buried across town, that painful realization teaches the mourner. When the bereaved mother hears the school bus but does not see her daughter step off of it, the searing agony she experiences teaches the mother. When the widow reaches out in the middle of the night to touch her husband, but her hand touches only air, her overwhelming loneliness teaches her. All such hurtful incidents teach the mourner the lesson he wants to resist—that the loved one is dead. Thus, the Confrontation Phase involves coming to grips cognitively with the loss—learning about it—as well as reacting psychologically, behaviorally, socially, and physically to it.

It will take a long time and hundreds, perhaps thousands, of these painful experiences of unfulfilled longing for the deceased before the mourner will be able to transfer to his gut what he knows in his head—that the loved one is really, truly, irrevocably gone. Yearning and searching continue for some time, despite being unrewarded. Repeated frustration of desires for the deceased and the unsuccessful conscious and unconscious attempts to recover the loved one ultimately lead to a gradual diminution of disbelief and denial and then to the depression, disorganization, and despair that signal the mourner's relinquishment of hope for reversing the loss and avoiding his reactions to its reality. Disbelief and denial continue to occur intermittently for a while and, in the most positive analysis, reflect the tenacity of the human spirit in persevering for reunion with the loved one. Persisting for too long, they reveal the mourner's inability to accept the reality and implications of the death and constitute a pathological response.

The Confrontation Phase has been described as a time of angry sadness. There are extremes of emotion. Some individuals want to express what they feel; some do not. Some are conflicted, wanting to express their feelings but being unable to do so. Frequently, needs and emotions are in conflict with each other. So, too, are thoughts about how to handle this situation. It is an overwhelming, confusing, and frightening time as the mourner experiences types, intensities, and vacillations of emotions that make him unrecognizable to himself, afraid of who and what he will become, and fearful of losing his mind. Most of the phenomena of grief—traditional psychological defenses, processes of cognitive completion with affective release, coping behaviors, and specific attempts at mitigating the pain of loss (i.e., disbelief, sense of the deceased's presence, hallucinations and illusions, linking objects and messages, dreams, avoidance of reminders, selective forgetting; Parkes, 1987)—serve an important function at this point. According to Parkes, they help to regulate the quantity of novel, unorganized, or in other respects disabling information the person handles at a given time. Parkes notes that the mourner oscillates between twin opposing tendencies. One is an inhibitory tendency, which by repression, avoidance, postponement, and so forth holds back or limits the mourner's perception of disturbing stimuli. The other is a facilitative or reality-testing tendency, which enhances the mourner's perception and thought about disturbing stimuli (Parkes, 1987). This process is identical to that described as the denial-intrusion cycle of the stress response syndrome, which develops after traumatic events (Horowitz, 1986a). This cycle regulates the individual's exposure to trauma-related material. The denial symptomatology is equivalent to Parkes' inhibitory tendency, and the intrusive symptomatology is the same as Parkes' facilitative tendency. In both schemas, the individual tries to maintain psychological equilibrium by alternately avoiding and approaching the material as he attempts to process it and work it through. The similarity between these two schemas supports the notion of acute grief as a form of traumatic stress reaction.

During the Confrontation Phase, the mourner may experience a number of psychological, behavioral, social, and physical responses. Some of these responses, discussed in greater detail in Rando (1984, 1988), are listed in Table 2.2. The reader will note that a number of these responses cross categories. As mentioned previously, any grief response expresses one or a combination of the mourner's feelings about the loss and its deprivation, protest at the loss and wish to reverse it, effects caused by the assault on the mourner as a result of the loss, and any personal actions stimulated by these reactions.

Table 2.2 Common Psychological, Behavioral, Social, and Physical Responses to Loss

PSYCHOLOGICAL RESPONSES

Affects

Separation pain, sadness, sorrow, anguish

Anxiety, panic, fear, vulnerability, insecurity

Yearning, pining, longing

Helplessness; powerlessness; feelings of being out of control, victimized, overwhelmed

Anger, hostility, irritability, intolerance, impatience

Guilt, self-reproach, regret

Depression, hopelessness, despair

Anhedonia, apathy, restricted range of affect

Frustration

Fear of going crazy

Emotional lability, hypersensitivity

Deprivation, mutilation, violation

Loneliness

Abandonment

Ambivalence

Relief

Cognitions

Disbelief

Bewilderment

Disorganization, confusion, distractibility

Preoccupation with the deceased, obsession, rumination

Impaired concentration, comprehension, mental functioning, memory, decision making

Cognitive dissonance, meaninglessness, senselessness, disillusionment, aimlessness

Spiritual confusion, alienation, rejection; increased spirituality

Lowered self-esteem, feelings of inadequacy

Pessimism

Diminished self-concern

Decreased interest, motivation, initiative, direction

Perceptions

Feelings of unreality, depersonalization, derealization, dissociation

Development of a perceptual set for the deceased

Paranormal experiences pertaining to the deceased (e.g., visual or auditory hallucinations, sense of presence)

Feeling as if something is about to happen

Defenses and/or Attempts at Coping

Shock, numbness, absence of emotions

Avoidance or repression of thoughts, feelings, or memories associated with the deceased or painful reactions to the loss

Denial

Searching behavior (for the deceased)

Protest

Regression

Search for meaning

Identification with the deceased

Dreams of the deceased

Feelings of unreality, depersonalization, derealization, dissociation

BEHAVIORAL RESPONSES

Searching behavior (for the deceased)

Restless hyperactivity, searching for something to do, heightened arousal, agitation, exaggerated startle response, hypervigilence, hypomanic behavior

Social withdrawal

Disorganized activity, absent-minded behavior

Increased intake of medicine and/or psychoactive substances

Loss of patterns of social interaction (e.g., dependency, clinginess, avoidance of being alone)

Crying and tearfulness

Anorexia or appetite disturbance leading to weight loss or gain

Sleep disturbance (too little, too much, interrupted)

Tendency to sigh

Decreased interest, motivation, initiative, direction, and energy for relationships and organized patterns of activity

Decreased effectiveness and productivity in functioning (personal, social, work)

Avoidance of or adherence to people, situations, and stimuli reminiscent of the deceased

Table 2.2 (cont'd)

Self-destructive behaviors (e.g., accident-prone behavior,
    high-risk behavior such as fast driving)
Acting-out behaviors, impulsive behaviors
Hyposexuality or hypersexuality
Change in life-style
Hiding grief for fear of driving others away
Clinging behavior
Grief spasms

SOCIAL RESPONSES

Lack of interest in other people and in usual activities due
    to preoccupation with the deceased
Social withdrawal
Decreased interest, motivation, initiative, direction, and energy
    for relationships and organized patterns of activity
Boredom
Criticality toward others and other manifestations of anger
    or irritation with others
Loss of patterns of social interaction
Feeling alienated, detached, or estranged from others
Jealousy of others without loss
Dependency on others, clinginess, and avoidance of being alone

PHYSICAL RESPONSES

Symptoms Indicative of Biological Signs of Depression

Anorexia or appetite disturbance leading to weight loss or gain
Decreased interest, motivation, initiative, direction, and energy
Depressed mood
Anhedonia, apathy, restricted range of affect
Impaired concentration, mental functioning, memory, decision making
Decreased sexual interest; hyposexuality or hypersexuality
Sleep disturbance (too little, too much, interrupted)
Crying and tearfulness
Tendency to sigh
Fatigue, lethargy
Lack of strength
Physical exhaustion
Feelings of emptiness and/or heaviness
Psychomotor retardation or agitation

Symptoms Indicative of Anxiety and Hyperarousal

Motor tension
Trembling, shaking, twitching
Muscle tension, aches, soreness
Easy fatigability
Headache
Restlessness and searching for something to do

Autonomic hyperactivity
Anxiety, tension, nervousness
Heart palpitations, tachycardia
Shortness of breath
Numbness, tingling sensations
Smothering sensations
Dizziness, unsteady feelings, faintness
Dry mouth
Sweating or cold, clammy hands
Hot flashes or chills
Chest pain, pressure, discomfort
Choking
Nausea, diarrhea, other abdominal distress
Frequent urination
Tightness in the throat, trouble swallowing, feeling of something stuck in the throat
Digestive disturbance

Vigilance and scanning
Heightened arousal
Agitation
Sense of being "geared up"
Exaggerated startle response
Irritability, outbursts of anger
Difficulty falling or staying asleep
Impaired concentration
Hypervigilance
Physiologic reactivity upon exposure to events that symbolize or resemble
    an aspect of the death or events associated with it

Other Symptoms Indicative of Physiological Response to Distress

In addition to the other physical symptoms already mentioned:

Hair loss
Constellation of vague, diffuse somatic complaints, sometimes
    experienced in waves lasting minutes to hours
Gastrointestinal symptoms
Cardiopulmonary symptoms
Pseudoneurologic symptoms

The psychological responses of the acutely bereaved mourner illustrate that the mourner's emotional, cognitive, perceptual, attitudinal, and religious/philosophical/spiritual domains are all seriously affected. The behavioral responses reveal the myriad actions and demeanor that can be stimulated by the loss and the reactions to it. The social responses of the acutely bereaved mourner indicate that the person is interested only in reuniting with the loved one and that all else is somewhat devalued. Acute grief also involves a state of great strain and physical risk (Osterweis et al., 1984), with significantly lowered resistance. Physical responses associated with heightened arousal and increased vulnerability have been well documented by both scientific studies and clinical observation to occur even with appropriate grieving as a concomitant of the uncomplicated mourning process. (See chapter 5 for more on physical illness secondary to loss.)

Accommodation Phase

In the Accommodation Phase, formerly called the *reestablishment phase* (Rando, 1984), there is a gradual decline of the symptoms of acute grief and the beginning of social and emotional reentry into the everyday world. However, the world is being reconstructed, as seen in the transformation of the relationship with the deceased and the mourner's revision of her assumptive world and establishment of a new identity. The mourner is learning to go on without the deceased, making necessary internal and external changes to accommodate the absence of that person, yet finding ways to keep the new relationship with the deceased appropriately alive. The deceased is not forgotten, nor is the loss; however, the mourner learns to live with cognizance of the death and its implications in a way that does not preclude healthy, life-affirming growth.

Other theorists have used the term *resolution* to refer to this phase. However, the type of once-and-for-all closure implied by this term does not actually occur after the death of a much-loved person. Certain aspects of the loss will remain until the mourner's own death, and, as discussed later in this chapter, the mourner will likely experience subsequent temporary upsurges of grief. The term *accommodation* connotes an adaptation of oneself to make room for a particular circumstance. As such, it captures more accurately the reality that the loss can be integrated appropriately into the rest of life but that a truly final closure usually cannot be obtained, nor is it even desirable. It has been rightly pointed out that *adaptation* could mean in some cases making the best of a bad situation, not changing, or not recovering lost functions (Osterweis et al., 1984). I perceive its synonym, accommodation, to be the single best term currently available. *Recovery* and *completion* carry the same inaccurate connotations as *resolution*. In contrast, *accommodation* implies making oneself fit or congruous, or reconciling the loss. The crucial action-oriented emphasis of mourning is retained in this term.

Accommodation of the loss waxes and wanes during the latter part of the Confrontation Phase and continues slowly thereafter. Many of the reactions from the Confrontation Phase coexist for some time with the initial aspects of this new one. One notable example is guilt, which often is a stumbling block. The mourner struggles to work through such issues as the mistaken belief that the intensity and duration of acute grief is a testimony to love for the deceased or that it is only by experiencing significant pain that a link can be maintained with the loved one. It is important that these conflicts be worked through. If not addressed, they may contribute to the development of complicated mourning.

The goal of accommodation is to learn to live with the loss and readjust one's new life accordingly. Adjustments must occur in the relationship with the deceased (developing a new relationship), in oneself (revising the assumptive world and forming a new identity), and in the external world (readjusting roles, skills, and behaviors and, at the appropriate time, reinvesting emotional energy in new people, objects, roles, hopes, beliefs, causes, ideals, goals, and other pursuits). Accommodation does not mean that the mourner would have chosen or wanted the loss. It merely means that she no longer has to fight it, but accepts it in the sense of learning to live with it as an inescapable fact of life.

Accommodation also means that the mourner can integrate the past with the present and the new person that exists. The mourner will never forget, but she will not always be acutely bereaved. Accommodating the loss will leave a psychic scar, similar to a scar that remains after a physical injury. This scar does not necessarily interfere with the mourner's overall functioning, but on certain days and under particular conditions it may ache or throb. It will remind the mourner of what she has been through and that she must tend to her feelings until the pain passes.

Mourning brings many changes. The mourner can expect to have an altered identity and redefined roles, relationships, skills, and behaviors. These changes can be either positive or negative. As someone who has loved and lost, the mourner can be richer or poorer because of the parts of herself that are irretrievably gone. Like physical scars, psychic scars can give one character or be sources of vulnerability. Although she may have had no control or choice over her loved one's dying, the mourner does have a choice over how she will let the loss affect her. This choice does not pertain to the acute period of grief, in which the mourner is inevitably subject to psychological, behavioral, social, and physical effects in all realms of her life. Rather, it pertains to the perspective or attitude she will take toward the rest of her life as her mourning brings her to a changed state. Will she make the most out of the rest of her life, or will she become bitter? Will she incorporate her loss and use it as a catalyst for growth, or will she never take risks again? Will the death cause her to make sure she never has any unfinished business with others she cares about, or will it give her the sense that the world owes her?

Countless bereaved individuals derive positive benefits from major loss. This fact illustrates that one can choose to recover from loss and capitalize on whatever good can come from the bad. This view does not deny the pain of grief and price of the loss of a loved one. Rather, it recognizes that, even in undergoing the pain of separation, a mourner can decide that loss will have some positive meaning for the remainder of life. Positive responses can be many and varied (e.g., new priorities, increased commitment to living life more fully and meaningfully, new awareness of life's preciousness and fragility, reduced unfinished business with loved ones, increased communication and commitment to family, greater sensitivity and fuller expression of feelings, increased religiousness and spirituality). Many have determined that social good should come from their losses and have channeled their pain and rage into meaningful endeavors assisting both themselves and society. Bereavement support groups have been established to help others. Some, such as Parents of Murdered Children or Mothers Against Drunk Driving, urge political changes to ensure that others do not suffer the same bereavement.

Many bereaved individuals have discovered and developed aspects of their identity that previously were unknown. They have realized new interests, found new relationships, or started living in ways that are in some cases more satisfactory and fulfilling than before. This does not mean that they were not grieved by the loss of their loved one, only that they responded to that loss after a period of grief and mourning in ways that enriched them. Indeed there are many who contend that bereavement is indispensable for growth (e.g., Cassem, 1975).

Just as one can decide what healthy accommodation will mean, one can decide what it will not mean. It need not mean that one is untouched by reminders, such as a certain song, particular smell, or special location. It need not mean that one does not experience the bittersweet combination of feelings that holidays can bring, as one rejoices with those who are still present and mourns for those no longer there. It does not mean that in certain events in life one will not painfully wish for the loved one to be alive to share one's joy or be proud of one. It does not mean that one no longer mourns; it only means that one learns to live with mourning in ways that do not interfere with the ongoing healthy functioning in the new life without the loved one. Indices of successful accommodation do not suggest that one must discard all connection with the deceased loved one or forget that person. Rather, they suggest that accommodation centers on learning to live with the fact of the loved one's absence and moving forward in the new world despite the fact that the psychic scar caused by the loss will remain and, on occasion, bring pain.

Caregivers can share with mourners this final perspective on bereavement:

> And, in the end, this moving forward with that scar is the
> very best that we could hope for. You would not want to

forget your loved one, as if she never existed or [had] not been an important part of your life. Those things that are important to you in your life are remembered and kept in the very special places of your heart and mind. This is no less true with regard to the loss of a beloved person. Keep this loss, treasure what you have learned from it, take the memories that you have from the person and the relationship and, in a healthy fashion, remember what should be remembered, hold on to what should be retained, and let go of that which must be relinquished. And then, as you continue on to invest emotionally in other people, goals, and pursuits, appropriately take your loved one with you, along with your new sense of self and new way of relating to the world, to enrich your present and future life without forgetting your important past. (Rando, 1988, p. 287)

THE SIX "R" PROCESSES OF MOURNING

Coinciding with these three phases, the mourner experiences six major mourning processes. This schema constitutes a refinement of the processes necessary in order to resolve grief and mourning, originally presented in Rando (1988). Chapter 9 discusses these six processes further and details treatment suggestions for complicated mourning resulting from them.

The reader may wonder why mourning is discussed here in terms of processes rather than tasks, as it is, for example, in Worden's (1982) well-received schema. Although the usefulness of Worden's approach is unquestioned, operationalizing mourning in terms of processes is preferable for three main reasons. First, knowledge of whether a task (i.e., a specific desired outcome) has been successfully completed is gained only at the end of the processes involved in completing the task. At that point, it may be too late to promote those processes easily. The mourner already has or has not accomplished the task and, if not, must be urged to readdress the requisite processes. In contrast, viewing mourning in terms of processes rather than outcomes allows the caregiver to focus on what the mourner currently is doing, thus providing more immediate feedback and the grounds for intervention. Second, processes can be evaluated, monitored, and influenced throughout the mourning experience. As is the case for other developmental sequences, keeping the spotlight on processes rather than outcomes enhances the chance that any necessary intervention will be timely and effective. The processes themselves are the very targets of that intervention. Third, processes provide a useful checklist for evaluating the precise status of the mourner and assessing grief and mourning. For example, a focus on where the mourner is in his mourning can reveal where he is stuck before he has failed at the task toward which he was progressing. In summary, processes better operationalize mourning because, as compared to tasks, they offer the caregiver more immediate feedback, the ability to intervene more quickly and appropriately, the specific targets for intervention, and improved assessment of the mourner's current experience. In addition, they provide a conceptual and experiential base from which to understand mourning.

Table 2.3 lists the six "R" processes of mourning, which must be undertaken for a loss to be accommodated in a healthy fashion, and indicates their relationship to the three phases of grief and mourning. Although these processes are interrelated and tend to build upon one another, a number of them may occur simultaneously (e.g., the second, third, and fourth "R" processes, which occur in the Confrontation Phase, and the fifth and sixth "R" processes, which occur in the Accommodation Phase). In addition, some elements or subprocesses may occur in more than one phase. The sequence is not invariant, although the order does reflect the typical course for a majority of mourners. Mourners may move back and forth among the processes, with such movement illustrating the nonlinear and fluctuating course of mourning.

Recognize the Loss

If the mourner is to commence active mourning, she needs to acknowledge that the death has occurred. Initially, this acceptance is on an intellectual level, involving only recognition and concession of the fact of the death. It will take much longer to internalize this fact and accept it emotionally. This can occur only after repeated and painful confrontations with the loved one's absence, which begin with the mourner's cognitive admission that the death has occurred. If the world is to continue to maintain some order for the mourner, she will also have to attain some understanding of the reasons for that death.

Acknowledge the death

If the mourner does not acknowledge the reality of the death or its implications, then there is no need to grieve. By not admitting the death or its irreversibility, the mourner is able to construe the loss as a temporary absence which, although causing sadness due to separation, does not demand the same type of reorientation and readaptation as does death.

It is only natural for the mourner to resist acknowledgment that the loved one has died. No one wants to admit that someone she has loved is gone forever. The natural urge is to deny death's reality and avoid confronting it. This is why confirmation of the death is so important and why so much time, money, and effort are spent attempting to recover bodies after airplane crashes, boating accidents, earthquakes, and so forth.

In the absence of sufficient evidence to confront mourners with the death—which in most cases is the body of the loved one—they can postpone their mourning or rationalize it away. A high percentage of

Table 2.3 The Six "R" Processes of Mourning in Relation to the Three Phases of Grief and Mourning

AVOIDANCE PHASE

1. Recognize the loss

- Acknowledge the death

- Understand the death

CONFRONTATION PHASE

2. React to the separation

- Experience the pain

- Feel, identify, accept, and give some form of expression to all the psychological reactions to the loss

- Identify and mourn secondary losses

3. Recollect and reexperience the deceased and the relationship

- Review and remember realistically

- Revive and reexperience the feelings

4. Relinquish the old attachments to the deceased and the old assumptive world

ACCOMMODATION PHASE

5. Readjust to move adaptively into the new world without forgetting the old

- Revise the assumptive world

- Develop a new relationship with the deceased

- Adopt new ways of being in the world

- Form a new identity

6. Reinvest

mourners who experience complications either have not viewed the body or have failed to participate in funeral rituals. Nothing opposes their need to deny and avoid. Especially in situations of sudden, unexpected death, the substantiation of the loss through the viewing of the body (or some part of it) is an important psychological requirement for bringing home the truth, confronting understandable urges to deny, challenging disbelief, and commencing healthy mourning.

If the status of the loved one is unknown, the mourner is left in a sort of limbo. In this situation, the following types of questions may plague the mourner: Is my loved one alive or dead? Is he out there somewhere but unable to come home? Did the accident leave him with amnesia so he cannot find his way back to us? Does he need my help? and, Should I be looking for him? This manner of questioning and other difficulties are witnessed in families of missing children, as well as in those whose loved ones are missing in action in the military or presumed dead but whose bodies have not been recovered.

Sometimes just a small piece of confirmatory evidence can help a person go on about the business of mourning. One woman felt that her husband "most probably" had died on a canoeing expedition when his raft overturned. However, for many months she could not make any changes in herself, her house, or her life-style. Although she "sort of knew" in her head, she could not allow herself to mourn. She felt it would be tantamount to giving up on her husband. The following spring, a set of dentures found on the riverbank was identified as her husband's. Once she knew this, she could plan a memorial service, start to grieve actively, and begin to make changes in her life. Prior to this, the absence of any physical confirmation of the death had kept her mourning on hold.

Understand the death

In addition to acknowledging that the death has occurred, the mourner will have to come to some understanding of the reasons for it. These are not philosophical or religious reasons; rather, they concern the facts contributing to the death and the circumstances surrounding it. The explanation needs to make sense intellectually, but it does not necessarily have to be acceptable to the survivor. It merely means that the mourner understands the reasons for the events leading to the death and has an account that explains how, why, and under what conditions the death happened as it did. It makes no difference whether or not this explanation is in accord with anyone else's—only that it satisfy the mourner. For example, the man who refuses to believe his son died by suicide, insisting the death was an accident, has achieved a personally satisfactory understanding of his son's death, even though his refusal to believe the truth may have implications in other areas.

Without a context for understanding a loved one's death or some sort of rationale for it, a mourner tends to become anxious and confused, wondering about what happened to her loved one and what potentially could happen to her. The death of the beloved person shatters the mourner's sense of the world's meaning, orderliness, and predictability, making it difficult for her to recover from the loss. Parents who have a child die from Sudden Infant Death Syndrome, in which no specific cause of death can be determined, often have particular problems in this regard.

React to the Separation

Once the reality of the death has been recognized, the mourner must react to and cope with that reality. Responses to the recognition of the death of the loved one are myriad, and they will occur on all levels of functioning. To the extent that the mourner grants himself permission to experience and express these reactions appropriately, healthy mourning is promoted.

Experience the pain

If the loss is to be accommodated successfully, the mourner must experience the pain of separation and the vicissitudes of the mourning process. Like acute grief, pain may be experienced across all dimensions of human functioning: the psychological (including the spiritual), behavioral, social, and physical. The type, intensity, and duration of that pain will be different for each individual, determined by the unique constellation of factors associated with the mourner and the loss.

Throughout healthy mourning, the survivor makes numerous attempts to reverse the reality of the death to avoid pain (e.g., by efforts to search for and recover the deceased). Such attempts to avoid or minimize pain are understandable and natural. They are important because ultimately it is their failure to reverse the loss that helps the mourner come to accept it. These frustrated attempts bring much pain, as does the separation from the loved one. Mitigations are employed (e.g., avoidance of reminders or perceiving certain events as "messages" from the deceased). Respites and diversions permit distance and allow for replenishment, reconnection with other parts of life, and a renewed sense of control. All of these things are necessary if the mourner is to carry on with mourning work; face the loss; and avoid the debilitation of constant, unremitting pain. However, pain eventually must be felt.

Feel, identify, accept, and give some form of expression to all the psychological reactions to the loss

Unacknowledged and unexpressed emotion is a major precipitant of pathology. Therefore, it is important that the mourner overcome personal, social, cultural, ethnic, or religious resistances to the processing of all of the psychological reactions to the loss and its implications. To deal properly with these reactions, the mourner must (a) accept and cope on a conscious level with the entire array of positive, negative, intense, and often unfamiliar emotional responses associated with the loss; (b) identify, label, and differentiate among these responses (to make painful stimuli more manageable); promote source identification, psychological processing, and problem solving to render greater control; and (c) find personally comfortable and appropriate avenues of verbal and nonverbal expression.

Identify and mourn secondary losses

The mourner reacts not only to the initial loss of the loved one, but also to secondary losses occasioned by the death. This means recognizing and mourning such losses as the roles filled by the deceased; the interaction, validation, reinforcement, and gratification once provided by her; the unfulfilled needs, feelings, hopes, wishes, fantasies, dreams, assumptions, expectations, and beliefs that now exist in her absence; the assumptive world that has been violated with her death; the parts of the self that have died with her; and the many other psychosocial and physical losses that accrue to the death.

Some of these secondary losses will be immediately apparent (e.g., the loss of the loved one's companionship), whereas others will become recognizable only over time as the mourner learns to be in the world without the deceased (e.g., the loss of the loved one's unique support when the mourner experiences a conflict with a difficult supervisor at work). Each of these individual secondary losses prompts its own mourning and adds to the survivor's total mourning experience.

Recollect and Reexperience the Deceased and the Relationship

Depending on how pivotal the deceased was in the mourner's world, the mourner will have to make many changes to adapt to the loved one's physical absence. Over time, the mourner must discover new ways of relating to the deceased, the external world, and even herself. However, prior to this, the mourner must alter her emotional attachments to and investments in the loved one in order to make way psychologically for these subsequent changes.

Previously, it was believed that this detachment demanded a complete decathexis from the deceased. However, as conceptualized here, successful mourning does not require a complete withdrawal of emotional investment. Rather, a modification of it and a transformation of the relationship from one of presence to one of memory (Irion, 1966) must be effected. Although the mourner may have no recognition of its ultimate benefit later on in mourning, reminiscing about the deceased and the relationship is necessary for this eventual change to occur—and, ultimately, for healthy accommodation of the loss.

The processes of recollection and reexperience also help the mourner identify any unfinished business she may have with the deceased. Specifically, they assist her in beginning to discern what issues remain to be addressed. At some point, the mourner will need to find appropriate vehicles for achieving closure on this unfinished business.

Review and remember realistically

In healthy mourning, the deceased must be remembered realistically. This means that *all* aspects of the person and the mutual relationship must be recalled—all of the positives, negatives, and neutrals. The mourner must repeatedly review the entire relationship, the expectations and needs that initially formed it, its ups and downs, its course and development, its crises and joys—all elements of it throughout the years. As these events and features of the relationship unfold, the mourner can examine associated feelings and thoughts: negative ones, such as anxiety, ambivalence, and guilt, as well as more positive ones, such as satisfaction, happiness, and meaning. Only by repeatedly reviewing the unique relationship in its totality (i.e., all of its component parts with all of the emotional and cognitive aspects that accrue to them) will the mourner be able to identify the feelings and thoughts that need to be processed in order ultimately to alter her emotional attachment to and investment in the deceased.

The mourner may resist recognizing or processing negative feelings and thoughts associated with the deceased. These produce guilt, anxiety, regret, and a host of other uncomfortable reactions. Nevertheless, this resistance must be worked through if mourning is to be successful. Although initially it is typical for the bereaved to idealize the deceased, this tendency usually passes with time. The mourner becomes more realistic and can recall less-than-positive parts of the person and relationship and deal with these along with the positive ones. The complete person must be recollected in order to develop the accurate composite image of the loved one necessary for healthy mourning to occur.

Revive and reexperience the feelings

The mourner is tied to the deceased by thousands of attachment bonds. Among these are needs for that special person, the unique relationship, and the gratification and meaning they provided; feelings, thoughts, behavior and interaction patterns, hopes, wishes, fantasies, and dreams about that person and the mutual relationship; and a host of assumptions, expectations, and beliefs. All of these bonds sustain the attachment and contribute to the mourner's assumptive view of self and the world.

In mourning, the ties binding the mourner to the deceased must be untied. Understandably, the mourner may resist redirecting her energy toward this end. It is only over time, when it becomes increasingly apparent that holding on is useless and even harmful, that the mourner starts to let go of old attachments and ultimately develop new ones. This release can be accomplished only after the mourner repeatedly processes all of the ties to the deceased and the relationship. Specifically, this means that all the needs, feelings, thoughts, memories, behavior and interaction patterns, hopes, wishes, fantasies, dreams, assumptions, expectations, and beliefs—and the feelings associated with them—must be revived and re-experienced, if not in actuality, then in memory. In this way, the emotional charge of each is defused a little each time, and the affect accompanying it lessens in intensity. This causes the ties to loosen. As the mourner repeatedly goes through this process, the feelings bonding the ties are reduced sufficiently so that the strength of the former attachment decreases. The connective emotion is spent and no longer connects. Basically, this process involves the reversing and undoing of the processes that had gone into building the relationship (Raphael, 1983). Along with the frustration of the mourner's desire to reunite with the deceased, this process eventually helps prompt the mourner to relinquish the attachment.

Untying the ties does not mean that the deceased is forgotten or unloved. Rather, it means that the ties are modified to reflect the change that the loved one is now dead and cannot return the mourner's emotional investment or gratify her needs as before. A new relationship ultimately must be developed because the old one is unworkable. (The section on developing a new relationship with the deceased spells out this process.)

Relinquish the Old Attachments to the Deceased and the Old Assumptive World

Before the mourner can transform the previous relationship with the deceased into something more appropriate to the loved one's new status, he must relinquish old attachments to that person. In addition, he must surrender his attachments to his old assumptive world, constructed on the basis of the loved one's existence. Only when these old attachments are let go can new ones reflecting the reality of the death be established.

The *assumptive world* is an organized schema containing everything a person assumes to be true about the world and the self on the basis of previous experience. It consists of all the assumptions (including expectations and beliefs) the individual sustains, with most of these becoming virtually automatic habits of cognition and behavior. In large part, the assumptive world determines the individual's needs, emotions, and behavior, and gives rise to hopes, wishes, fantasies, and dreams. It is the internal model against which the person constantly matches incoming sensory data in order to orient self, recognize what is happening, and plan behavior (Parkes, 1988). As conceptualized in this book, the assumptive world is viewed as being fueled by the individual's experiences, memories, and needs, and confirmed through experiences, behavior and interaction patterns, and role relationships.

The notion of an assumptive world is similar to that of Kelly's (1955) theory of personal constructs, which involves an individual system of constructed interpretations of self and events in the world by which a person anticipates, organizes, and attributes meaning and sense. This conceptualization pertains in bereavement. Indeed, Woodfield and Viney (1984–1985) propose that it is the changes in the mourner's assumptive world that specifically account for the psychological states characteristic of widowhood—shock and numbness, stress, anger, anxiety, guilt, sadness, despair, hostility, idealization, depression, and psychological reorganization. These responses are viewed as arising in response to the widow's attempts to adapt to the dislocation of her personal construct system.

Two types of assumptions exist: global and specific. *Global assumptions* pertain to the self, others, life, or the world in general. The circumstances of the death and the very fact that it occurred may violate global assumptions (e.g., murder of a loved one may shatter assumptions of invulnerability and views of the world as being meaningful or may invalidate the belief that God protects the innocent). Aspects of the mourner's assumptive world are assaulted, and the mourner must respond in a fashion to reduce cognitive dissonance and the distress, insecurity, and lack of meaning the loss brings.

In addition, the death of a loved one always violates the mourner's *specific assumptions* about the loved one's continued interactive presence and violates the countless expectations the mourner held for that person's forming a significant part of the world (e.g., "She will be there for me always"). With the loss of the person comes the loss of unique gratification, resources, and meaning. Each of the ties the mourner has to the deceased is represented in his assumptive world. All of these particular needs, feelings, thoughts, behavior and interaction patterns, hopes, wishes, fantasies, dreams, assumptions, expectations, and beliefs associated with the person are invalidated by the death. The mourner must learn to be without the particular interaction, validation, reinforcement, and role-fulfilling behaviors previously existing in the relationship. To continue to sustain the now out-of-date assumptive world when there is no possibility for the deceased to gratify the mourner's wishes for her presence only keeps the mourner trapped in a world of frustration and failed hopes for the loved one's return.

Parkes (1988) notes how readjusting one's assumptive world is mandated in mourning by the loss of a loved one and how the loss constitutes a *psychosocial transition* (PST), or a psychological change that occurs whenever an individual is confronted with the need to undertake a major revision of assumptions or expectations about the world. Parkes discusses this in terms of the woman who has lost her spouse:

> The death of a spouse invalidates assumptions that penetrate
> many aspects of life, from the moment of rising to going to
> sleep in an empty bed. Habits of action (setting the table for

two) and thought ("I must ask my husband about that") must be revised if the survivor is to live as a widow. . . . Grief following bereavement by death is aggravated if the person lost is the person to whom one would turn in times of trouble. Faced with the biggest trouble she has ever had, the widow repeatedly finds herself turning toward a person who is not there.

[This example begins] to explain why PSTs are so painful and take so much time and energy. For a long time it is necessary to take care in everything we think, say, or do; nothing can be taken for granted any more. The familiar world suddenly seems to have become unfamiliar, habits of thought and behavior let us down, and we lose confidence in our own internal world. (Parkes, 1988, pp. 56–57)

Readjust to Move Adaptively Into the New World Without Forgetting the Old

With the release of old connections to both the deceased and the old assumptive world, the mourner is able to establish new connections appropriate to the changes that have ensued. In this "R" process, the individual takes steps to accommodate the loss. Accommodation transpires in the internal realm, with revised assumptions about the world, an altered relationship with the deceased, and the formation of a new identity. It also takes place in the external realm, with adaptations in behavior.

Contrary to prevailing myth, it is clear that, if the mourner meets several criteria, she can retain certain connections with the old world that need not compromise healthy adjustment in the new one. Indeed, the phrase "moving adaptively into the new world without forgetting the old" best describes what would be considered the ideal in mourning. The operative words here are *moving* (which presumes a lack of stasis and suggests carrying on, operating, functioning, or working in a fashion so as to advance or grow) and *adaptively* (which connotes a suitable adjustment to and accommodation of change). As used here, the phrase is taken to indicate action that is healthy, life-affirming, and life-promoting.

Revise the assumptive world

The mourner must revise the assumptive world, which has been violated with the death. The extent of modification necessary depends on (a) the deceased's centrality and importance in all of the realms of the mourner's life; (b) the type and number of roles he occupied; (c) the meaning he provided; (d) the patterns of interaction established; (e) the death and its circumstances and the degree to which they violate other needs, feelings, thoughts, behavior and interaction patterns, hopes, wishes, fantasies, dreams, assumptions, expectations, and beliefs; and (f) the number, type, and quality of secondary losses. The more fundamental and numerous the violations occurring with and because of the death, the more the mourner's assumptive world will require reconstruction. The more reconstruction required, the more the mourner must contend with additional grief reactions stimulated by the secondary loss of elements of the assumptive world and must deal with the anxiety, insecurity, vulnerability, and questioned meaning such reconstruction inevitably brings.

The new assumptive world probably will contain many elements from the prior one. Additional elements may be novel in all respects (e.g., "I cannot expect my husband to take care of me anymore. I must learn to do it on my own."), or they may meld former assumptions with current reality (e.g., "I was naive when I believed that God protects the good. Now I realize that you can be good and still get cancer and die. I still believe in God, but I no longer expect that being good assures me of protection from adversity.").

There are times when revision of the assumptive world happens rather rapidly. When this occurs, it is frequently in direct response to the death and any crises or secondary losses arising from it. The more rapid and comprehensive the change, the more shocking and problematic the experience is to the mourner. (This is one reason why a sudden, unexpected death is so much more difficult to accommodate than a natural, expected one.) However, even after a sudden death, for the majority of mourners the revision process occurs gradually, spurred on as various events teach the lesson that certain expectations, beliefs, needs for the loved one, patterns of interaction, and so forth are now inappropriate. Sometimes the changes happen so subtly that it is only when confronted by a specific experience that the mourner recognizes she has adopted a new expectation. Many of the reactions attributed to grief over the death actually are reactions to the secondary losses contingent on the destructuring of the assumptive world following the death, or they are responses arising from the mourner's attempts to adapt to the death through the inseparable processes of assimilation and accommodation (Woodfield & Viney, 1984–1985).

Develop a new relationship with the deceased

The development of a healthy new relationship with the deceased is a crucial part of the mourning process when the person lost has been integral to the mourner's life. This is perhaps the area in which mourners and caregivers alike are the most misinformed. Countless individuals have been told, or themselves have told others, that "healthy" grief and mourning require that the mourner "put the past behind" and "get on with life." Adherents to this belief advocate thinking about the deceased during the acute processes of grief but erroneously believe that to deal successfully with a major loss one ultimately must break all connection with the person who died. However, to many mourners, this notion is tantamount to forgetting or denying the importance of the loved one. Such action is unacceptable: They resist it and, in the attempt to find ways to maintain the link, often develop connections that are not in their best interests. I believe that nothing else accounts more for the development of pathological ties to the deceased (as evidenced, for example, in chronic mourning) than the mourner's nontherapeutic attempts to retain an understandably desired connection with a lost loved one.

Mourners and caregivers must recognize that it is not unnatural, pathological, or indicative of inability to deal with reality if an individual does not want to sever all connection to one she has held dear. Especially if this person has been extremely important and close, the wish to have a link even in that person's absence is quite understandable. Human beings are symbolic creatures. We do not need a concrete presence to have a relationship. As such, it is not uncommon, nor does it disregard reality, to want to keep a special place in one's life for a special person and to want at times to interact symbolically with that loved one. The question should not be, Is wanting to maintain a connection with a deceased loved one wrong? but rather, What is an appropriate connection and what conditions promote it?

Ongoing relationships with deceased individuals occur not only in societies where worship of the dead is in an intrinsic part of the culture (e.g., ancestor worship in the Orient), but in our society as well. For example, in the United States a continuing infatuation exists with John F. Kennedy, Marilyn Monroe, James Dean, and Elvis Presley. The memory of these persons is kept alive by national interest, review of their accomplishments, conjecture, and curiosity. Healthy individuals in our society also purchase posters, read books, watch documentaries, take courses, and use postage stamps and currency—all of which feature deceased individuals. Holidays are reserved for honoring the dead. We build churches, synagogues, and mosques as special places in which we communicate with, have rituals for, and venerate the dead.

Why then is there such concern when an individual mourner wants to maintain a connection with a deceased loved one? Why, when pondering a particular moral question, might an individual be encouraged to go to the library and look up the thoughts of some long-dead philosopher but be discouraged from reflecting on what her deceased father would think about the subject? Overconcern with "pathological hanging on" appears to be the cause. People are so intent on the mourner's avoiding an unhealthy connection with the deceased that they interfere with the development of a healthy one. Unfortunately, because such prohibitions typically go against the needs of the mourner, in many cases the result is the establishment of inappropriate ties and, in far too many cases, some form of complicated mourning. Ironically, the individuals most committed to preventing pathology often end up creating it.

Although death has ended the life of the person the mourner has loved, it does not necessarily end the relationship. The literature includes a number of articles documenting the following: timeless attachment to a dead relative (Goin, Burgoyne, & Goin, 1979), the relationship of the bereaved to the deceased as the best determinant of whether mourning has been resolved (Rubin, 1982, 1984–1985, 1985), the continuing relationship with a dead spouse (Shuchter & Zisook, 1988), aspects of the elderly widow or widower's persistent tie with a deceased spouse (Moss & Moss, 1984–1985), and a continuing sense of the deceased's presence either as a constant companion or in some specific and appropriate location as a common feature of healthy mourning (Bowlby, 1980).

Despite the fears of some to the contrary, one can have a relationship with a deceased person that is not pathological and does not interfere with healthy and appropriate engagement in ongoing life. Attig (1986) notes that a relationship with a deceased loved one can be healthy and life affirming if the mourner relinquishes the concrete love of a person who is physically present and replaces it with the abstract love for an absent loved one. I personally believe that such a relationship is healthy if it simultaneously meets two criteria. First, the mourner must truly recognize that the person is dead and fully understand the implications of the death (i.e., her expectations of and abstract interactions with the deceased must reflect knowledge of this fact). Second, the mourner must continue to move forward adaptively into the new life, as previously described.

For instance, there is nothing wrong with a widow's reflecting on what her deceased husband would do in a particular situation and then considering this alternative in deciding how she will act. However, the situation would be different if felt she must do things her husband's way. In the latter case, she would be giving her husband ongoing control over her in death. Because her attitude and behavior do not reflect the recognition that her husband no longer has this sort of power over her, her relationship with him is unhealthy. She has failed to withdraw her former emotional investment in him as a person who once had this power. And, to the degree that she feels she must do what he wants, she continues to act as if he still were alive. Thus, she has failed to meet the first criterion for a healthy relationship with a deceased loved one—she has not truly recognized the implications of the death (i.e., that her husband no longer has power over her). This same woman might fully recognize that her husband is dead and no longer attribute any power to him but fail to move forward in her life, preferring to live it precisely in the manner she did when she shared it with him, not making any required adaptations, and/or not living life in a healthy way (e.g., remaining in chronic mourning for the rest of her life). In this case, she would be violating the second criterion—that she move forward adaptively into her new life without the deceased. Caregivers must recognize that at times it may erroneously appear that a mourner has met both criteria but actually has failed to meet one or both.

The image of the deceased with which the mourner interacts in the new relationship must be as accurate as possible. The same review process that assists the mourner in changing her emotional investment in that person also aids her in developing a realistic image of him. The good and bad, the happy and sad, the fulfilling and the unfulfilling—all aspects of the person, relationship, and experience must be reviewed, felt, and integrated. Based on all of this, the mourner develops a composite image of the loved one, reconciling all the different aspects of his personality and reflecting accurately all she has known and experienced with that person. Unrealistic composite images are not helpful because the truth presses on the mourner for acknowledgment. In such instances, the mourner's ability to have a genuine relationship with the deceased is as compromised as if she related unrealistically to a living person.

Healthy, life-affirming, and life-promoting ways of relating to the deceased are not fixed or stagnant. For instance, the mourner must relate to the loved one in a manner that is age-appropriate and suited to the present. The connection should offer a link to the past but should not bind the mourner to it or keep her from growth in the present. This would be the case if, for example, an adult woman who was a little girl when her mother died continued to perceive herself as a little girl and relate in this way to her mother. A more appropriate response would be for the mourner to wonder about and try to learn about the mother from an adult perspective. It would not be unusual for the mourner's understanding of her mother to grow as she reinterprets things her mother said or did or perceives them in a different light. If she is open, the mourner may even learn from her mother after the death: "Now I realize how she must have felt when I fought with my baby brother. Since I've become the mother of three, I know what it is like to have to play referee so often. This is what she must have meant. Perhaps if I try to do what she did, I can handle this whole situation better."

In this way, a loved one may be a continuing influence on a mourner and thus be kept alive appropriately. As the mourner matures and has new experiences, her appreciation for the person may grow along with her awareness of the person's influence on her and, through her, on others. It is not uncommon for events later in life to illustrate to a mourner just how much she has taken from her loved one. For example, after a particularly awkward social situation, she may be surprised at just how well she has learned from observing the loved one to put people at ease. Such experiences can affirm the "aliveness" and ongoing meaning of the loved one.

In maintaining a healthy relationship, the mourner must decide how much of the old life and relationship with the loved one can and should be retained. For example, she may choose to keep certain routines they shared, such as taking a walk on Sunday morning or having a quiet snack before bed. She may decide to display mementos of their relationship, such as artwork purchased on family vacations. Some things from the old life and relationship will need to be relinquished, however. For example, unless the mourner wants to see just how bereaved she can feel, she probably would be wise not to go alone to the place she and her loved one used to go ballroom dancing as a couple. Thus, the mourner determines what she can continue to do from the past to feel close to the loved one in a healthy way—keeping the person alive in memory without interfering with her mourning or progress in life.

It is not at all uncommon for healthy mourners to be connected to the deceased through hallucinatory experiences, a sense of the deceased's presence, and communication in the form of reviewing important events, asking for guidance about a problem, or prayer. Actively recalling memories, exposing oneself to memorabilia and other stimuli eliciting a sense of connection with the deceased (e.g., a special song or certain location), and dreaming are other ways in which mourners maintain and nourish their relationship with lost loved ones.

The mourner also can maintain a connection with the deceased through identification. Identification is a normal part of development and, in appropriate amounts, is not harmful. In fact, it is by identifying with significant others early in life that we take on many of the characteristics that make us who we are. Identification with the deceased occurs first as a way of perpetuating the mental image of the loved one to avoid feeling the pain of loss. By temporarily preserving the loved one, identification allows the mourner to work at the process of withdrawing and modifying emotional ties without being overwhelmed. Later, it helps to conserve the lost object while adding to the ego, thereby contributing to the enrichment of the personality. Just as the ego is constructed in childhood by the processes of incorporation of and identification with others, so the mourner's identity may be changed through identification with the deceased. Thus, through identification, the mourner can keep the loved one with her and expand her own identity. This can happen consciously or unconsciously and is healthy as long as the mourner's actions are appropriate to adult functioning and compatible with other roles. It is also important that identification not occur in areas where the mourner lacks competence, not happen too intensely, and not cause the mourner to lose a sense of personal identity.

Appropriate identification may take place in many ways. For example, the mourner may alter her personality and her sense of herself slightly by taking on the deceased's values, acting on some of his concerns, adopting some of his mannerisms, or feeling as he would have felt about certain issues. She may adopt some of his preferences, engage in some of his favorite activities, or take to quoting his little sayings. However, when incorporation and identification become ways to avoid appropriately experiencing the loss and relinquishing the loved one, the process has become complicated. A problem also can exist when the mourner has not differentiated herself appropriately from the deceased prior to the death.

In such an instance, she will be unable to relinquish the deceased because to do so would mean losing a primary part of herself.

Another way in which a loved one can be kept alive is through ritual. Participating in rituals provides the mourner with an opportunity to interact intensely with the memory of the loved one, as well as to do something symbolic in the loved one's name. Rituals include anniversary celebrations, specific commemorations or memorials, and symbolic activities related to the deceased—all of which provide connection and a way of relating to the loved one. Rituals do not have to be dramatic to serve this purpose. Some are simple and routine, such as mentioning the loved one at grace before meals; others are less frequent, such as perusing the family photograph album. (See chapter 7 for more discussion on the topic of therapeutic bereavement rituals.)

Tangible objects such as photographs, mementos, articles of clothing, or jewelry also may help keep the memory of the loved one alive and be a symbolic mark of his existence. So too can the deceased's creations (e.g., a painting or letter) or symbols of the relationship (e.g., the home that was shared). Not only may such objects stimulate recollection, their physical presence may represent the loved one's abstract presence in the mourner's life. These items are to be differentiated from linking objects (Volkan, 1972, 1981), which have a clearly pathological purpose. Certainly, the surviving family and/or social group of which the deceased was a part can be both a vehicle for, as well as an arena of, healthy continued symbolic existence of the deceased.

Finally, the most effective way of keeping a loved one alive is through one's own life and actions. In other words, because the mourner continues to exist despite the death, the loved one's influence continues through the mourner. In this fashion, children continue their parents' legacy by carrying on and embodying what their parents gave them. Ways of continuing the loved one's influence include talking about the loved one; acting on his values and concerns; thinking about him; considering his beliefs, feelings, and perspectives on matters when actions are necessary; enjoying and appreciating life because of having known, loved, and been influenced by him; and being and acting the person one is because of what one shared in the relationship.

Adopt new ways of being in the world

To be healthy, over the long term the mourner cannot continue to behave in the ways she did when the loved one was alive. She must begin to act in accordance with the fact that the loved one has died and must become accustomed to the new world without the deceased and move into it in ways that reflect the fact that he is no longer present as before. This entails the mourner's finding ways to fulfill needs the deceased previously had filled (i.e., meeting the need herself, finding someone else to meet the need, or determining other ways of getting the need met) or, alternatively, changing the desire for what is wanted or needed that is now unfulfilled with the death. For example, an individual mourning the death of her husband might meet a need once fulfilled by him by taking care of her own home maintenance, or she might find someone else to fill a psychosocial need once met by him by talking about her stress with her sister, with whom she has developed a closer relationship since the death. In her husband's absence, she might meet her need to be special to someone by volunteering as a buddy to a person with AIDS. In changing her desire for a need now unfulfilled with the death, the mourner may decide that she will be celibate until she can tolerate the idea of sexual activity with someone else.

To compensate for the loved one's absence and the loss of patterns of interaction and role-fulfilling behaviors, the mourner often must adopt new roles, skills, behaviors, and relationships. If mourning is healthy, and depending upon the previous involvement of the deceased in her life, the mourner will change in many different ways. She does not necessarily have to change aspects of her life that did not relate to the loved one because they are not directly affected by his absence, although they may be affected by the mourner's other personal changes as a consequence of it. Ways of behaving that did involve the deceased must be modified to reflect the reality of his absence. These changes in turn alter the mourner: She may gain new aspects (e.g., feel more competent because she has mastered new skills), lose old ones (e.g., shed passivity), and/or modify the ones she retains (e.g., recognize that she can have a career and be a good parent simultaneously).

Form a new identity

With a new assumptive world, a new relationship with the deceased, and the acquisition of new skills, behaviors, roles, and relationships, the mourner is no longer the same person she used to be. Her image of herself must change to reflect this reality. Also, part of this need for a new self-image concerns the fact that, in very close relationships, the interactions we have with loved ones help define our sense of self and identity. The part of the woman that was wife to the husband, the part of the man that was son to the father—these interactional selves contribute to an individual's unique personhood. When the husband dies, so too does the part of the woman that was a wife. Even if one day the woman marries again, it will be a new relationship. The part of her that was created in and validated by the relationship with the first husband no longer exists in reality, although it may continue on in memory. When coupled with the significant losses that may be sustained in the external and assumptive worlds, it is easy to see how much of the crisis of bereavement for the mourner actually stems from the loss of so much of the self.

The mourner's identity transforms slowly as she undergoes the gradual process of going from a "we" to an "I." A personal reorientation is mandated. To compensate for the losses of the loved one and the interactional self formed by the lost relationship, many changes take place. Some derive from gain (i.e., new roles, skills, behaviors, relationships, and aspects of the assumptive world are taken on). Some are the result of loss (i.e., certain hopes, expectations, experiences, attitudes, and ways of being are relinquished). Some are modifications and blendings of what was before. That which is changed (both positively and negatively) must be recognized and mourned, that which continues must be affirmed, and that which is new must be incorporated. The old and the new selves must be integrated. All of these changes in the internal and external worlds contribute to a new self and bring into being a new identity. However, movement is slow and halting, with many false starts and regressions.

Reinvest

It is unhealthy for an individual to lack appropriate and rewarding investments in life. Consequently, the emotional energy once invested in the relationship with the deceased eventually must be reinvested where it can be returned to the mourner. Some of this energy will be used in the new relationship with the loved one, but much more will require redirection. The relationship with the deceased should not sap all of the mourner's emotional resources—this would constitute a failure to meet the two criteria for a healthy relationship. Therefore, the emotional energy that had been directed toward the preservation and maintenance of the former relationship with the loved one must be redirected toward rewarding new investments in other people, objects, roles, hopes, beliefs, causes, ideals, goals, pursuits, and so forth. Although these new attachments definitely will not replace the loved one—no one and nothing can take that person's place—they can provide the mourner with the emotional gratification lost when the loved one died. The reinvestment need not be in a person having the same role as the one from whom energy was withdrawn. For example, a widower does not have to remarry to reinvest his emotional energy. He can do so by undertaking volunteer work or returning to school. The sole requirement is that he have an emotionally gratifying person, object, belief, or activity into which to put his energy and from which he receives satisfaction in return.

PERSPECTIVES ON THE DURATION AND COURSE OF MOURNING

Probably the most frequently asked questions about grief and mourning concern duration. Despite paying lip service to the notion that everyone's mourning is individual and that a complex of factors affect duration and course, almost everyone—from the mourner herself, to students, to care-givers, to media reporters—invariably returns to the question, How long does mourning take? Even when informed that the answer depends on the unique constellation of factors that determines any mourning response, the person posing the question often persists: "Yes, I realize that you would need much more information to be specific. Why don't you just give me a ballpark range?"

The search goes on for a limit, for a guidepost, for anything that can help to concretize this strange, intense, ambiguous, often unmanageable experience of mourning. Although the desire for an answer—a boundary for normalcy—is understandable, the caregiver must resist such a seduc-tion. Without sufficient information, it is wise to refrain from a specific response. Reasserting the complexity of the question will help the ques-tioner achieve a more genuine appreciation of the variability of the mourn-ing processes.

Certainly, the caregiver can point out that acute grief reactions *typically* end relatively early on within the six "R" processes of mourning. The care-giver also might stress that, depending on how mourning per se is concep-tualized, it may persist for years and, in some cases and in some ways, go on forever as subsequent life situations evoke aspects of the lost relationship.

The noted authors George Pollock and Lorraine Siggins comment separately on how, in some aspects, mourning continues forever:

> Sporadic episodes of mourning may still occur in connection with specific events or items, but these become fewer and less time-concentrated. New mourning experiences can serve to revive past mourning reactions that may still have bits of unresolved work present. In the instance of the loss of a very significant object, the total mourning process may never be completed. (Pollock, 1961, p. 354)

> Eventually [the mourning] process may be regarded as effectively complete. Yet in another sense mourning is never really over, for new life-situations may appear at any time which evoke for the mourner aspects of the lost relationship insignificant at the time of bereavement. For instance, this occasional resumption of mourning often occurs amongst those who lose a parent early in adolescence, but later become acutely aware of the parent's absence during the crises of later adolescence, when previously unexploited aspects of the remembered relationship assume a newly recognized importance. (Siggins, 1966, p. 18)

Note that neither author views continued mourning as necessarily pathological. This is not to say that unequivocal demonstrations of impaired functioning, complicated mourning, or recognized mental or physical disorders should be minimized, overlooked, or inappropriately depatholo-gized. What must be avoided is interpretation of the appropriateness of the duration of mourning or one of its manifestations in the absence of the data necessary to yield an accurate diagnosis (i.e., information on the unique constellation of factors associated with the mourner and the loss).

In fact, recent research has suggested that uncomplicated grief and mourning often persist much longer than believed, with some symptoms continuing for many years after the death (Zisook, DeVaul, & Click, 1982; Zisook & Shuchter, 1985, 1986). It is becoming increasingly evident that uncomplicated grief and mourning reactions can remain present for long periods of time without signifying pathology. Obviously, such data call into question the use of duration alone as a variable defining complicated mourning.

Despite the widespread societal, and unfortunately often clinical, myth that grief and mourning decline in a linear fashion over time, this simply is not the case. Grief and mourning fluctuate significantly over time and are affected by a host of variables that can augment or decrease their manifestations, as well as influence how specific responses may interact. For example, at certain times in the acute grief process, anger may be highly prominent; at others, the precedence of guilt may diminish the salience of anger as an issue. Because grief and mourning are processes, the mourner can be expected to undergo many changes and transitions. There will be changing prioritization of issues, concerns, and reactions. To treat either process as if it were a static state is to do a major disservice to the mourner.

Research also has corroborated that the intensity of grief and mourn-ing does not steadily decline over time. In an investigation with bereaved parents whose children had died of cancer, Rando (1983) initially found that 78 percent of the bereavement symptoms measured diminished from Year 1 to Year 2 after the death. However, they rose again during Year 2 to Year 3! Similar variations from the expected diminution in bereavement responses have been found by Levav (1982) and Fish (1986). For instance, Fish found some reactions in bereaved mothers (e.g., anger, guilt, and social isolation) to be higher after 2 years of bereavement. After 5 years, the intensities diminished to levels only slightly below those of the first 2 years (except in loss of control, which was higher, and rumination, which was significantly lower). In contrast, bereaved fathers showed a steady decrease in seven out of nine categories after 2 years and a decrease in all categories after 5 years. Clearly, before their responses become less dis-crepant, bereaved parents must contend with increased discrepancy, especially in the second through fourth years after the death. Such find-ings are important not only in dispelling myths about mourning but in forewarning bereaved individuals, who can benefit from this knowledge.

Another striking example of fluctuation in grief and mourning responses is commonly witnessed in reactions to sudden, unexpected death, as well as in some cases of anticipated death. Frequently, a mourner whose loved one has died without warning experiences acute grief after the loss. He then establishes what he perceives as a new equilibrium in coping. However, it is a false equilibrium, which usually is unbalanced somewhere around the sixth to ninth month after the death. Although this time period will vary according to individual circumstances, it is generally the point at which the mourner experiences an intensification of symptoms. The experience is quite disheartening, and the mourner may imagine himself to be regressing, losing his mind, or going out of control. Actually, three phenomena are occurring. One is that the mourner is emerging from the psychological and physiological daze he has been in during the early months following the death. Now that everyday life is recommencing and outside support is waning, the mourner is confronted with the loss in striking and unexpected ways that poignantly bring home its full measure. This may happen, for example, the first time the loved one is absent at the holidays or when the mourner struggles all alone to dress his little daughter in her Easter finery. Or it may happen when the mourner realizes he is having difficulty recalling his loved one's voice or picturing her in a room. Sometimes it happens when the family routine settles down enough to reflect the absence of the missing family member. Although the mourner may conclude erroneously that he is backsliding, in fact, he is only experiencing the loss and his reactions to it more strongly than ever. A second and related reason for the increase in distress can be found when the mourning response is observed as a form of the stress response syndrome (Horowitz, 1986a). In this scenario, denial creates a latency phase before the mourner experiences the onset of an intrusive phase. The symptomatology comes as a major surprise to this person, who believes himself to have "mastered" the event to a certain extent. Finally, this upsurge of symptomatology is also related to the mourner's abandonment of active searching for the deceased. The mourner's acute symptoms of grief escalate in response to his new observations about the permanence and finality of the loss. If Bowlby's (1980) notion of disbelief rather than denial is taken and the demise of disbelief is accepted as a casualty of the cessation of active searching, this view and Horowitz's may be seen as quite congruent. In both of these cases, when disbelief (or as Horowitz terms it, denial) is no longer maintained, the mourner confronts reality and its associated distressing affective, cognitive, behavioral, social, and somatic intrusions. These intrusions create, as well as manifest, other affective, cognitive, behavioral, social, and somatic concomitants and sequelae.

Such fluctuations in grief and mourning occur over both the short and long term. For instance, even an acutely bereaved individual cannot grieve 24 hours a day; grief sometimes must be suppressed for the ongoing demands of living. Depending upon the particular factors influencing the mourner at the time, some ups or downs will be longer than others (e.g., for a few weeks or months as opposed to a few hours).

SUBSEQUENT TEMPORARY UPSURGES OF GRIEF

A wide variety of circumstances can produce subsequent temporary upsurges of grief, or STUG reactions, long after a death. These are brief periods of acute grief for the loss of the loved one, which are catalyzed by a precipitant that underscores the absence of the deceased and/or resurrects memories of the death, the loved one, or feelings about the loss. Because complicated mourning is frequently defined as a prolongation of uncomplicated mourning, caregivers must appreciate the fact that, even many years after a death, mourners may commonly experience intense grief reactions. Too often, healthy and understandable STUG reactions have been misdiagnosed as pathological responses.

Although the majority of STUG reactions are part of uncomplicated mourning, it is important to note that such reactions can and sometimes do indicate unfinished or complicated mourning. A STUG reaction appropriate under one set of conditions may not be appropriate under another. On occasion, the symptoms, behaviors, or reactions will indeed represent unresolved aspects of the loss or pathological responses to it, or will contribute to undue pathology, distress, or dysfunction. By the same token, at times STUG reactions can help finish the unfinished business that remains in complicated mourning. In brief, the healthiness of a STUG reaction depends upon the following five factors.

1. The particular precipitant of the STUG reaction

2. The nature, duration, and intensity of the STUG reaction

3. The impact the STUG reaction has on the mourner and on her mourning and functioning

4. The impact of any coping or defense mechanisms summoned to contend with the STUG reaction

5. The unique constellation of factors influencing the mourner's response to the loss at that point in time

Current Thoughts on STUG Reactions

Despite the claims of previous authors that occurrences such as anniversary reactions reflect complicated mourning, recent writings suggest that they are not uncommon at all, but actually are expectable to a significant degree. Rosenblatt (1983), in examining the entries of 19th-century diarists to evaluate and amplify contemporary theories of grief and mourning, found that mentions of anniversary reactions were second only in frequency to the initial mention of the loss. Rosenblatt remarks that grief processes, like other thought processes, are linked to external events and persons and can be stimulated by them. This means that new or intensified grief can be sparked by reminders that elicit memories, ideas, and behavior patterns not previously detached fully from the deceased. He also notes that there are cognitive sources of discontinuity in grief work because not all hopes and memories will be salient at any one time and because life is too brief, memory too fallible, and consciousness too limited in scope for a mourner to disconnect within a short period of time all memories and hopes from the deceased. Consequently, grief will be resurrected periodically as fresh memories and hopes that have not been dealt with are encountered through reminders such as birthdays, anniversaries, holidays, significant family events, and so forth—each of which may bring with it a realization that could not have been understood before of what was lost.

Rosenblatt's arguments draw out those proposed by Johnson and Rosenblatt (1981), which differentiate *maturational grief* from *incomplete grief*. The former is grief arising from maturational events such as life-cycle milestones and from new experiences. This type of grief occurs in the presence of specific events or realizations that relate in some way to an earlier death but have not been carried directly forward since the time of that loss. Because the possibilities for encountering situations that may trigger temporary grief responses are vast, maturational grief is seen as universal for bereaved persons. In contrast, incomplete grief has continuity with the grief experience immediately after a loss. In such cases, acute grief persists with resistance to the formation of new relationships or to other major changes in behavior and often is accompanied by guilt, distortion of perception or memory, or feelings of inadequate closure. There are frequent surges of intense feeling, a sense of searching for the lost one, and obsessive attention to the loss. At times, the two types of grief are indistinguishable. However, treating maturational grief as though it were incomplete grief may be inappropriate and unproductive—perhaps even harmful, given the deleterious sequelae possible after misdiagnosis of pathology.

More recent support for the appropriateness of much subsequently experienced grief comes from Brabant (1989–1990), who argues that the onset of intense pain years after a loss actually may be a new response to a totally new loss. This new loss presents the mourner with aspects of the old loss not previously experienced (e.g., a special day or occasion on which the mourner would almost certainly have interacted with the deceased and that presents the mourner with a new loss that must be experienced, responded to, and resolved). Although the bereaved person may have anticipated the new loss intellectually, the existential loss can occur only at the point of action. It is the experiential loss that triggers the acute grief response. For instance, the bereaved parent loses the graduating senior (new loss) this year even though the child died 4 years ago at age 14. The child would have graduated this year if he had lived. Apropos of the new loss, the mourner grieves for the presently experienced loss of the high school senior, not the original loss per se. Thus, the response is not an anniversary reaction to an old loss, but a response to a new loss evoked by new pain.

Precipitants of STUG Reactions

As with any grief response, a STUG reaction may be manifested within the psychological, behavioral, social, and/or physical realms. Some of these responses may be welcomed because they signify that the deceased has not been forgotten or that the mourner is not unmoved by the loss. Other reactions may be dreaded and avoided. Some mourners fear that the reexperience of acute grief symptoms means that they are regressing or, worse still, that they will have to undergo all of their acute grief again. Clearly, meanings will be different for each mourner, and caregivers must attempt to understand these meanings. Clinically, it is not uncommon for mourners to be unaware of the precipitant of a STUG reaction or to be oblivious to its connection to the loss until it is pointed out.

As noted in Table 2.4, three main classes of STUG reaction precipitants exist, encompassing 14 categories. Some STUG reactions could legitimately fit into several of these categories. For example, a STUG reaction at Thanksgiving could be classified as a holiday reaction, a ritual-prompted reaction, a memory-based reaction, or, depending upon the anniversary dates and/or ages of the parties involved, an anniversary or age-correspondence reaction. Also, STUG reactions may combine with one another. For example, a woman might have a STUG reaction 5 years after her mother's death when she attends her cousin's wedding (ritual-prompted reaction) and hears the song "Mama" (reminder-inspired reaction). However, for ease of discussion, each category is briefly discussed independently of the others.

Cyclic precipitants

In this class are reactions that imply periodicity of the precipitant. Most individuals automatically think of yearly anniversaries in this regard; however, this is but one group of these reactions. The important element in this class is the expectation that the occasion will come again. The cycle may be of any duration—for example, every 4 years (e.g., at the time of the Presidential elections), annually (e.g., Mother's Day or a birthday), monthly (e.g., on the first of the month or at the full moon), weekly (e.g., on a Wednesday), daily (e.g., at dusk or noon), and so forth. Each of these categories involves a continual, repeated, cyclic rhythm of events.

Just as grief and mourning do not automatically decline linearly with time, neither do these cyclic events necessarily pass with the same or less distress. The changing context of the individual's life and mourning may on one occasion intensify the experience and on another lessen it. For instance, the mourner may fare better at the first anniversary than at the second.

Table 2.4 Classification of STUG Reactions According to Precipitants

Cyclic Precipitants

Anniversary reactions

Holiday reactions

Seasonal reactions

Ritual-prompted reactions (repetitive)

Linear Precipitants

Age-correspondence reactions

Experience-associated reactions

Transition-stimulated reactions

Developmentally determined reactions

Crisis-evoked reactions

Ritual-prompted reactions (single event)

Stimulus-Cued Precipitants

Memory-based reactions

Reminder-inspired reactions

Loss and/or reunion theme–aroused reactions

Music-elicited reactions

He may be prepared to experience great emotion and have significant support available. In addition, he still may be in some amount of shock and may focus attention on steeling himself to get through all the "firsts" rather than on experiencing the feelings that can accompany them. Although at the second anniversary the mourner may not experience as much fear, he may feel more pain. The loss usually cannot be denied as it could be the year before. The first time was novel; the second marks an ongoing and unchangeable reality, the awareness of which can bring additional agony and despair. Also, the expectation typically is that the reaction this time will be less intense. Often the mourner is shocked when this is not the case, which only adds to his emotional distress, fuels his fears that he will never be able to master the loss, and presents him with yet one more violation of his assumptive world. Finally, there usually is less support available at second and subsequent anniversaries—some people may even already have forgotten. Sometimes a particular anniversary may be problematic even years after relatively calm ones because it may coincide with other issues or other STUG reactions. Clearly, the caregiver needs to assess on an ongoing basis fluctuations in grief within the context of the mourner's life experience.

It is common for mourners to report that the anticipation of an upcoming cyclic event (e.g., Thanksgiving) is more stressful than the actual day. Caregivers can be quite helpful in sharing this information with mourners. The intent should not be to dismiss mourners' anxious suffering but to normalize it and afford a perspective to help them manage it. This phenomenon is not uncommon with the other types of precipitants, although it is less frequent.

Anniversary reactions. In the literature and in thanatological discussion, the term *anniversary reaction* has been a catchall for a variety of STUG phenomena, of which only some are stimulated by an actual anniversary date. As addressed here, these reactions are restricted to those stimulated by (a) a specific correspondence between the present and the time of loss (e.g., the first-year anniversary of a diagnosis or the second-month anniversary of the death) or (b) some periodic event (e.g., the Harvest Dance or the Army-Navy football game), occurrence (e.g., the first snowfall or migration of the birds), or special date (e.g., the birth date of the deceased or the date the mourner became engaged). As noted previously, the time periods can range from decades to days. Caregivers cannot assume which dates are most significant or meaningful for mourners or to which ones they will be the most reactive. For one, the date of the death may be more painful; for the other, the date of the loved one's birth may evoke the strongest response. Hence caregivers must inquire directly.

Holiday reactions. Many mourners fear going through the holidays without their loved one even more than approaching a particular anniversary. So great is this concern that bereavement support groups invariably make practical suggestions for coping with the holidays. National and local talk shows, magazine columns, and newspaper stories address the issue, and caregivers of all types hear about the building anxiety.

Holidays are the days on which the mourner is most reminded of the loss by the painful absence of the beloved person. In our society, the expectation is that loved ones gather harmoniously during the holidays. This expectation burdens many individuals, not just those who are mourning. Holiday programs, greeting cards, rituals, and social and work schedules fill the holiday season with unrealistic and unattainable expectations for intimacy, closeness, relaxation, and joy. Added to this are emotional, social, and financial pressures and demands, along with the depression, fatigue, and increased intake of alcohol, sugar, and other foods. Finally, the holiday season's nostalgia for "the good old days" (which may not really have been that good but become warmed in memory) creates a context that often inhibits rational thinking.

This, then, is the emotional and expectational set in which the mourner finds herself at the very time she is deprived of the presence of a dearly beloved one. Longing and separation pain are often made much worse by this situation. Holidays are the times when some mourners will begin to recognize most clearly the absence of the deceased and to learn the reality of the death. If the mourner and deceased lived apart, the holidays may have been one of the few times they would be together. Even if they lived close by, these times may have been among the most intense. As anniversaries of the times loved ones have been together and as occasions around which memories are made, holidays can thus be particularly poignant. It is not surprising that STUG reactions often take place at these times. Specific information about helping mourners handle the holidays is provided in Conley (1986) and Rando (1988), as well as in relevant publications provided by most national bereavement self-help groups and by many funeral directors.

Seasonal reactions. STUG reactions often are triggered by the seasons or particular events associated with them. Of course, what a particular season represents or triggers for one mourner may be different than for another. Therefore, even though the examples provided in the following discussion may be typical, in no way should they be considered exhaustive.

Spring is inordinately difficult for mourners. As one widow remarked in April, "I hate to see the flowers come up." This is the season of rebirth and new life. However, there is no new life for the deceased. The coming alive after the darkness of winter, the excitement of everything from love to baseball, and the jubilant plans made for the time of good weather contrast starkly with the experience of the individual struggling to cope with a death. The discrepancy between the mourner's feelings and those, apparently, of the rest of the world can be excruciating. Indeed, this contrast may in part explain why this time of year has the highest suicide rate of all. Many of the same dynamics that give rise to this statistic operate for the mourner as well.

Fall also can prove problematic. This is especially evident in September, traditionally the beginning of the school year and often perceived as a time of new beginnings even by adults long out of school. Parents mourning deceased children often find themselves experiencing STUG reactions as they witness preparation for school without their beloved child. Because school and play are a child's work, this time can be particularly poignant for bereaved parents, siblings, and peers. Sometimes they are not even aware of the reason for their feelings. As one bereaved mother remarked in mid-September, "I don't know why I've been so irritable and cranky these last few weeks." Holidays focusing on children—for example, Christmas and Hanukkah—share some of these same dynamics, although the reason or distress at these times is more commonly understood by mourners.

Sometimes late October, but usually mid- to late November and early December, may be quite painful to mourners and initiate STUG reactions. To quote one middle-aged man mourning the death of his sister, "It's like death is all around. I've become quite depressed lately. It's so dark and gloomy." These months are not only the harbingers of the holidays, they are also associated with the turning back of the clock, the shortening of days, and the coming of winter. In addition, these are the months known to precipitate the medical condition recently identified as Seasonal Affective Disorder, or SAD. It appears that the approach of the winter solstice and the short, dark days of winter leave some individuals feeling sad and depressed, with numerous psychosocial and physical symptoms, until spring brings longer, sunny days. SAD occurs in those not necessarily bereaved and may be an additional burden to those who are. Regardless of the existence of this disorder, there is a "death-y" feel that contrasts with the more pleasant, warm, and colorful fall. Thus, mourning for one's own dead may be stimulated by the symbolic death occurring in nature. It also can be fueled by the celebration of our contemporary holiday of Halloween, which still carries some remnants of ancient rituals for the dead.

Although STUG reactions may occur throughout the entire year, I have observed a greater number during spring and fall. At least three possible explanations for this exist. First, it may be that times of transition "hook" unresolved issues in human beings. To the extent that there is rarely total closure on mourning for a dearly loved person, periods of transition may serve as catalytic agents, just as crises have growth-producing potential despite the distress they cause. Second, the mourner's responses to change and advancing time may play a role. (See the subsequent discussion of transition-stimulated reactions for more on this issue.) Third, factors associated with the life-and-death aspects of these two seasons may be involved. The cyclic pattern of loss, death, and renewal prompts awareness of mortality and can potentiate mourning not only in winter, the season of symbolic death, but in spring, the season of symbolic life, given that life is intimately connected to death and being its obverse. Both seasons can potentiate mourning, even among those who have accommodated their loss fairly well.

Ritual-prompted reactions (repetitive). As noted in chapter 7, a ritual is a specific behavior or activity giving symbolic expression to certain feelings and thoughts. Rituals are part of everyday activities, events, and interaction patterns, as well as of periodic and once-in-a-lifetime happenings. There are two major types: rituals of transition and rituals of continuity. Rituals of transition are one-time occurrences involving rites of passage (e.g., a funeral or wedding) and focusing on change within the individual or subsystem, not within an entire group. Because they are not repetitive, they are discussed along with other linear precipitants. Rituals of continuity occur within a particular stage of the family's life cycle and are aimed at maintaining and confirming the stability of family life within that stage (van der Hart, 1983). They directly influence the entire group. Rituals of continuity may occur daily, weekly, annually, and so forth. They include telectic rites (i.e., acts undertaken when someone arrives or leaves, such as shaking hands on arrival or wishing someone well on departure) and intensification rites (i.e., collective ritualistic activities often coinciding with changes in natural surroundings, which intensify and tune the interactions of persons within the group, such as the communal evening meal).

Innumerable repetitive, secular rituals take place in everyday life. Such rituals include communal mealtime, Sunday dinner at Grandmother's, reading a story before bedtime, kissing family members before retiring for the night, playing cards on Saturday nights, having a cup of tea and discussing the day's events, and countless others. Other typical family rituals that take place less frequently include monthly trips to the library, Thanksgiving dinners, family reunions, summer picnics, vacations at the seashore, and so forth.

Experiencing a ritual in the absence of a deceased loved one may trigger a STUG reaction if that ritual had been a part of the relationship with the loved one or highlights what now is missing. Indeed, repeatedly in the Confrontation Phase of acute grief and less frequently thereafter, it is the mourner's experience of ritual in the absence of the deceased that teaches him that the deceased is in fact truly gone and, in the situation of healthy mourning, that accommodations will have to be made to reflect this reality. Initial confrontations with rituals without the deceased tend to prompt STUG reactions. So, too, can confrontations with rituals long after the death.

Linear precipitants

This grouping refers to STUG reactions stimulated by experiences, phenomena, and events that occur as a consequence of reaching a particular time, age, or state. These types involve the progression of time in a linear sense. There is no repetition or cycle implied; these reactions are related to one-time occurrences.

Another way of looking at this grouping is to note that its components give rise to so-called late-occurring grief reactions. These reactions are occasioned by experiences, phenomena, and events following the death that lend importance to aspects of the loss that may have been insignificant when the loved one died. In other words, the mourner has encountered something in her present life that brings home in a new way the fact that she is deprived of the deceased. The loved one's absence is particularly difficult to cope with at these times.

Age-correspondence reactions. Numbers are potent stimuli in bereavement, as they can be in other areas of psychic life. In this regard, coincidences are many times interpreted as related events, which the individual invests with significance (e.g., one family member died in 1975 and another died in 1985, so the mourner fears that another one will die in 1995). Similar beliefs may be associated with time (e.g., "knowing" that someone will die in August because other family members have died in that month); events (e.g., moving into a new home becomes associated with tragedy after the death of someone who had just moved); or age (e.g., the mourner cannot feel comfortable until the new baby passes the age at which another baby died).

The term *age-correspondence reaction* was coined by Birtchnell (1981) to describe the phenomenon of psychiatric breakdown occurring when a mourner reaches the age a parent was at death or when the mourner's child reaches the age of the mourner when a parent or significant other died. The empirical research has been mixed with regard to this phenomenon. Hilgard and Newman (1959) described the age-correspondence reaction and noted that in their sample it occurred frequently. According to Birtchnell, Hilgard and Newman misleadingly used the term *anniversary reaction*, which he feels should be reserved for incidents associated with intensification of mourning occurring in response to an anniversary of a significant event and not to a one-time occurrence that represents an age correspondence. Birtchnell finds a true age-correspondence phenomenon to be uncommon, despite observing that it can account in some measure for the time of onset and clinical characteristics observed in some reactions. I myself have observed that the age-correspondence phenomenon is not uncommon if one takes a broader perspective, analyzing other reactions besides psychiatric breakdown and looking at losses of significant figures other than parents. These other reactions include not only STUG reactions, but also the phenomenon witnessed in individuals for whom the age of the parent serves as a critically important benchmark in terms of chronological and personal time.

In any event, the age-correspondence phenomenon may involve either the mourner's conscious or unconscious awareness. It is not atypical to observe that an individual has serious, although often unexpressed, concerns about surviving past the age at which the loved one died. Usually, although not always, this loved one is a parent of the same sex. For many mourners, this may establish an expectation of death at that same age and a consequent living of life in accordance with that belief. For instance, on the belief "I don't expect to get out of my 40s—my father died at 49," the mourner may base such decisions as having children, choosing a career, or establishing other priorities.

In some mourners, it is easy to discern an onset of anxiety and/or other symptomatology in the months or years leading up to the age at which the loved one died. Where there is no other explanation for the timing or characteristics of symptomatology or dysfunction, the age-correspondence phenomenon should be explored. When mourners pass this turning point, some describe a sense of having a second life open to them. Only then may they realize or admit to themselves the extent of their trepidation or the degree to which they had made decisions on the belief that they would follow the script of the loved one. For some, especially those with certain psychological conflicts about the deceased, there may be feelings of guilt that they have surpassed the age at which their loved one died.

Age-correspondence reactions need not center exclusively on the individual's fears of his own mortality. A STUG reaction may center around reawakened or exacerbated grief over the initial loss of the loved one. Attaining the age of the loved one may highlight identification with that person or yield an appreciation of some of the issues, events, concerns, or experiences of that person. This can in turn allow the mourner to relate to or understand that individual better (e.g., "This is what it is like to be turning 50 and be concerned about my ability to advance in my profession. These were the issues my father was struggling with when he had his heart attack.").

As noted previously, a STUG reaction also can be precipitated when one's child attains the age the mourner was when the parent or significant other died. This may result in a focus on the possibility of the mourner's own death. It also may promote a resurgence of grief over the earlier loss. Essentially, this event involves reactivated memory of the loss and reactions to it, which are stimulated by observation and/or reminders of the personal developmental context within which the death of the loved one originally took place.

Another type of age-correspondence phenomenon occurs when a child approaches the age another child had been at death. STUG reactions can occur for bereaved parents as the coincidence of ages between the living and deceased child catalyzes memories, thoughts, emotions, and other reactions regarding the loss of the deceased child. This is typically an anxiety-provoking time for parents; some admit to being afraid to invest emotionally in the living child prior to her surpassing this particular age. It should be noted that, although this reaction is quite prevalent in parents who have another child or pregnancy after a loss, it is by no means exclusive to them. Any individual who has sustained the loss of a loved one may be concerned about other loved ones' surviving past the age of that death, whether or not those other loved ones are related. For example, one woman was quite concerned that her dearest friend would die around age 50 because that was the age of her father at the time of his sudden, unexpected death from a myocardial infarction. She did not attribute any magic to that particular number, but she had learned all too well that 50 is a time of vulnerability for cardiac conditions in men. Because her father's death had been sudden, she could have no assurance that there would be any warning if her friend had a heart attack, and she feared the unfinished business his death would leave if it repeated her father's. During the critical time period, she experienced both an upsurge of grief for her father and anticipatory grief for the potential loss of her friend.

Experience-associated reactions. STUG phenomena can take place when the mourner sustains an experience similar to one associated with the deceased. The association may be with experiences related to the loved one at the time of death (e.g., retirement) or perceived as symbolically related to the deceased person (e.g., playing softball). In both cases, experience and/or activities identified with the deceased stimulate the STUG reaction. These are similar to reminder-inspired reactions but are precipitated by experiences rather than specific stimuli. Although grouped under the category of linear precipitants, some of these reactions can occur more than once, and some may be cyclical.

Transition-stimulated reactions. Brief periods of acute grief may be stimulated during times of transition. As in the seasons of spring and fall, where the dynamics involved in a STUG reaction can pertain to the process of change, major transitions have the capacity to resurrect grief over a lost loved one. There are a number of possible reasons for this. Among many others, change may bring the following reactions.

1. Longing for the security of the deceased's presence

2. Painful awareness that life continues on in the absence of the deceased

3. Desire to cling to the psychologically, behaviorally, socially, and/or physically familiar because it serves as a connection to the deceased and is less anxiety-provoking than moving into the unknown without the loved one

4. Recognition that there is so much that the deceased is missing

5. Desire to hold onto what is changing, for change signals the mourner's movement into a new time and space that never will be shared by the deceased

6. Unwillingness to let time proceed because of fear that, with change, memories of the deceased will fade

7. Reluctance to see the time since the death become greater than the time the mourner was with the deceased

All of these issues pertain to time, and it is the passage of time that is signaled by transitions. These transitions may be external, social, or personal. Hence, grief responses may be potentiated at times associated with (a) the end of a decade (e.g., it may be difficult to let go of the 1990s if New Year's Eve marks the close of a decade in which the deceased had been alive and the beginning of a decade in which the deceased never will exist); (b) relocation to a new home (e.g., it might be painful to leave an environment that had been shared with the deceased for one in which the deceased had never been present); (c) cessation of an old relationship (e.g., ending a friendship may be hard if that person also had known the loved one or had assisted the mourner in coping with the loss); or (d) personal change (e.g., it may bring great sadness when a mourner gets married without the loved one's being able to witness this milestone).

Developmentally determined reactions. Developmentally determined STUG reactions arise because of developmental issues that (a) would be experienced by the deceased if she were alive or (b) are relevant to the mourner at the present juncture. For instance, with regard to the first type, one mourner was only able to have her son declared legally dead 8 years after he was presumed drowned. At that time he would have been 21, the age at which she considered him an adult. This mother simply could not bring herself to have the "child" declared dead but could manage, albeit with considerable distress, to have the "adult" declared dead. She felt that this would have coincided with her normal developmental role of letting go, which she would have had to do if he were alive. When all of this transpired, she experienced an acute exacerbation of grief as she prepared to relinquish her son once again. This example illustrates that, despite the physical death, mourners often keep track of the developmental processes and changes the deceased would be experiencing were that person alive. Mourners also may experience STUG reactions at the time there would have been an important event, process, or transition that would have been shared with the deceased (e.g., the time at which the couple would have been able to retire together to Florida). This could transpire even though there may have been many relatively grief-free years prior to the STUG reaction.

In the second type, the developmental issue prompting the STUG reaction pertains to the mourner. In this situation, aspects of the mourner's current life experience bring up grief reactions that may or may not have been undergone before. For example, when a mourner undergoes a mid-life crisis, he may become more reflective of past relationships and what they say about him. Contemplating the meaning and quality of the relationship he had with the one now dead may stimulate a STUG reaction. Similarly, the birth of one's first child may resurrect grief over the death of a parent who is not present to share in the experience.

Crisis-evoked reactions. Sometimes closely aligned to transition-stimulated reactions, crisis-evoked STUG reactions occur during times of flux. However, in addition to the flux, one usually finds some measure of distress and chaos, as well as concern, anxiety, or fear. At such times, the mourner may long for the security, comfort, protection, predictability, and meaning of the relationship with the deceased. Its absence stimulates the STUG reaction. Given that major loss tends to resurrect old losses, this reaction also can be catalyzed if elements of major loss exist in the crisis. Subsequent deaths, acute trauma, frightening situations, serious confrontations with failure, and threats to well-being are among the many possible crises that can precipitate such STUG reactions.

Ritual-prompted reactions (single event). Rituals that occur only once—typically rituals of transition—often tend to provoke STUG reactions. Examples of such rituals include graduations, weddings, and funerals. As noted previously, one dynamic arises from the element of transition, which can tug at unresolved or currently sensitive feelings, thoughts, and memories. Another comes from the mourner's reaction to change and what it may represent with regard to the loved one's loss (see the previous discussion of transition-stimulated reactions). Coinciding with these dynamics are some of the variables associated with holidays, anniversaries, and repetitive family rituals (e.g., the presence of other loved ones, which serves to highlight the deceased's absence). The issues salient for each of these other categories are equally pertinent here. The only difference is that this event will not be repeated.

Stimulus-cued precipitants

In this category are all of the STUG reactions precipitated by stimuli unrelated to time. These collapse into four groupings: (a) those that serve as actual reminders of the deceased, (b) those that symbolically remind the mourner of the deceased, (c) those that contain themes of loss and/or reunion, and (d) music eliciting emotion. These infinitely various stimuli can prompt recollection of the deceased and STUG reactions. They serve to trigger thoughts, feelings, and memories about the deceased, which in turn foster the grief reaction as the sense of absence and loss are aroused.

Memory-based reactions. STUG reactions often occur when the mourner encounters stimuli that had been shared in actual experience with the deceased (e.g., "our song," the smell of a particular cologne) or that bring back strong memories of that person (e.g., a photograph of the deceased, an article of clothing, a humorous story). In each case, the mourner's memory—whether of a shared experience or of the deceased—is heightened, and a STUG reaction may result.

Reminder-inspired reactions. STUG reactions may be instigated by stimuli that, although not actually experienced with or directly related to the deceased, symbolically remind the mourner of her. (These are to be differentiated from experience-associated reactions, which are precipitated by actual experiences and not by specific stimuli.) For instance, a woman whose husband had driven a Cadillac would well up with tears whenever she saw a similar model. Similarly, when the song "Daddy's Little Girl" is played at weddings, many women experience STUG reactions for deceased fathers.

Loss and/or reunion theme–aroused reactions. Observing, reading, or hearing about situations involving any type of loss or reunion can prod the mourner's own issues about loss to the fore and can catalyze strong wishes and fantasies for reunion with the deceased. STUG reactions based on this dynamic are associated with vicarious identification with those undergoing the loss and/or reunion experience. For instance, when the American hostages were released from Iran in 1981, I witnessed a tremendous impact on a number of mourners in treatment. Television coverage of the return of the hostages to their families and country reached some of these mourners at depths that nothing else had since the time of their losses. It sparked intense reactions to the recognition that they could not be reunited similarly with their loved ones.

Music-elicited reactions. Music is well known to reach profound depths in human beings; indeed, it even affects other species. STUG reactions may be elicited by the melody, dynamics, rhythm, tempo, and harmonics of particular musical pieces. Reactions of this sort are to be differentiated from those that can be categorized within the previous three types and in which the lyrics as well as the melody may be central. Here, the issue is the nonverbal engagement of emotions—in this case, emotions related to the loss.

CHAPTER 3

Theories of Complicated Mourning: A Historical Review

This chapter presents, in historical chronology, information on the philosophies, theories, and models used to explain complicated mourning. A proper understanding of the historical development of thinking about complicated mourning results in more than an interesting accumulation of facts. Both philosophy and history, as well as theory, are clinically relevant. Changes over time reflect broadening concepts of complicated mourning and have directly influenced the treatment strategies and techniques discussed in detail in later chapters of this book.

The discussion summarizes the works of 19 clinical observers, theorists, and practitioners. Their contributions regarding mourning in general and other issues pertinent to dying and death are not reviewed here. The focus is exclusively on complicated mourning and aspects related to it. Consequently, not all authors contributing to the field of thanatology are represented, and not all works of all authors are discussed. These necessary exclusions should not be construed as commentary on importance to the field.

Contributions have been selected on the basis of the following criteria: (a) historical primacy and significance of remarks, (b) significance of the contribution to fundamental knowledge about complicated mourning, (c) service as a wellspring for subsequent work, (d) degree of reference by later authors, and (e) professional acknowledgment as a "classic" in the field.

SIGMUND FREUD

It is the rare treatise or literature review on the topic of mourning that does not commence by citing Freud's (1917/1957c) classic paper "Mourning and Melancholia." Interestingly, like much subsequent psychoanalytic writing, Freud's analyses of mourning in this paper and in other works stemmed less from an interest in the topic in its own right than from its being an analogue and, not infrequently, a precipitant of clinical depression. At that time, discussions of mourning were used to elucidate not only depression but also an assortment of other mental processes and states of mind. Most of the initial examinations of mourning came about because the author used mourning to clarify or illustrate something else (Siggins, 1966).

Despite the special place accorded to it, "Mourning and Melancholia" was not the first work to examine aspects of bereavement. Pollock (1961) has outlined the precursors to this classic work, and his chronology and comments are relied upon heavily in the present review of Freud's contributions. Siggins' (1966) survey of the literature on mourning also must be acknowledged in this discussion, as well as in subsequent references to other early psychoanalytic writers.

In the early work "Studies on Hysteria," Freud describes a woman who had "nursed to the end three or four of those whom she loved" and who would

> shortly after her patient's death . . . begin . . . a work of reproduction which once more brought up before her eyes the scenes of the illness and death. Every day she would go through each impression once more, would weep over it and console herself. . . . In addition . . . this lady celebrated annual festivals of remembrance at the period of her various catastrophes. (Breuer & Freud, 1893/1955, p. 163)

This account anticipates Freud's later concept of the work of mourning and presents the first conceptualization of what now is termed an *anniversary reaction*.

Subsequent references to mourning are embedded in Freud's discussions of melancholia. In Draft G of the Fliess papers on melancholia, Freud (1895/1966a) speaks of the affect corresponding to melancholia as being "mourning—that is, longing for something lost" (p. 200) and comments that "uncoupling associations is always painful" (p. 205). In Draft N (Freud, 1897/1966b), when it seems that Freud was in the midst of working out his own mourning for his father's death 7 months previously, he again connects mourning with melancholia. He extends this comparison in "Contributions to a Discussion on Suicide" (Freud, 1910/1957a), in which he refers to the "affect of mourning" (p. 232).

Around this time, Freud proffers other comments on various aspects of mourning and its nature. In "Creative Writers and Day-Dreaming" (Freud, 1908/1959a), he comments on the fact that a loved object is never really relinquished:

> But whoever understands the human mind knows that hardly anything is harder for a man than to give up a pleasure which

he has once experienced. Actually, we can never give anything up; we only exchange one thing for another. What
appears to be a renunciation is really the formation of a
substitute or surrogate. (p. 145)

This statement on lack of relinquishment conflicts with material presented in "Mourning and Melancholia," in which Freud states that total
relinquishment is the goal of the mourner. Another comment, made
21 years later and in agreement with the one cited in "Creative Writers
and Day-Dreaming," is found in the often-quoted letter Freud wrote on
the anniversary of his deceased daughter's 36th birthday, to Ludwig
Binswanger, who had lost a son:

Although we know that after such a loss the acute state of
mourning will subside, we also know we shall remain in-
consolable and will never find a substitute. No matter what
may fill the gap, even if it be filled completely, it nevertheless
remains something else.
And, actually, this is how it should be, it is the only way
of perpetuating that love which we do not want to relinquish.
(Freud, 1929/1960, p. 386)

Both of these comments reveal Freud's belief that a lost object is never
really relinquished. Unfortunately, some interpreters have taken Freud's
contrary statement in "Mourning and Melancholia" too literally, using it
to support the view that the mourner ultimately must completely relinquish the lost object and that any continued relationship with the lost
object is pathological.

In "Notes Upon a Case of Obsessional Neurosis," Freud (1909/1955b)
states that the normal period of mourning lasts from 1 to 2 years. In "Five
Lectures on Psycho-Analysis" (Freud, 1910/1957b), he characterizes
mourning as a normal emotional process.

Further development of Freud's (1912/1955c) ideas on the mourning
process are next found in "Totem and Taboo," in which he elucidates the
function of the mourning process: "Mourning has a quite specific psychi-
cal task to perform: its function is to detach the survivors' memories and
hopes from the dead. When this has been achieved, the pain grows less
and with it the remorse and self-reproaches" (pp. 65–66). Also in this work,
Freud allows that human beings have ambivalence toward those they
love. Freud's acknowledgment of ambivalence here and in "Thoughts
for the Times on War and Death" (1915/1957e) are in interesting contrast
with his 1917 declaration in "Mourning and Melancholia" that ambivalence
in the relationship contributes to the lowering of self-esteem found in
melancholia and differentiates it from, and is presumed to be absent in,
healthy mourning. In the 1917 work, Freud states, "Melancholia contains

something more than normal mourning . . . the relation to the object is no simple one; it is complicated by the conflict due to ambivalence" (p. 256).

In "On Transience" (Freud, 1916/1957f), which was written after the death of his beloved brother and his painful split from Carl Jung and while his two sons and numerous close associates were serving in the military in World War I, Freud observes that the anticipated pain of losing a loved object interferes with present enjoyment. Again, Freud speaks to the issue of not wanting to relinquish a lost object as he also puzzles over the painfulness of the mourning process:

> But why it is that this detachment of libido from its objects should be such a painful process is a mystery to us. . . . We only see that libido clings to its objects and will not renounce those that are lost even when a substitute lies ready to hand. Such then is mourning. (pp. 306–307)

Further exploration of the pain of mourning takes place in Freud's (1926/1959b) addendum to "Inhibitions, Symptoms and Anxiety," entitled "Anxiety, Pain and Mourning." Here he notes a similarity between physical pain, which results in a high degree of narcissistic cathexis of the painful place, and mental pain after object loss. In this latter case, the pain of separation stems from the mounting and unsatisfiable cathexis of longing for the object, as the mourner undoes emotional ties to that object.

For many, the publication of Freud's (1917/1957c) classic work "Mourning and Melancholia" constitutes the beginning of formal investigation of the topic of mourning, despite the fact that others outside the discipline of psychology, as well as Freud himself, had written earlier on the topic. Freud essentially made eight main points about mourning in this famous text.

On the *recognition and definition of symbolic losses* (Rando, 1984), Freud writes that "Mourning is regularly the reaction to the loss of a loved person, or to the loss of some abstraction which has taken the place of one, such as one's country, liberty, an ideal, and so on" (p. 243).

In terms of a *perspective on mourning,* Freud notes that, "although mourning involves grave departures from the normal attitude to life, it never occurs to us to regard it as a pathological condition and to refer it to medical treatment. We rely on its being overcome after a certain lapse of time, and we look upon any interference with it as useless or even harmful" (pp. 243–244).

On the *distinguishing features of mourning,* he writes that

> The distinguishing mental features . . . are a profoundly painful dejection, cessation of interest in the outside world, loss of the capacity to love, [and] inhibition of all activity. . . . It is easy to see that this inhibition and circumscription of the ego

is the expression of an exclusive devotion to mourning which leaves nothing over for other purposes or other interests. It is really only because we know so well how to explain it that this attitude does not seem to us pathological. (p. 244)

Freud sees the *reason for initiating mourning* in terms of the need for detachment from the lost object. In particular, he writes that "reality-testing has shown that the loved object no longer exists, and it proceeds to demand that all libido shall be withdrawn from its attachments to that object" (p. 244) and that "mourning impels the ego to give up the object by declaring the object to be dead and offering the ego the inducement of continuing to live" (p. 257).

On the *reason mourning involves such struggle,* he comments as follows:

> This demand [to withdraw libidinal attachments] arouses understandable opposition—it is a matter of general observation that people never willingly abandon a libidinal position, not even, indeed, when a substitute is already beckoning to them. This opposition can be so intense that a turning away from reality takes place and a clinging to the object through the medium of a hallucinatory wishful psychosis. (p. 244)

The mourner's struggle ultimately promotes adaptation:

> Each single one of the memories and situations of expectancy which demonstrate the libido's attachment to the lost object is met by the verdict of reality that the object no longer exists; and the ego, confronted as it were with the question whether it shall share this fate, is persuaded by the sum of the narcissistic satisfactions it derives from being alive to sever its attachment to the object that has been abolished. (p. 255)

According to Freud, the *work of mourning* takes time and a great deal of energy:

> Normally, respect for reality gains the day [and complies with the demand to withdraw the libido from its attachments to the object despite opposition]. Nevertheless its orders cannot be obeyed at once. They are carried out bit by bit, at great expense of time and cathectic energy, and in the meantime the existence of the lost object is psychically prolonged. Each single one of the memories and expectations in which the libido is bound to the object is brought up and hypercathected, and detachment of the libido is accomplished in respect of it. (pp. 244–245)

The *indication of the end of mourning* is "when the work of mourning is completed [and] the ego becomes free and uninhibited again. . . . the ego will have succeeded in freeing its libido from the lost object" (pp. 245–252).

Finally, Freud points out with respect to the *development of pathological mourning,* as represented by melancholia, that "in some people the same influences produce melancholia instead of mourning and we consequently suspect them of a pathological disposition" (p. 243).

Also in "Mourning and Melancholia," Freud mentions the process of identification with the lost object strictly in connection with melancholia. At this point in his writing, he does not recognize identification as a normal component of mourning. He contrasts healthy mourning for a known lost object with melancholia, which appears to be unhealthy mourning for an unconscious lost object:

> An object-choice, an attachment of the libido to a particular person, had at one time existed; then, owing to a real slight or disappointment coming from this loved person, the object-relationship was shattered. The result was not the normal one of a withdrawal of the libido from this object and a displacement of it on to a new one, but something different. . . . The free libido was not displaced on to another object; it was withdrawn into the ego. There, however, it was not employed in any unspecified way, but served to establish an *identification* of the ego with the abandoned object. Thus the shadow of the object fell upon the ego. . . . The narcissistic identification with the object then becomes a substitute for the erotic cathexis, the result of which is that in spite of the conflict with the loved person the love-relation need not be given up. . . . Melancholia . . . is on the one hand, like mourning, a reaction to the real loss of a loved object; but over and above this, it is marked by a determinant [i.e., identification] which is absent in normal mourning or which, if it is present, transforms the latter into pathological mourning. (pp. 248–250)

In "The Ego and The Id," Freud (1923/1961) rectifies his association of identification with pathology and asserts the necessity of identification in mourning, noting that identification is the sole condition under which the id can give up its objects. He also observes the importance of the identification process in the formation and modification of the ego: "The ego is formed to a great extent out of identifications which take the place of abandoned cathexes by the id" (p. 48). In his "New Introductory Lectures on Psycho-Analysis," Freud (1933/1964) further clarifies that such identification, which subsequently enhances the ego, is compensatory after major loss: "If one has lost an object or has been obliged to give it up, one often compensates oneself by identifying oneself with it and by setting it up once more in one's ego" (p. 63).

Like his views on relinquishment of the lost object and ambivalence in mourning, Freud's changed viewpoint toward the process of identification underscores the need to integrate his writings in "Mourning and Melancholia" with his other works. Siggins (1966) is most helpful in putting Freud's commentary in "Mourning and Melancholia" in perspective. She points out that, in this paper, he creates an ideal account for discussion purposes but that in other writings he supplements this ideal account with further reflection upon the actual course of human mourning.

KARL ABRAHAM

In the early 1900s, Karl Abraham (1911/1949a) wrote an influential paper on the treatment of manic-depression and allied conditions. In it, he noted the similarity in psychic structure between manic-depressive depressions, involutional melancholia, and neurotic depressions, advancing the view that the depressive psychosis is a pathological variant of mourning.

It was partially in response to Abraham's paper that a number of Freud's (1917/1957c) comments in "Mourning and Melancholia" were made. Freud amplified Abraham's observations by delineating the similarities and differences between mourning and melancholia. In "A Short Study of the Development of the Libido, Viewed in the Light of Mental Disorders," Abraham (1924/1949b) in turn modified several of Freud's points. One concerned the relegation of lowered self-esteem exclusively to melancholia: Abraham asserts that melancholia is usually present to some extent as well in mourning, the amount being proportional to the strength of hostile feeling in the relationship.

Likewise, Abraham (1924/1949b) clarifies that identification is also an aspect of normal mourning, not pathological as originally assumed by Freud in "Mourning and Melancholia." He makes the additional claim that in the course of healthy mourning a temporary introjection of the object is effected, resulting in the consolation: "My loved object is not gone, for now I carry it within myself and can never lose it" (p. 437). He compares the mourning process in the normal individual, the neurotic, and the melancholiac. With regard to the normal individual, he writes:

> Introjection occurs in mourning in the healthy person. . . . In the normal person it is set in motion by real loss (death); and its main purpose is to preserve the person's relations to the dead object, or—what comes to the same thing—to compensate for his loss. (p. 438)

Finally, Abraham differentiates himself from Freud on the topic of ambivalence in mourning. He points out that, whereas ambivalent feelings toward the object definitely exist in melancholia or pathological mourning, they are not exclusive to those states. In other words, they are not necessarily diagnostic of pathology. Indeed, notes Abraham, such feelings also occur in healthy mourning. However, in contrast to the situation of the melancholiac, in the normal person the ambivalence is such that feelings of affection "easily oust the hostile ones in regard to an object he has (in reality) lost" (p. 442).

HELENE DEUTSCH

In her paper "Absence of Grief," Helene Deutsch (1937) described this phenomenon. In doing so, she appears to have identified the first type of complicated mourning not conceptualized as a specific variant of the manic-depressive conditions. She presents clinical observations supporting three main convictions:

> First, that the death of a beloved person must produce reactive expression of feeling in the normal course of events; second, that omission of such reactive responses is to be considered just as much a variation from the normal as excess in time or intensity; and third, that unmanifested grief will be found expressed to the full in some way or other. (p. 13)

Deutsch believes that, just as the ego of the child is not sufficiently developed to bear the strain of the work of mourning and therefore utilizes a mechanism of narcissistic self-protection to circumvent the process (e.g., one appears to be indifferent following the death of a loved one), so too is there a weakness in the ego of an adult who cannot permit mourning to occur. In the case of the child, the weak ego is the result of developmental immaturity; in the case of the adult, the weakness has been induced through previous or concurrent experiences.

Deutsch posits that two conditions existing within the ego are responsible for an absence of the grief reaction: (a) a relative inadequacy of the free and unoccupied portion of the ego (i.e., insufficient ego strength) and (b) a protective mechanism proceeding from the narcissistic cathexis of the ego (i.e., defense mechanisms mobilized to protect the ego from the dangers of mourning—painful affect, recognition of ambivalence, etc.).

Asserting that "suppressed affect following a loss seeks realization subsequently" (p. 21), Deutsch believes that every unresolved grief is given expression in one form or another and is convinced that "the unresolved process of mourning . . . must in some way be expressed in full" (p. 21). She interprets that many self-defeating behavior patterns, as well as many so-called unmotivated depressions, are the result of strivings toward expression that continue to exist in unexpressed grief, in latent readiness for discharge. Deutsch views the expediency of flight from the suffering of grief as "but a temporary gain, because . . . the necessity to mourn persists in the psychic apparatus" (p. 22).

Her comments on the necessity of mourning are unequivocal:

> The process of mourning as reaction to the real loss of a loved person *must be carried to completion.* As long as the early libidinal or aggressive attachments persist, the painful affect continues to flourish, and *vice versa,* the attachments are unresolved as long as the affective process of mourning has not been accomplished. (p. 21)

MELANIE KLEIN

Because of her concern with negative human emotions—rage, hatred, envy, and greed—Melanie Klein's work often seems bizarre to readers initially encountering it. However, further reading illustrates that Klein's theory offers an interesting entry into the unconscious and addresses universal elements of psychological functioning. The remainder of this discussion is based extensively on the most lucid exposition of Melanie Klein's work, recently put forth by Burch (1988).

Klein focuses on what are usually thought of as states of severe pathological functioning (e.g., paranoid, schizoid, and depressed states) but considers them characteristic of the world of normal infants. Yet, along with this, Klein argues for the innate unfolding of the more positive emotions or attitudes, such as love, empathy, gratitude, and a wish to preserve primary objects for their own sake rather than for one's own defensive need.

Klein theorizes an overlay of positions, or configurations of object relations, anxieties, and defenses. The first position is the *paranoid-schizoid position,* characterized by part-object relations in which the infant has his primary relationship with a part rather than a whole person or object (e.g., the mother's breast). Much of the more bizarre content of Klein's theory concerns this point in time. Klein believes that in this position, which occurs from birth until 3 or 4 months, oral aggressive impulses lead the child to fantasize sadistic biting and tearing attacks on the breast and anal aggressive fantasies of excreting or urinating on the mother. The child attempts to rid himself of the aggression by projecting it onto the part-objects (e.g., the breast wants to do him harm). However, these then need to be controlled, so they are introjected, becoming internal persecutors. Anxieties about persecution or overwhelming fears of being destroyed can cause disintegration in the fragile ego. Consequently, the ego splits off the bad object relationship to eliminate the source of danger and preserve the good object. Good experiences or fantasies of the breast are split off from bad ones and internalized, with the internalization of the good objects forming the core of the ego.

The second position, the *depressive position*, gradually begins to emerge at approximately 4 months and continues to dominate for the next 3 or 4 months. At this point, objects are now people and not parts. Splitting diminishes. The primary concern is for the object rather than the self. Fluctuating emotions of love and hate are experienced for the same person and create an ambivalent relationship.

The child's growing awareness of the mother as a person brings guilt over his fantasized attacks on her. The guilt is handled through reparation, sometimes fantasized and sometimes acted out in an effort to undo what has been done in fantasy and bring the infant in closer touch with reality as he observes repeatedly that his mother is still there. The infant faces many real losses in the course of development, with the first being the loss of the breast during the depressive period. The infant thinks his own angry attacks have destroyed it, and this state of loss, or feared loss, is the deepest source of painful conflicts. If attempts at reparation fail to alleviate the conflicts of the infantile depressive position, the child minimizes the sense of loss by fantasizing himself as omnipotent, denying the importance of the ego's good objects, and trying to control both good and bad ones by producing the hyperactivity of mania. When a good object is devalued successfully, a feeling of triumph over the parent is possible, often witnessed clinically through "disparagement of the object's importance and contempt for it" (Klein, 1935, p. 279). Alternately, or if manic defenses fail, the ego may become involved in obsessional repetition of efforts at reparation. The sense of triumph over the object prevents mourning and impedes internalization of the good object, and the healthy impulse toward reparation is denied because injury to that object is denied along with the child's own sorrow and guilt. These denials of the external world impair reality testing, while the internal world is left bereft of good objects.

According to Klein, severe pathology results from the inability to work through the anxieties of one or both of these positions. If the position has not been worked through adequately, crises in adult life trigger a return to the one at which anxieties were not worked through, even when more normal development has intervened. When the loss of a loved person cannot be mourned because an early sense of loss in the original depressive position is unresolved, complicated mourning develops.

In adulthood, losses recapitulate the early mourning process. The individual feels the good objects are lost again, and paranoid fears are revived and accompanied by a sense of persecution, often expressed by questions such as, Why is this happening to me? The inner world collapses and deteriorates, a condition termed by Klein (1940) as a mental illness, which usually goes unrecognized because it is so common. During mourning, passing states of elation occur between periods of sorrow and distress. The states are manic in character and result from fantasies of having incorporated the perfect or idealized object. Crying aids the process of mourning not only because it renders relief from tension, but also because it expels excreta or objects and represents a relaxation of manic control. The mourner's internal objects—when they are felt to be in mourning as well—share the grief as actual kind parents would and can be a source of further comfort.

The incapacity to mourn requires one to deny love for both internal and external objects. This leads to an overall blunting of emotional life or to an absence of feelings of love while hatred still has free reign. Whether grief will be normal or pathological depends on whether the mourner, as a child, has been able to establish his internal good objects and feel secure in his inner world.

In summary, adult mourning may be impaired or complicated by the revival of difficulties that originally arose during childhood, particularly those that developed at weaning, when the newly weaned child mourned the loss of the breast in the infantile depressive position.

ERICH LINDEMANN

Without question, Erich Lindemann's 1944 study "Symptomatology and Management of Acute Grief" is a classic in the field of loss. His work, along with Freud's, is cited continually in the literature and frequently forms the basis for other observers' comparisons, agreements, and disagreements. The points noted in the following discussion are directly relevant to the topic of complicated mourning.

Characteristics of Grief

Lindemann delineates five points that are pathognomonic for grief: somatic distress, preoccupation with the image of the deceased, guilt, hostile reactions, and loss of patterns of conduct. He notes that a sixth characteristic, quite striking but not as conspicuous as the other five, is often shown by individuals bordering on pathological reactions. This is the appearance in the bereaved's behavior of traits belonging to the deceased, especially symptoms of the deceased's final illness or behavior that may have been shown at the time of the tragedy. Lindemann theorizes that normal preoccupation with the deceased witnessed in acute grief is transformed into a preoccupation with the deceased's symptoms or personality traits and is then displaced to the bereaved's own body through the process of identification.

Grief Work

Lindemann proffers a definition of what is entailed in the work of grief (i.e., grief work). He operationalizes the concept by three tasks: emancipation from bondage to the deceased, readjustment to the environment in which the deceased is missing, and formation of new relationships. He asserts that the duration of grief depends on the success with which the bereaved undertakes this grief work. However, Lindemann notes that many individuals seek to avoid the intense distress connected with the grief experience and the expression of the emotion necessary for it, thereby creating major obstacles to the successful completion of grief work. Lindemann's work appears to have provided the first delineation of tasks of grief or mourning per se, and it has formed the basis for the six "R" processes of mourning described in this book.

Morbid Grief Reactions

Lindemann asserts that morbid grief reactions represent distortions of normal grief and that they can be transformed into normal reactions. He addresses two types of morbid reactions: a delay of reaction and a distorted reaction. A delay or postponement of a grief reaction may continue for years if the bereavement occurs at a time when the individual is confronted simultaneously with other important tasks or with maintaining the morale of others. A grief reaction ultimately may be precipitated by deliberate recall of circumstances surrounding the unmourned death, a spontaneous occurrence in the bereaved's life, or attainment of the age of the deceased.

Lindemann describes nine types of alterations that he considers manifestations of unresolved grief. Each of these distorted reactions, which he believes may respond to fairly simple and brief management, represents a special aspect of the grief syndrome and may take the place of the typical grief reaction. They include the following.

1. Overactivity without a sense of loss

2. The acquisition of symptoms belonging to the last illness of the deceased

3. A recognized medical disease of a psychosomatic nature

4. A conspicuous alteration in relationships to friends and relatives

5. Furious hostility against specific persons

6. Wooden and formal appearances, with affect and conduct resembling schizophrenic pictures

7. Lasting loss of patterns of social interaction

8. Actions detrimental to one's own social and economic existence

9. Agitated depression

It should be noted that a number of subsequent observers have taken the position that certain of these distorted reactions each represent a type of complicated mourning. At the very least, under certain conditions, they all can indicate the presence of diagnostic clues or symptoms of complicated mourning.

Personality and Circumstantial Factors

In delineating prognosticators, Lindemann has identified several important premorbid personality and circumstantial factors associated with complications of the mourning process. The following may predispose the bereaved to atypical responses.

1. An obsessive personality makeup

2. A history of past depressions

3. Being a mother who has lost a young child

4. Having had an intensely hostile relationship with the deceased

5. Disintegration of the bereaved's social system and profound alteration of the bereaved's living and social conditions following the loss

Interestingly, Lindemann notes that these factors are more influential in contributing to a morbid grief reaction than is previous neurosis. He strengthens this point by noting that, in his study, the most obvious pathological cases involved persons with no former history of neurosis.

Complicating Responses

In addressing the management of grief reactions, Lindemann notes that it is imperative to pay attention to a minimal or absent response because it can signal future complications:

> It is of the greatest importance to notice that not only over-reaction but under-reaction of the bereaved must be given attention, because delayed responses may occur at unpredictable moments and the dangerous distortions of the grief reaction, not conspicuous at first, be quite destructive later and these may be prevented. (p. 147)

Lindemann mentions several problematic responses mandating intervention beyond that prescribed for the typical grief response—that is, beyond the caregiver's "sharing the patient's grief work, namely, his efforts at extricating himself from the bondage to the deceased and at finding new patterns of rewarding interaction" (p. 147). For example, he predicts that special techniques will be needed if hostility is the most marked feature of the grief reaction, medication might be necessary if anxiety and depression are intolerable, and severe agitated depressions may defy all efforts at psychotherapy and require the somatic intervention of electroconvulsive therapy.

OTTO FENICHEL

Unlike Lindemann, Otto Fenichel is not noted primarily for his work on the topic of loss. Rather, he is best recognized for his contributions to psychoanalytic theory in his book *The Psychoanalytic Theory of Neurosis* (1945). The relevance of his work to the subject of complicated mourning stems from his clarification and articulation of the processes of introjection and decathexis in normal mourning; his exposition of mourning as a defense against the full impact of grief; his brief discussions of ambivalence, guilt, and remorse as normal components of mourning; and his comments about the conditions that predispose toward complicated responses. All four issues are particularly salient in the consideration of complicated mourning.

Fenichel writes of the adaptiveness of the bereaved's identification with and incorporation of the image of the deceased. Identification somewhat softens the pain of the demands for decathexis from the lost object (Freud, 1917/1957c) and mitigates the necessary process of loosening emotional ties. Specifically, after the loss the mourner avoids the overwhelming assault that would be experienced if the affects were released full strength by building up within herself a substitute object, via the process of incorporation, and then identifying with it. This promotes healthy mourning because, as Fenichel points out, "Apparently, for a normal person it is easier to loosen the ties with an introject than with an external object. The establishment of an introjection is a means of facilitating the final loosening" (p. 394). Thus, Fenichel views the essence of the mourning process as consisting of two acts, the first being the establishment of an introjection; the second, the loosening of binds to the introjected object.

The importance of assisting the bereaved to experience and work through mourning gradually is well explicated by Fenichel in his discussion regarding defenses against being overwhelmed by painful affects:

> In the affect of grief, postponement seems to be an essential component. What happens in mourning is nothing other than a gradual "working through" of an affect which, if released in its full strength, would overwhelm the ego, that is, the quantity of cathexes released by the loss of the object. What today is called grief is obviously a postponed and apportioned neutralization of a wild and self-destructive kind of affect which can still be observed in a child's panic upon the disappearance of his mother or in the uninhibited mourning reactions of primitives. (p. 162)

Like other clinical observers before and since, Fenichel notes that mourning becomes more complicated or even pathological when the relationship with the deceased has been an extremely ambivalent one. In such cases, Fenichel sees the introjection as acquiring a sadistic significance; the incorporation then represents not only an attempt to preserve the loved object but an attempt to destroy it as well. This can create new guilt feelings in the mourner.

Fenichel feels that death always will create some ambivalent feelings, even in relationships that have not been conflicted. He observes a number of reasons for the mobilization of ambivalence, with each creating guilt and remorse.

1. The death of a person for whom one had previously wished death may be perceived as a fulfillment of this wish.

2. The death of other persons may cause feelings of joy because death came to somebody else, not to oneself.

3. In the painful state of mourning, narcissistically oriented persons may tend unconsciously to reproach the deceased for having brought them into this painful state.

4. Identification with the dead may have punitive aspects ("Because you have wished the other person to die, you have to die yourself"), which contribute to fear of the dead's seeking revenge, eventuating in more ambivalence.

Fenichel summarizes as follows:

> It may be stated that mourning is characterized by an ambivalent introjection of the lost object, a continuation of feelings toward the introject that once had been directed toward the object, and the participation of guilt feelings throughout the process. (p. 395)

Finally, as pertains to complicated mourning, Fenichel lists conditions under which the narcissistic need and the conflicts around introjection in mourning will be more intense than usual. These conditions obtain when the relationship has been abnormally dependent or ambivalent and when the bereaved is orally fixated in character.

CHARLES ANDERSON

Charles Anderson's (1949) paper "Aspects of Pathological Grief and Mourning" appears to be the first quasi-empirical study of complicated mourning, a condition which he, like Lindemann, terms morbid grief. Anderson peppers his work with references to the grief and depression associated with World War II and appears particularly interested in aggression directed toward the introjected lost object, as well as in the combination of reproach, anxiety, and nightmares observed in mourners:

> There is a peculiarly painful and despairing quality of feeling both in grief and mourning: what has been loved seems to be irretrievably lost, and the mourner, as if responsible, reproaches himself, literally or symbolically rending his garments. These self-reproaches have their obverse for there is a plaint, an accusation against the dead person for having left and deserted the mourner. . . . Most painful of all, is the fusion of grief with depression, signal anxiety fear and triumph, a phenomenon which most of us have encountered in the course of our clinical work during the past few years, so full of loss. There are many people, especially in these recent years, who still have every cause to be sad, but are really not so; instead they are anxious, despairing and assailed by nightmares in which they are confronted with the images of dead, injured and avenging objects. The post-war scene is studded with innumerable Hamlets unable to live in peace without those they have lost, nor yet able to live in peace with the memories and images they carry within. It is among the most severe instances of chronic neurosis that there will be found those who are suffering from the extremities of morbid grief. (p. 48)

Anderson writes that he was drawn initially to the topic of loss both by its prevalence and by certain interesting clinical phenomena related to it. Such phenomena included events such as the violent reactions of some patients to cathartic treatment focusing on reliving repressed events (usually relating to an intensively ambivalent past relationship); dreams varying enormously in content and affect; reactivation of homosexual dreams, fantasies, or activity; and persistent hysterical symptoms reflecting the story of the loss and the lost object.

In an effort to formulate the relative incidence and shape of different responses to loss, Anderson reviewed the progress of 100 patients he had treated whom he considered ill as a consequence of morbid grief. These patients composed 9 percent of the total number of patients Anderson saw from 1944 to 1947. When initially treated, their responses to morbid grief had assumed the following clinical patterns: anxiety states (59 percent); hysterias (19 percent); obsessional tension states (7 percent); and manic-depressive responses (15 percent), of which 8 percent were agitated depressions, 4 percent were anergic depressions, and 3 percent were hypomanias. Anderson notes that these reactions were neither pure in type nor static; as the work of mourning proceeded, the clinical picture changed. It is his contention that neurotic responses are attempts to deal with and cure profound states of depression resulting from loss. As he writes, "Amongst adults, unresolved neurotic illnesses are often attempts to cure and master states of depression so intolerably painful and threatening to the ego that it utilizes all its resources to prevent itself from disintegrating and losing reality" (p. 49).

Anderson espouses the Kleinian philosophy that manic-depressives and those with pathological grief have never successfully overcome the infantile depressive position. He believes that successful mastery of grief only occurs in the mourner by

> reinstating within himself his lost object as something that is good, and this he manages to do out of temporary disharmony, because his inner world has been built on secure foundations and good object-relationships. In the *healthy* person there has been a successful working through of the infantile depressive situation. (p. 49)

The work of mourning is, he believes, "the gradual restoration of harmony into a disorganized inner world" (p. 51).

Anderson describes some of the individuals who exhibited several of the neurotic conditions he found among his patients. Those who appeared to be suffering from states of chronic anxiety had nightmares, fear, and outbursts of rage. Suicidal ideation was common; these individuals felt they had no right to be alive while the loved one was dead, and often their death was demanded of them in their nightmares. Theirs was a state of internal disintegration and disharmony. The ego now was threatened with the most intense and insatiable persecutory demands of the introjected love object(s):

> The phrase, "the bullet should have got me, not him" has been heard so often that it might appear to have become invested with the meaninglessness of a cliche; yet often enough those who say this are convinced they have no right to live while a comrade is dead and indeed make a travesty of their lives which epitomises an intense despair, a sense of inner badness on the one hand and on the other a reproach, an aggressive attack upon the object who has left them. Many cannot cry, much less feel genuine sadness, instead they are guilt-ridden and convinced of their utter unworthiness; others, though obviously ill, maintain with an almost hypo-manic fortitude that all is well with them, that unlike the foolish dead one, they have "got away with it" and experience bursts of elation, exaltation and triumph, usually interspersed into a background of depression; it is obvious that such states

of mind will pervert, distort and prolong the normal
process of grief. (p. 50)

Anderson describes a group of patients with hysterical symptoms,
who, unlike those with anxiety states, do not use words or reproach
themselves or the lost object. Rather, they demonstrate what has happened
by symbolically killing parts of their own soma by putting out of action
portions of their own ego (i.e., the "body speaks" and instructs that "the
story of what happened to the lost object and how the subject felt [and
feels] about his loss is expressed in mime"; p. 50). Although Anderson
notes varying degrees of awareness of what is occurring, there appears
to be an unconscious denial of an unacceptable notion:

> In all those who have developed symptoms of hysteria as
> a protection against the pain of grief there is the strongest
> denial of an unconscious conviction of personal responsibility
> for the loss, for the murder of the object. I think these
> hysterical reactions are an attempt to ward off something
> worse, a depressive attack and that a part of the organism is
> killed (and yet nursed and kept alive) to save the whole
> organism from self-destruction; a desperate quasi-suicide
> is enacted instead. (p. 50)

Other characteristics associated with morbid grief manifesting as
hysteria are a belle indifference to the hysterical symptom, depression,
hostility and suspiciousness, and great reluctance to talk about self or to
partake in any form of treatment. The symptom is so persistent and the
patient so recalcitrant, Anderson writes, that the psychiatrist can find
himself provoked into using violent countermeasures, such as electroconvulsive therapy or ether-induced cathartic treatments aimed at the
release of dammed-up affects by the forcible reenacting of the traumatic
situation. In Anderson's observations, the former tended to be ineffective;
the latter, capable of producing the most negative reactions.

Anderson attributes much to the bereaved's ambivalence in the relationship to the deceased. Thus, yet another clinical observer witnesses
ambivalence and ensuing guilt and self-devaluation as critical factors in
complicated mourning:

> The feelings of despair, guilt, unworthiness, and persecution
> which stamp the pathological mourner can be understood
> only in terms of the subject's general relationship with his
> objects and this is characterized by its precariousness and
> profound ambivalence; the mourner feels he has killed his
> object because of his unconscious aggression, because of his

malevolent instinctual drives, and is in despair that what he
has valued and loved has been destroyed by his badness. (p. 52)

The implication exists that such processes, although not necessarily to
this extreme, are present in less-conflicted forms of mourning. Anderson
describes a patient who was healthier than the others and who was able
to address his mourning successfully. Nevertheless, he had sought
psychiatric contact and evidenced some of the same issues and conflicts
seen more intensely in those with complicated mourning:

> This singular march of events occurring in a patient who can
> be looked upon as one of the most normal in my group, can
> be understood only in terms of instinctual ambivalence, of
> unconscious hatred against loved objects which have been
> internalized and incorporated into the subject's ego where
> they become internal persecutors with whom the ego is at
> war. At the same time the subject feels that he has killed his
> objects because of his unconscious aggression and depression
> emerges as the affective response to such a realization. (p. 53)

Anderson distinguishes two types of dreams in his mourning subjects. In the first type, the dead object (which Anderson asserts is dead
only in reality, not in the psychic world of the mourner) is injured or injur-
ing; persecuted or persecuting; wearing the garb of death, disease, or
injury; and bent upon the destruction of the dreamer. In other dreams of
this type, the dreamer is performing the most horrifying actions against
the already injured object. In the second type, the dead person is once
more alive, whole, and well, and happy past experiences are reenacted.
It is Anderson's contention that these two extremes represent the
mourner's love and hate and that many variations exist between them. The
nightmare of a mourner can change in content and affect, with the aggression passing away and the object's being restored. Anderson categorically
asserts that, where there has been a positive, mature relationship with the
object, the dreams never assume a ferocious quality; however, if the object
has been the target for unconscious aggression and the relationship was
infantile, then the dreams assume a nightmarish character.

Finally, Anderson examines hypomania. He asserts that, despite
appearing to be the converse of grief, hypomania is actually very much
related to mourning, as both a reaction to the "victory" over the object and
as a defense against despair and depression:

> A hypomanic response to loss undoubtedly appears to be the
> very antithesis of a real grief and sorrow, yet it can colour the
> pattern of mourning and add to it a feeling of triumph, of

exultation over internal persecution. Libidinal energy is used or rather misused to deny, triumph, exalt and a precarious victory is gained over what has been internalized so that feelings of despair there may be interpolated into phases of elation. Such hypomanic responses to grief represent a denial of depression and of all that has happened. "It doesn't matter, it hasn't happened, there is no need to undo what has been done" is the attitude implicit in such responses. (p. 54)

Anderson's observation provides a warning not to accept at face value the manifest appearances of the mourner and continues to illustrate the high frequency of symptoms that, contrary to stereotype, are associated less with vegetative, anergic, or retarded depression than with agitation (e.g., Lindemann, 1944), anxiety (e.g., Anderson, 1949), and aspects of mania (e.g., Freud, 1917/1957c). Both these observations, corroborated by the work of later authors, remain quite valid today.

SAMUEL LEHRMAN

Samuel Lehrman's 1956 exposition "Reactions to Untimely Death" appears to have been the first to offer an in-depth elucidation of the significance of anticipation, timing, and expectation as critical factors influencing mourning. His paper devotes itself to some variants of pathological reactions to untimely death and an analysis of their origin and meaning. He draws upon five case histories to illustrate his points.

Lehrman defines an *untimely death* as one occurring in a relatively young person. The term also implies disadvantageous timing in the death's occurrence. The loss may be an actual sudden, unexpected death, or it may be the diagnosis of a terminal illness. Frequently, there is surprise, shock, and lack of preparation. Lehrman separates these reactions from those in which the work of mourning can be accomplished more quickly because some detachment of the libido has already preceded the death (as in the case of anticipatory grief during a terminal illness), asserting that pathological reactions are more frequent when the death is untimely and sudden.

Lehrman considers reactions to untimely deaths to be variants of pathological grief and mourning. In outlining the conditions giving rise to these reactions, he contrasts them with normal reactions:

They differ from ordinary grief reactions in that the ego is less prepared for the loss, and in that the actual threat to the patient's ego is much greater. . . . Other conditions contributing to the formation of these pathological reactions are: previously existing psychopathology in the mourner, weakness of the ego, and absence of compensations in substitute love objects. Those patients who would tend to develop depressions (in the absence of death loss), or pathological grief reactions to expected or timely death, would inevitably develop pathological reactions to untimely death. It cannot be said, however, that pathological reactions to untimely death are only depressions or depression-equivalents, although prolonged dejection often appears as part of the clinical picture. (pp. 572–573)

In addition to identifying these reactions as forms of pathological grief and mourning, Lehrman draws the following conclusions after examining the literature and his own clinical material.

1. Reactions to untimely death may assume the form of an obsessive compulsive neurosis, anxiety state, hysteria, manic-depressive psychosis, or schizoid state. Clinical pictures are usually mixed. There is a similarity to traumatic neurosis.

2. A normal reaction to untimely death may occur where ego strength is sufficient.

3. Where the reaction to untimely death is pathological, the clinical picture is determined by the mourner's childhood conditioning and the extent to which the infantile neurosis has been mastered. If there is an actual threat to the ego (i.e., the loss of a caretaker), the trauma is felt more keenly. However, the internal fantasy trauma is more important than the actual one.

4. Reactions to untimely death tend to follow the typical pattern of grief reactions, which represent "a defense against unbearable, painful affect, or a defense against serious internal ego-threat such as suicide" (p. 576). The mechanism of denial is obtrusive in reactions to this type of death.

5. There is a marked similarity between reactions to untimely death of a nonaccidental kind and to traumatic neurosis (now called post-traumatic stress disorder). In both, there is a need to master psychological shock, with the mode of mastery being determined by childhood patterning.

6. Although reactions to untimely death should be treated as variants of grief reactions, they tend to be refractory and require therapy for an extended period of time. In psychotherapy, the dosage of affect expression needs to be controlled. Where drugs are employed, they ought to be sedative rather than abreacting. Treatment should proceed slowly.

JOHN BOWLBY

John Bowlby's voluminous work has contributed enormously to the literature on the topics of attachment, human development, childrearing, separation, loss, mourning, and psychopathology (Bowlby, 1960, 1961a, 1961b, 1963, 1969, 1973, 1980, 1982, 1988). As the chief architect of attachment theory, he was the first to articulate the relevance of attachment to mourning and ushered in a new school of thought now espoused by many other clinical observers. Because of the importance of John Bowlby's attachment theory for continuing clinical and empirical work on reactions to loss, his work is addressed in greater depth than that of other theorists. Few, despite having other philosophical or theoretical orientations, would object significantly to Bowlby's basic tenet that humans are profoundly affected and motivated by attachment and that they seek to maintain it. Much of Bowlby's work has been devoted to describing and explaining normal and so-called pathological reactions when attachments are severed.

Coming initially from a psychoanalytic perspective, Bowlby subsequently has incorporated principles from the disciplines of ethology and control theory. He has retained the aspects of psychoanalytic thinking that could be validated, dispensed with many of its abstract and unverifiable concepts, and forged links with cognitive psychology. The concepts of the attachment theory paradigm are compatible with those of neurophysiology and developmental psychology and are capable of meeting the requirements of a scientific discipline (Bowlby, 1980).

Framework of Attachment Theory

The conceptual framework Bowlby brings to the study of mourning enables him to explain the experiences, symptoms, behaviors, pain, and purpose of grief and mourning in human beings and to elucidate their analogues in other primates. Indeed, it is the similarity in responses to separation by human beings and higher order primates that convinces Bowlby that grief responses are instinctual, adaptational, and valuable for survival.

The following premises undergird Bowlby's theory of mourning:

(a) Attachment behaviour is conceived as any form of behaviour that results in a person attaining or retaining proximity to some other differentiated and preferred individual.*

---

* Excerpt from *Attachment and Loss: Vol. 3. Loss: Sadness and depression,* by John Bowlby. Copyright © 1980 by the Tavistock Institute for Human Relations. Reprinted by permission of Basic Books, a division of HarperCollins Publishers.

(b) As a class of behaviour with its own dynamic, attachment behaviour is conceived as distinct from feeding behaviour and sexual behaviour and of at least an equal significance in human life.

(c) During the course of healthy development attachment behaviour leads to the development of affectional bonds or attachments, initially between child and parent and later between adult and adult.

(d) Attachment behaviour, like other forms of instinctive behaviour, is mediated by behavioural systems which early in development become goal-corrected . . . continuous account is taken of any discrepancies there may be between initial instruction and current performance so that behaviour becomes modified accordingly. . . . The goal of attachment behaviour is to maintain certain degrees of proximity to, or of communication with, the discriminated attachment figure(s).

(e) Whereas an attachment bond endures, the various forms of attachment behaviour that contribute to it are active only when required . . . activated only by certain conditions, for example strangeness, fatigue, anything frightening, and un-availability or unresponsiveness of [the] attachment figure, and are terminated only by certain other conditions, for example a familiar environment and the ready availability and responsiveness of an attachment figure.

(f) Many of the most intense emotions arise during the formation, the maintenance, the disruption and the renewal of attachment relationships . . . threat of loss arouses anxiety and actual loss gives rise to sorrow; while each of these situations is likely to arouse anger. . . . Because such emotions are usually a reflection of the state of a person's affectional bonds, the psychology and psychopathology of emotion is found to be in large part the psychology and psychopathology of affectional bonds.

(g) Attachment behaviour has become a characteristic of many species during the course of their evolution because it con-tributes to the individual's survival by keeping him in touch with his caregiver(s), thereby reducing the risk of his coming to harm.

(h) Behaviour complementary to attachment behaviour and serving a complementary function, that of protecting the attached individual, is caregiving.

(i) In view of attachment behaviour being potentially active throughout life and also of its having the vital biological function proposed, it is held a grave error to suppose that, when active in an adult, attachment behaviour is indicative either of pathology or of regression to immature behaviour.

(j) Psychopathology is regarded as due to a person's psychological development having followed a deviant pathway, and not as due to his suffering a fixation at, or a regression to, some early stage of development.

(k) Disturbed patterns of attachment behaviour can be present at any age due to development having followed a deviant pathway. One of the commonest forms of disturbance is the over-ready elicitation of attachment behaviour, resulting in anxious attachment. Another . . . is a partial or complete deactivation of attachment behaviour.

(l) Principal determinants of the pathway along which an individual's attachment behaviour develops, and of the pattern in which it becomes organized, are the experiences he has with his attachment figures during his years of immaturity.

(m) On the way in which an individual's attachment behaviour becomes organized within his personality turns the pattern of affectional bonds he makes during his life. (Bowlby, 1980, pp. 39–41)

Normal and Pathological Mourning

In the context of these tenets of attachment theory, Bowlby's assertions about pathological mourning are well-supported. Pathological mourning is understood to be an exaggeration or distortion of the normal processes of mourning, with pathological variants resulting from defensive processes that have interfered with and diverted its course.

For Bowlby, mourning denotes a wide array of psychological processes, both conscious and unconscious, that are set in train by the loss of a loved person. There are four general phases through which bereaved individuals normally pass in their uncomplicated responses to the loss of a loved one: (a) numbing, (b) yearning and searching, (c) disorganization and despair, and (d) reorganization (Bowlby, 1980). The development of these phases constitutes a further refinement of the reactions Bowlby initially discerned in children temporarily separated from their mothers. In his investigations with children in the 1950s, he originally overlooked numbing but identified the sequence of protest (now yearning and searching), despair (now disorganization and despair), and detachment (now reorganization) as the typical course. He subsequently recognized its similarity to both normal and pathological mourning responses of adults (Bowlby, 1960, 1961a, 1961b, 1963).

With regard to complicated mourning, Bowlby has much to say. Regardless of whether one agrees with his conclusions, he is in a unique position to comment on the topic. Bowlby has offered more information about normal and abnormal response to loss in children and adults than any other investigator. Further, he has accomplished this in the context of making the major interdisciplinary contribution of attachment theory.

In the 1960s, Bowlby wrote a series of papers documenting the patterns of response typical of infants and young children following a significant loss (Bowlby, 1960, 1961a, 1961b, 1963). In these works, he emphasizes several previously undiscussed points. In terms of theory, he draws attention to mourning responses in lower species and highlights the primitive biological processes that humans, responding to separation, share with subhuman primates. This provides attachment theory with solid ethological grounding and anchors human mourning into a biological substrate:

> These records of mourning behaviour in sub-human species
> . . . make it fairly certain that each of the main behavioural
> features which we have listed as characteristics of mourning
> behaviour is in essential outline shared by man with lower
> animals. . . . In old and young, human and sub-human, loss
> of [a] loved object leads to a behavioural sequence which,
> varied though it be, is in some degree predictable. (Bowlby,
> 1961b, p. 331)

Bowlby presents evidence that the responses witnessed in infants and young children to the loss of the mother or primary attachment figure are, at a descriptive level, substantially the same as those observed when an older child or adult loses a loved one. He argues that these processes constitute mourning and that the subjective experience is one of grief. Bowlby (1963) further investigated the responses of the two age groups and discovered that "mourning responses that are commonly seen in infancy and early childhood bear many of the features which are the hallmarks of pathological mourning in the adult" (p. 504). These include unconscious yearning for the lost person, unconscious reproach against the lost person combined with conscious and often unremitting self-reproach, compulsive caring for other persons, and persistent disbelief that the loss is permanent (i.e., often referred to as denial).

Bowlby combines this clinical data with the observation that detachment processes in mourning children often develop prematurely to mask strong residual yearning and anger, which persist on an unconscious level ready for expression. In addition, he notes that early loss is apt to lead to personality disturbance and to leave the individual prone to respond to further loss with pathological mourning and psychiatric illness. In summarizing the case histories of individuals used to illustrate these dynamics, Bowlby (1963) writes:

> What appears . . . to have happened is that processes of mourning, having been evoked in early childhood, took a pathological turn in a way typical of them in that period of life; and that, over the years, the pathological processes have either persisted substantially unchanged or, having [been] temporarily modified, have been evoked afresh by a further loss. The extensive evidence . . . shows that loss of a parent in the early years is especially frequent in persons who later suffer from psychiatric illness. (p. 539)

Bowlby (1961a) elucidates the fashion in which childhood mourning and pathological mourning in adults differ from healthy adult mourning. This difference revolves around the types of defense used by the mourner to cope with the pain of the loss experience, particularly yearning for the lost person, which Bowlby identifies as a primary cause of pain. Such yearning is but one aspect of the critically important urges to recover and reproach the lost person manifested in Bowlby's phase of yearning and searching.

In contrast to Freud's (1917/1957c) earlier view, Bowlby asserts that anger—and its frequent companion, ambivalence—is a normal, integral part of healthy mourning. In discussing anger, he focuses less on its relationship to ambivalence than on its biological and psychological adaptiveness as a response to separation. In temporary situations, in both humans and subhuman primates, anger is useful. It helps the one left behind to overcome obstacles to reunion and to punish the one responsible, making subsequent separation less likely: "The function of this anger appears to be to add punch to the strenuous efforts both to recover the lost object and to dissuade it from deserting again that are the hallmarks of the first [protest] phase of mourning" (Bowlby, 1961a, p. 484).

Bowlby provides ethological evidence that instinctual behavior has evolved in such a way that, in the interests of both individual and group safety, human and animal responses to loss of a loved object always involve the urges first to recover it and then to scold it. This continues to be part of the human being's repertoire, even in those statistically rare cases where the separation is permanent (i.e., death).

When the loss is permanent, anger is futile. However, recognition of the permanence of the loss usually takes time, not only because statistically it is a rarer event than temporary separation, but also because the mourner has not yet learned that the loved one is gone. Indeed, in many instances it is only after repeated frustration of the urges to recover and reproach the lost loved one that the mourner comes to this realization. Going through this process is necessary in order for healthy mourning to proceed. Despite interpretations to the contrary, urges to find, recover, and reunite with the loved one and the feelings and behaviors accompanying these urges—anxiety, yearning, anger, protest, searching—are not pathological. Bowlby (1961a) writes:

> Because in cases of death an angry effort to recover the lost object is so obviously futile there has been a tendency to regard it as itself pathological. I believe this to be profoundly mistaken. So far from being pathological, the evidence suggests that the overt expression of this powerful urge, unrealistic and hopeless though it may be, is a necessary condition for mourning to run a healthy course. Only after every effort has been made to recover the lost object, it seems, is the individual in a mood to admit defeat and to orient himself afresh to a world from which the loved object is accepted as irretrievably missing. Protest, including an angry demand for the object's return and reproach against it for deserting, is as much a part of the *adult's* response to loss, especially a sudden loss, as of the young child's. (p. 485)

Therefore, the urges to recover and reproach the lost object, along with yearning for and anger at it, are critically important aspects of the healthy mourning process. It is a characteristic of pathological mourning that these urges and feelings are not expressed and that they become split off and repressed, thus causing "forms of character disturbance and neurotic illness" (Bowlby, 1961a, p. 485).

This means that, in both children and adults with pathological mourning, the experience of separation initiates defensive processes that lead yearning for the lost object and reproach for its desertion to become unconscious. Specifically, clinical data show that during the reorganization phase the responses that bind the mourner to the deceased and lead him to strive to recover the loved one are subject to a defensive process. In some manner they are removed from consciousness but nonetheless remain latent on an unconscious level, ready to become active again when circumstances change. What is necessary for this to occur varies with the stage to which the detachment, or reorganization, has progressed.

What differentiates these unhealthy mourning processes from healthy ones is that in healthy mourning the onset of these defensive processes is delayed. Consequently, the urges to recover the lost object and to reproach it have sufficient time for expression so that, through their repeated failure, they are extinguished. In childhood and in pathological mourning, the development of these defensive processes is accelerated, and the urges to recover and reproach the lost object have no chance to become extinguished. Instead, they persist unconsciously, with serious consequences.

The mechanisms involved in these processes are fixation and repression, and splitting of the ego. In fixation and repression, while the mourner unconsciously remains fixated on the lost object, his urges to recover and reproach it and the ambivalent emotions connected with these urges undergo repression. In splitting of the ego, one part of the personality, which is secret but conscious, denies that the object is really lost and maintains that there still is communication with it or that it soon will be recovered, whereas another part of the personality shares with the outside world the knowledge that the object is irretrievably lost. Although these views are incompatible, they can coexist for many years. Both repression and ego splitting can lead to psychiatric illness. This is why children with early losses are predisposed toward faulty personality development and why they, along with adults experiencing pathological mourning, are prone to psychiatric illness.

Two points of clarification must be made. First, Bowlby does not believe that early childhood loss inevitably leads to crippling of the personality. What he does maintain is that such loss can have sequelae that in later life too often lead to dysfunction. Second, he reiterates that the defensive processes in childhood and adult pathological mourning are pathological variants of those characterizing healthy mourning, the latter being of lesser degree and later onset. What is pathological is not the defenses themselves but their scope and intensity, the prematurity of their onset, and their tendency to persist.

Dispositional Factors in Complicated Mourning

Bowlby's work has led him to conclude that adults whose mourning takes a pathological course are likely before their bereavement to have made affectional relationships of certain kinds. In such persons, relationships are likely to be suffused with strong ambivalence, either overt or latent. Although not all those biased to make these kinds of relationships will respond to bereavement with disordered mourning, individuals with the following dispositions are more apt to do so.

1. *Disposition to make anxious and ambivalent relationships.* These individuals are often described as insecure, ambivalent, and having a low frustration tolerance.

2. *Disposition toward compulsive caregiving.* These individuals are often described as nervous, overdependent, clinging or temperamental, or neurotic.

3. *Disposition to assert independence of affectional ties.* These individuals are often described as self-sufficient, but their self-sufficiency seems precariously based.

Defensive Processes and the Defensive Exclusion
of Unwelcome Information

Bowlby translates the language associated with mental processes, defense mechanisms, and behaviors operating to mitigate the pain of mourning from traditional terminology (e.g., *repression, splitting, denial, dissociation, projection, displacement, identification,* and *reaction formation*) into terms consistent with his preference for a human information-processing model:

> My thesis is that the traditionally termed defensive processes can all be understood as examples of the defensive exclusion of unwelcome information; and that most of them differ from each other only in regard to the completeness and/or the persistence of the exclusion. Many are found in both healthy and disordered variants of mourning, but a few are confined to the disordered. (Bowlby, 1980, p. 140)

The duration and extent to which they influence mental functioning distinguish healthy forms of defensive process from pathological ones. Processes of defensive exclusion range from being clearly involuntary (e.g., numbing) to being totally voluntary (e.g., deliberate avoidance of places likely to evoke grief). They range from processes that are quite clear and of which the mourner is totally aware (e.g., a conscious belief that the loss is not permanent) to those that are so ill-defined and remote from consciousness as to require therapeutic work for the mourner to be made aware of them. Beliefs may be open to revision or rigidly held and resistant to alteration.

Bowlby lists a number of such processes, derived from Parkes (1970), that in almost any combination can be active in a given person, either simultaneously or successively. These include processes that (a) result in a bereaved person's feeling numbed and unable to think about what has happened; (b) direct attention and activity away from painful thoughts and reminders and toward neutral or pleasant ones; (c) maintain the belief that the loss is not permanent and that reunion is still possible; and (d) result in recognition that the loss has in fact occurred combined with a feeling that links with the dead still persist, often manifested in a comforting sense of the continuing presence of the lost person. Bowlby notes that processes associated with the feeling that links to the deceased still persist "so far from contributing to pathology, are an integral part of healthy mourning. . . . Processes of each of the other types may, however, take pathological forms" (Bowlby, 1980, p. 140).

Bowlby (1980) also points out two additional defensive processes that, unless present only briefly, appear to be incompatible with a healthy outcome. The first of these is a process (usually referred to in the psychoanalytic literature as displacement) in which the mourner redirects anger from the person who elicited it toward someone else. The second involves the mourner's cognitively disconnecting all of the emotional responses to the loss from the situation that elicited them (in traditional terminology, repression, splitting, or dissociation).

Cognitive Biases

Bowlby describes cognitive biases that influence how an individual responds to the world and events in it. These are representational models of the world and the self through which all incoming information is filtered and interpreted. What one perceives; how, in what way, and with what degree of awareness one perceives it; what one does with it and/or because of it; and its significance and meaning are all influenced by the cognitive structures through which information passes. These structures have been termed *cognitive biases*. These personal, internal biases interact with external conditions to affect one's response to a loss.

One of Bowlby's most insistent contentions, one further evidencing the role of attachment figures throughout life, is that cognitive biases are largely determined by early attachment figures and experiences with them:

> Plainly the directions in which an individual is cognitively biased are a function of the representational models of attachment figures and of self that he has built during his childhood and adolescence, and . . . these in turn are a function of the experiences he had in his family during those years. . . . In particular, I argue that the part played by the kinds of childhood experience a person has had are critical. For, through the medium of his representational models, they are in large part responsible, first, for the patterns of affectional relationship he makes during his life and, secondly, for the cognitive biases he brings to any loss he may sustain. (Bowlby, 1980, pp. 232–233)

Each individual processes loss in an idiosyncratic way depending on his own cognitive biases. These biases, therefore, are influential in determining the course mourning will take. Bowlby (1980) offers the following as examples of some of these influential biases: (a) how the bereaved construes the part played in the loss by the deceased, (b) how he construes his own part in the loss and the way the deceased might regard it, (c) what expectations he has regarding the way those who might lend assistance would treat him, (d) how aware he is of constructions he puts on past events and their influence on his present expectations, and (e) the extent to which whatever constructions and expectations he may have are open to revision.

Disordered Variants

Bowlby identifies two main disordered variants in adult mourning: chronic mourning and prolonged absence of conscious grieving. He also specifies a minor one, euphoria. About disordered variants in general, he writes:

Disordered variants of mourning lead to many forms of physical ill health as well as of mental ill health. Psychologically they result in a bereaved person's capacity to make and to maintain love relationships becoming more or less seriously impaired or, if already impaired, being left more impaired than it was before. Often they affect also a bereaved person's ability to organize the rest of his life. Disordered variants can be of every degree of severity from quite slight to extremely severe. In their lesser degrees they are not easily distinguished from healthy mourning. (Bowlby, 1980, p. 137)

Although they appear to be opposites, chronic mourning and the prolonged absence of conscious grieving share several important features. In both, the loss is believed, consciously or unconsciously, still to be reversible. Consequently, several aspects of mourning fail to come to closure:

The urge to search may therefore continue to possess the bereaved, either unceasingly or episodically, anger and/or self-reproach to be readily aroused, sorrow and sadness to be absent. In both variants the course of mourning remains uncompleted. Because the representational models [the mourner] has of himself and of the world about him remain unchanged his life is either planned on a false basis or else falls into unplanned disarray. (Bowlby, 1980, p. 138)

The fact that these two main variants of disordered mourning have a common thread is what explains the existence of clinical conditions containing features of both or representing an oscillation between them (e.g., the common combination in which, after a loss, a person for a few weeks or months shows an absence of conscious grieving only to become overwhelmed abruptly by intense emotions that lead to a state of chronic mourning).

Chronic mourning

Bowlby describes his first disordered variant, chronic mourning, in these terms:

The emotional responses to loss are unusually intense and prolonged, in many cases with anger or self-reproach dominant and persistent, and sorrow notably absent. So long as these responses continue the mourner is unable to plan his life, which commonly becomes and remains sadly disorganized. Depression is a principal symptom, often combined or alternating with anxiety, "agoraphobia" . . . hypochondria or alcoholism. (Bowlby, 1980, pp. 137–138)

In terms of the four phases of mourning delineated by Bowlby, the various forms of chronic mourning can be regarded as extended and distorted versions of the phases of yearning and searching and of disorganization and despair.

Personalities and predictors associated with chronic mourning. Two personalities that appear in Bowlby's works to be most prone to chronic mourning are those with a disposition to make anxious and ambivalent relationships and those with a disposition toward compulsive caregiving. Some early responses to loss that Bowlby believes are frequently predictive of chronic mourning include the following.

1. An abrupt and more intense and disruptive experience of mourning that begins after several months in which little or no response is evidenced

2. Acute disturbance, seen as early as 3 to 6 weeks after the loss, in the form of one or more of the following: unusually intense and continuous yearning, unusually deep despair expressed as welcoming the prospect of death, persistent anger and bitterness, and pronounced guilt and self-reproach

3. Recovery not commenced by the end of the first year

4. Anger and resentment persisting long after the early weeks, correlated with persistence of tension, restlessness, and intense yearning

5. The bereaved's reporting after a few weeks that he finds others unhelpful to him in his mourning

Mislocations of the lost person's presence. Although not exclusive to chronic mourning, mislocations of the lost person's presence occur most often in this form of mourning. Instead of the relatively common practice of locating the deceased somewhere appropriate (e.g., in the grave or a favorite chair) and experiencing the person as a companion, a minority of mourners locate the lost person somewhere quite inappropriate (e.g., within an animal, a physical object, another person, or the bereaved himself). Bowlby notes that inappropriate locations are pathological and seem always to be associated with incomplete or failed mourning.

Cognitive biases in chronic mourning. According to Bowlby, several biases contribute to the development of chronic mourning. Persons with this particular disordered variant tend to have representational models of attachment figures, and of the self, that often have incompatible features. These lead to specific biases about loss that promote chronic mourning.
      Bowlby describes the two pairs of models possessed by the chronic mourner:

Almost always, I infer, he will have a model of his parents
as above criticism and a complementary one of himself as a
more or less worthless person. He will believe himself a being
given to ingratitude and unjustifiable anger, who is fortunate
to have the self-sacrificing parents he has and to be in duty
bound to revere them. Coexistent with, but subordinate to,
this pair of models will be another pair in which his parents
are seen as grudging in their affection and attention and too
often unavailable, and he himself as being more justified in
his demands on his parents and in his anger when they fail
him than his parents allow, and also possessed of better feelings and intentions towards them than they ever credit him
with.
  The first pair of models, it is inferred, are derived from
what his parents have always told him, and the second,
subordinate, pair from his own first-hand experience.
Although the pairs are incompatible, both persist. . . .
Moreover, either one pair or the other or both are almost
certain to be applied unmodified whenever he embarks on
any new affectional relationship, for example marriage.
(Bowlby, 1980, pp. 234–235)

Bowlby breaks with tradition here by departing from the belief that
a depressed person idealizes his attachment figure as a consequence of
regression and/or response to aggression. Instead, Bowlby postulates that
an adult is strongly biased to view his attachment figure as being above
criticism "because one or both of his parents have insisted he do so" and
because they not infrequently would tend to "have backed their insistence
by threatening sanctions, mild, severe, or even terrifying, should he do
otherwise" (p. 236).

An inherent problem, however, is that the chronic mourner, by virtue
of his possessing two incompatible pairs of models, is in an unstable
mental situation. Because pairs may shift, the pair dominant during one
phase of life may become subordinate to the other pair in a different phase
of life. Notwithstanding this, even the subordinate pair of models exerts
a considerable effect on the individual's perceptions, feelings, and actions.

According to Bowlby, other features in addition to the ones already
described can predispose the individual to the development of chronic
mourning. Whether or not these are present in the mourner's cognitive
models depends upon his childhood experiences. For example, problems
may occur when the model of the self is pictured as being under total
obligation to provide care for the attachment figure. Or difficulties may
arise when an individual has been made to see his actions as constantly
jeopardizing the health—even the lives—of his parents. In this case the
person is strongly biased to construe the death of one of them as precisely
the catastrophe to which his alleged selfishness, thoughtlessness, and

deficient caregiving was bound to lead. The individual does not permit the thought that the deceased may on occasion have been at fault, thereby leading to idealization. In a third scenario, problems may be associated with a model of the attachment figure as someone who is more or less certain to react to any shortcomings of the self by threatening to desert or commit suicide. This situation leaves the mourner strongly biased to interpret the death as the long-awaited realization of these threats, with consequent anger and the misapprehension that, as in the past, the loved one can be recovered through coercion or supplication. These feelings account for the continuation over many years of angry protest and fruitless search. Whether the bereaved construes the death of the attachment figure as the result of punitive desertion or his own almost criminal negligence, the consequence is that he cannot help being convinced that he caused it and ultimately has only himself to blame. Insofar as he has a sense of the deceased's continuing presence, he will interpret that presence as plotting revenge. This accounts for his acute anxiety and alarming dreams.

Prolonged absence of conscious grieving

In this variant of pathological mourning, the bereaved's life continues to be organized much as before; however, he is apt to be afflicted with a number of psychological and physical ills, and he may suddenly and inexplicably become acutely depressed. Psychotherapy often reveals that the person sustains a number of disturbances that are derived from normal mourning, although strangely disconnected both cognitively and emotionally from the loss that gave rise to them. Individuals whose mourning is prone to take this pathological course are those with a disposition to assert independence of affectional ties.

In terms of Bowlby's four phases of mourning, the prolonged absence of conscious grieving can be regarded as a pathologically prolonged extension of the phase of numbing. Ever aware of the possibility for criticism, Bowlby takes pains to reassure the skeptic that the absence of conscious grieving reflects a variant of mourning and not simply a person's lack of cause to mourn. In delineating the telltale signs of impact on the bereaved, he paints the following clinical picture:

> Adults who show prolonged absence of conscious grieving are commonly self-sufficient people, proud of their independence and self-control, scornful of sentiment; tears they regard as weakness. After the loss they take a pride in carrying on as though nothing had happened, are busy and efficient, and may appear to be coping splendidly. But a sensitive observer notes that they are tense and often short-tempered. No references to the loss are volunteered, reminders are avoided and well-wishers allowed neither to sympathize nor to refer to the event. Physical symptoms may supervene:

headaches, palpitations, aches and pains. Insomnia is common, dreams unpleasant. . . . In some persons cheerfulness seems a little forced; others appear wooden and too formal. Some are more sociable than formerly, others withdrawn; in either case there may be excessive drinking. Bouts of tears or depression may come from what appears a clear sky. Certain topics are carefully avoided. Fear of emotional breakdown may be evident, whether admitted as it sometimes is or not. Grownup children become protective of a widowed parent, fearing lest reference to the loss by a thoughtless friend or visitor should disturb a precarious balance. Consolation is neither sought nor welcomed. (Bowlby, 1980, pp. 153–154)

Many of those who evidence a prolonged absence of conscious grieving avoid losing control. Others are less successful and, against their will, become tearful and upset at times. Although persons with this type of disordered variant tend not to dwell on their own loss, not infrequently they will become deeply and excessively concerned with the welfare of another, typically someone who has had or is having a difficult life, as a rule including a bereavement. They compulsively bestow care on this person whether welcomed or not, whether required or not. Acting as a compulsive caregiver may allow the mourner to care for the sadness and neediness in another that he is unable or unwilling to recognize and respond to in himself.

Consistent with their avoidance of the loss, these mourners often dispose of all tangible possessions that might remind them of the lost person. However, some may retain certain select items that serve as linking objects (Volkan, 1972, 1981), or objects perceived as having the power to magically reunite the mourner with the deceased.

It is Bowlby's belief that sooner or later at least some of those who consciously avoid grieving break down. Usually, they develop some form of depression. Bowlby identifies four classes of events that can precipitate such breakdowns: (a) an anniversary of the unmourned death; (b) another loss, often relatively minor; (c) reaching the age of the deceased when that person died; and (d) a loss suffered by a compulsively cared for person with whose experience the mourner may be identifying. Other individuals in this category may not suffer an actual breakdown but may have personal difficulties as a consequence of failed mourning. Empty personal relationships, a lack of concern or feelings, depersonalization, and a sense of unreality are just some of the prices paid for the prolonged absence of conscious grieving.

Cognitive biases in prolonged absence of conscious grieving. Cognitive biases contributing to a prolonged absence of conscious grieving appear to stem from childhood experiences of disparaging and sarcastic remarks made by parents when the child is in distress and seeking comfort. As a result of the child's learning that to cry and seek comfort brings rebuff and contempt, these culminate in cultivation of self-sufficiency and a self-protective shell. As much as possible, the individual learns to disavow the desire for love and support. In some, depending on the frequency of parental rejection and separation and the amount of anxiety and distress experienced, the shell becomes so thick that affectional relationships become blunted and the loss ceases to have much significance. Such a person may become proud of his self-reliance or may regret his lack of feeling; quite commonly, he oscillates between the two.

Despite the fact that Bowlby has spent much of his professional life providing evidence that childhood experiences play a major role in such reactions as the prolonged absence of conscious grieving following a loss, he does make the point that experiences of later life must not be overlooked. Adults consciously may distract themselves from grieving in response to the reactions of others or to respond to wishes or criticisms once made by the deceased.

Euphoria

Bowlby identifies euphoria as the third disordered variant of mourning. Although this response is uncommon and little studied, it is well recognized. There appear to be two types: In one, the euphoric response to a death is associated with an emphatic refusal to believe that the death has occurred and a vivid sense of the deceased's continuing presence. In the second type, the opposite of the first, the loss is acknowledged and claimed to be of great advantage to the bereaved. Although the euphoric mood in both is similar, the two types reflect very dissimilar dynamics:

> In the one, attachment desires continue to be directed towards
> the original figure who is claimed still to be meeting them. In
> the other, by contrast, desire for attachment is disowned and
> the claim to self-sufficiency is paramount. In these respects
> the condition has much in common with prolonged absence
> of grieving and its related condition of compulsive self-
> reliance. (Bowlby, 1980, p. 171)

GEORGE ENGEL

In his paper "Is Grief a Disease? A Challenge for Medical Research," George Engel (1961) first and most succinctly poses the quintessential philosophic question about the nature of grief, clarifying its oxymoronic quality (i.e., it is a normal abnormality). In further writings, he makes major contributions by delineating grief's characteristic features and six stages (Engel, 1964) and by elucidating its connection with biology and stress by associating object loss with both central nervous system activity and the conservation-withdrawal system (Engel, 1962a).

In terms of complicated mourning, Engel (1962b) identifies four forms that so-called unsuccessful or unresolved grief may take, in addition to those that constitute traditional psychopathological entities. These forms include denial of the death, denial of the loss or the affect (the death is acknowledged, but its significance is denied intellectually or affectively), use of a vicarious object (onto whom the mourner projects feelings of loss and who is taken as a replacement object unrealistically expected to fulfill the role of the lost object), and prolonged unresolved grief.

Engel appears to be one of the first, if not the first, to discriminate denial of the death from denial of the loss or affect. Many caregivers erroneously assume these two ideas are inextricably bound together, yet a mourner can acknowledge the death and not its emotional impact, its significance, or its implications. Both forms of denial can be found in complicated mourning. Denial of the fact of the death is more pathological and difficult to sustain; denial of the impact, significance, and implications of the death is often obscured under the external acknowledgment that the death did occur in reality.

Engel notes that the work of successful mourning usually takes from 6 to 12 months and that "the complete resolution of the grief is indicated by the ability to remember comfortably and realistically both the pleasures and disappointments of the lost relationship" (Engel, 1962b, p. 279). He believes that interference with the mourning process can lead to pathological consequences, noting that "like wound healing, successful mourning involves an orderly sequence and an irreducible interval of time, interference with which may distort the process of healing and lead to pathological consequences" (p. 274).

With regard to complicated mourning, Engel points out two harbingers of later difficulties. The first is the inability to cry. This inability is to be distinguished from the absence of crying in situations in which the person lost is not seriously missed or where voluntary suppression of crying complies with environmental or cultural demands. Rather, Engel refers to individuals who want to cry or feel that they should, yet are unable to. This is most likely to transpire when the relationship with the deceased has been highly ambivalent and when the survivor feels a good deal of guilt and shame. Ambivalence, usually not consciously acknowledged, is often expressed in the mourner's concern that others will see her as cold or hardhearted for her lack of tears. To avoid this possibility, she protests her devotion to the deceased. When the predominant affect is hopelessness, there are the additional elements of withdrawal, detachment, and apathy toward the death.

The second indicator of potential problems is when guilt causes the mourner to take on undesirable traits or symptoms of the deceased or to exaggerate the need to fulfill the wishes of that person. Identification with positive features is part of the normal mourning process. However, identification with negative features is a potential source of later pathology.

COLIN MURRAY PARKES

Providing clinical, theoretical, and empirical contributions to the literature since 1964, Colin Murray Parkes has been instrumental in increasing understanding of complicated mourning. His contributions over the past three decades have been published alone (Parkes, 1964, 1965, 1970, 1985, 1987, 1987–1988, 1988) and with others, most notably Robert Weiss (Parkes & Weiss, 1983) and Ira Glick (Glick et al., 1974).

Taking the posture that failure of recovery designates the bereavement reaction as abnormal, Parkes and Weiss (1983) suggest that "pathological variations are no more than extreme forms [of normal grief reactions] that appear in response to particularly unfavorable circumstances" (pp. 15–16). Dissatisfied with problems in using traditional psychiatric diagnostic categories to lend an understanding of grief, Parkes and Weiss have identified three main types of pathological grief syndromes associated with failure to recover from bereavement, combining both etiological and descriptive features: unanticipated grief, conflicted grief, and chronic grief. These three forms constitute a revision of Parkes' (1965) earlier categorization of pathological grief into inhibited, delayed, and chronic reactions, which he perceived to exist in addition to a variety of nonspecific reactions, such as psychosomatic and psychoneurotic disorders.

Unanticipated Grief

Unanticipated grief occurs after a sudden, unexpected, and untimely loss and is so disruptive that uncomplicated recovery can no longer be expected. Mourners are unable to grasp the full implications of the loss. Their adaptive capacities are seriously assaulted, and they suffer feelings of bewilderment, anxiety, self-reproach, depression, and despair so extreme as to render them unable to function normally in any areas of life. There is difficulty in accepting the loss, despite intellectual recognition of the death, and the death may continue to seem both inexplicable and unbelievable. There is avoidance of confrontation with the loss. Although some of these responses are seen in all mourners, it is the persistence of these reactions that constitutes the pathological grief syndrome. Typically, the mourner remains socially withdrawn, developing a sense of the continued presence of the loved one, to whom he feels bound. This feeling hampers the mourner's ability to function socially and occupationally.

The absence of forewarning appears to be a major disabling factor because it denies the survivor the opportunity to make gradual changes in world view (i.e., assumptive world). Along with this, the recognition of the unpredictability of the world and the insecurity it contains leads to significant anxiety, which undermines coping ability and adaptation.

Research on widows in Glick et al.'s (1974) Harvard Study suggests that this insecurity can persist in interesting ways. For example, widows whose husbands died suddenly were less likely to get remarried, appearing to fear putting themselves again in the same situation in which their loss had occurred. They were unwilling to subject themselves and their children to the possibility of another, similar unanticipated loss. Marriage became associated with great catastrophe, and they became phobic about it. Unlike widows whose husbands' deaths were anticipated and could confidently be ascribed to some disease process which thereafter might be feared, the widows whose husbands died without warning appeared thereafter to fear marriage itself.

Conflicted Grief

Conflicted grief arises after the loss of extremely troubled, ambivalent relationships. It evidences an unusual progression. Initially, the mourner exhibits a relative absence of expressed grief, often engaging in social activities and sometimes experiencing relief. However, this response is followed by a significant turnaround. The conflicted grief reaction pattern eventually becomes marked by severe grief: sadness, lack of acceptance of the loss, anxiety, self-doubt, guilt, remorse, and continued yearning and pining for the deceased associated with a persistent need for and sense of connection to the lost one.

Parkes and Weiss (1983) write that conflicted grief closely resembles the pathological reaction of delayed grief often observed in psychiatric settings, wherein the relative absence of overt grief in the early post-bereavement period is followed by a state of generalized anxiety, self-doubt, and distress. It is hypothesized that the ambivalence of the highly conflicted relationship contributes to this pattern of initial absence of grief followed by intense reaction. Parkes and Weiss note that in the early phase of bereavement these mourners repudiate their attachment to the deceased and assert that the conflicted relationship has left them with nothing to mourn. However, it appears that, notwithstanding the conflict and insecurity, a strong attachment existed. The strength of that attachment explains the difficulties that arise when initial attempts to avoid grieving fail.

These individuals experience problems inherent in mourning any ambivalent relationship: Previous experiences in the relationship leave them with more cause for guilt and self-reproach, and negative feelings interfere with necessary grief work, bring their own guilt and self-reproach, leave these persons few positive memories to support continued feelings of worth, and promote a sense of being hypocritical for expressing pain. In addition, grief exists for the loss of opportunity ever to resolve the conflicted relationship and for what could have been and was not.

Problems returning to effective functioning associated with this type of pathological grief pattern are also due to the premorbid personalities of the individuals involved. Those who would tolerate a conflicted relationship to begin with tend to have had the kind of early experiences that would predispose them to difficulty establishing satisfactory attachments and thus would be apt to be less capable of healthy recovery from loss.

Chronic Grief

The third type of pathological grief identified by Parkes and Weiss (1983) is chronic grief. This pattern, which they view as the most common of the pathological forms of grief response, is characterized by intractable grieving, low self-confidence, intense yearning for the deceased, feelings of helplessness, and anxiety. Chronic grief is most often associated with a highly and anxiously dependent relationship upon the deceased, as defined by "the inability to function adequately in the roles of ordinary life without the presence, emotional support, or actual help of the partner" (p. 135).

In the first few weeks after the death, the coincidence of intense yearning and a highly dependent relationship is an early indicator of what may become chronic grief. Parkes and Weiss regard the highly dependent relationship giving rise to chronic grief as a disorder of attachment that stimulates a loss reaction resistant to resolution. They postulate four factors associated with the persistence of this reaction.

1. The chronic griever's anxiously dependent personality, marked by fear of unfamiliar and potentially dangerous situations, leads to social withdrawal. This becomes a self-perpetuating situation because there is a consequent lack of the security, support, and reassurance of others that would lead to social reengagement.

2. The bereaved is able to maintain an illusion of security by continuing to turn toward the fantasy of a continued relationship with the deceased. Avoidance of recovery means the mourner does not have to relinquish this fantasy.

3. The mourner's lack of confidence in his own power to survive, or in the outside world as a safe place into which to venture, may make the security of an obsolescent world preferable to the anxiety of reality of the new world without the deceased.

4. Continuing in the role of mourner may garner the sympathy and support of others, which is quite attractive to the individual who views himself as helpless.

Parkes and Weiss conclude that the essential element of chronic grief is insecurity, observing that "it is insecurity that fosters emotional dependency and, later, a refusal to budge from a position of chronic mourning" (pp. 153–154).

Impediments to the Recovery Process

According to Parkes and Weiss (1983) there may be a rough correspondence between the main factor associated with each of these three pathological patterns and the part in their three-phase recovery process with which it interferes (i.e., intellectual recognition and explanation of the loss, emotional acceptance of the loss, and development of a new identity). It may be that a lack of forewarning (associated with unanticipated grief) compromises the ability to understand and explain the death because the death seems so disconnected with anything that preceded it. Ambivalence (associated with conflicted grief) appears to create problems in emotional acceptance of the death because of the complexity of feeling, intensity of guilt and remorse, and difficulty in acknowledging and accepting feelings and behaviors the mourner now would prefer to disown. Extreme dependence (associated with chronic grief) appears to interfere with the development of a new identity because of the mourner's continued linkage to the deceased and insufficient self-confidence or hope for the future. Other impediments to recovery include a tendency to doubt one's own capacities and be hopeless about the future and deathbed prohibitions of mourning issued by the loved one (e.g., "Don't grieve for me").

Similarities Between Normal and Pathological Grief

Parkes' 1965 study of the differences between bereaved individuals referred for psychiatric help (presumably persons with pathological grief responses) and a group of bereaved individuals who did not require psychiatric intervention (presumably persons with typical grief responses) reveals interesting data from which to extrapolate information about complicated mourning. Specifically, Parkes found that all subjects appeared to experience the same symptoms of grief. Only two symptoms were significantly more frequent in bereaved psychiatric patients: difficulty in accepting the fact of a loss and self-blame. To a lesser extent, hostility toward others associated with the loss was also reported more commonly in this group. Although both emotions were more frequent and seen more often as a major problem by those in the psychiatric group, there were no great differences between the two groups in the specific forms of guilt and anger expressed (Parkes, 1987). Among the psychiatric group—whose forms of atypical grieving most often were associated with panic attacks, persisting and intense guilt, or hypochondriacal symptoms of identification with the deceased's last illness—Parkes found two reactions: a tendency for grief to be prolonged and a tendency for grief to be delayed (with some delayed reactions also being prolonged). This presages Parkes' subsequent findings on chronic and conflicted grief.

In a related vein, Parkes identifies two invariants in atypical grief: intense separation anxiety and strong, but only partially successful, avoidance. As he writes:

These two features . . . were evident in all the forms of atypical grief I have come across. The degree of disbelief and avoidance varied considerably, but whatever its degree there was always an impression that the underlying separation anxiety was severe. (Parkes, 1987, p. 129)

From his studies, Parkes concludes that, in terms of the kind of reactions to bereavement, there are no differences between psychiatrically disturbed mourners and individuals appearing to evidence typical reactions and that no symptoms are peculiar to pathological grief per se, although extreme guilt, identification symptoms, and delay in grief do seem to indicate that pathology may develop:

The overall conclusion . . . must be that among the various mental disorders that can be precipitated by bereavement the most frequent are likely to comprise atypical forms of grief. Although these atypical forms differ in intensity and duration from the more usual reactions to bereavement, certain aspects of which may be exaggerated or distorted, they do not differ in kind. There are no symptoms that are peculiar to pathological grief although it seems reasonable to view extreme expressions of guilt, identification symptoms (as opposed to other phenomena of identification), and delay in the onset of grief of more than two weeks' duration, as indicators that the reaction to bereavement may take a pathological course. (Parkes, 1987, p. 134)

Believing that only if the underlying grief is resolved will the mourner reach genuine recovery and perceiving that failure to recover from bereavement may take the form of constriction and sadness associated with a wide variety of other conditions, Parkes (1987) and Parkes and Weiss (1983) urge that intervention be geared to the specific type of pathological reaction. The caregiver must discriminate among types because the intervention appropriate for one type may be inappropriate or even harmful for another. For example, encouraging overt expression of affect in conflicted grief may be quite helpful, but encouraging such expression in chronic grief will do nothing but perpetuate the problem.

LORRAINE SIGGINS

Lorraine Siggins' main contribution is not in adding new data to the field but in organizing and interpreting it in an especially clarifying fashion. Her synthesis of the sometimes confusing evolving work of the psychoanalytic writers, "Mourning: A Critical Survey of the Literature" (Siggins,

1966), is the most lucid exposition available on these conceptualizations of the processes of mourning. She also provides an excellent address of the components of grief—previously excluded by some in their emphasis on an ideal relationship—and presents a useful classification of the literature on mourning.

When Siggins discusses so-called pathological mourning reactions, she takes as her point of departure the normal reactions of mourning. Specifically, she brings up several clinical issues heretofore given insufficient attention and suggests that three situations indicate pathology. First, a persistent absence of emotion signals an undue delay in the beginning of the work of mourning. Siggins subscribes to the belief that unmanifested grief will be expressed in some fashion in pathological or disguised ways. She notes that absence of emotion is closely related to denial and may be present for a while in mourning considered healthy, serving to postpone pain until reality becomes unavoidable. She also finds this denial occasionally present after the initial strain of shock and grief, providing a brief respite to the mourner. For some individuals, the absence of emotion actually constitutes an identification with the deceased, who obviously now experiences no emotion. According to Siggins, the persistent absence of emotion indicates pathology. The important issue appears not to be that emotion is absent per se, but rather when and why such an absence occurs and the effects of it.

Second, a prolongation of mourning can provide an avenue for avoiding the difficult tasks of mourning. In this situation, the processes employed to assist in mourning actually interfere with it:

> The very processes by which the work of mourning is carried out are those that can be used to hold on to the illusion that the dead person lives, and so retard the work of mourning. These are the interrelated processes of hypercathexis of memories . . . introjection of the object . . . and identification. . . . These are all present normally and are the means of giving up the object by reducing the pain and allowing the process to take place gradually. However, if this internal grasping of the object ceases to be a means to an end—namely the first step in relinquishing the object—and becomes instead an end in itself, so as to hold on to the object, deny its loss, and avoid a fresh confrontation with reality, then it dislocates the process of mourning. In this situation reality is ignored. (Siggins, 1966, pp. 20–21)

Third, a distortion of mourning involves normal grief reactions of abnormal intensity, which not only are themselves pathological, but also prolong the process:

There is still a third group of reactions best dealt with under
the heading of pathological mourning . . . namely grief reactions of abnormal intensity. I have previously mentioned a list
of reactions that Freud did not include in his ideal description
of normal mourning, but which do in fact occur because of
the complexity of human relationships—anxiety, fear, guilt,
helplessness, anger, somatic symptoms and so on. Any one of
these may be exaggerated out of all proportion. Such exaggeration usually represents a conflict with the lost object.
These intensified reactions are themselves pathological, but
they may in addition cause an abnormal prolongation of the
mourning process. (Siggins, 1966, p. 21)

Siggins identifies four factors that predispose to pathological mourning: (a) sudden, unexpected occurrence of death, (b) the manner of death,
(c) a highly ambivalent relationship with the deceased, and (d) low tolerance of pain and anxiety.

In brief, Siggins characterizes pathological mourning as a situation
in which "the elements which ordinarily constitute mourning are present,
but the process is abnormally delayed, protracted, or intense" (Siggins,
1966, p. 21). In addition to normal and pathological mourning, Siggins
discusses a third major class of responses to the death of a loved one. She
holds that the pathology of this class is different and that it therefore may
be distinguished from mourning proper, either normal or abnormal. This
is the appearance of a recognizable psychiatric illness precipitated by
bereavement. Although she perceives such an illness as a pathological
response to loss, she does not view it as pathological mourning per se.

Siggins readily admits to overlap among normal mourning, pathological mourning, and psychiatric illness precipitated by loss. She illustrates how the same reaction can constitute an aspect of each of these three
different classes of response:

Among the three classifications I have suggested there is, of
course, some overlapping. For example, anxiety is a part of
the normal mourning process. If it becomes exaggerated, yet
is part of a recognizable picture of mourning which is still progressing even though retarded, it is classified as pathological
mourning. However, if anxiety is not merely exaggerated but
forms the predominant symptom without the other signs of
mourning, it is psychiatrically diagnosed as a psychoneurotic
reaction, anxiety type, precipitated by the death of a loved
one. (Siggins, 1966, p. 21)

The diagnostic and therapeutic implications of this overlap require the
caregiver to go beyond mere identification of the reaction by positioning

it in the more global context of pattern of response to the loss. In addition, the need for differential diagnosis is inherent in this observation.

CHARLES WAHL

Charles Wahl commences his 1970 article "The Differential Diagnosis of Normal and Neurotic Grief Following Bereavement" by putting into perspective one of the major issues at hand in complicated mourning: discrimination between normal and abnormal response to loss. In an effort to accomplish that task, Wahl examined 28 of his own cases of intense or protracted grief. From this he identified a set of criteria that he believes differentiates categories of normal and so-called neurotic grief reactions. Specifically, Wahl finds that, in contrast to normal grief, neurotic grief is distinguished by nine characteristics.

1. It is excessive and disproportionate in nature, as well as prolonged in duration.

2. It produces feelings of irrational despair and persistent hopelessness, along with a profound loss of personal identity.

3. It tends to evoke strong feelings of personal finitude and thanatophobia.

4. It is associated with the mourner's inability to accept or deal with ambivalent feelings toward the deceased.

5. It is associated with the mourner's personification of effect, in which there is a perception that the deceased has died purposely to reject, punish, or abandon, resulting in impaired self-esteem.

6. It is associated with the mourner's persistent irrational belief that the death was somehow her fault—in other words, a personification of causation.

7. It is associated with the mourner's inability to transfer emotional needs from the deceased to new persons or to give or receive intimacy or dependency. In addition, it accompanies diminished interest in and concern for others, as revealed by the tendency to become more self-engrossed and to evidence less interest in planning for the future for self and others.

8. It is associated with an exacerbation of antecedent neurotic symptomatology, along with symptoms of the deceased, in a kind of Law of Talion punishment for repressed and unacceptable death wishes toward the deceased.

9. It can lead to subsequent reactions of protracted apathy, heightened irritability, or aimless hyperactivity without appropriate affect.

VAMIK VOLKAN

Vamik Volkan is perhaps best known by therapists for his concept of the linking object, or object the mourner invests with the power to maintain the illusion of external contact with the deceased and with which the mourner can magically accomplish reunion (Volkan, 1972, 1981), as well as for his formulation of re-grief therapy (Volkan & Showalter, 1968). The procedures involved in re-grief therapy are discussed at length in chapter 7; presented in the following pages is an overview of Volkan's conceptualization of the grief and mourning process.

Stages and Complications of Mourning

Volkan divides the course of mourning into two stages: the initial stage and the work of mourning. The initial stage lasts from several weeks to a few months and involves acute reactions to the loss. A number of complications can occur during this time. One such complication involves an *exaggerated response* to the death, in which the normal signs and symptoms expected at the initial stage of mourning become magnified. Only time will determine whether they will persist. The two symptomatic behavior patterns most associated with this complication are denial and anger. Denial is very rare; Volkan (1985) reports seeing only two cases among the 150 mourners he studied. Anger, if extreme, may require psychiatric attention or hospitalization.

In the case of an *absent or minimal response,* expected signs and symptoms are missing or barely evidenced. Denial of a death is to be differentiated from acceptance of it with apparent equanimity. When the latter occurs, it points to the presence of complications and indicates that, sooner or later, a problematic reaction will occur.

With *protracted mourning,* the signs and symptoms of the initial stage fail to abate. When these symptoms occur frequently enough to disturb daily adjustment and reduce productivity, the complication has become chronic. Volkan sees chronicity in such a pure form as rare, instead usually witnessing the persistence of initial reactions combined with complications in the second stage, the work of mourning.

Finally, Volkan notes that *unusual new symptoms* may develop. These are recognizable psychological or psychosomatic illnesses, both of which demand professional treatment. Such illnesses appear for various reasons in different persons and must be formulated in psychodynamic terms with appropriate individualized treatment plans.

The second stage, the work of mourning, generally takes from 1 to 2 years to complete. As Volkan (1985) summarizes:

> The work of mourning . . . involves a slow-motion review of
> the mourner's relationship to the one mourned; a struggle
> between keeping or rejecting a close tie with representation of

the deceased; a painful awareness that no longer will the deceased be able to justify the mourner; and regressive disorganization, which is ultimately followed by a new inner organization able to test reality more fully for confirmation that the death, with all its psychological implications, has indeed taken place.

In the absence of complications, the mourner will identify during and at the end of mourning with selected aspects of the one mourned. Such aspects are depersonified and changed into functions; the mourner will assume some functions of the departed. When the work of mourning is successful, the mourner's ego can be expected to manifest enrichment due to the internalization of such new functions. Mourning thus ends with a new inner adaptation to the external loss. (pp. 271–272)

Complications in the healthy mourning process manifest themselves as either reactive depression or established pathological mourning. In both there are complications in the identification with and internalization of the deceased. In reactive depression, internalization of the lost object results in an almost total identification—the hated and dreaded traits of the deceased are internalized along with the loved and admired ones. In this case, the ambivalence with which the deceased had been regarded becomes an internal conflict: Love for the deceased promotes keeping the deceased within the self, whereas hate for the deceased promotes destruction (Fenichel, 1945). As a consequence, the depressed mourner's self-system becomes a battleground. Aggression preserved in the self through identification contributes to guilt and self-reproach.

In established pathological mourning, the deceased's representation is kept as an unassimilated introject, a special kind of object representation not entirely absorbed into or identified with the self-representation. The introject is described by mourners as an inner presence (Schafer, 1968) living inside the self where contact with it can be maintained. Although it strongly influences self-representation, it leads to no structural change and does not influence ego organization, as does identification. As Volkan (1985) points out:

> The ambivalent relationship of the past continues in the mourner's involvement with the introject; the mourner is torn between a strong yearning for the restored presence of the one mourned and an equally deep dread that the deceased might be confronted. The presence of the introject provides an illusion of choice, and in this way it reduces anxiety. (p. 279)

Signs of Established Pathological Mourning

Volkan considers the diagnosis of established pathological mourning when the mourner (a) displays an attitude toward the loss indicative of intellectual acknowledgment of its occurrence accompanied by emotional denial 6 months or more after the death and (b) maintains chronic hope for the deceased's return accompanied by simultaneous dread of that return.

In addition to these features and the presence of the unassimilated introject, numerous signs suggest the ambivalent yearning the mourner maintains for the deceased. These signs may take the form of interest in reincarnation, impulses to search for the lost loved one, and anxious pursuit and scrutiny of a stranger who resembles the deceased to establish or rule out the possibility that the one mourned continues to live.

Other behaviors reflecting the mourner's concerns include compulsive reading of obituaries, which reflects anxiety about one's own death, as well as the desire to support denial of the death through finding no mention of it. Using the present tense when speaking of the deceased (e.g., "My father *is* a tall man") illustrates the mourner's perception of the deceased's "aliveness." Preoccupation with death, including conversations focused on graveyards and tombs and references to people who are about to die or who have just died, gives the impression that the deceased and other figures representing that person via displacement populate the mourner's mind. Avoidance of visiting the grave of the deceased or providing a gravestone are additional manifestations, as is extreme preoccupation with the deceased to the point of losing the thread of daily life.

Finally, pathological mourning tends to have two major pathognomonic features: (a) dreams (frozen dreams, dreams of a life-and-death struggle, and dreams of the death as an illusion) and (b) linking objects and phenomena.

Dreams

Frozen dreams are composed of one tableau after another with no action. (Interestingly, *frozen,* the term often used spontaneously by mourners themselves, also connotes lifelessness.) Volkan (1981) reports how one patient likened his dreams to a slide series, whereas another compared his to slices of bread slipping out of their wrapping. These dreams reflect fixation in the work of mourning, which serves as a defense through which the mourner attempts to deny aggression toward the deceased while trying to find a way to bring the deceased back to life. The conflict between the wish to do so and the dread of success is handled by freezing the conflict, thereby averting resolution.

In dreams of a life-and-death struggle, the mourner sees the deceased as living but engaged in a mortal battle (e.g., on the point of drowning). The dreamer attempts to save the person but usually awakens with anxiety before succeeding. Such a dream confronts the mourner with "killing" versus "saving" the deceased.

Finally, dreams of death as an illusion involve seeing the deceased person as being dead but exhibiting signs of life (e.g., twitching or sweating). Consequently, doubt about the person's death persists.

Linking objects and phenomena

As noted earlier, linking objects and phenomena provide means by which the mourner may externally sustain a relationship with the deceased. Volkan (1985) writes:

> The individual in this state not only maintains internal contact with the representation of the one mourned through the introject but maintains also the illusion of external contact by means of a linking object. This object is used in a magical way to be, in metapsychological terms, a locus for meeting with the representation of the dead individual. Its employment facilitates the illusion that the mourner has full control of the choice between "killing" or "not killing" the one mourned, and thus need never resolve the dilemma of grief. . . . Linking phenomena are fantasies, sensations, or behavior patterns that perpetuate the possibility of contact between the mourner and the one mourned without reference to any tangible object. (p. 280)

With some overlap, linking objects can be grouped into five categories.

1. A personal possession of the deceased's (e.g., an article of clothing or a watch)

2. A gift from the deceased

3. Something the deceased used to extend senses or bodily functions (e.g., a camera—an extension of sight)

4. A realistic representation of the deceased (e.g., a photograph)

5. Something that was at hand when the mourner initially learned of the death or saw the body—in other words, something that could be considered a "last-minute object" (e.g., the record that was being played when the mourner received notification)

Volkan (1970) suggests that linking objects are tokens of triumph over the loss and that they mark a blurring of psychic boundaries between the mourner and the one mourned. It is as if representations of the two persons, or parts of them, merge externally through the use of these objects (Volkan, 1972).

An interesting phenomenon of distancing and avoidance occurs with the linking object that distinguishes it from either a fetish or a transitional object. Knowledge of the linking object's whereabouts is highly important, but it is as usual for the mourner to distance himself from the object as to embrace it. In this way, the ambivalence that characterized the relationship is symbolized and acted out in the way the mourner deals with the linking object. Volkan suggests that distancing and avoidance of the linking object derive from the mourner's use of the object to control expressions of anger arising from separation panic and from his investment of it with significantly more aggressive drive than in either the fetish or transitional object. The ambivalence condensed in the linking object, where the relationship with the deceased is externally maintained, represents both the wish to annihilate the deceased and the wish to keep the deceased alive. Therefore, the painful work of mourning has an external reference (i.e., the linking object) and remains unresolved.

Volkan (1985) also notes that something with sensory impact can serve as a linking phenomenon and provides the example of a mourner who had attended her father's funeral in the rain and who used the song "Raindrops Are Falling on My Head" as a linking phenomenon. For many years after the funeral, this song induced eerie feelings and helped perpetuate the illusion that the mourner could choose either to be in contact with her father or to bury him. Although this mourner's bereavement was complicated, it is important that the pathological use of such linking phenomena be discriminated from religious beliefs in an afterlife. In any culture in which these religious beliefs play a part, only an exaggerated application should be considered pathological.

GEORGE KRUPP

George Krupp's (1972) paper "Maladaptive Reactions to the Death of a Family Member" is the first to view death within a family systems perspective. Krupp focuses on the identification of so-called unresolved bereavement. Krupp defines this as the failure to complete the work of mourning successfully and to transfer interest from the dead loved object to the living world. As he points out, this situation "must be recognized because, if the maladjustment can be perceived, adjustment can be nurtured" (p. 429).

Noting how mourning can remain unresolved for years, with adults who have experienced bereavement in early childhood being more predisposed than others to subsequent mental illness, Krupp points to sequelae of unresolved loss in the family system, including poor mate choice, marital discord, children's behavior problems, and parents' irrational behavior. Referring to Bowlby's processes of mourning, Krupp asserts that it is only when mourning is incomplete—when the mourner remains in an early stage—that pathological mourning endangers subsequent adjustment.

Krupp identifies five forms of pathological mourning, stressing that, in mild forms, each may be an aspect of normal mourning.

1. *Exaggeration.* One of the most common forms of pathological mourning, this pattern is evidenced by a chronic bereavement reaction leading to clinical depression, which may be accompanied

by nightmares, outbursts of fear and anger, and strong guilt prompting the conviction that the mourner must be punished and make amends by dying, too. This form can lead to suicide.

2. *Complete ego breakdown.* In this form, intense rage is projected outward and erupts in paranoid and persecutory delusions. Panic arises from the ego's fear that the mourned object will return and harm it. Ego boundaries disintegrate; the distinction between self and object is blurred. The mourner may be dominated when awake and asleep by an hallucinatory world of internal and external evil objects attacking and counterattacking.

3. *Pathological identifications.* In this form, there is an intense reaction in which the mourner assumes the symptoms of the deceased. These symptoms permit the mourner to retain the dead one in fantasy as if alive. In one sense, the reaction is pleasurable, but in another it may represent a punishment for real or imagined wrongs done the deceased.

4. *Arrested psychosocial development.* This form of mourning occurs when the bereaved person remains fixated at an immature level and has problems developing beyond the stage when the loss took place. In a child, this may happen because dependency needs are very great at a young age. Fixation thus appears to be a method of denying the death. The absence of the socializing influence of the deceased parent makes it extremely difficult for the child to grow intellectually or emotionally.

5. *Absence of mourning.* Denial or postponement of emotion is one of the defense mechanisms most frequently used against anxiety or psychic pain, acting to safeguard the individual against complete disintegration. A normal part of the initial processes of mourning, denial becomes pathological only when the mourner remains in this phase and does not react to the loss at all.

In describing the difference between normal and pathological reactions to loss, Krupp (1972) points out that "mourning itself is a normal reaction to loss; it is only when unconscious factors predominate and hostility, guilt, anxiety, and depression are extreme both in degree and duration that the reaction becomes pathological" (p. 429). Krupp specifies four phenomena as indicating pathology. He observes that in each there is an incomplete admission of the death and only a changed communication with the deceased. These phenomena include (a) fantasies that promulgate denial of the loss; (b) maintenance of the lost object in awareness; (c) attempts at union with the lost object; and (d) symptomatic or personality identifications, which prolong the process by not permitting the relinquishing or restitution fantasies of normal mourning.

Conditions known to increase the probability of pathology include two factors: ambivalence (specifically, excessive hatred accompanied by guilt in the relationship) and guilt (which ultimately focuses attention back upon the mourner and prevents the necessary objective contemplation or acknowledgment of the loss).

As noted, Krupp takes his discussion beyond the intrapsychic into the familial and social realms. Discussing family systems dynamics, he makes it clear that inability to cope and unresolved mourning can characterize an entire family and that this may have a serious effect on both the individual members involved and the family as a unit. Citing Paul and Grosser (1965), he refers to clinical reports of how reaction to loss characteristic of one significant family member also tends to permeate the attitudes of other members.

Krupp proceeds to offer techniques for resolving unresolved mourning on both individual and family levels, then expands his view beyond the domain of the family. He articulates how recent social changes have had an impact on not only the family as a unit but also the individuals within it, specifically affecting their ability to contend with loss when it does occur. He concludes:

> In view of these juxtaposed societal influences, it is to be expected that many persons fail to adjust adequately to the stress of bereavement. People are enmeshed in conflict—dear ones have become fewer and less easily replaced, yet opportunities to express and resolve intense emotion have also diminished. (Krupp, 1972, p. 429)

Here we have one of the first, if not the first, mentions in the clinical literature of sociotechnological change as a factor in the development of complicated mourning.

BEVERLEY RAPHAEL

In 1983, Beverley Raphael published *The Anatomy of Bereavement*. This impressive tome, which reviews over 400 publications related to bereavement, sets a new standard by which to evaluate other contributions. Raphael integrates theory, research, and practice in her examination of how individuals cope with, understand, and eventually adapt to many different types of bereavements across the lifespan. In addition, she contributes to the interdisciplinary literature, especially by integrating concepts of grief and mourning with traumatic stress (Raphael, 1986) and by proposing the useful concept of personal disaster (Raphael, 1981). Raphael's (1975) paper "The Management of Pathological Grief" is one of the earliest to offer specific treatment strategies and interventions in this area. Her treatment approach for complicated mourning, focal psychotherapy, is discussed in chapter 7.

Raphael (1983) favors comprehension of morbid or pathological grief within the context of three general patterns, noting that overlap may exist among them because each is associated with denial or repression of aspects of the loss and an attempt to hold on to the lost relationship. These patterns are absent, delayed, or inhibited grief; distorted grief; and chronic grief. This classification does not include illnesses considered to represent bereavement decompensations and outcomes.

Absent, Delayed, or Inhibited Grief

In absent, delayed, or inhibited grief, the mourner avoids the pain of loss. The mourner may deny pining and yearning for the deceased and avoid review of the lost relationship because of the pain entailed in relinquishing it. In *absent grief*, no grief or mourning is manifested at all. This requires that the mourner completely deny the death or remain in a state of shock. Grief may be absent for a number of reasons (e.g., the mourner may be unable to acknowledge the loss or express feelings about it because of the belief that to do so would bring disastrous consequences). In the early months following a loss, it is difficult to distinguish this pattern of grief from that of delayed grief. Except in a few instances, this type of reaction to major loss appears clearly related to pathology.

The process of bereavement easily may be delayed. Such *delayed grief* may occur briefly or continue for an extended period. Delay is particularly likely when survival issues are present at the time of the death (e.g., when the mourner is injured at the same time the loved one is killed and must turn all attention toward surviving, putting the grief "on hold" until the danger has passed). In some cases, grief is delayed when the death is not really accepted—for example, when no body is available to confirm the event or when the body is not viewed by the mourner. If grief and mourning progress normally after relatively short delays, the prognosis usually is favorable. However, when delay is related to the mourner's avoidance of pain or to fears relating to loss of emotional control, guilt, or anger, more pathological outcomes are likely.

In the very common pathological reaction of *inhibited grief*, there is a partial or overall inhibition of grief expression. Normal aspects of mourning (e.g., angry protest) are suppressed or unconsciously repressed, as in the repression of yearning described by Bowlby (1980). The mourner is unwilling and unable to relinquish aspects of the relationship in the mourning process. A typical example of this occurs in the mourner who, out of fear of facing ambivalence toward and dependence on the deceased, mourns the positive aspects of the deceased but not the negative ones.

Distorted Grief

In distorted grief, some degree of inhibition or suppression of aspects of grief operates alongside powerful distortions. There are two common patterns: extreme anger and extreme guilt. Extreme anger, to the exclusion of other reactions, is often witnessed after the death of someone upon whom the bereaved has been pathologically dependent; the loss of a relationship that symbolized something special and irreplaceable; a sudden, unexpected death for which someone is blamed; and a violent death. It is most pronounced in those situations when there is a great sense of desertion, the bereaved feels her very survival is threatened by the event, or a symbolic link with earlier losses in childhood exists. The entire bereavement experience is taken up with intense and furious rage; there is little yearning and pining and no sorrow—only protest. Although such feelings may occur in the early stages of an uncomplicated bereavement, they are accompanied by other grief responses, such as yearning or sadness, and eventually pass. In contrast, in this reaction pattern anger persists, often becoming a destructive element in the mourner's life.

Extreme guilt, the second variation of distorted grief, tends to follow the loss of relationships that were intensely ambivalent and in which active fantasies about the death of the other were common. The connection in the relationship is strong but negative in whole or in part. When the death occurs, it appears to be a fulfillment of the mourner's aggressive wishes, and a need to self-punish becomes strong and persistent. This need is often associated with severe depression evolving out of the loss. Little direct anger is evident, although much hostility may be apparent. The bereavement experience is marked by ongoing self-blame and by continual, exaggerated guilty ruminations. There is no true mourning and sorrow, only guilt, which may be clung to in the attempt to placate the deceased. A subgroup of these mourners cannot bear their guilt personally, deny it, and project it by blaming others.

Chronic Grief

In this syndrome, intense grief continues unremittingly. Mourning does not draw to its natural conclusion; there is continued crying, preoccupation with the deceased, angry protest, and review of memories. It is as if the perpetuation of mourning keeps the loved one alive. Many times, life is maintained as if the deceased will return (e.g., keeping the deceased's room exactly as it was or his possessions close at hand). Some mourners alienate others as they adopt the permanent role of the grief-stricken one. This clinical picture may appear with full features of the acute grief response or as a chronic persistence of one of the other types of pathological grief. Chronic grief is typically seen after the death of one with whom the mourner had a dependent and irreplaceable relationship, often marked by an extraordinary and possibly pathological emotional investment; following a sudden, unexpected death; and subsequent to the death of a child.

By definition, chronic grief is not diagnosed until long after the loss, when acute responses fail to subside. By the time it is recognized, a pathologically defensive pattern and an entrenched role are often well established. There often is little motivation on the part of the mourner to relinquish either the chronic grief or the ongoing relationship with the deceased the grief symbolizes. At times, chronic grief becomes associated with the secondary gains of controlling and punishing others, as well as eliciting their care. Frequently, however, it ultimately alienates all sources of care, even professionals.

Need for Further Clarification in the Field

Raphael expresses the need for further research on pathological grief, noting that certain concepts are being accepted uncritically and that validation is lacking for types of pathological response to loss. In a recent review article on the current state of research in the field of bereavement, Raphael and Middleton (1987) argue that studies need to address the validity of stages and the way pathological grief reactions are conceptualized, as well as to develop valid operational criteria by which they may be defined. As they point out:

> Without any agreed-upon criteria of what is "resolution" and when, if at all, it may be expected to occur, it is difficult to validate concepts such as "delayed" grief. . . . It has now become very much accepted by both the public and workers in this field that it is "abnormal" not to react to the loss of a close relationship, yet there is not any systematic evidence that this is inevitably pathological. (p. 7)

Raphael and Middleton also argue that, to delineate normal from abnormal and shed some light on phases of response, such quantification needs to be more systematic throughout early and later stages after major loss. They stress that constructs of normal and abnormal have chiefly arisen from clinical grounds and that the criteria for and validity of these ideas need further phenomenological study. In addition, they underline the need to elucidate specific bereavement pathologies:

> As discussed previously these concepts, e.g., "chronic", "delayed", "inhibited", "distorted" are widely used by clinicians yet their validity and operational criteria specific to them have not been established. Nor has it been substantiated that they are different from other forms of psychiatric morbidity that may occur in association with bereavement such as depression, post-traumatic disorder, adjustment reaction or other illnesses. (p. 18)

AARON LAZARE

In a textbook he edited on outpatient psychiatry, Aaron Lazare (1979) included a gem of a work entitled simply "Unresolved Grief." Word quickly spread about its clinical usefulness, and it is one of the most often-cited references written in the last 15 years. Like other authors, Lazare discusses the history of unresolved grief and numerous clinical aspects related to it and uncomplicated grief. However, he departs from the rest in his particularly lucid and concise delineation of the causes, diagnosis, and treatment of unresolved grief.

Lazare divides the causes of unresolved grief into two categories: social and psychological factors. He specifies, discusses, and gives rich clinical examples of each. Under social factors, he addresses social negation of the loss, the socially unspeakable loss, social isolation, the social role of the strong one, and uncertainty over the loss. Under psychological factors he includes guilt, the loss of an extension of the self (narcissistic loss), reawakening of an old loss, the overwhelming impact of multiple loss, inadequate ego development, and idiosyncratic resistances to mourning.

Apparently sensitive to the clinician's desire for as much specificity as possible, Lazare delineates clear diagnostic criteria. When one or a combination of the following symptoms occurs after a death and continues beyond the usual period of bereavement (which according to Lazare is 6 months to 1 year), he considers the diagnosis of unresolved grief. The greater the number of the following symptoms and behaviors, the greater the likelihood of unresolved grief.

1. A depressive syndrome of varying severity beginning with the death, usually with symptoms so mild that treatment is not sought

2. A history of delayed or prolonged grief

3. Symptoms of guilt and self-reproach, panic attacks, and somatic expressions of fear, such as choking sensations and breathing attacks

4. Somatic symptoms representing identification with the dead person, often the symptoms of a terminal illness

5. Physical distress under the upper half of the sternum accompanied by statements such as "There is something stuck inside" or "I feel there is a demon inside of me"

6. Searching behavior

7. Recurrence of depressive symptoms and searching behavior on specific dates, such as anniversaries of the death, birthdays of the deceased, the age of the deceased at death, and holidays (especially Christmas)

8. A feeling that the death occurred yesterday, even though the loss took place months or years ago

9. Unwillingness to move the material possessions of the deceased

10. Change in relationships following the death

11. Diminished participation in religious and ritual activities

12. The inability to discuss the deceased without crying or the voice cracking, particularly when the death occurred over 1 year ago

13. Themes of loss

Lazare notes that the diagnosis is confirmed by two dimensions of the treatment process: (a) the symptoms and behaviors remit with specific treatment for unresolved grief (often within a relatively brief period of time—i.e., 2 to 12 months) and (b) the course of therapy is characterized by features of normal grief and the emergence of the following specific behaviors and feelings, which constitute criteria for successful treatment.

1. The depression of bereavement is resolved.

2. Patients verbalize how the clock of life has resumed after feeling for years that time has stood still (e.g., "I think I can begin to let time go on. But that is so hard because it means that I am going on without him.").

3. Patients experience and describe a different kind of sadness (e.g., "Before it was a bitter sadness; now it is a sweet sadness. The axe is out of my heart.").

4. The patient is able to discuss the deceased with relative equanimity and with nostalgia or the sweet sadness noted previously.

5. Holidays, particularly Christmas and Thanksgiving, become as enjoyable as they were prior to the loss.

6. Individuals who had expended considerable energy searching for the loved one discontinue their search.

7. The mourner often relates in a more healthy way to others.

8. The mourner discovers and identifies with positive aspects of the deceased.

Lazare is careful to note the difference between unresolved grief, which he estimates as being important in approximately 15 percent of psychiatric outpatient cases, and two conditions that may be mistaken for it. First, he differentiates it from the primary affective disorders and from schizophrenia, pointing out that, although these problems may be triggered by bereavement, their diagnosis, course, and treatment are distinct from that for unresolved grief. Second, he discriminates between unresolved grief and depression arising from the social deprivation and isolation that can be experienced after the death of a loved one. For individuals depressed by these factors as well as by their grief, treatment must include a restructuring of the social network.

MARDI HOROWITZ

Through in-depth examination of clinical, field, and experimental studies of individuals undergoing serious life events or vicarious simulations of such events, Mardi Horowitz has identified a predictable pattern of response, or *stress response syndrome* (see, for example, Horowitz, 1973, 1976, 1985, 1986a, 1986b; Horowitz, Wilner, Kaltreider, & Alvarez, 1980; Kanas, Kaltreider, & Horowitz, 1977). Events associated with this syndrome include military combat; concentration camp internment; nuclear holocaust; disasters; bereavement; personal illness, dying, and the threat of death; rape; medical illness; and mental illness. According to Horowitz, the response pattern tends to be present despite individual variations occasioned by personality differences; individual styles and capacities for coping and defense; and preexisting self-concepts, beliefs, conflicts or functional deficits. Horowitz's therapeutic approach based upon this conceptualization, time-limited dynamic psychotherapy for phase-oriented treatment of the stress response syndrome, is discussed in chapter 7.

The Stress Response Syndrome

By definition (Horowitz, 1986a), a stressful event contains news that is severely out of accord with the way an individual believes himself to be articulated with the surrounding world. This causes a sudden and powerful breach in the individual's security and violates his assumptive world. He is confronted with fear as well as with implications for short- and long-range personal meaning. The latter implications extend both into the past, joining with his personal life story, and into the future, prompting revisions in plans of both a practical and imaginative nature.

Horowitz asserts that, following a serious life event and immediate efforts at coping, the individual typically undergoes the following responses: outcry, denial and numbing, intrusion, working through, and completion. Figure 3.1 illustrates the relationship among these responses.

Outcry

Usually, there is an initial outcry accompanied by strong emotion—generally fear, but also sadness or rage—in reaction to the perception of the stressful event (e.g., "Oh, no!" or a scream, sob, or grimace of anguish). Some individuals evidence no outcry until their immediate coping efforts

Figure 3.1 Normal and Pathological Phases of Poststress Response

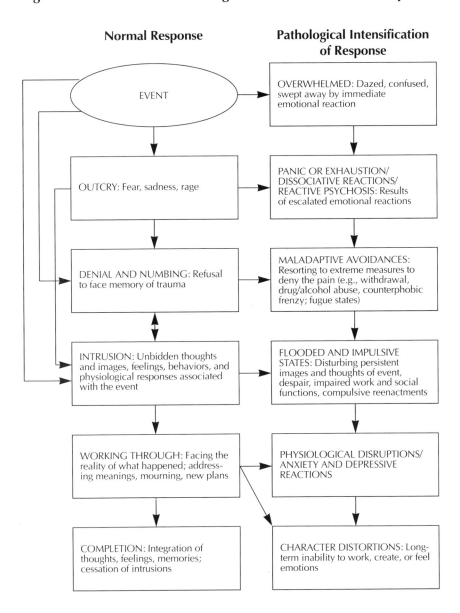

Normal Response

Pathological Intensification of Response

EVENT

OVERWHELMED: Dazed, confused, swept away by immediate emotional reaction

OUTCRY: Fear, sadness, rage

PANIC OR EXHAUSTION/ DISSOCIATIVE REACTIONS/ REACTIVE PSYCHOSIS: Results of escalated emotional reactions

DENIAL AND NUMBING: Refusal to face memory of trauma

MALADAPTIVE AVOIDANCES: Resorting to extreme measures to deny the pain (e.g., withdrawal, drug/alcohol abuse, counterphobic frenzy; fugue states)

INTRUSION: Unbidden thoughts and images, feelings, behaviors, and physiological responses associated with the event

FLOODED AND IMPULSIVE STATES: Disturbing persistent images and thoughts of event, despair, impaired work and social functions, compulsive reenactments

WORKING THROUGH: Facing the reality of what happened; address-ing meanings, mourning, new plans

PHYSIOLOGICAL DISRUPTIONS/ ANXIETY AND DEPRESSIVE REACTIONS

COMPLETION: Integration of thoughts, feelings, memories; cessation of intrusions

CHARACTER DISTORTIONS: Long-term inability to work, create, or feel emotions

Note. This figure has been adapted from M. J. Horowitz, "Disasters and Psycho-logical Responses to Stress," 1985, *Psychiatric Annals, 15,* p. 163; and *Stress Response Syndromes* (2nd ed., p. 41), 1986a, Northvale, NJ: Jason Aronson, Inc. Special thanks go to the author for his kind permission to include this figure here.

are no longer required. For instance, one might maneuver a careening car until it comes to a safe rest and only then, after no more action is required and one confronts the actual and potential trauma, cry out and become overwhelmed. Although outcry phenomena are normal in reaction to shocking news, abnormally intensified responses can occur. Such responses include exhaustion, panic, misdirected rageful destructiveness, sudden episodes of giving up, dissociative reactions, reactive psychosis, and other reactions in which the person is so overwhelmed or swept away by emotion that adaptive actions are neglected.

Denial and numbing

The signs and symptoms of response to a stressful life event are expressed in two predominant phases or states of mind, each characterized by a set of symptoms and each adaptive when not taken to extremes. The first state involves denial and numbing, in which the person tries to avoid facing the memory of the traumatic event. In this state, the person engages in ideational denial, ignores the implications of the threats or losses, and is emotionally numb, exhibiting both generalized withdrawal of interest in life and behavioral constriction (see Table 3.1). These symptoms serve to reestablish psychological equilibrium after the person has been overwhelmed by stress. They provide a way of modulating emotional reactions to the serious events by containing them within tolerable limits. However, when overused, denial and numbing can result in maladaptive avoidances such as withdrawal, suicide, drug and alcohol abuse, fugue states, and counterphobic frenzy.

Intrusion

Experiences of sudden intrusive repetitions of unbidden thoughts, images, emotional and physical feelings, and behaviors form the second state of mind (see Table 3.2). These are catalysts for the individual to perform the work of psychologically integrating the trauma. Unintegrated traumatic elements are stored in so-called active memory, which has an intrinsic tendency to repeat the representation of its contents via intrusive repetitions until those contents have been terminated by the completion of required cognitive processing. Essentially, because a lack of integration always brings stress, these traumatic elements knock on the door of the mourner's psyche, demanding to be given entrance. In situations of maladaptation, these can eventuate in flooded and impulsive states, disturbing persistence of trauma-related images and thoughts, despair, impaired work and social functions, and compulsive reenactments.

A number of common themes appear in the individual's intrusive, deliberately contemplated, or warded-off ideas: (a) fear of repetition, (b) fear of merger with victims, (c) shame and rage over vulnerability, (d) rage at the source, (e) rage at those exempted, (f) fear of loss of control

Table 3.1 Common Symptoms or Signs During Denial Phases of the Stress Response Syndrome

Perception and Attention

Daze
Selective inattention
Inability to appreciate significance of stimuli
Sleep disturbances (e.g., too little or too much)

Consciousness of Ideas and Feelings Related to the Event

Amnesia (complete or partial)
Nonexperience of themes that are consequences of the event

Conceptual Attributes

Disavowal of meanings of current stimuli in some way associated
    with the event
Loss of a realistic sense of appropriate connection with the ongoing world
Constriction of range of thought
Inflexibility of purpose
Major use of fantasies to counteract real conditions

Emotional Attributes

Numbness

Somatic Attributes

Tension-inhibition responses of the autonomic nervous system, with sen-
    sations such as bowel symptoms, fatigue, headache, and muscle pain

Activity Patterns

Frantic overactivity
Withdrawal
Failure to decide how to respond to consequences of the event

Note. From "Stress-Response Syndromes: A Review of Posttraumatic and Adjustment Disorders" by M. J. Horowitz, 1986b, *Hospital and Community Psychiatry, 37,* p. 242. Copyright 1986 by the American Psychiatric Association. Reprinted by permission.

Table 3.2 Common Symptoms or Signs During Intrusive Phases of the Stress Response Syndrome

Perception and Attention

Hypervigilance, startle reactions
Sleep and dream disturbances

Consciousness of Ideas and Feelings Related to the Event

Intrusive-repetitive thoughts, emotions, and behaviors (illusions, pseudohallucinations, nightmares, unbidden images, and ruminations)
Feelings of being pressured, confused, or disorganized when thinking about themes related to the event

Conceptual Attributes

Overgeneralization of stimuli so that they seem related to the event
Preoccupation with themes related to the event, with inability to concentrate on other topics

Emotional Attributes

Emotional "attacks" or "pangs" of affect related to the event

Somatic Attributes

Sensations or symptoms of flight or fight-readiness (or of exhaustion from chronic arousal), including tremor, diarrhea, and sweating (adrenergic, noradrenergic, or histaminic arousals) with sensations such as pounding heart, nausea, lump in throat, and weak legs

Activity Patterns

Compulsive repetitions of actions associated with the event or of searching for lost persons or situations

Note. From "Stress-Response Syndromes: A Review of Posttraumatic and Adjustment Disorders" by M. J. Horowitz, 1986b, *Hospital and Community Psychiatry, 37*, p. 242. Copyright 1986 by the American Psychiatric Association. Reprinted by permission.

of aggressive impulses, (g) guilt or shame over aggressive impulses, (h) guilt or shame over surviving, and (i) sadness over losses.

As with other trauma-related material, oscillating contemplation and suppression of these themes takes place. Inasmuch as contemplation of them may lead to intense emotional reactions and distressing states of mind—which themselves lead to unconscious regulatory processes inhibiting or facilitating thinking about the stress event, its meaning, and its implications—each theme provides grist for the therapeutic mill. Failure of regulatory processes can lead to emotional flooding, while the excessive use of defenses can interrupt and block the process of working through a theme to a level of relative completion.

At times, it is difficult to ascertain what belongs to the stress event and what belongs to past history. Any one of these themes can link present stress with prior conflicts over previous stress events. For example, the theme of guilt over hostile impulses is too common in everyone's past history to be unique to a current trauma; guilt over the current event is probably also emotionally associated with previous memories and fantasies of guilt over hostility. Needless to say, such blending of themes leads to diagnostic dilemmas.

Working through

After the initial outcry, either a denial or intrusive state may occur, although it is most common initially to witness denial. Following this, the individual oscillates between the two states. This process continues until working through—facing the reality of what has happened and integrating it with the rest of life—can be accomplished and the stress response reaction is completed. The working through process takes place not only with regard to the meanings of the event itself, but also with respect to its implications for one's relationships, self-images, and behaviors in the world. This entails the reappraisal of the event and the self, as well as revision of one's core inner models of self, role relationships, and future plans, all of which are significant parts of one's assumptive world. Failure to work through the new meanings of the event, undergo necessary mourning, and develop appropriate new plans frequently results in anxiety and depressive reactions, physiological disruptions and psychosomatic responses, or character distortions manifested by inability to work, create, act, or love.

Essentially, to work through the stress response syndrome to ultimate completion, the individual must process the emotional and ideational aspects of the stress experience and incorporate the experience into the existing mental models or schemata of his assumptive world. Old assumptions about the world and the self must be revised to accommodate the new reality imposed by the stressful experience. The process of incorporating the meaning and implications of the traumatic stress is initially resisted and can only occur piece by piece as the individual reviews, feels, and reacts to all aspects of the experience.

An information-processing model helps explain the specifics of the working through procedure: After any serious event, the individual must consider the meanings of the event and plan a response to it. He must take the new information about the self and the world gained from the trauma and find some way to incorporate it with his old information about the self and world. In essence, he must find a way to fit the new and the old together without cognitive dissonance. The need to match new information from the traumatic event with inner models based on older information, and the revision of both until they agree, is called the *completion tendency* (Horowitz, 1986a).

This completion tendency is what fuels the stress response. The basic cycle involves the individual's conscious and unconscious confrontation of trauma-related images, thoughts, feelings, and behaviors—and his attempts to make sense out of them and then to integrate them with the rest of his assumptive world. When there is a lack of accord between the new information related to the event and the old information in the person's usual inner working models or schemata (i.e., assumptive world), one of three things must happen: The new information must be reappraised so that it conforms to the old, the new information must be reappraised as unimportant so that cognitive dissonance is minimized, or the old inner schemata must be revised in order to match the new information conveyed by the event. Revision of inner models to the point of completion requires considerable cognitive change and extended time for information processing.

Problems develop when this working through process evokes emotional responses that are excessive or that threaten to overwhelm the person. Every recognition of discrepancy between the new state of affairs and old inner model can bring emotional reactions so painful that they interrupt the information processing. In reaction, to protect and defend himself, the individual may resort to controls to ward off pain (i.e., denial and numbing reactions). However, these do not permanently stop the pain because unintegrated traumatic material continually and involuntarily presents itself until it can be accommodated and mastered (i.e., through the repetition compulsion; Freud, 1920/1955a). Oscillations between intrusion and denial result. Intrusion stems from the repetition of the unprocessed and unintegrated traumatic material which, fueled by active memory, presses for external or internal action to stimulate continued revision and achieve completion. Denial results from inhibiting regulatory efforts to control the painful assimilation of stressful information gradually, dose by dose.

Completion

The working through cycle continues, spurred on by the tendency of active memory to present the traumatic material until the point of cognitive completion, when all relevant contents are processed and cleared from active memory storage. This occurs when all of the new information generated by the trauma has been integrated with the individual's schemata and organized memories, which themselves have been worked on to be made congruent with the new information. In an effort to reduce cognitive dissonance between the perceptions, feelings, thoughts, memories, or behaviors related to the trauma and the individual's assumptive world, both these preexisting models and the meanings given to the new trauma-related information are processed and modified repeatedly until such a congruence is achieved. This processing for fit results in a series of approximating representations of the stress event and the relevant inner schemata. Only when the fit is achieved can information processing cease and the process be viewed as complete. At this point, the trauma-related information is successfully integrated and accommodated into the individual's assumptive world.

Death and the Stress Response Model

In describing how this stress response model specifically relates to the loss of a loved one through death, Horowitz summarizes as follows:

> Completion requires the resolution of differences between new information and enduring mental models. Thus, the news of the death of a loved one is incongruent with an entire world picture that includes not only wishes and hopes but also habits and routine roles and self-images. Cognitive processing is reinitiated when representation occurs and may evoke unpleasant emotions such as fear or anxiety. Every repetition is a confrontation with a major difference between what is and what was gratifying and may invoke various responsive emotional states such as fear, anxiety, rage, panic, or guilt. If these emotional responses are likely to increase beyond the limits of toleration, the result may be distraught, overwhelmed states of mind. To avoid entry into such states of mind, therefore, controls [i.e., denial and numbing symptoms] are activated that will modify the cognitive processes (Horowitz, 1979). For example, the path from active memory storage to representation and processing can be inhibited. This reduction in processing reduces anxiety and, in turn, reduces the motivation for controls. With the reduction in control, the tendency of active memory toward representation then reasserts itself. Other immediate programs may be interrupted with the repeated representation of the stress-related information. The processing of the stress-related information resumes; the anxiety increases, the control increases; and the cycle continues. (1986a, pp. 95–96)

This process is precisely the same as that required by the six "R" processes of mourning. In this regard, mourning legitimately can be viewed as a stress response syndrome.

Horowitz has looked specifically at pathological grief following bereavement (Horowitz, Wilner, Marmar, & Krupnick, 1980), defined as "the intensification of grief to the level where the person is overwhelmed, resorts to maladaptive behavior, or remains interminably in the state of grief without progression of the mourning process toward completion" (p. 1157). Pathological mourning is held to involve "processes that do not move progressively toward assimilation or accommodation but, instead, lead to stereotyped repetitions or extensive interruptions of healing" (p. 1157).

Horowitz and colleagues identify three states of pathological grief—fear, rage, and deflation. Each is associated with prototypical self-images and role relationship models developed from early traumatic experiences in childhood. During the relationship with the deceased—a relationship that was compensatory—more competent self-images had been established. However, during mourning, the older and more negative latent self-images reemerge as the individual reviews the self-images and role relationship models of his assumptive world. Without the compensatory relationship to hold the competent self-image in check, those predisposed to pathological grief either experience unusually intense and interminable states of grief or develop excessive controls to prevent review of activated role relationship models. In either case, mourning remains incomplete.

Those predisposed to frighteningly sad states in response to loss tend originally to have been very needy and dependent. However, the self-images of weakness were held in check by the relationship with the strong, caring, and nurturant deceased loved one and were subordinate to the conceptualization of both the self and the other as strong. After the death, the person remains dependent and the need becomes frightening. The self-images shift back to those of a weak, helpless waif supplicating in vain to be rescued by the lost or abandoning loved one. This role relationship model is associated with a state of agitation, desperation, and intolerable sadness, leading to insistent demands for help.

Those mourners who respond with intensified rage states tend to have latent self-images that oscillate between perceptions of the self as, on the one hand, betrayed and needy or, on the other, evil, greedily consuming, and destructive. The relationship with the deceased had held these views in check and supported a conscious view of the self as kind and good, protecting the self from evil through mutual exchanges of a loving nature. After the death, the deceased is perceived as an evil deserter who has willfully betrayed the needy self. This perception leads to reactions of explosive rage and hostility diffusely expressed toward the deceased and everyone else. Alternatively, the deceased may be viewed as a victim of the evil, destructive self. This perception leads the mourner to guilt, remorse, self-loathing, and fearful expectation of accusation or punishment.

Oscillations between the two role models bring about shifts between anger and guilt. Such shifts result from defenses aimed at undoing or reducing the intensity of either affect. Sometimes impulsively self-destructive acts can occur.

Finally, mourners who develop excessively intense or prolonged deflated states tend to have preexisting tendencies to perceive themselves as worthless, defective, or disgusting. The previous relationship model was one between a scornful, superior critic and a contemptible, worthless inferior. In the relationship with the deceased, components of admiration and appreciation stabilized a worthwhile self-image, which was lost at the time of the death. Feelings of self-blame for inability to prevent the loss or scorn by the deceased fuel the sense of worthlessness. Due to the belief that the deceased left because of their own defects, these individuals experience feelings of deflation, shame, and dejection accompanied by withdrawal. In defense, these mourners move toward an illusion of self-sufficiency, numbing and insulating themselves emotionally.

SIDNEY ZISOOK AND COLLEAGUES

Since the mid-1970s, Sidney Zisook and his colleagues—most notably, Richard DeVaul, Stephen Shuchter, Thomas Faschingbauer, and Lucy Lyons—have contributed significantly to the literature on both uncomplicated and complicated grief and mourning. The writings of this group demonstrate a steady refinement of research investigating the parameters of bereavement.

In the course of their studies, Zisook and colleagues have dealt with three populations: a general group of bereaved people solicited via friends and colleagues of the investigators; widows and widowers in southern California; and psychiatric outpatients in southern California. In the process, they developed the Texas Inventory of Grief, which has been revised and is now called the Texas Revised Inventory of Grief (Faschingbauer, Zisook, & DeVaul, 1987). This is an assessment tool to describe, operationalize, and measure the process of grief and its changes over time.

Through both clinical observation and empirical work, Zisook and his colleagues are expanding the dimensions of uncomplicated mourning by documenting that aspects of the experience previously perceived as abnormal (e.g., anniversary reactions, chronic illness behavior, identification phenomena, anger and guilt, continued ties with the deceased) are actually typical reactions to the loss of a loved one. Their clarification of the multidimensional aspects of what they call normal grief and their delineation of psychosocial determinants, characteristics, and manifestations of what they term unresolved grief have made it abundantly clear that the old rules for differentiating the two experiences are no longer valid. Some of the most important findings of this research group are summarized in the following pages.

Normal Grief

Zisook and colleagues have clarified that a number of grief-related feelings, symptoms, and behaviors, as well as many aspects of grief work, continue indefinitely in a significant proportion of otherwise normal individuals. In fact, a significant number of bereaved individuals never completely resolve the death of their loved one as traditionally defined, with many still feeling a tie to the deceased.

For widows and widowers, the course of mourning is much more prolonged than generally expected. Although acute dysphoria was shown to peak between 1 and 2 years after the death, a number of symptoms persisted for over 10 years (Zisook et al., 1982). Apparently, many widows and widowers never fully accept the fact of their spouse's death and, in their own ways, indefinitely maintain a continuing relationship with that person (Zisook & Shuchter, 1985). In another study, Zisook and Shuchter (1986) also observed a discrepancy between the way many widows and widowers score on psychometric scales and how they view themselves. Self-assessments after 4 years revealed that the majority did not feel they had what they would call an excellent adjustment, despite the positive outcomes measured.

Unresolved Grief

With respect to incidence, one study (Zisook, Shuchter, & Shuckit, 1985) revealed that 17 percent of persons entering an outpatient psychiatric facility had unresolved grief according to self-report. These patients differed from other patients in that they had a higher incidence of multiple losses, a history of difficulty in getting along with their mothers, and greater difficulty with depression and physical distress. In a second outpatient study, Zisook and Lyons (1988, 1988–1989) found 21 percent to have unresolved grief. Unresolved grief was associated with increased intensity of affective symptomatology; past histories of depression, suicide attempts, and alcohol abuse; and family histories of depression. Incidence of unresolved grief was greatest among patients who had lost children and lowest among those who had lost parents.

As Zisook and colleagues point out, unresolved grief tends to be tenacious, persistent, and chronic unless treated. In addition, it is associated with increased medical and psychological morbidity (DeVaul, Zisook, & Faschingbauer, 1979). Individuals with unresolved grief tend to be younger, have failed to attend the funeral, are more disturbed both immediately and long after the loss, and are more depressed than individuals with resolved grief (Zisook & DeVaul, 1983). Interestingly, a self-rating of adjustment appears to be a highly reliable indicator of unresolved grief. Zisook and Lyons (1988) demonstrated that the answer to the single question, Are you now having trouble dealing with the death? is a simple, valid, and effective way to identify a clinically meaningful subgroup of bereaved individuals (i.e., those with unresolved grief).

Arrest of the grief process occurs most often in what this research team calls the acute mourning stage, a stage located between the stages of shock and resolution. Clinical presentations develop depending upon what aspect of the stage is unresolved (e.g., the clinical syndrome of agitated depression often develops when the intense feelings of acute mourning are unresolved; DeVaul & Zisook, 1976; DeVaul et al., 1979; Zisook, 1987). In particular, Zisook and DeVaul (1976–1977) have identified the clinical syndrome of grief-related facsimile illness. This is an arrest of the normal grief process in which there is a presentation of symptoms identical or nearly identical to those experienced by the deceased and for which previous treatment endeavors have been ineffective and inappropriate.

According to Zisook and colleagues, the two syndromes of depression and unresolved grief evidence some overlap (Zisook & DeVaul, 1983; Zisook & Lyons, 1988–1989). However, it seems that it is not simply loss through death that is associated with depression, but rather the way in which one deals with the loss (i.e., resolved versus unresolved grief; Zisook & Lyons, 1988–1989). These investigators also found evidence that unresolved grief is not equivalent to depression. They discovered that people who present as psychiatric outpatients with unresolved grief may not now be depressed or may never have been depressed and that some do not suffer more affective symptomatology than patients with resolved grief or those with no losses (Zisook & Lyons, 1988–1989). In addition, there appears to be a subgroup of bereaved individuals who qualify as nonsuppressors on the dexamethasone suppression test among a larger group meeting the Research Diagnostic Criteria for depression (Shuchter, Zisook, Kirkorowicz, & Risch, 1986). In the bereaved subgroup, nonsuppression appears related more to levels of anxiety than to depression. This raises interesting questions about the role of separation anxiety in depressive disorders following bereavement.

CHAPTER 4

Complicated Outcomes of Loss: Symptoms and Syndromes

DEFINITION OF COMPLICATED MOURNING

As used in this book, *complicated mourning* means that, given the amount of time since the death, there is some compromise, distortion, or failure of one or more of the six "R" processes of mourning (see Table 2.3). Even when the mourner successfully engages in only select subprocesses or only some elements of a given subprocess (e.g., expresses certain psychological reactions but not all of them), the "R" process as an entity is said to be compromised. All elements of each component of an "R" process must be completed successfully to avoid the designation of complicated mourning.

In all forms of complicated mourning, the mourner attempts to do two things: (a) deny, repress, or avoid aspects of the loss, its pain, and the full realization of its implications for the mourner and (b) hold on to and avoid relinquishing the lost loved one. These attempts, or some variation thereof, are what underlie and cause complications in the "R" processes of mourning. No matter what type of treatment is employed, it will need to address these two issues.

Complicated mourning always must be interpreted within time constraints. Incompletion of an "R" process due to insufficient time having passed since the death to permit the mourner to have worked through the process does not indicate complicated mourning, only that it is too soon to have addressed that specific "R" process. For instance, after a sudden, unexpected death most mourners find it impossible to complete the fourth "R" process (relinquish the old attachments to the deceased and the old assumptive world) within the first few months. If sufficient time has passed for a mourner to have addressed the "R" process of mourning for this particular loss and the process remains incomplete, then complicated mourning is present.

A loss can engender any of five specific outcomes: (a) uncomplicated mourning, (b) symptoms of complicated mourning, (c) a specific syndrome of complicated mourning, (d) a diagnosable mental or physical disorder, or (e) death. The last four outcomes represent the four forms complicated mourning may take. With the exception of death as an outcome, these patterns are not of an all-or-nothing nature, nor are they mutually exclusive. They may be permanent or temporary, and they may intermingle or follow one another in any sequence and without limit. Figure 4.1 illustrates the relationship among them.

As noted in chapter 1, seven high-risk factors are known to predispose any individual to complicated mourning. The typical genesis of complicated mourning is for one or more of these factors to contribute to a compromise, distortion, or failure of one or more of the six "R" processes of mourning, which then leads to one or more of the four forms of complicated mourning.

Uncomplicated mourning has been the topic of chapter 2 and therefore will not be discussed again here. The rest of this chapter focuses on symptoms and syndromes of complicated mourning. Chapter 5 details the interface of complicated mourning with mental or physical disorders recognized in the revised third edition of the *Diagnostic and Statistical Manual of Mental Disorders* (DSM-III-R; American Psychiatric Association, 1987) and briefly discusses death as a possible outcome of loss.

SYMPTOMS OF COMPLICATED MOURNING

At one level of response to loss, insufficient symptomatology exists to designate a full-blown syndrome of complicated mourning or a specific mental or physical disorder. Nonetheless, the mourner experiences some psychological, behavioral, social, or physical symptoms of distress, disability, dysfunction, pathology, or loss of freedom. Although inadequate in terms of number, intensity, duration, or type to meet the criteria for any of the other three forms of complicated mourning, these symptoms indicate that a vulnerability, conflict, or some unfinished business in mourning exists. By definition, they reveal a compromise, distortion, or failure in one or more of the "R" processes of mourning. Even though the mourner does not exhibit a specific complicated mourning syndrome or diagnosable mental or physical disorder, symptomatology may be equally severe, distressing, disabling, or dysfunctional. Without the particulars, one form of complicated mourning cannot automatically be assumed to be more harmful than another. For this reason, caregivers must comprehend what symptoms say about the individual's mourning, evaluate their impact on the mourner, and resist inference that in the absence of a diagnosable syndrome or disorder the consequences are minimal.

Like all elements of human function and dysfunction, symptoms of complicated mourning that are insufficient to qualify as a syndrome or

Figure 4.1 Potential Outcomes of Loss

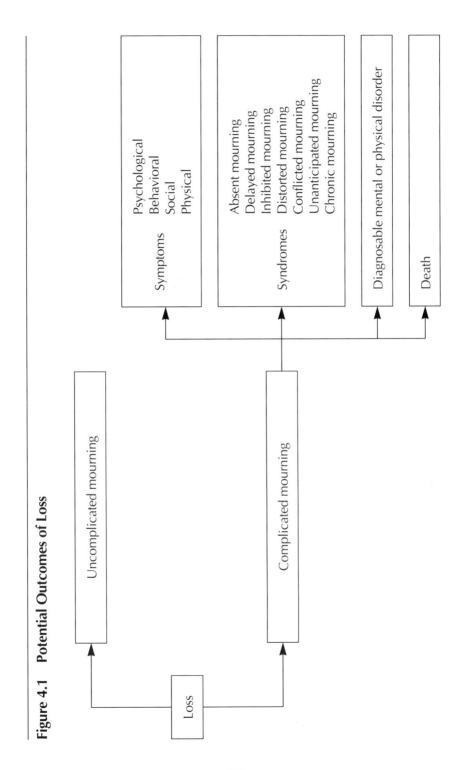

a mental or physical disorder can be classified into four categories: psychological, behavioral, social, or physical. Responses to loss identified as common in uncomplicated mourning (see Table 2.2) may be observed as symptoms of complicated mourning, although often these responses are more intense, prolonged, or distorted. Absence of some of these responses may itself constitute a symptom, as is suggested in the subsequent discussion of complicated mourning syndromes. With the exception of euphoria, there appear to be no symptoms that invariably indicate complicated mourning. Any symptom must be evaluated with regard to (a) the "R" processes of mourning (e.g., a symptom present when all "R" processes are complete does not necessarily signal complicated mourning, whereas the identical symptom present when "R" processes are incomplete does), (b) the factors circumscribing the mourner and the loss (see Table 2.1), and (c) the presence or absence of other symptoms.

Clinical Indicators of Complicated Mourning

It is important to recognize that many of the symptoms treated by mental health and health care professionals pertain to complicated mourning. I believe that the following symptoms—although in no way exhaustive—are particularly good clinical indicators of complicated mourning. However, as just noted, these must be evaluated in light of the status of the "R" processes of mourning, the constellation of factors circumscribing the particular mourner and loss, and other symptoms, as well as with regard to the time elapsed since the death.

1. A pattern of vulnerability to, sensitivity toward, or overreaction to experiences entailing loss and separation

2. Psychological and behavioral restlessness, oversensitivity, arousal, overreactivity, and perception of being "geared up," along with the need always to be occupied, as if cessation of movement would permit the surfacing of anxiety-provoking repressed or suppressed material

3. Unusually high death anxiety focusing on the self or loved ones

4. Excessive and persistent overidealization of the deceased and/or unrealistically positive recollections of the relationship

5. Rigid, compulsive, or ritualistic behavior sufficient to impinge on the mourner's freedom and well-being

6. Persistent obsessive thoughts and preoccupation with the deceased and elements of the loss

7. Inability to experience the various emotional reactions to loss typically found in the bereaved and/or uncharacteristically constricted affect

8. Inability to articulate, to whatever capacity the mourner has, existing feelings and thoughts about the deceased and the loss

9. Relationships with others marked by fear of intimacy and other indices of avoidance stemming primarily from fear of future loss

10. A pattern of self-destructive relationships commencing or escalating subsequent to the death, including compulsive caregiving and replacement relationships

11. The commencement or escalation after the death of self-defeating, self-destructive, or acting-out behavior, including psychoactive substance dependence or abuse

12. Chronic experience of numbness, alienation, depersonalization, or other affects and occurrences that isolate the mourner from herself and others

13. Chronic anger or some variation thereof (e.g., annoyance) or a combination of anger and depression (e.g., irritability, belligerence, intolerance)

Symptoms Misconstrued as Constituting Complicated Mourning

Some symptoms following the death of a loved one are frequently misconstrued as constituting complicated mourning. Of course, the particular constellation of factors involved in each individual case must be assessed in order to determine the importance of any particular symptom, and any symptom has the potential to progress to an unhealthy extent. However, the mere presence of the symptoms noted in the following list traditionally —and often erroneously—has been taken to indicate pathology.

1. Experiencing a resurrection of issues, feelings, and unresolved conflicts from past losses that either have or have not been accommodated successfully

2. Experiencing feelings other than sadness (e.g., anger or guilt) and reacting to the loss in other than psychological ways (e.g., behaviorally, socially, physically)

3. Feeling that part of the mourner has died along with the loved one

4. Feeling sorry for oneself to a certain extent

5. Having a continued relationship with the deceased

6. Maintaining parts of the environment in such a way as to stimulate memory of the deceased

7. Taking actions so that others will not forget the deceased

8. Feeling increased vulnerability about the possibility of one's own death or the deaths of other loved ones

9. Feeling some degree of reluctance to change things or have them be changed if the deceased had been a part of them, had been cognizant of them, or had been alive at the time they took place (e.g., not wanting the year to end or the decade to change, to relocate or take a new job, or to break up an old relationship)

10. Experiencing some aspects of mourning that continue for many years, if not forever and/or a course of mourning that does not decline linearly with time

11. Feeling resentment that others continue to live whereas the loved one has died, or that others are not mourning

12. Experiencing temporary periods of acute grief long after the death (see chapter 2 for discussion of STUG reactions)

SYNDROMES OF COMPLICATED MOURNING

According to the DSM-III-R, a *syndrome* is "a group of symptoms that occur together and that constitute a recognizable condition" (American Psychiatric Association, 1987, p. 405). Given the present state of knowledge about complicated mourning, this term appears preferable to others in describing certain factors and characteristics that cluster together after major loss. Complicated mourning symptoms may coalesce into seven complicated mourning syndromes. These syndromes may occur independently or concurrently. If only some of the symptoms are present, or if there is a combination of symptoms from several syndromes but they fail to meet the criteria for a particular complicated mourning syndrome, then they are considered complicated mourning symptoms. Only if specific criteria are met is a complicated mourning syndrome present. Again, the reader must be advised that a syndrome is not necessarily more pathological than a group of symptoms that does not fit these criteria.

The following discussion reorganizes information on the historical development of thinking on complicated mourning (see chapter 3) and combines it with my own personal observation. The classification of complicated mourning syndromes offered here is different from the atheoretical classification of mental disorders in the DSM-III-R, which understandably confines itself to behavioral description, minimizes criteria based on inference, and in many cases eliminates discussion of causality. Operating without these constraints, the present classification system provides information about etiological theories that have been cited in the DSM-III-R as being important in formulating treatment plans and designing research.

As Table 4.1 shows, each of the seven syndromes can be categorized according to whether it involves a problem in expression, skewed aspects, or closure. This table also indicates the particular "R" process or processes of mourning where difficulties initially arise; subsequent "R" processes can be expected to be compromised thereafter. In addition to showing the relationship of the syndromes of complicated mourning to the "R" processes, this schema suggests general philosophical approaches to treatment and can help the caregiver choose appropriate interventions for specific "R" processes, as will be detailed in chapter 9.

In general, for syndromes associated with problems in expression, the goal is to enable and promote complete processing of mourning. Syndromes associated with skewed aspects need to be approached with the aim of understanding and working these aspects through to convert the syndromes to uncomplicated mourning. The chronic mourning syndrome requires interventions to bring the acute grief to closure and to catalyze the latter mourning processes.

The remainder of this chapter identifies specific treatment issues for each syndrome and refers the reader to other chapters in the book where treatment suggestions pertaining to the various syndromes are detailed. Regardless of which specific approaches the caregiver chooses to use, all treatments should incorporate the generic philosophical perspectives and guidelines for treatment spelled out in chapter 8 and the specific approaches for intervention in the "R" processes of mourning described in chapter 9. As long as these perspectives and guidelines are respected, and the requisite "R" processes addressed, the caregiver is free to choose from among any number of his or her personally preferred techniques.

Absent Mourning

Absent mourning is perhaps the most misunderstood of all of the complicated mourning syndromes. It also is the one that clinicians and laypersons believe themselves to understand the best.

Usually, there is no discussion of absent mourning without reference to Deutsch's (1937) paper "Absence of Grief" (see chapter 3). However, the misconception arises when the assumption is made that the phenomenon Deutsch describes in the paper is absent mourning. Careful reading of Deutsch's work reveals that she is referring to the "complete absence of manifestations of mourning" (p. 13). In other words, she is addressing mourning that is publicly unexpressed, not mourning that is absent both externally and internally. In true absent mourning, it is as if the death had not occurred at all. What Deutsch describes is in fact a form of inhibited mourning.

True absent mourning appears to be rare because it requires that the mourner either maintain complete denial of the death or remain in a total state of shock—two quite difficult feats. To a variable extent and for variable

Table 4.1 Syndromes of Complicated Mourning in Relation to the Six "R" Processes

SYNDROMES	LOCATION OF INITIAL INTERFERENCE IN "R" PROCESSES
Problem in Expression	
Absent mourning	Recognize the loss (first "R" process)
Delayed mourning	React to the separation (second "R" process)
Inhibited mourning	React to the separation Recollect and reexperience the deceased and the relationship (second and third "R" processes)
Skewed Aspects	
Distorted mourning (extremely angry type, extremely guilty type)	React to the separation Recollect and reexperience the deceased and the relationship (second and third "R" processes)
Conflicted mourning	React to the separation Recollect and reexperience the deceased and the relationship (second and third "R" processes)
Unanticipated mourning	Recognize the loss (first "R" process)
Problem With Closure	
Chronic mourning	Relinquish the old attachments to the deceased and the old assumptive world Readjust to move adaptively into the new world without forgetting the old (fourth and fifth "R" processes)

lengths of time, both denial and shock are common in the earlier phases of the mourning processes and intermittently thereafter. It is only when they persist beyond the initial Avoidance Phase and the beginning of the Confrontation Phase that pathology is indicated. When assessment of psychological, behavioral, social, and physical factors indicates that an actual internal mourning experience is warranted, its absence is highly pathological.

Deutsch is not the only writer to have her words misinterpreted; similar misunderstanding has occurred with Bowlby's (1980) conception. Bowlby has written about prolonged absence of conscious grieving as one of the two main disordered variants of mourning (see chapter 3). Most readers have assumed he is talking about true absent mourning. However, like Deutsch, he describes a superficial absence of external indications of mourning. He notes that, despite the fact that the mourner's life appears superficially to continue as before, careful examination in psychotherapy typically reveals psychological and physical ills that the mourner disconnects cognitively and affectively from the death. Bowlby asserts that in fact these responses are derivatives of mourning. Therefore, he actually is describing a form of inhibited mourning.

Several discriminations must be made between true absent mourning and three other conditions. The first is lack of overt manifestations of mourning resulting from conscious or unconscious decisions on the part of the bereaved to refrain from public expression of emotional response. This pattern may be in response to environmental, sociocultural, ethnic, or religious/philosophical demands, or it may be the result of personality style or previous conditioning. In any case, the suppression is voluntary. The individual is experiencing reactions internally—these are simply not displayed. Thus, the absence is not of mourning per se, but of visible signs of it. A second condition that must be differentiated from true absent mourning is lack of overt manifestations of mourning that result from the mourner's reluctance or refusal to express emotional response as a consequence of that individual's psychological conflicts around the requirements of mourning the particular loss. In this case, mourning may not be manifested externally but is experienced internally in some form, although it may not necessarily be a healthy one or accompanied by conscious awareness. Both the first and second conditions culminate in a form of inhibited mourning. The third condition from which true absent mourning must be discriminated is the situation in which, given all the factors involved, the mourner understandably does not mourn because mourning is legitimately unnecessary. In other words, there may be no mourning after a particular death if the survivor had no emotional investment requiring such a response.

It is unlikely that most caregivers will ever see a case of true absent mourning as defined here. What usually is seen is severely inhibited mourning—so inhibited that there is no public or external manifestation of mourning despite there being some amount of private or internal recognition of the death and some amount of grief and/or mourning.

It should be noted that the delayed and conflicted mourning syndromes can in their early stages mimic absent mourning. However, in the delayed syndrome, mourning by definition eventually proceeds. In conflicted mourning, lack of response to the loss is soon followed by acute mourning. Until the mourning process begins, these three types may be indistinguishable.

Determinants and associated factors

As noted, genuine absent mourning, as opposed to the absence of the manifestations of mourning, is a very rare event. It occurs only under two conditions—either the mourner maintains complete denial of the death or remains in a total state of shock. Because these are two quite difficult processes to sustain, what commonly is seen is a severe or full inhibition of conscious and/or external responses while unconscious and/or internal responses occur to varying degrees. The mourner who exhibits genuine absent mourning must have a powerful ability to block out reality. Premorbid psychosis—or the tendency to become psychotic—can facilitate this ability, although it is not a prerequisite.

Treatment issues

Before undertaking treatment, it is important to differentiate absent mourning from delayed mourning, the beginning of conflicted mourning, severely inhibited mourning, and lack of expression due to insufficient reason to mourn. If absent mourning is judged present, the caregiver will have to focus interventions on breaking through the state of shock and/or reversing the denial. The following interventions will be helpful in this regard and should preface those borrowed as necessary from inhibited mourning.

1. Explore with the mourner the reasons he cannot accept the death.

2. Assist in the commencement of mourning by using the interventions suggested in chapter 9 for the first two "R" processes of mourning (i.e., recognize the loss; react to the separation). Pay special attention to mourners for whom there is an absence of confirmation of the death and mourners overwhelmed by multiple loss (see chapter 12 and interventions for bereavement overload in chapter 9 for discussion of the latter).

3. Convey to the mourner specific recognitions regarding his inner pain, defenses, reluctance to mourn, and wish to avoid the pain of loss (Raphael, 1983; see chapter 7).

4. Work with the mourner to reduce denial and numbing contributing to the absent mourning syndrome through the interventions suggested for the denial-numbing phase of the stress response syndrome (Horowitz, 1986a; see chapter 7).

5. As appropriate, utilize interventions suggested for inhibited mourning.

6. As appropriate, employ Raphael's (1983) suggestions for absent, delayed, or inhibited grief (see chapter 7).

Delayed Mourning

Delayed mourning perhaps better describes the mourner's status in the process of mourning than it serves to define a specific syndrome. An argument could be made for focusing on the general issue of delay as a nonspecific variable influencing complicated mourning. Certainly, evidence suggests that a delay or postponement of mourning (subject to the necessity to mourn, as noted earlier) is one of the strongest predictors of future complicated mourning (Lindemann, 1944; Parkes, 1987; Parkes & Weiss, 1983). It is also an important aspect of the conflicted mourning syndrome. Nevertheless, delayed mourning is included as a syndrome because of its clinical usefulness in describing not only the status of mourning, but also its underlying dynamics and etiology.

Uncomplicated mourning or any type of complicated mourning may be delayed for many years. Until such time as the delay is over, only absent or inhibited mourning may be exhibited. Therefore, during the interval prior to the commencement of some type of mourning (or more of it), it is impossible by observation alone to identify a particular response as being delayed. Unless there is knowledge of a conscious choice to delay mourning, delayed mourning is indistinguishable from absent or inhibited mourning until the delay is over, as well as from the initial phase of conflicted mourning, in which there is a relative absence of overt mourning prior to a state of acute mourning. In those situations where inhibited as opposed to absent mourning marks the interim prior to the commencement of fuller mourning, the delay is relative because some mourning is going on regardless of how inhibited it may be. The issue is that there will be an experience of mourning greater in terms of amount, intensity, kind, and/or activity after a period in which there has been comparatively less mourning.

In the delayed mourning syndrome, a full or partial mourning reaction is eventually triggered, bringing the period of delay or relative delay to an end. The elicitation of mourning may be intentional, such as when the mourner gives herself permission to mourn because she now has the time or feels it is safe enough. Mourning also may be stimulated unintentionally, as when the mourner experiences another loss or develops age-correspondence phenomena. Subsequent losses need not be death-related to bring delayed mourning to an end. It is not uncommon, for example, for a divorce to trigger the mourning of an older, unmourned loss, such as the death of a parent.

The real dynamic here is one of procrastination, or else the mourner's response could be identified as another form of mourning. To recapitulate, delay is a process variable. The content of the mourning, or lack thereof, during delayed mourning is actually better described by the absent or inhibited mourning syndromes.

Determinants and associated factors

A delay or relative delay in mourning may occur for any number of conscious or unconscious reasons. These can include the following.

1. The mourner needs to put mourning on hold to attend to other pressing responsibilities. These responsibilities may concern herself (e.g., her own needs for survival after injury) or others (e.g., their needs for comfort from her).

2. The mourner consciously evaluates that she cannot presently deal with the mourning process and so postpones it until a time when she thinks she can (e.g., the loss occurs when the mourner is suffering from stress overload).

3. The mourner cannot intellectually accept the fact that the death occurred because of lack of confirmation (e.g., there is no body or the mourner did not view it). This is to be differentiated from the situation in which there is a lack of acceptance because the survivor is still experiencing the shock and denial reactions of uncomplicated mourning and from the situation in which the absent mourning syndrome is present.

4. The mourner wants to avoid the pain and distress of mourning the loss and recognizing its implications.

5. The mourner has fears related to the process of mourning (e.g., confronting guilt and anger or losing emotional control).

6. The mourner lacks the social support to mourn.

7. The mourner sustains multiple bereavements simultaneously and cannot differentiate individual losses or discern where to begin mourning (e.g., three family members die in a fire).

It is not uncommon for there to be a brief period of delay before un-complicated mourning in those situations where the aforementioned conditions obtain. Certainly, some delays and the reasons for them are more problematic than others. Raphael (1983) has observed that where the delay is related to avoidance of the pain of loss or fears of guilt, anger, or losing emotional control, more pathological outcomes are likely. If the delay is kept relatively short and grief and mourning progress normally thereafter, the outcome usually is not pathological.

Delayed mourning can be diagnosed only under two conditions. The first condition is retrospection. When mourning finally proceeds, its lack or relative lack can be seen as a temporary situation. For example, when an individual begins to mourn 3 months after his wife's death, having had no experience of mourning in the interim period, it can be said that during those 3 months his mourning was delayed. If the evaluation had taken place at 2 months, all that could be said is that an absence of mourning currently exists. At that time, the mourner's experience could not legitimately be diagnosed as a delay because it remains to be seen whether mourning will commence at some point (signaling delayed mourning), whether no mourning will take place (signaling absent mourning), or whether extreme mourning responses will follow (signaling conflicted mourning).

The second condition under which delayed mourning can be diagnosed exists when it is evident that the mourner is consciously choosing to defer the mourning process and that this decision stems not from avoidance of pain, fear, or neurosis, but from an appropriate appraisal of and choice among available options. If the reasons for the delay are unconscious, avoidant, fearful, or neurotic, or if the decision is an unhealthy one, then, by definition, one is not dealing with a delayed mourning syndrome but one of the other complicated mourning syndromes.

The following example, although simplified for purposes of illustration, may help operationalize this idea: Suppose that, after being injured in an automobile accident that takes the life of his sister, an individual does not mourn because he must save his strength for his own battle to live. He postpones mourning until a later time, when he can deal with its processes. If the person otherwise has a history and/or characteristics suggestive of healthy coping with loss, the caregiver would be hard-pressed to interpret this sort of delay as a form of complicated mourning. In contrast, if the individual's delay of mourning stems from his desire to avoid unresolved anger at the deceased, this would be construed as less healthy. The situation might be seen as pathological if the delay persists beyond the period of time that, given the idiosyncratic nature of the situation and individual, reasonably could be expected to be required to address such ambivalence.

Bowlby's (1980) comments with regard to the determinants and associated factors of prolonged absence of conscious grieving, summarized in this chapter's discussion of inhibited mourning, are equally pertinent to this situation.

Treatment issues

Because by definition delayed mourning is a process variable, no specific interventions exist for it. Unless the delay is due to a conscious decision that the caregiver can support as healthy or in the best interests of the mourner, some other form or forms of complicated mourning are certainly involved. Depending on which type is involved, specific interventions can be applied. In all cases, interventions for the absent or inhibited mourning syndromes must be incorporated as appropriate whenever the reasons for delay are judged to be unhealthy.

If the mourner has made a conscious or unconscious decision in her own best interests to delay mourning temporarily, the caregiver's therapeutic focus must be as follows.

1. Work with the mourner to ensure that the reasons for the delay remain appropriate. If the reasons are inappropriate, confront them.

2. Ensure that during the period of delay the mourner undertakes necessary tasks and makes necessary decisions.

3. Support the mourner in dropping the delay and beginning to mourn when appropriate. In instances where specific factors are causing the delay, direct treatment accordingly. Such factors may include lack of confirmation of the death, insufficient social support, bereavement overload, or dilemmas posed by multiple deaths (see chapters 9, 10, and 12 for interventions in these situations). When the reasons for the delay no longer exist, or when another event triggers a full or partial mourning reaction, respond to facilitate uncomplicated mourning or move to intervene as appropriate for whatever form of complicated mourning exists.

Inhibited Mourning

The restraint of various mourning processes is very common in complicated mourning. It is present as well in some degree and for some time in uncomplicated mourning (e.g., the individual who initially idealizes the deceased and only gradually deals with less positive aspects). However, in complicated mourning, through inhibition the process consciously and/or unconsciously becomes and remains restricted to varying degrees. In some cases, there is full inhibition of external response despite the presence of internal responses indicative of varying amounts of awareness and pathology. These inhibitions are found in Deutsch's (1937) absence of grief and Bowlby's (1980) prolonged absence of conscious grieving. In the majority of cases of inhibited mourning, the inhibition is not complete but partial, and only certain parts of the loss are mourned. For example, a bereaved individual might refrain from review of the deceased and the lost relationship to avoid confrontation with aspects of that person and relationship previously eliciting anger. Because the mourner inhibits or suppresses these aspects, the response is then devoid of any manifestations of anger.

Although the inhibition of aspects of mourning is frequently discussed by those writing on complicated mourning, Raphael (1983) appears to be the first to conceptualize such inhibition as a clinical syndrome. Raphael describes inhibited mourning as a form of mourning in which expressions are "in some way or another toned down or shut off . . . [and which] may represent an overall inhibition of response or a partial inhibition" (p. 206). Normal aspects of mourning are suppressed, such as angry protest, or unconsciously repressed, as in the repression of yearning discussed by Bowlby (1980). Most often the mourner is able to relinquish and mourn only selected aspects of the deceased (e.g., the positive aspects but not the negative ones). A common pattern is intense idealization of the deceased with little review, acceptance, or relinquishment of the negative aspects of the relationship (Raphael, 1983).

In this syndrome, particular symptoms may tend to take the place of the inhibited aspects. For instance, somatization may occur, with numerous physical complaints being manifested instead of the inhibited affects of mourning (Averill, 1968). Worden (1982) employs the term *masked grief reactions* to describe the physical and psychiatric symptoms and maladaptive behaviors that are the masked expressions of repressed mourning. These reactions cause mourners difficulty, but mourners typically do not perceive or recognize them as being related to the loss. Bowlby (1980) has identified a similar phenomenon. He observes that in prolonged absence of conscious grieving, although life appears on the surface to continue as before, careful investigation in psychotherapy usually reveals psychological and physical ills—actual derivatives of mourning—that the mourner has disconnected cognitively and affectively from the death.

Determinants and associated factors

Deutsch (1937) speculates that the absence of external manifestations of mourning suggests the presence of two conditions: (a) insufficient ego strength to bear the work of mourning and (b) defensive mechanisms mobilized to protect the ego from the pain of mourning, recognition of ambivalence, and other associated dangers. Affect is excluded or displaced because of the survivor's inner awareness of the inability to master emotion.

Deutsch and many after her contend that unexpressed mourning will find expression in one way or another. It is important to note that this contention does not imply that all bereaved individuals must respond in similar fashion. Significant differences will be evident depending upon the particular constellation of factors influencing each mourner's response.

Recent criticism of the view that unexpressed mourning will eventually find expression misinterprets at least some of the literature by assuming that such expression invariably takes the form of depression or high distress (Wortman & Silver, 1987, 1989). Although in many cases the mourner does need to express depression and distress, in other cases this is not true. The crucial issue is whether what requires the mourner's processing, expression, and address—be it depression or any other response—receives sufficient attention for healthy accommodation of the loss. In other words, there is a distinct difference between not doing something that needs to be done and not having the need to begin with.

Many individuals who experience a prolonged absence of conscious grieving tend to have dispositions to assert independence from emotional ties (Bowlby, 1980). This disposition stems from childhood experiences that have taught them to cultivate self-sufficiency, encouraged the formation of a self-protective shell, and caused them to disavow desire for love and support. Many, although not all, avoid losing control, tend not to dwell on their own losses, and frequently act as compulsive caregivers for others in distress, often as a result of bereavement. Despite appearing to cope after an important loss, these mourners are often tense and short-tempered. Physical symptoms may supervene, and insomnia is common. A number of these individuals ultimately develop some form of depression or sustain empty personal and social experiences as a consequence of repressed mourning.

Bowlby also makes the interesting observation that, like its seeming opposite, chronic mourning, in prolonged absence of conscious grieving the loss is consciously or unconsciously believed still to be reversible. In both, the course of mourning remains incomplete, and the mourner's representational models maintained for self and the world remain unchanged and unaffected by reality. These commonalities explain why it is not unusual to see mourning with features of both syndromes or characterized by oscillation between the two syndromes.

When it comes to partial inhibition, to the extent that some aspects of inhibition can occur in each complicated mourning syndrome, the process of inhibition can be associated with all manner of determinants and factors. Often it has been related to difficulties on the part of the mourner in facing ambivalence toward and/or dependence upon the deceased loved one (Raphael, 1983). The impression conveyed is that acknowledging negative aspects of the relationship would bring forth guilt and anger, which are judged by the bereaved to be too great to bear.

Other factors that can be involved consciously or unconsciously in the inhibited mourning syndrome include the following.

1. The mourner's fear of intense affect

2. A personality style that encourages the inhibition of emotion or any response considered negative, conflictual, or unpleasant

3. Previous psychosocial conditioning

4. The tendency to somatize emotions and conflict

5. Environmental, sociocultural, ethnic, or religious/philosophical backgrounds that prohibit or restrict expressions of mourning

6. An unwillingness and/or inability to relinquish the lost relationship

7. Any of three types of death: (a) one the mourner might be uncomfortable admitting (e.g., suicide), (b) one that may be socially negated and for which the mourner receives subtle or blatant messages that mourning is unnecessary (e.g., stillbirth), or (c) one socially valued as a "low-grief" death (e.g., the death of an aged parent; Fulton, 1979)

8. A death resulting in the person's becoming a disenfranchised mourner (Doka, 1989), the characteristics of which predispose toward increased mourning complications

9. Being a child or an elderly person (Averill, 1968)

Treatment issues

The caregiver will find the following treatment suggestions helpful in intervening with inhibited mourning, especially for exploring reasons the mourner cannot accept the death or give himself permission to mourn and for dealing with fear of intense affect. The caregiver may also benefit by incorporating, as appropriate, interventions for delayed mourning.

1. Assist in the commencement of mourning by using the interventions suggested in chapter 9 for the first two "R" processes of mourning (i.e., recognize the loss; react to the separation). Pay special attention to mourners for whom there is an absence of confirmation of the death and mourners overwhelmed by multiple loss (see chapter 12 and interventions for bereavement overload in chapter 9 for discussion of the latter).

2. Explore with the mourner the reasons he cannot accept the death or give himself permission to mourn the loss and/or relinquish the lost relationship (e.g., fear of pain of grief, guilt, ambivalence, dependency) and work through these as defenses in order to remove them as obstructions to uncomplicated mourning. (See chapter 10 for specific instructions for dealing with problematic affects.)

3. To counteract the tendency to inhibit certain aspects of mourning (often the ambivalent or dependent part of the relationship), use interventions suggested in chapter 9 for the second and third "R"

processes of mourning (i.e., react to the separation; recollect and reexperience the deceased and the relationship) to promote identification—and ultimately processing—of all psychological reactions to the loss and all aspects of the deceased and the relationship.

4. Explore with the mourner why he is unwilling and/or unable to relinquish the lost relationship and work through the reasons that form obstacles to healthy mourning.

5. Convey to the mourner specific recognitions regarding his inner pain, defenses, reluctance to mourn, and wish to avoid the pain of loss (Raphael, 1983; see chapter 7).

6. Help the individual deal with fears that mourning will overwhelm him by lending support and strength via the therapeutic relationship, as well as by structuring and dosing the situation so that he is better able to confront it. As appropriate, follow the suggestions for intervention in the intrusive-repetitive phase of the stress response syndrome (Horowitz, 1986a; see chapter 7).

7. Work with the mourner to reduce denial and numbing through the interventions suggested for the denial-numbing phase of the stress response syndrome (Horowitz, 1986a; see chapter 7).

8. Legitimize the losses that have contributed to disenfranchising the mourner, encourage mourning of them, and mobilize support or network to enfranchise the mourner (see chapter 10).

9. If the mourner exhibits a personality style or conditioning encouraging inhibition of emotion or restriction of expressions of mourning, provide psychoeducational and normative information about healthy expression of affect, ambivalence, and the requirements of mourning. Work to identify personally acceptable and meaningful ways for the mourner to express feeling.

10. Recognize that those prone to inhibited mourning may have a predisposition to assert independence of affectional ties, as noted by Bowlby (1980) in his discussion of prolonged absence of conscious grieving. Frame the need for mourning in a fashion that stresses less its emotional aspects than its necessity as a mechanism to stabilize disequilibrium resulting from the loss. Do not neglect emotional aspects entirely, but be mindful that the need for mourning can be threatening to the person who protects himself by disavowing natural desires for love and support. This is not the time to attempt to remake the mourner into one who can tolerate intimacy, dependence, or expression of emotion. Rather, it is the time to help the mourner deal with these issues without shutting down or construing the experience as an expression of weakness.

11. If the mourner tends to somatize, intervene to support appropriate expression of affect and conflict.

12. With a child or an elderly mourner, work to promote the fullest expression of grief and mourning, recognizing society's tendency to disfranchise these two groups of mourners.

13. As applicable, incorporate interventions for delayed mourning.

14. As appropriate, employ Raphael's (1983) suggestions for absent, delayed, or inhibited grief (see chapter 7).

Distorted Mourning

The adjective *distorted* is used frequently in the literature on complicated mourning. Indeed, it describes one of the three primary dimensions that demarcate complicated responses from uncomplicated ones, the other two being covered by the terms *absent* and *prolonged*. One can easily see how absent and prolonged mourning are, in themselves, distortions of uncomplicated mourning. Thus, distortion is always involved to some extent in complicated mourning because, if no distortion exists, mourning is by definition uncomplicated. However, the present discussion concerns the specific syndrome of distorted mourning, which encompasses particular characteristics that distinguish it from the more general use of the term.

Lindemann (1944) identifies nine distorted reactions, each representing an aspect of acute grief:

1. Overactivity without a sense of loss

2. Acquisition of symptoms belonging to the last illness of the deceased

3. A recognized medical disease of a psychosomatic nature

4. A conspicuous alteration in relationship to friends and relatives

5. Furious hostility against specific persons

6. Wooden and formal appearances, with affect and conduct resembling schizophrenic pictures

7. Lasting loss of patterns of social interaction

8. Actions detrimental to one's own social and economic existence

9. Agitated depression

These appear most useful as symptoms of or diagnostic clues to complicated mourning in general because, with the exception of recognized psychosomatic disease and agitated depression, they are nonspecific behaviors and not syndromes in themselves.

Raphael (1983) has found that in distorted mourning certain aspects of uncomplicated mourning are exaggerated, whereas other aspects are inhibited. She has identified two patterns: extreme anger and extreme guilt. In the first pattern, intense and pervasive anger occurs in the absence of other reactions. Sorrow, yearning, pining, and even sadness are missing. In uncomplicated mourning, an individual may be intensely angry, but the anger either passes or coexists with other expected reactions to the loss. However, in distorted mourning of the extremely angry type, the entire response is taken up with protest and furious rage. For some, anger is accompanied by a great sense of desertion, the perception of threatened survival, a desire to punish the deceased for leaving the mourner deprived, or the resurrection of insecurity caused by earlier losses (usually of a parent in childhood). The anger persists and eventually can disrupt the mourner's whole life by destroying support systems and relationships.

The second pattern of distorted mourning is marked by extreme guilt. In this reaction, there is continual and exaggerated guilty rumination on the part of the bereaved, who is preoccupied with self-blame and self-punishment because of a conflicted premorbid relationship with the deceased. There is no genuine mourning and sorrow in this situation, only guilt. This exclusivity differentiates this type of complicated mourning from other types in which guilt is the predominant but not the only factor. Severe depression may occur. Although there is much hostility, there is little direct anger. If the guilt cannot be borne personally, it may be denied and projected onto others, especially other family members. If the guilt becomes unmanageable, these mourners can be at risk for full-blown depression and, if they fantasize reunion with the deceased or become extravagant in their need to self-punish, for suicide. Some of these mourners relish the painful nature of their guilt and use it in an attempt to appease the deceased.

Determinants and associated factors

The pattern of extreme anger has been identified by Raphael (1983) as a common response after the following types of loss: (a) the death of someone upon whom the bereaved was pathologically dependent, (b) the loss of a relationship that symbolized something special and irreplaceable, (c) a death where the mourner's sense of desertion by the deceased is great, (d) a sudden or unexpected death for which someone is blamed, and (e) a violent death. Another factor clinically associated with distorted mourning of the extremely angry type includes an angry predisposition on the part of the mourner. In this case, anger is the dominant and primary response, preferred over sadness and used to cover vulnerability, yearning, hurt, fear, and other painful or anxiety-provoking affects.

Raphael (1983) has noted that the pattern of extreme guilt tends to follow the loss of relationships that were intensely ambivalent and conflicted. Active fantasies about the death of the other may have occurred, and the actual death thus may appear to be a fulfillment of the mourner's aggressive wishes. This is what fuels the strong and persistent need to self-punish. Despite the fact that the relationship was wholly or significantly negative, the connection was strong, resulting in an intensification of responses. Other clinically associated factors I have observed include (a) the death of a child; (b) the mourner's actually having played a role in the individual's death (e.g., having driven the car in a fatal accident); (c) a tendency toward guilt feelings, perfectionism, or an unrealistic sense of responsibility for events occurring to others; and (d) the feeling that the mourner could have prevented the death but failed to do so.

Treatment issues

In the case of distorted mourning of the extremely angry type, the main treatment goal is to get underneath the anger and deal directly with its roots. Generally at the base of this response is the loss of a relationship that symbolized something special and irreplaceable to the mourner —usually one upon which she was pathologically dependent. In order to help the mourner accomplish this, the caregiver can do as follows.

1. Assist the mourner in identifying precisely and mourning all of the secondary losses inherent in the loss of the relationship, enabling her to specify the symbolic meanings of the person and relationship and to express the psychological reactions to these losses. Use interventions suggested for the second and third "R" processes (i.e., react to the separation; recollect and reexperience the deceased and the relationship; see chapter 9).

2. Address with the mourner the sequelae of the loss of this symbolic relationship so that they do not fuel further anger or become obscured by it. Intervene directly to work through these issues (e.g., the mourner's sense of desertion, perception of threatened survival, desire to punish the deceased, and resurrected insecurity).

3. Work with the mourner to address issues of dependency and codependency, using interventions such as those outlined in chapter 10. Give special focus to helping the mourner meet dependency needs in healthy fashions, increasing self-esteem and assertiveness, and avoiding displacement of anger that may alienate her support system.

4. Address anger in accordance with the therapeutic strategies and interventions delineated in chapter 10.

5. Where the personality of the mourner is such that anger is predominant and used to cover more painful or anxiety-provoking affects, intervene to access these affects and work through the anger as a defense, as well as an overlearned response or predisposition. Recognize that the goal here is to enable healthy mourning, not to make the mourner into a different person.

6. Using the previously mentioned techniques for inhibited mourning, help the mourner stimulate and work through any aspects of mourning besides anger that remain.

7. In cases of sudden, unexpected death in which someone is blamed or in which the death was traumatic, violent, or mutilating, employ interventions specific to the circumstances (see chapters 10 through 13). Where these circumstances transpire in the death of one upon whom the mourner was pathologically dependent, recognize and respond to the potential for increased severity of response.

8. Given the type of relationship the mourner had with the deceased and as necessary, spend additional time and effort working on the fourth and fifth "R" processes of mourning, as discussed in chapter 9 (i.e., relinquish the old attachments to the deceased and the old assumptive world; readjust to move adaptively into the new world without forgetting the old).

9. As appropriate, integrate Raphael's (1983) focal psychotherapy strategies and techniques for this form of complicated mourning (see chapter 7).

In the case of distorted mourning of the extremely guilty type, the main therapeutic issue is dealing directly with the roots of the guilt. Generally, the loss of a highly conflicted and ambivalent relationship is at the bottom of this response. In particular, the caregiver should attempt to intervene as follows.

1. By intervening in the second and third "R" processes of mourning (i.e., react to the separation; recollect and reexperience the deceased and the relationship), assist the mourner in identifying and processing all the emotions, thoughts, impulses, omissions and commissions, and other root causes of guilt in the relationship with the deceased (see chapter 9).

2. Review the relationship to identify and work through as much as possible any anger and ambivalence (see chapter 10).

3. Intervene in guilt stemming from the conflicted relationship and its assorted aspects (e.g., death wishes, links to earlier parent-child

relationships), as suggested in chapter 10. Ensure that guilt is channelled appropriately, not used as an appeasement of or a connection to the deceased, nor projected onto others. Recognize that guilt is in general problematic for human beings and that frequently it requires intervention even when not associated with a hate-filled relationship. Also, be aware that guilt may prevent the mourner from allowing further progress in the "R" processes (i.e., as a form of self-sabotage).

4. Using the previously mentioned techniques for inhibited mourning, assist the mourner in stimulating and working through any aspects of mourning besides guilt that remain.

5. Remain alert for signs of depression and self-destructive tendencies and behaviors that may be the sequelae of guilt, intervening as necessary.

6. Understand that the death of a child inherently provokes intense guilt that can be difficult to address therapeutically due to the nature of the parental role (see chapter 13).

7. Recognize that any problems resulting from loss of a conflicted premorbid relationship may be compounded if the death is sudden, violent, traumatic, or mutilating; follows an extended terminal illness; or involves a child. Employ specific interventions for these circumstances as appropriate (see chapters 11 through 13).

8. As appropriate, integrate Raphael's (1983) focal psychotherapy strategies and techniques for this form of complicated mourning (see chapter 7).

Conflicted Mourning

According to Parkes and Weiss (1983), who have identified this particular complicated mourning syndrome, conflicted mourning arises after the loss of highly troubled, ambivalent relationships. After a brief initial absence of grief—even relief—the mourner experiences severe grief, with sadness, lack of acceptance of the loss, anxiety, guilt, self-reproach, and continued yearning and pining for the deceased, along with a persistent need for and sense of connection to the lost person marked by remorse as well as by many of the same mixed feelings that had characterized the premorbid relationship. The response is clinically similar to that displayed in chronic mourning.

Although it appears somewhat related to Raphael's (1983) distorted mourning of the extremely guilty type, conflicted mourning differs in that many more of the affects and dynamics of uncomplicated mourning are experienced. In addition, this syndrome typically involves a delay in the onset of acute mourning and contains more intense elements of yearning, pining, and continued sense of connection. Thus, despite the fact that both syndromes are generated by ambivalent and conflicted relationships that leave the bereaved person with enormous remorse, the pattern of responses within them is different.

Determinants and associated factors

The primary determinant of conflicted mourning is the loss of an extremely ambivalent, conflict-ridden, and troubled relationship, over and above the ambivalence and conflict present in any normal human relationship. It could be predicted that those psychological qualities and early childhood experiences that lead to the formation of conflicted relationships would also be associated determinants (e.g., alcoholic parents, poor self-esteem).

Parkes and Weiss (1983) note that the ambivalence of the conflicted relationship creates problems in the emotional acceptance of the death because of the complexity of emotions, intensity of guilt and remorse, and difficulty in acknowledging and accepting feelings and behaviors the mourner now would prefer to disown. Essentially, what occurs is a brief period of relief and well-being, occasioned by the release from the conflict. However, relief cannot be maintained because of the consequences of the loss of the conflicted relationship. These consequences include guilt and self-reproach, lack of sufficient positive memories to support continued feelings of worth, sadness and anger that the relationship never was what the mourner might have wished it to be, a sense of hypocrisy for mourning what appears to have been such a negative relationship and surprise that the deceased is missed, and the loss of opportunity ever to resolve the conflicts.

Like relationships associated with distorted mourning of the extremely guilty type, severed relationships leading to conflicted mourning are strong in attachment despite being insecure and negative in content. It is precisely the strength of the attachment that causes the failure of initial attempts to avoid mourning. These attempts give rise to the initial delay as the mourner at first greatly enjoys the release from conflict and tries to repudiate the attachment to the deceased. However, the attachment then spawns difficulties: Problems are created by the ambivalence of the conflicted relationship, the relief is lost, and the repudiation fails. Conflicted mourning is experienced and becomes chronic in character.

The failure to recover coinciding with the conflicted mourning syndrome may stem not only from the traditional sequelae proposed to follow ambivalent relationships (i.e., atypical mourning, guilt and self-reproach, and identification). Parkes and Weiss note that this failure can be explained equally well by such phenomena as (a) continued inner dialogues with the criticizing deceased, (b) attempts to make restitution to the deceased through continued mourning, (c) inability to function better because the same personality dynamics and early experiences that permitted the mourner to tolerate the conflicted relationship interfere with successful recovery, and (d) the impedance of effective functioning and recovery by diminished self-esteem and self-confidence resulting from years in an unhappy relationship. This last point supports the observation of Rynearson (1990) that the mourner experiencing this syndrome perceives himself as numb and defective.

Treatment issues

In treating conflicted mourning, the caregiver must promote the overt expression of all the affects of mourning and must work through the particular problems posed by ambivalence and guilt. The following interventions should assist in this regard.

1. In the period of delayed mourning following the death, use strategies designed for the absent, delayed, or inhibited mourning syndromes in order to promote the overt expression of grief. This will entail focusing on the first, second, and third "R" processes of mourning (i.e., recognize the loss; react to the separation; recollect and reexperience the deceased and the relationship— see chapter 9).

2. Review the relationship to identify and work through any anger and ambivalence that had existed (see chapter 10).

3. Intervene in guilt stemming from the conflicted relationship (see chapter 10). Also, as appropriate, adapt strategies mentioned previously for distorted mourning of the extremely guilty type.

4. Given the dynamics of the premorbid relationship and how they, relevant personality characteristics, and early conditioning contribute to the failure to recover, employ intervention strategies focusing on dependency and codependency, as delineated in chapter 10.

5. Help the mourner understand that, despite the conflicted nature of the relationship, the attachment was nonetheless strong and that his need to mourn is not hypocritical. As appropriate, adapt explanations and interventions from chapter 10 on the need to mourn after victimizing relationships.

6. Identify and work through the special sadness, regret, and anger that the relationship was not what the mourner now wishes it could have been.

7. As necessary, intervene to deal with the anxiety present in this syndrome by using the strategies discussed in chapter 12 for anxiety associated with traumatic memories.

8. Where the mourner continues to experience inner dialogues of a criticizing nature with the deceased, work both to alter the internalized relationship and to formulate a more appropriate one, which will not interfere in healthy adaptation. Focus specifically on interventions spelled out in chapter 9 for the fourth and fifth "R" processes of mourning (i.e., relinquish the old attachments to the deceased and the old assumptive world; readjust to move adaptively into the new world without forgetting the old).

9. Given that conflicted mourning involves numerous aspects of the chronic mourning syndrome, use interventions identified for chronic mourning as appropriate.

10. Recognize that any problems resulting from loss of a conflicted premorbid relationship may be compounded if the death is sudden and unexpected, violent, traumatic, or mutilating; follows an extended terminal illness; or involves a child. Employ specific interventions for these circumstances as appropriate (see chapters 11 through 13).

11. To the extent that mourner liabilities in the form of previous or concurrent mental health problems, stresses, or crises interfere with mourning, intervene as suggested in chapter 10.

Unanticipated Mourning

Although sudden, unexpected death appears to be universally recognized as a significant factor predisposing the survivor to complicated mourning, only Lehrman (1956) and Parkes and Weiss (1983) identify the response following such a death as a specific syndrome. Lehrman (1956) notes that an untimely death is a death involving a relatively young person and implying disadvantageous timing in terms of an actual sudden death or diagnosis of incurability. He views reactions to untimely death as variants of pathological grief and mourning reactions, with the mourner's ego being less prepared for the loss and the threat to it being much greater. He asserts that pathological reactions are more frequent when the death has been untimely and sudden and notes that often there is surprise, shock, and lack of preparation.

Lehrman also points out that, as is the case in uncomplicated mourning, reactions to untimely death represent a defense against unbearable, painful affects. They may assume a variety of forms, such as obsessive compulsive neurosis, anxiety, hysteria, manic-depressive psychosis, or schizoid state. Denial is quite prominent. The clinical picture is usually mixed and atypical, in accordance with varying basic etiological factors, and is determined by the individual's childhood conditioning and the extent to which the infantile neurosis has been mastered. Lehrman's experience suggests that the mourner's reactions tend to be refractory and that treatment should proceed slowly. He also remarks on the striking similarity between reactions to untimely deaths and traumatic neurosis (i.e., post-traumatic stress disorder). In both conditions, the need exists to master the psychological shock, with the mode of mastery governing the clinical picture and being determined by childhood patterning. The response to untimely death need not always be pathological, however. Lehrman believes that, where ego strength is sufficient, an uncomplicated mourning reaction can occur.

One of Parkes and Weiss's (1983) most important contributions is their conceptualization of the unanticipated mourning syndrome, which they assert can have an impact so disruptive that uncomplicated recovery can no longer be expected. Although many of the reactions occurring in this syndrome are witnessed initially in all those whose loved ones die suddenly, it is the course and persistence of this reaction and its resulting consequences that constitute the unanticipated mourning syndrome. (I would add that there also must be a failure or complication in one or more of the "R" processes of mourning.) Parkes and Weiss observe that, in this syndrome, mourners are unable to grasp the full implications of the loss and have difficulty accepting that it happened despite intellectual recognition of its occurrence. The death continues to be both inexplicable and unbelievable, and mourners avoid confrontation with the loss. The adaptive capacities and coping abilities of these mourners are seriously assaulted. They suffer extreme feelings of bewilderment, anxiety, self-reproach, depression, and despair that render them incapable of functioning normally in any area of their lives. Grief symptomatology persists much longer than usual, and mourners typically remain socially withdrawn, developing a sense of the deceased's continued presence. This sense of continued presence binds them to the deceased and hampers their ability to function socially and occupationally.

The absence of forewarning compromises the ability to understand and explain the death because the loss seems so disconnected with anything that preceded it. The inability to prepare gradually for the loss and to make a less abrupt psychosocial transition appears to be a major disabling factor (Parkes, 1988). One's entire world, world view, and assumptions are violated instantly. This, plus the insecurity generated by recognition that tragedy could happen again without the mourner's being able to control it, leads to significant anxiety and loss of confidence in the world, which compromise the mourner's coping ability and adaptation. Subsequent relationships may be avoided in the desire to evade risk of future loss. Conversely, relationships that do exist can be compromised by the mourner's tendency to cling too tightly or control too much in an attempt to minimize the chances of experiencing further loss.

Having unfinished business with the deceased—often an inherent consequence of this type of loss—only exacerbates the mourner's problems. Such unfinished business is well known to exert significant psychological press upon the mourner, affectively and cognitively, through the repetition compulsion (Freud, 1920/1955a). As a result, the mourner may tend to experience the urge to act out in various ways to achieve a sense of closure.

Finally, it must be noted that experiencing a sudden, unexpected death in the context of a terminal illness or a recovery is also quite possible (see chapter 12). Too often, however, this type of loss is perceived by others as being an expected death, with resulting inappropriate expectations and the absence of proper support for the bereaved (see Rando, 1987b). This type of loss engenders the same reactions as other sudden deaths, along with some unique problems stemming from the inaccurate social evaluation of it.

Other complicating issues known to be inherent in sudden, unexpected death, by definition exacerbating difficulties, include persistence of physical and emotional shock, obsessive reconstruction of events in retrospect, highlighting of events at the time of death, increased intensity of emotional reactions, and overlap of post-traumatic symptomatology, which frequently develops secondary to traumatic overwhelming of the ego (see chapter 12).

Determinants and associated factors

As noted, the unanticipated mourning syndrome has as its primary determinant a sudden, unexpected loss (Parkes & Weiss, 1983). Lehrman (1956) has identified additional factors influencing the formation of pathological reactions to untimely death: previously existing psychopathology, weakness of the mourner's ego, and the absence of compensations in substitute love objects. Those persons prone to develop depressions in the absence of a loss through death or to evidence pathological reactions to an expected or timely death would also be likely to develop pathological reactions to an untimely death.

Clinical observation suggests that difficulty making psychosocial transitions in general and the preexistence of easily overwhelmed premorbid adaptive capacities also may be determinants of the unanticipated mourning syndrome. Situations after the death in which the mourner endures other losses that leave even less of the world she used to know (e.g., when the death forces a loss of possessions and immediate relocation) may be determinants as well. As discussed in chapter 10, such concurrent stresses are known to complicate any mourning process.

Treatment issues

In all cases in which the unanticipated mourning syndrome is present, the caregiver must spend considerable time facilitating the first and second "R" processes of mourning (i.e., recognize the loss; react to the separation —see chapter 9). There will be a need to intervene particularly in the fourth and fifth "R" processes as well (i.e., relinquish the old attachments to the deceased and the old assumptive world; readjust to move adaptively into the new world without forgetting the old). Chapter 12 includes extensive discussion of treatment issues associated with sudden, unexpected death, the precursor of the unanticipated mourning syndrome. The reader is referred there for the primary discussion of treatment of unanticipated mourning. Discussion in that chapter of treatment concerns relating to multiple death, traumatic death, and anxiety also will be pertinent, as will consideration of specific types of death that inherently involve a lack of anticipation: deaths from acute natural causes, accidents, disasters, war, suicides, and homicides (see chapter 11).

Chronic Mourning

Chronic mourning, also known as prolonged grief or protracted mourning, has been mentioned by nearly everyone writing on the topic of complicated mourning. This phenomenon, well recognized clinically, is acute mourning that persists interminably—that fails to draw to its natural conclusion and in which intense reactions do not abate over time. There is continued crying, sadness, angry protest, yearning and searching, review of the relationship, preoccupation with the deceased, depression, disorganization, anxiety, helplessness, and other reactions typical of the early responses to loss. In this regard, the phenomenon legitimately could be termed *chronic acute grief* because many chronic mourners never progress very far into the actual work of mourning—perhaps only to the third "R" process (i.e., recollecting and reexperiencing the deceased and the relationship). Nevertheless, for consistency the term *chronic mourning* will be retained.

Mourners with this syndrome present to a caregiver as if they had lost a loved one just days before, even though the loss may have taken place years ago. Such individuals may become permanently ensconced in the role of the grief-stricken one (Raphael, 1983). This may have one of two opposite outcomes: Chronic mourning may alienate others or may be the manner in which the mourner secures attention and sympathy (i.e., achieves secondary gain).

It may be that chronic mourning affords a kind of connection with the deceased. Not only does the perpetuation of mourning keep the person's memory alive, but the pain of mourning conveys to the mourner that he has not become inured to the loss—that he still feels strongly about the deceased.

Bowlby (1980) notes that, despite the fact that prolonged absence of conscious grieving may appear superficially to be the opposite of chronic mourning, in both the loss is consciously or unconsciously believed still to be reversible. The mourner continues to experience an urge to search for the deceased; anger and/or self-reproach is easily aroused while the course of mourning remains incomplete. These commonalities explain why it is not unusual to see a pattern of response with features of both types of mourning or oscillation between the two. They also account for the not uncommon progression of initial absence of conscious grieving, abrupt commencement of acute grief responses, and chronic mourning.

Bowlby conceptualizes chronic mourners as being stuck in extended and distorted phases of yearning and searching and of disorganization and despair. He identifies features such as persistent anger, resentment, and self-reproach as coinciding with the principal symptom of depression, often combined or alternating with anxiety, agoraphobia, hypochondria, or alcoholism. Interestingly, sorrow may be notably absent in many of these cases. Other components Bowlby witnesses include enduring tension, restlessness, intense yearning, and deep despair. It is also not uncommon to see anger directed at third parties, mummification (preserving the environment precisely the way it was prior to the death), the mourner's perception soon after the death that others are unhelpful, and mislocations of the lost person's presence.

Gorer (1965) differentiates between two types of chronic mourning. In the first type, the mourner suffers from chronic depressive reactions (i.e., the persistence of acute mourning). In the second type, the mourner says, "You never get over it," while leading an effective and reasonably satisfying life. Gorer regards this latter individual as one who believes unlimited mourning to be a duty to the dead and who evidences continued social expression of sorrow, although not truly experiencing deep or violent sadness. Parkes (1987) believes the distinction between these two types can be quite difficult to make and perceives considerable overlap. It is often pointed out that Queen Victoria, who chronically mourned the death of Prince Albert, still was able to function despite doing such things as continuing to have his clothes laid out. Parkes believes that it would be untrue to regard her perpetual mourning as nothing more than a duty to the dead.

Clearly, the caregiver must recognize that mourning can persist chronically in a number of different ways, which may or may not interfere with other functioning. Looking at the mourner's status with regard to the two criteria for a healthy relationship with the deceased will be the most helpful guide in this area. Briefly, this means that the mourner (a) truly recognizes that the loved one is dead and fully understands the implications of the death and (b) continues to move forward adaptively into the new life. It must be recognized that there may be some appropriate moving forward in the new life while other areas remain fixated.

Determinants and associated factors

Parkes and Weiss (1983) view chronic mourning as a disorder of attachment. It is their contention that chronic mourning, which they perceive as the most common form of complicated mourning, develops following the loss of a relationship in which the mourner was highly and anxiously dependent upon the deceased and in which the mourner required the deceased's presence, emotional support, or actual assistance in order to function adequately. They see this insecurity as the essential determinant of chronic mourning, first in its fostering of the mourner's emotional dependency and subsequently in its perpetuating his problems by making it difficult for him to relinquish the position of chronic mourning.

In addition to distinguishing personality traits of the individual prone to chronic mourning, Parkes and Weiss identify four factors that contribute to the persistence of chronic mourning.

1. The mourner's fearful personality leads to social withdrawal, which in turn leads to lack of support and encouragement, fostering additional withdrawal in a self-perpetuating cycle.

2. The mourner avoids recovery in order to maintain the security provided by the illusion of a continued relationship with the deceased.

3. The mourner lacks confidence in his power to survive and/or in the world as safe, which leads to preference for the obsolescent world over the new, anxiety-provoking world without the deceased.

4. Support garnered from others encourages the continuation of mourning.

Parkes and Weiss also note that, because of the mourner's insufficient self-confidence and hope for the future, the extreme dependence on the deceased associated with chronic mourning interferes with the development of the required new identity subsequent to the death. This view supports Rynearson's (1990) recent contention that the self-image of this type of mourner centers on helplessness. Parkes and Weiss observe that chronic mourning often can be predicted within the first few weeks by the coincidence of intense yearning and the loss of a highly dependent relationship.

According to Bowlby (1980), a person with a premorbid personality disposition toward compulsive caregiving is prone to develop chronic mourning. Bowlby also describes specific cognitive biases that coincide with chronic mourning (see chapter 3). The chronic mourner tends to have pairs of representational models of self and early attachment figures that often are incompatible, with one pair (derived from what his parents have told him) portraying the mourner's parents as above criticism and the mourner as worthless, given to ingratitude and unjustifiable anger and lucky to have the self-sacrificing parents he has. The second, and more frequently subordinate, pair of models (derived from the mourner's own experience) depicts the parents as begrudging in affection and attention and too often unavailable, and the mourner as more justified than his parents allow in his demands and anger toward them when they fail him. In addition, the mourner perceives himself as having better feelings and more positive intentions toward his parents than they credit him with.

Other features Bowlby delineates as having the potential to predispose an individual toward chronic mourning include a picture of the self as forever under total obligation to provide care for the attachment figure. A second feature stems from having been raised to see one's actions as constantly jeopardizing the health and even the lives of one's parents. In this situation, the individual will be strongly biased to construe the death of one of them as precisely the catastrophe to which his alleged selfishness, thoughtlessness, and deficient caregiving was bound to lead, with no thought permitted that the deceased might ever have been at fault. A third feature predisposing the individual toward chronic mourning is a model of the attachment figure as one more or less certain to react to the mourner's shortcomings with threats of desertion and suicide. When the death occurs, the mourner interprets it as the realization of these threats, bringing about extreme anger and raising the suspicion that, as has been successful in the past, the lost loved one can be recovered through coercion or supplication. This suspicion may precipitate many years of angry protest and fruitless search.

Each of these latter two features—construal of the death as due to his own negligence or to the deceased's desertion—convince the mourner that he is to blame. Insofar as the mourner has a sense of the deceased's continuing presence, he may take that presence to be plotting revenge. This may account for his acute anxiety and alarming dreams.

Finally, Bowlby identifies the following early features of a loss reaction as predictive of chronic mourning:

1. An abrupt commencement of intense and disruptive mourning following a period up to several months in which little or no response is evidenced

2. Acute disturbance early after the death, with unusually intense and continual yearning, unusually deep despair expressed as welcoming the prospect of death, persistent anger and bitterness, and/or pronounced guilt and self-reproach

3. Recovery not commenced by the end of the first year

4. Persistence of anger and resentment long after the early weeks, usually accompanied by continuing tension, restlessness, and intense yearning

5. The bereaved's reporting early after the death that others are not helpful

Raphael (1983) finds chronic mourning to be evidenced typically after the death of one with whom the mourner had a dependent and irreplaceable relationship and often to be marked by extraordinary and possibly pathological emotional investment in the deceased. She sees chronic mourning frequently after sudden, unexpected deaths and following the deaths of children. Bergler (1948) views chronic mourning, what he terms *prolonged mourning,* to be the mourner's acceptance of inappropriate guilt in order to diminish psychic conflict over repressed passivity.

I myself have observed that chronic mourning is often diagnosed inappropriately by caregivers. Most often, misconceptions about the resolution and duration of mourning account for this problem. First, some caregivers are unfamiliar with what resolution means or, to employ the terminology preferred throughout this text, what healthy accommodation of the loss entails. As a result, individuals are judged to be chronically mourning when, in fact, they are not—they are merely moving adaptively into the new world without forgetting the old. Until caregivers clarify both the natural and therapeutic aspects of the maintenance of a healthy relationship with the deceased, more individuals will have the misfortune to have their responses inappropriately pathologized. Second, caregivers are often misinformed about the duration of mourning. Research (e.g., Zisook & DeVaul, 1983; Zisook & Shuchter, 1985, 1986; Zisook et al., 1982) is only now making clear empirically what has been known for so long clinically: Mourning often persists for years, and it does not have to be complicated to do so. In addition, the typical course of mourning for certain kinds of losses can be expected to be significantly longer than for others. For instance, mourning following the death of a child usually is not only more intense and more complicated, but also more prolonged (Rando, 1985a, 1986f, 1986g). Thus, even relatively uncomplicated parental mourning has been viewed as both chronic and distorted. Other types of death and high-risk factors, discussed in chapters 11 through 13, present inherent complications that have prompted similar diagnoses.

Treatment issues

Before undertaking any interventions for chronic mourning, the caregiver must attempt to ascertain the reasons for the mourner's inability or unwillingness to move from the position of continual acute grief. Treatment then should be based on this determination. In each case, the caregiver will need to explore with the mourner the identity and roles he had with the lost loved one and the meaning of the relationship, recognizing that often little motivates the chronic mourner to change and that he may be reluctant to invest himself in treatment. The following specific guidelines for intervention may be helpful:

1. Inasmuch as the mourner's most significant problems are his inability, reluctance, or ignorance about how to proceed in the world without the deceased, use interventions suggested in chapter 9 for the fourth and fifth "R" processes of mourning

(i.e., relinquish the old attachments to the deceased and the old assumptive world; readjust to move adaptively into the new world without forgetting the old). The four subprocesses in the latter focus on the primary areas in which the mourner refuses to make readjustments. Interventions for the sixth "R" process (i.e., reinvest) are appropriate to provide new and better sources of gratification, which in this case may have to precede the prior two "R" processes in order to motivate the mourner to undertake them.

2. Given that the chronic mourning syndrome is defined as a disorder of attachment and is strongly associated with issues of dependence, helplessness, insecurity, and anxiety, employ relevant techniques and strategies as delineated in chapters 10 and 12 for the treatment of dependency, codependency, and anxiety.

3. Because social support can be pivotal in affecting chronic mourning, analyze the mourner's support system and intervene as required to eliminate misdirected reinforcement. If chronic mourning has alienated the individual from his support system, direct interventions toward both the system and the mourner to ameliorate this situation. In cases where mourning is erroneously considered chronic by support system members who underestimate the length of uncomplicated mourning or fail to recognize STUG phenomena, provide proper feedback and information.

4. Vigorously disabuse the mourner of any notion that the length of mourning is a testimony to love for the deceased, indicates the worth of the lost relationship, or is a duty owed to the deceased.

5. Where a significant purpose in this syndrome is to keep the deceased alive in the mourning, pay special attention to the interventions pertinent to the fourth "R" process of mourning (i.e., relinquish the old attachments to the deceased and the old assumptive world), as well as to the subprocess associated with developing a new relationship with the deceased in the fifth "R" process (i.e., readjust to move adaptively into the new world without forgetting the old—see chapter 9).

6. Understand that the caregiver's attitude in the treatment of the mourner will be an important intervention in itself. Following Parkes and Weiss's (1983) suggestions, move from building trust and giving support to providing encouragement, rewarding independence, and insisting on forward movement. Actively participate in helping the mourner to develop goals and make decisions.

7. Employ behavioral strategies as appropriate, setting the mourner a series of concrete tasks if necessary. Establish or take advantage

of the proper contingencies to help the mourner develop sources of reinforcement other than chronic mourning and roles other than that of chronic mourner.

8. If the individual is predisposed to chronic mourning because of the disposition toward compulsive caregiving or the specific cognitive biases outlined previously, intervene to work these through to the extent possible.

9. Because chronic mourning may occur after the loss of a special and irreplaceable relationship, help the mourner to identify precisely and mourn all of the secondary losses inherent in the loss and to specify the symbolic meanings of the person and relationship. As appropriate, employ interventions suggested for the subprocess concerning identification and mourning of secondary losses under the second "R" process (i.e., react to the separation— see chapter 9).

10. In cases of sudden, unexpected death and the death of a child, which are known to predispose towards chronic mourning, incorporate intervention strategies outlined in chapters 12 and 13, respectively.

11. As appropriate, employ Raphael's (1983) suggestions for chronic grief (see chapter 7).

CHAPTER 5

Complicated Outcomes of Loss: Mental Disorders, Physical Disorders, and Death

When the response to loss is not uncomplicated and does not result in complicated mourning symptoms or syndromes per se, it may eventuate in a mental disorder, a physical disorder, or death. This chapter explores these three potential outcomes of loss when they are associated with or develop from some compromise, distortion, or failure of one or more of the six "R" processes of mourning.

MENTAL DISORDERS

Since the earliest literature on complicated mourning, there has been great interest in the association among uncomplicated grief and mourning, complicated mourning, and recognized mental disorders. Indeed, as noted in chapter 3, much of the initial writing in this area compared complicated mourning with manic-depression.

There are two areas of focus centering on bereavement and mental illness. The first area pertains to the prevalence of psychiatric symptomatology during the uncomplicated grief and mourning experience; the second concerns the development of mental disorders as a consequence of bereavement. It is this second area that relates to complicated mourning, yet, given the continuum between uncomplicated and complicated response to loss, it is important to examine both. Until the patterns and responses of uncomplicated bereavement reactions are thoroughly understood, it is not possible to develop totally accurate criteria for complicated reactions.

Initial studies looking at psychiatric symptoms in mourning focused primarily on depressive symptomatology (Clayton & Darvish, 1979;

Clayton, Desmarais, & Winokur, 1968; Clayton, Halikas, & Maurice, 1971; Clayton, Herjanic, Murphy, & Woodruff, 1974; Maddison & Viola, 1968; Parkes, 1972; Paykel, Myers, Dienelt, Klerman, Lindenthal, & Pepper, 1969). All the studies reviewed by the Institute of Medicine's comprehensive study on the health consequences of bereavement document that distress and depressive symptoms dominate the emotional life of the bereaved during the first year (Osterweis et al., 1984). Yet, due to small sample sizes, the findings are inconsistent and inconclusive regarding how often the bereaved meet criteria for true psychiatric illnesses.

In their extensive review of the literature, Stroebe and Stroebe (1987) found only one study that did not report a significant increase in depression following bereavement (i.e., Heyman & Gianturco, 1973). They feel there is little doubt that recent bereavement is associated with heightened risk of depression and observe that responses during bereavement may meet the criteria for the diagnosis of clinical depression. For supportive evidence, they cite the long-accepted literature on stressful life and life-change events, which has consistently confirmed loss as a powerful predictor of mental disorder (Dohrenwend & Dohrenwend, 1974; Paykel et al., 1969; Rahe, 1979).

More recent studies on bereavement include examination of anxiety as well as depression (Faravelli & Pallanti, 1989; Jacobs, 1987; Jacobs et al., 1990; Jacobs & Kim, 1990; Sable, 1989). Although certainly other psychiatric disorders have been associated with bereavement, it appears that these two are most prevalent. Parkes (1987–1988) has distilled his view, writing that "My own experience indicates that the majority of people referred for psychiatric treatment after a bereavement are suffering from reactive depression, anxiety and their secondary effects (e.g., alcoholism) in association with atypical grief" (p. 368). The importance of delineating these pathological reactions derives from the fact that it is the first time psychiatric research has identified a group of psychiatric disorders with distinctive etiology, as well as clinical characteristics (Parkes, 1985).

Although most of the early research in this area focused on admissions to psychiatric hospitals, the development of disorders of mental health is not exclusive to psychiatric inpatients. Recent research suggests that the caregiver providing outpatient mental health treatment, as well as psychiatric consultation for medical hospitalizations, must be well aware of the impact of unresolved grief and complicated mourning. Although another reason may be given for referral, clinical experience and research investigation suggest that 15 to 21 percent of all individuals presenting for outpatient mental health services suffer from unresolved grief (Lazare, 1979; Zisook & Lyons, 1988–1989; Zisook et al., 1985), with the figures soaring to 53 percent when calculated for only outpatients who have experienced a loss (Zisook & Lyons, 1988–1989). In related areas, it has been determined that 25 percent of patients seen in psychiatric consultation on medical and surgical hospital wards have unresolved grief that antedates the medical problems for which they are hospitalized (DeVaul et al., 1979) and that 60 percent of patients with cancer referred for counseling or psychotherapy assessment sustain unresolved grief (Vachon, 1987b).

In conclusion, the clinical and empirical evidence suggests that uncomplicated grief and mourning are characterized by significant symptomatology indicating departure from normal mental health and that disturbances in mental health continue for longer periods of time than previously assumed. The impact of uncomplicated mourning is greater than originally believed. In addition, symptoms and syndromes of complicated mourning following the death of a loved one, including recognized mental disorders, are more prevalent than previously assumed. As succinctly noted by Bowlby (1980), "Clinical experience and a reading of the evidence leaves little doubt . . . that much psychiatric illness is an expression of pathological mourning" (p. 23).

Clearly, therefore, major loss can be an etiological cause or a concomitant variable in any mental disorder. With this as a given, the rest of this section presents the major categories of the *Diagnostic and Statistical Manual of Mental Disorders* (DSM-III-R; American Psychiatric Association, 1987) and, based on a review of the bereavement literature, delineates pertinent relationships with complicated mourning. In some of the studies reviewed, terminology used to indicate disorders was generic (i.e., *psychiatric disorder, mental illness, emotional disturbance, psychosis, neurosis, character pathology*), and the exact nature of the disorders was unspecified. Therefore, only references that mention a specific disorder are reported here. As greater comprehension of both uncomplicated and complicated mourning is achieved, one would expect more to be said about those disorders not yet the subject of empirical and clinical observation.

Three possible associations may exist between complicated mourning and a given diagnostic category: Mental disorders may (a) preexist (a high-risk factor), thus causing complications; (b) arise as a result of the loss; or (c) develop coincidentally with mourning (concurrent to it, not because of it). Surely, there is no diagnosis that has not at some time been associated with complicated mourning. Those relationships that are clinically most frequent are emphasized here, although it is recognized that idiosyncratic ones always can be discovered. Discussion frequently focuses on how complicated mourning predisposes to particular mental disorders. However, for some diagnostic categories, the focus is broadened to examine how the disorder itself can influence the development, severity, and form of complicated mourning by functioning as a provoking agent or vulnerability factor.

Disorders Usually First Evident in Infancy, Childhood, or Adolescence

Because the focus of this book is adult complicated mourning, most of the disorders usually first evident in infancy, childhood, or adolescence will not be discussed. However, research pertaining to two disorders in this category is of interest because of their presence in adulthood: developmental disorders and eating disorders. The reader also must be aware of the artificial dichotomy being drawn between childhood and adult bereavement and of the fact that investigation of adult mental disorders often presupposes that disorders in childhood, infancy, and adolescence have the same or similar etiology. In this regard, the anxiety disorders of childhood or adolescence and the disruptive behavior disorders, incorporated under conduct disorder and the oppositional defiant disorder, may be construed as bereavement-related sequelae of childhood that often persist as disorders of adulthood. The death of a loved one in childhood is itself a high-risk factor for complicated mourning both at the time and later in life. In addition, loss of attachment figures during these years may precipitate disorders that may only become manifested in adulthood.

Readers interested in further information about disorders usually first evident in infancy, childhood, or adolescence and their relationship with complicated mourning are advised to consult the works of the following authors: Anthony and Koupernik (1973); Bendiksen and Fulton (1975); Berlinsky and Biller (1982); Bloom-Feshbach and Bloom-Feshbach (1987); Bowlby (1980); Corr and McNeil (1986); E. Furman (1974); R. Furman (1973); Krupnick and Solomon (1987); Parkes and Stevenson-Hinde (1982); Raphael (1983); H. Rosen (1986); Schowalter, Patterson, Tallmer, Kutscher, Gullo, and Peretz (1983); and Wass and Corr (1984).

Developmental disorders

As defined by the DSM-III-R, the essential feature of this category is predominant disturbance in the acquisition of cognitive, language, motor, or social skills, with the disturbance involving a general delay (i.e., mental retardation), multiple areas of qualitative distortions of normal development (i.e., pervasive developmental disorders), or delay or failure to progress in a specific area of skill acquisition (i.e., specific developmental disorders). Especially as pertains to the first two types, different degrees of impairment exist. These must of course be taken into consideration in any assessment of bereavement response.

The following discussion focuses on how the particular disorder of mental retardation can predispose to complicated mourning. Little can be said at this juncture about the other disorders, with two exceptions. First, because the impairment in individuals with pervasive developmental disorders is even greater than that sustained by people with severe mental retardation, additional questions about how best to facilitate mourning in this group are raised. Second, it appears that some of the specific developmental disorders involving inadequate development of academic skills may be seen as concomitants of childhood mourning, both uncomplicated and complicated.

When an individual with mental retardation loses a loved one, that individual will have the same basic psychological, spiritual, behavioral, social, and physical needs as any other person. However, according to Lavin (1989), the person with retardation may also do as follows.

1. Demonstrate impaired mental abilities

2. Use less chronologically appropriate social behaviors

3. Function and have reactions below the level one would expect on the basis of chronological age

4. Be other-directed, thereby lacking confidence in her own ability to solve problems and relying on others to solve problems for her

5. Have an external locus of control, seeing fate or forces beyond her control as responsible for what happens and thereby being likely to interpret death as a result of a capricious fate

6. Experience difficulty with interpersonal relationships stemming from poor self-concept and limited social skills

7. Have a number of learning differences related to poor short-term memory

8. Have difficulty with abstract thinking and poor selective attention, tend to organize information poorly, and have difficulty generalizing information learned in one situation to a different situation

Often, strenuous efforts are exercised to shield the individual from life's losses and disappointments. In the effort to protect the person from the reality of death and the pain of mourning, parents and others tend to exclude her from wakes and funerals, thus preventing her from observing role models coping effectively with death. Ironically, this misguided protection excludes the person from access to experiences and information known to promote healthy mourning. At the other extreme, parents and caregivers mistakenly may assume that intellectual impairment means the individual will be unaffected by the loss. Regardless of the reason, when death education has been nonexistent, the person likely will be bewildered at the disappearance of the loved one.

Individuals with mental retardation also often experience inherent difficulties in comprehending the abstract concepts involved in death and in putting into words the myriad emotions mourning engenders. Indeed, their reactions to loss appear similar to those of young children, who experience pathological responses that contribute to further maladjustment (Bowlby, 1960, 1961a, 1963, 1980). Such problems combine with a lack of death education or other therapeutic experiences and the fact that other mental disorders are at least three to four times more prevalent among this group than among the general population (American Psychiatric Association, 1987). Clearly, numerous psychological, behavioral, social, and biological factors create significant potential for complicated mourning

in persons with mental retardation. These are exacerbated by the disenfranchisement of this population in their mourning.

Specific interventions for persons with mental retardation are described
by Hollins (1989), who delineates guided mourning group work, and Lavin
(1989), who has developed a four-stage approach for helping these individuals cope with death.

Eating disorders

Uncomplicated mourning often involves temporary disorders of appetite. Although one will see weight loss far more frequently than weight
gain, both do occur. To the extent that the mourner experiencing complications has severe appetite changes in conjunction with other diagnostic
indicators, the caregiver may possibly diagnose a substance dependence or
abuse disorder, mood disorder, somatoform disorder, factitious disorder,
adjustment disorder, psychological factor affecting physical condition, or
a V code condition.

Outside of the older psychoanalytic literature regarding the symbolic
meanings of eating in general, little has been written specifically on the
relationship between eating disorders and complicated mourning. However, Raphael (1983) mentions eating disorders as a specific pathological
outcome of bereavement, and the association is frequently demonstrated
clinically.

Citing mourning not from death but from the need to relinquish
parents as the primary source of emotional support in adolescence, Steele
(1974) has argued persuasively that overeating and obesity in adolescent
girls is a pathological attempt to cope with emotional loss. Steele's premise—
that overeating is a pathological form of coping with depression related to
mourning over the symbolic loss of parental objects—is bolstered by her
survey of the literature. This review includes literature asserting that obesity
generally accompanies depression or functions as a defense against it, that
object loss results in subsequent depression experienced by the individual as a vast emptiness and perceived by the ego as hunger, and that a relationship exists between eating and feelings of being cared for and loved.
Steele notes that the individual uses food to fill the psychological emptiness created by object loss. Another interpretation regarding overeating
stems from the observation that it may serve as a defense against a psychotic depression or other equally severe psychiatric disturbance.

Such interpretations are borne out in clinical writings such as those
offered by Robert Linder (1955) in his classic book of case studies, *The Fifty-
Minute Hour.* In the case Linder describes, the dynamics of bulimia for his
patient Laura are clearly and dramatically related to the loss of her father.
Such material coincides with that proffered by psychoanalysts who discuss introjection as a way of coping with object loss and mourning (e.g.,
Abraham, 1924/1949b; Fenichel, 1945).

These notions also offer a number of interesting hypotheses about the psychological dynamics behind substance dependence and abuse, over and above the oral gratification that has been postulated. Thus, this information could be relevant to the abuse of alcohol, nicotine, caffeine, and other drugs ingested orally.

Organic Mental Syndromes and Disorders

The present review of the bereavement literature did not uncover any empirical or clinical observations directly linking organic mental syndromes or disorders to complicated mourning. However, to the extent that it is associated with psychoactive substance dependence or abuse, complicated mourning can be related to the organic mental syndromes and disorders associated with those disorders.

Specifically, in the case of dementias arising in the senium and presenium, especially Alzheimer's disease, more may be extrapolated about mourning. Caregivers may be inclined to equate cognition with feelings and to believe that these processes decline simultaneously. In Alzheimer's disease, however, although the brain's functions are deteriorating, the emotions of the individual—including grief—remain intact. Harkulich and Calamita (1989) provide case examples to demonstrate the presence of grief in clients with Alzheimer's and to illustrate that there is emotional impact on even the most regressed clients. As they note, the client "is dealing with the life-long process of coping with loss and grief, and the incidence of dementia is just coincidental with this process. The challenge to the professional is to retrieve grief information and intervene in a therapeutic manner" (p. 5).

Although it is currently unclear to what extent complicated mourning could develop in these individuals, it is quite possible that the loss would lead to increased dementia. Harkulich and Calamita challenge caregivers in geriatric settings to intervene instead of ignoring behaviors that may indicate mourning in such individuals. In addition to this helpful perspective, the authors propose a 14-point treatment intervention plan.

In essence, caregivers must be mindful that, although cognitive dysfunction may complicate grief and mourning, it does not preclude the experience of pain. It will remain to be seen whether similar relationships exist between complicated mourning and the other syndromes and disorders in this category.

Psychoactive Substance Use Disorders

There are two classes of disorders in this category: psychoactive substance dependence and the residual category of psychoactive substance abuse. The former class is characterized by cognitive, behavioral, and physiologic symptoms indicating that the person has impaired control of substance use and continues use despite adverse consequences. The latter class is a category for maladaptive patterns of psychoactive substance use that do not meet the criteria for dependence.

When one considers the amount of pain inherent in the loss of a loved one, it is not surprising to discover the high incidence of prescribed medication—and self-medication—that occurs in both uncomplicated and complicated mourning. Licit and illicit substance use abounds. It is therefore prudent to inform caregivers, if they have not already learned through experience, that psychoactive substance dependence or abuse, either as a symptom or a syndrome, will affect a significant percentage of individuals seen for complicated mourning. It is imperative that caregivers not overlook this issue in favor of more dramatic aspects of the clinical picture (e.g., overwhelming pain, dysfunction, intense longing, denial of loss). Plainly, any use of psychoactive substances must be evaluated early in the treatment process.

Mourning as a predisposing factor in psychoactive substance use

Psychoactive substance dependence or abuse is a nonspecific symptom seen in many disorders. However, mourning does have certain characteristics that can serve as predisposing factors for substance use. The first is pain. It is well-known that, despite the initial attraction of euphoria, the avoidance of pain is the primary reason for chemical addiction.

The second predisposing factor is a social set conducive to tolerance. For example, alcohol is widely used as a form of self-medication. It is a socially acceptable drug, easily and legally procurable, and one that initially seems effective as a pain reducer or, in some cases, as a vehicle for acting out. For whatever purpose it is used, alcohol use is often tolerated by the mourner's family and friends. Typically, people are reluctant to confront the mourner when drinking turns into abuse because they feel that to do so would be unsympathetic, they want to avoid inflicting more pain or depriving the person of something perceived to alleviate pain, or they do not want to be accused of being insensitive or harsh for placing an additional burden on someone who already is so burdened or for taking something away from someone who has lost so much. Similar issues arise with regard to dependence on or abuse of other substances. In short, the condition of bereavement makes it difficult for family, friends, and caregivers to take the necessary "hard line" with abusers; it also makes it imperative that they do so.

A third factor predisposing to substance use is the entitlement often felt by the mourner and the emptiness that spawns it. The mourner has lost much and believes that some comfort is due him. When this feeling is combined with a heightened need for oral gratification to fill the void left by the deceased—as is also evident in eating disorders—the setting is ripe for substance dependence or abuse.

A fourth factor encouraging substance use stems from the reality that the symptoms of acute mourning cry out for relief. For many, that relief is sought through prescription and over-the-counter drugs. Many professional caregivers—as well as family, friends, and the bereaved themselves —look to medication as a palliative form of emotional control in the acute crisis after major loss. (This fact explains consistent findings on the increased prevalence of substance use in acute grief.) Nevertheless, professional controversy persists over the use of prescribed medication with the acutely bereaved.

The reader will note that, in the prevalence and rate statistics reported next, increases are for both prescribed and nonprescribed substances. Certainly, it is far from the case that all substance use in mourning is self-initiated: Not surprisingly, medication tends to be prescribed more liberally for female than for male mourners, particularly when acute grief responses are misperceived as being hysterical. In one of the more heartfelt passages of her book, Raphael (1983) describes how the prescription of tranquilizers and antidepressants often becomes part of a pattern of chronic use that appears to do little to help the bereaved's condition and adjustment. As she notes:

> Even when such drugs are not prescribed, a surprising
> number of bereaved people self-medicate either with the pills
> of other people or substances available without prescription.
> Self-medication . . . may be taken to induce sleep and block
> out pain and loneliness, or, may be a form of acting out in a
> self-destructive manner in response to guilt and conflicts
> aroused by the loss. (p. 214)

Although the bereaved may not have had a choice about the loss of the loved one, he does have a choice about what to put into his body as a response to that loss. For some, this type of control is better than nothing, especially when it comes with temporary relief of pain. However, these comments should not be construed to mean that medication is always harmful or contraindicated in bereavement. The reader is referred to the discussions of depression and anxiety in this chapter and to chapter 8 for information on the rationale for and clinical pragmatics involved in medicating mourners.

Finally, widespread self-medication for alleviation of psychic pain and bodily discomfort in the bereaved raises the question of whether vulnerability to substance use implies the existence of altered sensory and pain thresholds in mourning (Osterweis et al., 1984). Further research is necessary along these lines.

Prevalence of psychoactive substance use and rate increase in mourning

Elsewhere in this book a concerted effort has been made to discuss uncomplicated mourning only where it directly informs complicated mourning. Nonetheless, it is worthwhile here to note the prevalence of psychoactive substance use in uncomplicated mourning because such use invites serious problems in the mourner and predisposes toward recognized psychiatric disorders. It is not necessary to have complicated mourning to develop pathology in this area; however, substance dependence or abuse can complicate mourning, and whatever problems might be associated with substance dependence or abuse in uncomplicated mourning are significantly magnified in complicated mourning.

Some increase in psychotropic medicines, alcohol intake, and smoking is so commonplace in mourning as to be included in a listing of uncomplicated grief symptoms (Stroebe & Stroebe, 1987). This inclusion coincides with the observations of two parties who have conducted extensive reviews of the literature on mourning responses. Clayton (1982) concludes that "the startling outcome is that all studies show an increase in cigarette smoking, alcohol consumption and either tranquilliser or hypnotic use or both" (p. 407). The conclusions of the Institute of Medicine Study are similar:

> All studies document increases in alcohol consumption and smoking and greater use of tranquilizers or hypnotic medication (or both) among the bereaved. For the most part, these increases occur in people who already are using these substances; however, some of the increase is attributable to new users. (Osterweis et al., 1984, p. 40)

One of the most dramatic areas of difference between bereaved and nonbereaved individuals in Parkes and Weiss's (1983) study of widows and widowers was increased drug use in the bereaved sample. A total of 28 percent reported an increase in smoking, 28 percent reported an increase in alcohol consumption (32 percent of widowers and 27 percent of widows), and 26 percent had either begun taking tranquilizers or increased their use of them. In contrast, there was virtually no increased drug use in the married sample, with the exception of an unexplained increase in smoking among a fifth of the married men. Parkes and Brown (1972) found similar percentages: Twenty-eight percent of the bereaved reported an increase in smoking, as compared with 9 percent of the controls; 28 percent of the bereaved women reported increased consumption of alcohol, versus 3 percent of the controls. A first use of tranquilizers was reported by 26 percent of the widows and 4 percent of the controls. Parkes (1987) also cites dramatic findings from his investigation conducted with colleagues at the Harvard Medical School of physical and mental ill health in young, unselected widows and widowers. The study determined that 41 percent of the young widows and 37 percent of the young widowers were smoking more a year after bereavement and that 38 and 31 percent, respectively, were drinking more alcohol. Other findings of significant increases in substance use or in first use have been reported by, among others, Clayton and Darvish (1979); Glick et al. (1974), Maddison and Viola (1968); Parkes (1964, 1972); Thompson, Breckenridge, Gallagher, and Peterson (1984); and Zisook, Shuchter, and Mulvihill (1990).

Notwithstanding an expected increase in use and first use of substances in uncomplicated mourning, excessive consumption of alcohol and drugs should be taken as one sign that not all is going as it should (Parkes, 1987)—in other words, that mourning is complicated. Researchers have consistently noted that past and current abuse of alcohol and other substances is a risk factor for or category of poor outcome in mourning (Osterweis et al., 1984; Raphael, 1983). Such abuse has been identified as a specific factor contributing to unresolved grief (Zisook & DeVaul, 1983; Zisook & Lyons, 1988–1989; Zisook & Shuchter, 1985). It also has been associated with so-called incomplete mourning (Coleman, 1975, 1980, 1991; Coleman & Stanton, 1978) and with complicated mourning over prior losses, such as the death of a parent in childhood (Raphael, 1983) and adulthood (Birtchnell, 1975), as well as with the death of an alcoholic husband (Blankfield, 1989).

Finally, there appears to be a gender difference in the use of drugs and alcohol for coping with the problems of bereavement. After reviewing relevant studies, Stroebe and Stroebe (1983) suggest that more men than women use alcohol to cope with mourning. Rather than being diagnosed as depressed, men are more likely to end up with a diagnosis of alcoholism. Hence, as a reaction to events such as bereavement, depression may be the female equivalent of alcoholism in males (Seligman, 1975).

Substance dependence and abuse and complications of mourning

It is assumed that the reader already possesses the appropriate information about how substance dependence and abuse generally affect the psychological, behavioral, social, and physical functioning of the individual. It also is assumed that the reader is aware of the actual biological effects of drugs with abuse potential and knows how mourners are seduced into being promised relief by an agent that actually exacerbates distress. Such information will not be repeated here. What will be briefly sketched is a line of thought about the impact of substance dependence and abuse on the creation and maintenance of complicated mourning. This conceptualization appears to be generalizable to a variety of classes of substances.

In an interesting paper, Skolnick (1979) has put forth the notion that drug addiction is a symptom of pathological mourning in which the mourner resorts to chemically achieved relief to avoid the pain of mourning previous narcissistic losses. The addiction impairs mourning, which must be resolved if the addict is to relinquish the drug dependence. Skolnick writes as follows about her successful treatment process:

Over and beyond anything else that appears to cause the addiction, is the relief from anxiety—the repair of the loss, separation, rejection, anger, shame, guilt, and so forth. *Drugs become the instant defense against the pain and resolution of the mourning process.* There is an establishment of a chronic psychological hunger and craving for restitution of the narcissistic losses of the emotional needs and supports of a younger age. The ability to make oneself feel good and well through chemicals instills a false sense of mastery and control. . . . The quieting of the feelings of loss which engender rage, shame, guilt, and so on become the compulsive striving for the addict. . . . The addict has found in drugs a chemical solution to the psychic unbalance caused by the premature fixation of the mourning process. The feelings of loss create a psychic disequilibrium for which the addict seeks relief. . . . The normal completion of the mourning process is interrupted due to the chemical satisfaction and the mourning stages 3 and 4 are never attempted. . . . In withdrawal from the drug the addict must face the loss of chemical relief as well as the narcissistic loss and begin to make room for a real sense of self by decathecting from and mourning these losses. (pp. 285–287)

It can be seen how addiction, when viewed in these terms, not only indicates but actually perpetuates complicated mourning. Because in mourning the emotions are so deep, so intense, and so critical, the effects of drugs are elevated, as is the danger of addiction.

Heroin addiction also serves functional purposes in complicated mourning. In a series of papers, Coleman (Coleman, 1975, 1980, 1991; Coleman & Stanton, 1978) proposes that heroin addiction often is purposeful and productive as a social agent and facilitator of family integration following incompletely mourned traumatic or untimely deaths. She points to addiction as analogous to a process of slow death that facilitates the family's death-related participatory behavior and perpetuates the premature and unresolved death of a former family member.

Blankfield (1982–1983) describes variants of mourning that she found in a sample of alcoholics from an inpatient treatment center. Among her conclusions are the following.

1. Loss has various influences on the pattern of alcohol consumption: It commences intake, leaves it unaltered, or increases or decreases it.

2. The expression of grief clouded by alcohol withdrawal symptoms can be coped with in three ways: with a normal response, a pseudo-grief reaction, or a pathological response.

3. The form of presentation of pathological grief responses (evidenced by half the bereaved subjects) is frequently related to the premorbid personality, with more stable and conscientious personalities displaying guilt or depression and more egocentric and sociopathic personalities demonstrating acute situational behaviors, including homicidal and suicidal gestures.

4. Treatment is effective in the resolution of grief in the majority of patients, although it is not inevitably associated with containment of alcohol intake. Treatment must balance withdrawal from the substance of abuse, choice of medication, psychotherapy, and the individual personality and problem.

5. Documentation exists in the literature of increased suicide risk and the aggravating influence of loss in the alcoholic.

Blankfield's final point about suicide stems from studies such as those conducted by Chenoweth, Tonge, and Armstrong (1980); Murphy, Armstrong, Hermele, Fischer, and Clendenin (1979); and Murphy and Robins (1967). These studies reveal that alcoholics are at high risk for suicide after the loss of an affectional relationship. This risk is realized not only by consciously intentioned death. Additional information suggests that death for the substance abuser experiencing complicated mourning may be subintentioned (Shneidman, 1973), as is illustrated effectively by the following evaluation of the interaction between symptoms of complicated mourning (e.g., drug abuse and high-risk behaviors) and some of the pathological outcomes of that mourning:

> Potentially health-compromising behaviors, such as smoking and drinking, may become excessive following bereavement, especially in people who tended to use these substances before experiencing loss. Such behaviors may be considered normal in the bereaved because they occur with considerable frequency. Nevertheless, they are also psychologically and physically self-destructive, potentially leading to such illnesses as lung cancer and cirrhosis of the liver. Substance abuse and other dangerous activities, such as reckless driving, may not appear to be obviously suicidal, but they can serve the same purpose as more overt efforts. Risk-taking behavior may not appear to be directly associated with bereavement; such behavior is not readily expressive of grief but may instead be part of a defensive operation (Parkes & Weiss, 1983). So although they are endangering their lives and, in reality, struggling with grief, survivors may appear to be coping reasonably well. (Osterweis et al., 1984, p. 50)

Final confirmatory data regarding the association of complicated mourning, illness, and substance dependence and abuse comes from the literature on morbidity and mortality following bereavement. Sound data suggest that mortality, and presumably morbidity, in the recently bereaved may be increased by behavioral changes that compromise health maintenance or chronic disease management (Jacobs & Ostfeld, 1977). Therefore, increased alcohol consumption, smoking, and other drug use can exacerbate or precipitate illness. Excess mortality, especially in bereaved men, is explained in large part by deaths from suicide, cirrhosis, and cardiac arrest—all three having clinical antecedents influenced by substance use (i.e., depression, alcoholism, cardiovascular disease). This finding parallels Gove's (1973) conclusion that the excessive number of deaths in widowed individuals could be considered the result of a slow process of self-destruction.

Schizophrenia

Schizophrenia is not often discussed relative to complicated mourning. Parkes (1965) finds it a rare sequel of bereavement. Exceptions are found in a handful of studies addressing the death of a parent or sibling in childhood—a type of loss recognized to predispose the individual to complicated mourning.

Specifically, Watt and Nicholi (1979) examined three separate studies comparing adult schizophrenic patients with other psychiatric patients and concluded that the premature death of a parent may be a contributing factor in the etiology of schizophrenia. The deaths tended to be earlier than average in the lives of these patients and were more common in those with paranoid symptoms.

Similar findings pertinent to parental and sibling loss in childhood have been reported by Dennehy (1966), Hilgard (1969), Hilgard and Newman (1963), Huttunen and Niskanen (1979), and Rosenzweig and Bray (1943), but opposing findings have been suggested by Granville-Grossman (1966) and Gregory (1966).

Delusional (Paranoid) Disorder

Only one reference in the studies reviewed associated delusional disorder with complicated mourning. Evans, Jeckel, and Slott (1982) presented a case study of a woman with erotomania, a delusional belief sustained most often by a woman that a man—usually older and of higher social status—is intensely in love with her. In their case study, the authors postulated that the patient's symptomatology resulted from a complicated and pathological mourning process associated with the loss of the patient's father. Specifically, her unconscious yearning for him led to psychotic disorganization, which resulted in an initial psychiatric hospitalization. Later, she experienced a pathological reorganization marked by erotomanic delusions, which prompted three subsequent hospitalizations. Her symptoms were construed as her way of offering restitution for her father's death.

Psychotic Disorders Not Elsewhere Classified

In this diagnostic class are four specific disorders (brief reactive psychosis, schizophreniform disorder, schizoaffective disorder, induced psychotic disorder) and one residual category of psychotic disorder not otherwise specified.

Four sources in the literature reviewed associated psychotic disorders and complicated mourning: Raphael (1983) mentions in her review of pathological outcomes of bereavement that a range of psychiatric conditions have been described, briefly noting the schizophreniform disorder, among others, but not providing further information or documentation. Lindemann (1944) observes that one of the distorted reactions to mourning is the mourner's becoming wooden and formal, with affect and conduct resembling schizophrenic pictures. According to current DSM-III-R criteria, such reactions could reflect either a schizophreniform or schizoaffective disorder, although, depending on the particular symptoms, their timing in the illness, and their persistence, the diagnosis could be schizophrenia. Brief reactive psychoses are identified by Horowitz (1986a) as being a possible reaction to traumatic events. To the extent that traumatic events are risk factors for complicated mourning, brief reactive psychoses and complicated mourning may be associated. Finally, Krupp (1972) discusses complete ego breakdown as a form of complicated mourning. His short descriptions appear to fit best within the diagnostic categories of brief reactive psychosis or psychotic disorder not otherwise specified. No references pertaining to the induced psychotic disorder were found.

Mood Disorders

Recent studies have suggested that, whereas the anxiety disorders most frequently complicate widowhood in the first year, the mood disorder of depression has the greatest isomorphy with pathological grief (Jacobs & Kim, 1990). Although one may well argue with Jacobs and Kim's criteria for pathological grief—and therefore the isomorphy finding—and generalizability of findings is limited because the sample focused only on spousal bereavement, it appears that mood disorders are the category most often diagnosed in individuals experiencing either uncomplicated or complicated mourning.

There are two types of mood disorders. The first type, bipolar disorders, includes bipolar disorder, cyclothymia, and bipolar disorder not otherwise specified. The second type, depressive disorders, includes major depression, dysthymia, and depressive disorder not otherwise specified. This latter group of mood disorders are significantly and routinely associated with mourning.

Bipolar disorders

In 1944, Lindemann delineated certain distorted grief reactions indicative of unresolved grief. Two of these appear related to mania, although in his work Lindemann did not specify this relationship per se. These two reactions are overactivity without a sense of loss and actions detrimental to one's own social and economic existence.

Anderson (1949) found varieties of manic-depressive states to be the form assumed by 15 percent of his patients with morbid grief. Lehrman (1956) noted that a manic-depressive psychosis is one form that pathological grief and mourning may take after an untimely death. Parkes (1965) views mania as a rare sequel of bereavement. Those observers who do specifically mention mania most often refer to the paper by Rickarby (1977) in which four cases of mania associated with bereavement are presented to illustrate the relationship between the onset of an episode of illness with a known genetic predisposition and stress from the social environment. In all of these cases—each of which Rickarby believes exemplifies a different aspect of pathological grief—it appeared that mania was precipitated while the individuals were undergoing a state of persistent stress during their efforts to avoid the affects associated with the loss, its realities, and the need to give up the relationship with the deceased. The cases were construed to illustrate switch from stress into mania and to support strongly the theoretical considerations of Bunney, Goodwin, and Murphy (1972). The manic aspects of mourning in these cases (e.g., triumph, omnipotence, and massive denial) were found to be consistent with Klein's (1940) dynamic formulation of aspects of mania as part of the mourning process (i.e., triumph at the victory of survival and times of elation when feeling an internal possession of the idealized loved one). However, nothing suggested that such aspects were helpful in coming to terms with the loss or that they were associated with real resolution of depression, as had been suggested by Scott (1964). Rickarby notes Klein's and Scott's agreement, however, on the need to resolve the splitting inherent in the manic defense, accept both good and bad aspects of the deceased, and again trust the real world. He concludes that mania supervenes when stress is persistent and the pathological mourning unresolved and maladaptive, and that the sequence of pathological grief, distress, and mania supports the psychosomatic model of illness.

Certainly, hypomania is not unfamiliar to the experienced caregiver as a defense against the various "R" processes of mourning. At times, hypomania is difficult to differentiate from agitated depression and anxiety, especially from the former.

Depressive disorders

More investigation has been devoted to the association between loss and depression than to any other variable. Specifically, depression has been examined as a formal psychiatric disorder; a psychological, behavioral, social, or somatic symptom; and a physiological condition. As used here, the term *depression* incorporates symptomatology found in any of the depressive disorders.

Research relating to depression. Particularly helpful resources among the many that discuss depression as a typical consequence of loss in adults include Abrahms (1981); Akiskal and McKinney (1975); Arieti and Bemporad (1978); Belitsky and Jacobs (1986); Blanchard, Blanchard, and Becker (1976); Bornstein, Clayton, Halikas, Maurice, and Robins (1973); Bowlby (1980); Brown and Harris (1978); Bruce, Kim, Leaf, and Jacobs (1990); Carey (1977); Clayton (1974, 1979, 1982); Clayton and Darvish (1979); Clayton et al. (1968); Clayton, Halikas, and Maurice (1971, 1972); Clayton et al. (1974); Freud (1917/1957c); Frost and Clayton (1977); Gallagher, Breckenridge, Thompson, and Peterson (1983); Glick et al. (1974); Irwin, Daniels, Bloom, Smith, and Weiner (1987); Jacobs, Hansen, Berkman, Kasl, and Ostfeld (1989); Jacobs and Kim (1990); Jacobs and Lieberman (1987); Krause (1986); Lieberman and Videka-Sherman (1986); Maddison and Viola (1968); Marris (1958); Murrell and Himmelfarb (1989); Muskin and Rifkin (1986); Osterweis et al. (1984); Parkes (1964, 1965, 1970, 1987); Parkes and Brown (1972); Paykel et al. (1969); Radloff (1975); Raphael (1978, 1983); Robinson and Fleming (1989); Shuchter and Zisook (1987); Shuchter et al. (1986); Stroebe and Stroebe (1987); Stroebe, Stroebe, and Domittner (1985); van Rooijen (1979); Videka-Sherman and Lieberman (1985); Zisook and DeVaul (1983, 1984); Zisook and Lyons (1988–1989); Zisook and Shuchter (1986, 1991); Zisook, Shuchter, and Lyons (1987); and Zisook et al. (1985).

Unfortunately, as in all other aspects of the field, research on widows predominates in studies of depression and mourning. For this reason, the reader may want to review studies that consider depression in bereaved parents (e.g., Martinson, Davies, & McClowry, 1991; Rando, 1983, 1986g; Sanders, 1979–1980; Shanfield, 1987; Videka-Sherman & Lieberman, 1985). Resources examining the impact of childhood loss upon adult depression and childhood depression (often secondary to loss) adversely affecting subsequent bereavement in adulthood are reviewed by Berlinsky and Biller (1982); Bloom-Feshbach and Bloom-Feshbach (1987); Bowlby (1980); E. Furman (1974); R. Furman (1973); Papadatou and Papadatos (1991); Parkes and Stevenson-Hinde (1982); Paterson (1986); Raphael (1983); H. Rosen (1986); Schowalter et al. (1983); and Wass and Corr (1984). Studies involving the impact of stressful life events, including bereavement, on depression are reviewed by Dohrenwend and Dohrenwend (1974); Finlay-Jones (1981); Irwin et al. (1987); Krause (1986); and Rahe (1979).

In a helpful paper examining the psychiatric complications of bereavement, Jacobs and Kim (1990) review their own and other studies of bereaved spouses (often middle-aged and older) for data on the rate of major depression, anxiety disorders, and pathological grief in bereavement, additionally examining the potential risk factors for developing these syndromes and the comorbidity of the disorders. Jacobs and Kim report on Jacobs et al.'s (1989) interviews with 111 study participants at either 6 or 12 months after widowhood.

Using the Structured Clinical Interview for DSM-III (Spitzer, Williams, & Gibbon, 1985), Jacobs and colleagues discovered that 29 percent of the population met the criteria for major depression, with 32 percent of the subsample depressed at 6 months and 27 percent depressed at 12 months. The symptomatic picture of the depressed subset included melancholia in 21 percent, restlessness in 90 percent, guilt in 48 percent, psychomotor retardation in 90 percent, and thinking of death or hurting oneself in 59 percent. Risk factors for developing a major depression included unemployment and being female. Jacobs and Kim note that the 1-year figure of 27 percent for depression in bereaved spouses is much higher than the 17 percent figure obtained in the often-cited study by Bornstein et al. (1973). Jacobs and Kim also observe that the symptoms of depression reported did not differ materially from depressive syndromes typically seen in outpatient clinics and that in many cases they included melancholic features. Finally, they report that, whereas most of the depressive symptoms of widowhood resolved spontaneously, 33 percent of the depressions that commenced early in bereavement persisted throughout the first year and that, in one study (Zisook, 1989), 68 percent of early onset depressions did not remit spontaneously but continued to persist for at least 7 months. Combining all the statistics to that date, Jacobs and Kim speculate that the estimated rate of complications by unremitting depression at the end of the first year of bereavement is between 17 and 27 percent.

Other investigators recently have conducted more detailed investigations, with results similar to earlier findings. Zisook and Shuchter (1991) found the prevalence of widows and widowers who met the DSM-III-R criteria for depressive episodes to range from 24 percent at 2 months after the death to 16 percent at 13 months after the death, with the prevalence in each time period substantially above the 4 percent rate for depressive episodes observed in the comparison group. Those most likely to meet the criteria for depressive episodes at 13 months postdeath were younger, had past histories of major depression, were still grieving 2 months after the loss, and met DSM-III-R criteria for depressive episodes 2 and/or 7 months after the death. It should be noted that significant differences in methodology existed in the Jacobs et al. (1989) and Zisook and Shuchter (1991) investigations. The latter investigators feel these differences account for the discrepancy in prevalence rates for depression found at the end of the first year of bereavement.

In comparing the comorbidity of what was defined as pathologic grief (limited in this study to manifestations of separation distress) with depression, generalized anxiety disorder, and panic disorder, Jacobs and Kim share unpublished data (Jacobs & Kim, 1989) finding that isomorphy is greatest among those experiencing what they defined as pathologic grief (i.e., complicated mourning) and depression. Isomorphy was 84 percent, in contrast to isomorphy for pathological grief and generalized anxiety disorder (65 percent) or panic disorder (53 percent). This important finding suggests that the caregiver dealing with complicated mourning has a significant chance of working with the depressive disorders. For this reason, it is imperative that the caregiver be aware of (a) the areas of distinction between grief and depression and how to assess for them, (b) when and how to refer for psychopharmacologic evaluation and treatment, and (c) what treatment implications exist for the three possible associations between depressive symptoms and mourning (i.e., uncomplicated mourning with related depressive symptomatology, complicated mourning syndrome with depressive features, full-blown depressive disorder with or without an accompanying complicated mourning syndrome).

Significant overlap between depression and anxiety disorders in bereavement appears to be empirically evident (Jacobs et al., 1990). Of bereaved spouses with depression, 82.5 percent also met the criteria for an anxiety disorder, most frequently a generalized anxiety disorder. Of those who met the criteria for an anxiety disorder, 55.6 percent also reported a concurrent depressive syndrome. This rate was significantly higher than the rate of depression among those without anxiety disorder. All of the subjects who had a generalized anxiety disorder concomitantly met the criteria for a major depression; 60 percent of those with panic disorder met these criteria.

It must be noted that Paula Clayton, principal investigator in perhaps the best known and most-often quoted series of studies and publications examining depressive phenomena in the bereavement of widowhood (e.g., Bornstein et al., 1973; Clayton, 1974, 1979, 1982; Clayton & Darvish, 1979; Clayton et al., 1968; Clayton et al., 1971, 1972; Clayton et al., 1974; Frost & Clayton, 1977), puts forth data markedly different from that of most researchers. Despite depressive symptoms and significant increases in tranquilizer, sedative, and alcohol intake in the bereaved populations she studied, the individuals she studied had no more physician visits, hospitalizations, physical symptoms, or feelings of general poor health over a year than did control subjects. This discrepancy within the bereavement literature is especially noteworthy because much of Clayton's other data has been confirmed in subsequent investigations.

Differentiating between depression and mourning. The main issue with regard to any association between depression and mourning concerns the extent of isomorphy. This poses one of the thorniest problems in the diagnosis of depressive disorders subsequent to the death of a loved one. In many instances, it is unclear where depressive symptoms characteristic of uncomplicated mourning end and symptoms or syndromes associated with complicated mourning and/or the development of a recognized mental disorder begin.

Despite the absence of clear boundaries between uncomplicated grief and a depressive disorder, Stroebe and Stroebe (1987) assert that depressive symptoms can and should be differentiated—grief and depression must not be mistaken as one and the same. Three reasons support this contention: First, a number of symptoms are characteristic of acute grief but not depression (e.g., yearning for or identification with the deceased). Second, grief is not a set of symptoms that commences immediately after the loss and then fades away. Rather, it involves a succession of phases, with depression becoming the most salient characteristic of the grief reaction only after initial numbness has been replaced by pining and yearning, believed by many to reflect separation anxiety (Bowlby, 1980). And third, whereas clinical depression is certainly one form of complicated mourning, other forms are not characterized by depression. Stroebe and Stroebe (1987) conclude in this regard that "although depressive symptoms represent a 'final common path' (Akiskal & McKinney, 1973) between grief and depression, it should be remembered that, despite the overlap, grief and depression form two distinctive and distinguishable syndromes" (p. 25).

For the caregiver interested in complicated mourning, the differences between uncomplicated mourning and depression are of critical practical importance. Unless the caregiver is aware of them, he or she will be unable to diagnose complicated mourning when it appears in the guise of the normal depression of bereavement. Resources to which the caregiver can turn for specific criteria for accomplishing this clinical task include Abrahms (1981); Bowlby (1980); Briscoe and Smith (1975); Clayton et al. (1974); Freud (1917/1957c); Gallagher, Dessonville, Breckenridge, Thompson, and Amaral (1982); Jacobs and Lieberman (1987); Pedder (1982); Raphael (1983); Robinson and Fleming (1988, 1989); Schneider (1980); Shuchter and Zisook (1987); J. Smith (1971, 1975); and Stroebe and Stroebe (1987).

For the most part, these authors' findings are consistent with the realities of mourning. However, some beliefs do not appear to reflect the true nature of certain bereavements or the bereavement experience in general. For example, stemming back to Freud (1917/1957c) is the belief still held by some that self-esteem is adversely affected only in depression and not in healthy mourning. Certainly, the damage to self-esteem created by depression is much greater, more global, and more associated with an unrealistic sense of worthlessness and guilt than that resulting from major loss. Nevertheless, lowered self-esteem, albeit different in quality and intensity, is not an uncommon consequence of major loss. Perhaps like ambivalence, once thought to indicate only complicated mourning (Freud, 1917/1957c), problems in self-esteem will come to be perceived as pathological only when the type, extent, impact, and associated factors warrant.

Caregivers must keep in mind that depressive illness subsequent to bereavement may be more common for those with a personal or family history of affective disorder, although the evidence to confirm or refute this notion is currently lacking (Raphael, 1983). Certainly, preexisting genetic vulnerability can exacerbate problems, and previous depression and history of mental illness are typically associated with complicated mourning.

The mourner experiencing uncomplicated acute grief and the individual experiencing depression are both sad and depressed, in despair, confused, and uninterested in and unmotivated by the rest of the world, which seems insignificant and meaningless and in which time appears to stand still. Each tends to experience increased dependency, alterations in interpersonal relationships, inhibition of activities, and impaired psychosocial and occupational functioning. Often coinciding with all of this are nonspecific anxiety, fear of losing one's mind, spiritual estrangement, a longing for an end to the pain, behavioral changes, and somatic disturbances—this last including vegetative, physiological, and neuroendocrine and immunological symptoms.

Although the mourner and the depressive may appear superficially similar, the caregiver must compare the clinical picture for each with what is known to occur in uncomplicated and complicated mourning. To accomplish this, the caregiver must (a) get beneath the manifest layer and examine responses and their dynamics, (b) observe the timing of occurrence and course of depressive symptomatology, (c) evaluate the duration of depressive symptomatology, and (d) know when and to whom to refer the individual for a medication consultation.

Jacobs and Lieberman (1987) provide some criteria for discriminating between so-called normal depressions of bereavement and major depressive disorders. They contend that clinicians should be concerned if depressive syndromes persist longer than 6 months or a year; occur later (i.e., several months after the loss); include pervasive disturbance of self-esteem, psychomotor retardation, or suicidal gestures; cause severe subjective distress or impair social or occupational functioning (even in the absence of other symptomatic criteria); or are associated with personal or family history of depression. Criteria for intervention besides those suggesting a depressive disorder include depressive symptoms occurring in the context of pathological grief and a positive dexamethasone suppression test. Absence of any of these criteria need not preclude diagnosis and/or necessity to treat.

Observing that the major problem for the clinician is differentiating between the depression of mourning and a depressive disorder, Shuchter and Zisook (1987) propose two criteria for identifying a depressive disorder. First, the depression appears to have a life of its own and symptoms persist independently of day-to-day events, exposure to triggers, and the mourner's internal psychological processes. Symptoms may worsen in response to such factors, but, importantly, they persevere in their absence. Second, vegetative signs or symptoms persist beyond 2 months after the death. Continuation suggests that the experience goes beyond acute stress reactions to the loss, which may initially be the same, and that a clinical depression has evolved. However, the authors note that vegetative signs or symptoms less typical of acute stress reactions are also suggestive of clinical depression (e.g., hypersomnia, hyperphagia, and psychomotor retardation).

Numerous other writers refer to differences in the type, intensity, and prolongation of depressive symptoms. A synthesis of the most clinically relevant differences between uncomplicated mourning and depression includes the following points.

1. As noted by Clayton and her colleagues, whose work is cited earlier, mourners tend to define themselves differently than do depressed individuals. The latter are less likely to experience their condition as normal for their status and more likely to seek help and thereby define themselves as patients.

2. One of the major ways in which grief is different from depression is in level of pathology in cognitive functioning. Grief lacks the persistent, severe, distorted, and negative perceptions of self (including self-esteem), experience, world, and future (i.e., hopelessness) that is pathognomonic of depression. The clinical implication is that caregivers should go beyond assessment of depressive symptomatology to explore the personality factor of cognitive style and the personal meaning of the loss to the mourner (Robinson & Fleming, 1989).

3. In grief, the depression almost always is of the agitated, restless type. It tends to be transient and to occur earlier rather than later in the process. In a depressive disorder, depression is most often of the retarded, anergic type. In this case, the depression tends to persist and often occurs after a delay in grief.

4. Guilt in grief is relatively more often focused upon some specific aspect of the loss. In depression, the mourner experiences more of an overall sense of culpability, in which there is a preoccupation with one's badness, omissions or commissions, and worthlessness.

5. In grief, the loss is most often recognized and acknowledged; in depression, loss is often unrecognized and denied (J. Smith, 1975).

6. Grief is not humiliating or demoralizing, whereas depression is (J. Smith, 1975).

7. Suicidal gestures are rarely, if ever, observed in uncomplicated mourning but are not atypical in depression.

8. In grief, identification functions for healing and growth. In depression, it functions as a defense (J. Smith, 1975).

9. In grief, the individual mourns healthily; in depression, because there is usually no acknowledgment of the loss and grief is defended against, the person does not mourn (J. Smith, 1975).

10. In grief, pain is an acknowledgment of the loss, whereas in depression, pain is experienced as useless or meaningless (J. Smith, 1975).

11. In grief, there is more overt expression of anger than in depression.

12. In grief, the mourner has experienced in childhood "good-enough mothering" (Winnicott, 1965) such that a sufficient internal object has been established. This internal object and its ensuing good self-esteem keep the individual from being overwhelmed by the loss and facilitate mourning after it. In contrast, the experience of depression reveals some degree of childhood failure in this regard (Pedder, 1982).

13. Grief, as opposed to depression, is characterized by more fluctuation in mood and psychological reactions, along with more variability in activity levels, communication, appetite, cognitive and social functioning, and physical response.

14. In grief, preoccupation tends to be with the deceased, who also tends to be the focus of any hallucinations or delusions. In depression, preoccupation appears to be with the self, and any hallucinations or delusions tend to be congruent with depression, pessimism, and poor self-esteem.

15. In grief, the sex ratio for depression appears equal, and a past personal history of depression or family history of depression is rare. Depression affects more males, and past personal and familial histories of depression are common (Jacobs & Lieberman, 1987).

16. The mourner can often respond healthily and constructively to warmth, encouragement, and support; the depressed individual typically cannot (Schneider, 1980).

17. The mourner elicits sympathy, concern, and a desire to embrace, whereas the depressed individual frequently elicits irritation, frustration, and a desire to avoid (Schneider, 1980).

To know whether or not depressive symptomatology is associated with complicated mourning, the caregiver also must be cognizant of the evolution of that depressive symptomatology in mourning over time. The course of depression in mourning is such that different depressive aspects are expected to appear at different times.

In their retrospective examination of the patterns of abatement of depressive symptomatology in widows, Blanchard et al. (1976) provide helpful clinical information by illustrating the prevalence of certain depressive symptoms at distinct time periods within the mourning process. In the population they studied, the most severe initial symptoms of grief were physiological (i.e., appetite loss, weight loss, decreased speed of thinking, crying, fatigue, and sleep disturbance) and psychological (i.e., poor memory, difficulty concentrating, irritability, loss of interest, anger, hearing and seeing the deceased, and death thoughts). After a year, many of these physiological and psychological symptoms had declined. Symptoms such as weight loss, poor memory, and thoughts of death were at the same levels as experienced at the time of final interview, which was anywhere from 1 to 25 years after the death, with a mean time since death of 7.1 years. However, symptoms of crying, fatigue, sleep disturbance, and loss of interest, which had also declined during the first year, continued to do so until the time of final interview. This was taken as an indication that there is a longer time required for recovery from these symptoms. Finally, symptoms of depressed mood, restlessness, dreams of the deceased, hopelessness, and worthlessness did not appear to abate significantly in the year following the death but did lessen significantly between a year after the death and the final interview. Thus, these investigators found that certain physiological and psychological symptoms appear initially, with a decline in some occurring much sooner than others and with feelings of hopelessness and worthlessness surfacing as the mourner turns his attention from initial coping needs to future plans.

The general decline of depressive symptomatology is also perceived by Clayton (1982) in her review of the conclusions of her own investigations. Her general finding is that, whereas somatic symptoms of depression decrease significantly during the first year, psychological symptoms such as death wishes, hopelessness, suicidal thoughts, worthlessness, and angry feelings do not decrease and may even increase at 1 year after the death. For explanation, she turns to Parkes' (1987) work on the physiological responses of animals to stress, which identifies sympathetic stimulation, parasympathetic inhibition, and three distinct components of overall response (i.e., level of arousal, autonomic disturbance, and emotional reaction). She interprets her findings and those of Blanchard et al. (1976) as illustrating that the level of arousal and autonomic disturbance are prominent early in bereavement, with emotional reaction surfacing later in the process.

Corroborating this notion, as well as offering explanation for the so-called 6-month phenomenon often seen after sudden death, are Bowlby's (1980) and Parkes' (1987) phasic description of mourning. This phasic description asserts that it is only when continual frustration of yearning and searching for the deceased brings the mourner to the conclusion that the loss is permanent and irrevocable, and there is consequent abandonment of the search for the deceased, that disorganization, despair, and depression set in. Prior to that, there exists, at least deep in the mourner's mind, the belief that the deceased can be recovered. It is for this reason that one often sees intensely subjective symptoms of depression become more prominent at this point. Correspondingly, the somatic reactions of depression accompanying the physiological states of alarm and searching have subsided because neither state has brought about the desired reunion with the lost loved one. The subjective symptoms of depression are a reaction to this realization.

Without question, cases exist in which depressive symptomatology in mourning initially appears consistent with an uncomplicated scenario but then persists too long. Just as it is impossible to state how long acute grief will last without taking into consideration the various factors influencing it, so too is it impossible to determine how long is too long in the persistence of depressive symptomatology without an understanding of these same factors. In most instances, experienced caregivers develop their own internal norms for appropriate durations, beyond which they consider the depression to have become diagnostic of complicated mourning symptomatology, a complicated mourning syndrome, or a diagnosable mental or physical disorder. Some guidelines have been proffered by researchers in the field; however, it must be pointed out that practically all of this research has been conducted with widowed individuals. This means that those experiencing losses not well represented in the studies, such as the death of a child or a traumatic death, may appear to be abnormal when in fact they are not.

As noted earlier, Jacobs and Lieberman (1987) write that caregivers should be concerned if depressive syndromes persist longer than 6 months. They assert that such symptoms should be the target of intervention if they are still present 1 year postdeath. Shuchter and Zisook (1987) feel that vegetative signs and symptoms remaining beyond 2 months after the death suggest a clinical depression has developed. Yet findings offered by Blanchard et al. (1976) and Clayton (1982) make it clear that even in uncomplicated mourning a number of these symptoms remain for longer periods. Obviously, room exists for additional data to clarify these apparent contradictions. For the present, the caregiver in doubt about any of these issues would be wise to consult resources as specific as possible to the case at hand or peers who have had extensive experience in making these types of discriminations.

Finally, the caregiver must discriminate between a depressive disorder and depressive symptomatology in uncomplicated mourning because such information is essential in order to discern when to refer for medication consultation. The use of medication in bereavement is a complex issue. Located here are comments specific to the use of antidepressant medication. Chapter 8 provides a more general discussion of the rationale for and clinical pragmatics of medication in bereavement.

In delineating their multidimensional approach to the treatment of spousal bereavement, psychiatrists Shuchter and Zisook (1986) comment on treating depressions that emerge after 2 to 3 months of acute grief. They recommend that such depressions be treated with antidepressants whether evolved from the depressoid state of acute grief or not. Contrary to the popular view that such psychopharmacologic treatment interferes with mourning, their experience suggests that depression distorts mourning and increases maladaptation, whereas its treatment facilitates necessary adaptive processes.

In a subsequent work, Shuchter and Zisook (1987) assert that aggressive treatment of clinical depression is important (a) to lower the risk of medical sequelae to which the depressed are more vulnerable and (b) to make the bereaved better able to cope with their grief by limiting the dysfunction and intensified regression typically consequent to depression. Differentiating between clinical depression and grief in their view are persistent depressive symptoms that appear to a have a life of their own and to be unrelated to exposure to triggers, as well as vegetative signs and symptoms persisting beyond the first 2 months after the death. These investigators observe that antidepressants may be useful in the treatment of hypertrophied grief, where their action may be primarily anxiolytic, lowering separation anxiety.

Jacobs and Lieberman (1987) have developed clinical guidelines for prescription of antidepressants. If the depression is chronic, appears to interfere with bereavement, is associated with severe impairment in functioning, or is present with psychotic or certain endogenous symptoms, they feel that the use of antidepressants is often essential to initiate the healing process. For delusional depression, Jacobs and Lieberman advise that an antipsychotic agent be employed prior to commencing an antidepressant. They also suggest that, in dysthymia, antidepressants may have limited usefulness, noting in these cases that more structured therapeutic approaches, such as those proposed by Melges and DeMaso (1980) and Volkan (1975), may be in order.

In their review of psychopharmacologic treatment of bereavement, Kellner, Rada, and Winslow (1986) suggest prescribing psychotropic drugs when distress seems excessive or incapacitating and the mourner has not responded adequately to psychotherapy. They report seeing the typical clinical picture of an adjustment disorder with depressed mood and suggest that pharmacotherapy be the same in this case as when anxiety and depression coexist. Basically, treatment involves trying antianxiety medications first because of their rapid onset of action and because relief of anxiety in persons who are anxious and depressed tends also to lead to relief of depression. If the anxiety is relieved and the mourner is still markedly depressed or feels more depressed, these investigators advise considering the use of antidepressant drugs. They point out that an endogenous depression may be presenting itself or that the reaction may have been the consequence of a rare idiosyncratic side effect of the benzodiazepine, if one had been used. The authors believe that, although only a small proportion of mourners will experience a psychotic depressive reaction, the clinician should be on the alert for it, using the same diagnostic approach as for distinguishing between exogenous and endogenous depression. They note that early signs and symptoms heralding the physiologic shift to an endogenous depression include increase in psychomotor retardation, guilt and self-accusation, greater symptom severity in the morning, onset of suicidal ruminations, failure to react to changes in the environment, and increase in vegetative symptoms, especially loss of appetite and weight. If a psychotic depressive reaction occurs or if an endogenous component is suspected, they advise energetic treatment with tricyclic antidepressants in adequate doses. They also point out that suicide risk must be carefully assessed, with hospitalization being considered as necessary.

Hackett (1974) advises against giving antidepressants in acute uncomplicated grief, noting that "they rarely relieve normal grief symptoms, and they might pave the way for an abnormal grief response" (p. 56). Hackett does not reveal what he would prescribe if the depressive symptoms met his criteria for a depressive disorder requiring medication. However, the implication is that it is more appropriate to intervene with carefully prescribed medication early in bereavement to alleviate undue symptoms of restlessness, anxiety, and insomnia than it is to intervene in depressive symptoms.

Merlis (1972) discusses his preference for antianxiety over antidepressant medication, observing that, although grief has primarily been viewed as a depressive reaction, the variety of its symptoms and behavior patterns more often suggest an anxiety reaction. This fact—coupled with the generally slow onset of antidepressant effect, their side effects, and the frequent unpredictability of their action—makes antidepressants Merlis's second treatment choice. It is unknown what Merlis would prescribe in a situation of complicated mourning.

My own clinical experience bolsters the attitudes of these and other writers that symptoms of anxiety are more frequent and disabling than are symptoms of depression—and that they must be responded to earlier. However, a mandate definitely exists for using antidepressant medication in complicated mourning. It may be that the need for antidepressant medication to control symptoms of unremitting or endogenous depression is an indication that mourning has crossed from uncomplicated to complicated.

Among the many others who subscribe to the importance of antidepressant medication for enabling healthy mourning and preventing suicide, if threatened, are Arkin (1973); Belitsky and Jacobs (1986); Clayton

(1982); Goldberg, Kutscher, and Malitz (1986); Goldberg, Malitz, and Kutscher (1973); Hollister (1973); Jacobs and Kim (1990); Jacobs, Nelson, and Zisook (1987); Kübler-Ross (1973); Lazare (1979); Maddison and Raphael (1973); Muskin and Rifkin (1986); Parkes (1985); Shuchter and Zisook (1987); Wiener (1973); and Zisook et al. (1990). Kellner et al. (1986) present a review of literature and clinical intervention suggestions in this area. None of these authors, however, suggests that medication can replace the human contact necessary in the facilitation and support of mourning. In cases where the depression is especially severe, electroconvulsive therapy has been reported to be effective (Barnacle, 1949; Davis & Franklin, 1970; Lindemann, 1944; Lynn & Racy, 1969; Meyerson, 1944; Wretmark, 1959).

Anxiety Disorders

According to the DSM-III-R, recent studies document that anxiety disorders are the type most frequently found in the general population. These disorders include panic disorder (with and without agoraphobia), agoraphobia without a history of panic disorder, social phobia, simple phobia, obsessive compulsive disorder, post-traumatic stress disorder (PTSD), generalized anxiety disorder, and a residual category of anxiety disorder not otherwise specified.

Despite its prominence both generally and in bereavement, anxiety is perhaps one of the most misunderstood aspects of mourning. Its prevalence and function are seriously unappreciated, and its differing sources typically remain unidentified. The role it plays in the exacerbation of other bereavement sequelae is rarely addressed, and it is accorded little attention in the education and training of bereavement caregivers. Far greater emphasis is placed on depression, which superficially appears to be a logical consequence of the loss of a loved one. What fails to be appreciated is that anxiety is just as logical a consequence and is, in fact, more common in bereavement than depression and actually paves the way for it. It is beyond the scope of this work to review comprehensively the topic of anxiety and bereavement. However, two excellent resources on the topic are *The Meaning of Anxiety*, by May (1977) and the monograph series on stress and anxiety edited by Spielberger and Sarason (see, for example, Spielberger & Sarason, 1991). Chapter 12 includes discussion of some of the clinical manifestations and treatments of anxiety.

In the current absence of a recognized diagnostic category for complicated mourning, anxiety disorders appear to be, along with depression and adjustment disorders, one of the most common diagnoses given to individuals experiencing difficulties. This may be the case because two cardinal features of the anxiety disorders, symptoms of anxiety and avoidance behavior, are major symptoms of complicated mourning.

Perspectives on anxiety

At least six perspectives on anxiety can be identified. These perspectives encompass the viewpoints of psychology, philosophy, biology, history, and culture toward the very personal, existential, psychosocial, and pragmatic experience of mourning the loss of a loved one. Briefly, anxiety in mourning may be construed as any of the following.

1. A normal reaction to separation from a loved one (e.g., Bowlby, 1973)

2. A normal response to an external or internal threat (e.g., Freud, 1926/1959b, 1933/1964)

3. An inevitable aspect of the human condition of Being affirming itself against Nonbeing (e.g., May, 1977)

4. A consequence of confronting freedom and responsibility (e.g., Kierkegaard, 1844/1944)

5. A result of the psychological isolation of modern man, which has accompanied the individual freedom that emerged at the Renaissance (e.g., Fromm, 1941)

6. A biological response (e.g., Cannon, 1927; Goldstein, 1939; Parkes, 1987).

The particular generic issues around which anxiety concretizes itself in mourning have been identified as follows in Rando (1988).

1. Facing the unknown and unfamiliar (i.e., the new world without the loved one and one's own difficulty dealing with this new world)

2. Contending with insecurity inherent in psychosocial transitions

3. Managing labile emotions that sustain a terrifying degree of intensity and uncontrollability while simultaneously withstanding feelings of unreality, confusion, and incomprehensibility

4. Facing the panic of each new day when the reality of the loss reasserts itself and poses questions about the mourner's ability to respond to emotional and physical survival needs

5. Attempting to meet the extraordinarily painful requirements of the six "R" processes of mourning, which the mourner often initially resists

6. Coping with the feelings of helplessness, sense of victimization, and shattered assumptive world that result from the loss

7. Responding to the unsettling experiences of acute grief and one's perceptions of oneself and one's actions in it, especially if one perceives these as being significantly different than before

8. Being concerned about losing one's mind, being unable to adapt, and violating the expectations one has had for grief and mourning

9. Recognizing that one's usual coping patterns and problem-solving strategies cannot eliminate the problem

10. Encountering the altered sense of self arising from the loss of the loved one and the changes necessary to adapt to it

11. Confronting unacceptable or uncomfortable affects, thoughts, behaviors, impulses, wishes, needs, or images associated with the deceased, the self, the mutual relationship, or other foci of mourning

12. Struggling with the absence of role models, social guidelines, and realistic information about how to act, think, and feel as a mourner

Separation anxiety and bereavement

Anxiety assumes a prominent position in the works of two individuals most often cited in the bereavement field: John Bowlby and Colin Murray Parkes. The ethological grounding of their theories gives added significance to the critical functions and survival value of separation anxiety, upon which much of the rest of the mourning experience depends. The reader is urged to review chapter 3, as well as Bowlby (1973, 1980) and Parkes (1987) for rich and clear-cut clinical data about the role of anxiety in separation and loss.

Briefly, Bowlby (1980) advances Freud's (1926/1959b) view about anxiety: When a loved one is believed to be temporarily absent, the response is one of anxiety. When the loved one appears to be permanently absent, the response is one of pain and mourning. Therefore, before a loss is truly recognized as final, the mourner is anxious and initiates a series of attempts to find and recover the lost person (e.g., crying, searching, pining). After repeatedly frustrated attempts to reunite with the deceased have convinced the mourner that the person is not recoverable, hope is abandoned. Bowlby paraphrases Shand (1920) when he notes how fear presupposes hope; it is only when one is striving and hoping for better things that one is anxious about failing to obtain them. With no hope, there is nothing to fear. Because there is nothing to hope for, anxiety dissipates and the depression and despair of mourning ensue. Other sources of anxiety exist in the mourning experience (e.g., the threat of the new world or the confrontation with freedom and responsibility), but these are secondary to the mourning experience and are not the same as separation anxiety, which must be relinquished before mourning can progress.

The continuation of searching attempts revealed in the restlessness and agitation typical of complicated mourning indicates that the mourner has not truly acknowledged and internalized the reality of the loss. It only is when acknowledgment leads to the depression, despair, and disorganization of mourning that old patterns break down—a prerequisite for the revision and development of new patterns. In this regard, then, anxiety has a pivotal role in catalyzing searching for the deceased. The failure of this search brings about depression, despair, and disorganization, which ultimately propel the mourner into the relinquishment and change necessary to accommodate the loss in a healthy fashion.

There is perhaps little more interesting and challenging data for those relatively overfocused on the role of depression in loss than that provided by Shuchter and colleagues (1986). These investigators evaluated 19 widowed individuals and, along with diagnostic interviews and psychometric evaluations, administered dexamethasone suppression tests (DSTs) to assess the degree of biological depression present during acute grief. A total of 58 percent met the Research Diagnostic Criteria for depression; however, only 16 percent were nonsuppressors on the DST. This was the first test to demonstrate such findings. Kosten, Jacobs, and Mason (1984) had failed to find any nonsuppression among 13 widows and widowers, although they did note a modest correlation between Hamilton depression scores and post-DST cortisol levels. However, the striking news from Shuchter and colleagues' investigation concerned not the determination of nonsuppression, but rather the finding that nonsuppression was related more to levels of anxiety than to depression. The authors write:

> From our results, it is tempting to speculate that the pathophysiology of at least some grief-related "depressions" may be more related to separation anxiety than it is to primary affective disorder. . . . It may be that separation anxiety is a driving force which leads to both anxiety and depressive symptoms and, in some cases, a full-blown depressive disorder following bereavement; further, the abnormal DST results in a small percentage of such bereaved individuals may identify a subgroup who are "driven too hard or too far" and who show early biological evidence of disarray, possibly a forerunner or marker of further difficulties (i.e., unresolved grief). (Shuchter et al., 1986, pp. 880–881)

Thus, physiological data confirm the importance of anxiety in acute grief and support clinical data long supplied by Bowlby and Parkes. In all of these cases, it appears that anxiety in reaction to the separation initiates the specific processes that eventually culminate in the depressive symptomatology of bereavement.

Parkes (1987) elucidates both the problem and the reality of mis-interpreting the role of anxiety in bereavement:

> When asked how to classify a bereavement reaction, most psychiatrists say "reactive depression," and certainly depression is a prominent feature. Yet more prominent is a special kind of anxiety, separation anxiety. . . . In fact, I think it fair to say that the pining or yearning that constitutes separation anxiety is the characteristic feature of the pang of grief. If grief is to be forced into the Procrustean bed of traditional psychiatric diagnosis, therefore, it should probably become a subgroup of the anxiety states. But separation anxiety is not always the symptom that causes a bereaved person to seek help. (pp. 26–27)

The case made for the contribution of anxiety to complicated mourning is unequivocal:

> These two features, intense separation anxiety and strong but only partially successful attempts to avoid grieving, were evident in all the forms of atypical grief I have come across. The degree of disbelief and avoidance varied considerably, but whatever its degree there was always an impression that the underlying separation anxiety was severe. (Parkes, 1987, p. 129)

Parkes also observes that, in terms of increased use of the health care system, the bereaved seek treatment more frequently for anxiety than for organic physical disease.

Prevalence of anxiety disorders in bereavement

The anxiety of mourning—both separation anxiety and all other types—can eventuate in a full-blown anxiety disorder. These are more prevalent than most caregivers—with their overfocus on depression—realize. Jacobs et al. (1990) report the first systematic study of anxiety disorders during bereavement. (PTSD and the residual category were not included among the types covered in the DSM-III instrument used.) They interviewed 102 bereaved spouses either at 6 or 12 months after bereavement to evaluate the risk of anxiety disorders and compared their results to the epidemiologically established prevalence rates for the same metropolitan area. Among other findings, they determined that more than 40 percent of the bereaved reported an episode of anxiety disorder at some time during the first year. This percentage was significantly higher than the normal prevalence rate for the community from which the sample was drawn. A total of 10 percent met the criteria for panic disorder, and 30 percent met the criteria for generalized anxiety disorder, the two types of anxiety disorders that occurred significantly more often. In the first 6 months, 6.3 percent reported panic disorder, and 22.9 percent reported generalized anxiety disorder. In the second 6 months, prevalence almost doubled: Thirteen percent reported panic disorder, and 38.9 percent reported generalized anxiety disorder.

Jacobs and colleagues demonstrated empirically what had been well known clinically: A considerable overlap of and interrelationship between the anxiety disorders and depressive syndromes in bereavement exists. Of those who had an anxiety disorder, 55.6 percent reported a concomitant major depression. This figure is significantly higher than the rate of depression among those without anxiety. All of those with a generalized anxiety disorder met the criteria for a major depression; 60 percent of those with panic disorder met those criteria. The 55.6 percent figure contrasts with a figure of 82.5 percent for those with a major depression who also reported an anxiety disorder. In these individuals, most often there was a generalized anxiety disorder and less frequently another anxiety disorder.

For panic disorder, only a past personal history of panic disorder was a statistically significant risk factor. There was a trend for family history of anxiety disorder to be predictive. Analysis also determined that younger spouses, those with a family history of anxiety disorder, and those with a past personal history of depression or anxiety disorder were at statistically significant greater risk for experiencing generalized anxiety disorder. There was a trend for widows to be at higher risk. The risk factors of past personal and family history distinguish the anxiety disorders from depression; in some depression studies, they have been found not to influence risk during bereavement (e.g., Jacobs et al., 1989).

Jacobs and colleagues (1990) also determined empirically that anxiety disorders were significantly associated with more severe or unresolved grief, as well as with more depression. In a related investigation (Jacobs & Kim, 1989), anxiety disorders were found to have less isomorphy than did depression with what the authors defined as pathologic grief. They determined that isomorphy with pathologic grief was 84 percent for depression, as contrasted with 65 percent for generalized anxiety disorder and 53 percent for panic disorder.

Jacobs and Kim (1990), in reviewing the literature, conclude that in the first year of bereavement the estimated rate for complications from generalized anxiety disorder is 39 percent and that for panic disorder it is 14 percent. This contrasts with estimated rates of 4 to 34 percent for what they construe as pathologic grief and 17 to 27 percent for unremitting depression. These figures document the relatively greater frequency of anxiety over depression, despite the latter's greater isomorphy with what the authors perceived as pathologic grief and the popular notion of its greater prevalence in bereavement.

Relationship of anxiety to complicated mourning

Anxiety is known to be associated with complicated mourning both as a personality trait and as a determinant in the predispositions to make anxious and ambivalent attachments, engage in compulsive caregiving, or assert independence of affectional ties, all of which predispose to complicated mourning (Bowlby, 1980). As a generic ingredient in the fear and reluctance to confront the implications of the loss or pain of mourning, ambivalence or dependence in the premorbid relationship, or change in the relationship with the deceased, anxiety contributes to all of the symptoms and syndromes of complicated mourning. In addition, it interferes with the successful completion of the six "R" processes of mourning.

Although anxiety contributes in part to all types of complications in mourning, it plays the most prominent role in three specific complicated mourning syndromes. Specifically, anxiety is perceived as a chief cause of chronic mourning via its promotion of the disorder of attachment, hypothesized by Parkes and Weiss (1983) as fostering an emotional dependency that leaves the mourner ill-equipped to function without the deceased and contributes to the mourner's refusal to move forward. In distorted mourning of the extremely angry type (Raphael, 1983), anxiety is a chief and fueling feature of the response. Often such anxiety is manifested after the loss of an extremely dependent relationship through the mourner's perception of threatened survival and inordinate resurrection of the insecurity of earlier losses. Finally, in the unanticipated mourning syndrome (Parkes & Weiss, 1983), anxiety is not the chief cause, but rather the chief result. The lack of preparation for the loss stuns the mourner and illustrates powerlessness to protect oneself and one's loved ones. Thus, profound insecurity is a major consequence, underscoring impaired functioning following the loss.

Throughout the following analysis of the various anxiety disorders and their association with complicated mourning, the reader must remember that deaths that are sudden, random, traumatic, and/or violent and losses of highly dependent premorbid relationships function to increase anxiety, threat, vulnerability, helplessness, and violation of the mourner's assumptive world. Therefore, complicated mourning associated with the risk factors of suddenness, trauma, and dependency tends to be associated relatively more often with the anxiety disorders than with other types of disorders.

Types of anxiety disorders

The anxiety disorders are not discussed much in the thanatological literature as an outcome of loss because most emphasis is given to depression. This occurs despite the fact that anxiety symptoms routinely have been observed to be present in both uncomplicated and complicated mourning. Anxiety states in general, and phobias specifically, are mentioned in passing by Raphael (1983) in a listing of psychiatric conditions described as being outcomes following bereavement. Similarly, Raphael mentions panic, anxiety states, and agoraphobia as being some of the neurotic conditions identified by Jennings and France (1979) for which bereavement therapy has been used. Both Anderson (1949) and Lehrman (1956) mention anxiety states as a form in which complicated mourning presents itself, with Anderson finding that, in his patients with morbid grief, 59 percent had clinical patterns assuming anxiety states and 7 percent had obsessional tension states.

Despite this relative lack of recognition in the literature, all eight specific forms of anxiety disorder appear to have some association with complicated mourning. Simple phobia and social phobia are the most circumscribed. Some phobic aspects of uncomplicated mourning can either mimic a simple phobia (e.g., fear and avoidance of a death-related person, place, thing, or activity, such as phobic avoidance of the scene of the loved one's fatal car accident) or resemble a social phobia (e.g., fear of social embarrassment in the absence of the loved one's security and guidance). When these phobias persist for too long, assume an undue focus, or interfere too much with some aspect of the individual's functioning, then their diagnosis as an anxiety disorder—and therefore the diagnosis of complicated mourning—must be considered. However, the caregiver must bear in mind that many mourners will continue to avoid certain stimuli (e.g., the place of death) because of the association with the death. According to the DSM-III-R, sensitivity to certain stimuli or social situations after a death would not warrant diagnosis as a phobic disorder unless the avoidant behavior interferes with the person's functioning, normal routine, usual social activities, or relationships, or the individual experiences marked distress about having the fear. Jacobs et al. (1990) found that, as compared to community prevalence rates, the risk for social phobia was elevated in the second 6 months after bereavement; however, the level of impairment was minimal.

In cases where the phobia pertains to some stimulus related to a traumatic death, then the diagnosis of simple phobia is excluded under the DSM-III-R criteria. This symptomatology is better reflected by the category of PTSD or the residual category for anxiety disorders not otherwise specified.

In general, it must be remembered that phobic avoidance in recognizing the implications of the loss and undertaking the behaviors and processes necessary to accommodate it is a significant part of complicated mourning. The treatment of complicated mourning symptoms and syndromes inevitably involves working through some phobic aspects in a mourner's reactions.

According to Jacobs et al. (1990), panic disorders are among the two most frequently occurring anxiety disorders in bereavement. Panic disorder, with and without agoraphobia, has as a well-known predisposing factor the sudden loss of social supports or disruption of important interpersonal relationships. Indeed, episodes of panic disorder occur after losses and separations in about 50 percent of cases (Jacobs et al., 1990). Another predisposing factor is the existence of separation anxiety disorder in childhood. Both of these factors are consistent with the death of a loved one. As such, it is not surprising to see the development of a panic disorder as a consequence of bereavement and for it to be a common form of complicated mourning. Jacobs and Kim (1989) found that isomorphy for panic disorder and what they term pathologic grief to be 53 percent. The suddenness associated with unexpected deaths and the helplessness associated with both traumatic deaths and the disorder of attachment related to chronic mourning (Parkes & Weiss, 1983) raise the potential for panic disorder. Because of these dynamics, one would expect panic disorders to be more frequently associated with both the unanticipated mourning and chronic mourning syndromes than with other complicated mourning syndromes. Faravelli and Pallanti (1989) have recently documented that, when the role of all types of life events are evaluated, loss events have the strongest relationship to the development of panic disorder.

Jacobs et al. (1990) observed agoraphobia in 50 percent of the bereaved with panic disorder. When analyzed as an anxiety disorder regardless of the existence of panic, agoraphobia was found to be significantly elevated in the first 6 months of spousal bereavement. The anxiety disorder of agoraphobia without a history of panic disorder has been mentioned only in passing as a possible outcome of loss (e.g., Raphael, 1983). However, clinically it is not at all rare in the treatment of complicated mourning. Some agoraphobic symptoms are initially expected even in uncomplicated mourning, as the individual attempts to readjust without the security of the relationship with the deceased or the familiarity of the old world. In healthy mourning, such avoidance passes with time. To the extent that a mourner becomes dependent and fearful and remains this way, requiring the presence of others to function (e.g., to travel or to remain home alone), complicated mourning is suspect.

It stands to reason that agoraphobia would not be uncommon after the loss of a relationship upon which the mourner was extremely dependent. The symptoms of agoraphobia are also often consistent with behaviors found in the chronic mourner, who is frightened to proceed into the new world without the deceased. In addition, the disorder can be witnessed as a consequence of particular elements of a traumatic death (e.g., the death of a loved one in a car accident on the highway precipitates the mourner's refusal to travel on highways) or it may have a more general impact upon the individual (e.g., after a disastrous flood, the mourner feels uneasy about her ability to take care of herself and thereafter curtails activities requiring that she leave her home). To the extent that any death is sudden and precipitates unanticipated mourning reactions or the unanticipated mourning syndrome, the stage is set for increased anxiety and potentiated agoraphobic responses.

Loss has been identified as a precipitant of acute symtomatology in obsessive compulsive disorders (Capstick & Seldrup, 1973). Although little reference to the obsessive compulsive disorder has been made in the bereavement literature outside of its being mentioned under other terminology by Anderson (1949) and Lehrman (1956) as a form pathological grief may take, this disorder would not seem unexpected in an individual struggling to ward off the high degree of anxiety that can stem from the death of a loved one. In addition to anxiety resulting from the general sources previously outlined, the mourner often must contend with anxiety arising from confrontation with unacceptable and/or uncomfortable affects; thoughts, impulses, or images associated with the death (e.g., a terminal illness or funeral); and/or the premorbid relationship with the deceased. The mourner may respond to this anxiety with obsession, compulsion, or a mixture of both.

As with other elements of psychiatric disorder, some amount of obsession and compulsion is not abnormal in uncomplicated mourning. Indeed, the healthy bereaved individual is supposed to be somewhat obsessed with the deceased, events surrounding the death, and the premorbid relationship. Such a response is typical of the third "R" process, recollecting and reexperiencing the deceased and the relationship. It is also a normal response to sudden, unexpected death as the mourner attempts to attain some control and mastery over the situation. It may be that, for some mourners, the DSM-III-R criterion pertaining to the experience of obsessions as intrusive and senseless can differentiate, at least initially, between an uncomplicated and a complicated response. However, it is clear that a proportion of bereaved individuals experience as intrusive and senseless what others would construe as normal bereavement reactions (e.g., preoccupation with the deceased or reviewing and experiencing rage at the manner of notification of the death). In such instances, the criterion may be less useful in discriminating uncomplicated and complicated responses. (The reader should also see the discussion of obsessive compulsive personality disorder later in this chapter.)

Compulsive reactions develop in response to the conscious or unconscious awareness of certain emotions, thoughts, impulses, or behaviors that arise as consequences of the loss (e.g., anger about the death, anxiety about recognizing the implications of the death, desire to seek revenge upon the person held responsible). Compulsions arising in the effort to deal with and control the anxiety originating from the loss and reactions to it range from mild to severe and incapacitating.

It is not surprising that some amount of compulsivity emerges in bereavement as the mourner struggles to regain psychosocial, behavioral, physical, and spiritual balance in a world changed dramatically with the absence of the loved one. Certain personal bereavement rituals can provide comfort and enable a sense of control and focus in the midst of flux and chaos (see chapter 7). However, at question is the degree of benefit versus cost. Rechecking to ensure that the stove is turned off can give a mourner a sense of security and control in terms of minimizing vulnerability perceived after the sudden, unexpected death of a loved one. Such behaviors can become dysfunctional, however, when they impinge too greatly upon the mourner's ability to function (e.g., the mourner becomes so consumed with checking and rechecking the stove that it becomes impossible for him to leave the house). In my own practice, I have observed more true compulsions than true obsessions developing as a consequence of major loss. It would be interesting to see if this observation would be confirmed empirically.

Post-traumatic stress disorder, or PTSD, is significantly associated with complicated mourning and commonly found after traumatic and sudden deaths such as homicides, suicides, mutilating accidents, disasters, and war deaths, as well as after the death of a child and in circumstances where the mourner confronts violence or trauma or almost dies herself. In a perverse way, this disorder is both normal as well as abnormal when it arises under these conditions: It is known to follow traumatic deaths and is normal in the sense that it carries within its experience the necessary components for ultimate cognitive completion of the stress response syndrome (see Horowitz, 1986a). However, it represents a mourning reaction that is complicated and therefore simultaneously abnormal. Thus, oxymoronically, it is a "normal abnormality." PTSD appears to have been addressed in the thanatological literature in a rudimentary form in Lehrman's (1956) discussion on reactions to untimely death. It is extensively discussed in the consideration of traumatic death in chapter 12.

Certainly, the loss of a loved one and the alteration of one's assumptive world bring about the type of anxiety and worry inherent in a generalized anxiety disorder. For some period of time following the death of a loved one this is not an atypical response. The disorder contains a number of symptoms known to occur in uncomplicated mourning. Specifically, excessive anxiety and worry accompanied by motor tension, autonomic hyperactivity, and vigilance and scanning are representative of reactions present in the acute grief phase. Jacobs and colleagues (1990) found generalized anxiety disorder to be the most frequent type of anxiety disorder. This disorder is also associated with mild depressive symptoms, frequently a depressive disorder. In fact, Jacobs and colleagues found that virtually all of the bereaved who had this disorder met the criteria for major depression. To the extent that depression is also often associated with bereavement, the association between generalized anxiety disorder and complicated mourning is strengthened. Jacobs and Kim (1989) reported that isomorphy is 65 percent for generalized anxiety disorder and so-called pathologic grief.

Theoretically and clinically, the generalized anxiety disorder appears related to several complicated mourning syndromes. It is easily applicable to mourners who suffer the sequelae of sudden, unexpected death in the unanticipated mourning syndrome. In addition, this diagnostic category is descriptive of many of those whose psychodynamics and interpersonal relationships lead them to evidence chronic mourning and conflicted mourning. One might expect to see this disorder related to deaths that are traumatic, violent, and productive of significant feelings of helplessness; that are of the type to be especially disruptive to the mourner's assumptive world; and that sever a relationship upon which the mourner was especially dependent. All of these circumstances cause the mourner to be particularly anxious in the new world.

As is true for symptoms of depression, symptoms of anxiety must be evaluated for psychopharmacological intervention. Indeed, some have suggested that it may be more important to respond psychopharmacologically to symptoms of anxiety than to symptoms of depression (e.g., Hackett, 1974; Kellner et al., 1986; Merlis, 1972). Others advocate judicious prescription of whatever psychotropic medication is warranted by the symptoms (e.g., Jacobs & Kim, 1990; Shuchter & Zisook, 1987; Zisook et al., 1990). A number of other clinical writers have ascertained the necessity of responding to symptoms of anxiety through medication. These include, among others, Burnell and Burnell (1989), Ferguson (1973), Goldberg et al. (1986), Goldberg et al. (1973), Kellner (1975), Lazare (1979), and Lindemann (1944). When the bereavement is marked by significant elements of post-traumatic stress, the prevailing consensus is that medication is mandated. (See chapter 12 for more on post-traumatic stress.)

Somatoform Disorders

In somatoform disorders are found physical symptoms for which there are no demonstrable organic findings or physiological mechanisms and for which there is evidence or strong presumption of a link to psychological factors or conflicts. Mourning typically involves some amount of somatic symptoms and heightened somatic concerns. Myriad symptoms (e.g., preoccupation with the belief one has a serious disease based on interpretation of symptoms, pain, belief in one's shortened life, multiple somatic complaints, loss of physical function) are common in both uncomplicated and complicated mourning and across five of the somatoform disorders (i.e., conversion disorder, hypochondriasis, somatization disorder, somatoform pain disorder, and undifferentiated somatoform disorder). The sixth, body dysmorphic disorder, does not appear related to these symptoms or to mourning. There is a residual category as well. Issues of degree, intensity, type, and duration of such symptomatology are critically important areas of clinical discrimination because they pose inherent diagnostic problems. Clinically, I have observed far more cases of complicated mourning with a diffuse or polysymptomatic picture (i.e., hypochondriasis, somatization disorder, or undifferentiated somatoform disorder) than with a more differentiated symptom focus (i.e., conversion disorder or somatoform pain disorder). However, I am unaware of any data to confirm this difference in prevalence.

Raphael (1983), Stroebe and Stroebe (1987), and Osterweis et al. (1984) analyze the literature documenting general physical symptomatology and complaints as common in uncomplicated mourning. An increased number of such symptoms, undue preoccupation with them, or their intensification and/or prolongation are frequently associated with and indicative of complicated mourning.

Raphael (1983) notes that one finds ample clinical evidence of symptomatic patterns of bereavement in the areas of conversion reactions, hypochondriasis, and illness behavior. She identifies psychological issues related to them, such as the transient experience of the symptoms of the deceased's terminal illness. These symptoms may reflect the mourner's desire for identification with the deceased, the attempt to hold part of the deceased within, or even the attempt to punish oneself for surviving the loss by suffering the deceased's pain. Fantasies of reunion with the deceased also may exist.

Zisook and DeVaul (1976–1977) have identified a syndrome often witnessed clinically in which there is an arrest of the normal mourning process and a presentation of symptoms identical or nearly identical to those experienced by the deceased. In what these investigators refer to as grief-related facsimile illness, there usually is a history of previous ineffective and inappropriate treatment endeavors and psychiatric consultation for problems not related to the grief state. Often such referrals are for evaluation of persistent pain or disability out of keeping with clinical findings. Treatment of grief-related facsimile illness involves mobilization of arrested mourning, and the prognosis is good. In a related area, Melson and Rynearson (1982) observed how unresolved bereavement over the terminal illness and death of a mother stimulated in certain surviving daughters unconscious reenactments of the mother's illness.

Diagnosis of somatoform disorders can be complicated by the development of organically demonstrable psychosomatic illness and symptomatology, to which the bereaved are vulnerable. Raphael (1983) observes that further confusion is added by the fact that the mourner may find it easier to experience and ask for help for physical than for emotional pain. Hypochondriacal complaints may reflect the mourner's preoccupation with suffering or fear of death. Problems may be exacerbated in situations where the mourner has nursed a terminally ill person for a prolonged period and now feels contaminated by illness, receives secondary gain for the role of the sick one, or uses physical complaints to avoid contending with dependence upon the deceased and/or ambivalence about the relationship. Any of these reactions can become part of complicated mourning symptoms or syndromes.

Clinical experience reveals that somatoform disorders often are a consequence of complicated mourning. In particular, conversion disorder has been noted historically as being a form through which complicated mourning manifests itself (Lehrman, 1956), with Anderson (1949) finding that 19 percent of his patients with morbid grief evidenced it in this particular form. The five somatoform disorders mentioned in the beginning of this section are particularly apparent in the syndrome of inhibited mourning and to a lesser degree in delayed mourning. In these two syndromes, somatoform symptoms often mask the suppressed or repressed aspects of mourning. However, complicated mourning need not only precipitate somatic symptoms. It can be hypothesized that, to the extent that the mourner tends to somatize stress and conflict in general, this can predispose to complicated mourning.

Both conversion disorder and hypochondriasis are noted in the DSM-III-R as having as predisposing factors exposure to others with real physical illnesses and the experience of extreme psychosocial stress. Both of these factors are common components of terminal illness and death of a loved one. Indeed, overidentification with the last illness of the deceased has been noted as a pathological symptom of complicated mourning by numerous authors (e.g., Lindemann, 1944). Disorders strongly related to one or more of the somatization disorders (e.g., post-traumatic decline; Titchener, 1986) can develop subsequent to a sudden, traumatic, and/or unnatural death.

Dissociative Disorders

Each of the specified dissociative disorders (multiple personality disorder, psychogenic fugue, psychogenic amnesia, and depersonalization disorder), as well as the one residual category, involves a predisposing factor of severe psychosocial stress. In this regard, these disorders are associated with complicated mourning witnessed after traumatic deaths and in the mourning of those who have been victimized or abused. In particular, Putnam (1989) reports having seen a small number of cases in which the presentation of multiple personality disorder initially appeared to be a pathological grief reaction. In each case, an established and successful adult had a precipitous decline in functioning following the death of the primary abusive parent; the death seemed to activate dissociated affects and memories.

Frequent mention of dissociative disorders is made in the post-traumatic stress literature (e.g., van der Kolk, 1984, 1987b). Dissociation reactions and disorders also have been reported as a possible pathological outcome of bereavement by Jennings and France (1979) and Raphael (1983). It is common for most mourners to experience some amount of dissociation—especially, although not exclusively, depersonalization—in cases of acute grief, with relatively greater amounts in the case of sudden and traumatic deaths. The clinical issue therefore concerns the degree of such reactions.

In his examination of pathological mourning stemming from childhood bereavement, Bowlby (1980) provides a case study in which he refers to Stengel's (1939, 1941, 1943) work on compulsive wandering with amnesia. Bowlby observes that such psychogenic fugue states, although rare after childhood loss, do tend to involve in adults the antecedent loss of a parent during childhood. Bowlby also notes two closely connected features in the history of these patients, as identified by Stengel: (a) the high frequency of serious disturbance in these patients' childhood relationships with parents—in particular, losses due to death or separation and (b) the desire to seek the lost parent often present during the actual episodes of wandering. Bowlby conceptualizes such behavior as the activation of a previously deactivated principal system of behavior, which has been denied access to consciousness through complicated mourning.

Sexual Disorders

Although the present review of literature revealed no references associating the paraphilias and complicated mourning, significant mention occurs of both hyposexuality and hypersexuality as concomitants of acute grief and mourning, as well as signs of complicated mourning (e.g., Raphael, 1983). However, these responses and others grouped under the category of sexual dysfunction are not typically the major part of the clinical disturbance. Rather, they usually are components of a constellation of responses to the loss that may or may not reach the diagnostic criteria for a mental disorder (e.g., major depression). Sexual acting out is discussed in this chapter under the heading of impulse control disorders not elsewhere classified.

Sleep Disorders

Sleep disturbances are a common symptom of both uncomplicated and complicated grief and mourning. They may be protracted and frequently demand pharmacological intervention. Both dyssomnias and parasomnias usually occur in conjunction with other symptoms and are related to other mental disorders (e.g., major depression, PTSD).

   No associations appeared in the literature between sleep disturbance as the predominant complaint and complicated mourning, although some mourners' concerns about parasomnias (e.g., nightmares) may become so intense that they assume undue prominence. In such cases, even though the problem is associated with another mental disorder and a principal diagnosis would be difficult to justify, one might consider an additional diagnosis of parasomnia. The professional literature on depression and PTSD is a rich source of information about sleep disturbances.

Factitious Disorders

Factitious disorders may involve either physical or psychological symptoms. One report found in the literature associates complicated mourning with factitious disorders. Dopson (1979) describes a case of a 15-year-old girl with physical symptoms. The girl presented with chronic lymphedema of the right hand and arm as a way of identifying with the characteristics of the last illness of her beloved grandmother and of keeping the grandmother alive for herself and other members of her family.

Other reports also identify psychological symptoms. Specifically, Snowdon, Solomons, and Druce (1978) report 12 cases of feigned bereavement, and Raphael (1983) reports several others. In these cases, the patients appeared to feign bereavement in order to meet a number of conscious and unconscious needs ranging from allaying guilt and gratifying dependence to securing financial gain and achieving pleasure through lying. Many were depressed and/or manifested self-destructive behavior. In a number of cases, mourners exhibited obvious mental anguish even after gaining attention and hospitalization, suggesting that other losses or deprivations underlay their reactions. Sympathy routinely was sought.

Impulse Control Disorders Not Elsewhere Classified

Five specific forms of impulse control disorders comprise the residual diagnostic class for disorders of impulse control not classified in other categories. These include intermittent explosive disorder, kleptomania, pathological gambling, pyromania, and trichotillomania. Pathological gambling has been associated with complicated mourning, and evidence exists that an intermittent explosive disorder may at times describe certain individuals experiencing complicated mourning. The residual category for impulse disorders contains a number of other acting-out behaviors known to take place in both uncomplicated and complicated mourning.

In his study of gamblers, Whitman-Raymond (1988) identified pathological gambling as a defense against loss. According to this investigator, gamblers perceive their world as unsafe due to an abnormally formidable history of prior losses—which for them remain unresolved—and an inability to endure the threat of impending loss. Gambling activity distorts or eliminates the sense of time, makes all things seem possible, gives the sense that action is continuous, and dissolves normal parameters. This time distortion allows a denial of both past history and the inevitability of death while at the same time offering an adrenaline release that counters depression. It provides an illusion of the ability to predict the future and a sense of timelessness in the safety of ritual, furnishing the possibility of endless action and boundless winnings to anesthetize the fear of finite time and human mortality.

As for other diagnostic categories, the question of degree is important in determining whether symptoms reflect complicated mourning. For example, impulsive outbursts characteristic of the intermittent explosive disorder may accompany both uncomplicated and complicated grief and mourning because of the high amount of tension, anxiety, and anger present after a major loss. Post-traumatic stress symptoms can exacerbate these feelings further. Thus, discrete episodes of loss of control of aggressive impulses are not uncommon in complicated mourning, although they may not reach the level or frequency required for a strict diagnosis of intermittent explosive disorder. Most often, these explosions are symptomatic of another DSM-III-R disorder or can legitimately fit under the residual category here. In the absence of a diagnostic category for complicated mourning or a description of uncomplicated mourning that would include increased aggression and irritability, the caregiver would theoretically have little recourse but to use this category for mourners exhibiting strongly aggressive acting-out behaviors. Such a diagnosis would probably be most likely in deaths where anger is a prominent reaction (e.g., death of a child, accidental death for which someone is blamed, traumatic death) and in situations where anger is out of proportion to other reactions (e.g., distorted mourning of the extremely angry type).

A variety of other acting-out behaviors associated with complicated mourning do not meet the criteria for a specific impulse control disorder. These would be diagnosed under the residual category or as symptomatic of other disorders (e.g., depression). Behaviors mentioned frequently throughout the literature include, among others, antisocial acts, sexual acting out, alcohol and drug abuse, eating disorders, compulsive behaviors, accidents, suicidal gestures and acts, self-defeating behaviors, self-damaging behaviors, self-mutilation, and acting out in social/interpersonal relationships.

Raphael (1983) addresses the sexual impulsivity frequently seen clinically, identifying it as a "desperate measure to reestablish the symbiotic relationship on which the ego integrity depends. There is a need for comfort, bodily contact, and reassurance against the pain of the loss, the rejection, and the fear of being alone" (p. 214). Such sexual activity in response to the anxiety engendered by death or the threat of death is not uncommon (MacElveen-Hoehn, 1987).

The relationship between aborted mourning and abrupt changes in sexual behavior—often unrecognized because of the general cultural aversion to grief and death—is an important area of inquiry in family therapy because the procreative act, while representing the height of pleasure, also represents the symbolic expression of the parent's preparation for and participation in the next generation (Paul & Paul, 1982). In one study, intercourse and pregnancy-seeking behavior were identified as attempts to cope with the specific emotional pain of a loss or threatened loss, with the women involved desiring to reassert their being, vitality, potency, and ability to produce more life to counteract the loss, abandonment, wounded self-esteem, and tension caused by the death of a loved one (Swigar, Bowers, & Fleck, 1976). Those who had lost fathers were unaware of their intent to conceive in response to their stress at the time of conception, whereas those who had lost mothers actively considered pregnancy and fantasized about themselves in relation to their mothers and their fetuses, and about caring and being cared for.

Acting-out behaviors also may reflect a number of the ways in which new relationship patterns are developed subsequent to a loss. Some of these are positive and adaptive, whereas others are more pathological and indicate complicated mourning (e.g., Lindemann, 1944). Raphael (1983) has identified a number of the types of relationships reflecting complicated mourning: (a) fantasy relationships with the lost idealized loved one, (b) replacement relationships, (c) self-destructive relationships, (d) avoidant relationships, (e) compulsive caregiving relationships, (f) relationships based on power and aggression, and (g) relationships where old repetition-compulsions continue.

Adjustment Disorders

Along with disorders associated with depression and anxiety, the adjustment disorders appear to be one of the diagnostic categories most frequently employed for complicated mourning. According to the DSM-III-R, the essential feature of an adjustment disorder is a maladaptive reaction to an identifiable psychosocial stressor or stressors that occurs within 3 months after onset of the stressor and has persisted for no longer than 6 months.

Horowitz (1986b) has declared that, although adjustment disorder is a very open diagnostic category, it should not be regarded as a minor one. He points out that suicidal ideation may be high and that severe dysfunction found in work, social life, and parenting may cause great personal distress. Thus, in each case it is important to reach a specific formulation of the individual's predominant complaints.

Adjustment disorders are present with anxious mood, depressed mood, disturbance of conduct, mixed disturbance of emotions and conduct, mixed emotional features, physical complaints, withdrawal, and work (or academic) inhibition. In addition, one residual category is an adjustment disorder not otherwise specified. Together, these forms reflect all possible combinations of emotional, behavioral, and interpersonal dysfunction in life, as found across all areas of psychosocial, behavioral, interpersonal, and occupational functioning. Once again, the issue arises of which responses are expected in uncomplicated mourning and what responses constitute a diagnosable disorder indicating complicated mourning.

Psychological Factors Affecting Physical Condition

By its very nature, bereavement contributes to a wide range of physical symptoms and conditions. Clinical investigations repeatedly confirm the psychosomatic changes (i.e., actual physical conditions initiated or exacerbated by psychological factors) developing as a consequence of the loss of a loved one. Therefore, a strong association exists between this category and both uncomplicated and complicated mourning. Because the literature in this area is too broad to delineate here, the reader is referred to the following resources for reviews documenting specific findings: Clayton (1982); Jacobs and Douglas (1979); Jacobs and Ostfeld (1977); Klerman and Izen (1977); Lieberman and Jacobs (1987); Lund (1989); Osterweis et al. (1984); Parkes (1964, 1987); Raphael (1983); Stroebe and Stroebe (1987); Windholz, Marmar, and Horowitz (1985); and Zisook (1987). Specific studies documenting the relationship between particular medical disorders and complicated mourning include Levitan (1985), addressing the onset of asthma during acute complicated mourning; Paulley (1983), concluding that pathological mourning is a primary and invariably present precipitant of autoimmune disorders; and Stamm and Drapkin (1966), observing acute development of bronchial asthma as a manifestation of an abnormal mourning reaction and traumatic neurosis.

Other information about physical disorders associated with complicated mourning appears later in this chapter under the heading of physical disorders. The reader is also encouraged to examine the literature on psychosomatic illness, which frequently reports on the influence of loss and mourning on the development of disease (e.g., Baker & Brewerton, 1981; Day, 1951; Kissen, 1958; Morillo & Gardner, 1979; Paulley & Hughes, 1960; Stamm & Drapkin, 1966).

Personality Disorders

Although it would appear that personality and personality factors would be among the major determinants of adjustment to loss—and most theories of bereavement predict personality-related differences in individual reactions to loss—specific evidence from bereavement research has been minimal and inconclusive (Stroebe & Stroebe, 1987). Much discussion has focused on how relationships of extreme dependency predispose the individual to complicated mourning, implicating the dependent personality as a risk factor. In addition, some mention has been made of problems in mourning encountered by those with borderline, narcissistic, and obsessive compulsive personalities. However, with the exception of the several studies subsequently described, a relative dearth of clinical and empirical investigations on this topic exists. Perhaps this absence reflects a prior focus on commonalities in mourning and a lack of appreciation for individual differences. Or perhaps it reveals the significant difficulties involved in this type of research. In any event, the focus of the present section is on complicated mourning as a dependent variable, with personality as an independent variable.

Personality types and characteristics

In general, it has been observed that individuals with personality disorders are prone to complications in mourning. Alarcon (1984) reports on how personality disorders and characteristics serve as pathogenic factors in bereavement. Barry (1981) asserts the likelihood that all individuals suffering prolonged grief reactions have personality disorders requiring treatment beyond brief therapy for the grief reaction. Merlis (1972) writes that, in cases of pathological grief, evidence frequently exists to suggest a premorbid pathological personality disorder, which is aggravated and intensified by the bereavement process. It appears, however, that the only empirical and clinical investigation into the association between specific personality types (as opposed to personality characteristics) and bereavement has been conducted by Sanders (1979). Sanders used the Minnesota Multiphasic Personality Inventory (MMPI; Hathaway & McKinley, 1951) to determine premorbid personality profiles and the Grief Experience Inventory (GEI; Sanders, Mauger, & Strong, 1977) to reveal typologies of grief and mourning through self-report measures of experiences, feelings, symptoms, and behaviors of the mourning process. Comparing traits of the mourner with current states in the mourner allowed this investigator to determine the effect of bereavement on various types of personalities and coping patterns. The subjects, who were matched with a control group, were tested on the average of 2.2 months subsequent to bereavement and were followed up approximately 18 months after bereavement.

Sanders notes that four types of bereavement were correlated with four personalities: First, a disturbed bereavement group obtained a profile resembling a schizoid personality with depressive reactions. These individuals functioned premorbidly on the periphery of good mental health, with personality problems such as feelings of inadequacy, inferiority, and insecurity. When confronted with the emotional burden of acute grief, they had few resources upon which to draw. They experienced high levels of grief intensity—especially despair, helplessness, and a sense of unreality, with high inner turmoil and long-lasting desolation. On follow-up examination, they were grieving almost as deeply as indicated at the initial interview.

Second, a depressed high-grief group was composed of highly depressed, anxious, and oversensitive individuals who had a history of multiple losses and unusual concurrent crises. When they lost their loved one, upon whom they had been significantly dependent, these persons were subject to intense fear and emotionality, exhibiting a marked sense of helplessness, high depression, anxiety, somatization, and alienation. Although their GEI scores had decreased moderately at the follow-up and many indicated they felt somewhat better, these individuals still exhibited feelings of acute grief, and much reparation remained to be done. The learned helplessness they retained from their previous losses and their trait of anxiety contributed to a sense of loss of control over their universe and their own feelings, as well as to thoughts of failure and worthlessness.

Third, a denial group contained individuals who needed to employ strong defense mechanisms in order to survive crises, frequently using physical symptoms to occupy their thoughts and energies as a means of solving conflicts or avoiding responsibilities. Reluctant to admit to common human foibles, these individuals kept a "stiff upper lip" in their mourning, often surviving by a flight into activity and intensification of personal work, community activity, or church involvement. Despite sadness, they sped up their normal activities with determined optimism. Their denial was not of the death itself, but of the overt emotions surrounding it, and such denial appeared to be an adaptive defense in their crisis. At follow-up, they appeared as determined to survive their bereavement as they had initially, with little change in either MMPI or GEI profiles and continued focus on specific medical symptoms rather than on their life situation or emotional difficulties.

Fourth, a normal grief-contained group was composed of individuals whose MMPI profiles were considered normal and who revealed medium to high ego strength and good emotional control, with low depression, somatization, and anxiety. Although there was some loss of emotional control in their bereavement, there also was the need to maintain a high degree of socially desirable behavior. There was relatively little preoccupation with the deceased or feelings of unreality. These individuals felt their loss and expressed their sadness yet recognized the inevitability of loss in life and attempted to deal with it straightforwardly and openly, and the essence of their personalities was maintained in the crisis situation. At follow-up, although deeply wounded by their losses, their MMPI scores had changed only slightly, whereas their GEI profile reflected consistent reductions in the intensity on all the grief scales, indicating healthy and effective coping with the loss.

Sanders' research makes it clear that it is not necessarily the bereavement per se that causes complications, but also the psychodynamics of the personality. It is nonetheless important to note that some bereavement situations (e.g., traumatic events) can be expected to cause complications independently of the personality of the bereaved, although even so, responses are certainly influenced by personality. In addition, Sanders' findings suggest that core personality factors can facilitate positive coping or act to complicate mourning. This idea has important implications for treatment expectations and intervention, as spelled out in Sanders' original work. Similarly, this research supports the notion that no single intervention strategy meets the needs of all mourners and that a variety of approaches must be tailored for each individual. Finally, contrary to popular psychiatric opinion, findings indicate that denial (not of the death itself but of overt emotions surrounding it) is an adaptive defense that can serve some individuals well in their crisis.

Two studies on personality factors further clarify the associations between personality and mourning. In work over a 2-year period with a group of widows, Vachon, Sheldon, Lancee, Lyall, Rogers, and Freeman (1982) analyzed personality as measured on the 16 Personality Factor Questionnaire (Cattell, Eber, & Tatsuoka, 1970) and levels of distress as measured on the General Health Questionnaire (Goldberg, 1972). They found that a group exhibiting enduringly high distress had lower scores on ego strength and higher scores on guilt-proneness and anxiety. These women were found to be apprehensive, worrying, and highly anxious; in addition, they also experienced low social support. In contrast, women experiencing low distress were described as emotionally stable, mature, conscientious, conservative, and socially precise. Vachon and colleagues conclude that low distress can be best understood not as the absence of mourning but as the presence of personality characteristics that promote adaptation into a new role.

In their Tübingen study, Stroebe et al. (1985) measured emotional stability with the German version of the neuroticism scale of the Eysenck Personality Inventory (Eggert, 1983; Eysenck & Eysenck, 1964) and discovered that bereavement was associated with higher neuroticism scores (i.e., low emotional stability) and that those who scored high were more depressed. In addition, locus of control was assessed with the German version of the Interpersonal Control Scale devised by Levenson (Levenson, 1973). Bereavement was associated with an increased belief that events are controlled by chance. When expectedness of the loss was examined, it was discovered that individuals with low internal control beliefs reacted with greater depression to unexpected loss than those who believed they had control over their environment. There was little difference in depression among the two groups when the loss was expected. In reporting this study, Stroebe and Stroebe (1987) note that the amount of time between the loss and measurement of the depression may have provided the opportunity for those who believed in internal control to have adjusted better.

Parkes (Parkes, 1987; Parkes & Weiss, 1983) identifies the grief-prone personality as one who tends to react strongly to separations. This characteristic predisposes toward complicated mourning in the same way previous excessive grief and depression bode poorly for a current loss. Raphael (1983) observes that, although evidence relating personality variability to outcome is inconclusive and no specific risk factors have been demonstrated, four sets of personality variables appear to predispose toward complicated mourning: (a) characteristics leading to the formation of dependent, clinging, ambivalent relationships; (b) styles leading to relationships with others who are unable to accept the expression of feeling and review of the lost relationship (e.g., individuals with a so-called "plaintive set," which leads them to perceive their social group as inadequate and nonsupportive); (c) difficulty accepting the expression of negative affects or powerful feelings that generally may cause inhibition of mourning; and (d) increased vulnerability to loss or pathogenic focus resulting from early childhood loss, particularly parental loss. In addition, Raphael conjectures that if personality prior to bereavement is a variable, it may operate through such other factors as the patterns of affect expression and release permitted, whether the mourner has internalized good objects in his early stages of development, the preexisting relationship with the deceased, and the quality of social support available.

Others have come to conclusions similar to Raphael's about expression of affect. For instance, Maddison and Viola (1968) found that those who suppress affect are at high risk; Warnes (1985) observed how alexithymia complicates mourning; and Parkes (1979) noted that individuals whose family system discourages the expression of grief are at greater risk.

One other personality variable—hardiness—has been shown to be a significant predictor of grief in widows (Campbell, Swank, & Vincent, 1991). Hardy people are described as "committed to their activities, feeling they have a sense of control over their lives, and seeing life as a series of challenges. Additionally, time competence, the component of Maslow's description of the self-actualizing person related to living fully in the present, is an important factor" (p. 61). Mourners with a high degree of hardiness and time competence do better in adjusting to the loss of a spouse than those who have a lesser degree. In this study, hardiness significantly predicted resolution above and beyond general mental and other situational and sociodemographic variables (e.g., mode of death, age).

Specific personality disorders

Three clusters of personality disorders are noted in the DSM-III-R. Review of the bereavement literature reveals little discussion of the association of Cluster A (paranoid, schizoid, and schizotypal personalities) with complicated mourning. Two exceptions are Sanders' (1979) discussion of schizoid personality and its association with complicated mourning and Lehrman's (1956) mention of schizoid personality as a form that may be assumed by complicated mourning following untimely death. Clusters B (antisocial, borderline, histrionic, and narcissistic personalities) and C (avoidant, dependent, obsessive compulsive, and passive-aggressive personalities) have all been mentioned in association with complicated mourning, along with the residual category.

With regard to Cluster B, nothing in the literature specifically associates either antisocial or histrionic personality disorders with complicated mourning. However, clinical experience suggests that each disorder sustains characteristics that could contribute to or be associated with complicated mourning. For example, antisocial acting out is not uncommon in complicated mourning. The acting out may reveal an isolated reaction or represent either a symptom of the antisocial personality disorder or impulse control disorder not otherwise specified. A number of predisposing factors associated with the antisocial personality disorder are known also to be associated with complicated mourning (e.g., child abuse, early childhood losses, growing up without parental role models of both sexes). The features of the histrionic personality associate it with exacerbated and dramatic grief reactions, inadequate cognitive processing, poor impulse and affect controls, low frustration tolerance, intensified somatic complaints, and high demands for social attention and support. All of these factors are known to be associated with complicated mourning.

Practically all writers caution about the difficulties inherent in bereavement work with borderline patients (e.g., Lazare, 1979; Worden, 1982). Problems inherent in the mourning of individuals with narcissistic personality disorder are articulated by, among others, Anable (1978) and Gorkin (1984).

With regard to brief treatment of prolonged or particularly intense mourning reactions, Krupnick and Horowitz (1985) write that the specific vulnerabilities of those with borderline and narcissistic disorders must be taken into consideration to avoid precipitating regression into psychotic or self-destructive states. This does not mean, however, that such work should not be undertaken—only that treatment goals and strategies should reflect realistic limitations. Krupnick and Horowitz's study involved eight "vulnerable" patients seen in brief dynamic therapy after parental bereavement for symptoms including, among others, episodes of overwhelming intrusive symptomatology or an inability to mourn characterized by excessive avoidance. These investigators found that such treatment did not cause ongoing deterioration, although it may have been overly stressful or insufficiently sustaining in the three cases with the poorest outcomes. However, all the patients made significant strides in processing the parental death, and five reported general improvements in interpersonal relationships. The authors report three benefits for brief treatment of vulnerable patients experiencing complicated mourning: (a) its ability to serve as a trial for more extended treatment; (b) in the most successful cases, its provision of the opportunity to work through conflicts and serve as a vehicle for psychological growth; and (c) at the least, its ability to help vulnerable patients do sufficient psychotherapeutic work to prevent decline after a traumatic life event. Krupnick and Horowitz conclude that brief treatment may serve as a prologue to longer term therapies that initially would have been avoided, particularly by borderline patients, out of fears of excessive dependency, merger with the therapist, regression, or inability to separate from the relationship. It appears reasonable that these conclusions could be extrapolated for some other types of treatments as well.

Certainly, the caregiver must evaluate carefully and exercise caution, especially when treating borderline mourners and particularly when contemplating brief treatment (e.g., Davanloo, 1978; Mann, 1973; Sifneos, 1972). In general, the ability of these individuals to mourn is compromised by their inability to retain an internal image, separate, tolerate pain and intense affect, permit appropriate regression, deal with aggression, differentiate feelings, contend with suicidal ideation, exert impulse control, cope with feelings of emptiness and abandonment, permit temporary dependency, and engage in the six "R" processes of mourning. Often, their early childhood experiences are characterized by physical, sexual, and/or psychological abuse that places them at risk for complicated mourning both because of their personality development and often because of their relationship to the deceased. Despite these problems, their needs for processing loss demand intervention.

Cluster C's avoidant and dependent personality disorders entail features known to be associated with complicated mourning. According to the DSM-III-R, these two types frequently appear together. In the present discussion, they are collectively considered to involve pervasive patterns of dependence, fear of negative evaluation, social discomfort, and submissive behavior. They embody attributes of dependence and anxiety—both factors having been identified as high-risk variables for complicated mourning by such authors as Bowlby (1980), Fenichel (1945), Parkes (1987), Parkes and Weiss (1983), and Raphael (1983).

Specifically, extreme dependency has been found to be highly associated with distorted mourning of the extremely angry type and somewhat less associated with the inhibitory aspects found in the syndromes of absent, delayed, and inhibited mourning (Raphael, 1983). Raphael joins Parkes and Weiss (1983) in finding this dependence to be highly associated with chronic mourning. Parkes and Weiss see dependence and social avoidance to be essential determinants in the etiology of the disorder of attachment they perceive to underlie the chronic mourning syndrome.

As detailed in chapter 3, Bowlby (1980) classifies members of three groups prone to complicated mourning not according to personality, but according to the type of affectional relationships their personalities enable them to make. The first group is predisposed to make insecure and anxious attachments. In the second there is a strong disposition to engage in compulsive caregiving. The third group superficially appears opposite to the first two groups but actually acts from some of the same fears. This group incorporates those who protest a precariously based emotional self-sufficiency by asserting their independence from affectional ties. In all three groups, the relationships are likely to be suffused with overt or latent ambivalence that also complicates mourning.

Further confirmation of the role of dependence in complicated mourning is supplied by Horowitz, Wilner, Marmar et al. (1980). They observed the development of complicated mourning in survivors for whom the severed relationship had served to hold in check earlier latent negative self-images and role relationship models. With the death of the loved one, these feelings resurfaced and, in the absence of the relationship with the deceased to sustain a more positive self-image, caused mourners to experience pathological intensifications of acute grief, such as desperate, needy, and frightening sadness; out-of-control rage; or intense and prolonged deflation (i.e., shame, worthlessness, dejection, and withdrawal). Similar observations linking complicated mourning with the mourner's need for the deceased's representation to maintain a sense of self have been made by Lazare (1979) and Volkan (1985).

Often related to dependency is the passive-aggressive personality disorder. Although review of the bereavement literature netted no references associating this specific disorder with complicated mourning, abundant evidence exists that relationships with marked hostility, resentment, and ambivalence—whether overt or covert—predispose to complicated mourning. To the extent that those who tend to be passive aggressive in personality sustain relationships that are ambivalent and/or covertly aggressive, these individuals will be prone to complications. (See chapter 10 for further discussion of anger and ambivalence as risk factors.)

The obsessive compulsive personality disorder per se has been identified as having a significant association with complicated mourning by Lindemann (1944), who notes that the obsessive personality contributes to agitated depressions in mourning when it is associated with a history of previous depression. However, this is not the only way the obsessive personality is associated with complicated mourning. The pervasive pattern of perfectionism and inflexibility that characterizes this personality is often clinically observable in many individuals experiencing difficulty in mourning. The six "R" processes of mourning are significantly compromised by the dynamics of the obsessive compulsive personality. The unusual need for control, the preoccupation with productivity and details, and the inability to let things go all interfere with mourning. During mourning, especially during acute grief, a mourner experiences considerable chaos, unpredictability, flux, loss of control, emotional lability, and cognitive confusion. By its very nature, the mourning experience confronts obsessive compulsive individuals with the precise issues that are most difficult for them to contend with in any circumstance. Experiencing the failure of customary problem-solving strategies and attempts at perfectionism and control can be as difficult (or more so) for some of these mourners as the loss of the loved one. In brief, the loss simply cannot be managed or controlled to the degree required by this personality. (The reader should also consult the discussion of obsessive compulsive disorder in the section on anxiety disorders earlier in this chapter.)

The category for personality disorders not otherwise specified is used for a number of personality disorders known to predispose to complicated mourning. Individuals in this category would include, among others, those without other diagnoses who sustain inflexible and maladaptive personality traits (a) stemming from victimization (similar to the new diagnosis proposed for the DSM-IV, disorders of extreme stress not otherwise specified; Spitzer, 1990), (b) fitting the current criteria for identification as an adult child of an alcoholic (e.g., Woititz, 1983), or (c) meeting the definition of codependency (e.g., Wegscheider-Cruse & Cruse, 1990). In some instances, overlap may occur among some or all of these three categories. The reader is referred to chapter 10 for discussion of these personality characteristics and how they tend to complicate mourning.

V Codes for Conditions Not Attributable to a Mental Disorder That Are a Focus of Attention or Treatment

The clinical literature makes frequent mention of symptomatology secondary to the death of a loved one that legitimately could be classified in this category. Typically, these symptoms are nonspecific indications of the lack of healthy accommodation of the loss. Many of them are routinely cited (often without particular reference) as common areas in which complicated mourning evidences itself.

Twelve of the 13 conditions within this diagnostic grouping fall into four primary areas, in which both complicated and uncomplicated mourning are manifested:

1. Relationships (i.e., marital problem, parent-child problem, other interpersonal problem)

2. School or occupational areas (i.e., academic problem, occupational problem)

3. Acting-out behavior (i.e., adult antisocial behavior, child or adolescent antisocial behavior, malingering, noncompliance with medical treatment)

4. Secondary losses and/or concurrent crises (i.e., other specified family circumstances, phase of life or other life circumstance problem, uncomplicated bereavement)

The last condition, borderline intellectual functioning, is a premorbid characteristic of the mourner and does not appear related to complicated mourning except insofar as the mourning might consist of a temporary diminution of cognitive capacities secondary to the loss. Of course, as is the case for developmental disabilities and organic mental disorders, the preexistence of borderline intellectual functioning can complicate any mourning that does occur.

PHYSICAL DISORDERS

The development of a physical disorder is one of the potential outcomes of loss. At this point in the study of grief and mourning, significant research has been undertaken to evaluate the association between bereavement and physical ill health. For specific findings, the reader should consult the following relatively recent reviews: Clayton (1982); Jacobs and Douglas (1979); Klerman and Izen (1977); Lieberman and Jacobs (1987); Lund

(1989); Osterweis et al. (1984); Raphael (1983); Raphael and Middleton (1987); Stroebe and Stroebe (1987); Windholz, Marmar, et al. (1985); and Zisook (1987). Unfortunately, most of the research has been conducted with widows and widowers, and this is a serious impediment to generalization of findings. Nevertheless, the conclusions are significant in terms of creating greater appreciation for the role of physical distress in uncomplicated mourning and physical illness in complicated mourning.

In-depth discussion of this topic is beyond the scope of this book. However, several conclusions can be synthesized from the available studies and should be common knowledge for all bereavement caregivers:

1. Although complicated mourning may assume the form of physical disorder, uncomplicated grief and mourning inherently involve some measures of physical distress.

2. There is inconsistency among the findings regarding the morbidity associated with major loss. This inconsistency stems from methodological differences; the degree of health risk being examined; and differences in self-reported symptoms, perceived deterioration in health status, development of physical disorder, utilization of health care systems, and behaviors that influence health status.

3. Plenty of data demonstrate that bereavement can be and frequently is a great stressor and state of risk for physical disorder and morbidity. Observation suggests several types of associations between bereavement and disease (e.g., exacerbation of existing cardiovascular disease, vulnerability to certain infectious diseases, precipitation of depression leading to suicide, health-damaging behavioral changes; Osterweis et al., 1984). Jacobs and Douglas (1979) suggest that there are three conceptual levels of pathogenic mechanisms: (a) the physiologic level (e.g., autonomic changes characterized by the parasympathetic activation of the conservation-withdrawal reaction, altered immune function or changes in endocrine functioning and neurotransmitters), (b) the behavioral level (e.g., changes in health practices such as neglect of early signs of disease, neglect of proper management of disease, or excessive use of alcohol), and (c) the social level (e.g., loss of care by the deceased, social isolation of bereavement, or lowered economic resources to purchase medical care). Despite the documented association between loss and various types of morbidity and higher prevalence rates, direct causal links between bereavement and disease have not yet been established. However, promising data exist to suggest that grief is a mediating response between loss and illness (Jacobs & Douglas, 1979).

4. Clinical and empirical evidence suggests that complicated mourning may be manifested through the development of a diagnosable

physical disorder. Some of this evidence comes from direct clinical observation about complicated mourning (e.g., Paulley, 1983; Volkan, 1985), whereas much comes from work in the area of psychosomatic illness (e.g., Engel, 1967, 1968; Schmale, 1958) and stress (e.g., Lindemann, 1979).

Suffice it to say, complicated mourning may take the form of physical disorder or may exist in another form concomitant to it. Complicated mourning is present whenever the "normal" physical distress of uncomplicated mourning solidifies into a diagnosable physical disorder if, considering the amount of time that has transpired, there is a compromise, distortion, or failure of one or more of the "R" processes of mourning. One need not only sustain a personality predisposed to somatization to develop a physical disorder after the death of a loved one. Because even uncomplicated bereavement is known to be associated with the development of disease, the development of a physical disorder in itself cannot be taken as prima facie evidence that mourning is complicated. That can only be determined after considering the results of a comprehensive evaluation (see chapter 6) and integrating them with data about the evolution of the physical disorder.

DEATH

Although it is the least frequent of the potential outcomes of loss, death sometimes can be a consequence. This outcome may be the result of complicated mourning or a genuinely inadvertent consequence of the behavior of a person experiencing uncomplicated acute grief (e.g., accidentally falling down the stairs due to one's distress). The determination of whether a death is the result of complicated mourning or accident must be made only with regard to the individual's status vis-à-vis the six "R" processes of mourning.

Death as a form of complicated mourning may be consciously and specifically chosen (i.e., suicide), an immediate result of a complicated mourning reaction (e.g., an automobile crash resulting from the complicated mourning symptom of driving at excessive speed), or a long-term consequence of a complicated mourning reaction (e.g, cirrhosis of the liver after years of alcoholism). In these last two cases, the death may be subintentioned or unintentional but is secondary to the mourner's behavior (e.g., neglect of early disease warnings or change in health practices). The authors cited in the previous section on physical disorders also address the research on mortality after bereavement. Again, as in that area, the risk for increased mortality has been demonstrated. Despite some research problems, the relationship between bereavement and health seems more convincing here than in any other area (Stroebe & Strobe, 1987).

PART II

Assessment and Treatment

CHAPTER 6

Clinical Assessment of Grief and Mourning

All presenting problems require careful assessment. Indeed, the first step in any type of treatment is the evaluation. However, comprehensive assessment in the treatment of mourning—whether uncomplicated or complicated—is typically not accomplished. It is impossible to say exactly why this lack of rigorousness exists, even in experienced caregivers who usually are quite conscientious. However, it may in part be due to the caregiver's assumption that the index death is necessarily the stimulus for the mourner's current state. Unlike the unexplained depression or the diffuse anxiety with which another person may enter treatment, the source of the mourner's distress appears obvious. Further evaluation may therefore seem unnecessary.

In fact, however, the relationship between the index death and the mourner's response is not always so clear-cut. I once saw a woman for treatment whose referring psychiatrist had diagnosed her with a major depression as a result of her husband's death, which had occurred 8 months previously. In treatment, it became clear that her symptoms of complicated mourning were related not to her husband's death but rather to the death of her only child 19 years earlier. The psychiatrist had correctly diagnosed the problem but had attributed it to the wrong source! Obviously, until the proper assessment could be made, treatment in this case was unlikely to address relevant issues.

The fact that what one sees is not necessarily what one gets is not the only issue contributing to incomplete or inadequate assessment of grief and mourning. A second issue concerns the presumption that all that needs to be assessed is loss-related material—and of this loss-related material all that requires evaluation pertains to the index loss. However, bereavement transpires within the context of the complex existence of an individual who is more than merely a mourner, and the mourning response itself is influenced by myriad factors (see Table 2.1). All these factors must be assessed and understood for treatment to be effective.

Clinical experience and the literature repeatedly show three related points, each underscoring the need for proper assessment: (a) grief and mourning are highly idiosyncratic for each person; (b) the same symptom may have totally different meanings and implications for pathology, depending upon its context (e.g., in some cases an hallucination of the deceased is normal, whereas in other situations it is pathological); and (c) intervention is most effective for those mourners identified to be at high risk. In addition, many mourners cannot or do not make the connection between their symptoms and/or dysfunction and a loss and its grief and mourning processes. Caregivers must therefore make the connections for them. For all of these reasons, the importance of a thorough assessment cannot be overestimated.

Toward this end, the present chapter outlines some of the unique assessment issues associated with mourners and discusses various scenarios in which the caregiver might be asked to perform an assessment of a bereaved individual. It also describes the content and use of a structured clinical interview schedule and inventory for assessment, the Grief and Mourning Status Interview and Inventory (GAMSII). The GAMSII itself is provided as an appendix to this volume.

ASSESSMENT ISSUES

A number of unique assessment issues confront the caregiver working with bereaved individuals. Among these are the importance of continual assessment throughout the treatment process, factors relating to the mourner's state of mind, and the caregiver's orientation.

Importance of Continual Assessment

As noted, the mourning processes occur with great idiosyncrasy and much variation. Without an appreciation of all the factors involved, few judgments can be made about the health or pathology of a response, and little confidence can be placed in the efficacy of interventions. In addition, because of constant fluctuation in grief and mourning experiences, assessment must be an ongoing process. Grief and mourning do not necessarily decline in a linear fashion over time, especially over the short term; there are many twists and turns. Indeed, if there are no transitions, something is very wrong with the individual's response.

Although an initial assessment may accurately reveal a mourner's current status, it is only accurate insofar as nothing changes. Assumptions based on initial assessment, without continual monitoring, can be quite incorrect for the mourner down the line. Misinformation is likely to miscue the caregiver, thus contributing to ineffective or, worse yet, harmful interventions incompatible with the mourner's current treatment needs. The caregiver must be perpetually on the alert for fluctuations and changes experienced by the mourner over time and must respond to them throughout the entire treatment process. Very simply, if the caregiver does not know where the mourner is or what she requires at a given point, it is doubtful that interventions will be successful.

Influence of the Mourner's State of Mind on Assessment

Conducting an assessment of a mourner can be different from evaluating an individual under other circumstances because the mourner herself is different and the caregiver's responses to these differences often interfere with proper assessment. Such differences appear to derive chiefly from the mourner's explicit focus on the loss of the loved one, with a consequent devaluation of practically every other topic of discussion. The mourner is less inclined to respond favorably to the caregiver's assessment, and this reluctance can contribute to the typically witnessed scenario of an incomplete assessment.

A number of circumstances combine to place the mourner in this difficult psychological position. First, although other individuals certainly may be obsessed with issues that bring enormous pain or conflict, the mourner experiences additional agony because she has no choice regarding the death—it already has taken place. This is in contrast to the individual who can potentially work through an issue to avoid loss. For instance, in the case of marital difficulties, choices and options are available that might forestall or eliminate loss. This lack of choice regarding the death can make the mourner feel hopeless as well as bitter, and these emotions can interfere with necessary data gathering.

Another important difference between the mourner and another individual coming to treatment is that the state of loss initiating or perpetuating the difficulty is permanent. There will be no end to the problem, and the mourner may be unable to see an end to the pain. By definition, the actual death of the loved one is insoluble. The "correct" response, whatever that may be, will not make the problem (i.e., the loss) go away. Thus, in some ways, the mourner is powerless, impotent, helpless, and victimized. Again, these emotions are not the type that will facilitate the mourner's cooperation in the assessment. There may be a strong "What's the use?" attitude.

The loss may so violate the mourner's assumptive world that there is relatively little ongoing structure, order, stability, or meaning to sustain her. This may cause the mourner to experience even more threat or danger. To the degree that the death of the loved one leaves the mourner lacking a valuable therapeutic resource who normally would provide assistance and support, the mourner will face even more problems. The breadth and intensity of acute grief and the long-term impact of mourning under these circumstances may deplete the mourner of the necessary energy and strength to cope, as well as exacerbate stress, fear of loss of control, and anxiety about the meanings and consequences of often unexpected reactions. All of this can cause the mourner presenting for treatment to be more distressed and less willing to cooperate than an individual presenting for a different sort of problem.

Finally, the death of the loved one may resurrect unfinished business and feelings about old losses. These unresolved or resurrected issues often tend to complicate and aggravate the mourner's tribulations, in turn creating assessment difficulties.

Caregiver Orientation

In addition to factors relating to the mourner's state of mind, problems in the caregiver's orientation can result in a relatively poorer job of assessment of mourners. One central problem is assuming that all the reactions being witnessed in response to the current loss actually pertain exclusively to it and failing to realize that a number of them actually may relate to prior, concurrent, or secondary losses. The caregiver must identify and understand all of the specific losses associated with the death, each of which generates its own grief and mourning processes. Assessment is required to identify and differentiate among these other losses so that they may be addressed in treatment.

Another problem relates to the caregiver's failure to recognize that a good assessment is one of the most important parts of treatment and wish to proceed directly to "real" intervention. It is a mistake to assume that one has the luxury to discover information about the mourner in the course of whatever treatment has been initiated. Rather, one must tailor the treatment based on what is revealed in the assessment and, as noted earlier, carefully observe fluctuations and changes over time.

The caregiver's desire to reduce the mourner's pain as quickly as possible also can be a factor. In eagerness to be sensitive to and assist the bereaved individual, who is obviously suffering, the caregiver may allow insufficient time for proper assessment and proceed to comforting, facilitative, or confrontational treatment techniques before adequate comprehension can be gained of this distinct individual, mourning this specific loss, at this particular time, under these exact circumstances. The caregiver also may think that when a mourner says that she wants to eliminate pain she means it, not recognizing that she wants to maintain her pain as a connection to the deceased and wants to eliminate only what she perceives as the less functional parts.

The motive to reduce pain is laudatory. However, absent or incomplete assessment may actually hurt the mourner if the wrong treatment is applied. For example, Parkes and Weiss (1983) note that the most effective interventions for the conflicted mourning syndrome involve the promotion and facilitation of uncomplicated mourning. Expression of feeling and review of memories are urged. By contrast, in chronic mourning, attempts to promote expression of feelings and memories would only encourage the mourner to remain mired in her grief. Instead, insistence on forward movement and increased autonomy, as well as support for the mourner's taking a more active role in developing goals and making decisions, is appropriate. Yet another approach is warranted in response to the unanticipated mourning syndrome. In this case, the mourner requires repeated opportunities to talk through the implications of the loss and to react emotionally in order to make sense out of the death, bring order, and reduce feelings of being overwhelmed by stress and insecurity. Therefore, comprehensive assessment is necessary to assure that the correct diagnosis has been made and that proper treatment can be initiated.

Other concerns center on the caregiver's reticence to add to the mourner's pain. Specifically, the caregiver may be reluctant to burden the mourner by asking questions not focused specifically on the loss (in those cases where the mourner is unwilling to discuss other things) or by asking questions about the loss (if the mourner is particularly distressed about it). Such reticence also may manifest itself in the caregiver's indiscriminately allowing the mourner to take the lead and make all the choices in treatment to counteract the fact that she has had no control or choice about her loss. Certainly, there are times when such reticence is clinically appropriate. At other times, however, caregiver passivity is clinically unjustified and actually hurts the mourner.

The caregiver also may fail to recognize that mourners are more like themselves before a loss than they necessarily are like other mourners after a loss. Although mourners may have much in common with one another, especially if they have experienced similar losses, they share these commonalities only within the context of their own lives and idiosyncratic experiences of mourning. This is why it is imperative to gain accurate information on each mourner as an individual human being (e.g., personality style, coping resources, support system, psychosocial history) and not merely on that person in terms of her role as mourner.

Finally, the caregiver may mistakenly conclude that, because bereavement is not a "real" mental health problem but a normal reaction to a life change, there is no need to do a full assessment and that compassion, empathy, and support are all the mourner needs. Such an attitude is sometimes a reaction to the previous trend toward inappropriate pathologizing of uncomplicated mourning. In other words, the caregiver refuses to conduct a formal assessment of the problem in order to avoid approaching the mourner's reactions to the loss in the same way an identified psychiatric disorder would be approached. However, sacrificing clinical effectiveness for political reasons may be a case of throwing the baby out with the bathwater and does a significant disservice to the mourner.

FOUR ASSESSMENT SITUATIONS

The caregiver may be called upon to assess grief and mourning in any one of four situations: (a) during a time of crisis; (b) at the beginning of treatment; (c) within the context of ongoing treatment; and (d) for specific purposes, such as legal proceedings or determination of treatment disposition. Each situation has its own philosophy and implications for action. Although the depth and breadth of information gathered may be different and the purposes to which the data are put can vary, the goal and perspective in each situation is the same: to comprehend the grief and mourning experience within the context of the individual's unique past and present.

Regardless of the purpose for which assessment is undertaken, following the identification of the need to work on mourning, treatment may proceed according to a number of options. First, mourning issues may be separated from other treatment issues and addressed in isolation. In other words, treatment focuses exclusively on working to promote the healthy accommodation of the loss, with other topics reserved for subsequent address or identified and put aside. Second, mourning concerns may be integrated with other issues faced by the mourner and addressed as appropriate within the context of ongoing treatment. Here the primary focus is on the overall treatment, with mourning being just one topic of interest. Third, these issues may merely be taken into consideration in designing treatment for the current loss. Finally, the mourner may be referred elsewhere (e.g., to a bereavement specialist or support group) to complete treatment of mourning problems, with this outside treatment being assimilated with treatment provided by the original caregiver. This last option requires careful monitoring in order that splitting and other potential nontherapeutic consequences do not occur when the person is working in two therapeutic domains.

Assessment During Crisis

Assessment during a crisis situation may occur during initial intake, when an individual presents for some type of psychotherapeutic treatment (e.g., at a first session for counseling or therapy). It may take place as well when a caregiver performs a one-time assessment in the capacity of crisis worker (e.g., when an individual presents in the emergency room of a hospital). The issues discussed here are as applicable to an individual in an uncomplicated acute grief crisis as they are to the person who is experiencing a crisis in the context of complicated mourning.

In any event, crisis aspects must be the first priority. Very briefly, appropriate steps must be taken to assure the mourner's safety and the safety of others (e.g., considering the potential for suicide, homicide, unintentioned or subintentioned life-endangering acts or omissions) and to meet immediate needs for medical evaluation and treatment (e.g., providing medication, physical examination, medical testing and consultation, hospitalization). The topic of crisis management is beyond the scope of this work. For further information and guidance, the reader is directed to the writings of his or her own professional discipline or to specific resources, such as those by Aguilera (1990) and Slaby (1989).

By definition, crisis prohibits the comfortable, leisurely, and orderly collection of information. The mourner is simply too distressed. His overriding, immediate need is to articulate his reactions to the loss of his loved one, whether that loss transpired in the near or distant past. Certain basic questions must be asked, however. At the very least, demographic information must be secured, a brief mental status examination conducted, and a diagnostic impression formulated. In addition, the caregiver must attempt to obtain at least a brief account of the following.

1. The nature of the loss and the circumstances around it

2. Whether the loss was expected or unexpected and the degree of its suddenness

3. The meaning of the loss and the degree to which it will influence the mourner's life

4. The mourner's prior losses and how the mourner has coped with them

5. The mourner's current life circumstances and what resources and forms of support are available

A key issue for the caregiver is how to sensitively balance the need for assessment with the mourner's obvious needs. The task of collecting as much data as possible within the constraints posed is not an easy one, especially if the mourner is highly distressed. Frequently, asking direct questions, especially those that do not seem relevant to the mourner's immediate distress (e.g., about previous losses, psychosocial history, personality characteristics), will fail to garner the information the caregiver needs. The mourner is more concerned with telling his story and does not want or necessarily have the control to put aside his immediate upset to provide seemingly irrelevant background.

Given the mourner's attitude, the caregiver must ask the most important assessment questions within the context of attempting to understand and support the mourner and must make them seem relevant to the mourner and connected to his experiences. In other words, rather than asking a series of discrete questions in an interview style, the caregiver must frame the questions within a response to the mourner and gather the necessary data in bits and pieces throughout the interview. For example, instead of asking, "What is the nature and extent of your support system?" the caregiver might offer, "Clearly, this is an overwhelming experience to deal with. Is anyone helping you cope with all of this?" The indirect approach serves to collect the desired information at the same time it validates the mourner and sends the message—so important in crisis—that the mourner has been heard.

The caregiver will have to be quick to capitalize on assessment topics the mourner mentions in passing. For example, during discussion of the presenting problem, the mourner may mention a family member. The caregiver can then seize the opportunity to interrupt and inquire about family background. When the mourner mentions a prior loss or brings up an incident from the past, the caregiver can ask about other losses and past personal history. Many times, the caregiver will need to be creative in posing the necessary questions and inserting them comfortably within the flow of the conversation. Mandatory questions that might not fit within the context of a particular conversation (e.g., those concerning suicidal or homicidal ideation) can be brought up directly with an associative link, such as "You obviously are in a great deal of pain right now. Has that pain raised any thoughts about harming yourself or anyone else?"

In all assessment situations, but especially in a crisis situation, questions should be posed so as to make sense to the person being interviewed and to appear as if they flow logically from preceding comments. The caregiver who makes the mourner feel as though the interview is a game of "Twenty Questions" will lose valuable information. Often, out of concern for asking everything, the inexperienced caregiver rigidly adheres to a fixed order of questioning. This concern is admirable, but sometimes the caregiver can lose connection with the mourner in the attempt to follow an interview or assessment schedule. In such instances, the mourner may not return. Unless important reasons exist to conform strictly to a predetermined schedule (e.g., to achieve reliability in a research study), the caregiver should bear in mind that keeping the schedule at the price of losing the mourner is a poor trade-off.

In a crisis, much of the information that ideally would be requested in an initial meeting must be postponed until later. On some occasions, if the mourner is unable to provide the necessary information during the crisis, the caregiver will have to seek it from other sources, such as family members, medical charts, and so forth. If treatment continues with the same caregiver, questions can be posed at later meetings, when a more comfortable intermingling of assessment and treatment can take place.

Assessment at the Beginning of Treatment

Assessment of issues relating to loss at the beginning of treatment is perhaps the easiest situation for the caregiver, as well as for the mourner, although it is not devoid of difficulty. Assessment at this point is easy in the sense that it occurs simultaneously with the general assessment process that usually commences treatment. The mourner has the mental set to provide information that may or may not seem directly relevant to her reason for seeking intervention.

Clients coming to treatment for issues other than those relating to loss also often wonder about the relevance of assessment topics seemingly unrelated to their perceived focus of treatment (e.g., "I came here to talk about my anxiety about speaking in public. Why are you asking me about my relationship with my parents?"). Just as the caregiver educates the client in this case, so too must the caregiver educate the mourner who inquires about questions that do not appear to deal directly with the death of the loved one (e.g., "I'm coming here for assistance in coping with my sister's murder. Why do you expect me to discuss how I responded to my father's death 10 years ago?"). In both instances, the individual must be helped to understand that a comprehension of the person and her dynamics, as well as the context within which to place the current distress, is needed for treatment to be effective.

It appears that caregivers and mourners alike may be better able to comprehend the need for a global assessment when the issue is one other than death. Perhaps because death is such a dramatic and clear-cut event, it may seem not to need to be integrated with information about other aspects of a person's life. However, such integration is necessary in order to appreciate the meaning of the loss, the individual mourner, and the circumstances within which these two are found, as well as to determine the best course for treatment. With this rationale in mind, the caregiver must point out that the assessment will seek to clarify the influence of the past on the present and the interrelationships among all aspects of the person's life, both of which need to be understood to provide the best possible treatment.

Assessment During Ongoing Treatment

Ideally, a full loss history should be taken during all comprehensive intake evaluations and prior to the commencement of all types of interventions. However, because such a history is not always routinely obtained, at some point during treatment for an issue apparently unrelated to bereavement the need for a complete clinical assessment of grief and mourning may become clear. Perhaps it now is evident that mourning a particular loss is necessary, or that complicated mourning has contributed to, if not caused, the symptomatology that brings the individual to treatment.

The caregiver already may have accumulated much of the information required in work over time with the person. However, obtaining new information may be a bit awkward if it means that the caregiver must shift to a different role (i.e., suddenly becoming more of an interviewer after functioning more as a partner in the treatment process), and the shift must be undertaken with care. Sometimes the shift can be explicit (e.g., "I need to go back and ask you some specific questions about those losses"). At other times the caregiver may obtain the information without identifying a specific purpose. For example, the caregiver might ask about loss in general following a discussion of the mourner's current reactions to divorce.

The options for managing treatment of the now-identified mourning issue are the same as those available if the assessment takes place at the beginning of treatment. One may expect significant reactions from and implications for the mourner if he is sent away from the primary caregiver, with whom he has an established relationship, to focus on issues relating to mourning. Obviously, the need to change caregivers must be evaluated on a case-by-case basis and will be largely dependent on the individuals involved, the type of treatment being practiced, and the philosophy behind it.

Assessment for Specific Purposes

Numerous reasons exist for conducting a time-limited clinical assessment of grief and mourning. Such assessments include, among others, those for determining treatment disposition, obtaining psychiatric diagnosis, supporting legal action, determining suitability to adopt after child loss, and ascertaining the mourning status of caregivers who wish to work with the bereaved. In these circumstances, the mourner is cognizant of the rationale for the assessment and, in most cases, offers little resistance and minimal inquiry about reasons for particular questions. The goal of this type of assessment is the same as for other types: to generate an understanding of the mourner's individual experience. However, the goal may be easier to achieve because of the absence of complicating situational factors.

SPECIFIC AREAS OF ASSESSMENT: USING THE GRIEF AND MOURNING STATUS INTERVIEW AND INVENTORY (GAMSII)

The Grief and Mourning Status Interview and Inventory (GAMSII), a structured interview schedule and inventory for assessing grief and mourning, is a clinical tool. *In no way should it be construed to be a psychological instrument, test, or measurement of any kind.* Although it has been found clinically useful, it has not been subject to the rigorous development, standardization, or norming of a psychometric measure. Rather, it is an attempt to organize the material required in a comprehensive assessment of grief and mourning. It is hoped that continued honing of the GAMSII will further enhance its usefulness for caregivers.

As the following discussion details, the GAMSII is organized into three parts: Part I focuses on basic demographic information. Part II briefly lists the main points in obtaining a comprehensive evaluation of history, mental status, and selected premorbid characteristics. Part III offers a structured interview schedule providing questions in 10 separate loss-related topic areas. This information enables evaluation of the situation with regard to the six "R" processes of mourning and within the context of the factors circumscribing the particular loss and mourner. Treatment decisions and goals can be formulated accordingly.

Part I: Demographic Information

The section on demographic information is self-explanatory. It focuses on such areas as personal identifying information; residence; social, cultural, ethnic, and religious background; marital status; education; military history; occupation; income; religion; pregnancies; family; supports; prior losses; and date of identified current loss(es).

Part II: Comprehensive Evaluation of History, Mental Status, and Selected Premorbid Personality Characteristics

This part of the GAMSII aims to evaluate the overall status and functioning of the individual in order to place specific loss-related aspects in context. In order to make judgments about the person as a complete human being, not exclusively as a mourner, the caregiver must obtain the proper information on all factors influencing the individual in general, as well as on all factors influencing mourning in particular. If the assessment is restricted to loss-related areas, it will be impossible to determine how much of what is presented stems from a grief or mourning reaction and how much represents the individual's premorbid personality and functioning. Without the baseline data necessary to differentiate, to a reasonable level of certainty, grief and mourning from premorbid character, the caregiver's conclusions will be questionable. For example, without information to document that prior to her child's death a woman was a healthy, productive individual, a major depression following the loss might be seen as the result of the woman's characterological functioning and not as a result of the death. Conversely, a person's bizarre modes of thinking following the suicide of a sibling could be misjudged as a grief reaction when they actually reflect a thought disorder present long before the death. Clearly, proper treatment depends on the accurate interpretation of such symptomatology.

Of course, it must be acknowledged that information about predeath functioning can be contaminated by the mourner's current distress, as well as by retrospective distortion. However, problems of this nature are no different from those posed in any clinical situation in which an individual is asked to report on previous events or life history. In all such circumstances, the caregiver must be alert for (a) internal inconsistency; (b) past or present incongruence among thought, affect, and behavior; (c) data that do not corroborate the individual's reports; (d) unreliability of information over time; (e) violation of the caregiver's own norms for this population; and (f) evidence of psychiatric disturbance.

Because each discipline has its own preferred methods, the GAMSII does not provide specific instructions for conducting this portion of the assessment. For further guidance, the reader is referred to his or her own professional literature. However, the completion of Part II should result in a DSM-III-R diagnosis, including (even if there are no diagnoses on Axis I or II) assessment of physical disorders and conditions, severity of psychosocial stressors, and global functioning. The following areas must be covered in a comprehensive psychosocial/medical history.

- Presenting problem

- History of presenting problem

- Past personal history and current psychological functioning

    Psychosocial history and current functioning
    Occupational history and current functioning
    Past psychiatric history and current status
    Substance use history and current status
    Medical history and current status
    Financial history and current status

- Family history (psychosocial, psychiatric, medical, financial) and current status

- Concurrent stresses or crises

The mental status examination must evaluate the following 11 areas.

- Appearance

- Behavior and psychomotor activity

- Speech and language

- Mood and affect

- Thought process and content

- Perceptual disturbances

- Sensorium functions

- Insight and judgment

- Symptoms of depression

- Symptoms of anxiety and post-traumatic stress disorder (PTSD)

- Suicide and homicide risk

An assessment of selected premorbid personality characteristics must occur. Some of this information may be determined from the psychosocial/

medical history and the mental status examination. The remainder must be assessed directly by the caregiver according to his or her usual professional practice. Personality characteristics to be assessed are as follows.

- Ego functioning and strength
- Coping and defense mechanisms, styles, and abilities (specifically when dealing with stress, anxiety, threat, and feelings)
- Frustration tolerance
- Personality dynamics and conflicts
- Characterological scripts
- Sense of self, self-concept, and self-esteem
- Internal versus external locus of control and processing
- Cognitive style and biases
- Problem-solving skills
- Maturity
- Assumptive world components
- Sense of personal meaning and fulfillment in life
- Philosophy of life and values
- Spirituality
- Communication style
- Relationship patterns
- Characteristic ways of managing psychosocial transitions
- Specific strengths, skills, and assets
- Specific vulnerabilities and liabilities

A space to note diagnostic/clinical impressions based on data from Parts I and II is provided at this point.

Part III: Structured Interview Schedule

The individual's present loss is the area to which the majority of caregivers leap when they consider assessment. However, when conducted properly, assessment of loss is more comprehensive than most assume, addressing other current and past losses in addition to the particular death identified as the major stimulus for the present mourning reactions. Part III of the GAMSII provides a structured interview relating to all of the issues pertinent to the individual's present and previous losses. The 10 topic areas included in this section have a direct bearing on the mourner's functioning and experience relative to grief and mourning at the moment of interview and are known to influence long-term adaptation.

Each topic area includes several main questions and, where appropriate, follow-up questions. The caregiver should feel free to ask some or all of these questions depending on the mourner's responses. Inquiries need not be worded exactly as written, nor need the order of their presentation be rigidly followed. Language the mourner will likely understand may be substituted for more technical terminology. In brief, the caregiver should use these questions as general guidelines and tailor this portion of the GAMSII to meet the specific requirements of the situation.

This chapter lists a number of other areas for the caregiver to explore under each main topic. Although these areas are not included on the GAMSII, it is critically important for the caregiver to obtain data about them. The mourner's responses in these areas will be helpful in eliciting and refining the information requested in the larger topic areas. Often, the mourner will volunteer information about these areas. If not, the caregiver may develop specific questions to assess them.

Answers to the questions in the structured interview portion of the GAMSII are designed to enable the caregiver to (a) determine location and degree of progress in the six "R" processes of mourning, whether (and, if so, where) the mourner is fixated on certain mourning processes, and what complicating factors exist; (b) obtain a partial assessment of risk of developing complicated mourning and many of the factors contributing to it; (c) identify specific areas of success and difficulty in moving forward in the new life without forgetting the old; (d) assess type, range, extent, and intensity of grief and mourning reactions; and (e) identify treatment requirements to convert complicated mourning to uncomplicated mourning and facilitate successful accommodation of the loss.

The rest of this chapter examines in some detail the 10 topic areas in Part III of the GAMSII. Specifically, discussion identifies the main questions for each topic area, examines special issues relating to them, and identifies other critical areas for the caregiver to explore.

Topic Area A: Circumstances of the death; events that led up to and followed it

The immediate context for the death is an important area for assessment. Question A–1 for this topic area, "Tell me about the death and what led up to it," attempts to determine the circumstances before and at the death. Follow-up questions pertain to death after an illness.

Question A–2 is "What happened immediately after the death and in the few days thereafter?" (e.g., notifying relatives, making funeral arrangements). If the mourner does not mention such postdeath rituals as funerals, wakes, and memorial services, the caregiver should specifically ask about them and the mourner's reactions to them.

Other areas to explore

- Death surround and specific effects on the mourner: location of death, type of death, circumstances (e.g., traumatic, peaceful, violent, painful, loved one alone); reasons for the death; mourner's degree of preparation for the death; mourner's presence or absence at the death; mourner's degree of involvement at or participation in the death and/or responsibility for it; immediate effect of the death on the mourner

- Mourner's specific reactions to the death surround and its effects

- Circumstances prior to the death and/or context within which it occurred (e.g., after an argument, while the loved one was doing a favor for the mourner, after the mourner was kissed good-bye as usual)

- Mourner's perception of the death as anticipated or unexpected, as well as degree of suddenness

- Mourner's perception of the preventability of the death

- Mourner's perception of the timeliness of the death

- Manner and impact of death notification

- Degree of confirmation of the death

- Mourner's opportunity to see the body, spend time with it, and say good-bye

- Extent of the mourner's comfort with and participation in postdeath rituals; initial impact and subsequent effects of and reactions to them

- Mourner's degree of acceptance of the reality of the death and commencement of grief and mourning during postdeath activities and rituals

Topic Area B: Nature and meaning of what has been lost

Questions for this topic area are designed to determine exactly what the mourner experiences as lost in order to understand precisely what must be mourned. The mourner's answers will help the caregiver begin to identify the changes that must occur in the mourner, the mourner's behavior, and the mourner's assumptive world. Specifically, the mourner's answer to Question B–1, "Tell me about _____ ," helps the caregiver comprehend who and what the mourner has lost. Frequently, this question will lead into a direct discussion of the relationship that existed between the mourner and the loved one. If this topic does not come up spontaneously, the caregiver must ask specifically about the relationship, its history, and its course: "What type of relationship did the two of you have?" (Question B–2).

The caregiver will want to elicit both positive and negative recollections of the deceased and the relationship. Because the latter often are uncomfortable for the mourner, the caregiver must permit discussion of positive attributes prior to inquiring about less positive aspects: "You've told me a great deal about what was positive in the relationship. Could you tell me a little about the aspects that were not so positive?" (Question B–3).

Finally, it is important to have knowledge of the precise meaning of this loss to the mourner, the roles the deceased played in the life of the mourner, meaning of the relationship to the mourner, and any secondary losses experienced as a result of the deceased's absence or type of death, including altered assumptions in the mourner's assumptive world: "Exactly what did _____ and the relationship with him/her mean to you and give to you in your life?" (Question B–4) and "Specifically, what have you lost in your life physically or symbolically with _____'s death?" (Question B–5). The last question asks the mourner to identify any issues remaining with the deceased: "Do you have any unfinished business with _____? Anything you would have wanted to say or do that would have made you more comfortable with ending the relationship but that you never said or did and therefore lack closure on?" (Question B–6).

Other areas to explore

- Unique nature and meaning of the loss

- Characteristics of the relationship lost (i.e., the psychological qualities and nature of the relationship, its centrality to the mourner, the strength of the attachment and levels of ambivalence and dependence)

- History and course of the relationship

- Number, importance, and centrality of roles played and functions served by the deceased; behavior and role relationship patterns

- Secondary losses

- Mourner's perception of the deceased's fulfillment in life

- Ties relating to the deceased and the relationship (i.e., needs, feelings, thoughts, memories, behavior and interaction patterns, hopes, wishes, fantasies, dreams, assumptions, expectations, and beliefs)

- The relationship's fulfillments and disillusionments, disappointments, and frustrations

- Ability to realistically recollect and reexperience the deceased and the relationship

- Extent to which the continued physical presence of the deceased was necessary for the maintenance of the mourner's assumptive world

- Assumptive world changes specific to loss of the deceased and the relationship

- Unfinished business and lack of closure in the relationship with the deceased

Topic Area C: Mourner's reactions to the death and coping attempts

By asking Question C–1, "Please describe for me the type, quality, extent, and intensity of all the various reactions you have had since _____'s death," the caregiver prompts the mourner to consider and evaluate responses (i.e., responses to the death and responses to those responses) in all realms of life: psychological, behavioral, social, biological, occupational, financial, spiritual, and so forth. In addition, this question gives the mourner the opportunity to note any responses that were unexpected or frightening, or that affected the mourner's sense of self.

After getting a clear understanding of the individual's grief and mourning, the caregiver needs to determine which coping strategies and techniques the mourner has employed: "Tell me what you have done to cope with _____'s death" (Question C–2). It is also important to know how the mourner evaluates her success in coping. Toward this end, Question C–3 asks the mourner to complete the following sentence: "I feel that I am coping/have coped with this death . . ."

In order to facilitate intervention later on, it is helpful for the caregiver to determine precisely which are the most difficult aspects for the mourner in coping with the loss and what she has done that has helped her the most. Thus, Question C–4 asks the mourner to complete five additional sentences: (a) "The things that I do/did that help/helped me the most are/were . . ."; (b)"If I have/had problems related to this loss, they seem/seemed to be in the areas of . . ."; (c) "The most difficult parts of this for me are/have been . . ."; (d) "My most major concerns in all of this are . . ."; and (e) "What I have specifically done to try and help myself is . . ."

Other areas to explore

- Degree to which the mourner has completed the "R" processes of mourning

- Defenses against experiencing and expressing recognition of the implications of the death, painful affect, or negative emotions

- Coping strategies and techniques

- Ways of discriminating an undifferentiated mass of painful stimuli into specific components with different causes and demands

- Specific responses known to have profound consequences in bereavement: illogical or magical thinking; heightened guilt and responsibility; intrusive phenomena; high anxiety and/or avoidance; denial; yearning, searching, and hoping for the deceased's return; the two criteria for a healthy relationship with the deceased (i.e., recognition of the death and its implications; continued adaptive movement forward into the new life); depression

Topic Area D: Reactions of others in the mourner's world and perceived degree of support

The reactions of others profoundly affect the mourner, both negatively and positively. In some cases, especially within families, witnessing the distress of others exacerbates the mourner's pain or creates the additional burden of caring for other mourners. In other situations, the reactions of others comfort the mourner by allowing him to see that he is not alone and that others are also moved by the death. In still other situations, the mourner's relationships with others are altered after the death. Questions D–1 and D–2 tap into these areas: "How have others reacted to _____'s death?" and "How have they reacted to your reactions?" Question D–3 inquires about relationship changes: "Have your relationships with others changed since _____'s death?" Question D–4 assesses others' support of the mourner: "What types of support have you received from others to help you cope with _____'s death?"

Questions D–5 and D–6 then ask about the mourner's perception of whether the support and recognition received is sufficient and what effect this perception has had: "Were there any types of support or recognition you required but did not receive or any specific persons from whom you needed support or recognition but did not receive it?" and "How did the support or recognition you did and did not receive affect you and your grief and mourning?"

Finally, Question D–7 probes for missing support or recognition: "What needs for support or recognition remain unmet?"

Other areas to explore

- The acceptance and assistance of the mourner's support system

- Disenfranchised grief and mourning

- The bereaved individual's ability to ask for what he needs from others

- Dynamics of the family as a system and as a constellation of individual mourners

- Number, type, and quality of secondary losses related to social support

Topic Area E: Changes in the mourner and the mourner's life since the death

In general, answers to questions for this topic area help ascertain the extent of the mourner's readjustment and accommodation to the loss and identify the types and extent of changes brought about by the loss, as well as their repercussions. In particular, Question E–1 draws on the way the mourner's life has been altered and gives clues to the extent of secondary losses: "Please describe what has happened to you in the time since _____ died. For example, what changes (either gains or losses; internal or external; physical or psychosocial; psychological, behavioral, social, physical, spiritual, occupational, or financial), if any, have occurred to you, in you, and in your life since _____'s death?" Question E–2, "Do you feel changed by this death?" then attempts to judge the mourner's self-evaluation of change.

If these aspects have not already been brought out, the mourner needs to address the questions "If this death has affected the way you look at and live life, how has it done so?" (Question E–3) and "What, if anything, have you learned (positively or negatively) from this loss?" (Question E–4).

Other areas to explore

- Type and extent of grief and mourning reactions

- Degree to which the mourner has relinquished the old attachments to the deceased and the old assumptive world, including the old ways of relating to the deceased and being in the world

- Degree to which the mourner has readjusted to move adaptively into the new world without forgetting the old (i.e., revised the assumptive world; developed a new relationship with the deceased; adopted new ways of being in the world; formed a new identity)

- Changes occasioned by the death

- Number, type, quality, and effects of secondary losses experienced

- Search for meaning
- Degree to which the mourner has reinvested since the loss
- Positive outcomes or gains from the bereavement

Topic Area F: Mourner's relationship to the deceased and stimuli associated with the deceased

Questions for this topic area attempt to determine whether and how the mourner maintains an active relationship or sense of connection with the deceased and, if so, to provide an appreciation of the nature, quality, and impact of it. Question F–1 concerns the mourner's feelings about the relationship and/or connection with the deceased: "How would you describe _____'s role, if any, in your life at this time? In other words, do you have an ongoing sense of connection to _____ or does _____ play an active part in your ongoing life?"

The caregiver also must assess other ways in which the mourner may experience contact with the deceased. Question F–2 includes prefatory information to normalize unusual or paranormal experiences: "Many times after a person loses a loved one, he or she has some experiences in which there is a sense of the presence of the loved one. Sometimes the mourner takes these experiences as a 'sign' or as some form of communication from the loved one. Sometimes there are vivid dreams, or the mourner has an experience of seeing the image of the deceased or hearing that person's voice. Sometimes mourners are reluctant to talk about this because they think it makes them sound crazy, even though they are not. I know that this happens with many mourners, and I am wondering if anything like this has ever happened to you. Have you ever had any of these types of experiences or anything like them?"

After getting a description of what the existing relationship involves and any paranormal phenomena and the mourner's response to them, the caregiver should inquire, "How are you choosing to deal with _____'s room? Clothing? Other possessions?" (Question F–3). This question should be reframed to suit the mourner's relationship with the deceased (e.g., if a family member died, the mourner would be more likely to be confronted with making decisions about the room and the clothing than if the deceased were a dear friend whose family would take over this responsibility). This question and its follow-ups attempt to discern whether the mourner has saved any mementos and memorabilia and whether any of these are linking objects (Volkan, 1972).

The caregiver will want to get a sense of how the mourner handles and is affected by stimuli associated with the deceased and by memories in general. This includes not only physical or sensory stimuli such as mementos or fragrances, but also psychosocial stimuli (e.g., the types of events and experiences that give rise to STUG reactions—see chapter 2) and spontaneously occurring memories. Questions F–4 and F–5 focus on this aspect: "At this point, how is it for you when you come across things that remind you of _____ or bring back memories of him/her? For example, how may you react when you see pictures of him/her, suddenly remember a special time you shared, or go to an event and wish he/she would be there with you, such as a wedding or holiday gathering?" and "Have you noticed any responses on your part around the anniversary of the death, during other occasions, or under any other circumstances (i.e., STUG reactions)?"

Last, the caregiver needs information revealing whether the mourner's experience is being influenced by any promises, secrets, unfinished business, or contracts with the deceased. Such agreements, explicit or implicit, may have been made on the deathbed or earlier in the relationship. They may have been made directly with the deceased or be what the mourner believes the deceased would want. Question F–6, "How do you think _____ would want you to respond in your grief and mourning over him/her?" and its follow-ups are therefore designed to elicit this information.

Other areas to explore

- Degree to which the mourner has relinquished old attachments to the deceased

- Degree to which the mourner has developed a new relationship with the deceased

- Degree to which the mourner has met the two criteria for a healthy new relationship with the deceased (i.e., recognition of the death and its implications; continued adaptive movement forward into the new life)

- Degree and appropriateness of the mourner's reinvestment since the loss

- Use of personal bereavement rituals

- Identification with the deceased

- Healthy ways of keeping the deceased alive

- Content of memories

- Linking objects

- STUG reactions

- Intrusive repetitions of thought

Topic Area G: History, status, and influence of prior loss experiences, including mourner's methods of coping

The current influence of prior loss must be evaluated. Question G–1, "What other difficult physical or psychosocial losses have you experienced in your life?" pinpoints the mourner's prior loss experiences. As much as possible, the caregiver should attempt to obtain information about each particular loss, ascertain how it was coped with, and discern whether any unfinished business is associated with it. If losses are quite numerous, the caregiver may have to consider them as an aggregate or focus on only the most important ones. Question G–2, "What types of things did you do to cope with each loss?" and its follow-ups attempt to clarify particular aspects of each loss.

Other areas to explore

- The mourner's general coping behaviors, personality, and mental health

- Unfinished business

- Past experiences with loss and death, the mourner's success in coping, and the information and expectations derived from these experiences

- Resurrection of past losses by the current loss

Topic Area H: Mourner's self-assessment of healthy accommodation of the loss now and in the future

The mourner's self-assessment of healthy accommodation of the loss now and in the future is a gauge of the mourner's current interpretation of how the loss is being handled and the degree of hope that accompanies it. Information in this area is important because ultimately the caregiver may have to challenge any unrealistic expectations about what constitutes healthy accommodation (see Topic Area I). This topic focuses solely on the current evaluation, however. Several of the questions demand a numerical self-rating in order to compare responses. The questions for this area include "Compared to how you coped with and functioned in life in general prior to the death, how do you think you are doing now?" (Question H–1); "How do you think you are coping/have coped with this specific loss?" (Question H–2); "To what extent, if any, has the loss been integrated into your life?" (Question H–3); "How do you view the future?" (Question H–4); "How do you think you will ultimately do in your grief and mourning, and in learning to live without _____?" (Question H–5); "What remains for you to do or change in your grief and mourning and in your life to reach the point where you will be doing the best you can in coping with this loss and living without _____?" (Question H–6); "Have you made a decision to 'make it'?" (Question H–7); "In what areas is/will it be the hardest to re-build your life and/or to reinvest in it?" (Question H–8); "How do you, if you do, make sense out of this loss and its having occurred in your life?" (Question H–9); and "In retrospect thus far, is there anything you would do differently in your grief and mourning?" (Question H–10).

Other areas to explore

- Degree to which the mourner has readjusted to move adaptively into the new world without forgetting the old (i.e., revised the assumptive world; developed a new relationship with the deceased; adopted new ways of being in the world; formed a new identity)

- Degree to which the mourner has reinvested since the loss

- Criteria for successful accommodation of the loss

Topic Area I: Mourner's degree of realistic comprehension of and expectations for grief and mourning

The appropriateness of the mourner's information and expectations about grief and mourning will influence not only her self-evaluations, but also the permission she gives herself to experience and undertake the various processes of grief and mourning. Whereas the previous topic assessed how the mourner thought she was doing with her mourning, this topic assesses the accuracy and appropriateness of the mourner's knowledge and expectations about mourning, upon which the prior assessment was made. Questions designed to assess awareness of healthy mourning include "What do you think is necessary to cope with or survive a loss like this?" (Question I–1); "In your estimation, what is normal to experience after this kind of death?" (Question I–2); "In what ways do you think you have been a healthy and successful mourner?" (Question I–3); and "How do you anticipate the rest of your mourning will go?" (Question I–4).

It also will be helpful to know what the mourner feels is needed to arrive at a good future accommodation of the loss. Question I–5 focuses on this area: "What will indicate to you when you have achieved the best possible accommodation of this loss or are coping the very best you ever will be able to with _____'s death?"

Other areas to explore

- Degree to which the mourner has readjusted to move adaptively into the new life without forgetting the old (i.e., revised the assumptive world; developed a new relationship with the deceased; adopted new ways of being in the world; formed a new identity)

- Criteria for successful accommodation of the loss

- The harmful nature of myths and stereotypes about grief and mourning

- The mourner's past experiences with loss and death and the information and expectations derived from them

- How aspects of the mourner's social; cultural; ethnic; generational; and religious, philosophical, and spiritual background have influenced the mourner's knowledge and expectations

Topic Area J: Open topic

The open topic is included in order to ensure that the mourner has the opportunity to express what he feels is most important. Inquiries include "Are there any areas pertinent to your grief and mourning that we have not examined?" (Question J–1); "Are there any topics we have discussed that you feel we should consider further?" (Question J–2); and "What do you feel is the most important piece of information about your grief and mourning?" (Question J–3).

At the end of Part III, space is provided for noting diagnostic/clinical impressions derived from it. Subsequent to this, the caregiver is asked to summarize diagnostic/clinical impressions from all three parts of the GAMSII. This final synthesis of information is then used to help formulate treatment decisions and goals.

CHAPTER 7

Formal Therapeutic Approaches to Complicated Mourning

Although many authors have developed theoretical models of bereavement processes and have offered either general clinical suggestions for work with mourners or individualized suggestions for particular losses, far fewer have outlined concerted, specific approaches for intervention. This chapter examines five major therapeutic approaches to complicated mourning: focal psychotherapy; re-grief therapy; behavioral, cognitive, and social approaches; Gestalt therapy; and time-limited dynamic psychotherapy for phase-oriented treatment of the stress response syndrome. In addition, two more general approaches, useful within the context of any treatment paradigm, are described: Worden's treatment procedures for resolving pathological grief, and Rando's schema for creating therapeutic bereavement rituals.

FOCAL PSYCHOTHERAPY

Beverley Raphael's (1975, 1983) model of focal psychotherapy for the treatment of complicated mourning involves an assessment of the particular syndrome of complicated mourning, with specific treatment being dictated by the syndrome and its etiology. Detailed discussion of the syndromes identified by Raphael is presented in chapter 3.

In general, the goal of therapy is to convert the syndrome into a more normal pattern in which the individual is able to mourn appropriately. The strategies and techniques described may be conducted either in the immediate crisis, when inherent lowered defensiveness permits more rapid working through, or later, after pathological patterns have solidified and become shored up with more rigid defenses, making working through more difficult. The discussion here focuses on the latter perspective. However, Raphael maintains that treatment can be employed when assessment indicates bereavement is beginning to take a pathological course and need not wait until problems have existed for an extended period.

Raphael has discussed her treatment model in relation to the forms of complicated mourning described in the following pages. However, her techniques also can be extrapolated to other syndromes of complicated mourning.

Absent, Delayed, or Inhibited Grief

In absent, delayed, or inhibited grief, the caregiver's main tasks are to explore indirectly the reasons the bereaved cannot accept the death (e.g., dependence on the deceased, guilt about the death, fear of grief affects) and to review repeatedly the mourner's relationship with the deceased. In doing so, the mourner's defenses will be revealed and some aspects of mourning will be facilitated. The caregiver may interpret the absence of warranted affect as the mourner's fear of its release. If the emotional release begins but is then quickly covered up, the caregiver may interpret this as the mourner's fear of loss of control. When it appears that guilt over the lost relationship interferes with acceptance of the death, the caregiver may interpret this as the mourner's concern that previously held fantasies about killing the deceased now seem fulfilled by the death.

It may be necessary to return repeatedly to the lost relationship and its history, the death and its circumstances, and the social network (especially the family) and its response. Direct confrontation of denial rarely will succeed. It more often leads to a stalemate or control battle between mourner and caregiver, with the caregiver's believing the mourner must mourn and the mourner's adhering tenaciously to her denial and suppression because, for reasons neither has yet discovered, she cannot tolerate either recognition of the loss or affective release. It will be in the exploration of the death and the relationship that these reasons will be discovered and the denial ultimately relinquished.

In focal psychotherapy, the caregiver conveys certain recognized facts to the mourner, either explicitly through interpretation or more gradually as the treatment process unfolds. These include the following points.

1. The mourner's inner pain is obviously difficult to bear and express.

2. Inner pain and other fears are common among mourners, and the caregiver understands this.

3. The mourner's defenses serve a psychological purpose and therefore will not be torn down harshly or without due consideration of their function.

4. The mourner is reluctant, probably for a variety of reasons, to relinquish the deceased, and together the mourner and the caregiver will explore and understand the reasons and feelings associated with this reluctance.

5. The mourner, like many other mourners, dreads and wishes to avoid the pain of loss and other intense emotions that naturally occur at this time, especially anger, sadness, and guilt.

Distorted Grief

In distorted grief, some degree of inhibition or suppression operates alongside powerful distortions. There are two common patterns: extreme anger and extreme guilt. In grief distorted by extreme anger, the caregiver's aims and techniques are similar to those described for absent, delayed, or inhibited grief. However, particular emphasis is placed on helping the mourner work through the displacement aspects of the anger and the specific problems created by the loss of a relationship that was dependent or that symbolized something quite special and irreplaceable.

In grief distorted by extreme guilt, the dynamics reside in denied ambivalence and guilt. Here again, the caregiver will employ techniques described for absent, delayed, or inhibited grief in order to encourage and promote unexpressed mourning. The caregiver must explore the circumstances of the death, the lost relationship, and the support available to help the mourner resolve ambivalence. In addition, a special need exists to investigate the origins of the ambivalence in the relationship, its links to earlier repetition compulsions, and the mourner's parent-child relationships. As noted, a death wish toward the deceased may be discovered. When the mourner can voice this wish and face it with the caregiver, she has taken a major step toward resolution.

It is important that the caregiver abstain from too early a reassurance that the mourner did her best or all she could for the deceased. The mourner knows full well, consciously or unconsciously, the extent of any murderous fantasy she had entertained. She is genuinely reassured only when this destructive wish is brought out in the open and confronted by a caregiver or significant other who can be nonjudgmental in helping her come to terms with it. If the guilt is legitimate (i.e., linked to real behaviors and not originating purely in fantasy), the caregiver's role will be to help the mourner accept and live with this fact. Many individuals experiencing this type of complicated mourning hold on to their guilt in an attempt to appease the dead. If the guilt becomes unmanageable, these mourners may sink into clinical depression. If they also fantasize reunion with the deceased, they can become suicide risks. Needless to say, any suicidal preoccupations must be dealt with carefully in treatment.

Chronic Grief

Because chronic grief is only diagnosed when acute responses fail to subside, treatment may be complicated by the mourner's pathologically defensive pattern and entrenched role. Because of secondary gains associated with controlling and punishing others, as well as eliciting their care, the mourner may have little motivation to relinquish the grief or the ongoing relationship with the deceased it symbolizes. Frequently, however, chronic mourning ultimately alienates all members of the support system.

As is the case for the types of pathological grief previously described, the caregiver will need to focus on the lost relationship with the deceased, the nature of the death, and the perception of social support. In these cases, the particular work of treatment is to explore why the relationship has such special meaning to the mourner and why it cannot be relinquished. It also is necessary to explore what roles and identity the mourner had in relation to the deceased because it only may be with the adoption of new roles and identity that the deceased can be given up.

Behavioral strategies often can be useful in treating these mourners. Setting a series of concrete tasks—such as making fewer visits to the grave or sorting less often through the deceased's possessions—can help these individuals make some progress. The development of other sources of gratification and the establishment of a role alternate to that of chronic griever are two processes that can contribute to a more positive outcome. However, these individuals are notoriously difficult to treat and often hold on to mourning as if to keep the deceased alive through grief.

RE-GRIEF THERAPY

Many caregivers are familiar with Vamik Volkan's concept of the linking object, an object the mourner invests with the magical power to maintain an external relationship with the deceased. Therefore, his re-grief therapy is probably the best known treatment for complicated mourning. This treatment, originally developed to provide care for patients hospitalized briefly for established pathological mourning and reactive depression occasioned by a death (Volkan & Showalter, 1968), has been discussed frequently since then (Volkan, 1971, 1972, 1981, 1985, 1987; Volkan, Cillufo, & Sarvay, 1975; Volkan & Josephthal, 1979).

Volkan (1975) describes the purpose of re-grief therapy as follows:

> Re-grief therapy is designed to help the patient to bring into consciousness some time after the death his memories of the one he has lost and the experiences he had with her, in order to test them against reality, to accept with affect—especially appropriate anger—what has happened, and to free himself from excessive bondage to the dead. (p. 334)

An overview of Volkan's theory of grief and mourning is presented in chapter 3. The following summary of re-grief therapy is based on Volkan's (1985) delineation of the psychotherapy of complicated mourning. The steps described in the following pages reflect my own conceptualization of the treatment process; for a more detailed discussion, the reader is directed to the primary source.

The Re-Grief Treatment Process

According to Volkan, the entire re-griefing process can be completed successfully within 2 to 4 months, with sessions held three to four times weekly. In general, it involves the following eight steps.

Patient selection

Candidates for re-grief therapy have complications in the course of mourning that have led to either established pathological mourning or reactive depression. These two states can coexist, and some symptoms indicative of complications in the initial stage of mourning may appear in both. Although a mixed clinical picture may exist, there are ways to pinpoint established pathological mourning:

> One identifies established pathological mourning more clearly in the patient who uses a linking object and is preoccupied with longing for, yet dreads, the return of the one mourned, although the mourner may also have some degree of disruptive identification with the one mourned [as in reactive depression]. . . . The patient taken into re-grief therapy has a strong and persistent hope of seeing the deceased alive again, but still has a desire to "kill" the deceased in order to complete mourning . . . [and] places a high value on psychological contact with the deceased's representation, which may be perceived as an introject. Those able to externalize the representation onto their linking objects may not report an introject but, in any event, the patient is clearly trying to relate ambivalently to an unassimilated representation of the one lost. (Volkan, 1985, p. 286)

Other characteristics of pathological mourning are listed in the discussion of Volkan's work in chapter 3.

Demarcation

In the demarcation phase, the caregiver helps the mourner distinguish between what belongs to the mourner and what belongs to the deceased's representation. A detailed and empathic uncovering of the mourner's history provides the material necessary to accomplish this task. The caregiver must not question the mourner directly when taking the history. The development of a nondirective exchange is the vehicle through which the caregiver can help the mourner begin to differentiate his thoughts, attitudes, and feelings from those influenced by the introject of the deceased. Volkan asserts that the person suffering from established pathological mourning inevitably will broach the subject of death and the deceased. A focus on the history and associations pertaining to the lost relationship enables the caregiver to help the mourner see what has been taken in, evaluate feelings about the introject or representation of the deceased, and decide which aspects so bother the mourner that he wants to reject them. The manifest content of dreams helps illustrate how the mourning process became arrested and why the mourner feels he carries a special representation of the deceased, thus enabling him to understand the fixation.

The caregiver must avoid sharing too quickly the reasons formulated for the mourner's fixation. This can slow down the affective-cognitive process involved in the activation of a forward-moving mourning process. The demarcation phase may take several weeks, with mourner and caregiver meeting three to four times weekly. During this time, the caregiver does not encourage an outpouring of emotion but rather helps the mourner prepare for it. If the mourner feels unable to accommodate the rising flood of emotion, the caregiver may respond, "What is your hurry? We are still trying to learn about the circumstances of the death and the reasons why you can't grieve. When the time comes, you may allow yourself to grieve" (Volkan, 1985, p. 287).

In summary, during the demarcation phase, the caregiver expands the formulation that will guide future clarification and interpretation and learns more about the reasons for the patient's arrested mourning process and inability to grieve.

Review

During the review phase, the mourner is encouraged to reminisce about the deceased, circumstances of the final illness or accident, conditions within which the news of the death arrived, reactions to seeing the body, and particulars of the funeral. It is important for the caregiver to remember that direct questioning is much less productive than encouraging the patient to offer such topics himself and to display appropriate emotions while doing so.

Clarification of ambivalence

At this point, the caregiver expresses through therapeutic neutrality and empathy (not through verbal commentary) that ambivalence toward the deceased is normal. The caregiver also promotes both the mourner's curiosity about the ambivalence and the insight that it is largely responsible for the mourner's quandary over wanting to "save" the deceased as opposed to "kill" the deceased once and for all. Once the mourner can readily alternate between the negative and positive aspects of the ambivalence, he is apt to become angry.

Abreaction: Beginning to re-grieve

The anger the mourner experiences authenticates the reality of the death, although it may be diffused and directed toward others. It is as if the mourner had returned to the initial stage of the dilemma. The caregiver, understanding the mourner's need to keep the deceased alive symbolically, slowly clarifies the relationship between the mourner and the deceased and interprets it along with the reasons for the normal angry feelings. If everything is going well at this point, *abreaction,* or emotional reliving (Bibring, 1954) of certain past experiences connected with the deceased or the death, may occur. These reflect the revisiting of the initial response to death and the recommencement of the work of mourning. The mourner has thus begun to re-grieve. Volkan notes that certain impulses, such as death wishes, can be expected to surface and that the mourner's readiness to have them interpreted and to reduce guilt feelings can be assessed.

Revisiting and revising

Typically, the mourner with established pathological mourning employs the defense mechanism of splitting ego functions in the initial reaction to the death. The caregiver points this out by helping the mourner focus on the manner in which the deceased was perceived as being dead. This focus will be efficacious only if it occurs at an emotionally suitable time and is not merely an intellectual exercise. The mourner may reveal genuine surprise and blurt out something like "I thought he was not breathing any more. But I didn't really look!" (Volkan, 1985, p. 288). At this juncture, the caregiver has helped the mourner to revisit the point at which the ego splitting commenced and to reevaluate reality.

Many individuals suffering from established pathological mourning report problems at the funeral and that they did not actually witness the casket being lowered into the grave. When the caregiver inquires at the appropriate time, "How do you know that the dead person is buried?" the mourner is likely to be surprised to realize that one part of the self never did believe that the burial had been accomplished. It is not uncommon for a mourner then to feel anger at those who had stood in the way of his participation at the funeral ritual. The caregiver makes clear that, although the mourner felt and knew that the death had occurred, he paradoxically had continued to behave as though nothing had happened.

Working with the linking object

The most important part of the work of confrontation, clarification, and interpretation of death-related impulses, fantasies, and wishes toward the deceased—as well as of the defenses the mourner uses against them—is the focus on the linking object. Because it has physical existence and properties that reach the senses, the linking object has greater "magic" than the introject of the deceased. Once the mourner comprehends how the linking object has been used to maintain absolutely controlled contact with the image of the deceased, as well as to postpone (or "freeze") mourning, he can use it to activate mourning. The caregiver suggests that the linking object be brought into a session. Initially, the mourner usually avoids the object. Then the caregiver requests permission to keep it, pointing out that its magic exists solely in the mourner's perception of it. When it is ultimately introduced into a therapy session, it is placed between the mourner and caregiver long enough for the mourner to feel its spell. The mourner may be asked to touch it and say what comes to mind.

Volkan reports continuing to be astonished at the intensity of emotion congealed within the linking object, and he warns caregivers about it. This emotion serves to unlock the psychological processes that up until this point were contained in the linking object itself. The emotional storms triggered can continue for weeks. Initially diffuse, they eventually become differentiated. Together, mourner and caregiver can identify such emotions as anger, guilt, and sadness. The linking object finally loses its power irrespective of whether the mourner chooses to dispose of it.

Disorganization and reorganization

The clarifications and interpretations associated with the death and the deceased, along with the sharper focus on these subjects made possible by the use of the linking object, lead to the final phase of disorganization. This is then followed by reorganization and the appearance of sadness. Secondary-process thinking is then required to help heal the wound opened by the re-grief experience. Volkan reports that many individuals who had never before visited the grave of the deceased do so now, as if to say good-bye. Those who have been unable to arrange for a tombstone now can make the necessary arrangements. Many mourners at this point plan some memorial ritual. Many consult clergy for religious consolation as they begin accepting the death. They can feel sad but no longer need to feel guilty.

In some mourners coming to the end of treatment, Volkan uses the manifest content of serial dreams to indicate what point they have reached in their re-griefing. Many appear to feel that their introject has departed, leaving them in peace and feeling free, even excited, at the lifting of their burden and the seeking of new love objects.

Issues in Conducting Re-Grief Therapy

Volkan (1985) stresses that elucidation of the important meanings of the mourner's loss in re-grief therapy are of little help if emotions and ideation are not blended:

> Throughout the treatment, patients experience a variety of
> emotions as they gain insight into their inability to let the
> dead person die. This insight is reached by the clarifications
> and interpretations given, the therapy being designed to
> loosen up and reactivate the arrest of the mourning process.

The patient's resistance to acknowledging the fixation in the
work of mourning is interpreted. . . . The use of the linking
object brings about special emotional storms that are not cura-
tive without interpretation that engages the close scrutiny of
the patient's observing ego. Thus the link to the representation of the dead, externalized into the linking object, is
brought into the realm of the patient's inner experience.
(pp. 289–290)

Volkan also notes that, despite the use of the special device of the
linking object, the transference relationship is still the vehicle whereby
insight into ambivalence and the conflict between longing and dread may
be gained and resolution accomplished. As in psychoanalytic therapy, the
caregiver aims to develop a therapeutic alliance without encouraging
an infantile transference neurosis. To avoid potential development of a
ripened infantile transference neurosis, the caregiver prematurely interprets those transference phenomena that could lead to it (e.g., interrupt-
ing full displacement of the deceased's representation onto the caregiver
in order to keep the mourner aware of complications in mourning the loved
one). Nevertheless, the mourner's reactions to parallel situations of loss
involving the caregiver (e.g., separations at weekends) are interpreted in
due time. Such interpretations make it possible to work through past conflicts with the deceased in a focal way. The fresh grief stimulated by the
separation from the caregiver at termination also can be put to appropriate
use. Volkan (1985) concludes:

Transference reactions are inevitable but infantile transference
neurosis is not; selected reference to and interpretations of
the transference reactions may be therapeutic by providing
close and intimate contact within the therapeutic setting as
the patient's conflicts are understood. Thus, although re-grief
therapy is brief, lasting for months rather than years, it is
intense, intimate, and certainly not superficial. (p. 290)

Volkan offers two caveats in his discussion of established pathological
mourning and psychoanalysis. His comments have relevance for all types
of treatment. First, the individual with low level character organization
who presents characteristics of established pathological mourning is probably not a good candidate for re-grief therapy. Second, the presence of
established pathological mourning interferes with effective resolution of
other psychopathologies, especially when linking objects are used secretly.
Although it appears paradoxical, complicated mourning must be ameliorated before antecedent psychopathologies (e.g., dependence and aggression) can be treated, even though these preexisting psychopathologies
have caused the mourner to react to the loss in a pathological fashion.

Parenthetically, Volkan notes that some mourners with established pathological mourning may benefit greatly from long-term psychoanalytic treatment either instead of or after completing re-grief therapy.

Finally, Volkan states that the risk of suicide in those experiencing
established pathological mourning is not as great as it is in reactive depression. This appears to be because in established pathological mourning the
individual is protected from the impulse toward self-destruction by a stable
linking object or introject. The mourner maintains the illusion of contact
with a representation of the deceased; however, the illusion is not included
in the self-representation (as in depression), but remains exterior to it.
Thus, the mourner is aggressive toward the introject or the linking object
and not toward the self. More important, the illusion maintained mitigates
feelings of guilt because through it the mourner can, if he chooses, "bring
the dead back." When suicide is attempted by the person suffering from
established pathological mourning, the effort is not of the melancholic type
but reflects the wish for magical reunion with the representation of the
deceased. Suicide can seem a compelling prospect to the mourner when
anniversary reactions initiate a strong desire to merge with the representation of the loved one. However, complications in mourning also can lead
to unusual new symptoms (i.e., diagnosable mental or physical disorders).
These carry with them their own requirements for treatment, as well as
their own risks for suicide.

BEHAVIORAL, COGNITIVE, AND SOCIAL APPROACHES

Along with increased analysis of mourning outside of the realm of psychoanalytic thought, recent years have brought a corresponding increase in alternative treatments for both uncomplicated and complicated
mourning. A number of the treatments designed specifically for complicated mourning combine aspects of behavioral, cognitive, and social
approaches.

General Contributions of Learning Theory

In offering a behavioral analysis of the grief process, Brasted and Callahan
(1984) make several important points relevant to learning theory and response to loss. These investigators provide a complete explanation of uncomplicated grief and mourning in behavioral terms. Based upon this, the
caregiver would do well to bear the following ideas in mind when treating
complicated mourning.

1. Early exposure to loss appears to have the effect of sensitization.
   For this reason, those who have experienced the death of a significant other early in the lifespan appear to evidence more intense
   grief responses to subsequent significant deaths.

2. In behavioral theory, grief may be conceptualized as both anxiety and depression, and both anxiety and depression models of treatment are applicable in psychotherapy for pathological grief.

3. Pathological grieving appears to be a function of the mourner's successful or partially successful avoidance of normal grief stimuli. When the mourner is confronted with aversive stimuli generated by cues associated with the deceased, the avoidance that occurs prohibits the extinction of the mourner's experience of pain.

4. Because unrewarded responses must occur for a response to extinguish, mourners who distract themselves from experiencing the frustration of contact with stimuli associated with the deceased probably only delay their grief and mourning. Early avoidance of grieving may indicate future pathology.

5. Intensity of the grief response in and of itself cannot be construed as pathological, given that early losses can predispose mourners to grief that, although more intense than usual, is not necessarily pathological.

6. Treatment and prevention of pathological grief may involve skills training to enable effective coping with the new set of contingencies occasioned by the death of the loved one.

Applying the Behavioral Approach

In an article on behavioral approaches to grief, Averill and Wisocki (1981) discuss the application of behavioral techniques to the treatment of normal and pathological grief reactions. Although their focus was behavioral intervention for elderly individuals, their comments easily can be extrapolated to mourners of any age. Briefly, Averill and Wisocki note that behavior therapists tend not to focus on grief per se, but rather on the treatment of its specific reactions. Despite being occasioned by the loss of a loved one, the various components of grief cannot be attributed to any single cause. These observers therefore assert that grief cannot be alleviated by any single procedure and that treatment goals and procedures must be established depending on the component reactions that present difficulties. For this reason, they view assessment as critical in designing a treatment strategy.

In the treatment of pathological grief reactions, the application of a behavioral model yields three essential parts: a thorough assessment, the establishment of goals for therapeutic operations, and the selection of effective treatment procedures.

Assessment

Assessment is the most important aspect in the treatment of both normal and pathological grief reactions. In general, during the assessment, the caregiver must determine (a) the quality of the grief (e.g., whether it contains elements of pathology, has been unduly prolonged, follows a normal progression); (b) who is responsible for bringing the mourner into therapy and, therefore, who has defined the grieving behavior as requiring treatment; (c) the functional extent of the problem (e.g., how the grieving behavior may be affecting other life conditions); and (d) the mourner's cultural, generational, and personal values about grief.

Specifically, assessment must be made of the particular responses causing difficulties, including frequency of occurrence, intensity, duration, latency, and schedule of occurrence. In addition, consideration must be given to events that set the occasion for the behaviors (i.e., antecedents) and the events that maintain them (i.e., consequences), to be identified at both proximal and distal points. The most important distal antecedents concern the manner of bereavement (e.g., degree of suddenness of death, quality of premorbid relationship with deceased), and the most important distal consequences concern what it means to the mourner to relinquish the grieving behavior (e.g., loss of secondary gain).

Treatment goals

Treatment goals must be tailored to the specific responses presenting difficulty. Whatever the nature of the problem, goals should be established through discussion with the mourner and delineated in operational terms so both mourner and caregiver have a clear idea of the direction of the therapy. Depending upon the target behaviors, goals may address five broad categories.

1. *Physiological complaints.* Goals may be set to reduce specific somatic symptoms (e.g., insomnia or migraine headaches), increase physical activity, promote compliance with medical regimens and self-care programs, and so forth.

2. *Subjective (private) events.* Goals may focus on altering self-concepts, specific emotional experiences and desires (e.g., suicidal urges), disturbing fantasies, and maladaptive thought patterns.

3. *Overt behavior.* Goals may be set to change specific observable responses, including behavioral excesses (e.g., alcohol abuse), compulsions, avoidance reactions, and so forth.

4. *Interpersonal relationships.* Goals may seek to reduce isolation and improve the quality of social interaction.

5. *Environmental support.* Goals may be established to change either physical or social environmental structures to support or facilitate therapeutic gains.

Treatment procedures

Averill and Wisocki note that the caregiver can choose from a wide range of behavioral techniques in the treatment of pathological grief. They mention the following, noting that these are only a few among many: relaxation, systematic desensitization, covert conditioning, cognitive rehearsal, thought stopping, role-playing, contingency contracting, and skills training.

They perceive that, in many cases, application of these techniques to the symptoms of grief can be a relatively straightforward extension of ordinary clinical practice with behavioral approaches. For example, relaxation procedures may be used to help the mourner overcome general feelings of anxiety or to alleviate insomnia. Thought stopping can be used to reduce stress associated with troublesome cognitions. However, this last example points to one of the problems in treating grief reactions behaviorally. The technique of thought stopping should be used only for thoughts that impede the mourner's recovery (e.g., negative self-references contributing to depression), not necessarily for *all* painful thoughts. Shutting out all hurtful thoughts of the deceased would interfere with appropriate grief work.

Averill and Wisocki offer several clinical caveats associated with the use of behavioral techniques. First, because of their complex origins, grief symptoms may not yield to treatment as readily as other forms of distress. As illustrated by the previous example, deciding which symptoms of grief should be treated at which points in time is not always easy. Second, it cannot be assumed that a technique effective in treating a symptom in a nongrief context (e.g., insomnia) necessarily will be effective in treating the same symptom when occasioned by bereavement. Averill and Wisocki suggest the need for more research in this area. Finally, they point out that behavior therapy focuses on the antecedents and consequences of a reaction, with the time perspective typically limited even when distal events are taken into account. As a complex syndrome, grief cannot be understood without taking into account long-term historical causes and biological and sociocultural evolution. Because such issues are not usually the focus of behavior therapists, there tends to be a lack of involvement of these practitioners in the problem of grief, despite the skills and resources they have to offer for the treatment of specific grief reactions.

"Pure" Behavioral Therapy

The individual most identified with unadulterated, or "pure," behavior therapy is Ronald Ramsay (Ramsay, 1976, 1977, 1979; Ramsay & Happée, 1977). Ramsay (1977) compares unresolved grief with phobias, noting that both evidence anxiety and an avoidance of confrontation and difficult situations. He argues convincingly that the individual with unresolved grief exhibits the same type of avoidance behavior witnessed in phobics, only in bereavement the numerous stimuli and situations that evoke pain and anguish associated with the loss are avoided:

If we take it further and look at the behaviour of people
suffering from unresolved grief, we see avoidance behaviour

similar to that of phobics. Many of the former will not enter situations which will evoke the sense of loss; certain streets are avoided, personal belongings are not touched, "linking objects" . . . are locked away, certain tunes are never played. *The stimuli and situations which could get the grief work going, which could elicit the undesired responses so that extinction could take place, are avoided.* From Eysenck's theoretical explanation of how phobic reactions develop and are maintained, we would expect some grieving people to get "hung up" or even to become more depressed and miserable over time as they avoid and escape. (p. 133, emphasis added)

Ramsay would supplement this explanation of unresolved grief with behavioral conceptions of depression. Grief, containing many elements of depression, is seen as a natural consequence given (a) social reinforcement theory (Seitz, 1971), which predicts that the death of the loved one leads to depression as a function of the resulting inadequate or insufficient reinforcers occasioned by the loss of that person, and (b) learned helplessness theory (Seligman, 1975), which theorizes that depression results when the mourner confronts her powerlessness in the face of death and learns the futility of all action to relieve her suffering from the loss, bring gratification, or provide nurturance, resulting in a perception of helplessness and a consequent cessation of responses that eventually would alleviate stress and facilitate working through.

Ramsay (1977) summarizes the mourner's situation:

A person suffering from pathological grief has lost a major portion of the positive reinforcers in life, has learned that nothing helps to relieve the stress, and so either does nothing in the way of confronting himself with the situations which could lead to an extinction of the negative conditioned emotional responses, or, like the phobic, actively avoids those situations. (p. 134)

Although similarities exist in phobias and unresolved grief, the treatments differ. In both, there is a need to extinguish emotional reactions. Although treatment of phobias can sometimes be severe, as in the case of implosive therapy or emotional flooding, intervention may be accomplished gently through systematic desensitization. However, in unresolved grief, there appears to be no such gentle manner of treatment. Ramsay (1979) warns that "This is a difficult and harsh treatment . . . [and] the chances of suicide are high" and that "great care has to be taken in the way we use our techniques" (p. 246). For this reason, he has delineated specific criteria for this type of bereavement therapy. Unless circumstances are exceptional (e.g., joint threat of homicide and suicide), he advocates that within the first year after a loss the mourner be encouraged to work through the reactions on her own with help from others in the support system or from an empathic, nondirective caregiver. For those interested in treatment at least a year after the death, an assessment is required of (a) the mourner's ability to withstand the stress of treatment, (b) the efficacy of the social network in supporting the mourner during treatment, and (c) the possibilities open to the mourner for creating a new life. Where suicide is a danger, treatment must be carried out in an appropriate facility to safeguard the mourner. The mourner is apprised of the form of the treatment, its harshness, the alternatives available, and the fact that treatment is difficult and painful and will result in things getting worse before they get better. Ramsay lays down specific ground rules the mourner must abide by: (a) she cannot terminate prematurely or commit suicide during treatment, and if there is a danger of either she must be prepared for a brief hospitalization; (b) she may become angry at Ramsay but may not hit him or break up the furniture; and (c) she must tell him if he goes too fast or probes too painfully, for because they are working as a team she has as much say as he does. After this, Ramsay asks the mourner to include a significant other, whose support and involvement he considers vital. Both are given numerous opportunities to think over the decision to enter this type of treatment. Nothing is rushed.

Grief reactions by their nature force treatment toward the implosive end of the continuum (Ramsay & Happée, 1977). The caregiver can grade confrontations in roughly hierarchical fashion, yet the emotional reactions they precipitate are usually intense. In addition, the selection of stimuli to elicit phobic reactions is fairly straightforward, whereas it takes much searching to find the proper stimuli to elicit the mourner's conditioned emotional responses. The caregiver must know in advance what to expect in the nature and content of emotional responses to the loss of a loved one. Part of the caregiver's task is to help the mourner give structure to the process of feeling and expression—to relearn how to feel, code feelings correctly, and express them appropriately. Ramsay (1979) is quite clear that this type of intense treatment is not for the beginning caregiver and cautions against undertaking it without considerable experience with more conventional forms of therapy.

For Ramsay and other behaviorists, treatment of pathological mourning basically consists of the behavioral approaches of emotional flooding and repeated confrontation, with prolonged exposure and response prevention when the mourner attempts to escape or avoid. These techniques can seem quite brutal to those unused to them. The following excerpt from Ramsay and Happée's (1977) suggested intervention strategy for severe pathological bereavement reactions illustrates this point:

> The function of the therapist is to confront the client repeat-
> edly with the fact of the loss and all that it entails,

to break down the denial, to evoke the depression, guilt, anxieties, and aggressions, until these emotions are extinguished and there is no further reaction to the loss. This is usually done in lengthy sessions of enforced confrontation (usually 2 hours) [ideally three times a week] with no possibility of escape. Various items that can be expected to evoke a reaction are presented in imagination until one hits home and the client reacts. The caregiver then allows the reaction, be it a crying fit or an aggressive outburst, to take its course and subside. The therapist then presents that item again, and again, until no further reaction occurs. Then other items are tried out. For example, with a woman who has lost her husband, an item such as physical contact can be worked through in a hierarchical manner, from never again being able to hold his hand, through never being able to kiss him again, to never again feeling him stroking her breasts or his penis inside her. The therapist constantly has to bear in mind that he must work through all the gradations, as well as the various components, of the grief process.

Both the therapist and the client must be prepared for extremely painful emotional outbursts. As can be seen from the preceding example, the therapist hits hard, probing for where it hurts most; when he finds it, he keeps doggedly at it till the pain is burned out. In some cases, the therapy has to be carried out in a hospital, because chances of suicide are high. The task of the therapist is not made easy by the fact that he has to force the client to experience the pain, and he cannot lessen the pain; where the natural tendency is to comfort someone in distress, the therapist must make the distress worse before it will get better. This induction of pain and the frustration of not being allowed to ease it makes the carrying out of such a therapy extremely unpleasant. (pp. 60–61)

The goal of all of this is to evoke the various avoided emotions by means of appropriate stimuli (e.g., verbalization, imagination, recreation of events, Gestalt empty chair work, exposure to photographs or linking objects) and then to allow time for these feelings to extinguish subsequent to the mourner's personally chosen way of expressing them. Following this, the mourner is assisted to relinquish the deceased, often through sending that person away in some active fashion. The letting go must be absolute—no denial, complete acceptance, and permanent farewell—or else true reintegration cannot occur.

In light of the demands of the treatment, the caregiver must respond carefully or risk losing the mourner. The therapeutic relationship must be handled most delicately:

To keep the client motivated to continue, the therapist must alternate between being the hard taskmaster and a gentle, empathic, supportive person who understands how difficult it is for the client. Often, the therapist will have to discuss the rationale of the probing for a particular component before launching into the evocation of a painful emotional reaction. The therapist-client relationship is of vital importance, as it is in every therapy; without a good working relationship, the client will soon drop out of therapy or will be unwilling to make the necessary effort to confront the difficult tasks. The therapist needs consciously to build up and continually to maintain this working alliance, and to use it to help the client through difficult periods. Talking about the relationship, however, is kept to a minimum; such discussions are escape mechanisms to avoid further confrontation. (Ramsay & Happée, 1977, p. 61)

Cognitive-Behavioral Therapy

In 1977, Gauthier and Marshall first introduced a combination treatment of cognitive and behavioral therapy for pathological grief. According to their conceptualization, pathological grief is influenced by two factors: First, family and friends either fail to withdraw attention for grieving or do not provide consistent encouragement for more adaptive behavior, suggesting the necessity for a rearrangement of the social consequences of the mourner's behavior. Second, family and friends, or even the mourner himself, may decide to avoid the grief reaction completely, with social attention being given to behaviors that do not permit grief to occur. These behaviors include an avoidance of contact with thoughts, objects, or experiences that may remind the mourner of his loss and often involve a conspiracy of silence whereby friends and relatives withhold information about the death, avoid discussing the deceased, remove cues of the deceased (e.g., personal possessions, photographs), and forestall the involvement of the mourner in the funeral and burial rituals.

Even though grieving behavior may be circumvented, grieving thoughts are not so easily stopped. It is not uncommon for the mourner to have frequent thoughts about the deceased; it also is not uncommon for him to react by avoiding them. This avoidance stems from either the mourner's belief that it is not good to think about the deceased or his inability to withstand the pain provoked by such memories. However, the mourner's strategy does not avert sadness. Instead, it actually can increase distress through the *Napalkov phenomenon* (Napalkov, 1963). This phenomenon is associated with the tendency following a single pairing of a conditioned stimulus and an aversive unconditioned stimulus for repeated brief presentations of the conditioned stimulus alone at full intensity to produce a marked increase in conditioned blood pressure response. This phenomenon has been elaborated by Eysenck (1967, 1968) into a theory of the cognitive incubation of fear in humans. The person experiencing pathological mourning who experiences intrusive thoughts of the deceased and then immediately suppresses them matches Eysenck's ideal conditions for the incubation of distressed responses. In addition, the forced exclusion from contact with the deceased appears to make the mourner feel that he has neglected his duties, thereby adding guilt to the mourner's already distressed reaction.

Gauthier and Marshall (1977) synthesize these issues and suggest their necessary treatment:

> One implication of this analysis is that forced prolonged exposure to the distressing stimuli should reverse the growth in grief. . . . [T]here are at least two important factors in the maintenance and exacerbation of grief reactions. If grief responses are encouraged by social reinforcement, or if social reinforcement is not consistently given for alternative behavior, the grief will be maintained. Similarly, if attempts are made to inhibit the experience of grief, the result may very well be to produce ideal conditions for the cognitive incubation of grief as well as to further add to distress by introducing excessive guilt. Accordingly, treatment for grief reactions might take the form of a rescheduling of social reinforcement along with a procedure that encourages prolonged exposure at full intensity to the stimuli producing grief. (p. 42)

The authors claim remarkable success in their recent treatment of four cases of pathological grief, one with a 27-year duration. They required a maximum of three sessions for analysis of the problem and rearrangement of social contingencies, plus three flooding sessions, in order to produce marked changes in behavior. One case involved a woman whose son had died from an auto accident 3 years earlier. She presented with a variety of physical disorders and was psychiatrically evaluated as moderately to severely depressed in mood. Her treatment commenced with an explanation of the model and rationale for treatment. The first three sessions were spent obtaining a detailed description of the events surrounding the boy's death and factors maintaining the woman's grief reaction. During these sessions and for the remainder of the treatment, the woman's husband was advised to modify his behavior and that of the family to offer minimal sympathy for grief and considerable encouragement for alternative responses.

At the fourth session, flooding therapy commenced. This consisted of the caregiver's describing in detail the behaviors the mourner had engaged in at the time of the accident and after the death of her son (e.g., visiting the hospital, looking at and touching the body, and attending the funeral). The corresponding emotions she would have experienced also were described. The mourner was encouraged to imagine the details as vividly as she could and to experience the emotions realistically. At no point did the caregiver show any sympathy for the mourner's distress.

The mourner evidenced excessive grief throughout the first 30 to 40 minutes of her first 2-hour flooding session. After this, her distress subsided. At the two following sessions, the duration of the initial distress decreased markedly, and by the third session she displayed little or no grief. Both at the beginning and end of each flooding session, the mourner and her husband were encouraged gradually to reintroduce into their household articles of sentimental value associated with their deceased son (e.g., photographs, mementos).

At the subsequent interview, the mourner described herself as remarkably improved, and this was corroborated by her husband. She reported that she could think about her deceased son, examine his photograph, and engage in other such activities without depression. Although she felt sadness at times, it was not distressing to her. She could discuss her son without crying, and her symptomatology disappeared. At the 6-month follow-up, her improvement was maintained.

In a subsequent article, Gauthier and Pye (1979) advocate a modification of the aforementioned technique when (a) manipulation of social reinforcement is not possible or practical and (b) flooding cannot be implemented either because the mourner fears exposure for a prolonged time to grief-producing stimuli at full intensity or because the mourner's health does not permit the emotional impact of such sessions.

This modified treatment involves graduated self-exposure to the grief-producing stimuli, which the mourner has preselected and arranged in an ascending order of difficulty (e.g., walking by the door of the deceased's room, opening a closet in the room, sitting on the deceased's bed, listening to the deceased's voice on a tape recorder). The mourner is instructed to arrange exposure twice daily to these stimuli, starting with the least discomforting and progressing up the hierarchy until some measure of distress is felt. (In the grief-avoidant cardiac patient described by Gauthier and Pye, the distress was chest pain. Medical consultation and extreme caution are required when physical cues in a medically ill patient are used as indicators.) In addition, the mourner is instructed to employ positive coping self-statements whenever perceiving objects reminiscent of the deceased (e.g., "My son's years were good years. I am glad to have good memories"; "I can cope. Once I have gotten over grieving, I will be able to think comfortably about my son"; "I've had a loss, but this happens to others, and I can go on"). The mourner is advised to overcome distressing emotions and cease exposure to the grief-producing stimuli only when the feelings are ones of discomfort rather than distress. The caregiver praises any improvements, and the mourner is encouraged to extend these efforts continually.

Gauthier and Pye indicate that, in their case example, this modified treatment resulted in a marked reduction in avoidance behavior and subjective distress associated with grief-producing stimuli. Although the procedure involves brief exposure to grief-producing stimuli, the exposures are not to intensive stimuli. Therefore, the conditions described by Gauthier and Marshall (1977) for the incubation of distressed responses are not met. The implication from these two studies is that a treatment strategy involving either prolonged exposure to high intensity stimuli or brief exposure to low intensity stimuli should be helpful in dealing with grief.

Finally, a critical aspect of this work concerns the use of self-exposure and coping self-statements for the treatment of pathological grief. Their use suggests that grief is amenable to behavioral and verbal self-management: "Thus, it would appear that encouraging a patient to expose himself repeatedly in a graduated manner to stimuli producing grief and to rehearse coping self-statements in the presence of these stimuli may be an effective way of dealing with the problem of grief" (Gauthier & Pye, 1979, p. 207).

Guided Mourning

Guided mourning involves a series of interventions proposed by Mawson, Marks, Ramm, and Stern (1981). Unresolved grief is likened to phobic avoidance and treated by exposure to the avoided situation. In their investigation, Mawson and colleagues employed a number of behavioral strategies focused on the mourner's reactions to the loss. Specifically, this entailed (a) exposure to avoided or painful memories, ideas, or situations related to the loss, both in imagination and real life; (b) repeated description of difficult situations pertaining to the loss or its consequences (i.e., those associated with great sadness or guilt) until distress is diminished; (c) encouragement to visit places that have been avoided; (d) encouragement to say good-bye to the deceased verbally and behaviorally; and (e) assignments consisting of forced writing and thinking about the deceased, facing of the grief, and daily viewing of the deceased's photograph.

In their controlled study, the authors concluded that guided mourning is a useful ingredient in the management of morbid grief and is associated with improvement on a number of measures, although not on as many or to as great an extent as hoped. The effects of guided mourning were most evident on measures of approach to bereavement cues. In other words, the treatment decreased phobic avoidance. It was less successful in ameliorating depressed mood and general anxiety. Also, it did not attend to the social or biological features of morbid grief.

Two implications from these findings may be drawn: First, mood disturbance and avoidance of bereavement are less related than commonly thought. And, second, treatment effective for some forms of pathological grief is not necessarily effective for others. Guided mourning appears most helpful in instances where mourning has been avoided, repressed, or delayed. It is less useful where mourners can readily express their grief either in a self-punitive fashion or as an excuse to avoid developing a new lifestyle. Mourners who avoid life-style changes possibly would benefit more from a goal-oriented program.

The variable effect of treatment on different forms of pathological grief has been supported by S. Lieberman (1978), who studied the effect of forced mourning procedures on morbidly grieving patients. His treatment included a forced mourning procedure following the behavioral principles of systematic desensitization and implosion, coupled where practical with family involvement to maximize generalization. In working with mourners, Lieberman used the following procedures.

1. Requiring the mourner to speak of the deceased in positive and negative fashions; reviewing the relationship; and encouraging the expression of strong, painful, usually blocked emotions, verbally and nonverbally (e.g., through letter writing)

2. Focusing the mourner's attention on the topic of the deceased, bringing it back whenever it strays

3. Having the mourner bring in and face objects of avoidance (e.g., photographs, clothing)

4. Working with the mourner to put aside avoidance behavior and develop new relationships

5. Instructing the mourner to talk to family members about his feelings

6. Examining other important losses brought up by discussion of the target loss and addressing them in a similar fashion

Lieberman discerns three different patterns of morbid grief, each with its own requirements for intervention. The first pattern is phobic avoidance of persons, places, or things related to the deceased, coexisting with extreme guilt and anger about the deceased and circumstances surrounding the death. This pattern is usually related to a delay in the onset of grief longer than 2 weeks. A behaviorally inspired forced mourning procedure proves most effective.

The second pattern is associated with a total lack of grieving, usually with extreme anger about the deceased and circumstances surrounding the final illness and death. This pattern may first require venting of anger and hostility, which initially are not directed toward the deceased, who is idealized. Rather, this anger often tends to be directed at the caregiver. Later, the caregiver can encourage the understanding that these emotions are connected with the loss of the deceased, toward whom the anger ultimately can be directed.

The third pattern, prolonged grief, includes physical illness and recurrent nightmares. This pattern is similar to that exhibited by individuals diagnosed with reactive depression combined with physical illnesses. Interpretive psychotherapy and behavioral techniques, with an emphasis on dream work, appear to be the treatment of choice.

Lieberman perceives the family as being quite important in treatment because, clinically, it is common that morbid grieving is a family pattern. Other members of the family need to experience the forced mourning as much as the identified patient. When not included, family members tend to block the therapy by not allowing emotional expression of anger, grief, and loss.

Another clinician who has integrated various aspects of cognitive and behavioral therapies is Hodgkinson (1982). In an article reporting the use of cathartic therapy with 10 clients having severe but clear-cut grief problems, he delineates a number of points that easily can be extrapolated to other approaches toward complicated mourning. Hodgkinson indicates that simply asking the mourner to tell in detail the story of the loved one's death provides an assessment from which the caregiver can garner crucial information. For example, the caregiver can discover which of the emotional components of grief have been enhanced and which parts of the story elicit strong overt emotions or nonverbal indications of emotional pain or its avoidance. Hodgkinson asserts that the initial emotional outburst is important and that, during this time, the caregiver must avoid colluding with the mourner's avoidance of pain by indicating that the session is the place where the mourner can and must cry. He shares the experience of the woman who was, in the first session, on the verge of crying for the first time since her husband's death. The caregiver was unable to assist her full expression of emotion, the chance was lost, and the therapy was unsuccessful. By the end of the first session, the caregiver should have a picture of the circumstances of the death and the mourner's specific emotions attached to it. Ideally, the mourner is left with the impression that strong emotions are not totally overwhelming and that release engenders relief.

As a general rule, Hodgkinson's mourners were seen as inpatients or day patients in a supportive environment two or three times a week. This frequency ensured continued emotional facilitation but provided sufficient gaps to allow working through between sessions. Hodgkinson notes that outpatient therapies involving one session per week generally took longer. In addition, the less frequent schedule posed more danger for emotional catharsis to become disjointed.

The emotions in abnormal grief can be either inhibited or excessive. In either case, the formulation is the same: failure at some level to acknowledge and accept the death and to relinquish the deceased. The mourner may deny the death by inhibiting grief or may perpetuate grief as a link with the deceased. Whichever pertains, it is essential to focus elicited emotions repeatedly on the reality of the loved one's death. The initial phase of Hodgkinson's treatment stimulates these emotions. The caregiver begins by confronting the mourner with a photograph of the deceased. This creates a sense of the deceased's immediacy and makes avoidance of her absence difficult. Later, the caregiver focuses on the use of more individual linking objects. As in the forms of treatment previously addressed, negative emotions are stimulated repeatedly until they can no longer be elicited (i.e., they are extinguished) or are reduced to untroublesome proportions. In some cases, response prevention (Marks, Hodgson, & Rachman, 1974) on the part of the caregiver may be necessary to assist the mourner in relinquishing the deceased (e.g., redirecting the mourner from ritualistically stroking the deceased's clothing).

Conflicts will become apparent once emotional blocks have been breached. For example, the mourner will experience real or imagined guilt for omissions or commissions, and unfinished business with the deceased will come to the fore. These conflicts can be externalized through the use of Gestalt empty chair or third chair exercises, in which the mourner establishes a dialogue with the deceased.

With some mourners, the recession of feelings of depression suddenly precipitates intense feelings of anxiety. This can come from the transition from depressive preoccupation with the past to anxious appraisal of the future and represents an imperfect acceptance of the death, which must be addressed. Hodgkinson notes that the most dramatic acts of relinquishing the deceased tend to occur among these mourners.

Grief-Resolution Therapy: Reliving, Revising, and Revisiting

Grief-resolution therapy involves using guided imagery in order to remove obstacles and binds that previously inhibited grieving at the time of loss, while simultaneously assisting the mourner to reconstruct her personal future (Melges & DeMaso, 1980). It has been designed for individuals with unresolved grief—individuals who suffer from the wish to redo and reunite with the past, making the present and future seem hopeless.

Melges and DeMaso (1980) assert that diagnosis of unresolved grief reactions involves finding the dynamics that have inhibited the normal grieving processes. These dynamics usually can be detected by observing whether a person is bound to a loss that time has not and will not heal, with that person's hopes being pinned on the past rather than the present or future. The image of the significant other preoccupies the mourner a year or more after the death. Identifying the emotional reactions that have started shortly after the death, Melges and DeMaso begin to look for one or more of the following obstacles, which are likely to maintain the grief in an unresolved state.

1. Persistent yearning for recovery of the lost object

2. Overidentification with the deceased

3. The wish to cry or rage at the loss, coupled with an inability to do so

4. Misdirected anger and ambivalence toward the deceased

5. Interlocking grief reactions

6. Unspoken but powerful contracts with the deceased

7. Unrevealed secrets and unfinished business

8. Lack of a support group and alternative options

9. Secondary gain or reinforcement from others to remain grief stricken

According to Melges and DeMaso, the work of grief-resolution therapy is to help mourners resolve the process of mourning by removing one or more of these obstacles. The caregiver first identifies the obstacles, then helps the mourner remove them by revising in imagination scenes of the loss. The caregiver then has the mourner revisit and re-grieve the loss in present-time imagery with the obstacles removed. The intense work of grieving and giving up is supported by the concurrent building of new hopes and future plans.

Toward this end, there are three interrelated therapeutic phases: (a) cognitive structuring for the decision to re-grieve and for clarification of procedures; (b) guided imagery for reliving, revising, and revisiting scenes of the loss; and (c) future-oriented identity reconstruction.

Cognitive structuring

Cognitive structuring entails outlining the nature of the unresolved grief and procedures used for its treatment. Before the mourner is asked to make a decision to re-grieve, the caregiver must ensure that adequate rapport has been established. The caregiver then should acknowledge how difficult it will be for the mourner to relinquish the deceased. Melges and DeMaso offer a useful technique for empathizing with and sharing the meaning of attachment to the deceased. The mourner is directed to discuss positive exchanges that occurred with the deceased shortly before the death (e.g., kind words or an affectionate embrace). Then the mourner is asked to close her eyes and attempt to reexperience the reciprocal feelings stimulated by such exchanges. The caregiver seeks to reawaken the full yearning for the attachment and the emotions associated with the loss. Reexperiencing the depth of the attachment in this fashion often revives the mourner's lost sense of self. Although painful, it engenders hope for the reemergence of parts of her identity (Tooley, 1978).

Gradually, the caregiver introduces suggestions about the necessity for grieving until the mourner is prepared for a clear statement, such as "Many of your hopes for yourself are there buried with [the deceased] in the past. Do you think you can find the courage to grieve and let him go so that you can redirect yourself toward the present and the future?" (Melges & DeMaso, 1980, p. 55).

The mourner's decision to re-grieve is often therapeutic in and of itself. Cognitive structuring continues with the caregiver's explaining the procedures used in the guided imagery and indicating how the mourner will gradually go through grief-hope transitions. For example:

> I will ask you to review what you experienced when you lost your loved one by seeing in your "mind's eye" the events before and after his death. You will speak out loud in the present tense as though the events were happening right now. You will have your eyes closed but you will be able to see the happenings in your mind. I will be there listening to your feelings and what happened to you. We will spend about 20 minutes each session to deal separately with each of the following scenes: your awareness of your relationship to the deceased shortly before the news of his death, then the arrival of the news and how you felt, then the happenings at the funeral home, then the funeral, and finally you will say "goodbye" to him and walk away from the grave with the feeling that you can begin again. For each of these scenes, you will first relive what happened, then we'll rearrange the scene in your imagination so that you have removed obstacles to grieving, and after that you will revisit the scene and allow yourself to express feelings and deal with the conflicts which you previously have kept inside. Although your task will involve a lot of emotion—crying, perhaps anger—you also will experience feelings of increasing freedom and relief along with the awakening of parts of yourself that you have forgotten. (Melges & DeMaso, 1980, pp. 55–56)

Guided imagery

Three steps compose the part of the process involving guided imagery: reliving, revising, and revisiting. During each step, the caregiver must encourage active visualization and prevail upon the mourner to use the present tense.

Reliving entails the mourner's closing her eyes and viewing sequences of the loss in her mind's eye as if the scene were happening now (e.g., viewing the body at the funeral home). This gives opportunities for abreaction and provides important information about obstacles previously inhibiting grieving. The present-time imagery offers the quickest way to discover these obstacles because the mourner feels she actually is confronting them now instead of merely talking about them as past events.

Revising involves asking the mourner to remove barriers or binds that formerly inhibited full grieving (e.g., the mourner is alone at the funeral home instead of with a critical person whose presence had stifled her responses). It is quite typical for revising to require creating solitary scenes with the deceased in order that highly private material (e.g., anger, secrets, binds) can be worked out in the absence of competing relatives and social constraints. In some instances, the caregiver must actively rearrange the scene in order to make it therapeutic (e.g., suggest that the casket is open to let the mourner perceive that the loved one really is dead or indicate that the mourner is viewing the casket being lowered into the grave and the grave being filled with dirt after saying a final good-bye).

Revisiting the revised scene also takes place in the present tense, as if the scene were occurring in the here and now. The caregiver encourages the mourner to engage in dialogues with the deceased for a number of purposes.

1. To acknowledge the finality of the loss

2. To differentiate herself from the deceased

3. To express tears and rage

4. To deal with ambivalence and misdirected anger

5. To tease apart interlocking grief reactions

6. To emancipate herself from unspoken binds

7. To reveal secrets and deal with unfinished business

8. To express love and forgiveness

9. To obtain permission from the deceased to look for new relationships and options, especially those that seem to flow naturally from what the deceased would have wanted for the mourner

Near the end of each revised scene in which dialogues with the deceased have taken place, the caregiver encourages the mourner to exchange last words with the loved one and inquires as to whether the mourner is ready to say good-bye. Mourners often are unable to say good-bye in earlier scenes, such as viewing the body at the funeral home—the word appears to stick in their throats. The caregiver must recognize unreadiness and prompt the mourner to say good-bye for now while preparing her for the final good-bye, when the deceased is lowered into the grave and covered with dirt. This last scene usually has not been witnessed in reality by most mourners whose grief is unresolved; typically, it must be carried out exclusively in the imagination and there is no reliving per se.

Future-oriented identity reconstruction

After the final scene of lowering the body into the earth (or, in the case of cremation, disposition of the cremains), the caregiver asks the mourner to, in her mind's eye, walk about 50 yards away from the scene, then turn around and look back to feel if there are aspects of the deceased's personality she chooses to develop in herself. Most often, these are images of strength, strands from the past that can serve as bridges to the future. They are selective identifications that may be amplified for healthy identity reconstruction. In addition, the caregiver can inquire in what ways the mourner has grown and derived positive benefits from the experience of grieving and whether she wishes to continue to grow along these same dimensions. These choices may be reinforced further by future-oriented psychotherapy, which involves projections into the future in order to crystallize choices and internal values of one's becoming self. Melges and DeMaso note, parenthetically, that anticipatory guidance for coping with anniversary reactions can be carried out in this fashion as well.

Usually, grief-resolution therapy requires 6 to 10 sessions and is conducted as a focal treatment within the context of other types of therapy (e.g., cognitive, milieu, family therapy). The results are particularly good when the problem has been uncomplicated by long-standing personality conflicts, although even when such complications exist treatment identifies binds and offers clarifications that are constructive for subsequent therapeutic intervention. Because the present-tense focus of the guided imagery serves to highlight the obstacles and binds that the mourner often dimly perceives when discussing the loss in the past tense, the authors assert that grief-resolution therapy quickly gets at core issues. The time necessary depends on the clarity of the mourner's decision to re-grieve, the mourner's ego strength, and the extent of the mourner's binds to the deceased.

Melges and DeMaso suggest that there are a number of ways to test the adequacy of the re-grief work. Most obvious are the mourner's abreaction, her self-report of relief, and the comments of her family and social network. A specific test involves having the mourner project a year into the future and imagine herself returning alone to a place she and the deceased once cherished. In living through this future image, mourners who have undergone successful treatment often comment along the following lines: "He is gone; he is only a memory; yet knowing him has helped me to become who I am" (Melges & DeMaso, 1980, p. 57). Other tests involve the mourner's exposing herself to linking objects or revisiting the cemetery. In situations where there has been appropriate resolution of grief, the mourner reports experiencing distinctly different feelings than before treatment. Now the reactions are memories tinged with sadness rather than expectant yearnings for reunion.

Two situations may interfere with a successful response to these tests. In the first, due to inadequate expression of anger and ambivalence toward the deceased during the guided imagery, the mourner still clings to the deceased. This precludes the forgiveness that leads to the final giving up. In this case, the caregiver must go back with the mourner to selected scenes and have her rework them until the final good-bye is unfettered by unexpressed anger. In the second situation, entire families are stricken with unresolved grief, and there is no support for the mourner to let go of the deceased. In this case, family therapy is necessary. Melges and DeMaso suggest meeting with the mourner's family whenever possible prior to treatment to avoid this pitfall and to prepare them for the mourner's potentially heightened emotional reactivity.

Melges and DeMaso also report that, in their experience, there have been no lasting complications of this type of treatment. They note that short-term complications include (a) the mourner's resistance to undergo the necessary emotional turmoil of grieving (which usually can be managed by adequate pacing of the grief work); (b) the caregiver's emotional drain in empathizing with the relived scenes (which can be lessened by using a co-therapist); and (c) insufficient building of alternative relationships so that the mourner is left floundering after the re-grief work (which can be avoided by active restructuring of the mourner's social network). It is noted that all involved—the mourner, the caregiver, and the social and familial network—must be prepared for the mourner to get worse in terms of increased emotional turmoil before she gets better. Finally, the authors caution against the use of reactivation imagery with acutely manic or schizophrenic patients.

Social Systems Approach

An additional perspective for the treatment of so-called morbid grief reactions has been offered by Goalder (1985). Goalder puts forth a social systems framework for understanding the development of morbid grief reactions and for use in their assessment and treatment. This framework, one Goalder views as complementary to the psychodynamic approach, focuses on the adaptive responses of the mourner to the loss of the loved one. The psychodynamic approach assumes delusional attempts on the part of the mourner to maintain a continuing relationship with the deceased (e.g., attempting to recapture the missing resources that had been provided by the deceased through processes of denial and searching). This latter approach appears to Goalder to be of limited usefulness to the mourner in his task of psychological separation from the deceased. In contrast, the social psychological and social systems frameworks are particularly applicable to the mourner's tasks of readjustment to the new environment without the deceased and the mourner's formation of new relationships.

As Goalder points out, when a loved one dies, the mourner is cut off from major emotional, cognitive, social, and physical resources, although that mourner's needs remain at the same level. The mourner attempts to satisfy unmet needs by the aforementioned delusional attempts and by nondelusional attempts aimed at the individuals remaining in the social system. According to the social systems perspective, the nature of the reorganization of the social environment, destabilized by the death of the loved one, partly determines whether or not a mourner's response to the death will be healthy or morbid.

Treatment based on the social systems approach operates according to the following premises.

1. Dependency in relationships hinges on a balance between the needs and resources of the relationship members.

2. Needs and resources are of two kinds: either self-esteem (aimed at preventing social derogation) or security (functioning to prevent social abandonment).

3. Resources are defined as elements that satisfy social needs.

4. Relationships that are maintained strike a balance between the needs and resources among all members of a social system.

5. A system may consist of any number of individuals or subsystem relationships with an infinite variety of needs and resources.

6. Primary dependencies are subsystems that reflect a critical source of resource exchange for the members.

Goalder discusses three types of relationships in his analysis of grief reactions: the mourner/spouse subsystem, the mourner/person subsystems, and the person/relationship and relationship/relationship subsystems. The following discussion illustrates how these three types of relationships affect the mourner who has experienced the loss of a spouse. Comments here may inform about the loss of other loved ones, but their utility would appear to depend heavily on the closeness, centrality, and social legitimization of the relationship with that person.

Mourner/spouse subsystem

Goalder cites relevant social psychological literature documenting that a depressed individual appears to adopt a pattern of assuming personal responsibility for negative life events, with reduced self-esteem as a consequence of the critical attacks sustained on competence and integrity. With regard to loss of a spouse, the mourner experiences an inability to perform the necessary life roles previously assumed by the spouse in the complementary competencies of a primary dependent relationship. This leads, through social psychological processes, to attributions of personal incompetence, resulting in diminished self-esteem, assumption of personal responsibility for failure to meet one's own security needs, and sometimes to self-accusations for the death of the spouse and consequent definition of the self as evil. These alterations in attribution have a significant impact on the mourner. As Goalder (1985) summarizes: "Changes in patterns of attribution following the death of a significant other may crush an individual's self-esteem through challenges to his or her perceptions of personal competence and integrity, resulting in feelings of helplessness, worthlessness, and anger directed toward oneself" (p. 839).

Mourner/person subsystems

Mourner/person subsystems (e.g., relationships with children or friends) differ from the mourner/spouse subsystem in that the level of dependency is lower. However, when the spouse dies, important changes in these relationships occur as well. The social system balance that had existed prior to the death gives way to an imbalance of needs and resources afterwards, as the mourner's needs for esteem and security, formerly satisfied by the spouse, are now projected onto the other subsystems. There are two immediate results: (a) a heightened state of interpersonal stress as relationship partners attempt to find a new balance between needs and resources, with subsystems dissolving if their members are not highly interdependent, and (b) heightened influence attained by the nonmourning subsystem partners, primarily due to the increased reliance of the mourner on the mourner/person subsystems for satisfaction of needs previously satisfied by the deceased. The mourner's increased reliance on the social system may extend to norms and expectations for the grief experience. When these norms and expectations fail to follow the standards of the culture and derive instead from the idiosyncratic personal needs of other members of the social dependency system, morbid grief reactions may develop. In other words, because of increased dependency, the mourner becomes vulnerable to norms set by an altered social environment.

Person/relationship and relationship/relationship subsystems

Relationships in person/relationship and relationship/relationship subsystems exist to satisfy the joint needs of the mourner's primary dependency relationship. They may be between a child or friend and the mourner/spouse couple (i.e., person/relationship subsystem) or between the couple and another couple (i.e., relationship/relationship subsystem). There is limited focus on meeting individual needs because dependency in these relationships is focused on the needs of the relationship as an entity, rather than on those of individuals. Although the needs of the primary dependency relationship were promoted by these subsystems, there may be only an indirect relationship to the mourner's needs for personal security and esteem.

When the spouse dies and the mourner/spouse subsystem dissolves, the need and resource base for person/relationship and relationship/relationship subsystems changes. Individuals or relationships external to the mourner/spouse subsystem can no longer relate to it as an entity because it no longer exists. Dependencies based upon the mourner/spouse subsystem rather than on the mourner as an individual will go unmet and tend to disintegrate. The result is a significantly reduced social dependency system for the mourner. In brief, relationships associated primarily with the mourner's spouse and those having a person/relationship and relationship/relationship focus are no longer a part of the mourner's social system.

In summary, in morbid grief reactions barriers to adaptation to the death of a loved one fall into five domains: affect, self-esteem, social environment, competence, and behavior. These barriers have social systems roots characterized by the following.

1. Reduction of the social resource base through death and attrition

2. Application of pathology-inducing norms by those remaining in the social system

3. Self-attribution of traits of incompetence and/or wickedness

4. Active withdrawal from the social environment

The usefulness of the social systems approach for the treatment of complicated mourning stems not only from the assessment information it can yield but also from the clinical direction it provides for identifying the source and type of problem and treatment intervention. In comparison to a traditional intrapsychic or psychoanalytical approach, it allows a more comprehensive address of the mourner's range of responses to the death of a loved one. As Goalder (1985) concludes:

> Traditional approaches to a theory of bereavement tend to focus on delusional aspects, whereas the social systems approach stresses adaptational responses to grief. It is important to state that these theoretical perspectives are complimentary [sic] rather than duplicative and antagonistic. Each deals with a different aspect of grief response and each is valuable in its own right in identifying critical factors that contribute to MGR [Morbid Grief Reaction]. Any effective assessment and therapeutic strategy for those suffering from

MGR must take into account both delusional and adaptive strategies of individuals in their attempts to cope with loss of critical life resources. (p. 841)

GESTALT THERAPY

Although the Gestalt empty chair technique is widely used in the treatment of complicated mourning, little has been written focusing specifically on Gestalt intervention for problematic grief reactions. Yet, along with joy, orgasm, and anger, Gestalt theory considers grief one of the four primary emotions (Marcus, 1979). Loss and grief are viewed as inherent processes of life, component parts of the Gestalt processes of formation and destruction (Perls, Hefferline, & Goodman, 1951). Avoiding grief is perceived by Gestaltists as contributing to an abortion of the normal cycle, causing mourning to be retroflected into underlying and pervasive feelings of depression and resulting in unfinished business, unfinished relationships, unfinished endings, and distorted beginnings created by overlooking destructuring within the gestalt cycle of change, growth, and development (Clark, 1982).

The role of grief and mourning as essential elements of life is summarized by Clark (1982) in her discussion of principles and techniques of Gestalt psychotherapy in uncomplicated mourning:

Within the transition of change from one gestalt of our living to another, we contact both the process of separation (which is intrinsic to the disintegrating gestalt) and the process of connection (which is intrinsic to the forming gestalt). New beginnings slowly emerge as each level of loss is contacted and assimilated. Attention shifts. We find times of excitement, joy and passion as we restructure and reform our lives. The work of grieving allows us to move from the past through separation and loss to the present formings of the future. We know the "suffering of mourning, as a means of letting go the old self to change" (Perls, Hefferline, & Goodman, 1951, p. 360). We experience the deep paradox and mystery of change that the gestalt of the self is destructured as the gestalt of the self is formed. We find within ourselves the rhythm of gestalt formation and disintegration. We learn to say our goodbyes. We live our grief, our joys, our lives.

Within the rhythm of change, transition and growth— within the rhythm of our adult living and developing—we learn the pattern and rhythm of our grieving. . . . It is in and through the process of gestalt formation and destruction that we discover and create ourselves. (p. 62)

The reader is referred to Clark's original work for a full discussion of Gestalt therapy and uncomplicated mourning.

E. Smith (1985b) is the only Gestalt writer I have discovered to address issues of complicated mourning and its treatment specifically. He identifies the two types of situations in which caregivers can be especially helpful: those in which the mourner has sustained a loss but appears unable to mourn (i.e., in the absent, delayed, or inhibited mourning syndromes) and those in which mourning has commenced but has persisted for too long (i.e., in the chronic mourning syndrome).

In absent, delayed, or inhibited mourning, Smith distinguishes two dynamics, operating singly or together. The first is pain phobia. Its avoidance contributes to the creation of unfinished business:

> Losses demand grieving, a feeling of the loss, and a hurting
> with the loss in order to let go and move on with life. To
> refuse to do the hurting, to refuse to fully feel and express
> the sadness is to interrupt a natural organismic process and
> thereby create "unfinished business." (E. Smith, 1985b, p. 71)

The second dynamic Smith pinpoints as preventing full mourning is the "Be strong" script, exemplified by such notions as "Don't be weak," "Don't cry," "Don't show your emotions," "Don't show you're hurt," and "Be a man."

Both dynamics preventing full mourning are based on phobic behavior: In one case there is pain phobia, and in the other there is a phobia against breaking the old script. Smith asserts that the experience of loss sets up a state of tension that is only relieved through grieving. With the absence of full grieving, there is unfinished business—an incomplete task —that can remain as long as the grieving is avoided. To the extent that the task is incomplete, the mourner is left in a state of tension. Although with effort the unaddressed grief can be kept from awareness much of the time, the tension is still there, ready to break into awareness whenever the mourner's rigid vigil is not kept.

Mourning is a part of the resignation process necessary if the mourner is to overcome the clinging to the past (Perls, 1947), but unfinished business ties the mourner to the past. An interesting substantive observation made by Perls is that, in the analysis of the retrospective character (i.e., the individual obsessed with the past), there always is one distinct symptom— the suppression of crying. This lends further credence to the notion that suppressing mourning results in overinvestment in the past and insufficient investment in the present.

The absence of full grieving creates a condition of unfinished business, in which there is a refusal to enter fully into and experience the work of mourning. In contrast, chronic grieving maintains a condition of unfinished business—a refusal to finish the work, let go, and move on with one's life. Smith delineates two factors for the latter situation. First, grief may feed an underlying depression if one is characterologically predisposed to it. Second, grief may become a major source of meaning in the mourner's life and continue to be maintained through the phenomenon of secondary gain. In such cases, grief may seem more exciting than the alternatives in the mourner's life and can lend meaning to an otherwise drab existence. It may yield a sense of focus and importance, as well as increased attention from others.

Recognizing that both the absent, delayed, or inhibited complicated mourning syndromes and the chronic mourning syndrome involve unfinished business, the caregiver provides procedures for the completion of the processes. He or she supports grieving in any way needed while frustrating attempts to avoid it.

Smith delineates the Gestalt conceptualization of the grief cycle that underpins treatment procedures. In brief, loss creates a need to grieve, which gives rise to organismic tension or arousal, which causes the individual to feel sad, which calls forth the action of crying, which brings relief when the response is sufficient to meet the need at the time. Depending on the degree of loss, the grief cycle can vary in intensity, frequency, and number of repetitions. After the experience of relief from crying, some time may pass until the need to grieve builds up to the point where it is once again being experienced. With this cycle in mind, E. Smith (1985b) identifies awareness, arousal, and crying activity as the specific targets for intervention:

> Since the grief cycle requires awareness of the loss, awareness of the need to grieve, awareness and allowing of the tension or bodily arousal to build, awareness of sadness, and the activity of crying, the incompleteness of any of these decreases the amount of relief which can be experienced. So, the therapeutic focus is on any inadequacy of *awareness, arousal,* or *crying activity.* (p. 76)

It is toward the end of completing these experiences and finishing unfinished business that Smith uses the empty chair technique to encourage mourners to say good-bye. This technique involves the following four steps.

Step 1. The caregiver brings the deceased into the here-and-now experience of the mourner through psychodrama by inviting the mourner to imagine the deceased sitting in an empty chair. Depending on the degree of the mourner's experience with this type of work, the caregiver may have to increase the vividness of the deceased's image (e.g., suggesting seeing the person as clearly as possible; hearing the person say hello; smelling the odors associated with the person, such as perfume or pipe tobacco).

Step 2. When the mourner experiences the deceased with an adequate degree of vividness, the caregiver asks the mourner to sit for a few moments and observe what it is like to be with the deceased. The caregiver then may suggest that the mourner feel whatever emotions arise.

Step 3. The caregiver invites the mourner to tell the deceased whatever she is thinking and feeling, so long as these thoughts do not avoid the here-and-now experience. (The idea is to *talk to* the deceased rather than *talk about* that person.) Three important elements must be included in the expression, and the caregiver encourages full expression of each and calls attention to any that have not been expressed spontaneously. These include (a) appreciations, which reflect good memories and feelings and love for the deceased; (b) resentments, or unpleasant memories and negative feelings—sometimes hatred—for the deceased; and (c) regrets, or the acknowledgment of things not being or having been as the mourner would like. Healthy grieving requires expression of all three, or else some amount of unfinished business will remain.

Step 4. The caregiver then makes the empty chair monologue into an empty chair dialogue by inviting the mourner to switch chairs, become the deceased person, and respond to what the mourner has said. The mourner may shuttle back and forth between roles to amplify feelings and achieve a sense of completion and satisfaction. Obviously, appropriate timing of the switches is part of the caregiver's clinical art and skill.

Throughout these four steps, the caregiver must watch for any avoidance of full awareness, the buildup of arousal, or crying. On avoidance of full awareness, E. Smith (1985b) notes that points of avoidance are points for therapeutic intervention. Often, the intervention need only call attention to or encourage awareness of what is being avoided. Some examples include "Will you look at him when you say that?" "Stay with what you're experiencing," "Feel what you're feeling," and "Tell him you know he isn't coming back." Because arousal is quelled by inadequate breathing, the caregiver can deal with avoidance of the buildup of arousal by saying, "Don't hold your breath" or "Keep breathing." Finally, in order to frustrate the avoidance of crying, the caregiver could say, "Let that out," "Let your tears come," or "Make sound." When simply calling attention to avoidance or verbally encouraging the flow of the grief cycle is not potent enough, E. Smith (1985a) intervenes with body work aimed at increasing awareness, increasing breathing and therefore arousal, and reducing muscular tensions that inhibit crying.

TIME-LIMITED DYNAMIC PSYCHOTHERAPY FOR PHASE-ORIENTED TREATMENT OF THE STRESS RESPONSE SYNDROME

Mardi Horowitz and his colleagues at The Center for the Study of Neuroses at Langley Porter Psychiatric Institute have developed and researched a treatment following general principles for brief dynamic therapy (Malan, 1963, 1976; Mann, 1973; Sifneos, 1979). This treatment has been modified specifically for the phase-oriented working through of the stress response syndrome, the predictable pattern of response following any seriously stressful life event (Horowitz, 1973, 1976, 1986a; Horowitz & Kaltreider, 1979, 1980; Horowitz, Marmar, Krupnick, Wilner, Kaltreider, & Wallerstein, 1984; Horowitz, Marmar, Weiss, DeWitt, & Rosenbaum, 1984; Kanas et al., 1977; Windholz, Weiss, & Horowitz, 1985). Horowitz's conception of the stress response syndrome and its relationship to complicated mourning are described fully in chapter 3; the relevance of this conception to traumatic death is explored in chapter 12.

Very briefly, Horowitz asserts that following any stressful life event certain processes must occur in order for assimilation, accommodation, and healthy resumption of living to occur. The following five responses can be predicted: outcry, denial and numbing, intrusion, working through, and completion. In undergoing these responses, the individual must work through the meanings of the stressful event, as well as its implications for relationships, self-image, and behavior. This process entails reappraisal of the event and revision of core inner models of self, role relationships, and future plans (i.e., one's assumptive world). Interruption of necessary responses results in a stress response syndrome, most often diagnosed as post-traumatic stress disorder (PTSD), adjustment disorder, or brief reactive psychosis. Other diagnoses include phobic disorder, generalized anxiety disorder, major depressive disorder, and uncomplicated bereavement.

Overview of Treatment Procedures

Treatment of the stress response syndrome consists of a 12-session, once-a-week, time-limited dynamic psychotherapy. The main goal of intervention is to reduce the individual's need for controls that ward off stress-related ideas and the intolerable emotional states threatening to emerge if these ideas are not kept in check. Put simply, this is accomplished by helping the mourner complete the cycle of ideational and emotional responses to the stressful event. Completion demands the integration of the event's meanings and the development of appropriate adaptational responses, operationalized as being when the individual "is freely able to think about, or not think about, the event" (Horowitz, 1986a, p. 123).

Consciousness about the stressful event is valued not for the sake of awareness alone but because it is required to unlearn automatic associations and to resolve seemingly irreconcilable conflicts:

Change is accomplished by a combination of conscious and unconscious processes, by the revisions, learning, and the creation of new solutions required by the altered situation. In other words, change can be explained as decisions, both conscious and unconscious, that revise inner schemata and plans for action. The goal is continuity of the traumatic experience with other life memories, and the reintegration of personal aims. (Horowitz, 1986a, p. 99)

Interventions are dictated by the demands of the specific phase of the stress response the individual is experiencing. During the phase of denial and numbing, which is marked by overcontrol, abreactive-cathartic methods to reduce control are implemented (e.g., suggestion, social pressure, hypnosis, drugs). During the phase of intrusion, the therapeutic goal is to supplement relatively weak controls (i.e., take over some aspects of control operations and reduce the likelihood of emotional and ideational triggers to repeated representations). In general, intrusive symptomatology is the primary reason individuals enter treatment. Treatments for both phases of the stress response syndrome are noted in Table 7.1.

In many instances, the individual experiences both phases simultaneously, each demanding its own type of intervention. For example, after the death of a spouse, a mourner may have repetitive intrusive ideas and pangs of guilt over hostile attitudes toward the deceased but deny and ward off sadness and ideas related to loss. To the former state of relative undercontrol, the caregiver responds with interventions to supplement control. To the latter state of relative overcontrol, he or she responds to reduce controls.

Priorities in treatment are established according to the individual's current state. Table 7.2 shows the priorities of treatment for the stress response syndrome. When the stress event is ongoing, direct support is indicated. After the external event is over, if the individual swings between paralyzing denial and intolerable intrusions, the therapeutic aim is to decrease the amplitude of the swings; if the individual is frozen in a state of inhibited cognitive-emotional processing, the goal is to induce further thought and help dose subsequent responses.

Horowitz and colleagues' 12-session dynamic psychotherapy for the stress response syndrome generally follows the format illustrated in Table 7.3, although it may vary according to individual circumstances, characteristics, and responses. The initial therapeutic task is the establishment of a safe and communicative working alliance. This alliance facilitates the caregiver's ultimate goal of altering the status of the controls the individual uses to interrupt processing of the stress response so that he can complete the requisite information-processing cycles initiated by the stress event. A number of psychotherapeutic interventions assist the caregiver in doing so: analysis and interpretation of the person's defensive avoidances and the reasons for them; attention to warded-off material through identification, interpretation, and labeling of content; and the creation of evocative situations into which the person will bring the previously avoided ideas and feelings. Through these techniques, the caregiver works to help

Table 7.1 Treatments for Two Phases of the Stress Response Syndrome

Denial-Numbing Phase

Reduce controls
    Interpret defenses and attitudes that make
        controls necessary
    Suggest recollection

Encourage abreaction
Encourage description
    Association
    Speech
    Use of images rather than just words
        in recollection and fantasy
    Conceptual enactments, possibly also
        role-playing and art therapy
Reconstructions to prime memory and associations

Encourage catharsis
Explore emotional aspects of relationships and
    experiences of self during event
Supply support and encourage emotional
    relationships to counteract numbness

Intrusive-Repetitive Phase

Supply structure externally
    Structure time and events for patient when essential
        Organize information
Reduce external demand and stimulus levels
Rest
Provide identification models, group membership,
    good leadership, orienting values
Permit temporary idealization, dependency

Work through and reorganize by clarifying
    and educative interpretive work
Differentiate
    Reality from fantasy
    Past from current schemata
    Self-attributes from object attributes
Remove environmental reminders and triggers,
    interpret their meaning and effect
Teach "dosing" (e.g., attention on and away
    from stress-related information)

Support
Evoke other emotions (e.g., benevolent environment)
Suppress emotion (e.g., selective use of antianxiety agents)
Desensitization procedures and relaxation

Note. From *Stress Response Syndromes* (2nd ed., p. 124) by M.J. Horowitz, 1986a, Northvale, NJ: Jason Aronson. Copyright 1986 by Jason Aronson, Inc. Reprinted by permission.

Table 7.2 Priorities of Treatment for the Stress Response Syndrome

Patient's Current State	Treatment Goal
Under continuing impact of external stress event	Terminate external event or remove patient from contiguity with it Provide temporary relationship Help with decisions, plans, or working through
Swings to intolerable levels: Ideational-emotional attacks Paralyzing denial and numbness	Reduce amplitude of oscillations to swings of tolerable intensity of ideation and emotion Continue emotional and ideational support Selection of techniques cited for states of intrusion [in Table 7.1]
Frozen in overcontrol state of denial and numbness with or without intrusive repetitions	Help patient "dose" reexperience of event and implications that help patient remember for a time, put out of mind for a time, remember for a time, and so on—selection of denial techniques [from Table 7.1] During periods of recollection, help patient organize and express experience; increase sense of safety in therapeutic relationship so patient can resume processing the event
Able to experience and tolerate episodes of ideation and waves of emotion	Help patient work through associations: the conceptual, emotional, object relations, and self-image implications of the stress event Help patient relate this stress event to earlier threats, relationship models, self-concepts, and future plans
Able to work through ideas and emotions on one's own	Work through loss of therapeutic relationship Terminate treatment

Note. From *Stress Response Syndromes* (2nd ed., p. 125) by M.J. Horowitz, 1986a, Northvale, NJ: Jason Aronson. Copyright 1986 by Jason Aronson, Inc. Reprinted by permission.

Table 7.3 Sample 12-Session Dynamic Therapy for Stress Disorders

Session	Relationship Issues	Patient Activity	Therapist Activity
1	Initial positive feeling for helper	Patient tells story of event	Preliminary focus is discussed
2	Lull as sense of pressure is reduced	Event is related to previous life	Takes psychiatric history; gives patient realistic appraisal of syndrome
3	Patient testing therapist for various relationship possibilities	Patient adds associations to indicate expanded meaning of event	Focus is realigned; resistances to contemplating stress-related themes are interpreted
4	Therapeutic alliance deepened	Implications of event in the present are contemplated	Defenses and warded-off contents are interpreted, linking of latter to stress event and responses
5		Themes that have been avoided are worked on	Active confrontation with feared topics and reengagement in feared activities are encouraged
6		The future is contemplated	Time of termination is discussed
7–11	Transference reactions interpreted and linked to other configurations; acknowledgment of pending separation	The working through of central conflicts and issues of termination, as related to the life event and reactions to it, is continued	Central conflicts, termination, unfinished issues, and recommendations all are clarified and interpreted
12	Saying good-bye	Work to be continued on own and plans for the future are discussed	Real gains and summary of future work for patient to do on own are acknowledged

Note. From *Stress Response Syndromes* (2nd ed., p. 131) by M.J. Horowitz, 1986a, Northvale, NJ: Jason Aronson. Copyright 1986 by Jason Aronson, Inc. Reprinted by permission.

the individual appraise the serious life event and its associated meanings and make necessary revisions of inner models of the self and world to correspond with new external realities.

As the individual examines warded-off ideas, he may find that he is not as vulnerable or incapable of coping with stress as he previously had thought, and he may become aware of other resources. By examining the universal themes known to occur after stressful life events, he becomes able to deal with their meanings and their accompanying emotions. These themes include fear of repetition, fear of merger with victims, shame and rage over vulnerability, rage at the source, rage at those exempted, fear of loss of control over aggressive impulses, guilt or shame over aggressive impulses, guilt or shame over surviving, and sadness over losses.

As appraisal and revision take place, the individual becomes capable of making new decisions and engaging in adaptive actions. He practices these altered behavioral patterns until they become automatic. As he achieves new levels of awareness, the process is repeated and deepened. In essence, as the relationship with the caregiver deepens, he can modify his controls and assimilate more of the warded-off thoughts about the stressful event.

In addition to helping the individual work through his stress response reactions, the caregiver also may direct efforts toward modifying preexisting conflicts, developmental difficulties, and defensive styles that have caused unusual vulnerability to traumatization by this particular experience (e.g., weak self-image). In this paradigm, such work usually takes place during the middle of the therapeutic process.

Throughout treatment, the individual's state dictates shifts in therapeutic priorities and techniques, as indicated in Table 7.3. One shift in treatment focus is critically important for success. Initially, the caregiver and mourner agree to attenuate the presenting symptoms or problematic states or to avoid reentry into them, viewing these states in relation to the individual's other states of experience and behavior. During treatment, a broader analysis of the situation must occur, including an examination of the reasons for entering the problem states and the other even more threatening warded-off states. As painful symptoms decrease, the treatment focus is revised: Instead of focusing on the problem states themselves, treatment now explores when and why the individual enters into these painful states. This often involves focusing upon particular self-concepts and inner models of relationships (i.e., identity and the assumptive world). If this shift is not made at the proper time, the individual may terminate treatment once he achieves sufficient control to enter into a relatively stable denial phase. To end treatment at this point would be an error because the person has not worked through some of the most difficult and important parts of the stress response—and he may not do so on his own.

Even during this relatively brief treatment, the caregiver must attend to issues of characteristic defensive style and transference. Interpretations of defenses, core neurotic conflicts, and transference phenomena can be made; however, these phenomena must be interpreted according to their real relationship to the current stress and must be centered on the specific content of memories associated with the stressful event and on the usually negative transference reactions that interfere with treatment. In other words, interpretation in this context should be linked to the current event to maintain the treatment's stress-focused goals and priorities. At some point, if advisable, it may be possible to extend recognition of the individual's patterns of response to the transference, childhood relationships, and current interpersonal relationships, but there is no intent to allow a transference neurosis. Transference interpretations typically will be restricted to those negative responses that are likely to impede treatment.

Noting that recent stress events tend to bring character traits and pathology into sharp relief and that they activate latent conflicts and memories of past stress events, Horowitz (1976) crystallizes the divergence of views regarding whether treatment should be directed toward character (core neurotic conflict) analysis or completion of the stress response. Although he asserts that it is unlikely that therapeutic work associated with the stress event can proceed without some work on relevant character traits, activated conflicts, and memories, he contends that the decision as to how far to proceed in this direction must include consideration of the degree to which these and compulsive repetition of past traumas contribute to the occurrence of the recent stress event, the present reaction to the recent stress event, and difficulties in working through the recent events or in the therapeutic relationship. Additional areas to consider include the mourner's general maladaptation, his readiness and capacity to change, the ratio between the objective magnitude of the stress event and the degree of reaction, and cost and sufficiency factors.

Several sessions before the end, the topic of termination is introduced. This demands that the individual work through his reactions to the approaching loss of the caregiver and the therapy and leads to a reexperience of the original loss and frequently to a return of symptoms. However, in contrast to the actual precipitating loss or stressful event, this time the loss can be faced gradually rather than traumatically, actively rather than passively, and within a communicative and helping relationship rather than alone. During the final hours of treatment, the caregiver makes specific interpretations concerning the link between the termination experience and the stressful event.

Because of the time needed to process a major loss and anxiety about the loss of the therapeutic relationship, the individual usually still has some symptoms at termination. Despite these remaining symptoms, he has learned new psychological skills, developed reflective awareness, mastered new ways of thinking, gained insight, and modified habitual avoidances. Insofar as the individual practices these altered ways of feeling, thinking, and behaving—and uses newly acquired skills, techniques, and capacities—the learning that occurs with regard to the specific stress event may generalize to enhance overall coping. The person may identify and alter habitual defenses and attitudes, improve ongoing methods of coping, plan different ways of behaving, and in general respond to promote further psychological development. Thus, this type of treatment can result in significant changes within the person long after termination.

Despite the success of this time-limited procedure, sometimes psychotherapy without time limits will be the treatment of choice. This is usually the case with complex, delayed, or chronic stress response syndromes and for persons with PTSD in the context of a personality disorder, especially those characterized by vulnerability to the coherence and stability of self-organization. Nevertheless, even in such extended treatment, Horowitz asserts that a focus on working through traumatic events and reactions can be preserved. Regarding the use of interpretation, he advises an approach anchored in the traumatic event that begins at the surface, and then gradually extends to related issues at a pace tolerable and useful to the individual. Treatment interventions and decisions based on levels of interpretation about links between the current situation and current reactions and between the current situation and longstanding, individualized personality patterns are delineated in Horowitz (1986a).

Individual Factors in Treatment

Any person exposed to extreme stress can develop a stress response disorder. Thus, one should never assume that a person who has developed a stress response syndrome subsequent to a trauma is a person who was more impaired at the time of exposure to it. However, preexisting characteristics can interfere with adaptive response after a stressful event. As Horowitz (1985) notes, these characteristics include the following.

1. Belief in magical causation, leading to the view that past bad thoughts brought present harm

2. Active conflict with a theme similar to meanings contained in the traumatic event

3. An habitual tendency to use pathological defense mechanisms (e.g., extreme projection) in order to externalize personal emotional propensities, leading to memory distortions about the traumatic event

4. An habitual style of using fantasy-based reparations of injuries and losses, which hinders realistic appraisal of the personal implications of the traumatic event

5. Latent self-concepts of incompetency or relationship conflicts that are readily activated as a consequence of the traumatic event

6. Fatigue of biological substrates from acute and chronic stress, leading to a repetition of depressions

7. Activation of emergency response systems, exacerbating previous somatic reactions and thus hindering psychological adaptation and providing additional stress

Horowitz also stresses that, despite the general applicability of the stress response paradigm, each individual has a personal style for controlling the flow of ideas in order to avoid entry into painful states. He observes that even in focal therapy aimed at working through ideas and feelings associated with a serious life event, the caregiver's technique should be geared to these habitual modes and should accommodate personality differences and preexisting aspects of the individual. In-depth discussion regarding the treatment of individuals who use specific hysterical, obsessional, and narcissistic control styles to counter intrusive and painful emotional responses after trauma is offered in Horowitz (1986a).

WORDEN'S TREATMENT PROCEDURES FOR RESOLVING PATHOLOGICAL GRIEF

For Worden (1982), the goal of grief therapy (as distinct from grief counseling, which is intended to facilitate the normal process of mourning) is to resolve the conflicts of separation and assist the mourner in completing the tasks of mourning. The resolution of these conflicts necessarily will involve the mourner's experiencing thoughts and feelings that have been avoided.

The caregiver's responsibility is to provide the social support necessary for successful grief work and give the permission to mourn that previously had been denied. A positive therapeutic alliance is a prerequisite and can be enhanced by the caregiver's recognizing and acknowledging to the mourner the difficulty some individuals can have when they resurrect past losses. The greater the mourner's underlying conflict, the greater will be the resistance to exploring painful thoughts and feelings. The caregiver must constantly monitor and work with these resistances as an inherent part of the therapeutic process. For example, because the mourner may express resistance by raising issues unrelated to grief, it is important to keep sessions focused by reminding the mourner of the task and exploring the purpose for the resistance.

Worden's initial step in grief therapy is to establish a contract with the mourner to meet on a time-limited basis for 8 to 10 visits, during which they will explore the loss and its relationship to the present pain or distress.

He has found that most individuals presenting with what he calls a focused unresolved grief reaction, without unusual complications, generally can resolve their problem within this time frame. In some cases, serious underlying pathology is discovered during the contracted sequence of sessions, requiring a prolonged period of treatment unrelated to grief. The caregiver also may encounter an unresolved grief issue during a routine sequence of psychotherapy. In this instance, grief therapy also takes place within the context of a longer therapy.

Worden has outlined nine procedures for treating complicated mourning, with the assumption that "they will be applied within each therapist's own theoretical framework and level of professional competence" (p. 67). Briefly, these include the following.

Rule out physical disease. One should never commence treatment with an individual in which a physical symptom is the major presentation unless physical disease has been conclusively ruled out. Even if a mourner's physical symptoms quite clearly appear to be grief equivalents, it is important to exclude disease as a cause.

Set up the contract and establish an alliance. The mourner and the caregiver agree to reexplore the relationship with the deceased. The mourner's belief that this will be beneficial is reinforced by the caregiver, who agrees that this is a worthy area to explore. The focus is specifically the loss and what is directly related to it. Temporarily, the caregiver becomes a substitute for the lost person and works to render hope and comfort, remaining aware of the mourner's guilt and destructiveness but illustrating that this awareness does not diminish the compassion or concern felt for the mourner.

Revive memories of the deceased. The caregiver engages the mourner in discussion of the person who died—who he was, what he was like, what the mourner remembers about him, what they enjoyed doing together, and so forth. Initially, it is important to build a groundwork of positive memories in order to assist later on in balancing some of the negative ones. Gradually, the caregiver turns the conversation toward more ambivalent memories, and, finally, the mourner discusses memories filled with hurt, anger, and disappointment. If the mourner has come to treatment aware of only negative feelings, the process is reversed, with positive memories and affects revived, even if few in number. If the mourner is contending with multiple losses, each will need to be dealt with individually. (Worden believes that, generally, it is best to explore the loss believed to have the fewest complicating factors first.)

Assess which of four grief tasks are not completed. The four tasks identified by Worden as being necessary to accomplish grief resolution are as follows: Task I, accept the reality of the loss; Task II, experience the pain of grief; Task III, adjust to the environment in which the deceased is missing; and Task IV, withdraw emotional energy and reinvest it in another relationship. The caregiver must assess where the mourner has problems in the mourning process and intervene appropriately. If Task I is incomplete, and the mourner is saying to herself, "I won't have you dead. You are not dead but just away," therapy focuses on the reality of the death and the need to relinquish the deceased. If the mourner accepts the reality without expressing appropriate affect, thus evidencing problems in Task II, therapy stresses that it is safe for the mourner to experience both positive and negative feelings for the deceased and that she can come to a balance of these feelings. Here, a redefinition of the mourner's relationship with the deceased is needed. If the mourner has complications in Task III, problem solving becomes a major part of the treatment. The mourner is encouraged to get back to living and is taught to overcome helplessness by trying out new skills and developing new roles. Incompletion of Task IV requires that the caregiver help the mourner become emancipated from crippling attachment to the deceased in order to form new relationships. This entails giving the mourner permission to stop grieving, sanctioning new relationships, and exploring the difficulties involved in saying a final good-bye.

Deal with affect or lack of affect stimulated by memories. Often in grief therapy, the mourner idealizes the deceased, speaking in only the most glowingly positive terms. It is important for the caregiver to allow these descriptions early on. However, such overwhelming accolades often cover considerable unexpressed anger. This anger is worked through gradually by first exploring the more ambivalent feelings the mourner has and then helping her get in touch with angry feelings. Once these feelings are identified, the caregiver helps the mourner see that they do not obliterate positive feelings for the lost loved one and that they actually exist because the mourner did care for the deceased. In brief, the mourner needs to be left with a balance between positive and negative feelings. A second emotion frequently stimulated by memories of the deceased is guilt. As is the case for anger, guilt also is identified. It is important to help the mourner reality test the guilt; much is irrational and does not hold up under scrutiny. When dealing with guilt that has an actual basis in reality, therapy includes the seeking and granting of forgiveness between mourner and deceased. Role-playing techniques are quite useful in this regard.

Explore and defuse linking objects. In complicated mourning, the mourner's use of a linking object (Volkan, 1972, 1981) may impede resolution. It is important to inquire about what items a mourner has saved after a death and to determine whether they are linking objects, as opposed to keepsakes or mementos, which are not unhealthy. If the mourner is employing an item as a linking object, the caregiver encourages her to bring it into the session and discuss it. This can be most effective in facilitating mourning and in indicating conflicts causing problems in processing the loss. Often, as therapy progresses, the mourner spontaneously will put or give away these objects, even though previously such an action would have caused great anxiety.

Acknowledge the finality of the loss. When the mourner nurtures a chronic hope for reunion (Volkan, 1972), maintaining that the loss is not final and that the deceased is coming back in some form or another, the caregiver helps the individual assess precisely why she cannot acknowledge the finality of the loss. These reasons (e.g., the belief that acknowledgment means one must make one's own choices and be subject to one's own impulses) are then addressed therapeutically in order to prevent them from sustaining denial.

Deal with the fantasy of ending grieving. A very simple and fruitful procedure in treatment is to have the mourner explore the fantasy of what it would be like to complete the grieving (e.g., by evaluating what would be lost). This is an effective way of identifying interferences with grief resolution and secondary gains associated with remaining in mourning.

Help the mourner say a final good-bye. Saying good-bye is gradually done during the course of treatment. At each session, the mourner is encouraged to say a temporary good-bye (i.e., "Good-bye for now") to the deceased. Eventually, doing so will lead to saying a final good-bye at the conclusion of therapy. This usually comes out in statements like "I have to let you go," "I have to say good-bye," or "You're causing me too much pain, and I have to let you go." After being able to say this, the mourner often experiences a tremendous sense of relief, which is obvious at the following session. The caregiver allows the mourner to take the lead in this process by asking whether she is ready to say good-bye. When unfinished business is completed, the mourner will know she is ready to do so.

RANDO'S SCHEMA FOR CREATING THERAPEUTIC BEREAVEMENT RITUALS

Recent years have brought increased interest in therapeutic rituals in the treatment of both uncomplicated and complicated mourning (Kollar, 1989; Rando, 1985b; Reeves & Boersma, 1989–1990; van der Hart, 1983, 1988a, 1988b, 1988c, 1988d; van der Hart & Ebbers, 1981; van der Hart & Goossens, 1987). Given that rituals date back to time immemorial and are part of every social group, found in a dazzling variety of forms, and practiced in some manner by all societies, it seems surprising that scholarly appreciation for their use in treating the bereaved has been so late in coming. Certainly, mourners have always had therapeutic rituals, whether recognized as such or not. For example, appropriately designed funerals are one of the best and potentially most therapeutic rituals available (see Blauner, 1966; Irion, 1966, 1988; Kollar, 1983; Mandelbaum, 1959; Rando, 1984).

Rituals may involve an infinite number of behaviors or activities: "A ritual is defined as a specific behavior or activity which gives symbolic expression to certain feelings and thoughts of the actor(s) individually or as a group. It may be a habitually repetitive behavior or a one-time occurrence" (Rando, 1985b, p. 236). To this description, van der Hart and Ebbers (1981) would add the requirement of prescription: "We define rituals as formally prescribed symbolic acts that have to be enacted both in a specified manner and in a specified order. Sometimes a verbal formula accompanies the ritual, but this is dependent on the individual case" (p. 189). Rituals can provide powerful therapeutic experiences that symbolize transition, healing, and continuity (van der Hart, 1983).

For the individual mourner, therapeutic bereavement rituals can provide a structured way to affirm the death; recall the loved one; or explore, clarify, express, integrate, and subsequently make statements about the mourner's diverse feelings and thoughts about the loved one. They can assist the mourner in saying good-bye to the deceased and in encouraging the necessary formulation of a healthy new relationship with that person. Finally, they can symbolize the transition back into the new world.

In terms of the social group, therapeutic bereavement rituals can solidify family relationships and assist in the realignment of family roles and the healthy promotion of mourning. Provision of a commonly experienced symbolic behavior and an experience designed to help cope with and work through impediments to mourning strengthens the group's relational patterns and minimizes the divisive potential of complicated mourning within the family system.

The remainder of this chapter describes the specific therapeutic properties of rituals and details steps in creating therapeutic rituals appropriate for the bereaved. For additional information on secular rituals and the therapeutic value and societal functions and meanings of collective ceremony and ritual, the reader is urged to refer to the sources noted at the beginning of this chapter, as well as to d'Aquili, Laughlin, and McManus (1979); Drucker (1969); Gorer (1965); Imber-Black, Roberts, and Whiting (1988); Jackson (1983); Laughlin and d'Aquili (1979); Moore and Myerhoff (1977); and Toffler (1970).

Therapeutic Properties of Rituals

Rituals involve a number of specific healing properties that can be beneficial in promoting healthy mourning. These properties are described in the following pages.

Derivation of benefits from acting out

In this context, the term *acting out* refers to any purposeful behavioral expression of an internal thought or feeling. It is differentiated from the psychoanalytic use of the term, which describes a neurotic displacement of a behavioral response used to discharge some drive tension. Acting out through ritual makes a statement. In addition, it has the therapeutic benefit of enabling the individual to do something besides fall victim to the emptiness and powerlessness too frequently bestowed by bereavement. An activity is provided to challenge the passivity often found after victimization by loss, and this facilitates a sense of control. Acting out also cuts through intellectualization and other resistances to mourning and gets at the heart of affect. Rituals effectively put the subjective out into the objective world (Turner, 1977), providing a here-and-now focus on emotion, discouraging splitting and facilitating movement toward wholeness and integration, and providing a means of ventilation while offering appropriate channels for feelings. Acting out facilitates the expiation of guilt more effectively than does verbalization alone. In addition, acting out often reaches a person's unconscious levels more rapidly than verbalization because it appeals to the right side of the brain.

Legitimization of emotional and physical ventilation

Therapeutic ritual sanctions and validates the mourner's expression of feeling. In cases where there is personal or social conditioning against expression of affect, participation in therapeutic rituals—especially those prescribed by an authority figure such as a caregiver—provides both the forum and the means by which emotions can be released without violating previous conditioning or inviting idiosyncratic resistance. Rituals also promote physical release, which decreases intensity of emotion, promotes clearer thinking, and discharges pent-up tension. The psychological and physical movement in the ritual overcomes passivity in the face of loss, dissipates anxiety, increases a sense of personal power, and gives the person permission to go beyond a static state.

Provision of symbols and outlets to focus thoughts, feelings, and behaviors

Specific symbols and outlets in therapeutic bereavement rituals become for the mourner the tools for the expression of thoughts, feelings, and behaviors stimulated by the loss. The use of symbols concretizes thought and affect, which then can be manipulated by the mourner to convey a particular message. This provides the mourner with a tangible experience that would not be possible if abstractions alone were employed and, correspondingly, with the power to direct this experience. For example, lighting a candle might legitimize and define the special time during which the mourner reminisces about the deceased, and planting a tree might signal a mourner's forgiveness of the deceased.

Rendering of control

After undertaking a prescribed activity with symbolic meaning, the mourner often experiences emotional and physical release, along with a sense of the increased manageability of emotions. This increased sense of control can militate against the feeling of helplessness frequently experienced subsequent to major loss.

Delimitation of grief

Rituals can help channel feelings of mourning into a circumscribed behavior having a distinct beginning and end and a clear focus, thus helping the individual experience mourning in a less global, undifferentiated manner. Some mourners need external structure or authority to provide them permission to cease their particular expression of mourning. They may feel too guilty to stop by themselves, sometimes erroneously believing that chronicity of ritual, like chronicity of mourning, reveals the extent of their love for the deceased. For others, a structured end point is necessary to help them deal with their fear that they will be consumed by emotion. Rituals are especially salient for freeing up mourners from the need to demonstrate their feelings in an ongoing fashion. This is particularly true at holidays and anniversaries, when the bittersweet aspects of the day must be managed (Rando, 1988). For example, because they know that planting a tree on a deceased child's birthday will provide them with an activity in which they can demonstrate their love and illustrate to themselves and others that they have not forgotten the child, a family may feel it is less a betrayal if they do not feel constant pain on other days and may find it easier to permit themselves to experience whatever joy is possible.

Enhancement of an appropriate connection with the deceased

Rituals legitimize emotional exchanges. They can provide symbolic evidence of the continued existence of the deceased in the life of the mourner and at the same time clearly recognize the reality of the death and its implications. Therefore, participation in rituals may provide the mourner with an opportunity to interact intensely with the memory of the deceased for a delimited period of time without crossing over into pathological dimensions.

Enablement of the six "R" processes of mourning

Rituals provide assistance in confronting and working through mourning. They can help individuals confront painful stimuli associated with loss and can provide a framework for considering those stimuli and facilitating the mourning processes. Ritual behaviors are therapeutic in allowing an individual to state—consciously and unconsciously, implicitly and explicitly—that a loss has occurred and in promoting activities in which the mourner can experience, express, and channel feelings of grief. They can provide an opportunity for recollecting and reviewing, finishing unfinished business, and learning to relate to the deceased in a new fashion. In addition, repetition of rituals can promote working through and the required relinquishments, readjustments, and reinvestments by confronting the mourner multiple times with stimuli associated with the reality that must be incorporated, while simultaneously offering a healthy connection to the deceased. In essence, the assorted therapeutic benefits of rituals can stimulate and facilitate the six "R" processes of mourning, thus serving as transitional steps toward accommodating the loss.

Enhancement of learning gained through experience

Participation in ritual helps the mourner learn that the deceased truly is gone, provides the experience necessary to validate the loss, and helps him prepare for and readjust to the environment in which the deceased is missing. The active "doing" in ritual actualizes the learning most effectively, making it more real than abstract learning.

Provision of structure, form, and containment for ambivalent, nebulous, or poorly defined affect and cognition

Ritual is especially helpful in confronting the confusing disorganization and loss of control commonly experienced in grief. When emotions are labeled, they become more comprehensible. Similarly, acting out in the form of ritual can make emotions more understandable and manageable, thus placing them more within the control of the mourner. In other words, rituals actualize and concretize the abstract. They also serve to contain emotions by offering protection against overpowering feelings and excessive impulsiveness and to reduce anger and aggression in mourning (Rosenblatt, Jackson, & Walsh, 1972).

Prescription of actions for dealing with emotional or social chaos

Rituals can reduce stress overload, help conserve energy, concert behavior in a harmonious fashion, and provide structure and meaning through the prescription of particular behaviors during times of upheaval. The mourner can derive security in carrying out rituals that provide the conditions, arena, and format for the individual to feel grounded or safe while experiencing the intense reactions of grief.

Provision of experiences that allow the participation of other group members and affirm kinship and social solidarity

Collective rituals facilitate the social interaction critical for successful mourning and promote the mourner's ultimate reintegration into the social group. In addition, rituals can identify and define family, attest to its continuation in the absence of the deceased, strengthen relational patterns, promote unity, assist in realignment of roles, and express community solidarity and support.

Structuring of celebrations, anniversaries, and holidays

Although disturbing affects or cognitions associated with anniversaries and other special dates are a normal and essential part of the mourning process, such reactions are not always easily recognized or owned by mourners. Participation in ritual activities constructed to commemorate meaningful occasions are an unusually effective way of tapping into these affects or cognitions. They provide therapeutic experiences for eliciting, identifying, and channeling STUG reactions (see chapter 2).

Steps in Creating Therapeutic Bereavement Rituals

In order to ensure that a ritual is meaningful and therapeutic, the caregiver must ascertain precisely what the impediments to successful mourning are and then design the appropriate ritual or rituals to overcome these impediments. Specific rituals must be tailored to the individual needs of the mourner and must pertain to the specific loss experienced. Different types of loss may mandate diverse treatment rituals for the same individual. In designing such therapeutic bereavement rituals, it will be helpful to keep in mind the following 10 steps, which represent a synthesis of my own work with that of Onno van der Hart (1983, 1988a, 1988b, 1988c, 1988d).

Rituals may be incorporated into ongoing psychotherapeutic work of different philosophical orientations, may be ancillary to other work, or may comprise an independent treatment. If rituals are used as an independent treatment, care must be taken to address critical content and process variables in treatment (e.g., therapeutic alliance, safeguards). The discussion here assumes that all appropriate psychotherapeutic issues and/or concerns have been adequately raised and dealt with in the treatment design. A ritual is not a gimmick to be used out of context—hence use of the term *therapeutic bereavement rituals.*

Step 1: Assess

As in all other areas of intervention, assessment must precede intervention. The determinants that must be assessed in designing a ritual for therapeutic use include (a) the psychological, behavioral, social, physical, ethnic, generational, cultural, religious, philosophical, and spiritual characteristics of the mourner; (b) the mourner's previous relevant life experiences; (c) the nature and extent of psychosocial support; (d) characteristics specific to the loss (e.g., nature and meaning of the loss, circumstances and features of the death); (e) length of time since the death; and (f) the mourner's particular place in the mourning process and issues and possible conflicts attendant to it.

Step 2: Determine the focus and purpose with regard to mourning

A ritual may be created to facilitate the typical uncomplicated process of grief and mourning or to intervene with the individual whose mourning has become complicated. In either case, the caregiver must be clear on the specific purpose of the ritual. One does not suggest a ritual merely to have a ritual; its ultimate goal must be identified and serve to inform creation.

Step 3: Specify what message is to be conveyed

The purpose of a ritual is to give symbolic expression to certain feelings and thoughts. Before a ritual can be designed, the message embodying these feelings and thoughts must be identified to the degree possible. In some cases, the entire content of this message will not be apparent until the mourner has gone through part or all of the ritual. For example, the individual with conflicted mourning may only recognize the depth of her anger after she writes several letters to the deceased. In the absence of some knowledge of the message to be expressed, a ritual may be ineffective. An exception to this is when the ritual is designed to complete some particular unfinished business and to identify other remaining unfinished business (e.g., after expressing negative feelings, the mourner realizes she has positive feelings that also require expression).

Step 4: Choose the type of ritual

Depending upon the specific focus, purpose, and message to be conveyed, one of two types of rituals may be chosen: a ritual of transition or a ritual of continuity.

Rituals of transition. These rituals originally were termed *rites de passage* (van Gennep, 1960) and mark transitions undergone by individuals and groups during their development (e.g., marriage, birth, and death). Rituals of transition may encompass any of van Gennep's three phases of transition and ritual—separation, transition, and incorporation. This type is indicated in the treatment of mourning when the mourner is unable to relinquish the old attachments to the deceased or the old assumptive world, the old ways of being in the world, or the old identity.

The six "R" processes of mourning inherently involve van Gennep's three phases and leave taking. They represent the mourner's personal rite of passage in bereavement. In brief, the mourner progresses from the *separation phase,* in which interactions with the deceased are cut off by the death and in which the mourner responds by the processes of recognizing the loss and reacting to the separation, through the *transition phase.* In the transition phase, the old world no longer exists, but the mourner has not yet adapted to the new world. The mourner is preoccupied with the deceased and the mourning processes of recollecting and reexperiencing the deceased and the relationship and relinquishing the old attachments to the deceased and the old assumptive world. Adaptation to the new world ultimately will demand recognition of the deceased's absence; an altered relationship with that person; revision of the assumptive world; formation of a new identity; adjusted behavior in the new world; and reinvestment in other people, objects, roles, hopes, beliefs, causes, ideals, goals, and pursuits. The *incorporation phase* into the new world is accomplished when the mourner can make all the adaptations necessary to readjust to move adaptively into the new life without forgetting the old and subsequently reinvest in that new world.

The individual may sustain difficulties in any of the three phases. Each phase requires different rituals to work through. Table 7.4 outlines the choices for rituals of transition depending upon where in van Gennep's phases the individual requires assistance.

Leave-taking rituals (sometimes known generically as separation rituals) are indicated when the mourner has problems in the initial separation phase of transition. Frequently used in psychotherapy, they are characterized by van der Hart (1988d), the acknowledged expert in this area:

> The *therapeutic* leave-taking ritual . . . consists of symbolic actions which form an ordered whole, with the aid of which the person, the couple or the family can take their leave of something and make a new beginning in life. . . . The therapeutic leave-taking ritual is indicated not only for working through a loss, but sometimes, too, to obtain a perspective on other traumatic experiences: past experiences which haunt the person or persons and prevent them from orienting themselves to the present and the future. If it is successful, the ritual helps to wind up the past. (p. 5)

Van der Hart (1988b) comments further with specific regard to issues of concern in complicated mourning:

> Carrying out a leave-taking ritual is a sort of re-grief therapy in which a symbolic leave is taken of persons or situations from the past. If it is as it should be, the ritual also helps the client to make a new start in life, just as traditional mourning customs do. The therapeutic leave-taking ritual is a rite of passage with the aid of which the client leaves behind him a certain . . . situation and effects a new situation. (p. 15)

According to van der Hart (1983), more demand for these types of rituals exists than for rituals to help mourners with the transition and incorporation phases. However, problems do occur during these latter two phases.

In the transition phase, a person must alter his self-image, role, or definition of the relationship. A number of the difficulties at this phase can be defined as *threshold problems,* or problems arising because the

Table 7.4 Rituals of Transition Classified According to van Gennep's Three Phases

Separation

Leave-taking rituals

1. Preparatory phase

2. Reorganization phase

3. Finalization phase

    Leave-taking ceremony

    Cleansing rite

    Reunion rite

Transition

Seclusion rituals

Purification rituals

Incorporation

Reunion rituals

Rituals to strengthen ties

---

mourner is in a state of limbo—not in the past life anymore but not yet beyond it. The main characteristics of rituals designed to help the mourner with threshold problems are seclusion and purification. Seclusion prevents the process from being disturbed by the demands of everyday life. Such seclusion is similar to that undertaken by newlyweds going off on a honeymoon after separating from their individual lives but before presenting themselves as a couple in society. Purification is used to conclude the transition phase (e.g., taking a shower or bath, cleaning a house or room). Because purification activities are a common part of everyday life, the mourner must find a way to imbue them with special meaning.

The incorporation phase is the opposite of the separation phase, where ties have been loosened. In the incorporation phase, the mourner resumes contact with those from whom he has been separated. Ordinary life begins again. This phase is often symbolized by putting on new clothes, going to a party, or sharing a communal meal. All of these behaviors illustrate reunion and a strengthening of ties.

To summarize, the individual with complicated mourning who sustains difficulties in letting go of some aspects of the past may benefit from a ritual of transition. The problems may reside in the separation phase, in which case a comprehensive leave-taking ritual is recommended. (See Step 8 for discussion of implementing such a ritual.) Problems in the transition and/or incorporation phases benefit from more circumscribed rites devoted to promoting the particular phase. It must be realized that within each particular phase of the complex ritual of transition the whole of van Gennep's schema can be repeated one or more times.

Rituals of continuity. Rituals of continuity maintain and confirm the stability of life at a given point. They help participants adjust to change, define relationships, and provide security and protection. These include *telectic rites,* which are acts of greeting or farewell (e.g., shaking hands), and *intensification rites,* which are collective ritualistic activities coinciding with changes in the natural surroundings of the group, such as the alternation of day and night and the succession of seasons (e.g., the family dinner or Christmas holiday). As regards mourning, there appears to me to be a third type of continuity ritual. These might be termed *connection rites,* in which the mourner expresses an appropriate connection to the deceased. Rituals of this type include such activities as mentioning the deceased's name during grace, making a donation in memory of the deceased, or visiting the deceased's grave. In this regard, what is being continued—albeit in an altered fashion—is the expression of the mourner's love for and relationship with the deceased.

Rituals of continuity appear to develop on their own much more readily than do rituals of transition. As long as they reflect the two criteria for an appropriate relationship with the deceased (i.e., the mourner recognizes and understands the death and its implications and is continuing on in the new life in an adaptive fashion), such rituals are not unhealthy. Repetitive family, social, and holiday rituals are especially effective in prompting the mourner's awareness of the deceased's absence. Holidays may be a particularly important time to have a ritual of continuity, the purpose of which is to demonstrate that the deceased continues on as a memorable and special part of the mourner's life. (See Step 8 for discussion of implementing rituals of continuity.)

Step 5: Choose the elements of the ritual

Four key elements must be considered in constructing the ritual: who is involved, what symbols are to be used, what symbolic acts are to be undertaken, and what characteristics of the ritual are to be employed.

Who is involved. Rituals are appropriate if the focus of the individual's attention is a deceased person. However, if the focus is a living person, van der Hart (1983) suggests that it is better to choose a route other than performance of a ritual (e.g., to visit that person to talk things over or go into therapy together). He also notes that frequently the mourner mentions one person as being the focus of attention but later discovers that more people are involved. As in other aspects of therapy, it will be important for the mourner to be as specific as possible. If numerous people are involved, they are probably best dealt with one at a time.

Symbols used. Van der Hart (1983, 1988c) provides convincing evidence that the way in which one treats a symbol is analogous to the way in which one would treat what it symbolizes. The symbol is inseparably entwined with the feelings and thoughts fostered about the person or event symbolized, evoking new experiences and at the same time giving form to them. Symbols may be idiosyncratic or comprehensive. *Idiosyncratic symbols* are symbols that pertain to a single interactional event, whereas *comprehensive symbols* (sometimes termed *key symbols*) are condensed symbols evoking an emotional reaction greater than those referring to a single event.

Symbols are bound up with individuals or relationships on the basis of either similarity (e.g., symbols that connote some type of physical or symbolic resemblance) or contiguity (e.g., symbols that derive from, have been in contact with, and pertain to the relationship with the person). In addition, symbols may be created by the mourner (e.g., paintings, letters, drawings, poems, sculpture).

In using symbols, the principle of *pars pro toto* obtains: Whatever affects a part of the whole also influences the whole. This is how, in ritual behavior, a single symbol can represent an entire person. Thus, taking leave of a symbol becomes the same as taking leave of the person it represents. This does not mean that one must let go of all symbols. It may be that, whereas some objects are used in rituals and then relinquished (as in leave-taking ceremonies), others can be retained as keepsakes (van der Hart, 1988c). If reminders of the person to be separated from exist, a decision must be made as to what will happen to them, for they can continue to stimulate old responses.

Symbolic acts undertaken. In addition to the creation of symbols, symbolic acts may be undertaken. In leave-taking rituals, these acts are intended to diminish preoccupation with the other and bring about a farewell. In rituals of continuity, symbolic acts permit the individual to define the relationship with the other, provide security by permitting the individual to know where she stands in the situation, and help participants adjust to change.

It is important that the symbolic acts undertaken be consistent with the characteristics and needs of the mourner. For example, it is possible to go too far in using rituals with aggressive implications (e.g., destroying, burning, burying). Some mourners may regret too drastic a detachment from an object that reminds them of the other and might feel guilty or harm others as a result. In order to avoid going too far, van der Hart (1983) refers to the notion of doing such things as putting the symbol in a chest in the attic, then locking the chest and throwing away the key. Also less drastic than destroying an object is giving it away. As with the specific choice of symbolic behavior, the elements involved in the behavior must be compatible with the mourner. Examples of such elements might include transforming an object (e.g., melting down a wedding ring and having it made into another piece of jewelry), scattering the ashes of burned photographs, destroying a piece of furniture, or returning a gift. If, for example, an individual has problems with fire, it is preferable not to suggest burning old love letters as a symbolic act. Likewise, to suggest attendance at church for a mourner who eschews organized religion would be inappropriate. In brief, the manner in which the mourner continues to relate to the deceased must be ego-syntonic for that individual. This caveat applies not only to rituals of transition, but also to rituals of continuity.

Symbolic acts have various levels. The symbol may be transformed and then transformed again. With each transformation, the relationship is changed. In rituals of transition, a mourner may write numerous letters saying good-bye to a deceased loved one. Then the letters may be burned, with the mourner essentially saying good-bye to saying good-bye. The detachment is made real by the burning of the letters and may undergo yet further distancing by burial of the ashes. Rituals of continuity may contain many levels as well.

Characteristics employed. In designing a therapeutic bereavement ritual, seven specific characteristics must be considered. The caregiver must work to employ the characteristics that will make the experience personally meaningful and therapeutic for the individual mourner.

Specifically, there must be an appropriate *emotional distance* in any ritual in order for it to be effective. Rituals must involve a balanced experience allowing the individual to be both participant and observer (Scheff, 1977). Those that are too overwhelming (underdistancing) or do not have enough emotional meaning or content (overdistancing) will be nontherapeutic. The more absorbed the individual involved is in the performance, the more therapeutic the ritual.

Degree of *rigidity* refers to the amount of flexibility given to the mourner in the ritual. In some rituals, the mourner is allowed to reinterpret and/or revise any element she sees fit; in others, she must adhere to all the prescribed aspects. This element is differentiated from the closed and open aspects of a ritual, described subsequently, which concern the amount of structure imposed.

The amount of *repetition* is also a factor. Some rituals—or parts thereof —are designed to be performed only once, whereas others are designed to be repeated a specific number of times, over a particular period of time, or until a particular point is reached.

The greater its *multidimensionality*, the richer the ritual and the more unconscious levels of functioning will be influenced and play a role (van der Hart, 1983). Effective rituals evoke rich sensations (e.g., sounds, smells, tastes, images) and involve various activities (e.g., writing, cooking, eating, making music, singing, telling stories, praying, meditating).

The *complexity* of a ritual is also an issue. According to van der Hart (1983), when possible, it is preferable to employ a simple ritual in which key symbols are used. Although it is best for the caregiver to use symbols that are more rather than less comprehensive, identifying a cogent key symbol and a simple action to connect to the symbol may be difficult if the issues in the loss are complex. In such instances, more complex rituals can be considered.

Van der Hart (1983) points out that "ideally the ritual is performed until the necessary processing of the issue concerned and a reorganization of the personality have taken place; until the definitions of the relevant relationships are altered and the client has adjusted to that, emotionally and cognitively" (p. 135). Thus, *completeness* is a desirable goal. However, in reality the use of a ritual is often only part of a more comprehensive therapy in which the mourner progresses. It is advisable for the caregiver to ask the mourner about the outcomes of the ritual: its process, obstacles, frustrations, and deficiencies. The information provided can be used to do what is necessary to achieve completeness. As van der Hart (1983) writes:

> Especially where the "working through" of emotional problems is concerned, such as in grief work, the ritual must be complete, if possible. This means that in the ritual, a step— big or small—is actually taken. With a mourning ritual such as writing a "continuous" farewell letter, a relatively big step is aimed at. On the one hand, all relevant emotions have to be dealt with. On the other hand, sufficient room is required for the complete expression of those emotions; until they are "extinguished" and an emotional adjustment to a new situation, to the next stage of existence, can take place.
>
> Completeness also means that in therapy—of which the ritual can be a part—sufficient attention is paid to all three stages of the transition (separation, transition, [re]incorporation). This does not mean that those three stages have to be dealt with equally extensively, but that it is established that the client can go through the different stages—with or without help. (p. 136)

Finally, ritual may consist of a blend of *closed and open parts*. Including prescribed acts (closed) as well as parts that leave room for improvisation and in which the mourner can respond to the current situation (open) allow the mourner to incorporate aspects that otherwise would not receive attention. Thus, the mourner can shape her responses creatively to achieve completeness.

Step 6: Create the context

The context within which a ritual occurs adds to that ritual. Consequently, the caregiver and mourner must give thought to the ritual's location and atmosphere, as well as to whether or not others will be present. In some rituals, the location is fixed (e.g., visiting the cemetery). In others, the location can be anywhere (e.g., writing a letter to the deceased). It often is helpful to observe specific conditions at the time of the ritual. For instance, when poring over photograph albums, "talking" to the deceased, or writing a letter to the lost loved one, the mourner may light a candle to mark the time symbolically. The mourner may sit in a special chair while communicating with his lost loved one, or he may attend a church in order to participate in specific rituals in memory of the deceased. Essentially, creating the context properly identifies the ritual as such. It also can promote completion when the particular characteristics of the context facilitate the ritualistic behavior (e.g., being contemplative in a quiet church). The decision whether or not to include others should be made with recognition of the impact of issues such as the legitimization of the ritual or facilitation of the integration with others. If the mourner finds the ritual too difficult or painful to perform alone, the presence of others may be helpful.

Step 7: Prepare the mourner for the ritual

In preparing the mourner for the ritual, a number of points must be kept in mind. The first concerns timing. As in all aspects of therapy, timing is crucial to the success of the ritual as an intervention. For example, in leave-taking rituals, the ritual brings about a transformation, and the mourner must be at the proper psychological place to take that step. Van der Hart (1983) notes that it is not always possible to prepare the mourner to perform the ritual when that person is very fixed in the original condition. In such cases, the caregiver cannot wait until the mourner is "ripe" for the breakthrough but must be able to motivate the mourner to perform the ritual. Often preparation for the ritual is accomplished as a preliminary step or part of the ritual. Issues of proper timing do not generally arise with rituals of continuity, which serve to demonstrate the continued connection of the mourner to the deceased.

The second major point in preparing the mourner concerns the mourner's motivation. Again, this is much more of an issue in leave-taking rituals than in rituals of continuity. Because performing a ritual usually requires time, effort, and acknowledgment of emotion, it is important to motivate the mourner adequately. Van der Hart (1983) suggests that this can be done by undertaking such actions as (a) relating to the mourner examples of rituals used by others; (b) connecting with the mourner's mentality, culture and subculture, and private symbols; (c) capitalizing on the mourner's preferred mode of perception (i.e., visual, auditory, or kinesthetic); (d) ensuring proper timing; (e) reaching an agreement with the mourner over what should be done as opposed to prescribing the ritual authoritatively without the mourner's input; and (f) educating the mourner about rituals. In educating the mourner about rituals, the caregiver specifically conveys that the mourner first must regulate her external behavior and forget about her feelings and notes that if she actively performs what she has to do, her feelings also will change (van der Hart, 1983). In other words, the caregiver stresses that " 'pretending' can be just as effective as 'really doing' " (van der Hart, 1988c, p. 23). Obviously, trust in the caregiver, transference issues, and other nonspecific variables influencing any type of intervention also obtain here.

As with other strategies for intervention, a third point concerns the need for the caregiver to orient the mourner to this specific type of treatment according to the generic treatment suggestions provided in chapter 8. It is crucial for the caregiver to act with the recognition that much of the power of a ritual comes from the mourner's expectation. To the extent that proper motivation and orientation appropriately enhance the expectation, the ritual will be more therapeutic.

Knowing how to deal with mourner resistance is a fourth major point in preparing the mourner, and it is as critical in this type of intervention as in any other. One typically sees little resistance in rituals of continuity and great amounts in rituals of leave taking. As van der Hart (1983) points out, resistance to the separation is a legitimate feeling that must be dealt with extensively, with the ritual being aimed at proper processing of this feeling. In cases where resistance is not dealt with, the ritual can be sabotaged:

> In the case of José the therapist had neglected to acknowledge her "resistance" to saying farewell to her ex-husband by giving it a legitimate place in the ritual. When it was suggested that she should exchange her wedding ring at a jeweler's and buy a gold piece of jewelry in its place, she reacted with violent—and ambivalent—emotions. She wore the ring again, telephoned her ex-husband, and told him that she loved him; took the ring off again, almost threw it in the garbage can, and told him she hated him. The therapist should have given José more opportunity to cherish the ring—as a part of the total ritual. (van der Hart, 1983, p. 125)

Van der Hart (1983) suggests that in leave-taking rituals resistance actually should be incorporated into the ritual. Mourners can indicate that they are willing to say farewell but also that they find it very difficult to do so (e.g., saying, "I really don't want to let you go" as well as expressing the desire to relinquish). This can be done by producing a symbol and allowing it first to intensify the relationship. For example, a mourner might give a photograph a special place in the house before destroying it or putting it away.

Step 8: Implement the ritual

The procedures for implementing leave-taking rituals are more complex than those for undertaking rituals of continuity. As such, they are discussed first and at greater length.

As conceptualized by van der Hart (van der Hart, 1988a, 1988b; van der Hart & Goossens, 1987) and as indicated in Table 7.4, leave-taking rituals have three phases: preparatory, reorganization, and finalization. In the preparatory phase, as noted in Step 7, the caregiver explains how performing a ritual might help the individual deal with mourning and orients the mourner to work with rituals. The caregiver must ensure that the mourner is motivated to perform the ritual, as it typically will be an arduous emotional task. The mourner not only can experience strong emotions toward the deceased—and possibly toward those held responsible for the death—he can be torn between feelings of hope and despondency. Resistance must be anticipated and accounted for. Assistance and support should be solicited from the family, who must be informed of these matters and as a result may be stimulated to talk to one another about the loss. The caregiver and mourner conclude this phase with a definitive contract for treatment specifying what each has agreed on for the design of the leave-taking ritual and the nature of their joint work.

The working through of grief and other traumatic experiences occurs during the reorganization phase. For most individuals, this phase is associated with an increased number of dreams about the deceased and the past. The phase progresses with the mourner's experiencing deep despair and depression as he realizes that he no longer can derive the meaning of his existence from the deceased and that he must relinquish the ties that bind them together or at least give the deceased a less central place in his life. Because at this point no new perspective or objects exist from which to derive meaning, suicidal thoughts may predominate. Extra support from the caregiver in the form of more frequent contacts, explanation of the process and its course, and sometimes medication is often needed to help the mourner overcome this impasse without undue harm.

During this phase, the mourner may observe certain rules demarcating the mourning period from normal life (e.g., lighting a candle every evening, refraining from parties). The mourner carries out certain concrete tasks that stimulate the internal processes of working through toward a conclusion. To set mourning in motion or further encourage it, he is urged to take symbols of the relationship with the deceased and deal with them differently—for instance, to give them a more prominent place, both literally and figuratively, in order to reflect his changed way of dealing with his conscious experience of the deceased. The mourner may have chosen pre-existing key symbols, or he may have created them (e.g., drawings, sculpture, poetry), working on or altering them to increase their resemblance or connection to the deceased. The search for symbolic acts and objects takes place to discover what the mourner feels is fitting and meaningful.

Farewell letters are often used as symbols in the leave-taking ritual. This task is well suited to those with elements of conflicted mourning, who must express and integrate all their ambivalent feelings regarding the lost loved one. In one version of this procedure, three letters are written. In the first, the mourner's feelings are expressed in a direct and uncensored fashion. This letter is followed by a toned-down version, which in turn is followed by an even more dignified third letter. A common variation of this technique is the continuous letter, which typically is written in a circumscribed ritual setting under specific conditions. For example, writing may take place every day at a specific time and place. Having an established time makes the task more manageable and prevents the mourner from writing only when he feels good or only allowing one side of the ambivalent feelings to emerge. Having a specific place further marks the ritual. The ritual quality may be accentuated by the mourner's putting a picture of the deceased on the desk.

Rereading what has been committed already to paper is the best way to commence writing. Subsequent writing need not necessarily be new material. If at any point the mourner does not know what to write or is unable to put anything on paper, he still must remain seated. Unless the tension becomes unbearable, the mourner should not be allowed to walk away. The mourner must express not only the positive and negative feelings but the complete message. When the mourner's writing expresses less preoccupation with the past, his dreams imply the taking leave of the deceased, and he expresses growing interest in people and things in the present, the caregiver may view the process as coming to an end. The mourner should consult with the caregiver before terminating letter writing; otherwise he may risk stopping too soon and avoiding some painful but necessary experience.

It is not uncommon for writing to one person to potentiate writing to another as unfinished business is discovered. If more than one person is to be addressed in the writing, separate notebooks can be used for each. Alternatives to letter writing are making pottery, writing poetry, creating artwork, and so forth.

When it is clear that the reorganization phase has come to an end, the finalization phase may begin. This phase contains three subphases: a leave-taking ceremony, a cleansing rite, and a reunion rite. The reader will note how these phases provide yet another parallel to van Gennep's

(1960) three phases of transition (i.e., separation, transition, and incorporation). In the leave-taking ceremony, the mourner bids a solemn farewell to the symbols that were collected or created in the previous phase. Often this involves burying, or first burning and then burying, the objects. Sometimes the farewell is reflected in other acts, such as destroying a special piece of furniture, tearing a photograph, giving away a gift, burying clothes, or taking jewelry to have it melted down. What is important is that the act represents a letting go of the symbol and, by extension, the person and relationship it represented. Often the mourner himself knows best what symbolic form the farewell should take. Various levels of symbolic action may be involved, as is the case when continuous letters are burned and then buried. It also may be important to retain certain key symbols and relate to them differently. For example, a widower might remove the picture of his deceased wife from the bedroom and place it in the den. The objective is not to remove all existing symbols, nor to erase all memory of the deceased, but to let go of old ties that bind nontherapeutically to the past.

After the leave-taking ceremony, a cleansing rite may take place, which symbolically removes the vestiges of the leave-taking ceremony (e.g., taking a long shower or bath). Entry into the new life is marked by a reunion rite, which often takes the form of a special dinner with significant others and represents a strengthening of ties in the new world. The importance of the reunion rite, which gives symbolic expression to the most significant relationships in the new phase of the mourner's life, cannot be overemphasized.

After leave-taking rituals take place, follow-up sessions may be conducted. At times, a memorial ceremony may be suggested. It should be pointed out in advance that STUG reactions are not circumvented by the mourning work of a leave-taking ritual and that they can be anticipated.

There are times when the mourner wishes, or even needs, to undertake a ritual of continuity. As noted previously, this type involves telectic, intensification, and connection rites, each of which can be incorporated into bereavement rituals to facilitate healthy mourning. Implementing a ritual of continuity typically does not require as complex a process as does a leave-taking ritual. As van der Hart (1983) points out, rituals of continuity function primarily as conductors of situations in which the persons involved must adjust—especially in an emotional respect—to changed circumstances and new interactions. Adjustment takes place via the performance of prescribed sequences of actions and interactions. Through these rituals, existing definitions of relationships are strengthened and confirmed, in contrast to transition rituals, in which relationships are altered.

Without a doubt, connection rituals are the most prevalent. The caregiver must be prepared to help the mourner discover which particular symbolic actions are most appropriate, meaningful, and fulfilling to make desired statements about thoughts, sentiments, and significance; to mark remembrance of the lost loved one; and to enable the desired interaction and communication with the loved one in the context of a healthy new relationship (as developed in the fifth "R" process of mourning). When the connection rites are unhealthy—as they are in complicated mourning —the caregiver must turn to the "R" processes of mourning to ascertain precisely where the mourner is fixated, then work through the processes therapeutically to replace the unhealthy connection rites with healthy ones and to effect appropriate leave taking.

Step 9: Process the ritual experience

As with any other type of intervention, the caregiver must ascertain the impact of the ritual upon the mourner both during and after the ritual experience. The mourner must be encouraged to process the ritual in those manners most appropriate for the particular treatment. The central issue is that the mourner have the opportunity to achieve closure on the experience at all levels. If reactions or unfinished business are apparent, they must be identified and dealt with therapeutically in the context of the ritual, in a treatment modality ancillary to it, or in an appropriate therapeutic way after completion.

Step 10: Reevaluate and redecide

Finally, the mourner and caregiver must evaluate the effectiveness of the ritual and determine whether further rituals are necessary to achieve the established goals.

CHAPTER 8

Generic Issues in the Treatment of Complicated Mourning

Interventions in complicated mourning are, if nothing else, diverse. They may center on a particular problem issue for the mourner, an individual complicated mourning syndrome, a specific high-risk factor, or a distinct point in the processes of mourning where progress seems stalled. Likewise, caregivers differ in terms of their philosophical conceptualizations, theoretical orientations, and preferred intervention techniques. Despite this diversity, some principles and guidelines are generic—that is, they apply regardless of the point of departure for treatment or caregiver preference for treatment method. Following a brief overview of studies of treatment efficacy as regards mourning, the present chapter offers a philosophical context for treatment of complicated mourning and spells out general principles and guidelines for successful practice that should be incorporated within each caregiver's interventions.

As noted in chapter 1, most treatment for complicated mourning focuses on tertiary prevention. Specifically, *primary prevention* refers to efforts to reduce or eradicate the incidence of a disorder, ultimately preventing its occurrence. *Secondary prevention* refers to attempts to identify and treat a disorder as early as possible in order to reduce its length and severity. Finally, *tertiary prevention* deals with a disorder that already has occurred and attempts to minimize long-term impairment.

Primary prevention in the area of grief and mourning is practiced by those who facilitate the anticipatory grief experience for families of the terminally ill (Rando, 1986e). Interventions of this nature can prevent the experiences that can lead to the development of pathology after the loved one dies. Secondary prevention is provided by those who practice crisis intervention with populations at high risk either at the time of need or shortly thereafter (e.g., parents of children succumbing to Sudden Infant Death Syndrome, homicide survivors, disaster victims).

As noted, most of the treatment suggestions discussed in this book fall into the category of tertiary prevention in that they occur after the disorder of complicated mourning has started to develop or already has developed. However, the line distinguishing secondary from tertiary prevention can be quite blurry for the practicing caregiver, and certainly secondary prevention is a goal for many who treat mourners close to the time of loss. Suffice it to say that the suggestions offered here focus on treatment of a developing or already developed disorder, not on prevention.

By the time mourning has become complicated, mere grief facilitation is insufficient—the individual requires much more. The main therapeutic aim in complicated mourning is therefore to *intervene and convert complicated mourning into uncomplicated mourning, which then can be facilitated normally.* Obviously, this intervention is not a one-time event. The caregiver will need to continue to work on keeping the converted mourning uncomplicated or at least on continuing to convert as many aspects of it as possible. For example, some mourners may never mourn totally all aspects of the deceased. However, the caregiver can promote as much realistic mourning as is feasible and can facilitate uncomplicated mourning within these areas.

Intervention in complicated mourning therefore requires knowledge of (a) what is necessary to convert complicated to uncomplicated mourning (e.g., working through resistances, overcoming conditioning preventing parts of the process) and (b) ways to facilitate uncomplicated grief and mourning in order to promote healthy accommodation of loss, appropriate readjustment to move adaptively into the new world without forgetting the old, and meaningful reinvestment. As subsequent chapters detail, what is necessary to uncomplicate complicated mourning varies with the individual mourner and circumstances of the loss. For a review of the facilitation of uncomplicated mourning, the reader is referred to chapter 2 and the resources mentioned there.

EFFICACY OF INTERVENTION IN MOURNING

Research on treatment efficacy in mourning has generated some conclusions that have direct bearing on the work of every practicing caregiver. These are noted after the following brief review of the literature from which they derive.

In general, the literature can be divided according to a number of variables: positive versus negative outcomes; uncomplicated mourning versus complicated mourning; the specific loss experienced; individual versus group interventions; type and extent of intervention; use of a control group; and method of selection of subjects, type of evaluation, measures used, and duration of follow-up. An in-depth review of each pertinent study is beyond the scope of this chapter. Rather, a general overview of studies is provided with brief commentary. No critique is provided for any of these studies; conclusions stated are those provided by the investigators. For more extensive information on each study, the reader is referred to the original source. For critical analysis of general conclusions and specific studies, the reader is urged to consult Osterweis et al. (1984), Parkes (1980, 1987–1988), Raphael (1983), Raphael and Middleton (1987), and Stroebe and Stroebe (1987).

A Perspective on Intervention Studies

A general perspective with which to view the research is perhaps best established by comments included in the Institute of Medicine's study on the effectiveness of bereavement interventions (Osterweis et al., 1984). As the investigators note, for most individuals who experience uncomplicated mourning and who are not at particularly high risk for adverse consequences of bereavement, the support of family and friends, possibly augmented by the support of a self-help group, is generally sufficient. They comment as follows:

> There is no evidence that all bereaved people need or want formal interventions, though mutual support groups may fill a gap for those who have little other social support. There is some evidence to suggest that intervention programs help people to move faster through the grieving process, but ultimately most people get through it regardless of whether they have formal support. Still, shortening a process that is painful for an individual and for those around that person may be of considerable intrinsic value and deserves further study. (Osterweis et al., 1984, p. 273)

However, there is recognition that for others psychotherapeutic intervention will be necessary. With regard to this category of intervention, the authors observe that

> very little is known about the ability of any intervention to reduce the pain and stress of bereavement, to shorten the normal process, or to mitigate its long-term negative consequences. While the few controlled studies that have been conducted report contradictory findings, subjective reports attesting to the helpfulness of interventions abound. (Osterweis et al., 1984, p. 274)

This frequent discrepancy between empirical data and subjective reports is striking and cannot be discounted. Impressive examples are found in the research examining psychotherapy and self-help group intervention in bereavement. Although the data from a study by Videka-Sherman and

Lieberman (1985) revealed that neither psychotherapy nor self-help group intervention resulted in improvement in the mental health or social functioning of bereaved parents, 90 percent of those who had psychotherapy reported the experience to be helpful, 70 percent stated that they turned to their psychotherapist for help with the most pressing problems they faced after their child's deaths, and 25 percent named their therapist as the single most helpful person. In a similar study with widows, which analyzed the effects of psychotherapy and self-help group intervention on mental health, Lieberman and Videka-Sherman (1986) found significant positive changes to have occurred only for those who participated actively in self-help groups. However, 91 percent of those in therapy perceived their experience to be helpful, and 47 percent rated their therapist as the most useful among all types of supports (e.g., self-help groups, kin, and other professionals such as clergy). In terms of specific responses to a study request to indicate the frequency and importance of various therapeutic processes, Lieberman and Videka-Sherman (1986) report:

> The process most often cited was catharsis, "being able to say what bothers me instead of holding it in" (65%); after that came being understood (51%), insight (49%), being approved for the way they were handling their lives (42%), the inculcation of hope (35%), feeling comforted (34%), receiving advice and suggestions (30%), and help with decision making (25%). When asked to indicate which of these processes was the most helpful, the two that stood out were catharsis (69% saw this as extremely helpful) and insight (63% saw this as extremely helpful). (p. 443)

Early Intervention Studies

Early intervention studies have been mixed in results. In the first of a series of papers, Williams, Polak, and Vollman (1972) found that crisis intervention provided to families within hours following a sudden, unexpected death resulted in the treatment group's utilizing less denial in dealing with their feelings, as evidenced by their being more expressive of guilt, anger, and anxiety and their not finding it necessary to keep busier following the death. Despite this, there appeared to be no differences in physical and emotional health patterns between treatment and nontreatment groups at 6 months. Further investigation by Polak, Egan, Vandenbergh, and Williams (1975) concluded that, as of 6 months after the death, crisis intervention treatment following sudden death did not improve coping behavior nor decrease the risk of medical or psychiatric illness, disturbed family functioning, or increased social cost for families experiencing acute bereavement. Subsequently, it was observed that short-term crisis intervention focusing on strengthening adaptation to sudden death appeared to facilitate family decisions that more accurately reflected the individual desires of all family members (Williams, Lee, & Polak, 1976). However, not only did there seem to be no major impact 6 months postdeath, but those who did receive services reported more difficulty in coping with family and social readjustment problems, as well as a more acute sense of indirect economic loss. Some concerns were noted about subject differences in this study that could have influenced results. A further study found, as did the previous one, that sudden death is a major life crisis that has a major impact on surviving family members, which is influenced by knowledge of certain facts and circumstances at the time of death, and that crisis intervention strategies are not effective (Williams & Polak, 1979). Perhaps more important than these two findings, however, are the conclusions that in some cases immediate intervention actually is harmful and may delay or interfere with uncomplicated mourning processes and that to be effective intervention must take into account the interactive nature of specific environmental stresses and family/individual determinants. All of these controlled studies were conducted with subjects randomly assigned to treatment and control groups and with no determination of risk. Although these studies have been subject to criticism for methodological shortcomings, they effectively raise the issue of timing of intervention (Osterweis et al., 1984).

In contrast to these investigations, Gerber, Wiener, Battin, and Arkin (1975) used selected medical data to determine whether brief psychotherapy administered to elderly surviving spouses had a prophylactic effect on morbidity and maladjustment precipitated by a natural death in the family. A cautiously positive response was observed.

Interventions With High-Risk Mourners

Studies by Beverley Raphael and colleagues receive unanimous acclaim as the most well-controlled and methodologically sound investigations of bereavement intervention. These studies were the first to demonstrate the importance of identifying high-risk mourners and to illustrate the efficacy of treatment when offered to this select population. Among numerous other significant findings, Raphael (1977) found that perceived supportiveness of the social network is a key predictor of successful outcome, with those evaluating their social networks as very nonsupportive during the bereavement crisis experiencing the most positive impact from intervention. In addition, findings suggest that crisis support that facilitates the working through of ambivalence may prevent or lessen depressive morbidity (Raphael, 1978) and that those mourners who perceive their bereavement intervention as unhelpful do as badly as those who have none (Singh & Raphael, 1981).

Time-Limited Dynamic Psychotherapy

The work of Mardi Horowitz and colleagues consistently demonstrates the efficacy of time-limited dynamic psychotherapy (also known as brief psychotherapy) with individuals being treated for complicated mourning

(Horowitz, Marmar, Weiss et al., 1984; Horowitz, Marmar, Weiss, Kaltreider, & Wilner, 1986; Horowitz, Weiss et al., 1984; Krupnick & Horowitz, 1985; Marmar, Horowitz, Weiss, Wilner, & Kaltreider, 1988). With the exception of the study by Horowitz, Weiss et al. (1984), contrasting the reactions of patients and field subjects to the death of a parent, none of these studies included a control group. However, this research has generated important findings about a number of aspects of brief psychotherapy with bereaved individuals.

Horowitz, Weiss et al. (1984) determined that a patient group that sought and received time-limited dynamic psychotherapy for distress following the death of a parent reduced avoidant experiences more than did field subjects who presented initially with lower levels of distress and who had experienced parental death but had not sought treatment. Over a 13-month period, the treatment group's distress declined to a level comparable to that of field subjects. Horowitz, Marmar, Weiss et al. (1984) discovered a relationship between psychotherapeutic outcome and dispositional and process variables. Horowitz et al. (1986a, 1986b) analyzed change over the course of treatment, using comparisons of the different perspectives on outcome expressed by the patient, evaluating clinician, treating clinician, and independent judges and finding major symptom relief in the majority of patients but less change evidenced in adaptive abilities. Krupnick and Horowitz (1985) found that time-limited therapy was useful for some vulnerable bereaved persons (i.e., those with narcissistic and borderline personality disorders) as a conduit to more extended treatment, a vehicle to process mourning, and/or an intervention to prevent deterioration after a traumatic life event. Finally, Marmar et al. (1988) determined that, for widows, brief psychotherapy and mutual help group treatment seem about equally effective, with both treatments reducing stress-specific and general symptoms and, although to a lesser degree and at a slower pace than other brief treatments for other stressful life bereavements, improving social and work functioning.

Recent writing also identifies the acceptability and success of brief interventions conducted in a "piecemeal" fashion over several years (Shuchter & Zisook, 1990). In this approach toward treatment, the caregiver, cognizant of the multiple therapeutic processes that must be worked through over the years, intervenes at specific points in time with focused, practical, time-limited efforts. The principles of "hovering" over the bereaved will be new to many caregivers but may be timely given current practical and time constraints. Shuchter and Zisook plan to test this approach in research settings.

Cognitive-Behavioral and Behavioral Interventions

Three studies from the school of cognitive-behavioral treatment of complicated mourning address the effectiveness of these particular types of intervention. S. Lieberman (1978) treated 19 morbidly grieving patients with forced mourning procedures coupled with family involvement. After the completion of treatment, subjects were rated on symptomatic relief, ability to accept loss, and general life improvement. No control group was used. Lieberman notes that treatment resulted in major relief or disappearance of referral symptoms in 16 of the patients (84 percent), with one patient remaining unchanged and two actually suffering more severe symptoms. This study joins with the Williams and Polak (1979) investigation in raising the issue of iatrogenic effects of treatment, which Lieberman claims may be avoided by proper selection of treatment candidates. As he points out, forced mourning generally should be avoided with those who have fewer social supports combined with more economic and social problems.

Mawson et al. (1981) were spurred on by the S. Lieberman (1978) study to undertake a controlled investigation in which 12 patients with morbid grief were randomly assigned to a guided mourning treatment or to a control group in which they were encouraged to avoid thinking of the deceased and attending to other cues concerning their bereavement. Those who had the guided mourning intervention showed more improvement than did controls, who did not improve significantly or show any trend to do so. This confirmed to the investigators that guided mourning is useful in managing morbid grief, despite treatment effects not being as potent as originally predicted. That the superiority of the treatment was most evident on measures of approach to bereavement cues and less so on mood disturbance suggested to the authors that the two are less intimately linked than commonly believed.

Hodgkinson (1982) used a similar treatment, described as a cathartic approach to therapy, with an unselected population of 10 clients (i.e., the first 10 referred) having severe emotional problems related to grief. This investigator found that 7 of the clients were highly improved, 1 was moderately improved, and 1 each were slightly improved and unchanged.

A strictly behavioral approach based on emotional flooding and prolonged exposure, similar to treatment for phobias, has been used by Ramsay (Ramsay, 1976, 1977, 1979; Ramsay & Happée, 1977) in treatment of pathological grief. In reporting results to date on 23 cases, Ramsay (1979) subjectively rated the improvement of his clients as 9 highly improved, 9 moderately improved, 4 slightly improved, and 1 unchanged. Ramsay notes that clients' ratings of treatment effectiveness were higher than his. There was no control group.

Bereavement Support

Outcome evaluations for bereavement services associated with hospices or palliative care units have found that bereavement support is associated with decreased distress and symptomatology. After a controlled study,

Parkes (1981) determined that bereavement support reduced risk in a group of high-risk mourners whose family members had died at St. Christopher's Hospice. Cameron and Parkes (1983) discovered that relatives of individuals who had died at the Palliative Care Unit of the Royal Victoria Hospital, Montreal, were less symptomatic than families of those whose loved ones died elsewhere in the hospital. The former group had received predeath, at-death, and postdeath support.

Hypnotherapy, Trauma Desensitization, and Psychodynamic Therapy

In a controlled outcome study of pathological grief with elements of traumatic stress, Kleber and Brom (1987) examined the degree to which three different methods of treatment—hypnotherapy, trauma desensitization, and psychodynamic therapy—dealt with grief disorders and investigated whether the therapies produced different results. They found that, whereas none of the three therapies was significantly more effective than the others, all of the treatment groups evidenced more improvement than did the control group. The most significant changes were found in reduced symptoms of loss-related intrusions and avoidances. Anxiety, psychoneurotic complaints, and some aspects of self-esteem also were found to be affected. In a related study examining brief psychotherapy for post-traumatic stress disorders (of which a number were precipitated by deaths), Brom, Kleber, and Defares (1989) conducted a controlled study and reported that individuals treated with hypnotherapy, trauma desensitization, and psychodynamic therapy experienced a decline in symptoms as compared to the control group, with the major area of impact being a significantly lowered amount of trauma-related symptoms. In both studies, slight advantages of one treatment over another usually, although not exclusively, favored psychodynamic therapy.

Confiding and Confronting

Two additional studies illustrate the impact of confiding in others and confronting a traumatic event—actions inherent in most interventions for bereavement. Pennebaker and O'Heeron (1984) examined the degree to which confiding in others was associated with health problems in the year following the death of a spouse from suicide or motor vehicle accident. Results revealed that the sudden death of a spouse from accidental death or suicide is associated with increased health problems irrespective of the cause of death. Confiding in others appears to play a central role in the coping and health process, with not confiding about a traumatic event being associated with increased physiological activity and rumination. In addition, a significant negative correlation exists between confiding and ruminating: The more subjects discussed their spouse's death with friends and the less they ruminated about the death, the fewer health problems they reported, independent of their self-reported number of close friends. The authors assert that the physiological work of not confiding (i.e., behavioral inhibition) and of ruminating place cumulative stress on the body and increase the long-term probability of stress-related disease.

A related investigation with undergraduates found that writing about both the emotions and facts surrounding a personally traumatic event was associated with relatively higher blood pressure and negative moods following the essays but fewer health center visits in the 6 months following the experiment (Pennebaker & Beall, 1986). Although the authors of this controlled study perceive the outcome as promising rather than definitive, they contend that the findings beg for further research to validate their belief that one need not confide orally in another to receive the benefits suggested in the Pennebaker and O'Heeron (1984) study. Their tentative assertion is that the mere act of writing about an event and the emotions surrounding it is sufficient to reduce the long-term work of behavioral inhibition associated with disease. Interestingly, writing about the objective aspects of the traumatic event alone without the emotions was not arousing or particularly upsetting, but neither was it associated with long-term benefits, as was the case when emotions were integrated into the writing.

A subsequent investigation replicated the findings of the 1986 study and found that confronting and disclosing traumatic experiences by writing about them was associated with improved measures of cellular immune system function and physical health (Pennebaker, Kiecolt-Glaser, & Glaser, 1988). The authors believe the study strengthens their assertions that confronting trauma is beneficial from two perspectives: It reduces the necessity for inhibition and permits assimilation, reframing, or finding meaning in the event. They feel the results are important in (a) supporting an inhibitory model of psychosomatics, (b) pointing to the effectiveness of writing as a general preventive therapy, and (c) promoting awareness that psychotherapy can bring about direct and cost-effective improvements in health.

Self-Help and Other Groups

In a controlled outcome study combining both individual supportive intervention with self-help group intervention, Vachon, Lyall, Rogers, Freedman-Letofsky, and Freeman (1980) demonstrated reduced symptomatology and better adjustment for widows judged to have high distress. The intervention, which offered emotional, cognitive, and practical support, involved one-to-one supportive counseling with a widow who had received prior training in grief counseling, as well as a mutual support group experience. Some evidence suggests that intervention not only reduced risk but accelerated recovery.

Generally, studies of mutual help or support group treatment have netted mixed results. As previously mentioned, Marmar et al. (1988) found that women in mutual help group treatments experienced a reduction in stress-specific and general symptoms, as well as improvement in social and work functioning. In comparing women in mutual help groups with those receiving brief psychotherapy, this study determined that the treatments were equally effective. No control group was used.

In a study that some have criticized, Barrett (1978) compared three group treatments to a nontreatment control group of bereaved women who were recruited via newspaper announcements for discussion groups on widowhood issues. The three treatment groups included a self-help group, confidant group, and consciousness-raising group. The results showed no overall advantage for the treatment groups when compared with the control group. All four groups showed a statistically significant increase in self-esteem, an increase in grief intensity, and a decrease in negative attitudes toward remarriage, as well as a trend toward an increase in self-orientation. Some evidence suggested that the three treatment groups had better self-esteem and more intense grief at follow-up, with the author concluding that the consciousness-raising groups were the most effective and the self-help groups the least effective.

Walls and Meyers (1985) studied three therapeutic group interventions for normally grieving widows: a cognitive-restructuring group, a behavioral skills group, and a self-help group. When compared with a delayed treatment control group, the three intervention groups were found to have little effect on adjustment to widowhood. The authors concluded that cognitive therapy was somewhat more effective than the other treatments. It is important to note with regard to this small study that the subjects studied were low-risk at the outset.

In contrast, Lieberman and Videka-Sherman (1986) followed a group of widows over a 1-year period to determine the impact of self-help groups on their mental health and to compare them to similarly bereaved patients in psychotherapy and to those who sought no formal help. Significant positive changes were found to have occurred only for those widows who participated actively in the self-help groups.

Treatment for Bereaved Parents

Several studies have examined the effectiveness of treatment for bereaved parents. Forrest, Standish, and Baum (1982) investigated outcome differences in bereaved parents of stillborn babies. These parents were randomly assigned to either a support and counseling intervention or a control group of routine hospital care. At the 6-month follow-up, a significant difference in psychiatric symptoms favored the treatment group over the controls; however, this finding was not replicated at the 14-month follow-up.

Videka-Sherman and Lieberman (1985) compared bereaved parents who received psychotherapy with bereaved parents affiliated with The Compassionate Friends self-help group. They found no systematic effects of participation in either group, hypothesizing that the absence of a demonstrable effect in mental health or social functioning for bereaved parents—combined with their seriously inferior functioning as compared to those who had not lost a child—stems from the limits of any intervention to alter the devastating sequelae of losing a child. (See chapter 13 for further discussion of parental loss of a child.)

Conclusions

Several conclusions may be drawn from this brief review of the literature on the efficacy of bereavement interventions. First, evidence about the efficacy of interventions is mixed. The same problems that plague psychotherapy outcome research in general are present here. These include lack of comparability, shortage of appropriate and quantifiable measures of outcome, selection biases, and ethical issues concerning assignment of distressed individuals to control groups. Many studies are uncontrolled or poorly controlled and suffer in methodological design.

Well-controlled studies have demonstrated that intervention is most successful when it is directed toward bereaved individuals who have been identified as being at high risk either because of current high distress or as having high potential for distress due to specific risk factors. When offered to an unselected population or mourners experiencing little distress, efficacy appears to diminish. In concluding a review of studies directed toward the primary prevention of psychiatric disorders, including studies on intervention in bereavement, Raphael (1980a) declares:

> It is concluded that much work in this field represents a "call" for prevention; that diffuse interventions for diffuse population groups to achieve diffuse outcomes may not lead to demonstrable effects in prevention. Specific interventions directed towards high risk populations to achieve specific preventive goals have shown that primary prevention may be accomplished in some areas. (p. 163)

Despite the need to replicate studies and devise and implement more specific preventive services for those at high risk, interventions directed toward mourners at high risk and specifically tailored to address their particular risk factors (e.g., Parkes, 1980; Raphael, 1977) have been "shown to have demonstrable effectiveness in lessening postbereavement morbidity and thus represent one of the few positive outcomes in preventive psychiatry" (Raphael, 1983, p. 399).

Some research suggests that the timing of the intervention is crucial. Intervention provided too soon (e.g., within the first couple of weeks) may have no positive effects or, as illustrated in one study, even delay or interfere with uncomplicated bereavement (Osterweis et al., 1984). The optimal time for preventive intervention with those identified as being at high risk appears to be from the first 2 to 8 weeks up until 3 months postdeath (Raphael, 1983). Other conclusions suggest that, for intervention to be most effective, it must be comprehensive (i.e., covering the particular aspects of support for which there are deficits); extensive; and offered on an individual, rather than family or group, basis (Stroebe & Stroebe, 1987).

The few studies that have reported little or no impact of intervention do not seriously call into question the effectiveness of intervention programs; methodological shortcomings and idiosyncratic features appear responsible for the negative results (Stroebe & Stroebe, 1987). However, some studies note that a small group of mourners actually become worse after intervention (e.g., S. Lieberman, 1978; Williams & Polak, 1979). This raises important issues about iatrogenesis.

Notwithstanding the literature suggesting that treatment for complicated mourning can be effective, the difficulty of such psychotherapeutic work cannot be overestimated. Although Parkes (1987) interprets figures regarding the outcome of treatment of complicated bereavement as confirming for him "the impression that bereavement reactions carry a better prognosis than most other forms of mental illness" (p. 135), others speak specifically about the difficulty of treatment. For example, Rynearson (1987b) is somewhat pessimistic regarding mourners' responsiveness to treatment:

> A significant minority . . . of a nonpatient bereaved population may be presumed to develop intense and enduring pathologic grief responses. The promise of recovery with short-term, focused intervention appears to be misleading, as a sizeable proportion of patients with pathologic grief will be unresponsive to treatment. (p. 497)

He notes additional treatment difficulties:

> Peculiar to grief is the experience of a relationship that no longer exists, and it is the maladjustment to this lost relationship that forms the experiential nidus. This nidus does not welcome attention or change. It is rare that those with pathologic grief willingly present for treatment. Forming and maintaining a therapeutic alliance while struggling with the loss of a more crucial alliance promises dissonance and contradiction. The therapy of pathologic grief is slow and arduous. Failed recovery is not uncommon. (p. 487)

Barry (1981) also recognizes the difficulty of treating complicated mourning, significantly modifying his earlier (1973) conclusion that in most cases treatment (i.e., uncovering and abreaction of prolonged grief, held in abeyance) could be accomplished in a relatively brief period of time without much difficulty. The intervening 8 years provided him a number of cases "in which a direct attack on the resistances to grief has not been easily victorious" (Barry, 1981, p. 745). More specifically, he notes that

> experience since 1973 has shown more permutations of the [prolonged] grief reaction than originally described. Grief reactions are sometimes uncovered in the course of psychotherapy for other conditions and then require special consideration. Sometimes the proposed brief therapy of a grief reaction uncovers more serious underlying psychopathology needing more prolonged treatment. Probably all patients suffering prolonged grief reactions have personality disorders that may need further treatment. (Barry, 1981, p. 748)

Barry notes that often what is required is more than brief cathartic therapy. Implicit in this is his own approach to intervention, which is largely psychoanalytic. However, it seems to be more than mere philosophical bent that influences the length, pace, and depth of treatment. One must look specifically at the aims undertaken. Treatment decisions depend upon how many and which of the "R" processes of mourning the caregiver takes as targets in treatment (see chapter 9). For example, if the caregiver is concerned only with promoting the abreaction of acute grief by breaking down phobic avoidance—processes involving recognizing the loss and reacting to the separation—short-term behavioral intervention may be appropriate. If all six processes are targeted for intervention, more time and in-depth work will be required.

PHILOSOPHICAL PERSPECTIVES ON TREATMENT

One's philosophical perspective shapes and guides one's actions. For this reason, it is necessary to maintain the proper perspective in working with individuals experiencing complicated mourning. As with most other issues in complicated mourning, the proper perspective for treatment involves an understanding of the treatment of uncomplicated mourning as well. The points enumerated in Table 8.1, each revealing an aspect of the mindset and approach necessary for the facilitation of uncomplicated mourning, must be kept in mind. These points are adapted from Rando (1984), to which the reader is referred for further discussion.

In working with complicated mourning, the caregiver needs to keep in mind the following additional perspectives.

Table 8.1 Clinical Perspectives Necessary for Facilitating Uncomplicated Mourning

1. Remember that you cannot take away the pain from the bereaved.

2. Do not let your own sense of helplessness restrain you from reaching out to the bereaved.

3. Expect to have to tolerate volatile reactions from the bereaved.

4. Recognize the critical therapeutic value of your presence.

5. Make sure to view the loss from the bereaved's unique perspective.

6. Let genuine concern and caring show.

7. Do not let your personal needs determine the experience for the bereaved.

8. Do not attempt to explain the loss in religious or philosophical terms too early.

9. Do not suggest that the bereaved feel better because there are other loved ones still alive.

10. Do not attempt to minimize the situation.

11. Do not forget to plant the seeds of hope.

12. Do not encourage actions or responses antithetical to healthy mourning.

13. Maintain an appropriate therapeutic distance from the bereaved.

14. Do not fail to hold out the expectation that the bereaved ultimately will successfully accommodate the loss and that the pain will subside at some point.

The mourner who is experiencing complications is actually only attempting to mitigate the loss of the loved one

In all aspects of complicated mourning, there are two attempts (a) to deny, repress, or avoid aspects of the loss, its pain, and the full realization of its implications and (b) to hold on to and avoid relinquishing the lost loved one. Thus, the dysfunctional mourning witnessed actually consists of attempts to deal with or cope with the loss, albeit in an unhealthy fashion. Taking this perspective, the caregiver will recognize that complicated mourning really is not anything new; rather, it is a variation of the same processes witnessed in uncomplicated mourning despite different content or ways of being acted out.

Parkes (1987) has made it clear that what traditionally have been viewed as defenses are a normal part of mourning, with the goal being maintenance of appropriate distance between mourner and disturbing stimuli (i.e., recognition of the loss, reminders of the deceased, and responses to the loss) while the mourner buys time to integrate the loss by defending herself against complete realization of it. This is not to say that such defenses always enable the mourner to succeed in mastering the loss experience; many times they become distorted or pathological. Nevertheless, they have important biological and psychosocial functions that must be respected. For this reason, mourners must be approached with this perspective, and defenses must not be stripped away prematurely or too rapidly.

Indeed, defenses and resistance are to be anticipated and constitute the major content toward which therapeutic intervention is focused in complicated mourning. As mentioned previously, only if defenses can be worked through can the individual convert complicated to uncomplicated mourning and achieve the requisite accommodation of the loss through the "R" processes of mourning.

If mourning has become complicated, it can become uncomplicated

As opposed to the term *pathological*, the term *complicated* implies that, although something has gone wrong, it potentially can be corrected. Therefore, the caregiver's aim is to uncomplicate mourning by working through any resistances, defenses, and/or blocks to remove complicating factors and to permit a normal progression. This approach differs from the viewpoint that mourning has to be totally reworked because it is pathological or morbid. Traditionally, mourners have been blamed for complications resulting from factors related not necessarily to these individuals personally, but rather to the specific circumstances of the death. Focusing on complications in mourning and not the mourners themselves thus depathologizes such mourners.

The processes of mourning build upon themselves, and insufficient working through of earlier processes complicates subsequent ones

The caregiver must be aware of the sequential nature of the six "R" processes of mourning. With the exception of the second, third, and, on occasion, fourth processes (i.e., react to the separation; recollect and re-experience the deceased and the relationship; relinquish the old attachments to the deceased and the old assumptive world), which tend to occur somewhat simultaneously, and the fifth and sixth processes (i.e., readjust to move adaptively into the new world without forgetting the old; reinvest), which also can coincide in the Accommodation Phase, earlier processes tend to lay the foundation for subsequent ones. Even among those processes that may coincide, there is often an adherence to the chronological order. This is not to say that the mourner cannot vacillate among processes, only that, similar to stage theories of development (e.g., E. Erickson's, 1963, theory of psychosocial development), deficits in accomplishment of earlier processes compromise the ability to undergo later ones.

For instance, if the mourner fails to acknowledge the death of the loved one and admit to all the implications of this, he will never truly be able to relinquish old attachments and make necessary readjustments. He will not have come to the point where he needs to because hope still exists for the loved one's return. Therefore, these processes are unnecessary or, at most, premature. Similarly, if the mourner has not relinquished old attachments appropriately, his ability to develop a healthy new relationship with the deceased will be impaired. At least part of the new relationship will be unhealthy because it consists of inappropriate old attachments.

Briefly, in situations in which the mourner has insufficiently worked through processes prerequisite to a current mourning process, the caregiver will have to encourage the mourner to return to and address the earlier processes. However, the six "R" processes are not "all or nothing." The caregiver's task can be confusing when the mourner has partially completed a particular process but the incomplete part interferes with the ability to work through subsequent processes. For example, an individual might mourn enough of the deceased to relinquish old attachments to her positive aspects but remain invested in her negative ones. Ultimately, this lack of completion will interfere with the readjustment process.

The caregiver cannot trust external appearances to determine where the mourner actually is in the mourning processes. It is not uncommon for mourners to evidence some behaviors indicative of later mourning processes despite having insufficiently worked through earlier, prerequisite ones. For instance, a mourner may reinvest in new relationships but not have relinquished appropriately the old attachments to the deceased. Intervention must focus on the point at which the process became incomplete. A thorough assessment such as that provided by the Grief and Mourning

Status Interview and Inventory (GAMSII; see chapter 6 and the appendix), which incorporates, among other things, an examination of each "R" process, reduces the likelihood of this type of error.

Mourning involves cognitive processes to a much greater extent than generally acknowledged

From being taught the reality of the loss by pain, to attempting to make sense out of the loss, to revising the assumptive world and sense of self, cognitive processes and elements play a significant part in adaptation to loss. Along with all other elements of mourning, these factors deeply influence affective responses such as sadness, anxiety, anger, depression, guilt, and so forth. For this reason, caregivers must alter their relative overfocus on affect promotion and confrontation of avoidance to achieve a balance between these important tasks and support of the mourner in the process of learning about the loved one's absence, its implications, and what is necessary to survive in the intrapsychic and external worlds without that loved one. Without question, failure to do this is one of the major reasons for lack of success in the treatment of complicated mourning.

One set of cognitive processes is associated more with acute grief than with mourning. These processes relate to the mourner's learning about the reality of the loved one's death and appreciation of its implications. Much of what has been viewed as denial and/or resistance actually is the mourner's disbelief and inability up to that point to achieve clarity or comprehend the loss: The mourner gradually must learn the reality through pain, absence of the deceased, and frustration of desires to reunite with the deceased.

A second set of cognitive processes is associated more with mourning than with acute grief. These processes, pertaining specifically to revision of the assumptive world and formation of a new identity incorporating the changes necessitated by the loved one's death, are described by four theories of cognitive adaptation to threatening or traumatic events: (a) Parkes' (1988) revision of the assumptive world following psychosocial transitions and Woodfield and Viney's (1984–1985) work on personal construct dislocation and adaptation in bereavement; (b) Horowitz's (1986a) cognitive processing aspects of the stress response syndrome and integration of memories and responses, meanings, new assumptive world, and new sense of self; (c) Taylor's (1983) theory of cognitive adjustment to threatening events centering on search for meaning in the experience, attempt to regain mastery over the event in particular and over one's life in general, and an effort to restore self-esteem through self-enhancing evaluations; and (d) Janoff-Bulman's (1985) theory of the necessity to rebuild shattered assumptions following victimization, specifically the belief in personal invulnerability, the perception of the world as meaningful, and the perception of oneself as positive. Each of these theories must be incorporated in work with mourners.

Because most caregivers focus on assisting affective reaction to the perception of loss, chances are that many mourners receive insufficient support for and intervention in this critical realm of cognitive readjustment. The cognitive adjustment to loss influences affective adjustment (and vice versa), is just as necessary, and must receive equal clinical attention. Without appropriate cognitive change, the mourner simply cannot go on in a healthy way regardless of how much affective processing has been completed.

Treatment always must seek to address the underlying two attempts of complicated mourning

As mentioned previously, underlying all forms of complicated mourning are two attempts: (a) to deny, repress, or avoid aspects of the loss, its pain, and the full realization of its implications and (b) to hold on to and avoid relinquishing the lost loved one. Whatever else must be built into the treatment, interventions must be designed to address these two basic concerns.

Each mourner is unique and brings idiosyncrasies to the perception of and response to the loss, as well as an individual ability to contend with treatment

Despite commonalities with other mourners in similar situations or with similar characteristics, the mourner's experience is an individual one. Important corollaries to this fact are addressed in the following points, all of which reflect the need for the caregiver to comprehend the complicated mourning experience in the context of the particular mourner's life and life history. Lacking an understanding of the specific constellation of factors that circumscribe the mourner and the loss (see Table 2.1), the caregiver cannot diagnose or intervene with confidence.

First, complicated mourning occurs within the individual's established personality and in the context of idiosyncratic issues, conflicts, needs, defenses, and so forth. Treatment must be designed and implemented with this principle in mind. Although this point may seem self-evident, the fact is that too many caregivers evolve treatment plans on the basis of an identified complicated mourning syndrome, the presenting symptomatology, or psychiatric diagnosis. Instead, it is imperative to view the needs of the specific individual within the context of the type of idiosyncratically experienced complicated mourning. Each intervention ideally should be tailored to the particular mourner. For example, in one family the husband and teenage son were comfortable releasing their aggression subsequent to the preventable death of a teenage daughter by working out on a punching bag. This was unacceptable to the mother, who viewed the activity as too aggressive and unladylike. Therefore, she was advised each week to strip and change the sheets on all six double beds in the house within 20 minutes. This frenzied activity—one consistent with her image of herself—achieved the same goal of physical release of aggression in an ego-syntonic way.

Caregivers must recognize that many of the challenges confronting the mourner after a major loss would prove problematic for anyone: strong and painful emotions (e.g., anger, guilt, sadness), ambivalence, insecurity, shattered assumptions, the need to assume myriad new psychosocial roles and behaviors in a vastly changed world, the need to let go of a dearly loved one, increased vulnerability, and decreased sense of control. Therefore, it should come as no surprise if the mourner attempts to resist these confrontations and their accompanying demands for change. Most human beings would try to avoid these issues because of their inherently unpleasant nature. However, some issues may be more problematic than others to a particular mourner because of that person's previous experiences. Thus, although the fact that these issues may be universally disconcerting must be recognized, so too must any idiosyncratic issues, conflicts, or characterological difficulties they stimulate.

A broad perspective is needed for all mourners who, for whatever idiosyncratic psychosocial reasons, may have difficulty allowing themselves to yield to the necessary processes of mourning. The issue is not to change the mourner into a psychologically different person or the "ideal mourner," but to decondition just enough to enable the person to work through resistances to, or find alternative ways to deal with, the required processes of mourning. Certainly, in some cases working through earlier conflicts or issues prohibiting mourning will take time, energy, and effort, and can constitute a significant amount of the caregiver's work. Nevertheless, mourning will not progress properly until this is done.

All of this means the caregiver must conduct a thorough assessment of the mourner. This information is useful not only in comprehending the loss as experienced by the individual and any resistances to its therapeutic processing, but also in determining prior coping techniques and problem-solving behaviors so that they can be supported, refined, or supplanted as necessary. One should seek neither to reinvent the wheel nor to put it on a vehicle on which it does not belong.

Second, the mourner's relationship with the deceased and manner of coping with its loss reflect attachments that have been maintained over a long time. The caregiver must remember that long-term habits are usually fairly intractable. In this regard, the caregiver must respect the mourner's ways and types of attachment and consider these proclivities in establishing treatment expectations. For example, in conflicted mourning, the dynamics that allowed the mourner to remain in an abusive or unsatisfactory relationship in the first place are likely the same ones that interfere with her ability to recover from its loss. Again, assessment of such factors is a critical part of the intervention process.

Third, if the mourner did not perceive on some level the need for defenses, there would be none, and she would experience uncomplicated grief and mourning. Therefore, the caregiver must strive to understand and respect the idiosyncratic meaning and purposes of the mourner's defenses and then gently address them. They must be worked through one at a time: Smashing through them is usually ineffective and can be quite harmful. Indeed, dealing with defenses is the bulk of treatment for complicated mourning. Unfortunately, some caregivers view defenses as something to overcome in order to get to the "real work." Ironically, what they are attempting to dismiss is precisely the content of the work they seek to do. This somewhat psychoanalytic perspective appears valid also for those with other philosophical or theoretical inclinations. Even strict behaviorists (e.g., Ramsay, 1979) take defenses into account and work first to minimize them.

Finally, when the mourner is struggling with a major loss, quite often other old losses are catalyzed, and previous issues, conflicts, or unfinished business pertaining to them are called up from the past. Therefore, the caregiver must be aware that frequently the mourner contends not only with the death at hand, but also with the residue of past losses and issues. The individual's particular past experience influences reactions and responses to the present loss. This can increase the mourner's vulnerability and explains why caregivers often observe remarks, attitudes, thoughts, emotions, or behaviors that do not appear related to the current situation. Caregivers must be able to discern the impact of past issues on current mourning in order to know how best to intervene. Sometimes a previous loss must be addressed before a current one can be treated.

Male and female responses to loss are different and should be respected

Although it may seem unnecessary in the comparatively androgynous 1990s to talk about sex-role conditioning, significant differences between male and female approaches to the mourning experience clearly still exist. In general, these differences put males at a disadvantage (LaGrand, 1986; Rando, 1988). Because females experience relatively fewer conflicts between their traditional upbringing and the requirements of mourning (e.g., expression of emotion, acceptance of temporary regression, confiding in others), many caregivers strive to have male mourners respond to mourning as do their female counterparts. This is an unwise, to say nothing of almost always fruitless, goal. The caregiver would do better to direct energy toward translating what is required in grief and mourning into terms acceptable to the male mourner (e.g., discover methods by which the male mourner can release sorrow that do not violate his upbringing as much as sitting in a support group and crying). This is not to disparage appropriate attempts to make the male mourner more comfortable with those aspects of mourning that may be prohibited by male social conditioning but that are necessary for healthy accommodation of the loss. However, these attempts should not become ends in themselves or obscure the more important goal of assisting the individual in mourning the loss of his loved one. For example, some caregivers are determined to wring tears from male mourners, and doing so becomes the primary focus of the treatment and a major control issue for the caregiver.

Crying is not necessarily equivalent to mourning

A prevalent misconception held by caregivers, mourners, and the general public is that one's extent of and/or success in mourning is measurable by the amount of tears released. The desire on the part of caregivers to have an objective, quantifiable sign of mourning has caused a great many of them erroneously to operationalize grieving or mourning as crying. However, this is a mistake on several grounds.

1. Different individuals process affect differently based on their interpretation of the loss, their own personalities, their psychosocial and sexual conditioning (especially salient, although not exclusively, for males in our society), their support systems, and all of the other factors circumscribing them and their loss.

2. Although the shedding of tears is an extraordinarily effective release of sadness, it is not the sole one. People can deal with their sadness and hurt in other ways besides crying.

3. Sadness need not be the issue for which the mourner seeks and/or requires treatment. Focus on another issue (e.g., anger) may obviate the need for crying at a given point. Thus, the absence of crying should not automatically suggest that mourning is failing to progress appropriately.

4. A mourner may cry copiously but do no more than release tension. Mourning requires much more than a reaction to the loss, and to consider crying evidence of the occurrence of mourning is both inappropriate and invalid.

5. Abundant evidence documents that those most disturbed early after a loss are the ones heading for certain types of complicated mourning (Bornstein et al., 1973; Lund et al., 1985–1986; Parkes & Weiss, 1983). From this viewpoint, the amount, intensity, and duration of mourning may not so much signal that healthy mourning is taking place as provide forewarning of future complications. In many cases, persistent crying is actually a sign of the chronic mourning syndrome.

Often, even when external appearances are to the contrary, the mourner has not accepted the reality of the loved one's death

The caregiver must be aware of the possibility that underneath superficial appearances of acknowledgment the mourner has not actually accepted

the reality of the loved one's death but harbors a feeling that it can be reversed and that the deceased will return. Some components of complicated mourning, also seen to some degree in uncomplicated mourning,
may appear to indicate that the mourner has recognized the death. However, they actually reveal that the mourner still thinks or feels that there
is some chance to undo it. For example, in chronic mourning the survivor's
behavior would seem to indicate that the fact of death has been acknowledged. However, Bowlby (1980) points out that, like its seeming opposite,
prolonged absence of conscious grieving, chronic mourning expresses the
conscious or unconscious belief that the loss is still reversible. For this
reason, the chronic mourner may search unceasingly for the deceased,
and the course of mourning remains uncompleted. Many times, representational models of the self and world remain largely unchanged.

Bowlby also discusses anxiety in mourning and observes that some
of the anxiety witnessed in grief and mourning does not indicate a realization of the death but actually reveals a lack of acceptance of its finality. He
notes that only when there is hope that the separation is temporary is the
individual anxious lest it be permanent (i.e., separation anxiety). Anxiety
and fear presuppose hope; they arise when hope is threatened. It is only
when the permanence of the separation is truly recognized and hope is
gone that there is no anxiety. After the loss is perceived as a reality, the
response is no longer one of anxiety, but of pain, depression, and mourning. It is important to point out that anxiety also may develop in response
to the mourner's concerns about being alone, uncertainty about how to
handle new roles, and so forth. However, this is anxiety about the new
life without the deceased, not separation anxiety per se.

Raphael (1980b) writes about several types of complicated mourning
that also reveal a hidden lack of acceptance of death's reality. In distorted
mourning of the extremely angry type, the mourner is so fixed in angry
protest at the separation from the dependently loved person that she
cannot overcome her rage in order to relinquish the relationship. She continues to hope for, as well as demand, the return of the deceased. The deceased is kept alive in the perpetuation of mourning. Similarly, in distorted
mourning of the extremely guilty type, the deceased lives on in the
mourner's guilt. Identical dynamics occur in the chronic mourning syndrome as are found in both types of distorted mourning.

Frequently, it is only when the caregiver attempts to help the mourner
undertake the four subprocesses inherent in the "R" process of readjusting
to move adaptively into the new world without forgetting the old that it
becomes clear that progress in the earlier mourning processes has been
more apparent than real. For example, reluctance to adopt necessary new
ways of being in the world may be the first indication that, despite what
the mourner has said, she still anticipates the loved one's return. As noted
previously, this situation demands that the mourner return to work through
the earlier processes therapeutically before mourning can continue.

Related to this issue is the need for the caregiver to avoid assuming that what is on the surface reflects what is underneath. For example, a caregiver may perceive anger on the part of a mourner and construe it as a natural reaction to the accidental death of a loved one. However, unless this inference is verified by other data, the conclusion may be incorrect. The mourner actually may feel guilty for having had a fight with the deceased prior to the accident and may be using the anger to cover up guilt. This does not mean that the caregiver must doubt everything a mourner says, only that there must be an awareness that complicated mourning occasionally creates superficial manifestations that do not always reflect inner realities, as well as a willingness to pursue confirmatory data when necessary.

Unlike most other therapeutic situations, the person coming for treatment may not want the treatment to work

A mourner may not want treatment to work if it means he will lose the connection he maintains to the deceased. In most cases, it is the desire to perpetuate a link with the lost loved one that gives rise to the particular thoughts, feelings, or behaviors that define complicated mourning. This is why it is imperative that caregivers teach mourners how to sustain healthy and appropriate connections to the deceased (see chapter 2). However, before learning that there are healthy ways to maintain a connection with the deceased, mourners may mistakenly believe that their pathological way of holding on is the only way. In this regard, mourners may treasure pain for the link it provides to the deceased, although they may want to be rid of its discomfort. To try to bring them into therapy by stating that pain will be eliminated often pushes them away. In brief, mourners may not want therapy to work—or they may sabotage it—if they feel losing the connection with the deceased will be the result.

The mourner may avoid treatment if the caregiver speaks of it as taking away the pain or promises that the mourner will be out of pain. Better statements to entice mourners into treatment avoid threatening the connection with the deceased: "We can work on your learning to live with the pain of the loss" or "After our work together, you hopefully would be in less pain than you are now." Neither of these statements takes away the notion of having some amount of pain, which is often extremely important to maintain if the mourner perceives pain as an important tie to the deceased loved one. In cases where pain has other meanings (see the following section), it may be equally unwise to talk about taking away the pain as a reason for entering treatment until it is clear what the pain represents to that particular mourner.

Some mourners also may fear that getting better after therapy means that they will forget the loved one. Others worry that confronting the separation pain, anger, guilt, or dependency they seek to avoid will overwhelm them and cause them to break down psychologically. Still others may attempt to prove the strength of their love, want to avoid realizing the loss's implications, or feel a need to be punished and therefore secretly desire treatment to fail. These reasons, among others, often make mourners ambivalent about therapy despite their desire to escape discomfort and dysfunction. They also contribute to the resistance the mourner brings to the mourning processes in general and to therapy in particular.

This reality means that the caregiver must be prepared for the relative ineffectiveness of the usual inducements to therapy. Even for the willing, therapy demands confrontation with painful realities, hurtful emotions, and agonizing thoughts. Ambivalent mourners may require a good deal of support for participating in therapy, as well as additional reasons for undertaking it. Some of these reasons include the following.

1. Doing it for one's loved ones

2. Taking control over mourning so it does not control one

3. Discovering a better way to have a connection with the deceased

4. Gaining more access to oneself instead of being blocked off in certain areas

5. If the deceased would have wanted it, being able to go on in life in a healthy way

6. Learning how to live in the new world without the physical presence of the deceased

7. Learning how to revise the assumptive world and form a new identity

8. Becoming better able to remember the deceased and to recall, without pain, the memories shared

9. Removing mourning-related dysfunction from areas of one's life (e.g., psychosocial problems, occupational problems, physical problems)

Each caregiver will have to formulate those personally meaningful reasons that will persuade an individual to take the risk of entering treatment. Doing so does not imply that the caregiver should in any way "con" the mourner. Rather, it acknowledges that the inducement of improvement may be quite threatening and alerts the caregiver of the need to search for other legitimate and personally relevant incentives.

It is also important to point out that these concerns may surface many times during therapy. In addition, they may affect the nature of the treatment itself. For instance, unresolved grief may present as a repetitive negative therapeutic reaction (Nightingale, 1989). Throughout all treatment, the caregiver will need to monitor where the therapy is taking the mourner; how successful it is; and how it fits in with the mourner's current need to hold on to the deceased, maintain the pain, prevent relief from suffering, or in some other fashion perpetuate the complications or the mourning.

Pain is a multidimensional concept when it comes to the treatment of complicated mourning

As noted in the previous section, pain can be interpreted by the mourner as a link to the loved one. It also can serve a number of other purposes in the mourning process. Sometimes it is to be embraced; at other times, avoided. On some occasions, it is therapeutic and offers great service in coping with loss; at others, it signals pathological connection. For some it demonstrates a lack of resolution; for others, it constitutes proof of love. Some perceive it as punishment; others look on it as a natural consequence of loss.

No matter how it is perceived, after an individual loses a loved one, pain is generally found in some amount or, at the very least, lies at the root of defenses called upon to buffer the experience. By definition (Bowlby, 1980), as well as for the biological purpose of ensuring group cohesiveness (Averill, 1968), separation from attachment figures is extremely stressful and painful. The interpretation of and meaning attributed to that pain, however, varies from mourner to mourner. To deal effectively with the mourner's pain, the caregiver first must comprehend its idiosyncratic meaning. The following are some of the possible roles of pain.

1. Pain as healer: Pain is a process that cleans out the psychic wound caused by loss and promotes healing.

2. Pain as teacher: The pain felt when the desire to be reunited with the loved one is frustrated teaches the mourner that the loved one truly is gone.

3. Pain as connector: Pain is a link to the deceased, a bond that holds the loved one near.

4. Pain as testimonial: The amount of pain experienced provides a testimonial to the love the mourner has had or has for the deceased.

5. Pain as punishment: The unpleasant experience of pain is a form of punishment for the mourner's sins of omission or commission.

6. Pain as a normal consequence of loss: Loss happens, pain follows—period.

7. Pain as redeemer: Experiencing pain after loss will help the mourner atone for guilt over sins of omission or commission.

8. Pain as catalyst: The desire to avoid continued pain stimulates the mourner to acknowledge the reality of the loss and accommodate it within the self, the assumptive world, the relationship with the deceased, and the external world.

9. Pain as a signal that something is wrong: The experience of pain alerts the mourner to the fact that something requires attention.

10. Pain as a ticket to good things: Experiencing pain is a way of earning better things in the future.

11. Pain as the great equalizer: Pain equalizes people. No one escapes it, no matter what they do; how rich they are; or what their race, religion, or nationality is.

12. Pain as a symbol of strength: The person who endures pain— especially the person who endures pain stoically—is a strong, competent, and brave person.

The view of pain as teacher, healer, catalyst, signal of something wrong, and, sometimes, redeemer should be valued by both caregiver and mourner. Pain serves a useful function in each of these cases and must be experienced in order to achieve the positive benefits it can bring. Indeed, the person who never experiences any pain following a loss has no reason to make changes. Thus, pain has significant adaptive value. The caregiver must attempt to help the mourner achieve an optimum balance —enough to move forward and relinquish the past but not so much as to overwhelm adaptation.

When pain is perceived as punishment, a testimonial of love, or symbol of strength, the mourner can feel added distress. The caregiver will need to provide information about the normalcy of pain following major loss (i.e., pain occurs subsequent to a loss irrespective of whether there is any religious or philosophical interpretation of it as punishment or whether it is perceived as testimony or strength). Although it is not in the realm of most caregivers to convert or "deprogram" individuals of different religious or philosophical persuasions, it is within reason to address psychological issues regarding guilt and other secular sources for the mourner's perception of pain as punishment. Certainly, much literature has confirmed the tendency of individuals to attribute blame to themselves after a trauma (e.g., Janoff-Bulman, 1985), as well as to interpret negative events as a form of punishment (e.g., Bard & Sangrey, 1986). The notion that pain is a testimony to love for the deceased must be disabused in order to forestall the development of chronic mourning, among other reasons. The perception of pain as a symbol of strength requires similar reeducation to prevent secondary gain from fostering chronic mourning or the attachment of inappropriate or romanticized significance to pain. Thus, to the extent that psychological issues foster erroneous perceptions of pain, the caregiver must address them aggressively.

Pain conceptualized as a ticket to good things or as the great equalizer can be positive in the sense that these viewpoints give meaning to endurance and transcend current experience. However, they can be negative if employed as rationalizations for not addressing mourning work. Instances of the former should be supported; instances of the latter, confronted.

One of the hallmarks of emotional maturity and realistic acceptance of the limitations and vicissitudes of life is the mastery, acceptance, and tolerance of sadness, helplessness, and hopelessness (Dorpat, 1973). Therefore, it should be the caregiver's goal not to help the mourner avoid these affects, but to help her learn how best to live with their inevitable presence at certain times of life. This does not mean that the caregiver condones self-defeating or masochistic behaviors. Rather, it means helping the mourner learn how to cope. Dorpat's (1973) perspective on depressed and suicidal individuals clarifies this view and can be extrapolated to all mourners:

> What is meant by *mastering* mourning emotions? I definitely do not mean their dissolution as a desirable or even possible goal. Through intensive work with depressed and suicidal persons, I have changed my concept of the meaning and the adaptive function of the emotions in grief states.
>
> Ten years ago I thought differently. Then my aim was to assist the depressed patient to overcome and abolish feelings of hopelessness and helplessness. We know how overwhelming and potentially devastating such feelings are in the suicidal person.
>
> Certainly in the suicidal crisis phase of treatment, our offers of help and hope counteract such feelings. In later stages of treatment of suicidal persons, however, therapy should have an aim of fostering the patient's expression, mastery, and acceptance of *appropriate, reality-based* feelings of helplessness and hopelessness.
>
> As Gorer (1965) has shown, both English and American people tend to deny death, mourning, and the emotion of grief. Led by the example of our young people, we strive to become proficient in "turn on" emotions, such as hope, erotic feelings, and excitement. I submit that the mastery of *turn off* emotions such as grief, sadness, helplessness, and hopelessness deserves equal attention as they are potentially adaptive and constructive feelings. (p. 223)

Complete treatment of complicated mourning typically takes time

The caregiver needs to understand that the treatment of complicated mourning is often time consuming and involved. Certainly, one's theoretical or philosophical orientation will have a profound influence upon one's willingness to incorporate this notion into work with complicated mourning. The factor of pragmatics is also undeniable: Economic and time constraints frequently exert a strong and direct impact on the treatment process.

It is already clear that mourning, whether complicated or not, is insufficiently understood in the mental health system. This is evident in the way the problem is treated—or perhaps more accurately, not treated—in the DSM-III-R (American Psychiatric Association, 1987). Along with financial pressures, this lack of understanding contributes to treatment that may be briefer than warranted. Peer review recommendations, third-party insurer guidelines, and the session number limits of health maintenance and preferred provider organizations all conspire to keep treatment short term.

Obviously, this reality does not apply solely to treatment for complicated mourning. It is a serious and undeniable fact of life in mental health treatment in general. However, problems for intervention in complicated mourning increase because complicated mourning is poorly understood even by those in mental health, with this misunderstanding translating to a lack of appreciation of its impact, its frequent unresponsiveness to treatment, and its broad-range consequences. Professional and social expectations for the impact of and recovery from major loss are often inappropriate and characterized by myths and unrealistic stereotypes. In addition, given that death is a typical event, it is deemed that reactions should be manageable and short-lived, often with no recognition of the factors and sequelae that may circumscribe the particular event and the individual who survives it. Finally, the issues inherent in mourning the loss of a loved one tend to arouse relatively greater resistance than in other conditions (e.g., separation pain, reluctance to confront ambivalence, fear of losing connection to the deceased).

A number of schools of thought and practice do offer short-term treatment of complicated mourning. However, complicated mourning often requires more than brief treatment. The two crucial variables in selecting treatment are the extensiveness of the target goals and the number, type, and severity of complications that have interfered with mourning. For example, reduction of particular symptoms could be expected to take much less time than a complete address of all six "R" processes of mourning. Similarly, a basically healthy individual suffering from minor elements of post-traumatic stress associated with a relatively benign but sudden, unexpected death would present different treatment requirements than would someone whose lack of a support system and significant character pathology interfere with mourning for a murdered loved one.

Complicated mourning appears not to be relinquished easily, often due to the previously mentioned resistance to treatment, as well as to the desire to avoid (or, in some cases, refusal to relinquish) the pain it entails. Because the process commonly involves issues problematic for anyone at any time and often necessitates simultaneous major readjustments in the crucial areas of identity, roles, assumptive world, relationships, behaviors, and ways of being in the world, it is not at all surprising that this type of work would proceed more slowly than other types. Caregivers must be mindful of the variety and breadth of the work the mourner must accomplish, appreciate what this means in terms of demands on the individual in the context of that person's life history and these loss circumstances, and regulate the expectations and pace of treatment accordingly. The bottom line is to take the time necessary—don't rush.

The caregiver should be flexible in style and technique

Given the complexity of many situations of complicated mourning, the caregiver must be flexible in style and technique. For example, whereas it may be quite helpful to be nondirective in treatment as the mourner is recollecting the deceased and the mutual relationship, it would be less helpful to be nondirective if the mourner is dealing with severe traumatic reactions, in which case directed intervention is sorely needed. Similarly, flexibility in choice of techniques is critical. Cathartic techniques, as well as behavioral, cognitive, and insight-oriented techniques, all have been demonstrated to have utility in treating the bereaved. In most cases, even within the constraints of a particular theoretical perspective, it is possible— and advisable—to avail oneself of those methods known to be most effective in treating the multidimensional aspects of complicated mourning. Complicated mourning is less likely than other disorders to benefit from a solitary style or inflexible and insufficiently tailored interventions. Here true eclecticism is warranted.

Sanders (1989) provides one model. She suggests that a mixture of client-centered and psychoanalytic therapies is most helpful early on in mourning as the individual struggles with shock in confronting awareness of the loss and processing the feelings it generates. During what she terms the period of conservation and withdrawal, she perceives that the existential-humanistic approaches are most effective in helping the mourner achieve greater responsibility for the outcome of mourning, gain self-awareness, strive toward purpose and meaning, and contend with aloneness. Finally, Sanders identifies Gestalt therapy, as an extension of existential therapy, and behavior therapy as especially helpful in what she calls the healing and renewal phases. She notes that Gestalt therapy assists in the completion of unfinished business and the movement from dependency on others to oneself; behavior therapy directs itself toward specific behavior change, the acquisition of new behaviors, the elimination of maladaptive ones, and the promotion of desirable ones.

The main goal for caregivers is to recognize that complicated mourning benefits from a range of therapeutic styles, techniques, modalities, and philosophical approaches—and to take action accordingly. Caregivers must be aware of available helpful adjuncts to their armamentarium and use them when appropriately indicated and, of course, when prefaced by sufficient preparation, training, and mourner assessment.

Understanding timing can make or break treatment

Interventions in all kinds of treatment have been made or broken by timing. The abstract concept of timing inherently involves issues of readiness, appropriateness, defense and coping, ability, resources, perception, judgment, and fit. In fact, there is no such thing as an intervention by itself—it always is an intervention at some time. Time may be relative to the following.

1. The life of the person for whom the intervention is designed (specifically, the person's ongoing psychosocial and biological life at the precise time of the intervention, or his historical life as a whole from the time of birth until the intervention)

2. Where the individual is in time since the death

3. The point achieved in the mourning processes

4. Where the individual is in his relationship with the deceased

5. Where the individual is in his receipt of support from his support system

6. Where the individual is in any ongoing or anticipated involvement with the legal system

7. The point reached in the treatment process

Interventions appropriate and effective at one time will not necessarily be so at another. The caregiver must be attuned to the different dimensions of time and evaluate proposed interventions accordingly. Premature intervention can cause enormous resistance on the part of the mourner, even if the caregiver is correct in action or interpretation. To be told that one is denying rage toward the deceased may be a technically correct interpretation, but if it is offered too soon and causes the mourner to flee treatment, it has done little good. It is always useful to query oneself about the appropriateness of the timing of an intervention and the possible consequences it may have, just as one would about its overall appropriateness in terms of the mourner.

A related issue concerns the mourner's sense of time, which may be altered by the desire to hold on to the time the loved one was alive. Although it may have been 3 chronological years since the death, for the mourner it may be too soon to hear cold, hard facts without careful preparation. It is precisely because the mourner has an abnormal conception of time and life that she finds herself in treatment. For this reason, it is important for the caregiver to have a notion of the mourner's sense of time.

Another important issue concerns the fact that by the time some mourners finally begin to deal with their loss, there may be little support or understanding for what they are undergoing—and perhaps even intolerance and abuse. Worden (1982) has found that, to minimize adverse reactions, it is sometimes necessary to secure permission from the mourner to alert family members to possible changes in behavior that could cause misunderstanding. A number of other caregivers routinely involve family members or significant others in the treatment of complicated mourning to forestall these types of difficulties (e.g., S. Lieberman, 1978; Ramsay, 1979). Mourners need to be prepared to contend with family reactions and given assistance in finding the support they need. If support is not readily available, it will be incumbent upon the caregiver to provide as much as is possible.

The establishment of specific treatment goals is critical

As policies of peer review and increased demand for documentation of need and progress begin to pervade both treatment and record departments, mental health practitioners are beginning to target more specific treatment goals. However, it still is not uncommon for caregivers to lack concrete goals for their patients or clients. The issue of goals is especially important in the treatment of complicated mourning because of the nebulousness that often characterizes mourning processes, whether complicated or not.

The maintenance of specific treatment goals in complicated mourning will help keep the caregiver focused and provide criteria for evaluating change. These criteria can be established and operationalized in relation to the "R" processes of mourning. In addition, targeting objectives also will help separate issues of mourning from issues associated with mental or physical disorders. For example, in treating a mourner with a personality disorder, it will be important for the caregiver to remain clear on what is possible for loss accommodation within this particular individual's specific personality structure and on what constitutes healthy mourning within its context. The ability to mourn of an individual with a borderline personality disorder, for instance, would be expected to be quite different from that of one without such severe characterological impairments, and the expectations appropriate for each would be likewise dissimilar. Thus, the delineation of specific goals and objectives helps the caregiver remain both focused and realistic.

Treatment goals, like the specific interventions used to reach them, must be appropriate to the particular mourner, her mourning, and the constellation of factors circumscribing her and her loss. In any given situation, each high-risk and general factor influencing the mourner's response and each symptom of mourning presents its own issues and raises the need for its own type of intervention. When integrated, the interventions for all of these form the total treatment experience. The complexity of treatment required underscores the importance of a comprehensive assessment (see chapter 6 and the appendix).

The pace of progress must be realistic as well. Indeed, in working with complicated mourning, one must think in terms of small steps. To establish goals that are too large to begin with only sets the mourner up for failure. For example, the mourner may not be able to stop visiting the cemetery for a week at a time, but she may be able to decrease visits to once every other day. Sometimes the evidence of change will be small to the observer but significant to those who appreciate its idiosyncratic meaning (e.g., the symbolic importance of a widow's going to a movie alone). In other words, it is important to determine small initial goals that, over time, can lead to larger and more complex ones.

Physical release is a legitimate goal of intervention

Grief—whether it is uncomplicated or complicated—often makes the mourner feel angry, frustrated, victimized, guilty, anxious, depressed, sad, and helpless, along with myriad other reactions. These feelings are difficult to articulate and easily can become channeled into physical symptoms. In addition, restlessness produced by the inclination to search and recover the lost loved one often occurs in complicated mourning. Physical activity can reduce tension and anxiety, release aggression, relieve depression and other unpleasant feelings, decrease helplessness and lack of control, and provide constructive assertion of self in the face of victimization by loss—all components of grief and complicated mourning. Physical activity also can help prevent further physical and psychological problems. It can ground a person, work against shock, and increase feelings of personal power. The caregiver who believes that the treatment focus needs to be exclusively on psychosocial issues does the mourner a significant disservice. That person typically contends with great strain occasioned by both the loss and his nontherapeutic attempts to deal with it. For this reason, some form of physical activity appropriate and acceptable to the individual mourner should be incorporated into the treatment plan.

The caregiver's criteria for success must be both specific and general

Any formulation of criteria for success must take into account specific factors associated with where the person begins and what he has to work with (i.e., the factors influencing his response to loss—see Table 2.1). However, it also must address general issues (i.e., the mourner's progress in the six "R" processes of mourning). The key concern is to what extent and in what manner this particular mourner in these circumstances is able to readjust to move adaptively into the new world without forgetting the old in terms of the self, the assumptive world, the relationship with the deceased, and living in the new world without the loved one, as well as to reinvest in that new world. Thus, the caregiver formulates idiosyncratic goals for an individual mourner depending on the factors at hand (e.g., to be able to admit that a loved one's death was a suicide) along with general ones necessary for any person (i.e., to successfully complete the six "R" processes).

In judging the efficacy of treatment, both caregiver and mourner will need to consider large spans of time. Attempting to gauge treatment progress over the short term is like weighing oneself daily while dieting: In addition to causing distress about inevitable fluctuations, a too frequent assessment often does not reveal genuine, subtle changes that may be occurring. Although short-term changes must be identified, supported, and reinforced, it is advisable to take a longer term perspective (e.g., "You are much more actively involved with your family this fall than you were in the spring").

Transference and termination are critical issues in the treatment of complicated mourning

Being in treatment for the loss of a loved one will heighten for the mourner the importance of the transference relationship and termination from treatment. Regardless of whether or not the caregiver customarily works with these issues, their particular salience with regard to bereavement must be understood. Not all mourners will have the same issues or the same degree of intensity with regard to transference and termination. Typically, however, both phenomena can provide the caregiver with important opportunities to understand the loss and help the individual work through and adjust appropriately to it.

It is outside of the scope of this book to provide a comprehensive review of transference reactions and termination. For further discussion, the reader is directed to the professional literature in his or her own discipline or theoretical school. Although many resources are somewhat psychoanalytic in orientation (e.g., Brenner, 1976), this does not mean that the caregiver must subscribe to classical psychoanalytic treatment or philosophy to benefit from them (e.g., Sadock, 1989). Once sensitive to the importance of these experiences, the caregiver may integrate them into any perspective or mode of practice deemed suitable.

GENERIC GUIDELINES FOR TREATMENT

It is presumed that caregivers providing treatment for complicated mourning are well versed and clinically adept in the skills required in mental health intervention in general, as well as in techniques for facilitation of uncomplicated mourning. The reader is referred to Rando (1984) for a more comprehensive discussion of specific techniques. In addition to these skills and techniques, a number of generic guidelines for treatment of complicated mourning exist. These guidelines, listed in Table 8.2 and detailed in the following pages, are mandated throughout all phases of treatment

Table 8.2   Generic Guidelines for Treatment of Complicated Mourning

1. Orient the mourner to treatment.

2. Provide the mourner with explicit permission—indeed, a prescription—to mourn.

3. Support the mourner in coping with the mourning processes.

4. Promote social support of the mourner.

5. Maintain a family systems perspective in dealing with the mourner.

6. Ensure that the mourner has appropriate medical evaluation, medication, and treatment when symptoms warrant.

7. Do not necessarily accept what is on the surface; probe for underlying issues and impaired "R" processes.

8. Work with the mourner to recognize, actualize, and accept the reality of the death.

9. Normalize and legitimize appropriate affects, cognitions, wishes, fears, behaviors, experiences, and symptoms.

10. Assist the mourner in identifying, labeling, differentiating, and tracing affective experiences and their component parts.

11. Appreciate and enable the working through process.

12. Acknowledge that repetition is an inherent part of treatment, but ensure that repetition takes place in the service of working through.

13. Once affective experiences are identified, labeled, differentiated, and traced, enable the mourner to feel, accept, examine, give some form of expression to, and work through all of the feelings aroused by the loss.

14. Design and tailor treatment to address general and specific issues identified for the individual mourner.

15. Determine the symbolic meanings of persons, objects, experiences, and events to the mourner.

16. Identify, interpret, explore, and work through resistances to the mourning processes.

17. Identify any unfinished business with the deceased and discover or create appropriate ways to facilitate closure.

18. Help the mourner identify, label, differentiate, actualize, mourn, and accommodate secondary losses resulting from the death.

19. Recognize and respond to the importance of security afforded by the caregiver's availability to the mourner.

20. Recognize the dynamics of complicated mourning and adhere to the five "Ps" in work with the mourner.

21. When a normal, expectable emotion is absent, determine why and address the omission.

with each mourner and should be incorporated into the caregiver's own clinical perspective. All are intended to be employed toward the general goal of enabling the mourner to successfully complete the six "R" processes of mourning.

Orient the mourner to treatment

When taking an individual experiencing complicated mourning into treatment, it is helpful to provide an overall perspective along with information about what to expect, what the "rules" are, and how the process tends to go. Misinformation about mourning is rampant, and the mourner certainly has already had problems in processing the loss and most probably is ambivalent in some areas about achieving a successful outcome. For these reasons, it is essential that the caregiver familiarize the mourner with that treatment.

Throughout the orientation, the caregiver should present the mourner with a clear rationale for and description of therapy. The mourner should be able to feel that the caregiver knows what will happen and why—that everything has a purpose, even though the mourner might not be able to comprehend it at the time. This is especially important because of the natural tendency for the mourner to resist treatment in order to maintain a relationship with the deceased and to avoid the necessary pain of coming to grips with the loss and its implications. These feelings, coupled with lack of a sense of purpose, can promote a flight from therapy. Proper orientation can also clarify confusion about mourning in general and correct any misinformation the mourner might have in particular. To the extent that the mourner has faith in the caregiver, this will engender predictability, control, order, security, and confidence—things typically in short supply in this situation.

To achieve these goals, the orientation should focus on the following areas.

The caregiver's perspective on complicated mourning. The caregiver's perspective on complicated mourning provides (a) the bulk of the rationale for the interventions and processes the mourner will be experiencing in treatment; (b) a brief overview of treatment goals; (c) assurance that treatment can be beneficial; and (d) the framework within which the caregiver presents normative information about grief and mourning, along with specific facts to debunk the various myths, stereotypes, and misconceptions about grief and mourning that impede the individual's healthy experience of both.

Example: I believe that people often develop complicated mourning for two reasons: They are afraid they will lose their connection to their loved one if they mourn the death too well, and they are frightened that they will be unable to cope with the pain of the loss if they really face it. Both things are very scary, and understandably so. The ultimate purpose of treatment, as I see it, is to find special ways to maintain a connection with _____ but to make sure these are ways that won't bring you additional problems, as you are having now. We need to work together to find out how to do this and how to help you learn to live without _____'s being here as before. This means we will need to look very slowly at what the loss means to you and all the feelings it brings up in you. Most people think this is a simple process, but it really isn't. It's doable, but it takes work.

This sort of presentation gives the mourner an indication of what will occur and why. It also disabuses the common myth that mourning should not require very much work. Note the explicit and implicit empathic statements made in this context. These are important because the mourner is often quite fearful and needs reassurance that the caregiver recognizes her perspective.

The mourner also will need to receive information about grief and mourning. This information can be provided in a conversational, specific fashion. One need not lecture or present this information didactically but can interweave it as appropriate into the conversation.

Example: You are absolutely correct—many people do not understand your unique problems in this particular situation. Unfortunately, most folks think that all losses are the same. They fail to recognize that bereavement is determined by who and what the person lost, how the loved one died, and by the type of individual the person is, among many other things. Because no loss is ever exactly the same as another, mourning will be as individual and as different among people as are their fingerprints. Certainly, there are commonalities, but even these are experienced in idiosyncratic ways.

Information about the design and rules of this particular type of treatment. Information about the design and rules of treatment gives the mourner structure and a reason for undergoing this often painful process. Factual knowledge informs the mourner about what to expect, providing her with a sense of predictability, control, and participation.

Example: At this point I think it would be helpful for us to meet on a weekly basis. During these early meetings I will be asking you to tell me all about _____. I will be interested in what _____ was like, how you met, how you got along, what you did, and so forth. This is important for us to do because it helps me understand who the person was you are mourning and what your relationship was like so I can be most helpful to you. It will also give you opportunities to recall these things as well, which is a process you need to engage in right now.

Obviously, this type of example would not be appropriate for someone doing a different type of intervention (e.g., emotional flooding) or for certain mourners for whom such instructions would be contraindicated (e.g., a chronic mourner, who may require assistance in ceasing rumination about the deceased—although, in the beginning of that treatment, this is information that must be garnered even if the process is later to be attenuated). As for all the examples discussed here, the caregiver will have to tailor the message to the specific treatment and individual involved.

In any type of therapy, it is important to be specific about the rules to which the mourner must adhere. These must be clarified in order to ensure that the mourner understands what the caregiver expects and will tolerate and to provide the mourner with information she needs to make the decision whether or not to enter treatment. For this reason, clinical pragmatics such as the following must be addressed: length of sessions, fees and other financial obligations, limits of confidentiality, cancellation policies, emergency services, office policies, and the caregiver's clinical rules for treatment. The latter will vary according to the caregiver and the caregiver's philosophical orientation (e.g., eliciting free association, prohibiting physical aggression in the office, completing homework or maintaining a journal, asking the mourner to question the caregiver if necessary or giving the mourner responsibility for saying she disagrees with something).

Instructing the mourner about these rules should not be done in a cold, mechanical manner, as if reading a list of "Do's and Dont's." It must be done gently and with the stated purpose of providing the mourner with the information necessary for her to decide whether treatment with this particular caregiver is what she thinks she would like to attempt at this time. Laying the details out for the mourner's consideration shows respect, conveys that there is a structure in place (often very comforting to the mourner), and indicates that she has choices and is not helpless. This last aspect provides further ammunition to work against generalization of the powerlessness that may have occurred at the time of the loved one's death.

Predictions about resistances to, the course of, and the pitfalls of treatment. In orienting the mourner to treatment, the caregiver may carefully—and in a manner so as not to establish a self-fulfilling prophecy or frighten the mourner—offer some predictions about resistances to, the course of, and the pitfalls of treatment. The purpose in gently pointing out these resistances right away is to avoid having the mourner act them out and prematurely drop out of treatment. If done properly, providing this information also illustrates that the caregiver has listened and observed carefully and already is aware of potential problems. Although this generally tends to make the mourner feel more secure, depending upon the particular dynamics, it can make her feel more anxious. (If so, this problem should be addressed directly at the time.) It also demonstrates that issues will be handled in a straightforward manner and indicates that the caregiver appreciates the ambivalence with which the mourner approaches treatment. Finally, it provides a mechanism for discussing how the caregiver and mourner together can handle future resistances and defenses that may arise and for letting the mourner know what to expect.

> *Example:* In telling me about how you responded to previous deaths you said that whenever you became very sad you would literally run away from the situation. How should we handle it if that comes up here? Do you think we could make an agreement that if you feel as though you want to run out of my office when we are talking about _____ you could tell me as soon as you notice it? Then perhaps I can help you find a more effective way to cope with your sadness. If I notice that you look as if you want to bolt, I'll point that out to you, OK? It's understandable not to like to be so sad—you'd have to be a masochist to be unmoved—but maybe we can find better ways for you to cope with it.

Resistances will occur throughout all aspects of treatment, and issues of timing, interpretation, working through, and so forth should be dealt with as dictated by the caregiver's theoretical or philosophical orientation. Even if anticipated, problems still may occur, but at least the door has been opened to discussing them. After resistances or defenses have been discussed, the mourner will more likely understand them as such. Having had these resistances pointed out also can help the mourner prepare for them and not be frightened or disheartened by them. As in all types of treatment, however, the caregiver must remain nonjudgmental and must never predict outcomes in such a fashion as to set the mourner up for acting them out.

Predictions other than those pertinent to the mourner's resistances or defenses can be made early in the treatment of complicated mourning. For instance, the caregiver can convey that the course of treatment is usually a "Two steps forward, one step back" process and that the work it entails most probably (although not necessarily) will make the mourner feel somewhat worse before she feels better. This forewarning is designed to work against premature termination, but it must not be overemphasized or it may frighten the mourner away. A medical analogy often is quite useful.

Example: Sometimes it will be a little difficult as we talk about things that can bring up some pain. However, you need to know that it is pain in the service of healing. If you avoid it, you will never reap the benefits of working it through. To stop treatment is like stopping the physician in the middle of cleaning out an infected wound. If you stop then, the wound will only stay open and become more infected, and your pain will continue unabated—maybe even get worse. If you can tolerate the cleansing, then the wound will be able to heal afterwards. When you feel the pain, let's talk about it. That is one way pain can be reduced as you are undergoing this uncomfortable process. Finding ways to tolerate the pain so you can remain in treatment can help you get to the point where it does not hurt as much anymore and you can begin to heal.

Predictions can help prepare the mourner, place the mourning process in context, and eliminate unnecessary fear when certain events take place. An example of predicting a potential pitfall would be the caregiver's noting the tendency of some individuals to want to terminate treatment after an initial reduction in symptoms. The caregiver should warn the mourner about the inadvisability of terminating before treatment is completed. Any other predictions that may be made (e.g., about the occurrence of anniversary reactions or the possibility of treatment's causing family conflict) should be handled in a fashion to suggest to the mourner that certain things *may* occur.

Example: In a few weeks it is the anniversary of _____'s death. Sometimes, not always, people find that they get a little more symptomatic at these times because they are reminded consciously or unconsciously of what happened about the time of death. That may or may not happen to you.

When concerns are worded this way, the mourner is not forced to act out any self-fulfilling prophecy. Generally, predictions should be kept to a minimum and used only when it is in the mourner's best interests to be forewarned as opposed to discovering the reality herself. Obviously, caregivers must refrain from using predictions to impress mourners with their own knowledge.

Empowerment of the mourner through explicit provision of a number of aspects of control. It is important for the caregiver to orchestrate the empowerment of the mourner by providing a number of aspects of control. Empowering individuals in therapy is a critical goal for most types of treatment. In complicated mourning, where the mourner may feel—and is—victimized by the loss, empowerment is crucial. The mourner may be given explicit control of such issues as timing, content, pacing, depth, and so forth. In the frequent situation where resistance is high because of the fear of being overwhelmed by affect, empowerment is particularly necessary and fruitful. If mourners feel they have control, over time they will be more open to exploring dangerous or painful areas. Such control decreases the sense of helplessness, lack of control, and fear of being overwhelmed that the mourner often feels in the face of coping with the loss. It challenges passivity.

> *Example:* As we deal with _____'s death here, you can go as fast or as slow as you desire. You set the pace, and I will follow your lead. Some things may be comfortable to talk about, even pleasant. Some may be a little more uncomfortable. All I ask is that if things are difficult, you tell me. I will not force you to deal with anything you do not want to deal with—I could not even if I wanted to—but we can talk about how to make these things less difficult. We'll take it slow and easy as we look at this whole situation in little, tiny pieces, one at a time, until we've got the entire picture. Rome wasn't built in a day, and mourning doesn't happen all at once.

Explicit recognition of the mourner's pain and distress, as well as communication of the conviction that the mourner ultimately will be able to cope with the loss more effectively than at present. The caregiver must be sure to convey two important messages to the mourner early on in treatment. First, there must be an explicit recognition of the mourner's pain and distress. If the mourner fails to feel that the caregiver recognizes her pain and distress, not only will comfort be lacking, the necessary experience of empathy also will be absent. Needless to say, a feeling of empathy from the caregiver is a prerequisite if the mourner is to continue on in this exquisitely painful work. Of course, empathy must be conveyed in such a fashion as to communicate understanding and support, not to support avoidance of pain.

Second, the caregiver must communicate the conviction that the mourner ultimately will be able to cope with the loss relatively more effectively than at present. Hope is a necessary ingredient in getting through any adversity, and the mourning process is no exception. By sending the message that the work eventually will enable the mourner to cope with the loss more effectively, the caregiver essentially provides hope that at some point things will be better. Of course, one cannot promise a cure and certainly should not communicate the conviction that things will be better if one does not genuinely hold it. However, one can offer realistic hope for the future that still recognizes the currently intense experience of mourning and the permanent changes that come from major loss.

The hopes of each mourner will differ: One may hope for a decrease in pain, another may aspire to an eventual reunion with the deceased in an afterlife, and yet a third may hold onto the hope that in the future life will regain some meaning. The point is not for the caregiver to predict what will happen if the mourner pays attention to the work of mourning, but rather to assert that in the future the agony and anguish can be less than they are at the current time. This need not be set forth explicitly but may be communicated by implication. For instance, saying, "It must seem as if there's no light at the end of the tunnel" suggests that there is one, but the mourner just cannot get a sense of it yet.

> *Example:* I recognize that this is an excruciatingly painful time for you. Your loss brings many agonizing feelings and seemingly insurmountable tasks in learning to live without _____'s presence in your life as before. It won't always be this difficult —you will learn to cope with _____'s death and the pain it brings little by little over time—but for right now it probably does seem almost impossible, even though it isn't.

Enlistment of the mourner's commitment to treatment. The enlistment of the mourner's commitment to treatment is an often overlooked but important ingredient in therapy, both in the beginning and throughout the entire process. By definition, a commitment has the mourner "own" her involvement in the treatment and specifies that involvement, and the choice it inherently includes, as a required element of change.

Enlisting commitment entails the caregiver's directly asking the mourner whether she is willing to give treatment a chance to help her learn to live with her loss. The caregiver makes it clear that the mourner has the pivotal role in the therapy and helps her to see that, although she may have had no control or choice about the loss, she has both control and choice over how she will respond to it over the long term. This view pertains not so much to the acute period of grief, in which the mourner has been subjected to psychological, behavioral, social, and physical effects in all realms of life; rather, it pertains to the perspective or attitude she will assume thereafter.

> *Example:* I believe that with some hard work you can get to the point where you are in less pain and better able to tolerate living your life without _____'s presence. Are you willing to make the commitment to give this type of treatment a chance to help you get there? You are the only one who can determine whether it does. I can help you, but you are the one who must make the decision.

Provide the mourner with explicit permission— indeed, a prescription—to mourn

Most people experiencing uncomplicated as well as complicated mourning require both permission and encouragement (verbal and nonverbal) to mourn because of the traditionally unacceptable thoughts and feelings that become aroused and the personal and social discomfort such an experience brings. For many mourners experiencing difficulties, there is less need for permission and encouragement than for actual prescription. They often require an authority figure to inform them that they need to mourn and to mourn all aspects of the deceased person and the mutual relationship—even the "unacceptable" parts such as the deceased's negative qualities. They frequently require this direction in order to overcome their own resistances, which interfere with complete mourning, as well as to legitimize their struggle to free themselves from pain. As noted before, many mourners may view relinquishing their pain as severing all ties with the deceased. In this case, the professional prescription to mourn can help reduce guilt about doing so.

Support the mourner in coping with the mourning processes

Helping the mourner cope as best as possible with the vicissitudes of the mourning processes entails providing appropriate information and support. As in any other human situation, understanding makes the circumstances more tolerable. Therefore, normative psychoeducational information about mourning is very important. However, as is the case for normalization and legitimization, caregivers often fail to appreciate the therapeutic value and significance of providing psychoeducational material. This cognitive information is critically important in a number of ways.

1. It corrects misinformation held by the mourner and debunks myths establishing unrealistic expectations for mourning that, when unmet, eventuate in feelings such as guilt and failure. In this regard, it helps prevent further complications in mourning.

2. It provides a framework to help the mourner feel less overwhelmed, out of control, and helpless.

3. It offers specific data that promote healthy mourning (e.g., recognition that mourning reactions are unique to each person and will be experienced in many if not all realms of life, comprehension of appropriate expectations for time and course).

4. It normalizes and legitimizes aspects of mourning the individual erroneously may have interpreted as indicating negative things about himself (e.g., pathology, deficiency, worthlessness, that he is going crazy).

In addition to providing information, the caregiver can support the mourner in other ways by using interventions such as the following.

1. Instructing the mourner in how to "dose" himself (i.e., direct attention toward and then away from disturbing stimuli before they become intolerable) and control the pace of mourning by structuring respites

2. Helping the mourner discover ways to replenish himself following the severe emotional, social, physical, intellectual, and spiritual depletion resulting from the loss (e.g., rest, nutrition, social support, physical activity/sports, religion, philosophy, literature, media)

3. Encouraging physical activity or exercise to release pent-up emotion

4. Acknowledging pragmatic concerns and referring the mourner to the proper resources for assistance in these areas

5. Promoting appropriate support from others

6. Working with the mourner to maintain the proper balance between experiencing pain and other unpleasant affects and maintaining sufficient defenses to avoid being overwhelmed

7. Assisting the mourner to maintain good physical health and avoid or keep to a minimum use of drugs, sedatives, alcohol, caffeine, nicotine, and other self-medication

8. Helping the mourner develop the proper perspective on what accommodating the loss will mean

Promote social support of the mourner

A perceived failure in the area of social support is a high-risk factor for complicated mourning (see chapter 10). Sometimes the failure is global (i.e., there is no support at all for the mourner); sometimes it is specific (i.e., there is no support for certain aspects of mourning, such as the expression of anger or guilt, or a certain person does not offer a particular type of support). Consequently, the caregiver must do whatever possible to enable the mourner to receive the support that is lacking. This may involve teaching the mourner to be more assertive and effective in securing from the support system precisely what is needed. In other cases, it may mean meeting with family or other social system members to provide psychoeducational information about mourning, help them address their reasons for lack of support, and/or furnish them information on its importance in the mourning process. Depending on the caregiver's theoretical bent, some treatment may be provided in collateral visits in order to deal with the system dynamics interfering with appropriate support for the mourner. In cases of disenfranchised grief (Doka, 1989)—grief that is not socially acknowledged, validated, or supported—it may mean identifying alternate sources of support if a support system is unavailable or cannot or will not provide what is necessary. In instances where support is notably absent, the caregiver may work to help the mourner establish some type of network or system that can provide support (e.g., a self-help group). It is well recognized that connecting mourners with others who have sustained similar experiences is an important therapeutic contribution (see the previous section in this chapter concerning the efficacy of self-help and other groups).

Maintain a family systems perspective in dealing with the mourner

Regardless of whether the caregiver's philosophical or theoretical discipline or clinical practice includes family systems, it is important to remember that the family will influence the mourner and vice versa. Family members can potentiate reactions and conflicts among themselves that positively or negatively affect the mourner. The caregiver must take into account this multiplier effect (Rando, 1984) in families and also must be prepared to weigh the needs of a particular family member against the needs of another or against the needs of the family as a whole. Personal differences in mourning styles, idiosyncratic courses of bereavement, nonidentical needs, and the loss of different relationships despite the death of the same person all can complicate the individual family member's coping, the family's reorganization process, and the system's dynamics and ability to survive the loss. Closeness among family members can bring support but also can make them likely to displace blame, anger, and other hostile feelings onto one another; avoid communication for fear of upsetting one another; or place irrational demands on one another. The caregiver can promote support for the family but must be prepared to work with the mourner alone if this fails. Provision of information about the impact of mourning on families, the appropriate and inappropriate assumption of roles that influence adaptation, family reorganization after a death, the necessity for fair compromise, and so forth can help the individual cope with her own mourning within the context of the family system.

Ensure that the mourner has appropriate medical evaluation, medication, and treatment when symptoms warrant

Given the association between complicated mourning and physical morbidity, the mourner must receive appropriate medical evaluation, medication, and treatment when necessary. Theoretical issues relating to this topic are discussed here; specific clinical management issues relating to medication for depression and anxiety are provided in chapter 5.

For the caregiver to exclude attention to somatic symptoms in favor of psychosocial ones is to incompletely address the mourner's needs. Unless medically trained, the caregiver should never assume that physical symptomatology is merely a somatic manifestation of either uncomplicated or complicated mourning. This may well be the case, but the caregiver must make sure organic reasons are ruled out by a physician before commencing treatment.

The need for medical consultation is especially keen with regard to medication. In the past, physicians too readily prescribed too much medication for too many mourners with too little justification. Usually, antianxiety agents were prescribed to quell the symptoms of distress manifested in acute grief. Because the effect was often to retard the individual's experience of mourning, it was common to hear mourners later on express only the vaguest recollection of postdeath rituals and complain that, when they did come out of their drugged state, others expected them not to manifest acute distress. Their anguished cries, their wailing, their protest—all were silenced by drugs. Crucial opportunities to mourn were lost. For many of these individuals, complicated mourning was thus midwifed by benzodiazepines or anxiolytics. Later in the acute grief process, the drugs prescribed for many were antidepressants or sedatives. Sometimes, sedatives might be dispensed immediately after the death to help the mourner sleep.

Out of this overuse of medication grew a reactionary position condemning the use of any medication for grieving people. However, this extremist position meant that many of those who legitimately required medication were denied it. Notwithstanding the fact that in the past—and even currently—medication has been inappropriately prescribed, some mourners do require it. Failure to recognize and respond to this reality is every bit as harmful as forcing medication.

It is not the nonmedical caregiver's role to determine whether or not medication is actually needed, but rather to determine whether or not a consultation should be requested. In doing so, the caregiver should take great pains to find a psychiatrist or physician who is knowledgeable about psychotropic medication and comfortable with and interested in working with bereaved individuals. Unfortunately, too many psychiatrists and physicians are unfamiliar with uncomplicated reactions to loss and, as a result, misdiagnose and misprescribe. Many are actually frightened by mourners.

Both the caregiver and the physician who will consider prescribing medication must be aware of several important issues. First, as observed by Maddison and Raphael (1972), they must recognize the dynamic implications of psychopharmacotherapy for the bereaved. Specifically, these implications concern an unspoken message to stop expressing distress; a substitute object for the oral needs that are heightened by the loss of the loved one; suppression of anger and guilt, which can tip the balance of normal ambivalence to its pathological extreme and cause complications; and, in cases where the physician had cared for the deceased, a need to prescribe medication for the bereaved that may be motivated by the physician's desire to assuage guilt over the death, to give now what he or she could not give then, and to reaffirm his or her own potency. Maddison and Raphael also caution against pharmacotherapy that works to inhibit mourning.

Notwithstanding these caveats, the majority of those writing about the use of medication in bereavement draw the conclusion that, although studies are currently insufficient to provide conclusive data, medication probably should be considered when symptomatology is severe. The question then becomes what constitutes severe symptomatology.

Barton (1977b) believes that judicious amounts of tranquilizers and sleeping medications may be indicated during the early phase of uncomplicated grief but should be used only when medication would facilitate the mourner's reorganization, assist with overall coping, and intervene in disturbances of such important functions as sleep. He warns that medication should not be used in any fashion that would suppress the normal grief process and advises of the possibility of habituation to the medications as a means of forestalling the pain of grief. Like Maddison and Raphael (1972), he urges caregivers to be aware of the implicit communication in the prescription of drugs that the mourner's feeling state should not be present. This communication works against the legitimization of expression of feelings and acceptance of grief as a normal process. In some situations of complicated grief, Barton notes that psychiatric hospitalization or the use of medication in conjunction with psychotherapeutic efforts must be employed.

In the treatment of pathological grief, Parkes (1985) asserts that medication can have a place in conjunction with psychotherapy for those who are unable to communicate or are a serious suicide risk. Nevertheless, he voices the concern that medication is often misused to suppress grief and can become a means of self-destruction. He suggests that drugs of low toxicity are preferred, with brief hospitalizations as necessary.

Following extensive reviews of the literature, two separate investigating teams have concluded that, in instances of significant symptomatology or when symptoms meet criteria for mental disorders, medication can be beneficial. However, both groups urge great care in its prescription. Specifically, Stroebe and Stroebe (1987) identify the use of medication as a form of emotional control in the early part of grief as "dysfunctional," and Osterweis et al. (1984) stress that medication be prescribed for the bereaved with caution because of an absence of data about its usefulness and impact. Both teams note that, notwithstanding the view that interference with the grief process can result, use of psychotropic medication is widespread in bereavement. When medication is required, both teams suggest using the smallest effective dosage.

More positive views of medication, still stressing the care that must be exercised, appear in the writings of Sidney Zisook and his colleagues (e.g., Zisook et al., 1990), who observe:

> Although some might argue that the use of psychotropic medications during bereavement is maladaptive, in that these substances prevent the bereaved from "getting in touch with their true feelings" and thereby block the resolution of grief, this position has not been validated by empirical data. Alternatively,

these medications may be an effective tool in helping the bereaved individual cope with the overwhelming stress of widowhood, particularly initially, so that resolution might occur. (p. 325)

All of this still leaves the caregiver with a number of clinical issues to struggle with when considering medication for a bereaved person. Clearly, when symptoms are extreme, health or life is endangered, coping and functioning are unacceptably low, or mourning has evolved into a diagnosable mental disorder, the decision to use medication is more clear cut. Although issues of dynamic implications, dosage, and duration must be considered even in these scenarios, the more difficult cases by far are those in which the line between uncomplicated and complicated grief and mourning is less distinct. The following recommendations, which take into account both clinical experience and review of the literature, will be helpful in determining whether a medication consultation or prescription of medication is necessary. These recommendations presuppose the caregiver's understanding of what constitutes uncomplicated and complicated responses at a given point and for a given loss and knowledge of the appropriate use of various medications under different bereavement scenarios.

1. A thorough and accurate assessment must be made of the mourner and the factors surrounding the loss. Use of the GAMSII is encouraged (see chapter 6 and the appendix).

2. Mourners with preexisting psychological, psychophysiological, or physical disorders typically require continued attention to and medication for these disorders.

3. Mourners with post-traumatic stress symptoms usually require medication to address post-traumatic elements sufficiently such that mourning then can be accessed.

4. Grief and mourning can turn into a diagnosable mental disorder requiring medication (e.g., depression, anxiety disorder, adjustment disorder, brief reactive psychosis). Whenever this evolution occurs and diagnostic criteria are met, medication appropriate for that disorder is warranted. However, acute grief can account for many of the symptoms also typical of these disorders. Therefore, before medication is prescribed, caregivers must distinguish acute grief symptoms from mental disorder and be aware of which symptoms of uncomplicated acute grief can benefit from medication even before solidifying into these disorders. (See chapter 5 for more on recognized mental disorders.)

5. If the individual does not have the ability to mourn properly because coping is overwhelmed, functioning is compromised,

or symptomatology endangers health and/or life, it makes sense to do what is necessary to facilitate mourning. For example, even if in the absence of one of the aforementioned mental conditions the mourner experiences significant sleep deprivation, a mild sedative may be in order.

6. If the mourner evidences symptoms inconsistent with grief and mourning or that simply are not consonant with the caregiver's own internal norms, it may be wise to request a medical consultation.

7. If and when medications are prescribed, the caregiver must work with the mourner to ensure that they are used therapeutically and that they do not adversely interact with other drugs the mourner may be taking either by prescription or through self-medication. Both prescription and nonprescription use of drugs increases dramatically following bereavement. Nonprescription drugs used for self-medication may include illicit drugs as well as drugs whose use is socially sanctioned (e.g., alcohol, caffeine, nicotine, over-the-counter preparations).

8. The caregiver must remain alert for suicide (and, on occasion, homicide) potential in mourners receiving medication and must act according to usual and customary professional standards in evaluating and intervening in situations where threat to self or others exists.

9. The caregiver must appreciate and, where necessary, explicitly correct any messages implied by medication prescription that grief or mourning should be suppressed.

10. If suppression or interference with grief or mourning is suspected, the caregiver must reevaluate the drug used, dosage, and accompanying need for additional psychotherapeutic intervention. Consideration must be given to discontinuing the medication if reevaluation warrants.

11. The caregiver must use all medication as an adjunct to treatment or normal support, not as a replacement for it. Prescription must be time-limited, targeted to specific symptoms, and employ the lowest possible effective dosage to promote the mourner's coping and restorative processes.

Over time, the caregiver will develop internal norms about medication and mourning. When these have been established, they can be quite helpful in determining the need for a medication evaluation. Needless to say, whenever any significant doubt exists, the caregiver should err in the direction of requesting an evaluation.

Do not necessarily accept what is on the surface; probe for underlying issues and impaired "R" processes

The caregiver treating complicated mourning must look for hidden issues, latent needs, obscured reactions, and underlying dynamics. What is apparent on the surface may serve the function of camouflaging or defending against what is underneath (e.g., superficial guilt may cover deepseated helplessness). Ultimately, treatment must be directed toward the underlying issues, and the caregiver must intervene to enable the mourner to relinquish the superficial and address the more pivotal concerns beneath. As with resistances, this must be done gently and without stripping the mourner prematurely of needed defenses. In the same vein, in ascertaining which "R" processes have been impaired, the caregiver must not focus exclusively on the material presented superficially. In all cases, the caregiver must appreciate that there are manifest and latent levels to any mourner's response and must not exclude examination of either.

Work with the mourner to recognize, actualize, and accept the reality of the death

The ability to believe cognitively or to internalize affectively that the loved one is truly dead and to comprehend all of the implications of this is frequently hampered in complicated mourning. The caregiver's interventions must be geared toward helping the mourner come to grips with this reality. Many mourners superficially accept the loss but hold expectations to the contrary (e.g., the mourner "knows" his mother is dead but on some level continues to wait for her return). This situation is to be differentiated from the normal lag time that exists in uncomplicated mourning between intellectual and emotional acceptance of the death. In this latter circumstance, repeated confrontation with the deceased's absence and frustration of the mourner's wishes to be reunited with the loved one eventually teach the mourner that the loved one is irretrievably gone.

In complicated mourning, intellectual acknowledgment may be missing, disbelief may have the upper hand, and the mourner's own issues may prevent him from being able to allow himself to perceive the loss and its implications. Because intellectual acceptance is missing, it follows that affective acceptance will be absent as well. The caregiver's job is to work through resistances to the intellectual, and ultimately the affective, acceptance of this loss in order that mourning can progress. Anything that concretizes the loss for the mourner helps actualize it. The caregiver may encourage actualization of the loss by promoting actions such as the following. (All save the last also serve as evocative techniques to elicit the mourner's thoughts and expressions of grief.)

1. Talking about the deceased, the loss, and its meanings and implications

2. Recounting the circumstances of the death

3. Reviewing the relationship and reminiscing about its meanings and memories

4. Bringing into the session and interacting with tangible reminders and various memorabilia, such as photographs, special possessions, or, in some cases, linking objects (Volkan, 1972, 1981)

5. Identifying secondary losses accompanying and engendered by the death

6. Discussing the frustrating inability to gratify needs relating to the deceased

7. Finishing unfinished business with the deceased

8. Reality testing the loved one's absence and the mourner's expectations related to it

9. Confronting denial, resistances, and defenses

10. Visiting the cemetery or viewing other sources of confirmation of the death (e.g., death certificate, insurance payment voucher)

11. Using and making sure the mourner uses past tense verbs when discussing the deceased (except as involves the development of an appropriate new relationship)

12. Examining the altered assumptive and external worlds and the need for the mourner to change in regard to them and his identity

13. Assisting in the development of a healthy new relationship with the deceased that acknowledges the reality of the death and its implications and coincides with the mourner's going forth adaptively in the new world

Normalize and legitimize appropriate affects, cognitions, wishes, fears, behaviors, experiences, and symptoms

Normalizing and legitimizing the mourning process offer the mourner support, reassurance, and control. Doing so can eliminate additional stress and anxiety resulting from inappropriate self-evaluations based on erroneous interpretations about the mourning experience and general misinformation about grief and mourning. Normalizing and legitimizing minimize the mourner's concerns about going crazy and put things in a meaningful context, which in turn increases the ability to tolerate and cope. In addition, they tend to encourage further expression and release, which is so important in mourning. As is the case for providing psychoeducational information about mourning, normalization and legitimization are sometimes viewed by caregivers as unsophisticated techniques. However, they are critically important therapeutic interventions.

Assist the mourner in identifying, labeling, differentiating, and tracing affective experiences and their component parts

Complicated mourning often brings a confusing, undifferentiated mass of painful stimuli under which the mourner must labor. To the extent that components of this undifferentiated mass can be identified, named, distinguished from one another, traced back to original sources, and dealt with individually, the mourner will be better able to cope and experience a sense of control. It is vastly more difficult and discouraging to confront a vague, diffuse, oppressive accumulation of pain than it is to contend with specific components and then address their sources individually (e.g., anger at the loss, frustration at not being able to reach out and touch the deceased, fear of making it alone, or sadness at unfinished business). When a person identifies and names something, it becomes more manageable; when its source is identified, it becomes more grounded. Even if such awareness does not obviate problem solving, it helps give a sense of cognitive control and establish a direction for action. At the very least, it makes the experience more understandable and tolerable, thus decreasing emotional press upon the mourner. This type of differentiation also allows each feeling to be fully experienced and diminishes intellectual and affective confusion.

Appreciate and enable the working through process

One of the most important tenets of treatment in complicated mourning involves the need to work through its various aspects. Working through combines the three analytic techniques of confrontation, clarification, and interpretation (Karasu, 1989) and is an inherent objective of mourning. It involves repetition and continual elaboration or demonstration of the same defensive or instinctual behaviors in differing contexts, the goal being to make insight more effective and bring about significant and lasting changes. It entails overcoming resistances, expanding and modifying prior interpretations, identifying basic themes, or highlighting central issues to lead eventually to the inclusion in the conscious personality of previously warded-off components (Moore & Fine, 1990).

The repetition required in this working through process must be respected by the caregiver. It cannot be eliminated:

> The individual mental or emotional experiences . . . are, of course, part of the person's pattern of reacting and thinking, but they are interlocked with one another in multiple ways. Interpretive dissolution and understanding of some specific piece of dissociated material, therefore, can produce only a

certain degree of actual change. The extent to which any single piece of awareness and understanding affects a patient's many other known or dissociated interpersonal experiences, which are mutually interlocked with the first one and through them with his general patterns of reacting and thinking, will determine the extent of real change.

As a result, any understanding, any new piece of awareness which has been gained by interpretive clarification, has to be reconquered and tested time and again in new connections and contacts with other interlocking experiences, which may or may not have to be subsequently approached interpretively in their own right. That is the process to which psychoanalysts refer when speaking of the necessity of repeatedly "working through" the emotional experiences for the dynamics and contents of which awareness and understanding have been achieved, and when they speak of "working through" the elements which operated in the process of establishing this awareness and this understanding. (Fromm-Reichman, 1950, p. 141)

Caregivers need not espouse Fromm-Reichman's psychoanalytic perspective to appreciate her views on the working through process. Indeed, by other names this idea is also present in a majority of the other theoretical orientations. It is a pivotal concept inherently involved in the repetition compulsion principle (Freud, 1920/1955a) that underlies the generic processes of psychological adaptation to psychosocial change (e.g., psychosocial transitions and assumptive world changes, identified by Parkes, 1988) and trauma (e.g., the stress response syndrome, identified by Horowitz, 1986a), each of which is present to some degree in most bereavement reactions. Certainly, problems exist for which the working through process sustains less emphasis. In mourning, however, because of the extent of the readaptations of self that must occur, the complex interrelationships among the various parties involved, and the relative intractability of investment in loved objects, repetition and working through are a major portion of the experience. It is no coincidence that working through as a general process in psychotherapy has been compared with the work of mourning (Rado, 1925) and perceived as a process of mourning (Livingston, 1971).

It must be noted that simple recollection or intellectualized treatment of memories is insufficient. There also must be emotional catharsis and a review and reintegration of relevant past and present thoughts and beliefs, culminating in a revision of the assumptive world. Work must take place repeatedly over time and must clarify, interpret, and work through the present loss's links with earlier deprivations; fears of overwhelming, disintegrating emotions; and concerns about facing the future without the loved one (Raphael, 1986). In working with children traumatized by the Chowchilla school bus kidnapping, Terr (1979) observed that it was only when the children's traumatic dreams and play were interpreted—promoting both abreaction and understanding—that release occurred. Similarly, Pennebaker and Beall (1986) found that writing about the facts of a traumatic event and not the associated emotions was not upsetting but also did not lead to the same benefits as when emotions were addressed. Review of the literature on coming to terms with major negative life events suggests that cognitions and emotions are equally essential and that the working through process involves a dynamic interplay between them (Tait & Silver, 1989).

All "R" processes must be worked through, but several rely particularly upon this process for success. The "R" process of recollecting and reexperiencing the deceased and the relationship is ideally suited to working through, as are the four subprocesses associated with readjusting to move adaptively into the new world without forgetting the old (i.e., revising the assumptive world, developing a new relationship with the deceased, adopting new ways of being in the world, and forming a new identity).

Acknowledge that repetition is an inherent part of treatment, but ensure that repetition takes place in the service of working through

Repetition in order to master the loss—comprehend it, get new perspectives on it, achieve closure, work it through, and identify and express the feelings and thoughts to which it gives rise—is valuable and should be supported by the caregiver. Indeed, if a caregiver is not comfortable with repetition, he or she should focus on a different type of work, for repetition is an inherent part of the mourning process. Repetition should not be supported and encouraged, however, when it constitutes a resistance, a form of complicated mourning serving as a complex defense against therapeutically dealing with the death and moving forward (i.e., chronic mourning), a denial of the loss or some of its aspects, or an indication of being "stuck" in the mourning processes.

Once affective experiences are identified, labeled, differentiated, and traced, enable the mourner to feel, accept, examine, give some form of expression to, and work through all of the feelings aroused by the loss

It is not unusual for those experiencing complicated mourning to deny, inhibit, or distort some of their feelings after the loss of a loved one. The ultimate goal is for the mourner to feel, accept, examine, give some form of expression to, and work through each of these feelings. This is sometimes known as "processing the emotions." The mourner must deal with the entire spectrum of affect generated by the loss: feelings that are positive and negative, those with which the mourner is comfortable and those that make her uncomfortable, those that are socially validated, and those expected to be suppressed. If a feeling exists, it must be addressed in mourning. Failure to process applicable emotions as specifically noted here leaves mourning incomplete.

Design and tailor treatment to address general and specific issues identified for the individual mourner

Very simply, treatment of the mourner experiencing complications should take into account the general strategies and techniques to promote successful completion of the six "R" processes of mourning and address the two attempts of complicated mourning (i.e., to deny, repress or avoid aspects of the loss, its pain, and the full realization of its implications; to hold on to and avoid relinquishing the lost loved one). Treatment should also include specific interventions to address the mourner's idiosyncratic situation (e.g., high-risk factors, type of death, specific impediments to mourning). Designing and tailoring the treatment package in this fashion presupposes accurate and in-depth assessment.

Determine the symbolic meanings of persons, objects, experiences, and events to the mourner

Throughout the treatment process, the caregiver must work to understand the idiosyncratic experience of the mourner in order to know how best to intervene. This means the caregiver must continually process the meanings, symbolism, and significance the mourner attributes to specific persons, objects, experiences, and events. The fact that what may be true and required in one mourner's treatment may not be so for another is not unique to complicated mourning. It should be assumed for all types of problems and for all types of intervention. However, in complicated mourning the caregiver may be especially prone to attributions about the mourner—attributions that may or may not be accurate.

The most effective way of ensuring accuracy is to ask the mourner to clarify meaning (e.g., the meaning of displaying the deceased's photo, of engaging in a particular identification behavior, of admitting to previous feelings of rage). In all situations, the caregiver must be confident that his or her understanding of the meaning, symbolism, and significance attributed to a person, object, experience, or event accurately reflects that sustained by the mourner. If this is not the case, the caregiver is not operating within the phenomenological world of the mourner, and serious problems —or at least diminished therapeutic value—can ensue. For example, one caregiver made a serious blunder by failing to appreciate that the death of a deceased child's dog constituted for a particular bereaved parent an end of the connection to her son. The mourner's feeling of disconnectedness precipitated a suicide attempt.

Identify, interpret, explore, and work through resistances to the mourning processes

Like peeling an onion, the caregiver must gently remove layer after layer of resistance to the requisite processes of mourning. This is a crucial part of treatment, not something to be rushed through to get to the "underlying issues." Indeed, in complicated mourning, the resistances and defenses employed *are* the underlying issues and the therapeutic targets. Resistance can be seen in any thought, feeling, behavior, impulse, conflict, attitude, value, belief, issue, or conditioned response that contributes to complication in one or more of the six "R" processes of mourning.

It is ill-advised to assail defenses in an effort to force the individual to mourn. This strategy will only engender stronger resistance or overwhelm and/or traumatize the mourner and possibly lead to decompensation. Defenses and resistances are there for a purpose and must be respected, interpreted, and treated carefully. The caregiver gently works them through with the mourner so that he no longer needs them and can let them go. The mourner is never stripped of them, but rather permits himself to relinquish them. In brief, one never leaves the mourner without appropriate recourse to defense. Even in aggressive attacks upon mourning, such as those seen in some of the behavioral therapies, the caregiver accounts for and deals with resistances. For example, in Ramsay's (1979) controversial use of emotional flooding, discussed in some detail in chapter 7, the caregiver takes great pains to respect defenses and build in safeguards against the mourner's becoming overwhelmed.

Identify any unfinished business with the deceased and discover or create appropriate ways to facilitate closure

Unfinished business is anxiety provoking, presses upon the mourner for completion or closure, and tends to be acted out through the repetition compulsion. It can contribute to detrimental behaviors and relationships and can create significant pathology in all realms. For this reason, the caregiver must work to assure that the mourner in some fashion expresses all appreciations and positive feelings and thoughts, all resentments and negative feelings and thoughts, and all regrets and feelings and thoughts associated with the wish that things had been different. The caregiver may ask the mourner specifically what needs to be said or done to come to peace with the deceased and may create opportunities to achieve this closure. To the extent that the caregiver can assist the mourner in achieving closure with the deceased, there will be no unfinished business to prompt acting out, fewer complications of the "R" processes of mourning, fewer unrecognized secondary losses, and less emotional baggage from the past to interfere with current functioning.

Help the mourner identify, label, differentiate, actualize, mourn, and accommodate secondary losses resulting from the death

Just like the initial loss, secondary losses, whether physical or psychosocial, must be addressed. In this regard, *secondary* refers to consequence or time of occurrence, not degree of importance. Often secondary losses, especially psychosocial ones, fail to be legitimized as losses requiring grief work and are eclipsed by the more immediately visible death of the loved one. Nevertheless, such losses may be enormously significant. They can be even more problematic than the primary loss in terms of lack of social validation, support, or the mourner's preparation for them.

It is important to reiterate that secondary losses pertain not only to something once possessed but now lost (e.g., loss of a home because of financial problems, status because of widowhood, or security after a murder), but also to the loss of future plans or hopes (e.g., loss of the retirement to have been spent together, the opportunity to make amends with an ex-spouse, or a parent's presence at the marriage of a child). Secondary losses proliferate the more the mourner was tied to the deceased; the stronger the mourner's attachment to the deceased; the more numerous and central the roles the deceased played were in the life of the mourner; the more meanings that relationship embodied; the more behavior, interaction, and reinforcement patterns involved the deceased; the more integrated that person was in the assumptive world of the mourner; and the more investment, needs, feelings, thoughts, memories, hopes, wishes, fantasies, dreams, assumptions, expectations, and beliefs the mourner had relating to the deceased. Each loss requires its own mourning, despite the fact that often a number of such losses occur together. In fact, the total bereavement experience represents the accumulated sum of all of the grief and mourning for all of the losses engendered by the death. As is the case for feelings following the initial loss, feelings about each secondary loss must be processed, and ultimately each secondary loss must be mourned to the extent necessary. This is an area in which treatment is generally found lacking for individuals experiencing both uncomplicated and complicated mourning.

Recognize and respond to the importance of security afforded by the caregiver's availability to the mourner

Precisely because of dynamics contributing to complicated mourning (e.g., the mourner's insecurity without the deceased, avoidance of acknowledging aspects of the loss and its implications, fear of painful affects), the mourner typically will require assurance of the caregiver's psychological and physical availability. This does not mean that the caregiver must be available 24 hours a day; however, it does mean that the caregiver recognizes that the treatment is stressful, attempts to be as supportive as possible in helping the mourner undergo it gainfully, and will be as responsive as is therapeutically advisable when the mourner requires assistance.

Acting on the recognition of these needs does not mean that the caregiver never challenges, confronts, or nudges; it means rather that such actions are always undertaken in concert with the five "Ps": presence, permission, patience, predictability, and perseverance. These qualities are essential for successful work with this population.

Recognize the dynamics of complicated mourning and adhere to the five "Ps" in work with the mourner

Mourners experiencing difficulties are typically insecure, anxious, and phobic about acknowledging the loss, its implications, and/or the painful affects it brings. Therefore, the caregiver needs to ensure that all interventions are characterized by the five "Ps." *Presence* refers to the caregiver's commitment to be there for the mourner through the struggle with thoughts, feelings, and memories that may have frightened others away. *Permission* describes the attitude of the caregiver, which is open, interested, nonjudgmental, and nonprohibitive as regards the mourner's sharing of information, feelings, memories, and so forth. It does not mean that no boundaries or rules exist in the treatment, but it does mean that the mourner will not have to fear censorship or rejection if she expresses anger or other difficult emotions. *Patience* refers to the caregiver's attitude in putting into practice the recognition that the treatment process is painful, difficult, and often quite slow. The caregiver will act accordingly and be tolerant and imperturbable. If confrontations or limit setting are necessary for the good of the mourner (e.g., a chronic mourner may need to have a limit placed on how many times she can repeat the same story), they are accomplished without excitement or punitive attitude. *Predictability* means that the caregiver has demonstrated dependability, consistency, and trustworthiness and that the mourner has the security of knowing that the caregiver will act in a fashion consistent with those attributes. *Perseverance* is the quality of enduring through a treatment that can be long, painful, and frustrating at times. It implies the caregiver's commitment to see the treatment through to the end and not abandon the mourner.

When a normal, expectable emotion is absent, determine why and address the omission

In all of the forms of complicated mourning, by definition one or more aspects of healthy mourning are missing. The caregiver's responsibility is to rectify this situation—for instance, to help the mourner acknowledge the death, deal with the negative aspects of the relationship with the deceased, revise the assumptive world, and in short complete whatever "R" processes are incomplete. This principle also applies on a smaller scale: When the mourner describes a situation in which a normally expected emotion is lacking or minimized, the caregiver can rightfully wonder about this. For example, in the case of a bereaved parent who admits only to sadness at a police officer's "blaming the victim" after a drunk driving crash, the caregiver might note, "I wonder what other types of feelings you might have had when the officer said your daughter should have known better than to be crossing the street at that time of night." Depending upon the response, the caregiver can query why the normal response of anger was missing. This can lead to a discussion of reasons for denial and other defenses.

Of course, a danger exists in this type of questioning that the caregiver will insist upon the mourner's unconsciously having had emotions he never did have. Such absences may not necessarily be a consequence of a defense but may result from some aspect of personality or upbringing. For this reason, the caregiver always needs to pose hypotheses and statements in a fashion that is not global or absolute: "Most people would be somewhat disturbed about a comment like that" is preferable to "Anyone would be angry on hearing that statement."

Sometimes the caregiver can assist a mourner to own affect by presenting the same situation as if it had happened to someone else and inquiring about the mourner's reactions to it. Thus, in the situation described, the caregiver might ask, "What do you think you would feel if some police officer blamed your best friend's daughter for being on the street instead of the drunk driver who hit her?" Frequently, distancing a situation in this way enables the caregiver to circumvent personal restrictions or perfectionistic standards the mourner might apply to himself but not necessarily to anyone else. Sometimes the same effect can be achieved by the caregiver's minimizing the situation to dramatize to the mourner precisely what he may be doing and to make a point (e.g., "I see. It was nothing. Just the funeral of your best friend."). This always must be done with care to avoid being perceived as mockery instead of illustration by understatement.

CHAPTER 9

Intervening in the Six "R" Processes of Mourning

One way of conceptualizing the treatment of complicated mourning is to view the mourner's problems as arising from some compromise, distortion, or failure of one or more of the uncomplicated mourning processes. Looking at the issue in this light can provide an overall context for treatment and enhance the likelihood that interventions will be appropriate and effective. This chapter therefore expands the theoretical overview of the six "R" processes of mourning presented in chapter 2 and listed in Table 2.3. The information in chapter 2 provides a necessary context and foundation for understanding the material here, and the reader is urged to consider it first. Specifically, the discussion in this chapter identifies particular reasons for complications in each of the mourning processes and suggests appropriate therapeutic interventions. As noted earlier, the caregiver's goal is to uncomplicate any complications in these mourning processes; once this is accomplished, a full range of facilitation techniques can be employed.

RECOGNIZE THE LOSS

Complications stemming from this point in mourning are caused by an inability or unwillingness either to (a) acknowledge the death or (b) understand it. Failure to acknowledge the death compromises the mourner's ability to go on in mourning by obviating the need for mourning. Inability to understand the death creates difficulties because the mourner experiences the world as being anxiety provoking and without order or sense.

Acknowledge the Death

If there is no acknowledgment that the death has occurred, the mourner has nothing to mourn, only a separation to endure. In essence, the mourner lacks the pivotal stimulus to catalyze mourning. The lack of this stimulus suits quite well those parts of the mourner that very understandably want to resist believing that the loved one is actually dead. As long as the mourner can avoid confronting reality, she is spared the pain of having to respond to this recognition, as well as the stress of mourning.

Reasons for complications

There are three reasons why a mourner may not acknowledge the death of a loved one after an appropriate amount of time: (a) the mourner does not have the necessary confirmation of the death, (b) the mourner has the necessary confirmation of the death but because of psychological dynamics denies its reality or refuses to accept it, and (c) the mourner has access to but chooses to avoid confirmatory evidence of the death.

In the first case, the mourner is unable to acknowledge the death because no evidence exists to confirm its reality (e.g., no body is found, or the mourner did not view the body for some reason). In this situation, there is no proof of the loved one's death to confront the mourner's normal desire for this terrible reality not to be true or to force commencement of the painful processes of mourning. There is only the loved one's absence, which can be explained in other ways (e.g., "My wife was rescued from the boating accident but has amnesia and so cannot find her way home or call us for assistance. This is why she has not returned."). A lack of confirmation precisely fits the mourner's understandable need for the death not to be true. Having no physical confirmation of the death thus disadvantages the mourner significantly.

In the second case, the mourner has confirmation of the death (i.e., has viewed the body and even participated in the postdeath rituals) but is unwilling to acknowledge it for internal psychological reasons. In such a situation, common in complicated mourning, there may be total denial of acknowledgment of the death, simultaneous partial acceptance and denial, or a vacillation between both poles. Total denial is enormously difficult to maintain and is usually quite rare. As is true for other types of distressing information, it is possible for the mourner simultaneously to deny and accept the existence of a threat (i.e., acknowledgment of the death), usually on different levels or in different areas of the psyche. This typically is illustrated by intellectual acknowledgment of the death in the absence of emotional acceptance. In uncomplicated mourning, there is often a delay between intellectual acknowledgment and emotional acceptance; however, the phenomenon discussed here is a more long-term state that inhibits the mourner's progress toward eventual acceptance and internalization of the loved one's death. Finally, the mourner may vacillate between denial and acceptance. The best examples of degrees of denial have been provided in the unparalleled work of Weisman (1972a), who has documented the complex dance between denial and acceptance in erminal illness. A similar choreography exists in the mourner's approach to the acknowledgment of a loved one's death. Readers familiar with Weisman's work will recall his clarification that the purpose of denial is not simply to avoid a danger, but to prevent the loss of a significant relationship (Weisman & Hackett, 1967). Similar dynamics apply here, with the relationship the denier seeks not to lose being the previous relationship with the deceased. Rather than admit that the former relationship with the deceased is over, the mourner denies the fact of the death.

In the third case, the mourner exhibits a pattern between that exhibited by individuals who do not acknowledge the death because they lack the necessary confirmation and that exhibited by individuals who have confirmed the death but cannot psychologically accept it. This mourner could confirm the death if she wanted to but does not in order to avoid confronting the loss. This is the case with the mourner who refuses to view the body even though it is available or to participate in postdeath rituals. Sometimes the refusal is quite blunt (e.g., "I do not want to go to a funeral. It is a barbaric custom."). Often, however, more subtle excuses are offered (e.g., "I want to remember him the way he was" or "A funeral really is unnecessary at this point").

It is well known that mourners who do not participate in rituals that would be appropriate for them to take part in tend to have more difficulty believing the death actually occurred (e.g., Volkan, 1975, 1985, 1987) and poorer adjustment afterwards (e.g., Fulton, 1976). The need for participation appears to be especially keen when the death is sudden and unexpected. In this case, confirmation is crucial in helping the mourner comprehend the world, which has changed dramatically without any warning (Rando, 1984, 1988; Raphael, 1983, 1986; Worden, 1982).

Despite the absence of confirmation, many individuals ultimately are capable of acknowledging that their loved one has died. Although they would like to believe their loved one has, for example, been rescued following an accident, they realize that this is a fantasy. They recognize its improbability and, confronted by the absence of the loved one over a period of time, begin to learn the lesson that the loved one has indeed died. What makes the difference between mourners who acknowledge the death without confirmation and those who do not is unclear: Some carefully designed research into the determinants of acceptance or nonacceptance would certainly be welcome.

Therapeutic interventions

The goal of interventions at this point is to enable the mourner to recognize and acknowledge that the loved one is dead (i.e., comprehend that the loss is permanent and irreversible and understand the implications that has). Interventions involve both a general strategy to help the mourner actualize the loss and specific strategies chosen on the basis of the mourner's reasons for failure to acknowledge the death. Interventions designed to help the mourner actualize the loss are intended to make the loss more real. In general, these can be broken down into three categories, although they certainly also can be combined.

First, *verbal interventions* involve (a) having the mourner talk about what others are calling the death and the circumstances surrounding it; (b) discussing the absence of the loved one and how it is interpreted, along with the mourner's frustrated needs for that loved one, feelings about the separation, concerns it generates, and meanings and implications were the separation to be permanent; (c) addressing other issues or circumstances that may be placing demands upon the mourner's ego such that it cannot allow itself to acknowledge the loss (Deutsch, 1937); or (d) sharing thoughts and feelings with others who believe the death to have occurred. It will be important to ask the mourner why she thinks she is not acknowledging something acknowledged by everyone else. This questioning is intended not to coerce her into changing her perspective but to address resistances that may be interfering with her ability to acknowledge the death (e.g., "If I were to allow that he really is dead, that would mean I am all alone"). In this way, the caregiver can determine which blocks must be addressed.

Second, *behavioral interventions* encompass techniques to confront avoidance of the loved one's absence. For example, working with stimuli associated with the deceased (e.g., photographs, memorabilia, personal possessions) can create a sense of immediacy within the situation and bring the deceased more directly into the experience of the mourner and caregiver. In vivo techniques, such as going to the cemetery, having the loved one declared legally dead, and so forth also may help make the loss more real for the mourner. Therapeutic bereavement rituals can achieve the same purpose when they are designed to confront the mourner with the reality of the loss. (See chapter 7 for more on the use of such rituals.)

Third, *cognitive interventions* include techniques such as imagery, visualization, cognitive restructuring, and cognitive rehearsal. Although cognitive interventions may be used less frequently at this point than at others in the mourning process, these techniques can be helpful.

Treatment strategies for the absent, delayed, and inhibited syndromes of complicated mourning (see chapter 4) may be helpful for mourners who have confirmatory evidence but for psychological reasons cannot accept the death and for mourners who avoid confirmatory evidence. In such cases, particular attention should be given to the reasons the mourner cannot accept the reality of the death. Verbal and behavioral interventions may be especially helpful in understanding and dealing with avoidance. In the situation in which there is an actual absence of confirmatory evidence of the death, the caregiver has three choices: help the mourner to know, help the mourner to know without knowing, or help the mourner to live without knowing. In implementing any of these three approaches, the caregiver must take into consideration the generic suggestions for treatment presented in chapter 8.

Help the mourner to know.   The caregiver can encourage the mourner to seek as much information as possible or practical and work with the mourner to discover and analyze any available data that could confirm or disconfirm the death. For example, the caregiver might suggest that dental records be examined to ascertain the identity of a body that has been discovered. Essentially, the caregiver supports appropriate information seeking in the hope that it will assist the mourner in acknowledging the death. The key word here is *appropriate*—wild goose chases should be avoided.

Help the mourner to know without knowing.   The caregiver can assist the mourner in looking at all of the facts and probabilities and in determining that objective evidence suggests the loved one truly has died and that the mourner needs to deal with this reality. This is very difficult because of concerns about abandoning the loved one. For this reason, the caregiver must acknowledge the fact that the death has not been confirmed 100 percent and deal with the mourner's feelings that going on may seem to be "giving up" on the loved one. We know from families of missing children and those missing in military action that tremendous stress results from the lack of confirmation of the death, the continuing absence of the loved one, and the demand for an end of mourning and the resumption of normal life. Enormous psychological issues confront any mourner in assuming a death prior to its confirmation: guilt, self-condemnation, frustration, anxiety, chronic uncertainty, helplessness, anger, and chronic mourning.

Help the mourner to live without knowing.   If the mourner feels it is unacceptable to know without knowing (i.e., acknowledge the death without absolute certainty) or she truly cannot conceive of the loved one as dead in the absence of proof, the caregiver may be reduced to the option of assisting the mourner to live without ever knowing for sure that the loved one is dead. Treatment focuses on developing the most effective coping strategies; processing specific affects, thoughts, and fantasies; reducing anxiety; and coping with practical and emotional concerns (e.g., celebrating the holidays or dealing with the magical belief that if one stops mourning or looking for the loved one then that person really will die). In any event, failure to acknowledge the death because of a lack of confirmation should not be taken as a form of denial, unwillingness, or defense. Rather, this group of individuals is missing something routinely required in order to mourn. The fact that they require this evidence is not their fault; rather, they are victimized by circumstances.

In some cases, the mourner must adapt to chronic uncertainty and, in some respects, chronic mourning for the separation from the loved one. In this situation, mourning does not lead to a healthy and integrated accommodation of the loss, nor does it ever end. The mourner learns to live with the situation but does not make the type of readjustments necessary for healthy accommodation of the loss. In other cases, the mourner actually knows without knowing but will not admit it. A relatively better chance of adjustment exists in this latter situation, although the mourner's equilibrium can be disturbed when life events point out that she is living as though the death were confirmed, thus causing her guilt, or when she desires to move on in some area of life but cannot because the burden of unfinished business and complicated mourning is too great.

Understand the Death

Human beings have a powerful need for comprehension—for cognitive mastery, predictability, and control—and the security provided by what is logical and sensible. The world needs to be perceived as having some order if the individual is to go on in a healthy way. Similarly, the death of a loved one must make logical sense if the mourner is to cope with and readjust well to it. In order to understand the death, the mourner must be able to construct a causal account of the events that led to it. It does not matter whether the mourner's explanation is the same as everyone else's, or even if it is realistic, only that it answers questions about what caused the death. Thus, a mourner's belief that a death was an accident and not a suicide may run counter to prevailing thought and evidence but nevertheless be quite adequate for the purpose. If the mourner is unable to construct an account explaining how and why the death transpired, he will likely have problems recovering from and adjusting to major loss. The lack of closure inherent in not knowing the reason for the death adds to these problems.

Reasons for complications

Complications may develop in this portion of mourning when no cause of death can be found. Lacking an explanation and unable to fit the loved one's death into a logical context, the mourner experiences the world as devoid of sense and order. This violation of the assumption that one lives in an orderly and comprehensible world tends to cause the mourner to become confused and anxious, and to wonder about what potentially could happen to him.

Mourners stalled at this point can develop a general insecurity not unlike that experienced by individuals suffering from the unanticipated mourning syndrome associated with sudden, unexpected death. However, these mourners are additionally burdened by the fact that there is no explanation at all for the death, whereas in most cases of sudden death a reason exists, even if it does not make sense (e.g., a freak accident or suicide).

Therapeutic interventions

When understanding is lacking, the caregiver needs to work with the mourner to gather as much information as possible about the antecedents, context, and events associated with the death and to develop as complete as possible an account of why and how the death occurred. If, after the available data are secured, important gaps still remain, interventions should attempt to help the mourner cope with the anxiety, lack of closure, and frustration of not knowing, as well as with any consequent reactions (e.g., insecurity, confusion, anger).

What the mourner can and does know needs to be identified and labeled clearly; what he cannot know also needs to be pinpointed. This process is similar to helping a dying person cope with fear of the unknown (Rando, 1984). In accomplishing the latter, the caregiver and mourner separate what can be known from what cannot and identify questions for which answers can be given immediately (e.g., "What will happen to my body after death?"), after some time has passed (e.g., "How will my loved ones respond to my dying?"), or not in this lifetime (e.g., "Is there life after death?").

As appropriate, the caregiver also may employ specific interventions for helping mourners who have experienced the sudden, unexpected death of a loved one (see chapter 12). Strategies for revising the assumptive world, discussed later in this chapter, address the mourner's need to make sense of and in the world. These also may be quite useful.

REACT TO THE SEPARATION

Complications in this "R" process occur because the mourner is thwarted in (a) experiencing the pain; (b) feeling, identifying, accepting, and giving some form of expression to all the psychological reactions to the loss; and (c) identifying and mourning secondary losses. In addition, mourning may be complicated at this point if there has been a failure in the first "R" process (i.e., recognize the loss). Thus, to the extent that the mourner fails to grant herself permission to experience and express the myriad reactions to the recognition of the loved one's death and the subsequent secondary losses generated by it, healthy mourning is compromised.

Experience the Pain

Healthy mourning necessitates coming to grips with and working through pain. By avoiding pain, the mourner also avoids those experiences that ultimately will teach him that the loved one is truly gone and indicate that adaptations must be made to contend with the loss and integrate it appropriately in present and future life. In brief, then, the caregiver must help the mourner confront the pain successfully, all the while recognizing that its experience and meaning differ for different people.

Reasons for complications

Complications at this point stem from the mourner's desire to avoid pain. In itself, this is an understandable and healthy reaction. Only a masochist enjoys pain, and the enjoyment of pain constitutes significant pathology. Concerns about being overwhelmed and anxiety about dealing with guilt-producing emotions are other common reasons for avoiding mourning at this point. Each has, at its basis, the mourner's desire to avoid the pain he perceives the loss to involve. Such avoidance is a common component in complications of most of the other "R" processes as well.

Mourners may develop additional complications if they overcompensate for their fear of pain. These complications often center around fears of being overwhelmed by mental suffering and loss of control (e.g., "If I really allow myself to feel the pain, it will destroy me" or "If I start to cry I will never be able to stop"). Thus, mourners attempt to avoid being touched by their sadness, pain, and anguish over losing the loved one. Rather than deal with these affects directly, they may resort to aggressive or controlling actions to hide their true vulnerability. Alternatively, they may manufacture an attitude of dispassion and indifference to camouflage their feelings from others as well as from themselves. This approach can coincide with the development of absent, delayed, inhibited, or distorted complicated mourning syndromes.

It is not uncommon to observe a mourner who minimizes a loss to reduce the intensity of pain experienced (e.g., "I really didn't know my grandmother all that well. It's no big deal."). Intellectualization also may limit the mourner's reactions (e.g., "It's really better that she died in this fashion at age 40. God knows, she never would have wanted to become elderly and end up in a nursing home."). Rationalization may function similarly (e.g., "If he wanted to kill himself, who am I to mourn over him? He must have wanted it, so I shouldn't be upset at his death."). All of these are attempts at defending against the pain, and all interfere with mourning.

Finally, many mourners have internalized the message from social, cultural, ethnic, generational, or religious/philosophical conditioning that they should not mourn or need not experience the pain of their loss. Such teachings can combine with individual needs to avoid and can set up additional blocks to the healthy, and ultimately finite, experience of pain.

Therapeutic interventions

In a sense, the caregiver who advocates facing the pain of loss is asking the mourner to go against nature. Therefore, it is important that the caregiver explicitly recognize the mourner's pain and natural desire to avoid dealing with that pain. However, the caregiver also must stress that avoidance will bring only more pain and that it is in the mourner's best interests to deal with this distress straightforwardly. The mourner must be helped to appreciate that only by contending with the painful reality—whatever this means in terms of the individual loss situation—will healing occur. The caregiver also must hold out the expectation that, although the situation is difficult and the emotions hurtful, the mourner will be able to bear them and that, at some future time, will experience less pain.

The mourner can be helped to make the decision to address the pain if the caregiver provides the proper perspective. The caregiver needs to legitimize it (pain is real, intense, and frightening—something one would want to avoid), normalize it (pain is an expectable consequence of loss despite its appearing so extraordinary), and place it in a context of a natural reaction that necessarily occurs after the loss but before healing. If pain can be perceived as having meaning and purpose—which it does in healthy mourning—it can be borne better. The mourner needs to understand that pain arises in reaction to the severance of a bond and that suffering arises from the "challenges that threaten the intactness of the person as a complex social and psychological entity" (Cassel, 1982, p. 639). The purpose of the pain is found in its expressing the reactions to that severance and, ultimately, in its teaching the mourner that he must change his assumptions about and relationship with the deceased and look elsewhere for gratification.

It is not consistently true that pain will be interpreted and reacted to as an aversive stimulus. Pain has different meanings to different people, and the way the mourner perceives pain will influence that mourner's response profoundly. For example, sometimes the mourner endures pain to maintain a tie with the deceased. In this case, what one typically might expect in terms of a response (i.e., the desire to reduce or avoid pain) is lacking. A promise or premature attempt to eliminate pain serves only to raise resistance to treatment. Failure to explore the specific meanings pain may have for each individual can result in the caregiver's adopting an inappropriate, perhaps even harmful, strategy. For instance, in the example given in which pain is valued as a connection to the deceased, the usual inducement to help the mourner achieve pain reduction will not work because the mourner's real pain comes from the thought of *not* having pain (i.e., losing the tie to the loved one). Until the mourner can be taught how to have a healthier connection to the deceased, treatment must focus on learning to live with the pain or lessening it so it can be more bearable. Progress is revealed when such mourners no longer need to have pain to have a connection to the lost loved one. (See chapter 8 for more on the idiosyncratic meanings of pain.)

The caregiver must explore what specifically frightens the mourner about or causes him to avoid pain. Although the common thread is to keep from discomfort, idiosyncratic elements must be distinguished. In this way, the particular resistances or blocks to healthy mourning are identified for further work. For example, the mourner who has a history of pain avoidance probably never has had the experience of mastering pain. In this case, the caregiver can expose the mourner gradually to avoided painful stimuli in order to extinguish anxiety and help the mourner learn that he can indeed manage pain and that his catastrophizing has been unrealistic. This can be accomplished through any one or combination of behavioral techniques for avoidance, as well as through the use of therapeutic bereavement rituals (see chapter 7), with interventions being chosen on the basis of need and caregiver preference.

The caregiver may undertake a number of actions to help the mourner in dealing with fears of losing control and being overwhelmed.

1. Inform the mourner that he can go as rapidly or as slowly as he wishes and that he can stop whenever he begins to feel overwhelmed (unless a particular technique contraindicates this—e.g., emotional flooding).

2. Break down the pain into its component parts; identify, label, differentiate among, and trace each one; and work on only one aspect at a time to make the distress more understandable and manageable (e.g., sadness at the deprivation, fear of being alone).

3. Separate the pain from this loss from that stemming from prior losses or conflicts that may be resurrected here. Label the source (i.e., which affects belong to which experiences) in order to make the distress more understandable and manageable.

4. Address the mourner's fear that he is not strong enough to undergo the experience of the pain by serving as an ego-prosthesis. Through personal presence, support, encouragement, and the five "Ps" (see chapter 8), work to make it safe enough for the mourner to allow himself to get in contact with the pain. Recognize throughout that it may take quite a while for a mourner to feel safe enough to discuss some or all aspects of his pain.

5. Redefine the terms *lose control* or *break down*, acknowledging the intensity of the feelings but reframing them more positively, using such terms as *emotional release* or *intense feelings*. Legitimize the normalcy of such feelings by pointing out that situations of major loss prompt reactions that require strong expression and follow different norms than usual.

6. Help the mourner understand that it is precisely those emotions that go unexpressed that prompt loss of control and that there is great value in expressing a little emotion at a time in order to avoid an accumulation that will explode later on.

7. Enable the mourner to recognize that, although the processing of emotions must take place in order for healthy mourning and accommodation of the loss, he can choose how and when. Teach him how to "dose" his own exposure to painful affects, thoughts, memories, and so forth.

8. Encourage expression of feelings with those people and in those places that are comfortable and without threat. If none exist, work to establish them (e.g., enlist the aid of an appropriate family member or provide referral to a support group). Given that social support is critical in the mourning process, it is inadvisable for the mourner to remain isolated.

9. Be mindful of the limits and capabilities of individual mourners. For example, recognize when one may require gentle closure, need a slower pace in treatment, benefit from a respite, or in some way require a modification of the treatment and mourning experience in order to maximize coping and minimize the chance that he will become overwhelmed and close off.

10. Be aware of the possibility of flight. Some mourners will attempt to cope by physical flight (e.g., moving to a new home or taking a vacation) or psychosocial flight (e.g., changing lovers or getting a new job). The purpose is to keep moving so that the pain does not have a chance to catch up to the mourner. Especially with mourners who experience significantly increased arousal, restlessness, and anxiety, this moving about can become chronic. Unfortunately, it can strip the mourner of roots that could be therapeutic in lending security, engender additional secondary losses and concurrent stresses, and become a chronic behavior pattern in which the mourner must never stop if the defense against experiencing affects is to work. In addition, this response leaves the mourner without respite, peace, or quiet time to mourn.

11. Encourage the mourner to find appropriate ways to take breaks from mourning and replenish. Unremitting mourning will debilitate anyone. Backing off from the pain is healthy at times and need not constitute avoidance. Diversions like going to a movie can provide the break the psyche needs in order to re-address the work of mourning. Others—for example, cleaning the house—can provide a break but also render a sense of control and accomplishment. In addition, diversions serve as channels for restless energy. All mourners need to turn away from pain at times to reconnect with the living, growing parts of themselves and others. Problems occur only when there is too much focus on respites and insufficient attention paid to mourning.

12. Educate the mourner about the price of mourning if not properly addressed and explain how pain will only increase if he fails to deal with it.

Finally, if there has been a failure in the previous "R" process of recognizing the loss, this will obviate the need for contending with pain. Interventions must be geared toward achieving recognition before dealing with issues of affect.

Feel, Identify, Accept, and Give Some Form of Expression to All the Psychological Reactions to the Loss

Failure to express as personally necessary all of the psychological reactions to a loss leaves mourning incomplete and consequently complicated. Therefore, the caregiver's goals are to promote the identification and appropriate expression of all the mourner's psychological reactions to the loss and to enable the mourner to work through any resistances that may impede this.

Reasons for complications

The most frequent complication observed in the mourner stuck in this subprocess is the failure to address and express the entire range of feelings generated by the loss. Often, the mourner deems some feelings unacceptable, and these are suppressed, given partial expression (usually through somatic equivalents or psychosocial symptoms), or avoided entirely.

The desire to evade the recognition of feelings, thoughts, or memories that prompt guilt is paramount for a majority of mourners. Guilt is frequently related to remembered acts of omission or commission, recollection of hostile feelings, or the perceived failure to live up to specific expectations or standards. The intensity and strength of guilt cannot be overstated. It also leads to a restricted review of the relationship and a consequent lack of completion of the subsequent mourning process of recollecting and reexperiencing the deceased and the relationship.

Another impediment stems from the mourner's desire to avoid recognition of dependency upon the deceased. This avoidance may be because such recognition could violate the mourner's self-image as an independent person. More likely, it reflects the fear of having to confront the extent and depth of dependency and what implications exist now that the loved one is no longer present. It can be enormously frightening to recognize that one's security and stability are gone—so much so that one may choose not to recognize, examine, or express such feelings as fear, anger, and helplessness. Or one's energies may be directed instead toward defending against these painful feelings by overcompensating with others. This is exemplified in distorted mourning of the extremely angry type, in which the mourner experiences extreme anger over the perceived abandonment by the loved one in place of the fragile vulnerability that gave rise to it.

Once again, the caregiver must be cognizant of the mourner's fear of being overwhelmed by painful affects. In an attempt to avoid this possibility, the mourner may not deal with the affects at all, distort their expression, permit them expression solely via symptomatology, respond by over-compensation or counterphobic behaviors, or engage any of a number of psychological defense and/or coping mechanisms. These may include any one of a number of defense mechanisms categorized as being narcissistic, immature, neurotic, or mature (Wong, 1989).

Other complications in this subprocess may derive from the personality and self-image of the mourner, especially as they affect the mourner's ability to accept and express certain necessary psychological responses to loss. For example, certain personality characteristics may thwart the expression of any affect (e.g., as witnessed in the overcontrolled, intellectualized person) and/or may disallow the expression of certain types of affect (e.g., hostile feelings). Social, cultural, ethnic, generational, or religious/philosophical conditioning about having hostile or negative feelings also can close off this crucial area and predispose the mourner to a variety of the forms of complicated mourning, especially the syndromes of inhibited mourning, conflicted mourning, and distorted mourning of the extremely guilty type. So, too, can the mourner's role, which may preclude dealing with particular reactions to the death deemed inconsistent (e.g., the widowed military officer who cannot permit himself to get in touch with the limited amount of dependency he allowed himself on his wife). In all of these situations, some characteristic of the mourner interferes with full experience, identification, acceptance, and expression of emotions related to the loss. To the extent that necessary working through is prohibited, the individual's mourning becomes complicated.

During this subprocess the mourner also must give expression to the urges to recover and reproach the loved one for leaving and to associated yearning, longing, and pining. As with children, repression and splitting of these feelings from conscious awareness so that they exist only as secret wishes cause mourning to take a pathological turn (Bowlby, 1980).

Finally, a failure in the previous "R" process of recognizing the loss and/or the subprocess of experiencing the pain, under the main process of reacting to the separation, will complicate this work.

Therapeutic interventions

The caregiver should convey a desire to understand and process the entire spectrum of reactions the mourner sustains—or might be expected to sustain—and should communicate that failure to do so will leave mourning complicated. Compassionate interest, coupled with the idea that exploration in this area needs to be thorough, must be expressed. The caregiver should listen to and treat the mourner in a fashion that communicates trustworthiness, permissiveness, and acceptance. The mourner must be able to feel safe. Without this type of atmosphere, few mourners will open up to a caregiver or even to themselves. For many, disclosure to self or others requires security and confidence in the caregiver, who is functioning as an ego-prosthesis. The time it takes to establish conditions of safety and trust will vary depending upon the mourner's needs; caregivers must remember that this process is slow and does not respond to urgency.

Although similar conditions are required in most forms of treatment, they are especially necessary in cases of complicated mourning when the following circumstances exist.

1. Affects are unusually threatening or overwhelming to the mourner.

2. The mourner is unusually fragile.

3. Affects stem from long-term trauma (e.g., child abuse) or a traumatic event (e.g., homicide), either of which contributes to a post-traumatic stress disorder or a related constellation of symptoms.

4. The mourner's history reveals betrayal or victimization by those in authority who should have protected the mourner (e.g., sexual abuse by a previous therapist).

5. The mourner's personality, self-image, conditioning, roles, other attributes, or desire for social approval strongly prohibit the expression of the very emotions the caregiver seeks to facilitate.

If a mourner has difficulty processing affects or admitting to yearning for or urges to find and recover the deceased, the caregiver must (a) use the strategies outlined for the previous subprocess to enable confrontation with painful emotions and (b) stimulate the affects that are not being addressed. The latter may be done verbally by having the mourner review the relationship and recall the person, the circumstances of the death, and the events around it. There should be discussion of the meanings of the loss to the mourner, the subsequent responses of others, and the secondary losses and ensuing changes. All of this is designed to put the mourner in touch with thoughts, feelings, and memories related to the loss and its consequences. (Interventions for specific emotions are described in chapter 10.)

Other techniques besides verbal discussion can put the mourner in touch with unexpressed affects. Many generic techniques of the behavioral therapies (e.g., guided mourning or grief-resolution therapy) and therapeutic bereavement rituals can expose the mourner to avoided stimuli, encourage mourning behaviors, or prompt the appropriate acting out of necessary communications and/or adaptive new ways of being in the world. A number of cognitive, evocative, and expressive techniques (e.g., guided imagery, Gestalt role-playing, painting) are useful as well for stimulating affect. They can expose the mourner to emotion circumvented by avoiding particular thoughts, memories, behaviors, circumstances, or tangible reminders. Then, if appropriate, the caregiver can identify, normalize, and legitimize the reaction and help the mourner in feeling, identifying, understanding, accepting, and choosing how best to express the response in a personally meaningful and congruent fashion.

The absence of expected feelings can be queried with statements like "People often seem worried about things that didn't go right at a time like this—an argument or misunderstanding or something they meant to do and didn't before the person died. Have there been any concerns like this for you?" (Raphael, 1980b, p. 163). Sometimes asking what the mourner would do differently if she knew then what she knows now can help the mourner identify regrets and concerns about various omissions or commissions. Care should be taken in this regard to avoid encouraging the mourner to feel responsible for not having had, at that time, knowledge it would have been impossible to have. Directly asking about the existence of other emotions can also stimulate recall or reexamination of the events and lead to a discerning of affects that might have been denied or suppressed, or that were not part of the mourner's reality at that time.

If the individual is unfamiliar with dealing with emotions, the caregiver can give examples of what a mourner might have to deal with in order to illustrate the range of emotions possible, model how to differentiate among them and label their causes, and normalize a variety of affects. For example, a caregiver could say, "I can imagine that a person in your situation might have a number of feelings. For example, to name just a couple, I would think that such a person might be quite saddened by the death of his sister—the family member to whom he has been the closest—as well as somewhat angry that it was caused by a driver who was so intoxicated that he never should have been allowed to get behind the wheel of a car." The caregiver also can use the technique of distancing by describing the very same situation and then asking how the mourner would feel if that situation happened to a dear friend.

Such interventions always must be used cautiously. First, the caregiver should not use the pronoun *you*. This avoids the appearance of telling the mourner what she is, or should be, feeling—a scenario that tends to anger many individuals. In addition, the distance maintained by not personalizing the comments may permit the mourner to view any emotions perceived or discussed as less of a personal threat. Second, unless circumstances specifically call for it, at this point guilt should not be mentioned as an emotion with which the mourner might need to contend. This can be too threatening and may interfere with the discovery of other emotions if the mourner feels they might be "manufactured" out of the guilt. Unless the mourner brings it up, guilt is better dealt with after other emotions have been prompted and the mourner has had more experience being in contact with and dealing with affects. Finally, speculations about affects must not be phrased as certainties, but rather offered as possibilities for the mourner to consider. When presented in this fashion, the notion of having these feelings is likely to generate much less resistance.

The caregiver should not overuse this type of intervention, for it tends to close down the mourner's options. It is always preferable to see whether the mourner can generate the possible feelings independently and then comment on them as they might pertain to herself. Notwithstanding this, there are cases where the mourner does have to be prompted to consider affects that might require processing. Doing so judiciously can be therapeutic as long as the caregiver remembers that the mourner may not be able to acknowledge an emotion despite its clear presence to the caregiver. The mourner may feel it "just doesn't fit," be resistant due to defensiveness or a control struggle with the caregiver, or be unable to grasp the experience and/or notion of this emotion in these circumstances. Feelings cannot be demanded from mourners; any resistances to them have to be worked through first. And, of course, it is always possible for the caregiver to be incorrect.

Intellectualized treatment of the emotion will do little good; the mourner must experience and own the feeling. It must be processed affectively, not merely talked about. Research demonstrates that intellectual confrontation with a traumatic event fails to achieve the type of adjustment reached when there is an integration of both intellectual and emotional confrontation (Pennebaker & Beall, 1986; Pennebaker et al., 1988; Tait & Silver, 1989; Terr, 1979). This finding confirms the work of clinicians and researchers in the general area of stress response (e.g., Horowitz, 1986a) and in the specific area of victimization (e.g., incest, war, physical assault), where the goal is integration of affect, memory, cognition, behavior, and, in some cases, physiology (e.g., Courtois, 1988; Herman, 1990; Keane, 1990). Such integration is also the goal of the caregiver working with complicated mourning.

In a related vein, research suggests that merely ruminating about a spouse's death does not help individuals cope with loss; in fact, it is associated with increased health problems (Pennebaker & O'Heeron, 1984). To be successful as a cognitive strategy, the intellectual work of coping with threatening events must depart from the passive process of ruminating by involving a search for meaning in the experience, an attempt to gain mastery over one's life, and an effort to enhance self-esteem (Taylor, 1983). This notion gives further credence to the difference between grief and mourning (i.e., grief is reactive, whereas mourning is proactive) by supporting the insufficiency of grief to bring forth healthy adaptation in the absence of mourning.

It is important to point out that the target of the caregiver's interventions in promoting expression of affects is not exclusively emotion the mourner is consciously or subconsciously inhibiting or suppressing. Aim must be taken as well at those reactions that are not there to begin with, because of (a) repression or denial; (b) conditioning, values, beliefs, prior mental health status, condition at the time of the event in question, or other idiosyncratic aspects that have interfered with the development of the expected emotion; or (c) current mental health (e.g., alexithymia). In these situations, the caregiver may work to promote affect in the manner previously described. However, in many instances the caregiver must first help the mourner reconstruct parts of the past in order now to experience the proper emotion and/or establish appropriate emotional links with experiences that for some reason were devoid of them. The goal is not to have the mourner "make up" the emotion or pretend at feeling. Rather, it is to foster the normal development and ultimate processing of emotions that could not grow because of the infertility of the mourner's psyche at that time (i.e., emotions that could not be experienced or recognized because of the mourner's state). This might occur in situations where a person is traumatized and in shock, has dissociated, or experiences the particular emotion as being foreign. As an example of the latter, it might be too much at the time of an accident for an individual to recognize that she is angry at a disaster worker for hurting her while in the process of saving her life.

In cases of unfinished emotional business, the caregiver may have to take the mourner back to the time the affect was generated and facilitate its expression through a psychotherapeutic technique of personal ch
(e.g., psychodrama or the reliving, revising, and re
resolution therapy; Melges & DeMaso, 1980). A
may provide appropriate psychotherapeutic expe
expressing the affect and finishing the unfinish
writing, Gestalt empty chair work, creation of a t
ritual).

The caregiver must be on the alert for resistai
mourning processes. However, this particular
generates a greater amount of resistance than any
ing. This resistance arises primarily from the mou   pain,
losing control, or breaking down in processing these emotions; (b) desire to avoid having to discover and/or contend with guilt, anger, or dependency; or (c) previous personal, societal, cultural, ethnic, generational, religious/philosophical, or role-related conditioning. With regard to this last factor, the caregiver must be aware that various sources of conditioning can lead to resistance or inability to accept certain feelings as tolerable, normal, or permissible. Unless the mourner can be made more comfortable with certain emotions, she will be incapable of dealing with their having been present in the prior relationship with the deceased (e.g., anger at her father before he died) or present in the here and now (e.g., anger because her father has died and left her).

The caregiver must give considerable attention to the working through of resistance. Resistance can be handled in whatever psychotherapeutic fashion is acceptable to the caregiver, provided that it is not incompatible with other goals or interventions for the treatment of complicated mourning. Dealing with resistance inherently involves exploring the defenses employed in the service of that resistance in order to discover the particular reasons behind them, then working these defenses through. The most effective and meaningful avenues of expression must be identified for each mourner; what works for one will not necessarily work for another. This is where creativity in caregiving will be apparent.

In complicated mourning, one observes far more restlessness, agitation, and other signs of hyperarousal than opposite signs of psychomotor retardation. This should not be surprising, given that complicated mourning inherently involves something that is not being dealt with, as well as a number of uncomfortable emotions. All of these responses place stress upon the mourner and manufacture the emotional and physiological anxiety and arousal commonly seen in all seven syndromes and most symptom constellations of complicated mourning. This appears true even in situations lacking a component of post-traumatic stress, which by definition contains physiological manifestations of increased arousal.

Although most caregivers claim to appreciate the importance of physical activity, far fewer incorporate it into their treatment regimes. So often, mourners are victimized in the sense that they have been robbed of their loved ones, can exert no control in retrieving those loved ones, are powerless against fate, and, in many cases, are forced to contend with enormous rage. They must face an assumptive world that will never be the same again. The point is that much of what happens to a mourner contributes to feelings of frustration, tension, anger, helplessness, powerlessness, and being out of control. These feelings are stored in the body, as well as in the mind and heart.

Although physical activity is therapeutic in uncomplicated mourning, it is crucial in complicated mourning because it permits release of pent-up feelings, assumption of control, externalization of aggression, channeling of frustration and other negative feelings, reduction of anxiety, and modulation of arousal. In addition, it promotes clearer thinking, expression of feelings that may be difficult to articulate, and an increased sense of self-possession and well-being. All of these gains surpass those offered solely by verbalization. The type of physical activity can vary according to the needs, interests, and capacities of the mourner.

Finally, when there has been a failure to complete the prior "R" process or subprocesses, the caregiver must turn attention to the successful working through of these in order to facilitate mourning.

Identify and Mourn Secondary Losses

When a loved one dies, the survivors lose much more than that individual. They also sustain a number of physical and psychosocial losses as a consequence of the death and the deceased's inability to participate in their lives as before. These secondary losses generate a need for grief and mourning no less than the actual death, and success or lack thereof in mourning them can have a profound influence on the overall course of mourning. Complications in mourning secondary losses can be just as malignant as complications in mourning the death itself. The total bereavement experience for the mourner actually is the sum of *all* of the losses associated with this death.

Reasons for complications

Reasons for complications in this area of mourning are similar to those that interfere in the other mourning processes because what occurs with regard to secondary losses tends to be a microcosm of what occurs in the overall process. In other words, what is necessary to mourn secondary losses is the same as what is necessary to mourn the death of the loved one. In fact, an argument can be made against differentiating between secondary losses and the primary loss of the death. (Here the term *primary* refers to chronology, not necessarily impact.) This argument rests on the observation that dealing with the death inherently involves dealing with at least some of the secondary losses generated by it. Although this is undoubtedly true, the distinction between the death and secondary losses is useful in clarifying issues of causality (i.e., secondary losses occur only as a consequence of the death) and timing (i.e., some secondary losses are not coincident with the death and may not be perceived or even exist until some time after the death).

The same fears, concerns, and resistances one has about mourning the death can influence mourning secondary losses. For instance, if a mourner does not want to confront anger at the death of his mother, upon whom he was excessively dependent, he most likely also will resist dealing with losing the role of son. If a mourner is fearful of being overwhelmed by sadness and feelings of helplessness in the face of separation from the deceased, it might be anticipated that he would have similar concerns about focusing on secondary losses that would prompt these same emotions. He could be expected to employ many of the same strategies he uses to avoid mourning the death (e.g., minimizing the loss, denial, isolation of affect, intellectualization).

It is important to note that the mourner may not mourn specific secondary losses in order to avoid mourning in general. For instance, the individual may not mourn the loss of her daughter's adored grandmother if it means getting in touch with her own feelings about the loss of her mother. Conversely, complications can develop when the mourner focuses on a secondary loss to avoid contending with the primary one. Both of these problems raise the issue of the mourner's evaluation of the secondary loss, which is personal and arbitrary but critical for the caregiver to understand. Many times the mourner experiences secondary losses as being more troublesome than the death itself (e.g., losing the social role of wife to a prominent person may be more problematic for a woman to deal with than the actual loss of her husband). On the other hand, many secondary losses are insignificant to the mourner. Again, the caregiver must understand the importance of each loss from the idiosyncratic perspective of the mourner.

Problems also can arise in this phase of mourning when secondary losses accumulate and threaten the mourner with bereavement overload (Kastenbaum, 1969), or when the mourner feels as if he is experiencing a nonstop chain of losses. If the mourner is overloaded or senses the potential to become so, he may be reluctant to address the additional deprivation and pain of secondary losses, preferring instead to avoid them and the reactions they bring. If important aspects of these losses remain unprocessed, they can exert an emotional press upon the mourner. The depletion and stress caused by these secondary losses can become in itself a concurrent stressor—one of the high-risk factors for complicated mourning.

Problems also develop because a majority of secondary losses tend to be psychosocial in nature. Consequently, they are less likely than physical losses to be identified as such and to be recognized as requiring mourning. For each loss that is not validated, the mourner is disenfranchised (see chapter 10). The mourner who cannot recognize, acknowledge, and legitimize secondary losses will never be able to mourn them, and failure to mourn them complicates mourning in general. Readjustments that must come about in the mourner's assumptive world, relationship with the deceased, ways of being in the world, and identity inherently involve secondary losses. This means that, although the mourner should strive for adaptive, healthy changes in these areas, these changes themselves create additional demands for mourning.

Therapeutic interventions

Many of the interventions employed for complicated mourning in general are equally effective for identifying and mourning secondary losses. These may be readily extrapolated. However, it is important to point out that effective intervention mandates that the caregiver know the mourner well enough to be able to help identify idiosyncratic secondary losses. It may be relatively easy to point out those that are more generic (e.g., the death of a spouse causes the secondary loss of a sexual partner and coparent). Yet such losses should never be assumed. Only with careful listening and comprehension will the caregiver be able to discern the specific losses peculiar to the mourner.

In cases of bereavement overload, the caregiver can take a number of steps to help the mourner cope with the simultaneous experience of losses.

1. Decrease immediate stress, external demands, and stimuli; provide rest, time out, and structure to calm the mourner down.

2. Provide the proper perspective on bereavement overload and label it as such.

3. Lighten the usual therapeutic pressure in addressing the issues, but remain supportive and nonabandoning. Gently stress the need for the mourner's slower but continued movement in healthy mourning.

4. Triage the stressors (i.e., losses) and prioritize them. Give the most basic needs attention first. Identify issues that require immediate attention and discuss problem-solving strategies as specifically and concretely as possible.

5. Help the mourner recognize his overwhelmed state and identify, label, differentiate, and specify the sources of the losses and all the reactions they spur.

6. Use treatment strategies discussed under the subprocess of experiencing the pain to enable confrontation with painful emotions.

7. Help the mourner regain control by identifying and supporting appropriate coping mechanisms while suggesting alternatives to nonconstructive ones.

8. When appropriate, normalize the helplessness, discouragement, anxiety, frustration, and so forth typical of stress-overloaded individuals.

9. Formulate with the mourner a general approach to the overload and construct viable short- and long-range plans for reducing it.

10. Convey that these kinds of situations can be handled with time, patience, and commitment to follow through; provide information about stress, secondary losses, concurrent stresses, and their interaction with mourning.

11. Institute stress management strategies as needed.

12. Make sure the mourner is receiving proper rest, nutrition, and exercise, and is refraining from inappropriate drug, alcohol, tobacco, caffeine, and food intake.

To assist the mourner in identifying and mourning secondary losses, the caregiver must provide the proper information about psychosocial and secondary losses to facilitate their identification and serious consideration. The caregiver also needs to enfranchise the mourner with regard to major secondary losses (i.e., identifying, legitimizing, processing, and looking for supports in mourning them). For example, the support group Parents Without Partners addresses secondary losses pertinent to single parents.

The issues of timing and dosing are critical with regard to identifying secondary losses. Although in most cases it is therapeutic throughout treatment to help the mourner gradually recognize secondary losses as (and even before) they occur, premature and/or multiple identification can overwhelm the mourner. This situation can precipitate an iatrogenic crisis that may interfere with treatment and the mourning process by causing cessation or major complications in one or both. In one instance, a caregiver listed too many of a mourner's secondary losses too early in treatment, nearly prompting a flight from treatment. This mourner was flooded with an unmanageable amount of deprivation and anxiety, which then caused him to shut down emotionally to protect himself from being overwhelmed. Gradual identification of secondary losses over time, and as pertinent to both the bereavement and treatment experiences, will ensure that the intervention remains therapeutic and does not cause the mourner to become an iatrogenic casualty.

By receiving too much focus, secondary losses can divert attention away from the general mourning processes. If processing secondary losses becomes a way of avoiding coping with the necessary mourning tasks instead of being one of them, the caregiver must work to right the emphasis. Despite this caution, the caregiver should be aware that many times successfully addressing secondary losses first can help the mourner cope with the death by teaching him that he can manage the affects and readjustments he may have avoided and by indicating that he can survive. For example, one caregiver encouraged a mourner to approach the pain and helplessness associated with the death of her husband by first helping her to become more assertive and effective in caring for herself. Once the mourner recognized that she had managed to survive a work crisis and some problems with her son, she realized that she was stronger than she ever had believed. This realization gave her the ability to face the fear and other painful affects she had sought to avoid by inhibiting her mourning.

Finally, if the mourner has not been successful in addressing the previous "R" process or subprocesses, he will have difficulty in this one. Therefore, the caregiver will need to direct their completion.

RECOLLECT AND REEXPERIENCE THE DECEASED AND THE RELATIONSHIP

Before mourners are able to relinquish old attachments and subsequently readjust to move adaptively into the new world without forgetting the old, they first must (a) review and remember realistically and (b) revive and reexperience the feelings associated with the deceased and the relationship. Many mourners resist this process; it is painful, underscores their loss, reminds them of things they would rather forget, and appears to violate the social message to move forward rather than look backward. However, inability to achieve the two goals of the process has serious consequences. It interferes with the development of a realistic composite image of the deceased and leaves mourners unable to undo the emotional connections bonding them to the loved one and the relationship. By default, mourners are left emotionally connected to the deceased as if that person were still living. Such circumstances significantly complicate mourning.

This process merges into the subsequent process of relinquishing the old attachments to the deceased and the old assumptive world. Other theories (e.g., notions of decathexis) combine these two processes. The two processes have been separated here for ease of discussion. However, it is important for the reader to note that, in reality, they are not so amenable to dissection.

Review and Remember Realistically

Remembering realistically involves a complete review of all recollections about the deceased and the mutual relationship. *All* means precisely what it says: the full range of memories of needs, feelings, thoughts, behavior and interaction patterns, hopes, wishes, fantasies, dreams, assumptions, expectations, and beliefs. It also means all of the aspects of each of these memories and all of the feelings about them—good and bad, happy and sad, fulfilling and unfulfilling, comfortable and uncomfortable, and so forth. The mourner must review completely all of what she knows and feels about the deceased and her experiences with him. This review—stretching back to the very beginning of the relationship—is necessary to put the mourner in touch with the entire range of memories and emotions that must be processed. Along with this must come a review of all of the meanings that various aspects of the deceased and the relationship, alone or in combination, held for the mourner.

In the initial stages of mourning, the deceased and the relationship are usually idealized. This is why the focus of repressed memories most often is on negative aspects. However, in some cases the reverse is true. For example, after the death of someone with whom the mourner had an unusually ambivalent relationship (even in the absence of distorted mourning of the extremely angry type), the mourner may approach treatment with a great deal of anger at the deceased. Only over time will positive aspects be identified and mourned.

Whether views of the relationship are initially positive or negative, as the review process continues and if mourning is progressing in a healthy fashion, additional elements are incorporated. A more realistic picture of the loved one emerges, one containing a mixture of positive and negative aspects, with the latter arising from the normal ambivalence contained to some extent in any relationship. It is important that the mourner ultimately develop a realistic composite image of the deceased that adequately represents the real person and the real good-bad relationship (Raphael, 1983), one that accurately reflects all the mourner has known, felt, and experienced about the deceased. It is with this composite image that the mourner later will interact in the new relationship with the deceased. When the individual mourns only selected aspects of the relationship, complicated mourning invariably ensues.

Reasons for complications

To maintain an unrealistic image of the deceased or the relationship, whether positive or negative, the mourner must expend enormous energy. Such an image does not permit the mourner to review and process the ambivalent thoughts, memories, and feelings that exist in all human relationships. It also leaves an inaccurate composite picture of the deceased with which the mourner will have to deal thereafter. Untruths press upon the mourner, who is aware on some level that the image does not reflect the way it was. The stress of defending against the conscious recognition of the truth can interfere with the mourner's ability to recall her life with the deceased properly; compromise the development of a healthy new relationship with him; or cause her to mistrust her own reality testing, judgments, and perceptions. Despite the high costs of incomplete and inaccurate recollections, the mourner may persist in avoiding the reality of who and what the deceased was, how they related, what the mourner thought and felt about the situation, and what all of this says about her. This is especially true if the mourner perceives herself, the deceased, or their relationship to have been negative in some way.

At times, the reluctance of a mourner to address what she construes as negative aspects reflects that mourner's lack of appreciation for and knowledge about the existence of some amount of ambivalence in all relationships. If so, her judgment of these negative reactions may be inappropriate and overly harsh. Or she may tend to overgeneralize to the extreme and believe that a few negative things mean that the entire person or relationship was bad. At other times, a mourner's judgment may be quite accurate, and the negative reactions she experiences but would prefer to disown are appropriate to the situation (e.g., the deceased was indeed cruel and the relationship abusive). Nevertheless, being justified about feeling hostile or having an accurate negative perception does not obviate the complications posed for mourning by anger, ambivalence, conflict, or victimization.

Fear of recognizing the existence or extent of dependency keeps some mourners from remembering the deceased and their relationship fully. Such memories may be too painful, underscore how alone the mourner is now, or raise anxiety about how to cope or even survive without the deceased. This may generate feelings of insecurity, helplessness, and anger in response—all of which are often avoided.

In addition to the fear of confronting anger and/or dependency and the feelings they engender, the mourner may avoid realistic recollection of the relationship in order to evade facing her own acts of omission or commission and thoughts, feelings, and fantasies she now feels guilty about in light of the loved one's death. Some of these may involve angry responses to the deceased or the relationship; others can represent a wide variety of affect, cognition, and behavior unrelated to aggressive feelings. In themselves, these acts are not necessarily guilt producing, yet they may haunt the mourner after the death. For example, the mourner may have wondered what it would be like to have sex with someone other than her partner, wished that her mother would not always call right when she was trying to get the children to bed, or rescheduled a date to take her younger sister shopping. This sort of illegitimate guilt can become a major contributing factor in the mourner's refusal to remember the deceased and the relationship realistically.

Other reasons for complications in the process of reviewing and realistically remembering the deceased and the relationship include the following.

1. The mourner desires and/or needs to maintain a particular view and fears that realistic appraisal would compromise that view. A discrepancy develops between the image the mourner sustains and the reality that will have to be confronted if the mourner reviews too much (e.g., the mourner does not want to look too closely at the character of her idol for fear of discovering that he has feet of clay).

2. Certain aspects of the deceased or the mutual relationship might imply things about the mourner that the mourner would prefer to avoid (e.g., if the deceased only gravitated toward losers, what does that say about the mourner's having been in a relationship with him?).

3. The mourner may be inexperienced and/or uncomfortable looking at the person in certain dimensions that require processing (e.g., she never permitted herself to think about her father as a sexual being).

4. The mourner fears discovering something distressing that could contaminate her perceptions of the relationship (e.g., the mourner limits her recollections out of concern that if something negative is discovered in the deceased or the relationship it would indicate that everything was bad).

5. The mourner holds the magical belief that if one tries to remember, one will tend to forget. This belief is reflected by statements such as "If I try to make myself think of her, I just go blank. Don't ask me to try to think about her."

6. The mourner fears she will not be able to remember as precisely or comprehensively as possible. Given that the mourner already has lost a great deal, the recognition that certain memories may be lost can be excruciatingly painful. This fear can cause the mourner not to review or recollect at all in order to avoid discovering that she cannot remember something.

7. Social admonitions against focusing on the past instead of looking forward prevent recollection (e.g., the mourner wants to talk about her brother, but her relatives keep telling her she must get on with her life).

8. The mourner fears that thinking about negative aspects of the deceased or the relationship will interfere with or override the positive ones (e.g., a mourner works hard to repress memories of her son as a troublesome adolescent out of fear she will lose her memories of him as an angelic toddler).

9. The mourner feels she has no time to sit and dwell but must be more "productive" (e.g., the mourner wants to hurry and get better but will not take the time to reflect or reminisce in order to achieve that goal). This belief is prevalent in bereaved males.

10. Extreme anger at the deceased and/or the desire to pull away from the relationship even in thought interferes with recollection (e.g., the mourner wants to punish the deceased for having committed suicide and so refuses to think about him or the relationship).

Therapeutic interventions

The first task of the caregiver is to ascertain what the impediment is in the review and recollection process. Where the impediment is in some way a fear of what will be discovered, the caregiver must address that fear, determine what the fantasies about it are, and minimize or work through it.

When the reluctance to engage in this part of mourning pertains to concerns about the discovery of guilt-producing material, the caregiver can follow the suggestions offered in chapter 10 on guilt and its complication of mourning. The same is true with regard to anger and dependency. In those cases where traumatic memories prevail, the caregiver can employ some of the techniques addressed in chapter 12 for treatment of mourning characterized by elements of post-traumatic stress.

When fear of recollection is related to fears of increasing the sadness or pain of separation, the caregiver should first gently encourage those reminiscences that can be tolerated most easily and gradually permit desensitization to occur. Relatively simple yes-or-no questions can be posed, such as "Was your father employed at the time of his death?" When the mourner answers a question, the caregiver can prompt for additional information, progressing very slowly and adhering to less emotional areas (e.g., "So he was teaching at the time of his death. Can you tell me a little about his areas of interest?"). The answers to these questions help in putting together a picture of the deceased and encouraging the flow of more information. In giving them, the mourner learns that reminiscing can be accomplished successfully. The caregiver may have to work diligently to elicit such information from mourners who are very resistant to reviewing and remembering.

Mourners can be helped enormously by being given a rationale for why the caregiver wants them to undergo these processes. It is important to remember that for some, such processes are in direct opposition to what is suggested by their social, cultural, ethnic, generational, or religious/philosophical conditioning. The caregiver can acknowledge the existence of these teachings but offer what is known to be true about coping with loss (i.e., mourning must not be short-circuited or problems develop; reminiscing and developing an accurate composite image are necessary parts of the mourning process). At this point, the caregiver does not necessarily want to mention withdrawing or modifying the emotional investment in the deceased because this may threaten the mourner who has not yet developed healthy new ties. Rather, the caregiver should refer to the process as learning to live with the loss by getting in touch with who the deceased was, what the relationship was like, and what meaning it had for the mourner. If necessary, the caregiver must explicitly label this process as work. Some mourners think that sitting and remembering is akin to doing nothing and do not construe it as productive. The process for these individuals must be legitimized as a necessary task, as important as any other.

The caregiver must normalize the sadness the mourner may experience at this point. If the mourner is concerned about being overwhelmed, previously discussed strategies for confrontation with painful emotions and for coping with bereavement overload may be employed. At an appropriate time (i.e., when it will not be viewed as diminishing or minimizing the extent and/or severity of the pain of the loss), the caregiver can introduce the concept of some memories being *bittersweet*. This notion recognizes both the sadness at being parted from the person who is lost (*bitter*) and the pleasure and warmth of the memory of an experience belonging to or shared with the loved one (*sweet*).

In undertaking this work, the mourner may become very concerned about the interaction between positive and negative memories, fearing that a realistic recollection will put her in touch with negative memories that will either neutralize or overwhelm the positive ones or be so painful as to drive her insane. Several responses are possible in this case. First, there must be an acknowledgment of the mourner's concern. Second, the caregiver must reassure the mourner that painful memories, while temporarily taking precedence until they are worked through and integrated, do not have the power to erase positive ones. They may have a transitory power to attract more attention and be more disruptive (especially when they are experienced intrusively, as in post-traumatic stress responses), but their demand for attention can be redirected with training and obviated with treatment. Third, the caregiver can help the mourner realize that memories have more strength when repressed. If examined and integrated with thought and affect, memories have much less power, cause less (if any) symptomatology, are less likely to be intrusively experienced, and prompt less (if any) behavioral acting out. Fourth, it will be helpful to share with the mourner that, in general, painful images tend to decrease over time. It is not unusual for mourners to fear that they will be unable to recollect the face of their loved one or to recall the sound of his voice, his touch, his scent. They may fear that all they will be left with are lingering images of illness, accident, or the deceased in the casket. In reality, this is uncommon. For most mourners, painful images are subsumed over time, and the pleasant ones come more readily to mind. Yet, for a while, negative memories may predominate. This is a natural consequence of the attention that has been focused on them, the mourner's attempts to push them out of mind, and the difficulty in integrating all of the images of someone who has been experienced in thousands of separate ways. Like anything else, that which we try the hardest to forget, we remember because of the attention we pay to it. That which we try the hardest to remember often eludes us because we struggle too intensely and inhibit our own thinking. Usually, over time, as less effort is expended to force memories and especially if the loved one and the relationship are discussed, recollections not focused on the illness, death, or funeral return. It is in an atmosphere of free access to all thoughts and feelings about the person and the relationship—the very atmosphere that the caregiver tries to stimulate in treatment—that the mourner is able to remember the loved one best.

The caregiver should undertake all of these suggested interventions with the assumption that what is necessary is to review the mourner's life story with the deceased, looking at what each character was and wasn't and feeling what it was like to be a player then and now. If the caregiver frames the mourner's task as trying to remember everything and not omitting a single detail, the process of recollection may well appear to the mourner to be an excruciating, anxiety-provoking, inhibiting burden. Although such detail is essentially what is desired, success will not be achieved if the goal is stated this way.

Finally, problems in working through the previous mourning processes may become evident at this point. If so, the caregiver's task is to return to and help the mourner deal with them.

Revive and Reexperience the Feelings

Feelings—positive, negative, and ambivalent—are what keep us connected. The characteristics of the feelings are less important than their strength in bonding people. Negative feelings can bond just as tightly as positive ones. Deep feelings, like a psychological electromagnetic current, provide the ongoing magnetism between us and our loved ones. They attach us, and whenever there is an attachment—even if negative—mourning is demanded. If there is no attachment, mourning is unnecessary even if negative feelings exist. For example, if a person hates a family member but is still attached in some fashion to that individual, mourning is mandated at the time of death. If a person hates someone to whom he is not attached (e.g., a public figure) or to whom he is no longer attached (e.g., an estranged relative), mourning is not necessary at death because there is no attachment that requires changing.

In order for mourning to proceed, the feelings accompanying what has been remembered about the deceased and the relationship must be revived and reexperienced. To put it simply, they must be felt. Feeling the feelings allows them to be discharged and released, which lowers the intensity of affect. The mourner requires this reduction in the feelings attaching him to the loved one if he is to alter his bonds to reflect the reality that the loved one now is dead and cannot interact with him as before. He must do this because to stay intensely and vitally connected to someone or something that now is not connected back is unhealthy. Therefore, the goal of reviving and reexperiencing the feelings is to reduce the strength of the affect perpetuating attachment bonds or ties (i.e., needs, feelings, thoughts, memories, behavior and interaction patterns, hopes, wishes, fantasies, dreams, assumptions, expectations, and beliefs). In addition, this process helps the mourner identify unfinished business he may have with the deceased and discern what issues remain to be addressed.

With enough psychological work, the emotion maintaining the attachment bonds or ties between mourner and deceased is significantly diminished or spent. Although the memory of the tie will remain, the emotion that kept the loved one vitally connected to the deceased will dissipate. This weakens the bond so that the attachments can be loosened from the deceased. In a subsequent "R" process, the old ties will be relinquished in order to free the mourner to make new attachments and ties with other persons or reinvestment objects and to forge new and more appropriate connections with the deceased.

The best analogy for this process of emotional diminution to facilitate the ultimate alteration of bonds with the deceased has been provided by A. Viscione (personal communication, August 20, 1990), who likens the change to the dimming of lights. Early in the mourning process, it is as if all of the lights (i.e., the emotions sustaining the ties, attachments, or bonds) are blazing. The dimmer switch is up all the way as the mourner experiences heightened emotion about the loved one. The intensity of affect is provoked by longing, yearning, and pining for the loved one, from whom separation brings acute agony, and by the painful but requisite process of review and remembrance. Over time, however, the intensity of the lights diminishes. The dimmer switch is turned down as the mourner expends his emotions, and the lights dim naturally as a consequence of the reduced affect caused by readjustments to the absence of the deceased. In many cases, as mourning progresses toward accommodation of the loss, although the lights are still on, they are quite subdued. They are softer, less fiery—more warm, less intense. Depending upon the mourner and the circumstances, they may be extinguished entirely in some places and left on in varying intensities in others.

The mourner will want to resist this process. No one willingly gives up connections to a person to whom he is emotionally attached. However, the strength of that attachment will lessen as memories are relived, emotions are shared, tears are cried, stories are retold, expectations for gratification are continually frustrated, and readjustments are made. All of the specific ties that bound the mourner to the deceased—the needs, feelings, thoughts, memories, behavior and interaction patterns, hopes, wishes, fantasies, dreams, assumptions, expectations, and beliefs—gradually are worked through by being revived, reexperienced, and processed. In the case of behavior and interaction patterns, the ties are reexperienced in memory if not in actuality.

Ties to the deceased do not have to be abandoned entirely, but they must be sufficiently modified so that new ties with others and the deceased can be established. The mourner still may have many feelings for the lost loved one, but in healthy mourning these are feelings for what used to be and for the meaning and significance that person still may hold in the mourner's life. If the mourner has experienced sufficient opportunities to change those feelings into ones appropriate to a relationship of memory and not of presence, but feelings remain of the sort that keep living people connected, then mourning has become complicated.

Reasons for complications

Reasons for complications in the process of reviving and reexperiencing feelings related to the deceased and the mutual relationship are an amalgamation of those found in virtually all of the other "R" processes of mourning. The caregiver can expect to see variations on the following causes: (a) fear of pain and desire to avoid it; (b) fear of encountering unacceptable memories, feelings, or thoughts; (c) fear of being overwhelmed by sadness; and (d) desire to avoid doing anything to alter ties with the deceased in order to maintain prior connections and avoid recognition of the loss and its implications.

In addition, difficulties can be expected if the mourner has not worked through earlier "R" processes, especially those involving acknowledging the death; experiencing the pain; and feeling, identifying, accepting, and giving some form of expression to all the psychological reactions to the loss.

Therapeutic interventions

Interventions for this process are similar to those for others in which emotions are evoked and memories stimulated. The reader is referred especially to the treatment sections for the "R" process of reacting to the separation and the subprocess of reviewing and remembering realistically, under the main process of recollecting and reexperiencing the deceased and the relationship.

What is somewhat different here is the unparalleled poignancy of this subprocess. It occurs during the Confrontation Phase of mourning (see chapter 2) and transpires coincidentally with (a) the second "R" process (i.e., reacting to the separation); (b) the subprocess of reviewing and remembering realistically, under the third "R" process (i.e., recollecting and reexperiencing the deceased and the relationship); and sometimes with (c) the fourth "R" process (i.e., relinquishing the old attachments to the deceased and the old assumptive world). As a result, the mourner may experience enormous strain. The pain is usually intense, and, of course, resistances are high. To be expected to scratch psychologically at the wound caused by the loss by reviving and reexperiencing the feelings essentially asks the mourner to be masochistic. However, it is masochism in the service of healing. Although the caregiver cannot fault the mourner for attempting to circumvent the process, avoidance cannot be supported. This is often an excruciating time for both caregiver and mourner because acute grief reactions fuel and are fueled by reminiscence and reexperience. The caregiver should expect to pay an emotional toll for standing for the healthy response.

RELINQUISH THE OLD ATTACHMENTS TO THE DECEASED AND THE OLD ASSUMPTIVE WORLD

An inherent part of adapting to the loss of a loved one in a healthy way is relinquishing former attachments to both the deceased and the assumptive world of which he was a part. Successful completion of this process gives the mourner the freedom to form new attachments, appropriate to the reality of the death. When the mourner is unable or unwilling to make these necessary changes, mourning becomes complicated, and the death cannot be accommodated.

Relinquish the Old Attachments to the Deceased

Attachments to the deceased can be many and varied. These are represented in hundreds or thousands of separate needs, feelings, thoughts, memories, behavior and interaction patterns, hopes, wishes, fantasies, dreams, assumptions, expectations, and beliefs. Each will have to be disconnected from the loved one, who no longer can respond as before. Only then can attachments appropriate to the reality of the death and the mourner's existence without the loved one be developed. If the old attachments are not withdrawn, complicated mourning will result.

Reasons for complications

The major complication interfering with a mourner's relinquishment of former attachments to the deceased is that the mourner does not want to. She does not want to because she fears that then she will have no connection to the loved one and that to do so means he really is dead. She does not want to because it makes her feel insecure and anxious, and because she cannot imagine life without him. She does not want to because she does not think she can manage to do it and because her ties to the deceased defined parts of herself. She does not want to be different now, but wants to go back to the old world, the old life, the old relationship, and the old self. She does not want to because this was not the way her life was supposed to go. And so on.

Therapeutic interventions

Because this subprocess of mourning is so intricately interwoven with the previous process of recollection and reexperience, interventions are similar. Treatment suggestions to assist the subprocess of developing a new relationship with the deceased, subsequently discussed, are also applicable. Specifically, it will be helpful for the caregiver to explain the process of relinquishment and subsequent reformation of a relationship with the deceased. This explanation should provide a purpose to the pain, assurance that the mourner's relinquishment will not strip her of everything, and a framework for comprehending the confusing and distressing experiences the mourner is undergoing to provide some measure of predictability and control. This type of explanation should help alleviate some of the anxiety and insecurity caused by the mourner's lack of information or experience in this type of situation.

Another important thing a caregiver can do to assist in the relinquishment of old attachments is to help the mourner recognize precisely what these attachments were in the first place. The following interventions can help actualize each attachment or group of attachments.

1. Explicit identification of each of the attachments

2. Exploration of how each attachment developed

3. Interpretation of the meanings and significance to the mourner of each attachment

4. Discussion and processing of the needs, feelings, thoughts, memories, behavior and interaction patterns, hopes, wishes,

fantasies, dreams, assumptions, expectations, and beliefs generated by each attachment and of the reactions and frustrations consequent to their loss

5. Discussion of how each attachment has a corresponding element in the assumptive world

These interventions are designed to accomplish the following goals.

1. Identify precisely what is being lost and encourage the mourning processes via the exploration, emotional processing, and working through of attachments.

2. Make each attachment tangible enough so that feelings about it can be discussed and plans made for what to do about it. Concretizing the attachments makes the process of relinquishing them more understandable and manageable, and actualizes them as secondary losses.

3. Illustrate how the needs, feelings, thoughts, behavior and interaction patterns, hopes, wishes, fantasies, dreams, assumptions, expectations, and beliefs that had mandated or involved the physical presence of the deceased must be relinquished because they can no longer be gratified. This helps the mourner perceive the process in terms of learning not to need all the different and unique types of interaction, gratification, validation, and reinforcement the loved one had provided.

4. Enable the mourner to understand how specific attachments to her loved one (e.g., the assumptions, expectations, and beliefs regarding him) have influenced her global assumptive world and now mandate alterations in it to reflect his absence. Global elements that may need to be changed because of the death include assumptions about security, expectations about certain needs being fulfilled, beliefs that the world is fair, and so forth.

In identifying and characterizing the ties that must be relinquished, the caregiver often must deal with intense resistance. The mourner's pain and overwhelming desire to avoid letting go must be normalized. This is not to insinuate that the caregiver fails to hold out the expectation that letting go of the way things were ultimately can be accomplished. While empathizing and legitimizing the mourner's wish to have things different, the caregiver still must provide the reality testing that they are not.

It also is important for the caregiver to realize that often the relinquishment of old ties can be recognized only in retrospect. For instance, it may become apparent that the mourner is letting go of her reliance upon the deceased only after she has taken a particular risk on her own. The caregiver needs to point this out to the mourner in a fashion that will not scare her into thinking that she is abandoning the deceased, has forgotten him, or, worse still, feels that he has become insignificant. Statements should recognize the change, place it in a context of the transformation necessary for the relationship with the deceased to continue, and help the mourner process her feelings about it. For example, the caregiver might say, "It seems you have learned to place some of the reliance you used to place on Tom on yourself. What is that like for you? How do you think he would feel? You are taking what he once gave you externally and giving it to yourself internally. As with other aspects of your relationship with him, you still can have some of these precious connections to and gifts from him, only now they come from your memories of what he was like for you."

If the proper perspective is established, mourners can be receptive to the idea of establishing a new relationship with the deceased and can work toward this and other readjustment goals. However, this willingness does not preclude their sadness, pain, and other reactions at what they do have to give up. Having a relationship in mind, heart, and memory is certainly better than nothing; it pales, however, next to a relationship based on the physical presence of the loved one. The feelings, thoughts, and other reactions to the reality of a diminished relationship and all of its secondary losses must be processed at this point.

To the extent that any prior "R" processes are not worked through, treatment demands the caregiver return and address them. To attempt to work on relinquishing attachments without having processed feelings about the attachments puts the cart before the horse. In both cases, there will be no forward movement.

Relinquish the Old Attachments to the Old Assumptive World

In order to accommodate the death of the loved one and cope with assumptions (including expectations and beliefs) violated or modified by the death and its consequences, the mourner must revise the assumptive world. Before this is possible, however, the mourner must relinquish old attachments to the old assumptive world, which was based in part on the loved one's existence and how her interactions with the mourner maintained his assumptions, gratified his needs, fulfilled his expectations, met his hopes, confirmed his beliefs, and so forth. Such relinquishment involves major secondary losses. If the mourner continues to operate with an out-of-date and invalid construct system, healthy mourning and necessary readjustment processes will become complicated.

Reasons for complications

Complicating factors in the relinquishment of attachments to the old assumptive world arise from several quarters and pose mourners with dilemmas too often seriously underestimated by their caregivers. The human being's need for meaning and for cognitive control—understanding, sense, security, and predictability—cannot be overstated. Those working in the field of post-traumatic stress and victimization have long recognized this fact and have incorporated into their treatment plans and self-help strategies the need to rebuild the assumptive world and regain lost cognitive control and meaning (see chapter 12). Caregivers of those victimized by the loss of a loved one, whether or not through traumatic circumstances, must do no less.

The human being is attached emotionally to each assumption about the world in general and about the deceased and the relationship in particular, as well as to the needs and desires that nurture and spring from them. Some global assumptions have been with the individual for as long as he can remember (e.g., "Be good and you will be rewarded" or "Life is fair"). When these notions are shattered by the death of a loved one, beliefs and expectations almost as old the mourner are dissolved. Even in the face of profound evidence that these ideas are invalid (e.g., the mourner's brother was good, but that did not protect him from his fatal accident), the mourner may resist relinquishing them. The same is true for specific assumptions (e.g., the mourner's brother will always be there for him). If the mourner is to adhere to these views of the old assumptive world, he must find some way to resolve the cognitive dissonance he experiences about them in light of the new realities brought by the death. This can prove to be quite a dilemma.

Thus, for mourners, as for all human beings, life has been predicated on certain assumptions. Some of the major ones revolve around meaning, security, fairness, control, predictability, and invulnerability. When one or several of these must be reconsidered after the death of a loved one, the others may become suspect as well. Mourners fear that, like a house of cards, the whole assumptive world will come tumbling down. If fundamental beliefs are discarded, what is left? What will take their place? For some, there may be modified assumptions. These can come from revamping old beliefs or incorporating some of them with new realities in the aftermath of the death. This can prove to be a time of great flux, putting demands on mourners for adaptation for which they might have neither energy nor interest. For others, after the loss of certain important assumptions nothing but cynicism remains. This can be terrifying to mourners, who feel adrift, insecure, and directionless. In fact, many of the emotions that occur in bereavement and are automatically assumed to stem from the loss of the loved one actually may derive from the secondary losses of important parts of the assumptive world.

After losing a loved one, a mourner is not anxious to lose more, and this also may play a part in reluctance to relinquish the old assumptive world. The mourner, who has been deprived of so much, does not want further deprivation. He wants the security of the old world back. Part of his tenacity in holding on to the old attachments is his "digging in his heels" to try to prevent further loss. The mourner also may become frustrated and want to give up when he discovers the new world can no longer support the old assumptions which had been so meaningful and gratifying. Like well-worn shoes, these assumptions were quite comfortable. The death of the loved one—and the caregiver's prompting to identify and respond to the lack of fit that now exists—challenges longstanding beliefs.

Like other habits, our ways of perceiving things, our expectations, and our beliefs are ingrained. It may take considerable time to change them. Especially if they have been suddenly and traumatically shattered (e.g., by homicide, mutilating accident, loss of a child, suicide), shock may interfere with the necessary search for and/or substitution of alternate assumptions or beliefs that can reorder and reexplain the world.

Therapeutic interventions

A number of interventions can be undertaken to help the mourner relinquish the old attachments to the old assumptive world. First, the caregiver needs to recognize explicitly that the mourner has already lost a great deal. Then the caregiver must acknowledge the losses inherent in relinquishing the attachments to the old assumptive world and identify them as secondary losses requiring processing. The mourner's reactions to these losses (e.g., anger, fear, confusion) must be identified, differentiated, traced, legitimized, and normalized by the caregiver so they can be appropriately processed, given some form of expression, and worked through. An explanation of the need for relinquishing attachments to the old assumptive world can provide the mourner a reason to continue to reshape his world. He can be helped to see that he has to relearn how to be in the world without the deceased and to understand what that world now means to him. This is not to say that the mourner will be able to rebuild his assumptive world quickly. The process is lengthy because only by bumping up against the new world and discovering that the old assumptions, expectations, and beliefs—and the needs, feelings, thoughts, behavior and interaction patterns, hopes, wishes, fantasies, and dreams that coincide with them—no longer fit does the mourner learn the lesson that they must be changed.

Violations in the mourner's assumptive world that are relatively few and minor will not necessarily compromise the structural integrity of a strong foundation (i.e., the individual's personality, coping ability, and mental health). However, if the foundation is unsteady to begin with, or if assaults are too numerous, the caregiver must decide whether to repair (i.e., change a few things but leave most of the basic structure intact) or rebuild (i.e., start over from scratch because so much must be changed). The four theories of cognitive readjustment that play a major role in this subprocess are, as noted in chapter 8, (a) Parkes' (1988) revision of the assumptive world following psychosocial transitions and Woodfield and Viney's (1984–1985) work on personal construct dislocation and adaptation in bereavement; (b) Horowitz's (1986a) cognitive processing aspects of the stress response syndrome and integration of memories and responses, meanings, new assumptive world, and new sense of self; (c) Taylor's (1983) theory of cognitive adjustment to threatening events centering on search for meaning in the experience, attempt to regain mastery over the event in particular and over one's life in general, and effort to restore self-esteem through self-enhancing evaluations; and (d) Janoff-Bulman's (1985) theory of the necessity to rebuild shattered assumptions following victimization, specifically the belief in personal invulnerability, the perception of the world as meaningful, and the perception of oneself as positive.

Once again, if earlier mourning processes have not been worked through, the caregiver must return to address them in order for the mourner to be successful at this point.

READJUST TO MOVE ADAPTIVELY INTO THE NEW WORLD WITHOUT FORGETTING THE OLD

The name of this mourning process reflects the main criterion for successful adaptation in mourning: Is the mourner able to move adaptively into the new life while simultaneously having a healthy connection with the old? The key word here is *adaptively*. It is on the definition of this term that the diagnosis of complicated mourning often turns. Similarly, the caregiver's interpretation of what constitutes a healthy connection with the old world—specifically, the deceased—will influence evaluation.

Usually, the mourner wants to try to recapture the world as it once was. Over time, she learns that this cannot happen and slowly ceases in her attempts to bring the old world back, eases her resistance to the new world, then actively participates in the creation of that new world by (a) revising the assumptive world, (b) developing a new relationship with the deceased, (c) adopting new ways of being in the world, and (d) forming a new identity. Ultimately, the mourner will need to reinvest in that new world (i.e., complete the sixth "R" process). Where any one or a combination of the four subprocesses essential for readjustment is compromised, mourning becomes complicated.

The four subprocesses interrelate with and influence one another. For example, changes in the assumptive world may lead to changed behaviors, which can lead to an altered identity. Likewise, changes in one's identity may cause one to perceive the world differently (i.e., revise the assumptive world) as well as conduct oneself differently in it (i.e., adopt new ways of being). For this reason, the caregiver should regard these four subprocesses as parts of a whole. For the most part, treatment approaches, interventions, and strategies can be used interchangeably. In all cases, failure to deal with prerequisite "R" processes will necessitate working through of these earlier issues.

Revise the Assumptive World

When a loved one dies, the world—both physical and assumptive—is no longer the same. To adjust to that fact and accommodate to the deceased's absence, the mourner must change both behavior in the altered physical world and elements of the assumptive world. After a period of time, to continue to operate in either world as if the deceased were still alive not only constitutes pathology, but also causes continual frustration for the mourner. For this reason, the mourner must revise the assumptive world or continue to be pained by the violation of its components.

As noted in the discussion of relinquishing the old attachments to the old assumptive world, global elements of the assumptive world as well as elements specific to the loved one may be shattered by the death. Revisions of assumptions specific to the deceased always are required with that person's death because of their violation; global assumptions may or may not be violated and therefore may not require revision in all cases. In the latter situation, basic, general assumptions about such things as fairness in the world, personal invulnerability, the trustworthiness of others, and so forth may be attacked, given the circumstances of the death (e.g., one no longer feels invulnerable after a loved one is murdered), its meaning to the mourner (e.g., the mourner may no longer be able to believe in the goodness of God after the death of her little girl), or the consequences of it (e.g., when others avoid the mourner after the AIDS-related death of her brother, she may become cynical about their compassion). Conceptualizations about the self, others, life, or the world as a whole may undergo modification as well. Revisions of the assumptive world must also reflect the new realities specifically consequent to the loved one's absence (e.g., a mourner can no longer rely on the comfort of his wife's solace at the end of a hard day).

Reasons for complications

As is the case for relinquishing the old attachments to the deceased and the old assumptive world, the mourner's inclination at this point is to avoid changes. In addition to this desire, there often exists a type of magical thinking: "If I keep the world the same, then nothing has changed. My loved one really didn't die." To perpetuate this belief, the mourner may strive for minimal changes in either the physical or assumptive worlds. A latent lack of acceptance of the death may be revealed by an unwillingness at this point to perceive the need for change or refusal to change even if a need is perceived.

Another reason for complications is that, frequently, the mourner does not believe she can function without the deceased. She feels helpless being in the world without his protection, guidance, and security. She is reluctant to change not because she can't, but because she *thinks* she can't. She also may want to save herself from having to contend with anything new. Often, one observes this reaction in chronic mourners of the type described by Parkes and Weiss (1983) as having a disorder of attachment. In such individuals, marked insecurity after the death of a person upon whom they were extremely dependent fosters a refusal to budge from chronic mourning. It is simply safer and more comfortable to live in an obsolescent world than to contend with the anxiety of the present one. These dynamics are also pertinent for mourners reluctant to make changes in the other three readjustment subprocesses.

Some mourners may experience complications because they feel the need to be punished for previous acts (of omission or commission), feelings (most usually aggressive), or thoughts (typically negative) directed toward the deceased and/or the mutual relationship. They seek to expiate their guilt through punishment and self-sabotage. Thus, their refusal to readjust themselves and their world in a healthy fashion is a form of self-punishment. It also may be a way they can indicate to the deceased, as well as to themselves, how much they wish things to be the way they were when the deceased was alive.

The instability experienced at this point may be very distressing for those whose assumptive worlds require extensive revision or whose necessary changes are dramatic or difficult. This may be the case for the mourner who has numerous fundamental changes to make, who sustains insufficient ego strength, or who experiences a loss so traumatic that it overwhelms the ability to cope. Everything can appear unfamiliar and frightening as the foundation on which the individual's life has been built crumbles. These secondary losses—as well as the apprehension; anxiety; fear; and consequent psychological, behavioral, social, and physical reactions—require attention and intervention. They further destabilize the mourner, who already is in the midst of flux. Many reactions that have been attributed solely to the death itself could in many instances legitimately be interpreted either as reactions to secondary losses associated with the destructuring of the assumptive world or as responses arising from the mourner's attempts to adapt to the death through the two inseparable processes of assimilation and accommodation (Woodfield & Viney, 1984–1985).

Finally, a lack of social support can hamper the mourner in all areas of readjustment. This lack may manifest itself as an absence of emotional support from positive relationships (i.e., consolation, encouragement, nurturance, expressed concern, empathy) or other types of support (e.g., instrumental, validational, informational; see chapter 10) sufficient to enable the mourner to bear the pain, undergo the complex processes of mourning, and stimulate and facilitate review, expression of affect, and gradual readjustment. If others do not support reality testing and provide feedback, it will be difficult for the mourner to alter emotions, cognitions, expectations, and behaviors. Similarly, problems may arise from a lack of instrumental or practical assistance to manage tasks necessary for daily living or for readjusting to the death. For all of these reasons, the mourner may refuse or simply be unable to manage this or any of the other readjustment subprocesses.

Therapeutic interventions

Interventions appropriate for relinquishing the old attachments to the old assumptive world are applicable here. In addition to implementing these interventions, the caregiver can help clarify which elements of the old assumptive world can be retained, which must be relinquished, which must be modified, which must be added, and why. For example, a mourner might retain the belief that honesty is the best policy but, to avoid compromising a pending lawsuit, might modify this belief when it comes to granting media interviews about the loved one's death. By the same token, the belief that justice always prevails may be totally overthrown for the new belief that the pursuit of truth in the criminal justice system often is a farce.

Similarly, specific assumptions, expectations, beliefs, and so forth pertaining to the deceased and the self may be altered. Some may be retained (e.g., "I still believe John and I had the best marriage ever"), relinquished (e.g., "I no longer can expect John to run interference for me with those troublesome neighbors"), modified (e.g., "Although I always thought John was the best one to deal with our daughter, I now see that I do a very good job myself"), or added (e.g., "Since John's accident, I firmly believe that if you love someone very much you had better make sure you say so, or else one day you may lose them for good without having had a chance to express how you felt").

The caregiver can point out what the new world is teaching the mourner about her assumptions and note indications of a current lack of fit. For example, a mourner may assume erroneously that others will rescue her as her parents always did. Painful though it may be, when new situations leave the mourner without rescuers she will learn that she must rescue herself, find someone else to rescue her, or avoid the types of situations from which she would require rescuing. In this and similar scenarios, readjustments concern both the assumptive world and the adoption of new ways of being. Often, although not always, the two go hand in hand. Such coincidence illustrates just how integrated the assumptive world is with the individual's behaviors. The mourner's new behaviors and assumptive world in turn have a profound impact on the individual's identity. Eventually, they all must be integrated.

Although some revisions of the assumptive world happen quite quickly (e.g., the suicide of one's mother likely would cause a rapid change in feelings about self, others, and general security in the world), other changes take place more gradually as the mourner learns new truths about the world without the deceased and responds to the numerous secondary losses that ensue over time. The caregiver must recognize these secondary losses, help to identify and label them, process and work through the reactions associated with them, and help the mourner integrate them into her life. The mourner will need to take time to test out revised or new assumptions, expectations, beliefs, and so forth to determine their validity. For instance, after the loss of a loved one from a sudden heart attack, the mourner may believe existing in the world is impossible without constant anxiety about having another loved one die at any moment. Treatment may involve much time, effort, and work before the mourner can acknowledge the possibility of such an event without constantly ruminating about it. The caregiver's continued support, identification, interpretation, and ongoing clarification of the meaning of the process and its content will be most therapeutic.

Helping the mourner perceive what has remained the same in the context of change also can be a potent intervention. It is reassuring to note that, despite the major loss of the loved one and the altered assumptive world, some things are unchanged (e.g., the mourner still has a dry sense of humor or continues to work diligently at whatever task she undertakes). Recognition and affirmation of continuity can provide stability in the face of change and lend the security needed to make the types of changes required after the loved one's death. The endurance these stable elements reflect is quite reassuring to any mourner.

Spiritual, religious, philosophical, and existential issues are critical components of an individual's assumptive world, and they play a large part in the readjustment processes after a loved one's death. The search for meaning can be a major part of mourning, especially, but not exclusively, after the death of a child (because the death of a child violates the very order of nature) and after sudden, unexpected deaths; suicides; homicides; or deaths occurring under other very traumatic or mutilating circumstances. Overwhelming questions of this nature may preoccupy the mourner for a long time, if not forever. Some of these questions can be answered (e.g., those about the circumstances of the loved one's death). However, some questions, particularly those pertaining to the philosophical reasons for the death and how it fits into the scheme of life, are more difficult. Why loved ones must suffer and die is a question that few, if any, can answer satisfactorily. However, it is the caregiver's job to assist the mourner in contending with these questions. Questions that cannot be answered may have to be accepted as being unanswerable or at least tolerated. Accepting that there is a reason, although unknown, can help some mourners cope a little better with an otherwise unfathomable event.

The quest to answer these questions, make sense out of the death, and ultimately find meaning in the new life can result in a profound sense of injustice and disillusionment if values and beliefs that once were comforting and promised security become hollow and useless. The mourner may look at her principles and standards and wonder, What's the use? Things that once were important to her can become meaningless; she can feel confused and adrift, without any emotional anchors. Such secondary losses, obviously related to the demand to revise the assumptive world, must be recognized, identified, and mourned.

Whether the secondary losses associated with revisions in the assumptive world are permanent or temporary will depend on how the mourner reconciles the death of her loved one and the new life it thrusts upon her with her other values, beliefs, standards, assumptions, expectations, and so forth. Mourners whose assumptive worlds are shattered can become embittered, enraged, cynical, and mistrustful; they can experience a crisis of faith in previously held religious or philosophical beliefs or in other aspects of their assumptive worlds. Because everyone needs a reason to live, the caregiver's task will be to help the mourner identify the beliefs and actions that will provide a new sense of purpose or restore meaning in life. It is well known that mourners who find ways to make their loved ones' deaths meaningful discover ways to survive and do so better than those who do not derive any meaning. To the extent that the caregiver can enable the mourner to reestablish a system of belief, find new meaning, or actively create meaning out of the meaningless event of the loved one's death, that caregiver has helped the mourner revise the assumptive world, which in turn assists the mourner in coping in the physical world. As Nietzsche said, "A person who has a 'why' to live can find a 'how' to survive."

The caregiver can take some specific steps to assist the mourner in rebuilding the assumptive world. The following suggestions are taken from Janoff-Bulman's (1985) work on rebuilding shattered assumptions in the aftermath of victimization. They seem especially pertinent after very traumatic deaths, suicides, homicides, or the deaths of children. To the extent that any major bereavement is a victimization, the caregiver may extrapolate them. He or she must be careful, however, that these causes of action do not preclude necessary processing of the event and the feelings engendered by it.

Redefine the event to be consistent with the assumptive world. Redefining the event minimizes the threat to the mourner's assumptive world by maximizing the possibility of maintaining prior theories of reality. Five mechanisms have been identified to minimize the perceived impact of the victimizing event and reduce the likelihood of perceiving oneself as a victim (Taylor, Wood, & Lichtman, 1983): (a) comparing with less fortunate others, (b) comparing on the basis of a favorable attribute, (c) creating hypothetical worse worlds, (d) construing benefit from the experience, and (e) manufacturing normative standards of adjustment.

Find meaning by attempting to make sense of the experience. Those who can make sense or find meaning after victimization tend to be less psychologically distressed and better socially adjusted, and appear to have more effectively integrated the experience with their assumptive worlds. This is often done by making causal attributions that explain what happened and allow the victim to reestablish a belief in an orderly and comprehensible world, satisfying the need for a view of the world that makes sense. Behavioral (as opposed to characterological) self-blame, frequently seen after victimization, is one such causal attribution.

Change behaviors. Direct actions to adapt to the changes wrought by victimization can provide victims with a sense of control that can minimize the perception of vulnerability; assist in reestablishing a view of the world that is not wholly unresponsive to one's efforts; and help rebuild a positive self-image, including perceptions of personal strength and autonomy.

Seek social support. A common response to victimization is to turn to others for emotional support and other forms of help. Sometimes these goals are achieved, and the victim is helped to recover and adjust by being provided the opportunity to talk about the event, ventilate emotions, and receive assistance in problem solving. An immediate social environment that is safe and secure challenges the victim's newfound perception of the world as malevolent and threatening. At other times, people may not be helpful, or worse, they may make things more difficult. In the absence of supportive family and friends, peer support groups are therapeutic in reducing the victim's self-perception of deviance, thereby enhancing a generally weakened self-image. Although in some cases victimization does not adversely affect the mourner's self-perceptions, the caregiver should attempt to rebuild positive self-perceptions as appropriate (Krupnick, 1980).

Taylor's (1983) work on cognitive adaptation to threatening events is equally pertinent. She asserts that the adjustment process centers around three themes and involves three types of cognitively adaptive efforts to enable persons to return to or exceed their previous level of functioning after experiencing personal tragedy. These ideas were originally discussed with respect to the experience of cancer but are extrapolated here—as they have been in other contexts—for threats associated with mourning. First, a search for meaning entails the effort to understand why the crisis occurred; comprehend what its impact has been; and make causal attributions to understand, predict, and control the environment (Wong & Weiner, 1981).

Often there is a rethinking of attitudes and priorities to restructure life along more satisfying lines. Second, an effort to gain mastery involves working to achieve a feeling of control over the threatening event to keep it from occurring again. Attempts to attain a sense of mastery may be behavioral (i.e., behaviors are altered to minimize reoccurrence), cognitive (i.e., the event is thought about in a way that lends control), or psychological (e.g., meditation, self-hypnosis, positive thinking). Attempts to control sequelae of threat-related events are another way of gaining mastery. Third, the process of self-enhancement takes the form of coping efforts designed to enhance the self and restore self-esteem following victimization by events beyond the individual's control. It includes esteem-enhancing cognitions such as making downward social comparisons (i.e., evaluating oneself as doing better than someone else or being more fortunate than another). Such operations may instill motivation and provide information.

Other specific interventions for rebuilding the assumptive world are found in chapter 12, where they are addressed in the context of the post-traumatic stress response. Because the six "R" processes of mourning—especially as associated with complicated mourning—are a form of stress response syndrome, these interventions can be extrapolated even if no post-traumatic stress elements are present in the death or mourning experience.

Develop a New Relationship With the Deceased

Although the death of the loved one separates the mourner from the deceased, it does not constitute the end of their relationship. The mourner can have an appropriate, sustained, loving, and symbolic relationship with the lost loved one provided two criteria are met simultaneously: (a) the mourner must truly recognize that the loved one is dead and fully understand the implications of this (i.e., his expectations of and interactions with the deceased must reflect knowledge of this fact) and (b) the mourner must continue to move forward adaptively into the new life. Mourners will differ in their need for the type, quality, and intensity of a new relationship with the deceased depending on the particular factors circumscribing them and their loss. The remainder of this section presumes a desire for a strong connection with the deceased. The caregiver will need to extrapolate the information provided as a given mourner departs from this pattern.

There appears to be less resistance to this subprocess than to any other aspect of mourning. This is probably because it permits the mourner to have some of what he wants (i.e., a connection with the loved one). What may be resisted is the fact that this is the sole type of connection or relationship now possible. In most cases, resistance is due less to the idea of having a new relationship with the deceased than it is to the notion that the new relationship must be an abstract one.

Arguments for the development of a new relationship with the deceased, and for its appropriateness and lack of pathology, have been articulated in chapter 2 and will not be repeated here. However, it is absolutely crucial that caregivers understand the mourner's need to maintain a connection to the deceased. It is precisely because mourners are not provided a means of having a healthy connection that they continue to hang on in unhealthy ways. As caregivers, we have two choices: Either we help mourners achieve healthy connections with those they have lost, or we watch them develop their own connections, which may or may not be adaptive. A good deal of complicated mourning derives from mourners' attempts to maintain connections with the deceased. Therefore, facilitating healthy connections can be expected to reduce the amount of complicated mourning.

Reasons for complications

In addition to failure to address prior "R" processes, four main reasons exist for complications in this subprocess: First, the mourner is unwilling to accept the need to form a new relationship with the deceased because he wants the return of the old relationship, in which the loved one was physically present. Second, the mourner fails in simultaneously meeting the two criteria for a healthy relationship with the deceased (i.e., recognition of the loss and its implications and adaptive forward movement into the new life). Third, the mourner's support system or caregivers fail to support and/or passively or actively discourage the development of a new relationship with the deceased. Fourth, the mourner uses identification with the deceased to avoid appropriate relinquishment, or the identification itself is inappropriate.

Therapeutic interventions

If the caregiver enters the picture after a pathological connection has already been established, the task will be to find a better and more appropriate way to maintain a tie so that the mourner can relinquish the inappropriate one. In this regard, all therapeutic interventions are built around the caregiver's educating the mourner about the establishment of a healthy new relationship with the deceased. The caregiver must first disabuse the mourner of the prevailing myth that connections to the dead are unhealthy and provide explicit permission to reconnect with the loved one under the two conditions necessary for an appropriate relationship with the deceased. The caregiver's next goal is to promote a healthy new relationship in those ways that are as personally meaningful as possible for the mourner. Working with the mourner to create this relationship can increase feelings of power and control and decrease some of the helplessness and passivity with which many mourners struggle.

In the process of reorganization, the mourner forms a new relationship based largely on recollection, memory, and past experience (Irion, 1966). In other words, there is a relinquishment of the concrete loving of the physically present person and a replacement with the abstract loving of the absent loved one (Attig, 1986). Therefore, part of the caregiver's task is to engage the mourner in an active exploratory process to decide in which particular ways he wants to keep the deceased's memory alive. This means first helping the mourner decide what the new relationship with the lost loved one will be like, a goal predicated on the deceased's being remembered in context as someone who lived and died (Irion, 1966). Before this will be possible, the mourner must possess a clear, realistic composite image of the deceased—an image that reconciles all the differing aspects of the deceased's personality and all the experiences the mourner had with that person. It is also necessary for the mourner to decide consciously which parts of the old life and relationship should be retained (e.g., special activities, routines, or mementos) and which must be relinquished.

As spelled out in chapter 2, healthy ways of retaining the connection involve remembering the deceased as life continues, choosing life-promoting rather than death-denying reminiscences, and continuing to maintain the new relationship with the deceased without jeopardizing subsequent reinvestment in others. Through such actions as anniversary celebrations, prayers, memorializations and commemorative activities, personal and collective rituals, donations, mementos, maintenance of certain parts of the relationship, mention during grace over dinner, healthy identification, and one's own actions it is possible for the mourner to relate to the deceased and keep her appropriately "alive" while maintaining the proper perspective on the new relationship.

The mourner may experience problems if he uses identification—an important way of keeping some connection to the loved one—to avoid appropriate relinquishment of the old relationship or if the identification is inappropriate. The latter circumstance exists when the identification occurs too intensely (e.g., the mourner loses a sense of personal identity), when it is inappropriate to adult functioning (e.g., a bereaved parent acts immaturely), when it occurs in areas in which the mourner lacks competence (e.g., when the physically limited mourner tries to become the star athlete his brother was), or when it is incompatible with other roles (e.g., the adult child of an alcoholic becomes irresponsible like his deceased father and no longer assumes parental responsibility for his own young children). In each of these instances, the identification is unhealthy, and the caregiver should help the mourner discover more appropriate ways to identify with the loved one.

When resistance is present to the creation of a new relationship with the deceased because the mourner demands the return of the loved one, the caregiver deals with this situation in the same fashion as for all other protests at the loss and wishes for a different reality. Doing so involves first acknowledging, identifying, and labeling the mourner's response as a wish or protest and then reality testing it. Although it is important to support the mourner for ventilating the wish or protest, the mourner's unwillingness to relinquish the deceased must be dissected to identify the source of the difficulty. If there is protest at the death, this suggests that the loss has not yet been accepted and that the caregiver and mourner need to go back and work through an earlier "R" process. Once the reasons for not relinquishing the deceased are clear, the next step is to work through the accompanying emotions until the loss can be acknowledged and to ensure that any anger remaining about the loss of the former relationship with the deceased does not compromise the development of a new relationship.

If the mourner fails to meet one or both of the criteria for a healthy relationship with the deceased, the caregiver needs to intervene by identifying and working through the blocks to the achievement of that criterion. If the mourner does not truly recognize the death and its implications, the caregiver must return to the point where difficulties began and facilitate such recognition. The caregiver must be alert for evidence of latent thoughts, feelings, expectations, behaviors, and attitudes that reveal that recognition of the death is superficial and that a deeper refusal to accept the reality of the loss and its implications exists. Especially at this point in the mourning processes, the caregiver must not be seduced into taking superficial behaviors as true indications of underlying feelings and thoughts.

If the mourner is not moving forward adaptively into the new life, the caregiver must assess the source of the failure, then deal with this situation. Specifically, problems in this area may be due to failure in a preceding "R" process; the need to go through the process just described for dealing with protests and wishes; or complications associated with the parallel subprocesses of revising the assumptive world, adopting new ways of being in the world, and forming a new identity, and/or the coincidental "R" process of reinvesting in the new life.

Sometimes connections with the deceased may be marked by the violation of both criteria for a healthy relationship. Such individuals are relatively easy to spot because they act as if the loved one still is alive and make no changes in their lives. However, there are some in this group—as well as some who fail at only one of the criteria—who are more difficult to identify. They give the appearance of having recognized the reality of the death and/or of moving forth in a healthy way. Closer examination reveals that many or all of the cognitive, emotional, behavioral, or social adaptations are superficial rather than real. In fact, on a deep level these mourners have not accepted the reality and/or have not made the proper adjustments to accommodate it. For example, a young woman once professed to me that she had accomplished her grief work and indeed had gone through the motions of making changes following her father's death from leukemia. A discussion of incongruities in her reports of her emotions and the affect displayed during therapy led to a number of inconsistencies and ultimately to the recognition that she was playing a role. In truth, she could not believe her father was dead (he was only "away" for an extended time). In the deepest regions of her psyche, she expected him to return and comment on how good a performance she had been giving. She never truly internalized the fact that he was gone forever and that she now had to live her life without his protection.

In the event that social support is lacking for the development of a new relationship with the deceased, the caregiver may consider having a collateral meeting with the mourner's significant others to discuss this specific aspect of mourning and other readjustment processes. This meeting also can be helpful in educating the mourner's important others about long-term issues involved in mourning and in dispelling prevailing myths. If it becomes clear that the source of difficulties is family members or other associates, the caregiver can adopt an appropriate approach to address family systems issues. If working with significant others is not an option—or if it fails—the mourner can be helped to find a support group or other sympathetic individuals who can facilitate the development of a new relationship with the deceased, as well as the rest of the readjustment subprocesses of mourning.

Adopt New Ways of Being in the World

To live life in a healthy way, the mourner must adopt new ways of being in the world after the loved one is no longer there. New roles, skills, behaviors, and even relationships must be undertaken to compensate for the absence if the loved one had been an integral part of the mourner's life and/or his presence met her needs. In other words, the mourner must respond to or eliminate needs the deceased formerly met and must add, relinquish, or change aspects of her life to accommodate the specific losses his death brings. To the extent that the mourner fails to make requisite readjustments in the mourning processes after a sufficient time has passed, continues to behave in the world as if the deceased were still present or will return, or significantly reduces interaction in the world because it does not contain the deceased, that individual can be said to experience complicated mourning.

Reasons for complications

A number of reasons exist for complications at this juncture. First, as with other mourning processes, the mourner may resist engagement to deny the implications of the loss. Frequently, magical thinking is involved, with the mourner believing that keeping the world the same as it used to be somehow means that the loved one is not really dead.

Another reason for the reluctance to assume new behaviors is the feeling that the old ones are the sole ties remaining to the deceased. To behave as if the deceased is still alive and to perpetuate old ways of being can make some mourners feel that they have, through their own actions, retained a connection. The persistence of old behaviors therefore asserts a desire not to let the world go on without the loved one. In this case, it is imperative that the caregiver help the mourner develop appropriate and healthy new ties to the deceased in order to forestall the development of pathological ones that would interfere with healthy adaptation to the new life and world.

Anxiety and a poor self-image also may interfere with moving forth in the new world. Parkes and Weiss (1983) talk about the chronic mourner, whose problems with dependency, insecurity, and anxiety interfere with the relinquishment of the old relationship and keep her from trying out new behaviors in the world without the deceased. Secondary gain from others to remain grief-stricken, either due to misguided sympathy or the desire to keep the mourner from moving forward, also can contribute to the mourner's reluctance to adopt new behaviors and move forward.

A serious lack of psychosocial, behavioral, vocational, or other skills can impede the adoption of new behaviors appropriate to the new life without the deceased. For instance, the mourner may experience significant problems in taking on the roles needed to keep the family functioning (e.g., finding a job) or get her own needs met (e.g., developing new friendships with individuals who can validate her widowed status and support her new identity in ways older friends cannot). A lack of proper skills definitely impedes the mourner's undertaking of new behaviors. Related to the individual's lack of social skills is a lack of social support. Perhaps even more than for other mourning processes, the absence of such support will impede the mourner's ability to take on the new behaviors demanded by healthy readjustment to the loved one's death.

Mourners who experience significant trauma, anxiety, insecurity, vulnerability, and fear for their own well-being may restrict their world in the attempt to ensure control and protection. This is not unusual after deaths that are associated with homicide, accident, disaster, and sometimes war, or that involve mutilation, violence, and trauma. Sometimes these dynamics apply in suicide deaths as well. Whenever these factors are present, they force the mourner to contend with post-traumatic stress, a factor that can seriously impair the ability to go on in the new world in an adaptive fashion.

A final complication concerns the element of time. The death of a loved one demands major adaptations in all realms; it is a monumental psychosocial transition. Changes in the assumptive world, relationship with the deceased, and identity directly influence the person's ability to undertake new ways of being in the world. If an insufficient amount of time has transpired to allow these changes to occur and be integrated, no evidence will be seen of new ways of being. In this case, the complication exists not in the mourner but in the demands of the process.

Therapeutic interventions

As noted previously, a great deal of interrelationship exists among the four readjustment subprocesses. The assumption of new skills, roles, and behaviors necessitated in the absence of the deceased influence and are influenced by the revised assumptive world and the new relationship with the lost loved one. The mourner's identity is affected by all of these changes and, in turn, exerts a profound impact on them. Therefore, it should not be surprising that considerable overlap exists among the required therapeutic interventions. Ultimately, all will need to be integrated.

Specific interventions to deal with the magical belief that maintaining things as they are somehow will keep the loved one alive have been discussed as they relate to previous mourning processes. To summarize briefly, these interventions assist the mourner in recognizing and ultimately working through reluctance to admit the reality. Reality testing can help the mourner internalize what she probably already knows but represses (i.e., that no matter how she chooses to construe the world, none of her cognitive and affective maneuvering can change reality).

If the mourner's failure to adopt appropriate behaviors in the new world stems from a desire to maintain previous behavioral connections with the deceased, the caregiver can work with the mourner to supplant unhealthy connections.

When anxiety compromises the mourner's ability to go on appropriately in the new world, the caregiver needs to investigate the source of the affect; identify and label its component parts and specific fears; process, problem solve, and work through each part and each specific fear; and teach stress management strategies. Cognitive and behavioral treatments are frequently employed with success to help the mourner better tolerate the anxiety that occurs at this point, as is the provision of psychoeducational information on the meaning and management of anxiety reactions. The caregiver is urged to have realistic expectations for the mourner whose anxiety is characterological and/or coexists with extreme dependency, passivity, or any other concurrent psychological condition. Such a mourner may require longer treatment or other types of in-depth intervention. The reader is referred to chapter 10 for more on intervention strategies for these associated areas. In cases where anxiety is an independent response or associated with a post-traumatic stress response syndrome, the caregiver is urged to look to the treatment strategies recommended in chapter 12.

If the mourner's failure to move forward with new behaviors stems from a lack of appropriate skills or knowledge, the caregiver can work with the mourner to secure proper training in order to develop those skills and gain that knowledge (e.g., vocational retraining or enrollment in a night course). If psychosocial skills (e.g., assertiveness or communication skills) are lacking, the caregiver may devote treatment time to these. Problems with social support may be addressed with appropriate family or social systems education and/or intervention. When the social support system is supplying secondary gain for the mourner to maintain old ways of behaving, the caregiver must point this out to the mourner, explain its disadvantages, and work with the mourner to find alternate ways of receiving gratification.

In addition to these specific recommendations, it is important for the caregiver to keep some general points in mind. As with all other forms of mental health intervention, events and behaviors may have symbolic meaning to the mourner. The mourner thus may resist the adoption of new behaviors not from any desire to thwart the process, but in response to what she perceives the new behaviors to mean. For example, one widow absolutely refused to do anything on her own after her husband died—go shopping, go to church, attend a high school reunion at a local restaurant. Her caregiver initially thought she had become agoraphobic. However, further exploration revealed that, due to her upbringing with a quite lascivious father, she firmly believed that any unmarried woman who went out alone anywhere would be perceived as being "on the make." Because she did not want to send this message, she would not leave her home alone. Her response stemmed not from her husband's death, but from her father's conditioning. This example underscores the importance of ascertaining the particular meanings assigned and interpretations made by the mourner.

The caregiver also must instill in the mourner the proper perspective on this part of the mourning process. In particular, the mourner needs to appreciate that trying out new behaviors in the new world can be anxiety provoking and unsettling. This fact must be recognized explicitly by both parties, and account must be taken of it in the expectations each maintains. The mourner must understand that changing behaviors takes time and that only gradually does an individual acquire new modes of behaving, especially when what prompts the necessity for change is the loss of a loved one. In educating the mourner about normal aspects of grief and mourning, the caregiver should convey the message that these aspects manifest themselves across all realms of one's existence. Therefore, the mourner can expect reactions and possibly need to make changes in all different areas of life (e.g., psychologically, behaviorally, socially, physically, spiritually, occupationally—even financially or politically). These changes can be expected to be greater or lesser depending on the deceased's significance in these areas and/or the amount of adaptation demanded as a consequence of the impact of other changes.

Finally, the caregiver must help the mourner see that the adoption of new behaviors requires trial and error and that progress is often "two steps forward, one step back." The mourner must expect disappointments, mistakes, frustrations, and embarrassments. However, these are important in teaching the mourner about the new life and what is required to act in a healthy fashion in it. It is wise to stress that new behaviors are experimental rather than cast in concrete; the mourner is free to change her mind and course of action in the future. In general, the caregiver must convey the need to adopt a "live and learn" strategy in any attempt to go forth in the new world without forgetting the old. To the extent that the mourner is not encumbered by personality characteristics such as perfectionism, rigidity, compulsiveness, obsessiveness, and so forth, she will be better able to tolerate this often ambiguous and chaotic process.

Form a New Identity

The death of an individual who was an important part of the mourner's life inevitably will change that mourner. The more and deeper the involvement between the two individuals, the greater the impact on the mourner the loved one's death will bring. This is because human beings define themselves by, among other things, the interactions they have with others. These contribute to one's sense of self and reality. Even when the role defining a relationship is replaced, as is the case when a widower remarries, what was unique to the original relationship cannot be replaced. In this regard, parts of the mourner invariably die when the loved one dies. This does not mean that the mourner cannot continue to exist or can never change. Rather, it means that he will never reexperience what it takes for his previous relationship with the deceased to continue. He can no longer interrelate with the loved one as before—and interrelating is necessary for the relationship and the parts of the mourner formed and validated by that interrelationship to survive. Although roles can be replaced, the people in them cannot.

Another major transition the mourner must undertake at this time involves the change from a "we" to an "I." The need to modify or give up preexisting views predicated on the "we," caused by the need to respond to the new world without the deceased, demands that the mourner take on new ways of thinking, feeling, and being to reflect the reality that the loved one is dead.

The new views developed during the revision of the assumptive world—the different expectations, beliefs, assumptions, knowledge, hopes, and so forth taken on to reflect the fact that the loved one is gone— also help form the new identity. As the mourner starts to see and experience the world in a new way, as he continues to learn through painful encounters with reality that the loved one truly is gone despite his wishes to the contrary, he will eventually see and experience himself in a new light. Thus, a changed sense of self gives birth to a changed identity. Further changes in that identity also occur as a consequence of the mourner's identification with the deceased, as noted previously. All of these aspects need to be integrated for healthy accommodation of loss.

Over time, the mourner must develop a perspective on what has been lost or gained in the self. That which has been changed (either positively or negatively) must be recognized and mourned; that which continues must be affirmed; that which is new must be incorporated. The mourner will then need to integrate the new and old selves. He will have a corresponding need for new friends to validate the new identity (e.g., as a single parent). New relationships with others who share important elements of the new identity are important to provide information and role-modeling and to prevent feelings of alienation. Old friends can provide support, continuity, and important resources for reminiscence, but they may be unable to support the new elements of the mourner's identity.

In summary, all of the processes of mourning contribute to changing the mourner. To be healthy and make proper adjustments to the loss, the mourner must change. Not to change means that the mourner has not observed the real differences in the world consequent to the death and has not compensated for them. These compensations involve how the mourner thinks, feels, and behaves. In effect, they cause him to be a different person than before—sometimes better, sometimes worse, and sometimes just different. Despite an initial reluctance to modify his view of the world or his needs, feelings, thoughts, behavior and interaction patterns, hopes, wishes, fantasies, dreams, assumptions, expectations, and beliefs, the healthy mourner eventually does so. In brief, anyone who sustains a major loss and does not change in some fashion either was not that close to the loved one to begin with or has mourned ineffectively.

Reasons for complications

An individual can experience complications at this point for a variety of reasons. First, it can be very frightening for the mourner to watch himself changing. If the changes are perceived as positive, healthy, and leading to better things, they may be more readily accepted. However, as is clearly witnessed in psychotherapy, even when positive changes are achieved or in the process of being achieved the individual often becomes anxious, asking questions such as, Who will I be if I am not the me I was? What will I be like, and what will my life be like, if I give up the way that I have been? How do I know that this will be a better way to be? What guarantees do I have? and, Will life be boring without some pain? Natural resistance to change, fear of the unknown, and insecurity over possible consequences all come into play at this time. A disinclination to contend with any more secondary losses often operates here whether changes are positive or negative. The person who must change as the result of a loss has an extra issue with which to contend: The changes are unwanted. He is forced to adapt to a reality that (unless he has murdered his loved one) he has not chosen. Some mourners may simply refuse to change, passively reacting to the loss but doing no more (i.e., grieving but not mourning).

The refusal to make changes, or to integrate those changes when they have been forced by external reality (e.g., the deceased's absence), may be especially strong in persons who have been quite dependent upon the deceased, who have little else to define themselves and so feel they cannot change, who have borderline personality organizations, who are immature in their psychological development in ways other than borderline pathology (e.g., individuals with developmental disabilities, immature personalities, children), or who feel the relationship was the best thing in their less than satisfactory lives.

Others may run into complications in this aspect of mourning because they are unable to accept the angry, vulnerable, anxious, or other parts of themselves that the death has created. These aspects of self are not in their self-image (i.e., they are ego-dystonic) and may be difficult to integrate into a new identity. For example, the previously sensitive mourner whose loved one was murdered becomes embittered, or the formerly hopeful individual whose loved one commits suicide becomes cynical. In addition, those who split off or otherwise fail to accommodate new aspects of themselves run a high risk of developing psychological problems that complicate mourning.

The mourner who has problems with identification can also become stuck at this point. If the identification is too intense or incompatible with adult functioning, occurs in areas in which the mourner lacks competence, or is incongruent with other roles, difficulties may arise. A lack of access to individuals who will validate aspects of the new identity can stymie its ultimate formation as well.

For some individuals, the new identity may be that of chronic mourner. In this case, the new identity solidifies a way of life in which mourning for the loved one is perpetuated and failure is evident in the relinquishing, readjusting, and reinvesting demanded by healthy mourning.

As with all other mourning processes, the degree of success in the previous processes will influence this one. As one of the four readjustment subprocesses, the formation of a new identity is significantly determined by the revision of the assumptive world, the development of a new relationship with the deceased, and the adoption of new ways of being in the world. Again, a desire to maintain the old connections with the deceased and to keep the world as much as possible as it was before the loss may interfere with appropriate changes in identity by obviating the need for revision of the assumptive world and adoption of new ways of being.

Therapeutic interventions

In general, the caregiver can help the mourner discover aspects of his new identity by inquiring what needs, feelings, thoughts, behavior and interaction patterns, roles, skills, hopes, wishes, fantasies, dreams, assumptions, expectations, and beliefs he has had to give up or modify and what new ones have had to be assumed to readjust to the death of the loved one. The mourner can be asked to consider how identification with the deceased has added to or changed his previous identity. Over time, the mourner must operationalize these changes so they can be owned and understood more easily in the context of normal reorganization following major loss. After identifying both positive and negative changes, the individual must mourn them as secondary losses and integrate all the new and old components of his identity. The caregiver can help provide a much-needed sense of security and continuity during this time of transformation by pointing out what has remained constant despite the loss.

The mourner's anxiety over changes in the self must be acknowledged, legitimized, normalized, given verbal expression, and differentiated into component fears. These component fears must then be labeled, processed, and subjected to problem solving, if necessary. For example, if a mourner is afraid that her new view of herself as an independent woman compromises her femininity, the caregiver will need to work with her to help her see that this is not necessarily true. As this example illustrates, the caregiver first must understand the personal symbolic meanings of the changes in the mourner's self in order to give maximum therapeutic assistance.

When working with mourners whose personality organizations contribute to problems in identity formation, the caregiver must enable mourning issues to be addressed as completely as possible. However, individual limitations should be considered when setting goals and expectations. This does not mean that people with preexisting mental health problems cannot be treated successfully for complicated mourning: The reader is referred to chapter 10 for further discussion on this point.

If the mourner has difficulty integrating unacceptable or ego-dystonic parts of himself into a new identity, the caregiver should focus on working through these unacceptable sequelae to the extent possible. However, reactions may never be worked through to the point where they are no longer salient. For example, after the mutilating death of a loved one who was sitting in the passenger side of an automobile, the mourner may always feel the need to be the driver. It may not be possible to eliminate this need, even with a variety of psychotherapeutic interventions and approaches. If this is the case, the caregiver should help the mourner learn to live with these sequelae as well as possible and to avoid punishing himself or developing related symptomatology. Like learning to live without the loved one, the mourner must learn to integrate this reality into his life. Even if he is not pleased with it, he can accept that it is a part of him. As long as any necessary compartmentalization is done with conscious awareness and minimization of consequences, it need not be pathological. It is far more dangerous to split off the undesired or unacceptable parts of the self—better to acknowledge, understand, label, and account for these within the psyche.

If inappropriate identification with the deceased creates problems for the mourner in forming a new identity, the caregiver must interpret this, acknowledge the desire to remain connected to the loved one, and suggest that the mourner discover healthier ways to maintain this connection. Interventions suggested in chapter 2 and earlier in this chapter for helping the mourner develop a new relationship with the deceased are therefore applicable.

In situations where the formation of a new identity is compromised by the lack of appropriate social support, the caregiver must work to identify available resources and then refer the mourner to them. To the extent that work with the family or others in the mourner's social system is indicated, possible, and within the expertise of the caregiver, education and treatment can take place there as well.

For mourners whose identity is based on the perpetuation of acute grief, the caregiver must initiate an overall intervention for chronic mourning. The assumption of the identity of chronic mourner is only one of the characteristic issues of this type of complicated mourning, albeit a major one. Treatment must therefore be undertaken in the context of the chronic mourning syndrome as an entity (see chapter 4).

To the extent that complications arise in the formation of a new identity as a consequence of unfinished business in the prior mourning processes, the caregiver must go back and work through those previous processes. Certainly, for example, one is not going to form a new identity successfully without moving past the expressions of protest, guilt, sadness, confusion, and so forth that characterize acute grief and require expression in the process of reacting to the separation. Healthy movement in the subprocesses of revising the assumptive world and adopting new ways of being is most closely related to success in integrating a new self-image. Problems in these two subprocesses are therefore most influential in complicating the formation of a new identity.

REINVEST

When a loved one dies, the mourner loses the gratification that the deceased had provided through the mutual relationship. The absence of this person and the needs, expectations, desires, assumptions, and so forth that are unfulfilled with the loved one's death stimulate the processes of mourning. As noted previously, a number of these processes involve reexperiencing then letting go of the feelings that bind the mourner to the deceased, then modifying these feelings in order to create a new relationship with the deceased loved one. Part of this process mandates that the emotional energy that once was placed in the relationship with the deceased be withdrawn. To be healthy, the mourner cannot continue to direct all of her energy toward one who cannot return it. Some of it will be used to keep alive the new relationship with the deceased, but the rest of it must go toward establishing and maintaining other rewarding investments.

This redirection of energies will not, of course, replace the loved one. However, it can reconnect the mourner with new people, objects, activities, roles, pursuits, hopes, beliefs, ideals, goals, or causes that can provide emotional gratification to compensate for that which was lost with the death of the loved one. The object of reinvestment may be tangible (e.g., another person, a house, an art collection) or psychosocial (e.g., a relationship, a dream of becoming a teacher, being president of the chamber of commerce). Energy does not have to be reinvested in precisely the same object or role from which it was withdrawn (i.e., a widower does not have to remarry). The sole requirement for healthy reinvestment is that the mourner place the emotional energy and involvement in a source that will return it.

Reasons for complications

In addition to failure in one or more of the previous "R" processes, a main cause of complication in the reinvestment process of mourning is misinformation. Many mourners equate the length and amount of their suffering with their love for the deceased. For them, reinvestment suggests that they no longer miss the loved one or that the relationship was not meaningful or important. Still others believe that it is an insult to the memory of the loved one to enjoy life again. These and other myths block healthy reinvestment.

Reinvestment may be avoided by mourners who fear either being hurt again by loving another who also could be lost or others' perceptions that they have not loved or mourned the deceased enough. Other mourners may be fearful as a concomitant of personality characteristics of extreme dependency and anxiety or because of unfamiliarity with the new world and a lack of social or communication skills. Yet others fear the unknown or that their reinvestment in life signals the end of their involvement with the loved one.

The type of death experienced by the loved one can have an adverse impact on reinvestment, which can in turn complicate mourning. Some individuals have been through long-term illnesses with their loved ones. After so much time devoted to caretaking, they often are so depleted and unused to living a life for themselves that they have difficulty readjusting. Other mourners may experience complications in reinvestment because the nature of the death precludes social support and/or makes it embarrassing or painful for the bereaved to reinvest as they otherwise would. This is especially true after suicide, murder, AIDS-related deaths, autoerotic asphyxiation, and other types of deaths that tend to disenfranchise the mourner. What little support does exist for these types of deaths can be negated by the mourner, who may be so discomforted as to withdraw even if it is offered.

Therapeutic interventions

Problems associated with erroneous beliefs, myths, and incorrect interpretations about the meaning of reinvestment can be managed relatively easily by the caregiver. Misinformation can be corrected by the provision of accurate psychoeducational information. Usually, discussion will involve the caregiver's providing proper information on what the accommodation of loss really entails.

The mourner's specific fears need to be identified and dealt with separately. As is the case for other concerns, the caregiver must comprehend their meaning and symbolic significance to the mourner. At this point, problem solving may be as important as the more abstract process of working through. Problems in reinvestment associated with negative reactions by the support system can be addressed by stimulating social support or therapeutically working through blocks via family or social systems intervention and the dissemination of psychoeducational information.

Interventions with those depleted from a loved one's terminal illness will center around redefining new goals, reestablishing the self as a central focus, and replenishing physical and psychosocial (including spiritual) needs. Also critical are assistance with family reorganization and working through of the conflicts inherently generated in terminal illness (see Rando, 1984, 1986e, 1988).

Finally, the factor of time plays a part in the reinvestment process. The caregiver will need to be able to discern how much, if any, resistance to reinvestment is due to complicated mourning and how much results from an insufficient amount of time and working through. Mourners will vary significantly in what is needed for both.

PART III

Specific Clinical Problems

CHAPTER 10

Risks and Therapeutic Implications Associated With Individual, Relationship, and System Factors

The potential for a death to bring on complications in mourning depends on the unique constellation of factors associated with each individual situation. Indeed, as noted in chapter 2, numerous sets of variables may influence any mourner's response. In turn, each set may contain a number of aspects, further increasing the total number of variables that can affect grief and mourning. Despite this range of variables, the literature is remarkably consistent in identifying factors predictive of complicated mourning. These factors fall generally into two categories. First are factors associated with the specific death.

1. Sudden, unexpected death (especially when traumatic, violent, mutilating, or random)

2. Death from an overly lengthy illness

3. Loss of a child

4. The mourner's perception of the death as preventable

The next category includes the following antecedent and subsequent variables.

1. A premorbid relationship with the deceased that was markedly (a) angry or ambivalent or (b) dependent

2. Prior or concurrent mourner liabilities, including (a) unaccommodated losses and/or stresses and (b) mental health problems

3. The mourner's perceived lack of social support

This chapter and chapters 11, 12, and 13 organize discussion of these and other high-risk factors along the following lines: The present chapter describes and offers treatment suggestions for dealing with high-risk factors pertaining to the individual, relationship with the deceased, or social system. Specifically, these include the mourner's liabilities, anger, ambivalence, guilt, dependency and codependency, and degree of social support. Additional risks, examined in chapter 11, are associated with the mode of death: natural death, accident—including death resulting from disaster and war—suicide, or homicide. Also discussed in this chapter is the mourner's perception of the death as preventable. Yet other risks, outlined in chapter 12, are linked with particular circumstances of the death (i.e., sudden, unexpected death; multiple death; or traumatic death). Finally, chapter 13 includes discussion of risks associated with death of a child and AIDS-related death.

The treatment suggestions presented in this chapter, as well as in chapters 11 through 13, are in addition to the philosophical perspectives on treatment and the generic treatment guidelines discussed in chapter 8 and the specific strategies for intervening in the six "R" processes of mourning outlined in chapter 9. These earlier chapters must be read first because they form a matrix for understanding the interventions suggested in this and subsequent chapters.

INTERRELATIONSHIP AMONG HIGH-RISK FACTORS

In the vast majority of complicated mourning experiences, more than one high-risk factor exists. Generally, the existence of more factors increases the risk of complications. Not all risk factors are equal, however. For example, in many cases the mourner who has lost a child (risk factor) by suicide (risk factor) would likely be at greater risk for complications than the mourner whose spouse dies suddenly and unexpectedly (risk factor) from a heart attack and who believes the death to have been preventable (risk factor). Nonetheless, it is important to point out that assumptions of this sort always must be qualified by individual circumstances. Perhaps the mourner in the latter situation has additional risk factors associated with mental health problems, concurrent stresses, or perceived lack of social support. If so, that mourner might be at relatively greater risk than the one who has lost a child by suicide. Sometimes the addition of certain factors increases risk exponentially rather than additively. In any event, predictions must be based on careful consideration of the cumulative effect of all risk factors and any moderating influences. It is helpful to remember that Andrews, Tennant, Hewson, and Vaillant (1978) have proposed that prediction of risk of psychological impairment after life event stress improves by taking into account meaning of the event to the individual, effectiveness of coping style, personality attributes, and adequacy of social support during the crisis.

It is crucial that the caregiver recognize the different sources of complications in mourning, as well as the interrelationships among them. Historically, according to the assumptions of the psychoanalytic viewpoint, the reactions of the mourner experiencing complications indicate problematic internal psychodynamics and conflicts. However, such attributions of individual weakness or psychopathology too often ignore factors inherent in the particular circumstances of the death. This attitude results in the pathologizing of many understandable and statistically normal responses after specific types of death.

Similarly, the impact of inadequate social validation of the loss and/or social support during and after it also has been seriously overlooked in favor of attributing responses to the influence of the individual mourner's psychology. Erroneous assumptions of this sort interfere with appropriate treatment and potentially hurt the mourner by increasing negative self-evaluations. It must be clearly understood that there are more risk factors for complicated mourning that are external to the individual mourner than involve the mourner's direct contribution.

These caveats do not belie the importance of the individual mourner's liabilities when it comes to mourning. Although the nature and circumstances of the death or the degree of social validation for the loss and/or social support may prompt their own inherent reactions, these will be experienced idiosyncratically as a function of the individual mourner's psychology. In addition, there are times when mourner liabilities such as mental health problems and effects of past or concurrent stresses may overshadow the impact of circumstances surrounding the death or social response.

Although some factors can be identified as predisposing the mourner to complicated mourning, their interpretation is always relative. Factors must be examined in relation to one another because their potency and impact vary over circumstances; one factor cannot always be presumed to be more influential than another. In brief, then, the caregiver's goal is to know how much weight to assign any particular variable, and when. Certainly, this determination will have a profound bearing on treatment. Integrating all of this information is where the caregiver's art and previous experience will come into play.

MOURNER LIABILITIES

Overview

Liabilities either preexist within the mourner and the mourner's life or occur simultaneously with the bereavement. In other words, two areas may complicate mourning: (a) the mourner's prior and concurrent losses and stresses and (b) the mourner's prior and concurrent mental health. Because these factors are intrinsic to the mourner, more than any other variables they cut across temporal dimensions of the loss experience and are pivotal antecedent, concurrent, and subsequent determinants of bereavement outcome. It is axiomatic that prior and concurrent losses and stresses and prior and concurrent mental health are powerful determinants of individual mourning. This perception is shared by the following authors, who, among many others, identify both factors as critical variables influencing mourning: Barnes (1987), Bowlby (1980), Clayton (1982), Osterweis et al. (1984), Parkes (1965, 1987), Parkes and Weiss (1983), Rando (1984), Raphael (1983), Raphael and Maddison (1976), Sanders (1989), Shanfield (1987), Stroebe and Stroebe (1987), Worden (1982), Zisook and Shuchter (1985), and Zisook et al. (1985).

Prior and concurrent losses or stresses

Research findings. The literature in this area is somewhat inconsistent. In widows, previous life crises have been found to be significantly related to poorer bereavement outcomes, especially when a close temporal relationship has existed between the crisis and the death (Maddison, 1968; Maddison & Walker, 1967; Parkes, 1975, 1987). Corroborating this result without including the variable of temporal relationships, Rando (1983) found that previous physical and psychosocial loss tended to be associated with poorer bereavement outcomes and lower anticipatory grief among parents whose children had died from cancer. Representing alternate findings are Bornstein et al. (1973), Huston (1971), Shanfield and Swain (1984), and Vachon (1976), all of whom suggest that coping with a prior bereavement appears to facilitate better outcomes following bereavement.

Differential impacts of previous losses may in part account for such inconsistency. On the one hand, Rando (1983) found that the total amount of previous loss judged by the mourner as having been successfully coped with influenced adjustment after bereavement, with better bereavement outcomes tending to be associated with fewer previous losses. On the other hand, Worden (1982) observed that it is not just the number of life crises that is important, but which life crises they are and how the individual undergoing them perceives them. Stroebe and Stroebe (1987) examined a number of studies and suggested that antecedent losses are likely to have differing effects on bereavement outcome depending upon when they occur, whom they involve, and their frequency.

In attempting to integrate the disparate literature, Stroebe and Stroebe (1987) offer three hypotheses: First, an antecedent bereavement experience would increase risk of poor outcome if it entailed the loss of a key attachment figure during childhood. Second, if the antecedent loss occurred during adulthood, the experience could prepare the individual for subsequent bereavements. Third, someone who has suffered multiple losses of very close persons, possibly in rapid succession, could be at particularly high risk, given that cumulative experiences might lead to loss of the feeling of control over events, hopelessness, depression, social withdrawal from others for fear of losing them also, and consequent loneliness. They note the similarity of the third hypothesis to Kastenbaum's (1969) concept of bereavement overload and conclude, "In short, in assessing the impact of prior losses on bereavement reactions, one needs to look at the specific type and timing of these experiences" (p. 201).

Integrating the ideas presented by Rando (1983), Worden (1982), and Stroebe and Stroebe (1987) may help to resolve discrepant findings. Each loss or stress must be identified and note must be taken of when it occurred, whom it involved, and what it meant to the mourner. The individual's evaluation of success in coping with the loss or stress must be taken into consideration, as should his comparison of it with the current loss. The total sum of these prior losses and stresses would constitute another variable affecting mourning. It appears that if there is not an overload of losses and stresses, and if the mourner has coped with them successfully, this may inoculate the mourner somewhat from the toxicity of a subsequent major loss. If the number of prior losses and stresses is excessive, or if the mourner has coped with them unsuccessfully, then they may constitute a more negative factor. Clearly, more research is required to clarify any relationship between prior loss and stress, and ability to cope with current loss. Such research must take into account the clinical reality that it is less the experience of having undergone a loss or stress per se than the degree of successful accommodation that influences a person.

Another important issue in interpreting findings about previous loss concerns the difference between a death and a nondeath loss or stress. A number of studies have grouped these occurrences together. Only the mourner can determine the degree of difficulty inherent in either type of crisis. However, for many individuals, certain stresses may be more difficult to adjust to than a death. For instance, many individuals who have experienced both divorce and death of a loved one would assert that the divorce is more difficult, inasmuch as death precludes some of the hanging-on and fantasy that often complicate post-divorce adjustment and insofar as death may constitute less of a purposeful rejection. Unlike death, the pain of divorce may be exacerbated by the potential for its reversal, the need to interact "for the children's sake" or other reasons, or the prospect of witnessing the former spouse with someone else. These factors can complicate mourning the loss of the marriage and subsequent adjustment. Conversely, nondeath losses or stresses may pale next to the death of a loved one.

Plainly, the caregiver cannot merely look at category of event (e.g., death versus nondeath stress) or total number of events to determine the degree of influence exerted on the current bereavement experience. Previous losses and stresses place differential demands for coping on the individual depending upon intensity, type, meaning, requirements, and number. In addition, to the extent that any prior losses and/or stresses have depleted the mourner or interfered with healthy adaptation to the current death, these crises would constitute high-risk factors.

Notwithstanding inconsistency in the literature resulting from the mixing of deaths with nondeath losses and stresses, it appears clinically that prior loss often can leave the individual at high risk for complicated mourning. This seems especially true if the loss occurred in childhood and was not appropriately integrated. The main reason for this is that early, unresolved loss interferes with appropriate personality development and compromises mental health, leaving the mourner less able to cope with subsequent losses (e.g., Bowlby, 1980; Brown, 1982; Caplan, 1964; Raphael, 1983). However, early unresolved loss is not the only type that can predispose the mourner to complications. Prior losses occurring after childhood and prior and concurrent stresses impinging upon the mourner at the time of the death also may pose problems.

Types of concurrent stresses. Five types of concurrent stresses exist. The first involves an event that happens to coincide with bereavement over the loss of the loved one. No direct cause and effect relationship exists between this event and the death, although events associated with the death certainly could be the same as those providing the concurrent stress (e.g., severe economic hardship). The stress places demands on the bereaved that interfere with her ability to do the proper work of mourning (e.g., she is so busy holding down two jobs that she cannot take the time to mourn).

The second type of concurrent stress occurs when the same circumstances that caused the death of the loved one cause the mourner to be unable to attend to mourning processes (e.g., the explosion that killed one brother simultaneously seriously injures another brother, who must delay his mourning to concentrate on his own survival).

The third type of concurrent stress is observable in cases of multiple loss, where the death of one individual cannot be mourned properly because mourning is also required for others at the same time (e.g., three family members die in an automobile crash, and the survivor cannot cope with the loss of all three simultaneously). Sometimes such losses occur not at the same time but close enough to another death that incomplete mourning over the first loss interferes with mourning for the current death (e.g., a man's mother dies 2 weeks before his son, and the man is unable to do justice to either in his mourning). These types of concurrent bereavements are sometimes so overwhelming that they lead to inhibition of mourning, chronic mourning, or psychiatric decompensation (Raphael, 1983). (For more on the topic of multiple death, see chapter 12.)

The fourth type of concurrent stress occurs when the death creates secondary losses or circumstances that interfere with the mourning of that death. A secondary loss functioning as a concurrent stress is seen in the example of the widow who was forced by financial difficulties to move from her home within weeks after her husband's sudden, unexpected death. Her relocation confounded her mourning by giving her additional stress with which to contend. In this case, it also robbed her of the family support she needed in light of the suddenness of her husband's death and made it more difficult for her to recognize her loss, given that she was in a new environment devoid of triggers to reveal her husband's absence. Another problematic circumstance might arise if the current death triggers a STUG reaction to a prior loss (see chapter 2). The STUG reaction might become a concurrent stress, further hindering mourning.

To the extent that remnants of any earlier loss or crisis persist, the bereaved individual can be expected to face additional difficulties in mourning the current loss. In this regard, the unfinished business of earlier losses legitimately might be viewed as the fifth type of concurrent stress.

Effect of prior and concurrent losses and stresses on mourning. Prior and concurrent losses and/or stresses compromise the mourning of a current death in a number of ways.

1. Prior loss may exert an impact on the individual's subsequent loss responses. A lack of resolution and the psychological press of unfinished business, which typically push for closure through the repetition compulsion (Freud, 1920/1955a), and intrusive thoughts (e.g., Horowitz, 1986a) can directly affect the mourner's ability to contend with the current loss. If this situation is not worked through, it can hinder effective mourning. A desire to avoid confronting previous losses also may prevent dealing with a current loss if a pattern of avoidance has become firmly entrenched.

2. Bereavement overload (Kastenbaum, 1969) stemming from a number of simultaneous bereavements (e.g., multiple deaths in one disaster or serial losses over a brief time) may leave the mourner emotionally depleted and often physically exhausted, unable to mourn the current loss adequately. Also, in some cases, the deaths may leave the mourner without the support necessary to cope because the resources to whom the mourner would have turned for assistance are the individuals who have died (Lazare, 1979).

3. A depletion of the ego can occur because of the demands of prior or concurrent losses or stresses. In this situation, the ego is impaired, an insufficient amount of ego is available for current mourning (Deutsch, 1937), or the ego is unable to tolerate the affects aroused (E. Furman, 1974).

4. A mourner's prior experiences with losses and stresses may establish expectations regarding future loss and influence the coping strategies and defense mechanisms adopted. If previous

experiences with losses and/or stresses have been negative or have not been accommodated, this can adversely affect the present experience of loss both through specific learning (e.g., the mourner may feel his friends will think him foolish if he shares his guilty feelings because that is what happened before) and through the sequelae of the loss (e.g., the mourner is left mentally or physically vulnerable or damaged and is thus more easily stressed). Conversely, prior losses and stresses can be therapeutic in teaching the mourner what is necessary to cope, which strategies are most helpful or harmful, or that the distress will eventually diminish. It must be pointed out that an absence of prior losses and stresses can be problematic as well. In such cases, early experiences are so positive that the loss and its consequences represent a particularly devastating violation of the mourner's assumptive world. One person summed up this situation by calling it "the curse of too good a childhood." Caregivers must recognize that, despite having greater ego strength and optimism, these individuals may be just as overwhelmed as those who come from very negative backgrounds. Their being unaccustomed to being as effective as desired and their lack of practice in defending their assumptions (Janoff-Bulman, 1985) also contribute to their pain and must be addressed.

5. When other crises impinge on the crisis of bereavement, the mourner may be able to do little more than survive. For instance, if the mourner has been injured at the same time the death occurred or has a health crisis during the period of acute grief, these additional concurrent demands for survival usually will take precedence over mourning. Nonetheless, mourning will be in the background, clearly affected by the circumstances.

Sometimes bereavement occurs at a time when the adaptive resources of the mourner already are at a minimum, and the death contributes to the mourner's increased feelings of vulnerability and helplessness. For example, a person may have been undergoing a very difficult and draining divorce when her sister dies. This person, already overwhelmed and depleted, will likely not be able to mourn the loss initially and/or in the proper fashion, although these problems can be remedied with proper attention. This situation may in part explain the phenomenon of poor adjustment following lengthy terminal illnesses (Rando, 1983, 1986e). The requirements of caring for the loved one and dealing with other aspects of the terminal illness experience so deplete the mourner that when the death finally arrives the individual is exhausted and less able to cope. In such cases, as well as in those where multiple and as yet unaccommodated losses have occurred over a relatively brief period of time, the mourner may evidence psychic numbing, which, as described by Lifton (1976), often occurs after disasters. The survivor, overwhelmed with loss and death, shuts off or blunts emotion to defend against the trauma and the feelings of helplessness and pain it brings. Although in the face of major loss this defense initially may be adaptive, if it persists, it is quite unhealthy.

Clearly, concurrent stresses take up important coping resources and create extra strain, thus hindering processing and accommodation of the loss. Individuals experiencing such stresses are therefore at a significantly greater risk for complicated mourning than those who are not so assailed.

Prior and concurrent mental health

It is evident that the mourner's mental health will influence the mourning process because, inasmuch as it describes the mourner, it will also define mourning. No other factor so accurately describes and delimits who is affected by loss, how loss is experienced, or what is available for a response to it. Very simply, everything the mourner experiences and does depends upon his perceptions and coping abilities. To the extent that the mourner brings sound mental health, achievement of appropriate object relations, good ego strength, hardiness, healthy self-esteem, effective communication skills, emotional resilience, appropriate coping resources, capacity to express emotion, a mature personality, optimism, and a transcendent belief system to bear upon mourning, it appears clear that the individual will have an advantage. Often a history of depression or anxiety is a significantly negative influence. (See chapter 5 for discussion of specific mental disorders and personality characteristics as related to complicated mourning.)

Treatment Implications

Both prior and concurrent losses and stresses and the mourner's mental health require address in addition to complicated mourning. A good loss history must determine the timing, cause, type, location, and other factors circumscribing prior or concurrent losses and stresses, as well as pinpoint the mourner's reactions to and lessons learned from them. The mourner's expectations and/or manner of coping with these losses and stresses and her evaluation of success will affect her response to the present circumstances. Therefore, it is important that the caregiver determine, to the extent possible, what belongs to the current situation, what belongs to previous situations, and how present and previous losses and stresses compare (see chapter 6, on assessment). If complications in mourning exist due to unfinished business relating to prior or concurrent losses or stresses, the caregiver must find a way to address these issues in treatment. Depending on the degree of involvement with or vulnerability due to a particular prior or concurrent loss or stress (e.g., unmourned prior loss or disclosure of sexual abuse), the caregiver may decide to (a) focus exclusively on these issues, (b) incorporate work on these issues with work focused on the current loss, (c) merely take these issues into consideration in designing treatment for the current loss, or (d) refer the individual to another caregiver for concurrent treatment before undertaking or continuing treatment for the current loss. Each loss and/or stress must be legitimized, and continued reassessment will be required to ensure the ongoing applicability of the treatment. Treatment suggestions for multiple death, outlined in chapter 12, may be pertinent, as will suggestions for dealing with bereavement overload, offered in chapter 9.

Clearly, treatment also must take into account any preexisting mental health problems. Current mourning may not be affected if these mental health problems have been resolved or are of a type that does not interfere with the mourner's ability to process the current loss. Any impairment must be reflected in the treatment plan, goals, and expectations. For the caregiver, this may mean expanding treatment that has as its primary focus mourning for the current loss to include treating the concurrent mental health problem, modifying treatment to attend exclusively to the concurrent mental illness, or providing referral to another caregiver to attend to concurrent mental health problems while the initial caregiver focuses on mourning.

ANGER

Overview

As used here, *anger* refers to any amount of hostile or aggressive emotion, whether minor (e.g., annoyance) or major (e.g., rage). In addition to the general conception of anger as a nonspecific issue in mourning and as a characteristic of the mourner's personality influencing interpretations of and responses to life, anger in mourning may be any one of the following.

1. A normal reaction to loss

2. A reaction witnessed after the death of one upon whom the mourner had been extremely dependent (i.e., in the context of distorted mourning of the extremely angry type; Raphael, 1983)

3. A reaction witnessed after particular types of deaths, most notably violent deaths; sudden, unexpected deaths for which someone is blamed; deaths where the mourner's sense of desertion is great; and/or deaths in which a relationship symbolizing something special and irreplaceable to the mourner is lost (Raphael, 1983)

4. A major, if not definitive, characteristic of the premorbid relationship

In brief, the caregiver may be called upon to work with anger of two major kinds: (a) anger stimulated by the particular death and/or its circumstances and consequences or (b) anger as a component of the premorbid relationship between mourner and deceased. Of course, many situations reflect both types of anger, as well as a mixture of elements in the premorbid relationship (e.g., a mourner may have had a relationship with the deceased that was both conflicted and dependent). It is important to point out that a one-to-one correspondence between antecedents and consequences of anger does not exist. For instance, a premorbid relationship in which the mourner was highly dependent on the deceased can give rise to either distorted mourning of the extremely angry type (Raphael, 1983) or chronic mourning (Bowlby, 1980; Parkes & Weiss, 1983; Raphael, 1983).

Anger as a normal consequence of loss

As discussed earlier in this book, anger is a normal reaction to loss stemming from the biological predisposition to attempt to find and recover the lost loved one and ensure that no further separations ensue (Bowlby, 1969, 1973; Parkes, 1987) and an emotional consequence of being deprived of something valued. There is always some dimension of anger present at some point in grief.

Anger following the loss of a dependent relationship

As described by Raphael (1983), distorted mourning of the extremely angry type typically is the result of the loss of a relationship upon which the mourner was extremely dependent, often to a pathological extent. It reflects protest at the loss and often is accompanied by a sense of desertion and the perception of threatened survival. Intense bitterness is present. Anger is directed at everyone and often is displaced onto others, either from feelings about the deceased, the perceived abandonment, or the self. This intense anger occurs in the absence of reactions such as sorrow, yearning, and pining; the mourner is consumed with anger at the loss and desire to punish those he holds responsible. The persistence and intensity of such feelings can eventually ruin relationships and destroy the mourner's support system.

The death of the loved one frequently appears to resurrect insecurity caused by earlier, often childhood, losses. The rage catalyzed in the present often appears to stem from the childhood rage at an earlier loss. Once again, the mourner is left feeling helpless. The high degree of dependency—often infantile in nature—fuels the mourner's protest at the loss and exacerbates the uncontainable fury at being left with so many unmet needs.

Although such feelings are normal for a while following a loss, their intransigence and exclusivity characterize this type of complicated mourning and differentiate it from uncomplicated bereavement. In addition, perseverance in protesting the loss indicates that on some level the mourner feels the loss is reversible and is attempting unconsciously to bring about the return of the deceased.

Anger following particular types of death

As noted previously, Raphael (1983) has observed that intense anger can be expected following violent deaths; sudden, unexpected deaths for which someone is blamed; deaths where the mourner's sense of desertion is great; and deaths where a very special and irreplaceable relationship is lost. The latter two types are associated with relationships of extreme dependency. These particular circumstances also would suggest that the following types of death might precipitate extreme anger: deaths of children, homicides, suicides, deaths resulting from accidents or disaster, deaths during war, preventable deaths, and deaths from natural causes that are blamed on the omissions or commissions of the deceased and/or those influencing the deceased. Each of these deaths inherently contains anger-producing dimensions influencing mourning, whether complicated or uncomplicated.

Anger as a major characteristic of the premorbid relationship

Two complicated mourning syndromes are seen to derive from a contentious premorbid relationship: conflicted mourning (Parkes & Weiss, 1983) and distorted mourning of the extremely guilty type (Raphael, 1983). Also, to the extent that the mourner seeks to avoid encountering negative or conflicted aspects of the relationship with the deceased and therefore permits only the mourning of positive aspects of the relationship, anger is taken as a primary determinant in the inhibited mourning syndrome (Raphael, 1983). Anger existing in the relationship with the deceased prior to the death may or may not coincide with anger stemming from the circumstances of the death and/or its consequences.

Treatment Implications

Anger poses problems for mourners—indeed for a majority of persons—for several reasons. Despite impressive evidence that unacknowledged anger causes psychological, behavioral, social, and physical problems, anger is a poorly tolerated and often misunderstood emotion in Western societies. As a consequence of anger's illegitimate status, few models exist for its successful expression, and many inappropriate interpretations are made of it. Clearly, the caregiver must take into account this general view of anger in undertaking any treatment.

The following discussion highlights treatment concerns when anger results from loss of an extremely dependent relationship, the particular circumstances of the death, or contentiousness in the premorbid relationship. Interventions for problems stemming from anger as a personality characteristic of the mourner are not addressed here; for resources on this general issue, the reader should consult his or her own professional literature.

Prerequisites for treatment

Before beginning to design any kind of treatment for mourning complicated by anger, the caregiver first must understand the purposes of anger and be able to promote healthy psychological, behavioral, social, and physiological processing and management of this emotion. It also is important to determine when the presence of anger reveals a lack of acceptance of the death (e.g., when it is associated with distorted mourning of the extremely angry type arising after the loss of a dependent relationship) and when it indicates acceptance (e.g., when the mourner accepts the permanent loss of the loved one in a drunk driving crash yet is angry about the senselessness of the event).

Recognizing anger, hostility, and frustration in the mourner is sometimes difficult because these emotions may take myriad forms: negative verbalizations, aggressive behavior, sarcasm, intolerance, negativity, irritability, tension, anxiety, obstinacy, belligerence, criticism, self-reproach, passive aggressiveness, withholding, withdrawal, jealousy of others, stinginess, and so forth. A careful assessment of all such responses is therefore worthwhile.

Assuming which aspects of a death or premorbid situation constitute the mourner's worst problems may not result in an accurate picture. For example, it is not safe to assume that a mutilating accident would be the major factor contributing to a mourner's anger; it may be that her refusal to reconcile with the deceased before the accident is causing immense guilt, covered superficially with anger. A specific inquiry is in order.

The caregiver must realize that some mourners may squelch their anger. For those who find admitting to anger at the deceased or other individuals difficult, the caregiver can employ less emotionally charged words, such as *irritation* or *annoyance* (Lazare, 1979). Essentially, relabeling feelings makes them more tolerable. Another way of facilitating expression is to ask first what is missed about the deceased and then what is not missed (Worden, 1982). Other mourners may experience intense rage reactions (e.g., those seen after a homicide or death of a child). In most cases, the caregiver should not fear such intense reactions; often, they are normal sequelae of particular kinds of death.

Finally, the caregiver must realize that working through may take some time, especially after victimization. Repetition in processing and expressing anger, often through a variety of modalities, will be required before anger is exhausted or diminished to the degree possible.

Components of effective treatment

To intervene effectively, the caregiver will need to work specifically to accomplish the following.

Provide psychoeducational and normative information about anger.
First clarify that it is normal to have angry feelings. Because this is such
an important issue, it must be stated explicitly: "You are not a bad person
for having angry thoughts or feelings. You can be judged and indeed will
be held accountable for your actions, but your thoughts and feelings are
neither right nor wrong—they just are." This concept may be difficult for
some mourners to comprehend, especially those who hold religious,
philosophical, or sociocultural beliefs prescribing what is proper to think
and feel. Nevertheless, the caregiver must be clear in distinguishing between a feeling or thought and an action or behavior. So long as they do
not conflict with the achievement of healthy mourning, any number of
strategies may be useful in helping mourners exercise a full range of
thoughts and emotions and distinguish them from behavior. It may be
particularly helpful to share with the mourner Lifton's (1979) conceptualization of anger as a way of asserting vitality. In this view, anger and
the desire to attack one's victimizer serve as an alternative to living in the
realm of inner deadness caused by the victimization. Acknowledgment
of this notion empowers the mourner and permits her to experience her
reactions.

Work through the mourner's individual resistances. There may be
myriad idiosyncratic reasons why the mourner resists dealing with anger.
For instance, it is not unusual for the mourner to fear that his anger means
there was nothing good about the relationship or to be reluctant to relinquish anger because it is a connection to the deceased he does not want
to lose. Address these resistances as appropriate.

If the mourner resists dealing with anger because of its ego-dystonic
nature, work to find ways for him to accommodate the aggression in this
situation (e.g., support the desire to consider oneself a nonviolent person
but normalize aggressive fantasies toward a victimizer, pointing out that
such fantasies are not necessarily a generalized, permanent aspect of the
personality but can remain specific to an individual person and situation).

When extreme idealization appears to be covering anger of any sort,
allow the mourner to maintain the idealization until it appears fully
expressed and has had sufficient opportunity to be worked through. If
idealization persists, at an appropriate point inquiry may be directed
toward negative aspects of the relationship (e.g., "You have told me about
so many wonderful aspects of your father. I assume, because he was
human, that there were some that were not so wonderful. Let's talk a little
about those, too, because I want to see all facets of him, and I know that
no one really is ever perfect, despite what one may say."). Such inquiry
can also educate the mourner about the normalcy of negative attributes
and ease any concerns that he or the deceased will be judged unfavorably
if negative elements are discussed. If such an approach fails to reveal anything less than perfect about the deceased, more confrontational inquiries

can be posed (e.g., "I do not believe that any human being is perfect. It simply is not possible. That is why you have me wondering why you are attempting so diligently to portray your father to me as if he were perfect. Let's look at why that might be so important to you."). In this case and others like it, a power struggle with the mourner about the deceased's perfection will not be profitable; it will be much more productive to understand and work through defenses and resistances first.

Help the mourner identify and understand the true sources and causes of anger. The mourner will need to recognize that different sources and causes of anger can coexist (e.g., anger at the deceased may be present along with anger at the type of death) and that different emotions may be camouflaged by anger (e.g., anxiety, depression, dependency). Problem-solve and address each source or cause where possible (e.g., anger resulting from a feeling of lack of control after the accidental death of a loved one might be minimized by pressing for an investigation into the incident). If anger covers up important issues, recognize that it serves as the mourner's protection from dealing with deeper concerns and gently help her to admit to and address these underlying areas. Stripping away the defense of anger prematurely will only traumatize the mourner and cause her to engage other defenses.

In situations where a strong need exists to understand the reasons for the anger, help the mourner identify the most probable causes and make the most appropriate attributions. Although some behavioral self-blame (i.e., blaming one's behavior, not oneself) appears adaptive at times in restoring a sense of order in the world (Janoff-Bulman, 1985), discourage beliefs that will only make things worse for the mourner.

Help the mourner process the anger. The mourner must acknowledge the existence of anger and feel, identify, label, differentiate into component parts, trace, give some form of expression to, and work through all of the emotions that may be hidden under the facade of anger (e.g., grief, anxiety, frustration, impotence, sadness, depression). Evocative techniques, both verbal and nonverbal, will be especially useful. After processing the anger, ask the mourner to respond both philosophically and practically to the questions, What do you want to do with your anger? What do you need to do with it? and, What can you allow yourself to do with it?

Give the mourner permission to ventilate and channel aggressive feelings in appropriate ways. Bottling up anger prevents it from being properly released, diffused, sublimated, extinguished, or contained. In addition, it interferes with cognitive and emotional processing. Encourage the mourner to make anger constructive by taking the position that anger is energy and can be put to work for the mourner. Help him see that, because he already has been through so much, he needs to discover how anger can be expressed in ways that will not add to his distress. Support identification of the most meaningful ways to channel anger and frustration (e.g., working for stiffer drunk driving legislation after an alcohol-related crash or pressing a civil suit when criminal charges are not filed after the collapse of a building). Conversely, help the mourner set limits on acting out aggressive feelings (e.g., acknowledge anger at the criminal justice system after a perpetrator is released but confront and put limits on the mourner's attempts to seek revenge).

Address the mourner's concerns that expressions of anger will potentiate another survivor's anger or cause the entire family or social group to erupt (i.e., the multiplier effect; Rando, 1984). Help reduce anger to avoid inappropriate displacement or an explosion because of a lack of outlets; encourage negotiation and compromise regarding conflicting needs of family members.

Finally, take care that the mourner not turn anger back upon himself in the absence of any other target. This can cause depression and other psychosocial and physical consequences. In mourners whose experiences with the deceased have led to the development of any type of victimization sequelae, counter the process of perpetuating self-victimization.

Identify and enable the mourner to work through the "R" processes of mourning compromised by the anger.   Anger can compromise a number of the "R" processes and thereby cause complicated mourning. The role of the caregiver is to ascertain in which ways anger—in any one or more of its myriad manifestations and functions—interferes with the successful completion of the "R" processes; address it as a defense, resistance, or impediment; and work to promote healthy completion of the specific process(es) that have been compromised.

Provide vehicles for resolving unfinished business.   If a significant amount of anger stems from unfinished business, put current issues on hold and work through the unfinished business first in order to decrease the potential for complicated mourning or acting out. Useful techniques for expressing current emotion and for completing unfinished business include, among others, therapeutic bereavement rituals (see chapter 7), Gestalt exercises (e.g., role-playing, the empty chair technique), writing, art, and psychodrama. Suggest physical as well as verbal and intellectual outlets for discharging aggression (e.g., exercise or pounding a pillow).

Help the mourner minimize secondary victimization.   After some types of deaths, anger may result from secondary victimization (e.g., exploitation by the media after a murder or suicide). Providing information about how to avoid such secondary victimization can help the mourner cope.

AMBIVALENCE

Overview

Even though ambivalence is an inherent part of all relationships, it often is difficult for mourners to be comfortable with the human reality of the simultaneous existence and impact of both negative and positive feelings or attitudes. In ambivalence, anger invariably coexists with another, more positive feeling to create contradictory cognitions, emotions, attitudes, or behaviors. One therefore cannot address ambivalence without inherently dealing with anger or one of its derivatives (e.g., contention, hostility, annoyance, frustration, intolerance). As used in regard to mourning, the term *ambivalence,* while acknowledging both positive and negative components, focuses attention on the negative aspect and/or the conflict experienced by the mourner's having opposing thoughts, feelings, attitudes, or behaviors.

In particular, five main problems complicate mourning when ambivalence is present. First, mourners are often reluctant to acknowledge that negative emotions—particularly anger—play a part in a relationship. Difficulty dealing with anger will therefore translate into difficulty dealing with ambivalence. Prohibitions against and misinformation about negative feelings thus can compromise the individual's ability to develop a realistic picture of the deceased and the relationship. Just as important, failure to incorporate less than positive feelings into the relationship with the deceased results by definition in denial, repression, or suppression of some aspects of mourning. This leaves the mourner tied in an unhealthy way to the deceased in those areas not processed.

Second, when it comes to emotional issues, human beings tend to think discretely, in a dichotomous "either-or" fashion that belies the complexity of human relationships. For this reason, people tend to have problems handling the simultaneous experience of two opposing emotions, especially when they erroneously assume that the experience of one precludes the existence of the other (e.g., if one is angry one cannot love a person and vice versa). Additional stress is created in the form of intrapsychic conflict between two diametrically opposed feelings, each exerting pressure on the mourner to behave in a contradictory fashion or causing overfocus on one to the detriment of the other. Often this type of conflict causes confusion, immobilization, or attempts to suppress one or both sets of feelings. It also can result in a skewed image of the deceased and the relationship.

Third, there is a general failure to appreciate that negative feelings bond people together no less than positive ones. Sometimes individuals erroneously believe that because there is hostility in a relationship there is no connection. Yet, in some cases, hostility actually *is* the bond. In most instances, individuals fail to recognize that ambivalence implies that an attachment is present, however insecure it may be.

Fourth, after a death the recognition of the hostility within the ambivalence prompts guilt, which the mourner tries to evade by avoiding recollecting and reexperiencing the deceased and the relationship (i.e., the third "R" process). Some sources of this guilt may be the mourner's recollection of rage and murderous wishes toward the deceased; fear that wishes for the death of the deceased have come true and the mourner is responsible and may be punished for the death; or relief at termination of the relationship, satisfaction that her own death was not demanded, or delight in survival over the deceased.

Fifth, intense ambivalence may complicate mourning by leaving the mourner not knowing the world or unable to adjust to it adaptively without the negative experience(s) that may have characterized it previously. This can further cause the mourner to be chronically angry, mistrustful, alienated, or in some other way adversely affected. In turn, these reactions impede appropriate reinvestment in others, contaminate the new relationship with the deceased such that it constitutes an unhealthy recapitulation of the old abusive relationship and compromises readjustment and reinvestment, and leave the mourner without the opportunity to rectify the relationship or finish unfinished business. All of these factors can lead to a reluctance to continue the mourning processes.

The following discussion focuses on the general and specific problems posed by ambivalence in mourning. The special issue of complicated mourning in those who have been victimized exemplifies the difficulties encountered when an individual confronts the death of a highly ambivalently loved other. In interpreting the suggestions presented here, the caregiver must recognize that degrees of attachment as well as conflict exist. When little or no attachment is present, the death will call for little if any mourning, even if the relationship has been characterized by much conflict. For instance, the death of a spouse who had no connection to the mourner outside of sharing a house may require little mourning, even if what little relationship did exist was quite ambivalent. Certainly, not all conflicted relationships sustain a similar degree of anger or ambivalence. Similarly, not all victimized persons have the same type of relationship with their abusers. Varying degrees of ambivalence and strength of attachment bond can be expected; these will combine with other variables to characterize each mourning experience.

Treatment Implications

The caregiver's basic treatment strategy for ambivalence involves (a) educating the mourner about ambivalence in relationships in general and in mourning specifically, (b) stimulating and promoting a full range of affects, (c) providing opportunities for appropriate expression and channeling of emotions, and (d) working through and integrating feelings and memories of the deceased and the relationship to achieve a realistic composite image.

The caregiver does so in order to help the mourner complete the last three "R" processes: relinquish the old attachments to the deceased and the old assumptive world, readjust to move adaptively into the new world without forgetting the old, and ultimately reinvest in the new world. Insofar as anger is an inherent component of ambivalence, treatment recommendations discussed for anger must be taken along with those presented here.

Evocative techniques are especially useful in provoking affect. These may be verbal or nonverbal, structured or unstructured. The caregiver will need to employ strategies similar to those discussed under interventions proposed for the "R" processes of reacting to the separation and recollecting and reexperiencing the deceased and the relationship (see chapter 9). In addition, techniques advocated by Gauthier and Marshall (1977), Gauthier and Pye (1979), Mawson et al. (1981), Melges and DeMaso (1980), Ramsay (1979), Volkan (1985), and the Gestaltists (e.g., Smith, 1985b) also will be useful.

In situations where ambivalence is extreme, the caregiver will have to process with the mourner the various reasons for conflict, normalize such emotions when they are appropriate, and work them through as much as possible in order to defuse their intensity and the bonds they serve to perpetuate. Sometimes guilt associated with aggressive feelings or thoughts is not ameliorated through the normalization process; the provision of information about ambivalence, reasons for guilt, or experiences and consequences of victimization; or the opportunity for ventilation in the presence of a nonjudgmental person. In this case, the caregiver must incorporate specific interventions for guilt, as discussed later in this chapter.

Raphael (1978) has demonstrated in research with widows how those mourning conflicted relationships require specific types of support to deal with their ambivalence and has shown that, when these needs are unmet, the risk of complicated mourning increases. In Raphael's study, such support included (a) permission and encouragement to talk about their guilt, (b) help in talking about problems in their relationships or the deceased's bad points, (c) help from supporters who knew how the widows were feeling, (d) help in releasing their feelings, and (e) reassurance about their own capacities to cope and good points. Each of these areas points toward a specific target of intervention. Insofar as these areas are relevant to other mourners, the caregiver should ensure that they are addressed either in treatment or by the support system. In addition, it is important to stress that, along with processing negative feelings and memories, the widows in Raphael's study required empathy and reassurance about their own good points. This underscores the need for the caregiver to bear in mind that aggressive feelings and thoughts, poorly tolerated by most individuals in our society, indicate to the mourner that she is "bad." Failure to appreciate and respond to this type of perception and to social injunctions against anger, and to provide both sufficient information about the normalcy of ambivalence and support for dealing with it, can interrupt the treatment process.

In general, Raphael (1983) suggests encouraging grief tainted with significant ambivalence by examining the circumstances of the death, the lost relationship, and the support available to help resolve ambivalence; exploring the origins of the ambivalence in the relationship and its psychodynamic links; dealing with the death wish toward the deceased; and helping the mourner come to terms with guilt. Chapter 7 offers a more detailed application of Raphael's focal psychotherapy for mourning conflicted relationships.

Ambivalence in Mourning a Conflicted Relationship Following Chronic Victimization

A major area of complicated mourning concerns those who mourn the death of a loved one with whom they have had a markedly conflicted relationship. Such relationships have been identified as the primary cause of conflicted mourning (Parkes & Weiss, 1983) and distorted mourning of the extremely guilty type, as well as a determinant of inhibited mourning (Raphael, 1983). However, even if a full-blown complicated mourning syndrome is not the result, conflicted relationships can be costly to any mourner. The complexity of feelings, intensity of guilt and remorse, and difficulty acknowledging and accepting feelings and behaviors the mourner would prefer to disown create problems in the emotional acceptance and ultimate accommodation of the death (Parkes & Weiss, 1983).

This section therefore addresses problematic issues arising when an individual is called upon to mourn the death of a loved one with whom he has had a markedly conflicted and ambivalent relationship as a consequence of some form of victimization. Parental abuse of a child is discussed as a preeminent example of victimization. Inasmuch as the dynamics of such a relationship exist in less intense form in other types of conflicted relationships, the caregiver may extrapolate to meet other mourners' needs.

Sources of conflict from victimization

It must be pointed out that nearly all of the literature discussing ambivalence in conflicted relationships concerns the marital relationship. This is no doubt the case because researchers have had better access to widows than to other bereaved individuals. When other examples are given, they tend to pertain to parent-child relationships. Still, their number is small, leaving the reader with the incorrect impression that individuals with complicated mourning because of conflicted premorbid relationships tend to be bereaved spouses. My own clinical observation suggests that an increasing number of individuals coming to treatment have had conflicted premorbid relationships with individuals other than spouses.

Complicated mourning appears not uncommon in those who have been physically, sexually, or psychologically abused and victimized by a parent or another adult responsible for giving care (e.g., guardian, relative, friend, authority figure). Other forms of victimization also give rise to psychological damage that will later influence mourning. These include, among others, chemical dependency and substance abuse, dysfunctional family relationships, neglect, mental or physical illness, adverse socioeconomic conditions, and broken relationships. Factors influencing the ambivalence created by the victimization include the specifics of the victimization and the characteristics of the victim and the perpetrator. If there is a non-offending parent or caretaker who did not intervene or believe the child when informed, the relationship with that individual is most probably ambivalent as well and can be expected to be problematic when mourning is required.

Before proceeding, it is important to note that victimization is not exclusive to children who grow up with abusive parents or other adult figures, although more severe consequences result when abuse is at the hands of such individuals. Victimization also takes place under such conditions as spouse abuse, imprisonment, war, captivity, institutionalization, political torture, and terrorism. The interpersonal victimization discussed here for both adults and children involves prolonged periods of involuntary dependency and helplessness. Events acutely victimizing the individual and forcing briefer periods of dependency and/or helplessness include, among others, rape, criminal assault, accident, disaster, hostage taking, disability, and sudden unemployment. According to *Webster's Ninth New Collegiate Dictionary*, a victim is "one that is acted on and usually adversely affected by a force or agent." According to Janoff-Bulman (1985) the suffering of the victim generally is the result of physical and/or psychological loss, and his psychological distress is due largely to the shattering of three basic assumptions: the belief in personal invulnerability, the perception of the world as meaningful, and the view of the self as positive. For more in-depth material on victimization and its treatment, the reader is referred to Bard and Sangrey (1986), Courtois (1988), Danieli (1988), Figley (1985b, 1986), Figley and McCubbin (1983), Herman (1981), Horowitz (1986a), Hunter (1983), Janoff-Bulman (1985), Janoff-Bulman and Frieze (1983), Kluft (1990), Krystal (1968), Lifton (1979), McCann and Pearlman (1990a), Ochberg (1988a), Putnam (1989), Raphael (1986), Segal (1986), Spitzer (1990), Tait and Silver (1989), Taylor (1983), Terr (1979), Ulman and Brothers (1988), VandenBos and Bryant (1987), van der Kolk (1984, 1987b), and Wilson (1989).

Victimization of a child: An example

Any type of abuse or neglect experienced by a child victimizes that child in some fashion and affects attachment and other areas of development to varying degrees. Chronic victimization also creates significant conflict in the relationship with the abuser, whether or not accompanied by disclosure, and usually is associated with development of disturbances in mental and physical health or development of victimization symptoms (e.g., identity confusion, substance abuse, poor self-esteem, repetition of victim role in subsequent relationships), a particular mental disorder or constellation of personality traits (e.g., post-traumatic stress disorder, borderline personality diagnosis, ACOA personality), and many other sequelae. Typically, there is anger and ambivalence, whether manifest or latent. The ambivalence is exacerbated in many cases by self-blame and the inappropriate idealization of the perpetrator.

Chronic victimization and endurance of extreme stress may result in longstanding sequelae with manifestations similar to those evident in personality disorder. These sequelae differ in their intractability and complicate the "R" processes of mourning that must be undertaken to help ameliorate them. According to Spitzer (1990), symptomatology after extreme stress may include alterations in the following areas.

1. Affect or impulse regulation (e.g., chronic and pervasive depressed mood or sense of emptiness or deadness, physically self-destructive acts, chronic suicidal preoccupation, overinhibition or excessive expression of anger and/or sexual drive, excessive risk taking associated with persistent feelings of invulnerability)

2. Attention or consciousness (e.g., transient dissociative episodes, depersonalization or derealization, amnesia for traumatic events, persistent preoccupation with the victimization experience)

3. Self-perception (e.g., a generalized sense of being ineffective in dealing with one's environment, not limited to the traumatic experience; the belief that one has been permanently damaged by the stress; exaggerated sense of guilt or responsibility for the trauma; persistent shame, embarrassment, or humiliation regarding others' knowledge of the traumatic experience; the feeling that nobody else can understand the traumatic experience; inappropriate minimizing of injuries)

4. Perception of the perpetrator (e.g., adopting the distorted beliefs of the perpetrator with regard to interpersonal behavior, inappropriate idealization of the perpetrator or paradoxical gratitude, persistent preoccupation with hurting or humiliating the perpetrator)

5. Relations with others (e.g., inability to trust or be intimate with others, increased vulnerability to being revictimized by a different perpetrator or traumatic event, victimizing others in the same way one was victimized)

6. Systems of meaning (e.g., despair and hopelessness about the future, loss of previously sustaining beliefs without a replacement)

When the abuser dies, the mourner can become revictimized by the death if she fails to work through the mourning properly to become free of the bonds, concomitants, and sequelae of the abusive relationship. This is the height of injustice: The mourner, who already has suffered at the hands of the deceased, suffers additionally from the consequences of complicated mourning. It is extremely difficult to mourn someone who has victimized one. Yet it is absolutely imperative to do so in order to free oneself from the ties of the relationship and, as much as possible, the unhealthy sense of self, assumptions, beliefs, behaviors, feelings, and so forth that the relationship has nurtured.

Victimization from the consequences of complicated mourning after the death of the abuser may come not only from the mourner's refusal to mourn fully—although that is quite common—but also from reactions to the previous abuse. For example, Putnam (1989) reports on a handful of cases in which he observed what initially appeared to be a pathological grief reaction following the death of the primary abusive parent. In each of the four cases, the individual was an established and successful adult in whom a multiple personality disorder (MPD) became apparent during the precipitous decline in functioning following the death of the parent. It appeared that the current stress (i.e., the death of the abuser) activated previously dissociated affects and memories associated with the abuse, which in turn prompted MPD reactions.

Intervening with the conflicted mourner

Individuals having had a conflicted and victimizing premorbid relationship with a loved one may present with symptoms along a continuum of response. At one extreme are mourners who focus only on positive aspects of the deceased and relationship. They may gloss over negative aspects, sometimes even to the point of idealizing the deceased. Their unwillingness to admit that there might be any less than positive feelings is a clue to the strength of their need to avoid confronting the reality of the abuse and their feelings around it. Interventions for this group will be similar to those delineated for the second and third "R" processes of mourning (i.e., react to the separation and recollect and reexperience the deceased and the relationship; see chapter 9).

At the other extreme are mourners who overfocus on negative aspects of the deceased and the relationship. Typically, they come to treatment not for assistance in mourning but for problems such as depression, anxiety, self-defeating relationships, or one of the many sequelae known to develop from a long-term abusive relationship. Many times, these individuals deny the need for mourning. Very simply, they do not think they have anything to mourn. They point out their relief at being free of the con-flicted relationship, asserting that it was totally negative and that there is nothing to be sad about. They perceive review of the relationship as useless and, out of anger, may refuse even to dignify the death of the abuser by "wasting any time or tears." Sometimes, if they do become aware that they miss the deceased in some way or that there had been times in the rela-tionship that were not so negative, their resulting feelings of hypocrisy can cause them to repudiate further the need to mourn.

Most mourners fall somewhere between these two extremes. Care-givers must comprehend that mourners who exhibit responses more typical of those who assert that there is nothing to mourn do so because of the high amount of ambivalence that had existed in the relationship, which often was accompanied by a wish for the death of the person. All mourners, but especially those who deny the need to mourn, must be edu-cated about the unique issues inherent in mourning an extremely con-flicted relationship.

1. Mourning the death of an abusive individual does not invalidate the abuse, lessen the culpability of the perpetrator or victimization of the mourner, or mean the mourner wishes the deceased were alive to resume the relationship.

2. Negative ties can bind just as strongly as positive ones, with the degree of bonding being determined by the strength of attach-ment, not its characteristics. Characteristics of the bond determine only the quality of the attachment.

3. Extremely negative ties—even those that predominate in number and intensity—can coexist with some positive ties (e.g., from a time prior to abuse, from a time when abuse was not occurring, from an idealization of the abuser).

4. All ties, whether positive or negative, must be relinquished. This demands mourning.

5. Contrary to popular assumption, mourning negative ties does not mean that the mourner is sad that the deceased has died or experi-ences unwanted deprivation. There is nothing in the definition or requirements of mourning that mandates sadness over the loss. In reality, mourning only means that whatever ties existed are worked through in order for the mourner to be free from them and that the mourner adapts suitably to their absence. Not to free oneself is a form of continued victimization.

6. Much of the mourning that must take place after the death of an abuser focuses on mourning for what that abuser has taken away from the mourner (e.g., innocence, autonomy, a happy childhood, trust).

7. The six "R" processes of mourning illustrate that much alteration must be done in the assumptive world, the self, and one's behaviors in the world after the death. Thus, the mourner should not focus exclusively on the deceased. He must be helped to see that the major purpose of mourning is to free himself, and, only if appropriate, to express sadness and other emotions over the loss.

8. The consequences of victimization frequently leave post-traumatic stress sequelae. Therefore, treatment of complicated mourning associated with the death of a victimizer typically entails therapeutic strategies and techniques delineated in chapter 12 as helpful in intervention with traumatic losses.

The mourner is at high risk for complications in the third "R" process of mourning (i.e., recollect and reexperience the deceased and the relationship). For this reason, he must be made comfortable with the notion of ambivalence in order that those aspects of the deceased and the relationship that were positive (if he is overly focused on the negative) or negative (if he is overly focused on the positive) can be mourned appropriately. All mourning of victimizing relationships inherently involves dealing with both anger and ambivalence; therefore, interventions delineated previously for anger are necessary.

Sometimes mourners who overfocus on the negative fear feeling anything positive for the deceased abuser. Many times this posture evaporates as the mourner learns that he does not have to abandon his anger merely because there is a positive memory or feeling. Whatever his feelings, he must be helped to understand the need for reviewing and feeling all of his emotions and memories pertaining to the deceased. No less than any other mourner, he must experience all of the "R" processes of mourning.

The mourner also must be helped to realize that he must relearn the world and reshape his image of himself without continuing to incorporate abuse and victimized ways of thinking, feeling, and behaving, and that he must learn how to have healthy and appropriately trusting relationships with others. Both of these goals are enabled via mourning.

In some cases, the caregiver will need to legitimize the mourner's desire not to think about the relationship with the abuser while still encouraging him and helping him work through resistances to doing so. The mourner can be told that if he wants to bury the unpleasant memories, that is fine—however, he needs to bury them dead (i.e., worked through), not alive. Again, in many cases, therapeutic strategies outlined for intervention with traumatized mourners are applicable here.

In brief, the ultimate goal in treating an individual who has been victimized is to address both the victimization and complicated mourning. With regard to victimization, the caregiver must help the mourner integrate memories, thoughts, images, feelings, behaviors, and sometimes physiological responses concerning the trauma—a process inherently involving mourning. The caregiver must also help the mourner incorporate these aspects into the totality of his life, developing an appropriate perspective on what happened and reconnecting in a healthy way with others and with newly created meaning in life. This will entail blending the treatment for complicated mourning with that suggested for victimization and post-traumatic stress. The resources on victimization noted earlier in this chapter provide specific information on doing so.

GUILT

Overview

Intricately interwoven with anger and ambivalence is guilt. The existence of the former two often gives rise to the latter. Problematic enough in uncomplicated mourning, guilt can take on major destructive dimensions in complicated mourning. It is a primary characteristic in the complicated mourning syndromes of conflicted mourning (Parkes & Weiss, 1983) and distorted mourning of the extremely guilty type (Raphael, 1983). In addition, because guilt suppresses certain necessary aspects of mourning, it may be a primary determinant of the absent, delayed, and inhibited mourning syndromes.

As defined here, *guilt* is the feeling of culpability deriving from perceived offenses or a sense of inadequacy. Typically, it is accompanied by regret, remorse, negative self-evaluation, and feelings that one should atone. A certain amount of guilt is healthy and promotes appropriate behavior by producing anxiety when the conscience and/or ego ideal has been violated; a complete absence of the ability to feel guilt (e.g., as occurs in the antisocial personality) is pathological. The person who cannot feel guilt lacks the internal mechanism that governs behavior in order to conform to social or personal standards. Some individuals are, on the other hand, predisposed to abnormally high amounts of guilt. Among other characteristics, these persons tend to exhibit an overly strict and rigid conscience, poor self-esteem, high anxiety, depression, or obsessive compulsiveness.

According to Opp and Samson (1987), guilt has two latent functions besides its function as a behavior regulator. One is to defend against helplessness, and the other is to serve as self-punishment and a tool for retribution. They argue that, as a consequence for one's "bad behavior," guilt obviates the feeling of being socially disenfranchised and allows the individual to continue to be part of society. In addition, guilt keeps the individual from forgetting an event and thus keeps the event from becoming dishonored or meaningless. This continued sense of meaning is crucial after events in which others have died while the mourner survives. Thus, the powerful effects of guilt in defending against helplessness, fulfilling the need for self-punishment, and enhancing meaning may explain the guilty person's resistance to therapeutic intervention. Opp and Samson also present an interesting taxonomy of guilt and offer treatment suggestions based on it. They identify five types of guilt: survivor guilt, demonic guilt, moral/spiritual guilt, betraying/abandoning guilt, and superman guilt. Although their suggestions pertain to combat veterans, caregivers will find the bulk of the information helpful for a more general group of mourners experiencing complications.

Guilt and shame are related but often confused conceptually. Although the theoretical differences between guilt and shame are quite important, they extend beyond the scope of this discussion. Very briefly, in guilt the individual perceives her *behavior* as bad, whereas in shame the individual perceives *herself* as bad. In guilt, one fears punishment; in shame, one fears abandonment by loved ones. Shame develops earlier than guilt and appears to be less correctable or forgivable (Whitfield, 1987). Both responses can be stimulated by the loss of a loved one and ensuing mourning. Guilt is quite common in mourning; shame is not as frequent. Certainly, there are developmental experiences, personality characteristics, and circumstances (e.g., death of a child, suicide, helplessness during trauma) that can increase the mourner's propensity to experience shame. These topics are discussed elsewhere in the book. The rest of the present discussion focuses on the more common element of guilt. For further information on the conceptual and therapeutic distinctions between guilt and shame, see Bradshaw (1988b), E. Erikson (1963), Kaufman (1980), Lewis (1971), Madow (1988), Piers and Singer (1953), and Whitfield (1987).

Although some elements of guilt are typically present in each mourner's bereavement experience, certain circumstances give rise to particularly intense and complex guilt. In addition to its occurrence among individuals who tend to be guilt-prone and unrealistically assume responsibility for events occurring to others, circumstances that generate high guilt are associated with specific characteristics of the loss, including the loss of an ambivalent or extremely conflicted relationship, a death in which the mourner truly holds some degree of responsibility, the mourner's perception that she could have prevented the death but failed to do so, and helplessness during the trauma that took a loved one's life. Guilt is also associated with distinct types of death, including suicide, death after a long-term illness, death where the mourner also might have or should have died, death of a child, and sudden, unexpected death. (Chapters 11 through 13 provide discussion of a number of these types of death.)

Sources of guilt

Four main sources are pertinent in the development of a sense of guilt: evolution, religion, law, and the psychological and emotional development of the child (Madow, 1988). However, clinically, guilt may derive from any one or combination of six primary occurrences: (a) falling short of one's self-image, (b) violation of a conscious or unconscious personal standard, (c) ambivalence, (d) imperfection in relationships, (e) surviving when others have died, and (f) feeling one contributed in some way to the death. Although technically these all could be subsumed under the second occurrence, violation of a personal standard, differentiating them here will help illuminate their clinical manifestations.

Falling short of one's self-image.   Whenever a person falls short of his own self-image, the discrepancy usually causes him to feel guilt and sometimes shame. In guilt, the self-image serves as a standard against which the person's feelings, thoughts, and behaviors are measured. For example, the individual who considers himself strong and in control will feel guilty when he perceives himself to be acting weak and out of control.

Violation of a personal standard.   The healthy individual also feels guilt when he perceives that a conscious or unconscious personal standard has been violated. There is a judgment of wrongdoing and a consequent sense of badness or lowering of self-esteem, with a fear or expectation of punishment and typically a feeling that one should make retribution. Many of these standards have been incorporated into the conscience. As Madow (1988) writes, "True guilt feelings come from the internal disapproval of a wish or act measured against our own conscience" (p. 36).

A major difficulty stems from the fact that many individuals hold essentially unrealistic and inappropriate standards for themselves and feel guilty whenever they fail to live up to them. Because these standards and the expectations based upon them are often unreasonable, the individual may be "set up" to experience guilt. If, for example, the person believes that he must never be angry at someone he loves (an unrealistic standard), he inevitably will have to confront guilt after a loved one's death because some dimension of ambivalence exists in all relationships and memories of it typically surface after a death. This is one of the reasons bereaved parents sustain such intense guilt: They maintain for themselves in the parental role the most inappropriate and unrealistic standards. When the child dies, these standards, along with the parental role, are viciously violated. The subsequent guilt is enormous, although often totally unwarranted. (See chapter 13 for more on the topic of parental loss of a child.)

Ambivalence.   Given that many, if not most, individuals have problems tolerating negative feelings toward one they love and frequently believe it is wrong to have such feelings to begin with, ambivalence tends to lead to guilt. In mourning—especially in the early period after the death when the mourner idealizes the deceased and the relationship and overfocuses on his own negative contributions—the ability to view ambivalence as normal in the relationship is especially compromised. Guilt is often experienced at this point. Raphael (1980b) observes that when there has been overt hostility in the premorbid relationship with the deceased, the mourner is likely to express guilt more readily. When hostility has been previously repressed or denied, the mourner may have more difficulty recognizing the existence and emotional meaning of guilt.

Imperfection in relationships. Another reason for guilt is that our relationships, as ourselves, are imperfect. Consequently, an individual will always be able to point to omissions, commissions, "if onlys," and "should haves" that transpired in the relationship. No matter how much one loved another person or how consistently loving or good one was, after a death it is normal to remember the time one was not as good, as patient, as loving, or as what have you as one could have been. It is a cruel trick of human nature that, in the early phases of mourning, in contrast to the way the deceased is remembered, individuals tend to recall everything negative on their part in the relationship and fail to remember their more positive contributions. This lack of balance, along with the recognition of what was or was not done, contributes to guilt.

Surviving when others have died. Survival guilt (Lifton, 1976) is not uncommon in bereaved parents, after an incident causing multiple deaths, or subsequent to the deaths of those to whom the mourner felt especially connected. It is also possible after the deaths of siblings because of the dynamics of this particular relationship. Quite frequently, it is observed in situations in which the survivor could have died but did not, whereas others did lose their lives (e.g., disasters or war). Issues of perceived debts owed to the dead arise here and complicate mourning. (See chapter 12 for more on guilt associated with traumatic circumstances.)

Feeling one contributed to the death. Guilt may be associated with what one did (e.g., driving the car in a fatal accident, being supportive of the job at which the loved one was murdered) or did not do (e.g., failing to force the loved one to go to the doctor earlier or break up the relationship with the person whose rejection ultimately drove the loved one to suicide). Whenever a death is perceived as having been preventable but was not prevented, reactions and complications of the mourning processes tend to be exacerbated.

Other specific sources of guilt in mourning include having postponed occasions for enjoyment with the deceased out of selfishness or feeling the missed occasion could be made up later; feeling discomfort over the emotions or behaviors of grief and mourning (e.g., anger or crying) if these emotions or behaviors are perceived as ego-dystonic; experiencing relief after a death following a long-term illness or at the end of a conflicted relationship; experiencing thoughts, feelings, and behaviors that are a natural outgrowth of living with a dying person (Rando, 1984, 1986e); engaging in magical thinking (believing that one's aggressive thoughts, wishes, or impulses killed the deceased); and experiencing pleasure that someone else died and not oneself. These sources are basically variations on the main sources already delineated.

Types of guilt

Two basic types of guilt exist: illegitimate (or neurotic) guilt and legitimate (or appropriate) guilt. *Illegitimate guilt* comes from inappropriate self-condemnation associated with vulnerabilities derived from parental admonitions during childhood (Lifton, 1979) or from the sources of guilt cited previously. It is out of proportion to the event (Rando, 1984). *Legitimate guilt* arises from actual wrongdoing and thus is appropriate to the situation. It occurs when a direct cause and effect relationship exists between what a person did or failed to do and serious wrong or harm.

In addition, Lifton (1979) discriminates between static and animating guilt. This differentiation is useful in pointing up directions for intervention. *Static guilt* refers to guilt resulting in a deadening immobilization of the self. It has two forms. The first, self-lacerating guilt, is a sustained self-condemnation preventing actual knowledge of the guilt and resulting in a continual "killing" of the self. This type is similar to that seen in Parkes and Weiss's (1983) conflicted mourning or Raphael's (1983) distorted mourning of the extremely guilty type. The second, numbed guilt, is characterized by a series of maneuvers designed to avoid the experience of the guilt, such as a "freezing" of the self as anesthesia against experience in general. Both of these forms of static guilt are important to Lifton's concept of neurosis.

In contrast to these two types of static guilt is *animating guilt,* in which one derives from the imagery of self-condemnation the energy to move toward renewal and change. Animating guilt involves a revitalization that draws upon past experience for the capacity to feel uneasy in the face of wrong but does not reflect the immobilization found in static forms of guilt. Caregivers may choose to facilitate such a response in their work with mourners whose guilt does not abate with mere discussion. Lifton (1979) exemplifies animating guilt in Vietnam veterans:

> This kind of guilt is the anxiety of responsibility, as it is
> characterized by a continuous transformation of self-condem-
> nation into the feeling that one must, should, and can act
> against the wrong and toward an alternative. For certain
> Vietnam veterans, an animating relationship to guilt meant
> transforming mere self-condemnation over what one did in
> Vietnam into (still self-critical) explorations of why one acted
> that way (including not only one's past psychological tendencies

but the nature of the society that created these tendencies and pursued the war itself). This also resulted in various kinds of action against the war and toward social change. An animating relationship to guilt thus requires imagery of possibility beyond the guilt itself, imagery that is no less social than individual. (p. 139)

There is another genre of guilt that must be appreciated and respected. For lack of a better term, I call it *functional guilt*. Many times guilt serves a crucial protective function—for instance, helping the mourner defend against having been helpless in a disaster situation, meting out self-punishment, or sustaining the meaning of an event. Guilt is the price paid to avoid contending with something perceived as even more threatening. If the guilt is functional, the caregiver must respond differently than if it does not serve a therapeutic purpose. To take guilt away without understanding its underlying function can do serious harm to the mourner. The caregiver must not strip the mourner of guilt until he or she knows what is being defended against and how to establish the situation therapeutically so that the real issue can be gently worked through. This is especially necessary when the mourner has experienced or lost a loved one to traumatic circumstances in which he was helpless himself or unable to intervene on behalf of the loved one.

Problems posed by guilt

Five main problems in mourning are posed by guilt. Each can turn uncomplicated into complicated mourning. First, out of concern for what she may discover that may make her feel guilty, the mourner may inhibit the second and third "R" processes of mourning (i.e., react to the separation; recollect and reexperience the deceased and the relationship). This suppression can contribute to absent, delayed, or inhibited mourning syndromes. In brief, the mourner is unable to undertake those aspects of mourning that would confront her with the thoughts, feelings, or actions she now wants to avoid in order to escape feeling guilty and suffering remorse. When the individual only processes the positive aspects, mourning becomes skewed and incomplete.

Second, unresolved guilt can cause the mourner to sabotage the "R" processes of mourning, often, although not exclusively, the fifth and sixth "R" processes (i.e., readjust to move adaptively into the new world without forgetting the old; reinvest). The unfinished nature of the guilt interferes with the mourner's ability to grant herself permission to make necessary adaptations and instead keeps the mourner bound to the past.

Third, problems arise when the mourner uses guilt as a form of connection to the deceased. Chronic and extreme guilt may represent a mechanism for keeping the deceased alive. Thus, the mourner may be unwilling to relinquish guilt because of the purpose it serves. Especially after the loss of a conflicted relationship, about which the mourner was highly ambivalent, guilt may become a way of appeasing the deceased (Raphael, 1983) and perpetuating abuse that occurred within the relationship.

Fourth, difficulties arise when guilt is employed as a specific resistance to what is required by the "R" processes of mourning. For instance, extreme guilt after the death of a loved one with whom the mourner did not necessarily experience a conflicted relationship can reflect a redirected focus undertaken to avoid either the reality of the death or relinquishment of the deceased. In other situations, extreme guilt with suppression of other affects may reveal a belief that the death can be reversed or the notion that the guilt will earn something for the mourner: "'Perhaps if I decry my badness it will save me being punished further', or, '[perhaps] he will be given back', or '[perhaps] I can prevent it from happening again'" (Raphael, 1975, p. 178).

Fifth, in cases of functional guilt, the guilt masks other emotions or issues, and/or it meets specific needs that must be identified and worked through if mourning is to be successful. If these underlying concerns are not addressed, complications will persist. In situations where the mourner experiences functional guilt, there is often great ambivalence about relinquishing it because of the functions it serves.

In all cases, extreme guilt is dangerous because it may lead to punitive and self-destructive behaviors, including suicide, and may precipitate severe depression. Also, as noted by Raphael (1983), when guilt cannot be borne personally, it may be projected onto family members, and this can contribute to significant disruption.

Treatment Implications

As an emotion, guilt must be processed and worked through like all other emotions in mourning. For details on this, the reader is referred to chapter 9 for discussion of the "R" processes of mourning, specifically to interventions promoting the processes of reacting to the separation and to recollecting and reexperiencing the deceased and the relationship. In general, the caregiver must help the mourner discuss the guilty feelings and the behaviors, omissions, thoughts, attitudes, emotions, wishes, fantasies, or impulses that have generated them. In cases where guilt camouflages other feelings and issues, these must be gently addressed over time. The mourner must be helped to see the positives in the relationship and cautioned against overemphasizing the negatives. The mourner will need to alter any unrealistic standards or irrational beliefs that contribute to guilt, find constructive ways to expiate it, and forgive himself.

This process involves the caregiver's working to enable the mourner ultimately to accomplish the following goals.

1. Recognize and accept guilt feelings, which are often unconscious.

2. Adopt the proper perspective about ambivalence, human error and imperfection, and normalcy of guilt feelings after loss.

3. Process guilt by acknowledging the impact of the omissions, commissions, emotions, thoughts, attitudes, wishes, fantasies, and impulses giving rise to it; understand how and why these things occurred and work through their origins in the relationship; therapeutically address guilt feelings so that they do not inhibit or sabotage any of the "R" processes of mourning or mask any underlying issues; and feel and express remorse or other feelings that arise.

4. Share the guilt with another or others in a supportive relationship. When permitted by nonjudgmental persons, this very important process can diffuse and reduce guilt, normalize it, and help the mourner learn to live with it. Parkes and Weiss (1983) note that encouraging the guilty mourner to share feelings of self-reproach and the pain of grief decreases guilt by combining the functions of confession and ordeal. However, as observed by Raphael (1978), it may be difficult to receive support from others to address one's guilt. In such instances, the caregiver may intervene to connect the mourner with people or groups that will permit the address of guilt.

In helping the mourner cope with guilt, the caregiver will need to identify the sources of the guilt, its type, and the functions, if any, it serves, then problem-solve or work it through to the extent possible. For instance, if the mourner sustains unrealistic expectations about ambivalence or perfection in the relationship, the caregiver must provide normative and psychoeducational information to correct the misinformation, then work to obviate or redefine the guilt. If the mourner sustains the magical belief that his own aggressive wishes killed the loved one, the caregiver must work to dispute this notion. If the mourner adheres to guilt in order to maintain the illusion that by atonement the death can be undone, or if he uses guilt to serve as an unhealthy connection to the deceased, these resistances must be identified and worked through. If the mourner uses guilt as a means of honoring the memory of his fellow comrades in war, the caregiver will need to help him find a healthier way to keep their memory alive, after first gently working through the guilt as a functional mechanism.

The caregiver also must identify in what specific ways guilt affects the "R" processes of mourning and incorporate interventions to facilitate these along with interventions to work through guilt as a resistance. Problems especially, although not exclusively, tend to be found in the second and third "R" processes (i.e., react to the separation; recollect and reexperience the deceased and the relationship), where guilt often inhibits full processing of feelings and memories, and in the fifth and sixth "R" processes (i.e., readjust to move adaptively into the new world without forgetting the old; reinvest), where guilt can tend to sabotage the mourner's breaking from the past and reestablishing himself in terms of the new reality of the loved one's death. This is not to say that guilt is overlooked in favor of specific interventions to promote these processes, only that such interventions may have to be incorporated with or introduced shortly thereafter those designed to facilitate working through of guilt itself.

In cases where guilt serves the functional purpose of protecting the mourner from other feelings or issues or of meeting latent needs, the caregiver must work gently to enable the mourner to perceive the underlying concerns (e.g., that the mourner was powerless to save the loved one in the disaster and that guilt protects him from experiencing that feeling by making it seem that he had the power to act but just did not). Gradually, the mourner is allowed to discover the real issue as the guilt is examined and understood in terms of the purposes served. This process cannot be forced, nor the guilt taken away, because such action may overwhelm the mourner. The caregiver's goal is to enable this confrontation and therapeutically assist the mourner in addressing the central issue. Guilt must be handled as a defense or resistance (i.e., worked through, not smashed through).

To determine whether more rational beliefs are appropriate, the caregiver must help the mourner reality test the self-image and/or the standards, expectations, and elements of conscience against which he judges himself deficient. Doing so will help the mourner see whether the sources of guilt actually are inappropriate and unrealistic standards, as opposed to the mourner's wrongdoing, and whether more appropriate and realistic standards are required. The caregiver can help the mourner verbalize and evaluate the appropriateness of conscious or unconscious self-condemning statements in order to raise his awareness of what he is doing to himself. The mourner must examine the events in question rationally to determine if, given the amount of information available at the time, he did in fact have good intentions and act appropriately. He will have to be reminded at the same time that he is human and that human beings make mistakes, cannot predict the future, do not always have the control they might desire, and have ambivalent feelings.

Especially after a sudden, unexpected death, guilt may be heightened by the mourner's focus on the relationship at the moment of loss to the exclusion of the relationship as a whole. In this case, the caregiver should encourage in-depth ventilation and working through, along with exploration of deeper origins of ambivalence, if needed. Where persistent and extreme guilt serves as a vehicle for connection with the deceased, the mourner can be helped to embrace more appropriate connections within a healthy new relationship. As needed, the caregiver will need to integrate interventions appropriate to the circumstances or type of death giving rise to the guilt (e.g., death after a conflicted relationship or suicide, death of a child).

In order to complete the composite situation realistically, at the appropriate time the caregiver will need to point out without minimizing the mourner's guilt the positive intents and actions in the mourner's relationship with the deceased. However, premature reassurance that the mourner should not feel guilty or emphasis on positives may deny the mourner the necessary opportunity to ventilate guilty feelings. Especially when there has been extreme ambivalence or legitimate reasons for guilt, the mourner will not be aided by the caregiver's attempts to explain away guilt. This will likely make the mourner feel worse, as well as misunderstood by and disconnected from the caregiver. It is only when the mourner is able to address the ambivalence and any associated hostile wishes, thoughts, or impulses (e.g., a death wish toward the deceased) that there is a chance for favorable resolution. The caregiver will need to determine when and how to intervene, being extremely careful not to be manipulated by the mourner into being judgmental or dismissing the mourner's guilt. This is particularly difficult when witnessing a person's pain or inappropriate self-castigation due to illegitimate guilt. Nevertheless, caregivers must not attempt to rescue the mourner from guilt, but must work through the reasons for it.

Frequently, guilt can be alleviated by understanding its source, working through related issues and feelings, and/or addressing the underlying concerns it camouflages. However, more may be demanded from the mourner when guilt is legitimate. The mourner will need to find appropriate ways to atone in order to expiate guilt. In this case, the caregiver can work to enable the mourner to change static guilt to animating guilt (Lifton, 1979) or to mitigate guilt by doing something meaningful to help others or contribute to society. Guilt that cannot be expiated must be accommodated; the individual must learn to live with it and not perpetuate self-punishment.

The following strategies will be helpful in working with a mourner whose guilt requires more than emotional processing and working through.

1. Help the mourner recognize that, although guilt often can be worked through, at times it cannot. In such cases, it must be reduced to the extent possible, owned, and integrated into the rest of life (e.g., "I realize I made a mistake. I am truly sorry for it and take responsibility for it. I must live with it without letting it be destructive to me.").

2. Enable the mourner to engage in appropriate symbolic experiences to make amends, provide relief, illustrate to himself and others his

feelings about the deceased, or offer opportunities for atoning behavior (e.g., Gestalt exercises, psychodrama). At some point, the mourner may also wish to create a therapeutic ritual in which he can say good-bye to guilt (see chapter 7).

3. Aid the mourner in discovering constructive ways to make restitution and expiate guilt. Assist the mourner in avoiding the destructive use of guilt as self-punishment.

4. Help the mourner forgive himself. Self-forgiveness may only be possible after the mourner has done a number of things to atone for his guilt (e.g., completed a particular project undertaken as a form of retribution) or if he continues to live in a fashion demonstrating a state of atonement (e.g., staying sober).

DEPENDENCY AND CODEPENDENCY

Overview

Issues of dependency and codependency surface as causes, concomitants, and consequences of complicated mourning in several ways. First, the loss of relationships in which the mourner has been extremely dependent is well known to contribute to the development of three complicated mourning syndromes: distorted mourning of the extremely angry type (Raphael, 1983), chronic mourning (Bowlby, 1980; Parkes & Weiss, 1983; Raphael, 1983), and inhibited mourning (Raphael, 1983).

Second, dependency is strongly associated with other factors highly correlated with complicated mourning—specifically, early prior losses, depression, and anger and ambivalence at the dependency (sometimes eventuating in what is known as hostile dependency).

Third, high dependency tends to result in problematic mourning because of a number of its inherent elements and associated aspects.

1. High dependency suggests an excessive need for the deceased, whose death simultaneously leaves the mourner with more losses and fewer resources.

2. High dependency signals insecurity, which usually suggests that times of transition will be avoided as much as possible. The dependent mourner will not want to let the deceased go or struggle with mourning processes mandating a change in the relationship with the deceased or in her own assumptive world, behaviors, or sense of self.

3. High dependency indicates a lack of feelings of competence and confidence in the ability to cope or take care of the self. These perceived deficits may make the mourner fearful of going on after the death.

4. Previous dependency upon the deceased may have left the mourner unprepared and unskilled in assertiveness and initiative, resulting in her having little confidence in her ability to move forward in the new world.

5. Overreliance on the deceased may have reinforced the mourner's sense of helplessness, thus limiting her ability to readjust to the new world without him.

6. Overdependency on the deceased may cement the mourner's belief in her inability to function in the loved one's absence and may inhibit her from relinquishing her old attachments to him and the old assumptive world.

7. Extreme dependency on the deceased may make it difficult for the mourner to allow herself to recognize the reality of the loss and its implications for fear of what this will mean for her. The desire to avoid acknowledging the implications of the loss may compromise the mourner's remembering and review processes and inhibit the development of a new relationship with the deceased.

8. High dependency upon the deceased may cause the mourner to overreact to the separation, fulfilling the prophecy of her inability to function without the deceased.

9. High dependency associated with fear of the inability to handle pain and with the belief that the mourner cannot make it on her own without the deceased interferes with acknowledgment of the separation and the loss, acceptance of the need to react and adjust to the loss, and reinvestment in the new world.

Fourth, codependency appears to derive from dysfunctional family experiences. These experiences tend to foster specific unhealthy myths, distortions, and personality traits, engendering conflicts, beliefs, attitudes, feelings, and behavior patterns that not only result in self-defeating behaviors and relationships but also interfere with the requisite "R" processes of mourning and the development of appropriate support systems.

As used here, the term *codependency* refers to "a pattern of painful dependency on compulsive behaviors and on approval from others in an attempt to find safety, self-worth and identity" (Wegscheider-Cruse & Cruse, 1990, p. 8). This definition expands upon the narrower interpretation held early on in the field of addiction that a codependent person maintains a relationship with an alcoholic or an addict, often manifesting problems with dependent relationships, undertaking excessive caretaking, and enabling the alcoholic or addict. The key issue in the broader definition is the individual's self-defeating dependency upon other people or behaviors for self-worth. Codependency need not be associated with addiction: Any parent, partner, or significant other with behavior that somehow diminishes or shames a person puts that person at risk for, or reinforces, codependency (Snow & Willard, 1990).

Wegscheider-Cruse and Cruse (1990) conceptualize codependency as a brain disorder that stimulates self-defeating behaviors. They delineate the symptom groups of the basic disease of codependency as follows.

1. Distorted thinking (denial, delusion, and dissociation)

2. Distorted feeling (emotional repression)

3. Distorted behavior (compulsive behavior used for self-medication), including behavioral addictions (relationship dependency, care-taking, workaholism, eating or not eating, sexual acting out, con-trolling, spending and gambling, etc.) and chemical addictions (drugs, alcohol, nicotine, caffeine, sugar, etc.)

One can readily discern that the codependent as described here sustains many of the same dynamics and characteristics as the individual experiencing complicated mourning. In brief, a number of the elements known to complicate mourning are present in the codependent. Thus, the concept of codependency is an umbrella under which many mourners legitimately can be housed. It provides a perspective on the development and maintenance of self-defeating thoughts, feelings, and behaviors, and points to intervention strategies that are useful in contending with indi-viduals whose mourning is compromised by these dynamics.

Readers familiar with the literature on ACOAs will see how that group fits automatically within this classification (e.g., Black, 1987; Wegsheider-Cruise, 1989; Whitfield, 1987, 1990; Wholey, 1988; Woititz, 1983, 1985). However, today it is clear that much of what is true for ACOAs is equally valid for individuals from other types of dysfunctional families. Such fami-lies are characterized by, among other things, one or both parents being physically or sexually abusive, psychiatrically disturbed, or ACOA and/or codependent. Alternatively, such parents might sustain rigid religious be-liefs or engage in compulsive behaviors such as workaholism, gambling, drug abuse, or overeating. Codependency has been found in individuals who were adopted or in foster care, who had a chronically ill family member, or who themselves were chronically ill.

Three perspectives on dependency and codependency

When it comes to complicated mourning, the issues of dependency and codependency can be addressed from any one of three perspectives: First, the mourner may have experienced an unusually dependent rela-tionship with the deceased. The key word here is *unusual*; it is common and healthy to have a certain amount of interdependency with a beloved person. As described here, the dependency is extreme. Second, the mourner may have been the one upon whom the deceased had been extremely dependent. And third, the death may cause the mourner to become either dependent or codependent.

Unusual dependency upon the deceased. Extreme dependency is characterized by overreliance upon another in order to feel secure, achieve gratification, make decisions, and manage in life. Dependent persons tend to feel uncomfortable and helpless when not with others, often going to great lengths to avoid being alone. They have difficulty initiating activities on their own and are easily hurt by disapproval or criticism. Frequently, in an attempt to get others to like them, they undertake unpleasant tasks. In general, they relinquish their own control, subordinate themselves to others for fear of rejection, and are preoccupied by fears of being abandoned and by feeling devastated or helpless when close relationships end (American Psychiatric Association, 1987).

When a mourner maintains an unhealthy dependency upon the deceased, the severing of that relationship by death leaves the mourner with a number of unfulfilled needs. The mourner lacks both the experience in taking care of himself and the conviction that he can attend to his own needs.

One can see how the death of a person upon whom the mourner was extremely dependent delivers an assaultive narcissistic injury beyond what would normally be experienced after the loss of a loved one. This blow to the already dependent person both enrages and overwhelms, with both reactions compromising the ability to cope with the loss and its consequences. Rage is evidenced most clearly in the syndrome of distorted mourning of the extremely angry type (Raphael, 1983), whereas the inability to cope is witnessed best in the chronic mourning syndrome (Bowlby, 1980; Parkes & Weiss, 1983; Raphael, 1983). Although dependency is not necessarily a definitive factor in inhibited mourning, the effects of the desire to avoid acknowledging dependency upon the deceased also may be seen in this syndrome (Raphael, 1983).

Parkes and Weiss (1983) assert that extreme dependency in the premorbid relationship with the deceased leads, after the death, to chronic mourning and amounts to a disorder of attachment in which the normal bonds that ensure mutual security and effectiveness become distorted to the point where security and effectiveness are impaired. Insecurity fosters emotional dependency, and extreme anxiety in the absence of the other person tends to be characteristic. In such a relationship, the mourner has required the presence, emotional support, or actual assistance of the deceased in order to function adequately. Such insecurity and the resulting dependency—along with personality traits, lack of confidence, anxiety, and secondary gain—account for the dependent mourner's chronic refusal to relinquish mourning for the deceased. Bowlby (1980) notes how dependency leading to chronic mourning is evidenced in two dispositions on the part of the mourner: the disposition to make anxious and ambivalent relationships (the former being pathognomonic of dependency) and the disposition toward compulsive caregiving. The latter disposition is a strong trait of codependents. These associations further solidify the link between dependency, codependency, and complicated mourning.

Raphael (1983) notes that the death of one with whom the mourner had a dependent and irreplaceable relationship, often marked by extraordinary and possibly pathological emotional investment, is one of three factors predisposing the mourner toward chronic mourning. (The other two factors are sudden, unexpected death and the death of a child.) Agreeing with Parkes and Weiss (1983) and Bowlby (1980), Raphael points out that a highly dependent premorbid relationship with the deceased often initiates chronic mourning. She also asserts that it can give rise to distorted mourning of the extremely angry type. In fact, aspects of these two syndromes often occur together and share such dynamics as anger, the belief that the loss is reversible, interest in keeping the deceased "alive," insecurity, and persistence of reactions. An associated determinant for both concerns the fact that the loss is of an individual upon whom the mourner was pathologically dependent and whose relationship represented something special and irreplaceable to the mourner.

With regard to the death of a child, the child's dependency upon the parent is definitely an issue, as described in the following discussion of the deceased's dependency upon the mourner. Yet one could also argue that many adults are codependent upon their children and the role of parent for their self-esteem and identity. Excessive dependency of this type may complicate mourning.

Deceased's dependency upon the mourner. When the deceased is the one who has been dependent, the death may bring numerous difficulties to the mourner. These often center on the mourner's perception that she has in some sense failed the deceased by permitting that individual to die. In this way, the mourner feels that she has not been there for someone who relied upon her. In the situation where an individual cares for an elderly parent, dependency has shifted in that the child now takes care of the parent. When death comes, the mourner may feel uncomfortable and somewhat guilty because the parent always could make things better for her but she could not do so for the parent (Rando, 1988).

Although individuals in many roles may be dependent upon one another (e.g., disabled siblings, infirm in-laws, or dear friends lacking other supports), problems after the death of one who was dependent reach their zenith when the deceased was the mourner's child. Here, the dependency dynamic combines with myriad other issues inherent in the death of a child (see chapter 13). Grief and mourning reach their highest intensities here and appear more complicated than in any other scenario (Rando, 1986f, 1986g).

Dependency or codependency caused by the death. The last perspective concerns the situation in which the death causes the mourner to become dependent or codependent. The loss and its consequences for the mourner, the circumstances of the death, and/or the reactions of the social support system contribute to excessive dependency on other people and on certain distorted ways of thinking, feeling, and behaving (e.g., behavioral or chemical addictions) in order to cope. Although a certain amount of dependency is appropriate and even therapeutic in mourning, too much compromises the process. The mourner can actually become codependent upon mourning itself. This is exemplified clearly in chronic mourning and to a less dramatic extent in certain distortions of thinking, feeling, and behaving that interfere with the "R" processes of mourning (e.g., compulsively caring for others who are mourning instead of caring for oneself; feeling so stigmatized by the loved one's death that one withdraws socially or turns to alcohol to medicate pain). In the circumstance of sudden, unexpected death, noted by Raphael (1983) to be a factor predisposing an individual to chronic mourning, the many sequelae of lack of preparation and assaulted capacities for adaptation certainly may result in the mourner's greater dependency on others after the death.

Treatment Implications

Treatment involves two main sets of interventions: those that pertain to issues of dependency and codependency and those that pertain to how these issues interface with mourning. Although presented here in two categories for the purpose of discussion, in reality these interventions often overlap.

Treatment for dependency or codependency

A basic perspective for treating dependency and codependency has been outlined by Wegscheider-Cruse and Cruse (1990). This perspective incorporates the following points:

1. Effective treatment confronts self-delusion with new information. With learning comes understanding and insight and from that comes a reality-based commitment to heal.

2. It creates a safe atmosphere where feelings can surface, to be expressed and discharged so healing can take place. We can't heal what we can't feel.

3. It provides an atmosphere where it is safe and possible to recognize, detox, and detach from compulsive medicating behaviors. We can't feel what is medicated. (p. 65)

Specific interventions include increasing appropriate autonomy and independence through psychological work (e.g., improving self-esteem, decreasing anxiety and helplessness, increasing assertiveness) and appropriate skill development. The caregiver also may help the mourner work through unhealthy, self-defeating dependency and codependency by addressing the following: the codependency trap, denial, emotional repression, compulsive behavior (i.e., self-defeating behaviors and chemical dependence), low self-worth, relationship difficulties, medical problems, choices and risks, forgiveness and amends, and recovery and living (Wegscheider-Cruse & Cruse, 1990). Finally, interventions should be designed to heal the so-called wounded child within. This involves a host of strategies and techniques beyond the scope of this book. For further information on treating dependency, codependency, and the child within, the reader is referred to Beattie (1987), Bradshaw (1988a), Cermak (1986), Wegscheider-Cruse (1989), Whitfield (1987, 1990), Wholey (1988), Woititz (1983, 1985), Woititz and Garner (1990), and Wolfelt (1990a, 1990b.)

Treatment for complicated mourning impaired by dependency or codependency

In addition to considering the previously mentioned interventions, the caregiver needs to intervene in specific ways with the individual whose mourning is complicated by dependency or codependency. Depending on the presentation of the individual's mourning, it also is useful to employ the strategies and techniques recommended for chronic mourning and/or distorted mourning of the extremely angry type (see chapter 4). To the extent that inhibition is present, the caregiver can employ interventions suggested in that chapter for the inhibited mourning syndrome.

To help the mourner confront issues specifically relevant to dependency and/or codependency, the caregiver may do as follows.

1. Promote recognition of reality of the loss, especially its permanence and irreversibility.

2. Identify the meaning of the relationship and why the mourner feels it cannot be relinquished, exploring the identity and roles the mourner had with the deceased.

3. Promote identification of aspects of the mourner's dependency upon the deceased, expression of feelings about losing each aspect, and discussion of what needs to be done to take care of the self without the help of the deceased. In collaboration with the mourner, plan a program to put these actions into effect.

4. Identify and work through problems created by the loss of the dependent relationship, being sure to identify them as major secondary losses and intervening as directed in chapter 9 for the subprocess of identifying and mourning secondary losses, under the "R" process of reacting to the separation.

5. Initially, offer unqualified support in order to build trust. Once a therapeutic relationship has been established, gradually shift the

emphasis from support to encouragement, discouraging the tendency to cling to the role of mourner and insisting on and reinforcing forward movement (Parkes & Weiss, 1983).

6. Place particular emphasis on the last three "R" processes of relinquishing the old attachments to the deceased and the old assumptive world, readjusting to move adaptively into the new world without forgetting the old, and reinvesting.

7. Assist the mourner in the subprocess of developing a new relationship with the deceased, under the "R" process of readjusting to move adaptively into the new world without forgetting the old, so chronic mourning or distorted mourning of the extremely angry type as a connection to the deceased can be relinquished.

8. Use behavioral strategies to put limits upon chronic mourning.

9. According to Raphael (1980b), where distorted mourning of the extremely angry type exists, work on the displacement of anger, recognizing that anger at the deceased for desertion may be particularly difficult for the mourner to acknowledge when the loved one is perceived as having been perfect. Initiate discussion of the difficulties that occur when a presumably perfect person is gone and enable the mourner to confront and ventilate anger. If possible, deal in the ways discussed earlier in this chapter with the denied ambivalence and repressed anger that usually are involved.

SOCIAL SUPPORT

Overview

One of the most consistent findings in the clinical and empirical literature is the salience of the mourner's perception of social support. If the mourner perceives the world as providing support for mourning, that perception is an extremely positive factor. If the mourner perceives that support is unavailable, that it is available and not forthcoming, or that his loss is not socially acknowledged, that perception can have a profound impact on coping and may constitute a high-risk factor for complicated mourning. To the extent that a perceived lack of social support constitutes a concurrent stress or crisis, in itself a high-risk factor, the mourner is further disadvantaged.

Types of social support and relationship to bereavement outcome

The mourner may need or want any one or combination of the following types of support.

1. Emotional support (e.g., encouraging expression of feelings and review of the lost relationship or demonstrating and expressing concern or caring for the mourner)

2. Instrumental support (e.g., helping with tasks posed specifically by the death, such as making funeral arrangements; basic survival needs, such as cooking meals; or required tasks of daily living, such as washing clothes)

3. Validational support (e.g., acknowledging the mourner's loss and its pain)

4. Informational support (e.g., providing necessary information or feedback, such as telling the mourner how to secure insurance benefits or giving him feedback about how he is responding to his bereaved child)

5. Support of presence (e.g., being physically present with and for the mourner)

6. Relational support (e.g., providing emotional interrelationship and intimacy, serving as an emotional anchor during stress)

7. Social activities support (e.g., involving the mourner in social activities to provide diversion, respite, replenishment, or opportunities for reinvestment)

Research has found that, because of fluctuating mourner needs, different sources and types of support are useful at different times during bereavement. For example, Bankoff (1981, 1983a, 1983b) demonstrated that for young widows, parents were most helpful early in bereavement, whereas later on single or other widowed friends provided the best assistance. In addition, when a mourner fails to receive required assistance from an appropriate helper at a particular time, other sources of support that are received may become meaningless (M. Lieberman, 1986). One of the difficulties for caregivers is therefore tuning in to the mourner's idiosyncratic timetable and needs. In a related vein, recent research suggests that mourners experience significantly more negative interactions or difficulty in receiving social support from another person when the loss is shared by both parties than when the loss is not shared (Rosenblatt, Spoentgen, Karis, Dahl, Kaiser, & Elde, 1991).

Significant research has been done relating to the impact on bereavement outcome of the influence, type, source, amount, focus, differential impact, and timing of social support and the prerequisite process of social validation. The following references are among many that focus specifically on the impact of social support on bereavement: Bahr and Harvey (1979, 1980); Bankoff (1981, 1983a, 1983b); Davidowitz and Myrick (1984); Doka (1989); Hughes and Fleming (1991); Lehman, Ellard, and Wortman

(1986); Lopata (1979); Lowenthal and Haven (1968); Maddison and Walker (1967); Pihlblad and Adams (1972); Rosenblatt et al. (1991); Sheldon, Cochrane, Vachon, Lyall, Rogers, and Freeman (1981); Vachon, Sheldon et al. (1982); and Walker, McBride, and Vachon (1977). Resources addressing the impact of social validation or support on coping in general or on physical or emotional health in particular are beyond the scope of this review. Issues of social validation and social support pertinent to specific types of high-risk deaths are discussed in chapters 11 through 13.

Need for social support

A number of possibilities exist with regard to the availability of social support.

1. Support is not available because the mourner is socially or geographically isolated or has no available resources.

2. Support is available and others recognize that it should be given, but they do not give it.

3. Support is available, others recognize that it should be given and give it, but it is insufficient. This may be the case because the mourner requires more than it is possible for others to give (e.g., the death was so traumatic that it requires support beyond what is available) or because the mourner is so psychologically needy that her requirements are insatiable. It is also possible that, despite good intentions, the amount and type of support do not meet the mourner's legitimate needs (e.g., those offering support do not allow the mourner to talk about the deceased).

4. Support is available, but others do not recognize that it is needed and hence do not give it (i.e., the mourner is disenfranchised, as discussed in the next section).

5. Support is available, others recognize it is needed, and it is given sufficiently to meet the mourner's needs.

The needs of the mourner for social support after the death of a loved one will vary depending on a number of factors. One such determinant concerns the mourner's personal characteristics (e.g., personality; mental health; coping abilities; maturity; age; sex-role conditioning; social, cultural, ethnic, generational, and religious/philosophical background; physiological factors influencing mourning). The mourner's expectations for assistance from others, derived from past experiences, also will be a factor, as will the nature, meaning, and characteristics of the loss (e.g., who died, what the loss means to the mourner, and what the relationship was like). The nature and circumstances of the death (e.g., degree of anticipation, cause of death) will also have an impact, along with the type, nature, severity, and consequences of any concurrent stresses. Finally, outcomes may be affected by other resources available to the mourner.

In all cases, it is the mourner's perception of social support received that determines the degree of complication, not the objective receipt of support. Therefore, the caregiver cannot assess the impact of support without taking into account the individual mourner's subjective appraisal. One mourner may have a single good friend to offer support and judge that to be quite adequate. Another mourner may have an extended and responsive support network yet feel that it is insufficient.

Disenfranchised grief

In order for an individual to support a mourner in bereavement, there must first be the recognition that such support is necessary. A lack of social validation and recognition of a loss leaves the person mourning that loss in a state of *disenfranchised grief*, or grief experienced when a loss is not or cannot be openly acknowledged, publicly mourned, or socially supported (Doka, 1989). For example, such a situation is too often typical in the case of a death related to AIDS (see chapter 13).

Doka (1989) observes that, in our society, mourners are cast into disenfranchised grief for a number of reasons: First, the relationship is not recognized. Lack of recognition may occur because the relationship is not based on traditional kin ties (e.g., friend, coworker, cohabitant partner), is not publicly recognized or socially sanctioned (e.g., homosexual relationship, extramarital affair), or existed primarily in the past (e.g., ex-spouse, former friend). Second, the loss is not recognized. This situation may arise when the loss itself is not socially defined as significant (e.g., perinatal death, abortion, death of a pet) or the reality of the loss is not socially validated (e.g., death of the personality in Alzheimer's disease despite ongoing biological vitality). Third, the mourner is not recognized. The characteristics of some bereaved individuals disenfranchise their grief because they are not defined as capable of grief (e.g., children, the elderly, persons with developmental disabilities). Therefore, there is little if any recognition of their loss or need to mourn.

To this list may be added a fourth reason, which concerns aspects of the situation that determine whether the loss, once recognized, will be supported by the mourner's social group. In particular, the social group may respond minimally because members are defensive or wish to protect themselves against anxiety (e.g., the death is too horrible to contend with, such as a mutilating death or the death of a child) or from embarrassment (e.g., after a stigmatized death, such as autoerotic asphyxiation). Support also may be withheld to punish one of the parties involved (e.g., after a death associated with AIDS or a criminal act). Finally, others may hold the misapprehension that loss of a person they devalued should not elicit grief in the survivors (e.g., death of an alcoholic or a person with a disability). In all these cases, even though the mourner's social group may recognize the loss, they respond as though they do not.

Clinically, it appears that difficulties nearly always arise when a mourner's perceived needs for support are not met. However, problems are exacerbated when the disenfranchised mourner recognizes that the support is available but is being withheld for some reason. The simultaneous availability of support and lack of receipt is worse than complete unavailability because it tends to increase secondary loss and intensify such normal grief feelings as despair, depression, anger, abandonment, shame, victimization, anxiety, guilt, search for meaning, and social withdrawal. At the same time, disenfranchisement removes or minimizes sources of support by excluding the mourner from an active role in the dying and/or funeral rituals (Doka, 1989).

Treatment Implications

If the mourner is socially disenfranchised, the caregiver must first work to enfranchise that person. Only when the mourner has been enfranchised to the degree possible can the caregiver facilitate uncomplicated mourning or address aspects of complicated mourning. Enfranchising the mourner requires legitimizing his status as a mourner, helping him actualize his loss (if necessary), and conveying the importance of undertaking the "R" processes of mourning.

Regardless of the amount of support available to the mourner, the caregiver must identify the mourner's loss as legitimate. It is important to teach the mourner about the concept of disenfranchised mourning and help him articulate the importance and special meaning of the relationship lost. The caregiver may also need to provide ways to ritualize the loss if these have been absent (see chapter 7) and intervene when reactions to secondary losses occur as a consequence of disenfranchisement (e.g., anger because one could not attend the funeral).

Whatever social validation and acceptance of the loss can be secured from others in the environment should be promoted in the ways previously discussed. Sometimes such support cannot be secured, either because circumstances of the particular loss prevent it (e.g., continued confidentiality is required after the death of a secret lover) or because the nature or extent of the support is simply inadequate. If either situation is the case, the mourner must be helped to identify and use whatever support is available. Perhaps the mourner must rely on only one person instead of an entire network or must turn to other resources, such as audiovisual or printed materials.

Mourning in the elderly, people with developmental disabilities, and children must not be ignored or dismissed. In educating others, the caregiver must make it clear that the loss is in the eye of the beholder and that others' social evaluation of the loss does not necessarily reflect the individual's experience. Also, information about the importance of non-death losses and losses of those who are unrelated to the mourner (e.g., friends, ex-in-laws, pets) can be helpful both to the mourner and to members of the mourner's support system.

In cases where the issue is less one of disenfranchisement than one of absent or insufficient social support, the caregiver must work to ensure that social connections are available to meet the mourner's needs. Specifically, the caregiver must undertake the following.

1. Identify the precise type of support the mourner requires and what specifically in that type of support is desired and not possessed. (This may mean identifying the particular resource or individual who is not providing the support.)

2. Work with the mourner to identify unmet needs as secondary losses and process them as suggested according to the treatment suggestions for the subprocess of identifying and mourning secondary losses, under the "R" process of reacting to the separation (see chapter 9).

3. Deal with the mourner's feelings about not getting needs for support met and/or why those needs are not getting met. (This is especially salient if a specific person or persons were expected to provide support in particular ways but support is not forthcoming.)

4. Review the mourner's expectations for support to ascertain whether they are appropriate. If they are inappropriate, help the mourner readjust them as necessary.

5. Assess the lack of support to determine whether it is due to a lack of assertiveness or another psychological issue on the mourner's part. If so, address these obstacles.

6. Recognize that support for particular losses often can be found in self-help groups and printed resources. Refer the mourner as necessary to these groups and resources.

7. Intervene to provide proper psychoeducational information to members of the mourner's support system if they have unrealistic expectations or incorrect information about the mourner's needs.

Throughout intervention, the caregiver must keep in mind the following important points: First, because of fluctuating mourner needs, different sources and types of support will be required at different times. This means that needs will not remain static but will require reappraisal. Second, the individual mourner's—not the caregiver's—subjective appraisal of the nature and extent of support required must constitute the basis for actions taken. Finally, because the needs of the mourner for social support vary depending on a number of factors, issues of support consistently must be perceived within the context of the constellation of factors influencing the particular mourner and loss. What supports one may be insignificant to another.

CHAPTER 11

Risks and Therapeutic Implications Associated With Mode of Death

The nature and circumstances of a death can be so powerful as to bring complications to even the healthiest mourner. This is not to say that hardiness of personality does not stand the mourner in good stead, even under the direst of situations. In any adversity, some individuals will do better than others. However, some circumstances have the ability to complicate the mourning of most if not all human beings, at least to some degree. The danger in not recognizing that complications may arise out of the particular mode of death is that the caregiver may incorrectly pathologize the mourner for responses automatically set in train by the loss itself.

Although there are many distinct causes of death, there are only four modes: natural death, accidental death, suicide, or homicide. Shneidman (1963) has offered the NASH acronym to identify these four modes. This chapter discusses specific complications associated with the four modes of death and offers suggestions for appropriate intervention. Discussed under homicide is the issue of preventability, a high-risk factor in any circumstance but one that raises special questions in this type of death.

All of the treatment suggestions presented in this chapter are in addition to the philosophical perspectives on treatment and the generic treatment guidelines proposed in chapter 8 and the specific suggestions for intervening in the six "R" processes of mourning detailed in chapter 9. Chapters 12 and 13 go on to describe complications resulting from traumatic characteristics of the death, death of a child, and AIDS-related death.

NATURAL VERSUS UNNATURAL DEATH

In the case of natural death, the mourner usually is spared having to deal with problems associated with a personal agent's direct responsibility for the death, as is the case in homicide, suicide, and some accidents or disasters. Nonetheless, complications may arise when the mourner feels that the death was in some way preventable, with a large part of the risk this type of death poses to the mourner being determined by the extent to which the death is viewed as preventable. The death might have been subintentioned by the deceased or at least attributed to his carelessness or neglect, as in the case where the loved one's lung cancer is linked to his refusal to stop smoking cigarettes. Alternatively, it might be blamed on a third party—for instance, holding the loved one's mother responsible for discouraging a diet that might have prevented a fatal heart attack. The mourner also may blame herself for acts of omission or commission that she feels played a part in the death—for example, not taking the loved one to the doctor sooner. Despite the fact that some issues of blame may be pertinent in this type of death, they are usually less intense than when the death was completely avoidable.

Often the death surround (i.e., the location; type of death; reasons for it; mourner's presence at it; and mourner's degree of preparation, participation, and confirmation of it) in natural deaths is less distressing than in other types of death. For example, accepting the death of a loved one if she dies in her sleep might be expected to be easier than if she were shot during a robbery. Yet certain circumstances in natural death can present problems. A case in point would be when a man has a sudden heart attack, loses control of his vehicle, and smashes into a telephone pole. The additional elements of trauma, violence, and mutilation heighten the risk factors of this death, regardless of the fact that it stems from natural causes. Similarly, in the case where there has been an intense medical battle for life, the loved one's family may have pushed aside the possibility of death during the fight for survival, only to be shocked when the loved one dies after emergency surgery. Likewise, in cases where no specific cause can be determined, as is true for Sudden Infant Death Syndrome, mourners may be left with painful complications associated with the lack of a reason for the death.

In contrast to natural death, Rynearson (1987a) addresses psychological adjustment to unnatural death, which is "characterized by horror, brutality, and calamity—abhorrent acts that are psychosocially dissonant and to some degree unacceptable" (p. 77). Rynearson notes that unnatural death presents at least three phenomenologic peculiarities that influence outcomes: violence, violation, and volition. He asserts the following:

> These three Vs of unnatural dying . . . are far from inert or neutral phenomena. Each of them catalyzes a strong psychosocial aftermath. . . . This is so obvious—the peaceful dying of someone ringed by nurturing relatives is categorically distinct from the brutal dying of someone who is stabbed repeatedly by an assaultive thief or someone who is hit in a crosswalk by

a drunk driver, or someone who is partially decapitated by a self-inflicted gunshot wound. It is the form and context of dying rather than death itself that lends meaning and structure to the psychologic recapitulation and assimilation of death by the bereaved . . . unnatural dying demands not only normal and/or pathologic bereavement, but adjustment to a death that is to some degree characterized by violence, violation, and volition. (Rynearson, 1987a, p. 78)

Rynearson illustrates that adjustment to unnatural death involves a variable combination of violence, violation, and volition, and stresses that each is associated with a compensatory psychological response: Violence is associated with post-traumatic stress, violation is associated with victimization, and volition is associated with compulsive inquiry. In definitively separating these responses, which stem from the character of unnatural death, from those stimulated by intrapsychic dynamics, he does something most caregivers forget to do, much to the mourner's detriment:

This syndromal combination of post-traumatic stress, victimization, and compulsive inquiry is specifically associated with the variables of unnatural dying and *occurs independent of antecedent psychopathology or an ambivalent relationship with the deceased*. Presumably, certain antecedent psychologic conditions might render survivors more vulnerable; that is, phobic disorders to post-traumatic stress, paranoid disorders to victimization, or obsessive disorders to compulsive inquiry. . . . While antecedent and direct variables may mutually influence adjustment, it would be misleading to postulate (as Lindemann did from Freud's speculation) that post-traumatic stress, victimization, and compulsive inquiry are reflections of unconscious conflict. Rather, they appear to be the psychologic consequences of overwhelming affect and defensive collapse. (Rynearson, 1987a, p. 86, emphasis added)

NATURAL DEATH

Two causes of natural death place the survivor at particular risk for complicated mourning: death caused by acute natural causes and death caused by an overly lengthy terminal illness.

Acute Natural Causes

A death from acute natural causes is a sudden, unexpected death, with lack of anticipation constituting the critical risk factor. Treatment suggestions provided in chapter 12 for sudden, unexpected death are therefore pertinent. Examples of this type include a loved one's dying in his sleep from a stroke, dropping dead from a heart attack, or succumbing during emergency surgery required after a hemorrhage. More than in other types of sudden death, the mourner who loses a loved one from acute natural causes may feel consolation that the deceased did not suffer. However, the impact of lack of forewarning must be added to other risk factors when evaluating the potential for complicated mourning.

In working with mourners who have lost loved ones to acute natural death, the caregiver must be aware of the difficulty in determining when a death is anticipated and when it is not. The duration required for a death to be anticipated varies from research study to research study and from mourner to mourner. Depending upon the particular study, periods of anticipation from hours to weeks have been interpreted as brief. Mourners likewise vary in their interpretations. The caregiver, left without an objective guideline for what constitutes an unanticipated or anticipated death, must view all deaths from the survivor's idiosyncratic perspective and plan intervention accordingly.

Overly Lengthy Terminal Illness

Although many negative sequelae of sudden, unexpected death interfere with healthy mourning, it is also possible at the other extreme for mourning to be complicated by circumstances in the dying process or by too lengthy a period of illness preceding death. Specifically, problems in mourning tend to arise when (a) certain interrelated processes necessary for anticipatory grief are not undertaken appropriately (Rando, 1986a, 1986e), (b) the "normal" negative experiences of the illness are insufficiently appreciated and integrated or are undergone in a manner so as to complicate the postdeath experience, or (c) the illness persists too long and therapeutic benefits are obscured by the additional stresses of the experience. To the extent that healthy behaviors, interactions, and anticipatory grief processes can be promoted during this time, the mourner's postdeath bereavement can be made relatively easier than it would be if the experience of terminal illness lacked these therapeutic benefits (Rando, 1986e).

For a comprehensive analysis and clinical suggestions for the experience of anticipatory grief and terminal illness of both patient and family members, the reader is referred to Rando (1984, 1986e). Other suggested resources on the topic include Barton (1977a); Fulton and Fulton (1971); Fulton and Gottesman (1980); Garfield (1978); Glaser and Strauss (1965); Kalish (1970); Kübler-Ross (1969); Moos and Tsu (1977); Pattison (1969, 1977, 1978); Pearson (1969); Saunders (1975); Schoenberg, Carr, Peretz, and Kutscher (1970); Shneidman (1978); Siegel and Weinstein (1983); Sobel and Worden (1982); van Bommel (1987); Weisman (1972a, 1972b, 1975, 1977); Weisman and Hackett (1961); and Weisman and Worden (1975).

In the past, terminal illnesses were usually brief and characterized by a steady decline in the patient's well-being. Medical advancements have increased the duration of many terminal illnesses, and more often the course of such illnesses is unpredictable. Problems the mourner, his family, and others may experience in this regard leave them with sequelae that encumber them during the illness and can complicate postdeath mourning (Rando, 1986e, 1986h). These problems include the following.

1. Coping with the stress of remissions and relapses, as well as with the sights, sounds, smells, and demands of debilitating illness and with the many psychological reactions arising from these experiences

2. Managing the effects of lengthened periods of anticipatory grief, uncertainty, anxiety, and the consequences of chronic and unremitting stress

3. Contending with aspects of chronicity: an uncertain, up-and-down course; confusion magnified by situations breeding inconsistency, resentment, and ambivalence; lack of norms and clearly specified expectations and responsibilities; and depletion secondary to demands for major readaptation and investment of self, time, and finances

4. Dealing with the demands of responding to dying as a gradual process in which family members, on a long-term basis, must contend with and balance opposing tasks, clashing responsibilities, discordant roles, and a loved one who while still living is also slowly dying

5. Handling increased financial, social, physical, time, and emotional demands

6. Surviving long-term family disruption and disorganization

7. Witnessing the overall progressive decline of the loved one and coping with the emotional responses of family members to that decline and their inability to stem it

8. Coping with consequences commonly observed in families of the dying: psychological conflicts, emotional exhaustion, physical debilitation, social isolation, and family discord, as well as with the typical emotional reactions of guilt, anxiety, sorrow, depression, anger, and hostility

9. Managing intensive treatment regimens and their side effects

10. Confronting dilemmas about decision making and treatment choices

In optimum amounts and for an optimum period of time, these experiences teach the family about the loved one's impending death (e.g., a relapse provides more evidence that the illness cannot be controlled). As such, they can be useful in promoting anticipatory grief processes and in keeping the mourner from the deleterious effects of a sudden, unexpected death. However, if they persist for too long, they lose their therapeutic value, causing the family to become overwhelmed and depleted, precluding healthy mourning, diminishing or destroying adaptive coping capacities, and impeding appropriate mourning. In addition, family members may be unable to perceive the normalcy and universality of the guilt that is the natural outgrowth of living with a dying person, and this causes additional guilt, anxiety, depression, and feelings of loss of control. They may become increasingly angry that there is no relief from the oppression of the illness and its demands. Indeed, they may become entrenched in a cycle of anger, which produces guilt, which promotes increased involvement, which results in further depletion and anger, which begins the cycle again. Finally, after devoting their lives to the patient, they may be confused after the death about what to do in life besides care for a dying person. All of these outcomes serve to complicate the mourning process.

Research bears out that an optimum length of time exists for an illness as relates to survivors' postdeath grief and mourning. In studies that may account for the contradictory results of previous investigations examining the impact of the length of an illness, both Rando (1983) and Sanders (1982–1983) found that illnesses that were too long, as well as those that were too short, predisposed survivors to poorer outcomes.

Rando (1983) specifically investigated the grief and adaptation of parents whose children had died from cancer. In the study, family members whose loved ones had died from an illness lasting less than 6 months or more than 18 months appeared to be least prepared for the death. Those whose loved ones experienced longer illnesses were the least prepared and reported the poorest subsequent adjustment. In contrast, those whose loved ones had undergone illnesses in the interim range were most prepared at the time of death and adjusted most satisfactorily following it. Although the 18-month time period for study here was arbitrarily chosen and might be different in another investigation, the main issue is that at some point the illness simply becomes too long, affecting the mourner negatively. Because these findings have been corroborated clinically and by other studies (e.g., Sanders, 1982–1983), they are judged applicable to mourners other than those experiencing the loss of a child.

Rando's conclusions have been supported by Sanders (1982–1983), who found that survivors whose loved ones died from a short-term chronic illness (defined as being less than 6 months in duration) fared better afterward than those whose loved ones died suddenly or from a long-term chronic illness. Interestingly, when initially interviewed, the group whose loved ones experienced short-term illness was similar in level of postdeath grief symptomatology to the groups whose loved ones had experienced either sudden or long-term illness. It was only on follow-up 18 months later that the short-term group was observed to be less symptomatic. These data should prompt caregivers to recognize that comparisons of types of death, as well as evaluations of adjustment to bereavement, should take into account the length of time since the death. This factor must be considered in evaluating research findings and designing appropriate research methodologies.

In the Rando (1983) study, a clear pattern emerged to suggest that, as the length of illness increases, the percentage of family members with higher indices of postdeath anger and hostility, and of abnormal grief, increases. It was hypothesized that when the illness was too short, family members were unable to prepare themselves adequately. When it was too long, the experience and stress associated with the illness appeared to exacerbate disturbed reactions following the death, increased the intensity of feelings of anger and hostility, and militated against adequate preparation for the death. It is also important to consider the hypothesis that family members became conditioned over the long, up-and-down course of the illness to expect that their loved ones would survive despite the odds because they had done so consistently in the past. An alternate and not incompatible theory is that the arduous experience of lengthy illness sapped family members of their abilities to cope, compromising their ability to prepare for the death and adjust afterward. The anger and hostility, and the abnormal grief that steadily intensified as the illness continued, also may have precluded better therapeutic readiness and subsequent adjustment.

Together, Rando's and Sanders' findings document the risk potential of sudden, unexpected death and death following a lengthy illness. Previous research often collapsed data into two categories (i.e., short-term and long-term illness) and precluded observation of the pattern evident when discriminating among short, medium, and long durations of illness. However, information about the optimum length of an illness is critical in identifying high-risk mourners. Such knowledge will help caregivers recognize a family's need for increased support after too long an illness, appreciate their decreased coping abilities, and understand the escalating burden of their experience and its interference with preparation at death and adjustment thereafter. In addition, it will help them determine the family's postdeath requirements for education, intervention, and reintegration.

The following suggestions for intervention are appropriate for the mourner whose loved one has died after a lengthy illness.

1. Provide the mourner with psychoeducational information to promote understanding of this type of loss and legitimize any complications that may develop. Remember that complications may be unexpected because the mourner may have believed herself to have been doing the "right" thing by tending to the loved one during the illness.

2. Help address and work through the various reasons for and types of guilt and ambivalence that come from the experience of an extended terminal illness, using interventions delineated in chapter 10. Guilt also may play a particular role when mourners must alter plans for the death, either because of depletion from the illness (e.g., the loved one can no longer be cared for at home because the spouse is herself exhausted or ill) or from fear of the approaching death (e.g., the family calls the ambulance and the loved one dies in the hospital instead of in his own home).

3. Explain that it is not uncommon for family members to feel surprised when the end comes, even though they may have been preparing for it all along. Caregivers should remember that it is not only denial or conditioning through prior recoveries that leaves loved ones unprepared at the last minute; sometimes disbelief reflects the human inability to comprehend reactions to and implications of death prior to experiencing them.

4. If the extended illness had in any way created lingering anger or caused the mourner to become codependent, employ appropriate interventions, as described in chapter 10.

5. Recognize that an extended terminal illness leaves the mourner depleted in many areas and with lowered defensiveness, stressed coping mechanisms, and a life perhaps now empty because it previously revolved around the care of the loved one. Provide extra support; assist in the mourner's finding and permitting replenishment; facilitate the assumption of new roles and connections to others to provide sources of gratification; and enable family role reassignment and redistribution while identifying and responding therapeutically to the interrupted development of family members and/or their adoption of unhealthy attitudes, behaviors, thoughts, and feelings.

6. Bear in mind that, whereas the experience of caring for a dying person eliminates some problems in postdeath mourning, it can create other difficulties (e.g., increased hurt, more memories and emotional involvement from which to disengage, the shattering of daily routines, the apparent invalidation of one's efforts; Rosenblatt, 1983).

As discussed at some length in chapter 12, it is quite possible for a death occurring in the context of terminal illness or recovery to be sudden, even though such a situation may seem contradictory. In fact, whether a loss is sudden or expected depends not on an objective time span but on its subjective psychosocial timing for the mourner. Interventions spelled out in chapter 12 for sudden, unexpected death are therefore applicable.

Along with these are recommendations for mourners whose loved ones die from sudden, unexpected death in the context of terminal illness or recovery. In general, interventions are designed to (a) provide appropriate information about how this type of loss differs from both sudden and anticipated deaths occurring in other contexts, (b) offer assistance and direction in how to cope with the sequelae of this very different type of loss, (c) help the mourner secure social support from others who erroneously may construe the loss to be expected, and (d) manage the increased anger and guilt that often arise under these circumstances.

ACCIDENTAL DEATH

This section provides discussion of death resulting from accident, disaster, and war. Technically, a war death is classified as just that and is not viewed as an accident. Despite this fact, war deaths appear clinically to share much in common with disaster and are therefore included here. In each of these three kinds of deaths, the dynamics of suddenness, violence, trauma, and preventability contribute to mourners' typical reactions; in many cases, so too do the factors of loss of a child and multiple death. Typical reactions include, among others, post-traumatic stress; helplessness; guilt and anger; search for assignment of blame as well as meaning; and, many times, bereavement overload.

Risk Factors Associated With Accidental Death

Accidental deaths can be either sudden or anticipated. For instance, a person can be killed instantly in a car crash or can linger in a hospital for months. The same reality obtains for disaster or war deaths: An individual may be killed on impact during a plane crash or initially survive battle wounds only to die from injuries later on. The unanticipated nature of these deaths is a significant risk factor in many cases, contributing to confusion, anxiety, incomprehensibility, bewilderment, self-reproach, depression, and overwhelming states of psychological and physical shock. Where events lead to a sudden or relatively sudden death, the mourner can be expected to experience an unanticipated grief reaction, which may or may not evolve into a full-blown unanticipated mourning syndrome. The following resources are recommended for more comprehensive information about bereavement sequelae and interventions for sudden accidental deaths: Bowlby (1980); Glick et al. (1974); Hodgkinson (1989); Lehman, Wortman, and Williams (1987); Lehrman (1956); Lord (1987); Lundin (1984a, 1984b); Mancini (1986); Rando (1983, 1984, 1988); Raphael (1983, 1986); Rynearson (1987a); Sanders (1982–1983, 1986); Weisman (1973); and Worden (1982). The reader also will want to refer to the discussion in chapter 12 of sudden, unexpected death.

Accidents occur in disproportionately higher rates among children, adolescents, and young adults and are the leading cause of death among all persons ages 1 to 37 (National Safety Council, 1991). This means that there is a relatively higher chance that those mourning accidental deaths will also have to deal with the loss of a young individual, perhaps a child, with such untimely deaths invariably bringing on more complicated mourning. One often sees in accidental deaths the constellation of youth, lack of anticipation, violence, and preventability. When these particular high-risk factors occur together, the risk of complicated mourning escalates dramatically.

A high correlation also exists between accidental death and violence, mutilation, and destruction, as is witnessed in such traumatic events as automobile accidents and air disasters. Such aspects tend to leave survivors with a greater sense of helplessness and threat, as well as with intense feelings of vulnerability, insecurity, fear, and lack of protection. Such losses are more shocking and difficult to assimilate.

One recent study on reactions to the death of a spouse or child from a motor vehicle crash provides convincing evidence that such losses engender long-lasting distress that must be perceived not as a sign of individual coping failure but as a common response to the situation (Lehman et al., 1987). These investigators found that, even after 4 to 7 years had elapsed, a significant percentage of mourners (from 30 to 85 percent, depending upon the question asked) were still dealing actively with the death in terms of thoughts, memories, and feelings. The majority were still searching for some meaning in what had happened.

Additional problems are caused by traumatic memories of the event or imagined scenes of what transpired (often worse than the reality). These can haunt the bereaved through thoughts, images, dreams, and the sudden feeling that the trauma is recurring. Such responses can take on the repetitive and intrusive qualities seen in post-traumatic stress disorders. (For more on issues associated with traumatic death, see chapter 12.)

The violence of an accidental death also can raise destructive fantasies, and, in the mourner's mind, link the death consciously or unconsciously to violent feelings or thoughts or to ambivalence that might have been felt toward the deceased (Raphael, 1983). The mourner may interpret these feelings or thoughts as having caused the death and can experience heightened guilt and other guilt-related reactions as a result. This can cause significant complications in the mourning process.

Guilt may be intensified beyond what is typically seen postdeath as a result of the strong need to assign blame and responsibility in accidental deaths. It is not uncommon for mourners to interrogate themselves endlessly to determine whether they were responsible for the death or to obsess guiltily about their decisions, omissions, or commissions (e.g., Why did I let her borrow the car? Why didn't I go and visit her instead of suggesting she fly out here? and, Maybe if I hadn't bought him that bicycle for his birthday he would be alive now.). This increased concern with and sense of guilt and responsibility, whether realistic or not, can interfere with healthy mourning and generate its own treatment demands. In instances where mourners correctly or incorrectly perceive that others blame them for the death, further complications may arise in terms of interference with the request for and/or receipt of social support.

Mourners also are often preoccupied with issues of suffering and, if this is the case, not being with the loved one at the time of death. They are frequently concerned about the loved one's last moments of life, asking questions such as, Did she suffer? What was the death like? Did she know it was happening? Was she alone? and, Did she call out for me? If the mourner was not present at the death, he may replay scenes he believes to have occurred and imagine the worst. The experience can end up being far more painful for him than it actually was for the deceased. Imagined scenes can be most traumatizing and can constitute a major stumbling block if not adequately worked through. Sometimes accurate medical information can be helpful (e.g., knowledge that the loved one died instantly and did not suffer or that she was in shock and had no awareness of what was happening). If such comforting information is unavailable, the mourner must find a way to cope with unanswered questions and concerns about the loved one's final moments.

In the quest to answer questions and understand the reasons for, circumstances of, and meaning in the tragic event, mourners may have a pressing need to find out from survivors of the accident what their loved ones were doing when they died (e.g., whether they were rescuing others, which may give the death more meaning; Hodgkinson, 1989). They may attempt to retrace the loved one's final steps in order to understand what he experienced. One family who had lost a son in the Zebrugge, Belgium, ferry disaster pieced together all the information they could from the inquest, postmortems, and witness statements, and were ultimately able to stand at the point where their son met his death on an identical ship (Hodgkinson, 1989). This was most important for them and their mourning.

The issue of preventability often is inextricably linked with accidental death. The mourner tends to cope better if the death is construed as unpreventable, whereas the perception of death as preventable appears to increase the duration and severity of grief and mourning (Bugen, 1979). For example, those whose loved ones die in natural disasters (e.g., earthquake or hurricane) fare better than those whose loved ones die from disasters that are the result of avoidable human error (e.g., airplane crash or train derailment). If it is unclear whether or not the death could have been prevented, or if the mourner assumes responsibility for having had the power to prevent it but did not, grief and mourning will be greater, and more guilt probably will arise to provoke further complications.

Central to the question of preventability is the issue of blame and responsibility. If the death could have been avoided, mourners must contend with anger at the fact that it occurred when it was not inevitable, as well as with anger at the agent responsible, if there is one. In these instances, mourners tend to spend great time and effort searching for the cause of death and attempting to determine who or what is to blame, trying to find some meaning in the death, and striving to regain some sense of control. To these mourners, the death is utterly senseless and unnecessary, and they must struggle to cope with this fact and with feelings about the unfairness and injustice of a death that did not have to happen.

Accidental deaths frequently demand that the mourner deal with this sense of unfairness and injustice. The fact that a mourner's loved one died solely because she was in the wrong place on the highway at the wrong time or because she chose the wrong tour bus can be infuriating. Recognition of such a reality can leave the mourner feeling impotent to protect other loved ones and himself. The limits of one's power and the fact that humans are at the mercy of fate are brought home all too well in these circumstances. The fact that the loss fails to make sense often interferes with the mourner's perception of the death as timely, acceptable, or appropriate. Such interference contributes to problems in the accommodation of the loss.

Typically, it is important for the mourner that any agent involved in the death be identified and held accountable. Even though doing so will not bring the loved one back, for many mourners this is a way to make clear to the world that the death should not have happened, a wrong has been done, and that it must not go unnoticed or unpunished. The time and energy that goes into litigation or advocacy work, for example, can offer some critically important psychological benefits. The desire to address the issue of preventability also explains why the self-help group Mothers Against Drunk Driving (MADD) refuses to use the term *drunk driving accident*, instead insisting on recognition of the volition exercised by the driver through use of the term *drunk driving crash*. Thus, they differentiate the event from a genuine accident that was unpreventable and unpredictable.

In cases where the agents involved are those to whom the well-being of the loved one has been entrusted (e.g., physicians), reactions are intensified. This stems from the violation of expectations and trust inherent in such betrayals as malpractice or criminal negligence. The breaking of faith by someone in whose hands one has literally put the life of a loved one leaves the mourner enraged and distraught. As in homicide, fantasies of vengeance and retribution are not uncommon when such an agent has been identified.

If the deceased is perceived as having contributed in any fashion to her own death (e.g., driven too fast or ignored hurricane warnings), the mourner may feel anger that the loved one has in part caused the losses eliciting painful mourning. If such emotion is admitted, it can lack an appropriate target or outlet and can remain as unfinished business, which complicates mourning. The mourner also may feel guilty for entertaining such angry thoughts.

Losing a loved one from an unpreventable accident or a natural disaster does not mean there are no issues of anger, causality, or attribution of responsibility. Such a death has its own type of stress: Precisely because there is no one to blame, mourners may find it difficult to cope. Many assert that it would be easier if they could direct their anger toward someone because pointing it toward such agents as fate, God, or the weather is unsatisfying. Lack of a particular target can thus interfere with the necessary and healthy experience, expression, and channeling of anger. Such mourners often feel powerless and frustrated. Without a specific target, they may feel that they should not be angry or that they have no recourse but to turn the anger inward, where enormous rage boils with no outlet. Some of these mourners actually assume blame for the death because they find it easier to cope with the event's being their own responsibility—and thus within their own control—than to contend with the fact that it was truly random. The assumption of blame is the price they pay to maintain their needed sense that the world is not random and unpredictable, but orderly and dependable. Truly random events are terrifying because they are uncontrollable and individuals cannot protect themselves against them.

Accidents also can prove problematic for healthy mourning in that the victim's body may not be readily available. It may be mutilated beyond recognition or to the point where others conspire to protect the mourner from viewing it. Alternatively, the mourner may be so inhibited by his own fears that he refrains from looking at it (Raphael, 1983). To the extent that viewing the body is critical to confirm the loss (especially in cases of sudden, unexpected death), confront denial, and ultimately promote mourning, these aspects of accidental death cause complications.

In situations where death is not instantaneous, the loved one and the mourner sometimes are put through additional trauma, which can increase the burden the mourner must bear during the grief and mourning processes. Images of extensive, traumatic, mutilating, dehumanizing, or aggressive actions undertaken by health care workers to save the life of the loved one can remain emblazoned in the mourner's memory. Although the mourner may be consoled that everything possible was done, it still may be painful to recall the use of heroic medical measures (e.g., the jolting of the body when cardiac paddles were applied). Some mourners are further enraged and frustrated by the fact that the loved one had to endure these procedures but died anyway.

Another factor associated with accidental deaths known to have the potential for complicating mourning is the manner of notification of the death. Unfortunately, this arduous task often falls to those least prepared to perform it. In some circumstances, notification itself is so traumatic that the mourner may have accommodated the loss for some time before feelings about the notification and the notifier are calmed. Weisman (1973) describes a particularly brutal example of "hard tell," noting that "long after the woman recovered from her bereavement, she dwelt upon the calamitous way in which the news broke up her life. Not only did she repeat that moment over and over in her mind, but she hated the nameless voice that first called her" (p. 271). Suitable forms of notification to minimize additional suffering are offered by Hogshead (1976), Mancini (1986), Robinson (1981, 1982), Schultz (1980), Soreff (1979), and Weisman (1973).

Accidental deaths, especially those associated with disasters, frequently call into play the legal and insurance systems. Conflicts in these areas can complicate mourning over both the short and long term, although for some, involvement with these systems ultimately can prove therapeutic. Basically, this type of involvement engages issues associated with judgment, blame, responsibility, guilt, retribution, punishment, vengeance, and the psychosocial and financial worth of the deceased and the survivors' suffering. All of these issues are salient in mourning.

Bereavement in accidental and disaster deaths also can be complicated by the continued replay of the destruction, which is visibly portrayed in the media. The bereaved cannot deny the trauma because it is so publicly aired, and it may be very difficult for them to shut out, even temporarily, the reality of the loss and its implications (Raphael, 1983).

Finally, caregivers should remember that in situations where the mourner also has been injured, the struggle for survival may interfere with the commencement of appropriate grief and mourning and can contribute to the development of the delayed mourning syndrome. If this is the case, the caregiver must be prepared to support the mourner, gradually building a relationship of security and trust until the time when the mourner can face the pain of the losses and undertake active mourning (Raphael, 1986). Specific discussion of delayed mourning and its treatment is found in chapter 4.

Additional Risk Factors in Disaster Deaths

In addition to all the problematic elements of accidental deaths, disaster deaths are associated with other high-risk factors. In assessing the impact of these combined risk factors, Raphael (1986) concludes, "Whatever the losses, the bereavements of disaster are rarely uncomplicated" (p. 100). Two sets of factors are relevant: The first set focuses on common issues in disaster deaths, whereas the second addresses issues arising from three scenarios of disaster-related bereavement.

Common issues in disaster deaths

Several common issues cut across all disaster deaths. Raphael (1986) has identified these as described in the following discussion, with my own elaborations. The reader will note that a number of these issues are also pertinent in other kinds of accidental deaths.

First, identification of the dead may cause problems contributing to complications in mourning. Dismemberment may make it difficult to piece remains into human form, and often bodies may be so charred or mutilated that identification is compromised or can be accomplished only through forensic means. When remains are poorly distinguishable, mourners are left with intense fears about the suffering that must have accompanied the death.

The tendency to expect victims of disasters to be more damaged because of the violence and mutilation involved may cause the expectation that viewing the body will be inherently damaging. Stating that there is very little evidence to support this fear, Raphael (1986) cites several studies indicating that mourners who view the body do not regret it, whereas not being able to do so contributes to bereavement difficulties. Despite this evidence, mourners are frequently advised not to see the body by well-meaning others who seek to protect them. It may also be difficult to arrange to see the body even if the survivor so desires. Bureaucratic processes (e.g., coroner's inquests and legal and political intervention) often involved after disaster deaths can also delay, irritate, and complicate the commencement of the grief and mourning processes. There may be an extended period of time before the cause of death is substantiated and/or the body released to the family. Even then, the body may not be in a recognizable state.

Because many mourners are unable to see and recognize the body of the loved one after this type of death, they must contend with uncertainty. This may fuel mourners' natural denial, as well as represent the wish to undo the death and have it not be true. When the loved one was last seen alive, well, and whole but is then never seen again—dead or alive—mourners may wonder about the accuracy of the identification and ask whether the remains they buried were really those of their loved one: Was it really him? Could there have been some sort of mistake? and, How do I know for sure? In the absence of a clear visual confirmation of the death, mourning may not commence. Thus, the first of the "R" processes (i.e., recognize the loss) is compromised, interfering with the remainder of the mourning processes contingent upon it. Raphael (1986) offers the example of the widow who felt she had sinned in remarrying until the day she saw her husband's grave in Greece 30 years after his death. As Raphael summarizes, "In general, failure to see and say good-bye to the dead person may make it hard to give up the commitment" (p. 103).

Confirmation of the death often is followed by the need to have the loved one's remains brought home, where survivors may give them proper treatment. For example, in the aftermath of one airplane crash resulting in severely mutilated and indistinguishable bodies, rather than have their loved ones buried anonymously, families agreed to a unique solution. The bodies of all of the victims were cremated, the remains were commingled, and each family received a portion of the commingled remains. Although the remains were mixed, each family knew that they had a portion of the remains of their own loved one. To the surprise of those around them who were unfamiliar with the often critical need to regain possession of a loved one's remains, the survivors found this most gratifying.

Finally, inherent in disasters affecting an entire community or taking the lives of a number of loved ones, the mourner must contend with the problem of multiple death (see chapter 12). Multiple loss not only increases the number of loved ones for which mourning must be accomplished, it also decreases the number of loved ones available to offer support. The breakdown of social networks that frequently occurs after a disaster also robs the mourner of needed social support and increases the risk of complications. Other secondary losses after community disasters add to those experienced as a consequence of the loss of loved ones. These specifically include losses of home, "communality" (K. Erickson, 1976b), fellowship, neighborhood, environment, material possessions, money, and work. All of these are aspects of or symbols of one's identity and one's past and present. Thus, symbolic secondary losses can be enormous and must be appreciated by mourner and caregiver alike.

Additional complications in disaster bereavement may stem from family separation and relocation stress; anger at the helpers and political, social, and economic agencies if perceived to be ineffective, overly bureaucratic, or too slow; victimization by the media; and problems resulting from food or water shortages or contamination, unsanitary conditions, and poor medical care.

Issues in three scenarios of disaster-related bereavement

Raphael (1986) has identified three different scenarios of disaster-related bereavement: (a) deaths that occur from a disaster in a far and mysterious place, (b) deaths that occur in a disaster in the individual's own country or town but in which the mourner was not involved, and (c) deaths that occur in a disaster that affected the mourner as well. Each scenario has inherent risk factors that come into play in addition to those associated with sudden, accidental, and disaster deaths in general. These specific factors can influence the experience and course of the survivor's grief and mourning.

Deaths occurring from a disaster in a far and mysterious place separate survivors from the loved one at the time of occurrence. Mourners are not themselves personally involved in the disaster, yet they certainly suffer its effects. Frequently, there is a period of anxious waiting for news of the disaster, during which the worst is feared but hope is maintained. When the death is confirmed, geographic distance may prevent transformation of this confirmation into personal reality: Mourners may be unable to travel to the disaster site or may be unable to secure identification of the body or view it because of its mutilation. Consequently, there is a legacy of uncertainty and doubt about the death; no opportunity to spend time with the deceased and say good-bye or take in images of the reality of the death; and, because they are so spread out, little chance for mutual support from other survivors.

Some disaster deaths occur in the individual's own country or town but do not involve the mourner. In this scenario, there is also a period of waiting accompanied by great uncertainty and fear. Typically, there is a greater sense of immediacy and involvement in this type of disaster, as contrasted with the first type. This is because the mourner is exposed to media coverage and often undertakes active attempts to deny or confirm the worst fears by calling hospitals, going to the disaster site, and so forth. This situation is quite difficult because, even though survivors are close enough to see and hear the horror in graphic detail, they often cannot get needed information. They must live in terrible anxiety until they can ascertain what has happened to their loved ones, with each piece of information and misinformation being added to the picture in an attempt to construct what has happened. Without knowledge of their loved ones' status, the passage of time increases survivors' frustration and powerlessness. Often the waiting is punctuated by intense praying, bargaining with God or fate, and other attempts to purchase the welfare of the loved one. Even though they are not present, survivors are intimately involved in the disaster through identification with the loved one.

In disasters affecting the mourner along with the deceased, the mourner may or may not have been with the loved one at the time of death. The mourner may have desperately attempted to reach or save the loved one or may have witnessed the death or discovered the body. Unless the mourner has witnessed the death, there still may be a period of waiting until the reality of the death is confirmed, either because the loved one cannot be found or her status is unknown. In addition, the state of the body and types of morgue facilities available may influence whether, for how long, and in what manner the mourner may be able to be with the body of the deceased and say good-bye.

The degree to which postdeath grief is experienced will be determined greatly by the extent of emotional shock, threat, and exposure to trauma suffered personally by the mourner during the disaster impact. If the mourner had been saved by the deceased, had competed with her for survival, or feels responsible for omissions or commissions resulting in the loved one's death, this can complicate mourning, as can guilt that the mourner survived whereas the loved one did not.

In situations where the mourner was also injured in the disaster, these injuries may have prevented him from viewing the body or participating in funeral rituals. Concerned family members and health care workers may add to the mourner's distress by withholding information out of concern for her condition or because it is difficult for them to discuss such trauma with one already so victimized. The mourner may be left alone to deal with bereavement without the proper information or the necessary support. In addition, her own injuries may leave her confused and unable to process the information she does receive, or the energy demanded for her own survival may preclude her being able to grieve.

Even if not physically injured, the mourner may be preoccupied with trying to cope with her own traumatic reactions to the disaster, attempting to master and make sense out of her own encounter with death, and working toward getting her life and world back together. Sometimes others must be cared for first (e.g., children, the elderly). As a result, members of the mourner's support system may mistakenly believe that the mourner is unaffected by the death of the loved one or is coping well with it. In reality, the mourner is only becoming stable enough to deal with the loss. Like the individual who, as explained by Maslow's (1962) hierarchy of needs, must meet basic physical requirements before addressing higher level psychosocial ones, the mourner often unconsciously prioritizes and delays mourning until the time she judges herself strong enough to confront the experience. Survival issues take precedence; it may only be much later that the full impact of her losses, and her grief and mourning over them, will surface.

Additional Risk Factors in War Deaths

In war, one confronts massive numbers of casualties, threat to person and country, the violence of modern weapons—all of which lead to massive threat of death and destruction for large numbers (Raphael, 1983). Stress-related combat disorders are well documented for combatants (e.g., Opp & Samson, 1987) but are outside the purview of this discussion. Less well documented but often severe in consequence are the disorders of mourning that can follow the death of a loved one in war.

There has been a relative absence of work devoted to analyzing war bereavement. The work of Anderson (1949) and Milgram (1982) is an exception, although the latter focuses exclusively on wartime bereavement in Israel. Reporting to the World Federation for Mental Health, Sanua (1977) notes that, after an exhaustive literature search and correspondence with the United States Department of Defense, investigators were stunned to find that no systematic studies on war bereavement were available or had ever been undertaken in the United States. (Some research had been undertaken with relatives of soldiers missing in action, however.) Sanua provides some data contrasting war bereaved families in the United States with war bereaved families in Israel. Focusing solely on Israeli mourning after the war death of a loved one, Palgi (1973) observes in general that, because the death of a soldier has symbolic meaning for the entire society, the extent of the mourner's adjustment not only depends on personal strengths or psychic vulnerability but also is integrally linked to the cultural content and value system of that society.

War deaths typically embody all of the risk factors and issues found in accidental and disaster deaths, as well as homicides. To these must be added factors inherent in traumatic death (see chapter 12). Yet this still does not account for the entire spectrum of factors that can complicate a survivor's mourning of a loved one killed in war. Other factors include the following.

1. The service person's and mourner's philosophical agreement with war in general and the specific reasons for this war

2. The service person's attitude about going to war (i.e., whether the individual believed in the cause and volunteered or was reluctant to serve)

3. The type of death and the circumstances of it (e.g., in battle, through torture, in a noncombat situation)

4. The country's political climate and its citizens' degree of support for the war and the troops

5. The service person's and mourner's degree of agreement with particular military actions and battle strategy

6. The nature of the war and the combat experiences it contained for the service person

7. The stress of separation experienced by the mourner while the service person was deployed, congruence between expectations for and the reality of this experience, and the length of deployment

8. The impact of the media on the survivor's awareness of war events, personal and social stress, and sense of helplessness

9. The extent of support available

Depending on the length and nature of the stress of the separation and the degree to which the service person's death is anticipated, some mourners may experience postdeath reactions similar to those seen after the loss of a loved one from an illness that has persisted too long. If the death occurs after hostilities have ceased, mourners may experience a situation similar to that caused by sudden, unexpected death in the context of recovery from near-death (see chapter 12). In brief, the death can leave them without adequate recognition and social support.

In both disasters and war, the encounter with death, violence, and mutilation often has profound and long-lasting effects. Particularly sensitive to this is Raphael (1983, 1986), who describes vividly the sights, sounds, and smells victims and rescuers must confront (and ultimately integrate) at the same time they are coping with the shocking personal threat of death. Depending on the degree of exposure to death and bodily mutilation, the mourner may experience psychic numbing (Lifton, 1976). For a brief time, the mourner experiences a massive shutting out of emotion in defense against death anxiety and guilt. At the time of trauma, this numbing helps the survivor protect against overwhelming helplessness and emotional pain. However, when chronic, this response may become maladaptive in that it closes the person off from all feeling. Psychic numbing has been observed in victims of concentration camps and Hiroshima as well as in survivors of other disasters (e.g., the Buffalo Creek flood; K. Erickson, 1976a, 1979). Sometimes the survivor is marked by the death imprint (Lifton, 1976a), in which the survivor has experienced a jarring awareness of the fact of death, as well as of its extent and violence, and appears locked into a death encounter, with its compelling, indelible image dominating his subsequent life. At times, the survivor may reflect his identification with death and the dead via the manifestation of an image of death in life (Raphael, 1983). In many cases, post-traumatic stress responses or a full-blown post-traumatic stress disorder may result.

Without question, the death of a loved one in war is an unusual mixture of both sudden and anticipated loss characterized by an abnormally great number of high-risk variables. Inasmuch as this scenario combines factors present in other types of high-risk deaths, the interventions suggested for each of these can be extrapolated to meet the mourner's needs.

SUICIDE

The literature on suicide generally is devoted to understanding the phenomenon (i.e., reasons underlying it, epidemiology, etc.), suicide prevention, and treatment of suicide survivors. This last category—by far the smallest of the three—is the source of references relevant to suicide as a risk factor contributing to complicated mourning. The present section reviews those aspects of bereavement following suicide that potentiate risk. For more information on suicide, most notably its clinical and treatment aspects, the reader is referred to the following sources: Appel and Wrobleski (1987); Bolton (1986); Bolton and Mitchell (1983); Cain (1972); Calhoun, Selby, and Selby (1982); Demi (1984); Dunne (1987); Dunne, McIntosh, and Dunne-Maxim (1987); Hauser (1987); Lindemann and Greer (1953); McIntosh and Wrobleski (1988); Ness and Pfeffer (1990); Resnik (1969); Rogers, Sheldon, Barwick, Letofsky, and Lancee (1982); Rudestam (1977a, 1977b); Rudestam and Imbroll (1983); Rynearson (1981, 1987a); Schuyler (1973); Shepherd and Barraclough (1974, 1976); Sheskin and Wallace (1976); Shneidman (1973, 1981); van der Wal (1989–1990); Warren (1972); Welu (1975); and Wrobleski and McIntosh (1987).

In addition to the intervention suggestions made throughout this discussion, the caregiver will want to consider interventions delineated for guilt, anger, and socially disenfranchised death (chapter 10) as well as for sudden, unexpected death and traumatic death (chapter 12). It is also especially important for the caregiver to provide appropriate psychoeducational information to help the mourner understand the dynamics of this type of loss and to legitimize resulting complications.

For the most part, the literature has revealed little if any dispute that suicide is—along with sudden accidental death and homicide—one of the most difficult deaths with which a mourner must contend. The majority of authors assert that suicide is the precipitant for the worst kind of bereavement experience and the most disturbed mourning (e.g., Cain, 1972; Stroebe & Stroebe, 1987; Worden, 1982), placing survivors at a risk for physical and mental health problems greater than that for individuals bereaved due to other causes of death (e.g., Gonda, 1989; Osterweis et al., 1984).

Recently, this long-held belief has come under some attack. After reviewing the literature, van der Wal (1989–1990) concluded that "there is no empirical evidence to support the popular notion that survivors of suicide show more pathological reactions, a more complicated and prolonged grief process, than other survivor groups" (p. 149), although he did find support for the thesis that bereavement after suicide is qualitatively different from that following other causes of death. Barrett and Scott (1986) concluded that at 2 to 4 years postdeath there were no differences in measures of recovery between mourners whose loved ones had committed suicide and those whose loved ones had experienced other types of death. Barrett and Scott argue that longitudinal research should compare more closely the grief reactions and courses of suicide survivors and other mourners. Finally, following their critical review of the sequelae of bereavement resulting from suicide, Ness and Pfeffer (1990) note that, notwithstanding the differences in bereavement after suicide and other types of death, data are far from conclusive and the field suffers from a relative lack of well-controlled, empirical studies with sound methodologies.

Although clinical evidence overwhelmingly favors the conclusion that death by suicide predisposes the mourner to extreme difficulty, insufficient empirical evidence exists to confirm or disconfirm this conclusion. The difficulty of researching the topic fuels the problem. What is generally agreed upon is that a number of distinctive aspects of a death by suicide lend mourning a unique complexion. Part of the problem is aptly described by Shneidman (1972):

> I believe that the person who commits suicide puts his psychological skeleton in the survivor's emotional closet— he sentences the survivor to deal with many negative feelings and, more, to become obsessed with thoughts regarding his own actual or possible role in having precipitated the suicidal act or having failed to abort it. It can be a heavy load. (p. x)

In cases where suicide is deemed acceptable or even assisted by survivors (e.g., in the face of terminal illness), one might expect that survivors' negative reactions would be mitigated. It is my contention that, except in this instance, suicide does indeed complicate mourning for survivors. The exact cause of death; its degree of violence; the emotions, problems, and images left for mourners to contend with; and the existence and content of a suicide note (especially when guilt producing) all influence the psychic trauma survivors experience. The following discussion examines factors associated with bereavement outcomes, synthesizing findings of the references cited earlier.

Factors Complicating Mourning After Suicide

Before specific factors are discussed, it first must be pointed out that issues relating to degree of anticipation, timeliness, preventability, violence, and the death surround usually play an important part in the mourner's response to a death by suicide. Insofar as these issues, discussed earlier in this chapter and in chapter 12, are pertinent to a specific situation, the caregiver must consider them. In addition to these factors, certain other reactions following a death by suicide can prove problematic. These are of two types: individual psychological reactions and familial and social reactions.

Individual psychological reactions

Even when a death was not by suicide and the mourner understands that the deceased's departure was not by choice, the cessation of interaction is frequently associated with, among other natural reactions, feelings of rejection, abandonment, shame, and/or personal diminishment. When suicide has severed the relationship, the mourner is deprived of any comfort in knowing the departure was not by design. Rather, the loved one has consciously and deliberately chosen death over life with the mourner. The rejection is not symbolic; it is actual. Abandonment, dishonor, humiliation, and feelings of personal diminishment are reality-based sequelae following the purposeful desertion of one who is loved and needed. Clearly, the dynamics of a loved one's choosing to die set the mourner up for intense feelings toward the deceased and the self. These feelings can arise not only from having been unable to prevent the death, but also from how little the mourner construes himself to have meant to the deceased, given the deceased's choice to end life. Lowered self-esteem; shattered self-worth; and feelings of inadequacy, deficiency, and failure are typical. Indeed, because suicide often erodes the capacity to trust that this type of rejection will not happen again, the caregiver may have to work with the mourner to prevent emotional withdrawal from others and acting out associated with fears of intimacy.

Anger, guilt, and shame. Following a suicide, mourners often experience heightened feelings of anger, guilt, and shame. The intensity of these feelings sets them apart from survivors whose loved ones experienced other types of death. Normal anger is intensified after a suicide into rage at the betrayal inherent in the loved one's abandonment, the emotional and social predicaments the mourner now faces, and the enormous amount of unfinished business remaining in the relationship. Unfortunately, the mourner lacks the best and most obvious target toward which to direct this anger and rage (i.e., the deceased). That individual is now at peace while the mourner is left to cope with the intense pain and stigma of the death.

The anger the suicide survivor feels toward the deceased, God, or the world is often more torturous and vehement because of the deliberateness of the rejection by the deceased. During mourning, this emotion must be vigorously addressed, with an emphasis on appropriate externalization. The internalization of anger, coupled with intense guilt, can lead to unhealthy acting out.

The unavailability of the deceased increases the feelings of frustration, powerlessness, and being out of control already present in such a tremendous victimization. Because the absence of the loved one leaves the mourner without an accessible target, her aggressive feelings may become self-directed, resulting in depression or self-destructive behaviors and relationships. Alternatively, she may act out these feelings. The mourner can feel quite guilty when she becomes aware of the depth of her anger toward her loved one. At times, blame and anger directed at others is, in fact, a true projection of the mourner's own unacceptable feelings. Yet such feelings also may be a direct expression of the mourner's perception of others' irresponsibility or failure. Therapists and physicians are common objects of such feelings and often are held accountable for failure to predict or prevent the death.

Despite the tendency on the part of some to assign responsibility in this way, it would be inaccurate to assume that the mourner always will blame others for the suicide. In many cases, the mourner is all too aware that only the deceased could have prevented the death. Especially in situations where the mourner has witnessed long-term depression, stress, and failed efforts to intervene, she may have felt the suicide was inevitable or even wished for the end of suffering that death could bring. Notwithstanding this, in some persons the recognition of such thoughts can provoke guilt feelings after the suicide actually comes to pass. Efforts to deal with these feelings can then lead to blame projected onto others.

Genuine sorrow over the loss often complicates the acute and long-lasting rage seen after suicide, pushing it underground only to make it more virulent and less amenable to healthy expression and treatment. In ordinary circumstances it is difficult for a mourner to contend with the combination of anger and sorrow; in this scenario, it becomes monumentally burdensome. Interfering even further with the appropriate processing of these emotions may be the mourner's guilt over having such strong rage.

In modest amounts, guilt characterizes most mourning experiences; however, in mourning after suicide, it is infinitely stronger and more persistent. Obsession about one's part in the death and what one might have done to prevent it, endless concerns about responsibility for omissions or commissions that might have influenced the ultimate outcome, constant rumination about past experiences and conversations with the deceased now reinterpreted in light of the suicide, and the clarity of 20/20 hindsight all churn away, intensifying the mourner's experience. Could something have been done? What clues should the mourner have seen? Why wasn't she more patient? Is it her fault? The contents of any suicide note can inflame matters even more.

The primary causes of guilt in grief (i.e., falling short of one's self-image, violation of a personal standard, ambivalence, imperfection in relationships, surviving when others have died, and feeling one contributed to the death) are intensified in this scenario. Precisely because the death was preventable, the situation predisposes the mourner to problems known to develop in the presence of intense guilt (e.g., increased depression or anxiety).

Guilt and torturous self-blame, whether realistic or unrealistic, may lead to a need to be punished, as is evidenced by acting out that cries for a punitive response from others (e.g., socially deviant behavior such as larceny). Alternatively, these reactions may reveal the individual's attempts at self-punishment (e.g., self-destructive relationships that reenact the loved one's abandonment).

As is the case for any mourner, guilt must be constructively addressed, not dismissed. In the search for understanding and the effort to put the suicide in a logical chronology, the survivor may look back and see clues to the impending suicide that now make sense but then were imperceptible or unrecognizable. The caregiver must challenge the mourner about whether it is realistic to have expected herself to have noticed these clues and must work with her to keep her from assuming undue guilt over not having acted on them to prevent the suicide. In addition, in normalizing and dealing therapeutically with guilt, the caregiver should be aware that the mourner frequently assumes especially intense and unrealistic guilt. Therefore, the caregiver should watch for behavior indicating self-punishment, self-sabotage, or unhealthy attempts at expiation and atonement, helping the survivor see that, regardless of what she did or did not do, she is not responsible for or in control of another's choices.

When combined with a negative social reaction to the suicide, the loved one's choosing to die sets the survivor up for intense feelings of shame. The sense of personal rejection wrought by suicide is profound. The caregiver must help the survivor identify this and any feelings of unworthiness or badness that may develop as the survivor struggles to understand why she has been so viciously rejected. Ripple effects of these types of negative thoughts are common and, like secondary losses, must be identified and worked through.

Finally, it is noteworthy that following their extensive review of the literature on suicide, Ness and Pfeffer (1990) caution caregivers to avoid overly ambitious goals for suicide survivors. They note that these mourners "never resolve their feelings entirely . . . [and that] overly ambitious therapeutic goals in this direction may frustrate rather than help the bereaved individual" (p. 284).

Concern for one's own suicidality. Depression, self-reproach, despair, and regression are frequent manifestations of guilt and anger not channelled therapeutically. These reactions ultimately can contribute to the increased suicidal behaviors and thoughts seen in such mourners, thus adding to their frequently expressed concerns about contagion and genetic transmission of the predisposition toward suicide, mental illness, and self-destructive impulses. Cain (1972) and Worden (1982) report how sons of fathers who had committed suicide are particularly, although not exclusively, vulnerable to the belief that suicide will be their own ultimate fate.

A number of facts increase the risk for subsequent suicides among survivors of suicide:

1. Often the same social, environmental, and psychological conditions obtain for the survivor as for the deceased (e.g., abuse, alcoholism, depression, poverty).

2. Suicide usually occurs in a family experiencing stress or multiple crises.

3. Suicide survivors can identify with the deceased via suicidal behaviors.

4. In some situations, the suicide of one removes its taboo for others.

The caregiver should be aware of these dynamics yet take care to explain to the mourner that suicide is based on choice, not heredity or inevitability.

The search for understanding. The personalized, agonizing question, Why did she do this to me? is usually found underneath the more global question, Why, why, why? (Worden, 1982). Frustratingly, however, the survivor has no way to explore this issue with the deceased but must find a way to live with both the question and associated affects unless a response can be hypothesized and accepted. This is no small task. Not only must the mourner try to understand the deceased's rationale and fit her actions into the context of the relationship without benefit of her input, he must strive over time to integrate abandonment and betrayal into that relationship. What does the suicide say about the deceased's feelings about the mourner? Does the suicide invalidate everything else positive that had transpired in the relationship? Is the act a statement about the deceased or the mourner? Does the suicide mean the mourner is unlovable? What did he do to deserve this? Such questioning is common.

The mourner desperately seeks to make sense of the death. However, self-exoneration is only one of the motives for the search. The mourner also needs to comprehend the reasons the loved one chose to end life in order to be able to understand and learn to live with the suicide. This is particularly difficult when there has been no prior indication that the loved one had been contemplating such drastic action.

A search for meaning also is fueled because a suicide can so destabilize the mourner's assumptive world that its healthy recreation depends on the development of a new meaning system. This meaning system must incorporate the reality of this type of loss and its attendant rejection and guilt, as well as the "goodness" or "lack of badness" of the mourner, who may have internalized many negative feelings secondary to both the rejection and guilt for not having prevented the death. Sometimes the mourner's inability to predict the suicide contributes not only to the shattering of the assumptive world, but also to the mourner's distrust of himself.

The mourner must contend with the reactions he has to his loved one's choice and will need to make sense of and accommodate any resulting feelings with other emotions about the loved one. For example, he may struggle with disillusionment. He may question the loved one's once unquestionable decision-making abilities. He may have second thoughts about the loved one's strength. Or he may perceive the loved one as ill. Reconciling current feelings or thoughts about the deceased with previous ones can be problematic. Cognitive dissonance, confusion, and insecurity, along with questioning of one's own judgment, can result from the inconsistency between prior beliefs, assumptions, and expectations about the deceased and the reality of the suicide.

As is true for other sudden, unexpected deaths, the mourner attempts to understand the motives for the death, its cause, what contributed to it, and what led up to it. In other words, the mourner attempts to accomplish the first "R" process of mourning (i.e., recognize the loss) and becomes particularly involved in the subprocess of understanding the death. To facilitate this, Shneidman (1969) has proposed the *psychological autopsy,* a method to reconstruct the behavioral and psychological events leading to a suicide in order to determine why the individual committed suicide, how the individual died and why she died at that particular time, and the most probable cause of death. This is one example of *postvention* (Shneidman, 1981), an approach involving intervention through activities designed to reduce the effects of a traumatic event such as suicide on the lives of survivors.

In helping the survivor come to some understanding of why the deceased chose the option of dying, the caregiver should allow him to play out different scenarios about the deceased's frame of mind, choice of method, reasoning, and decision-making process. Although the mourner may disagree with the loved one's taking her own life, he can be helped to see that he is not responsible. Suicide was the loved one's choice—perhaps the last and only option she perceived at that time. Whether or not the mourner accepts the notion that the deceased had a right to end her own life, he must recognize that it was her choice, not his. It will be beneficial to point out that the survivor may recognize this fact intellectually long before he can accept it emotionally. The caregiver also must anticipate and recognize the psychologically important functions of the mourner's compulsive inquiry into events, need to assign blame and responsibility, and struggle for understanding and meaning. Intricately related to the need to restore some control, predictability, and justice in the world, these processes require support and, if nontherapeutic, appropriate intervention.

Unfinished business. The absence of sufficient understanding of the death is not only unsettling but also provides the enormous stress of unfinished business, which presses upon the mourner for resolution and increases anxiety. One of the caregiver's primary goals is therefore to help the survivor identify and deal with any unfinished business that remains and cope with the sequelae of being unprepared and lacking the opportunity to say good-bye (e.g., heightened sense of unreality, intensified feelings, obsessive rumination, propensity to act out in an attempt to achieve closure).

The voluntary choosing of death, and at times the violent nature of the death, may prevent the survivor from remembering the deceased realistically. The survivor needs to have a realistic composite image of the deceased in order to recover, but this usually cannot be achieved until many of the emotions associated with the death have been worked through. The caregiver should therefore work with the survivor to see clearly both the deceased's positive and negative aspects.

When the death follows significant conflict, ambivalence, or hostility in the relationship or concludes a long-term history of stress (e.g., depression, previous suicide attempts, alcohol problems, marital separation), the mourner often finds herself in a difficult position. The suicide, often representing the final act of conflict, is followed by relief that the demands posed by the relationship have ceased. However, this relief coincides with a sense of failure, sadness, anger, shame, and guilt that the mourner could not solve the previous problems. The mixture of relief intermingled with these other reactions is unexpected, shameful, and guilt producing. In brief, the mourner is damned if she allows herself to experience relief and, because she must deny the existence of a real emotion, damned if she does not. In such situations, the dynamics of the conflicted mourning syndrome (Parkes & Weiss, 1983) often come to the fore and are exacerbated by other aspects of this type of death.

In working through the unfinished business in such a relationship, the caregiver can normalize the sense of relief that frequently comes when suicide ends a life that had placed onerous burdens and worries on the survivor. It also may be helpful to suggest that relief always follows the end of an unhappy situation, that it need not create more guilt, and, most important, that one may feel relieved that something is over and still mourn.

Familial and social reactions

A number of adverse familial and social reactions frequently occur following a suicide. Many of these responses are undertaken in an attempt to minimize the guilt and pain experienced after this kind of death. As Rudestam (1987) observes, studies repeatedly confirm that survivors whose loved ones committed suicide are viewed more negatively and with more blame than are survivors whose loved ones experienced other types of death.

Among the family dynamics that demand intervention or referral are communication dysfunction, social isolation, projection of guilt and blaming of others, and scapegoating. Families frequently identify a scapegoat as a way of coping with feelings of guilt and responsibility (Lindemann & Greer, 1953). Often, the scapegoat is held accountable for failing to observe the signs of impending suicide or otherwise meet the needs of the deceased.

Another way families cope with guilt and concomitant feelings of shame is by denying that the death was a suicide and constructing a family myth to rationalize the death to themselves as well as to the outside world (Warren, 1972). Denial of the cause of death by calling the suicide an accident or a natural death allows the family to avoid feelings of responsibility and guilt, as well as the pain of the rejection, abandonment, and deliberateness implicit in the death. Often this type of distortion is defended on the basis of protecting the children in the family. However, this type of secret is known to produce severe family and individual pathology. In this regard, the legacy of suicide (Cain, 1972) surpasses intrapersonal uncertainty, guilt, blame, and hostility and can send an emotional shock wave causing "a network of underground 'after shocks' of serious life events that can occur anywhere in the extended family system in the months or years following serious emotional events in a family" (Bowen, 1976, p. 339). Bowen identifies two of the key elements in determining the impact of a death on the family: the degree to which surviving family members deny the death and communication among family members. Thus, the emotional costs of a secret of this nature take a heavy toll on family members' psychological, social, and physical health. In particular, the secret and the fear that the truth will be discovered form the basis for a weighty conspiracy of silence; foster reluctance to share grief and feelings about the death; and aid in the development of strained relationships predicated on doing whatever is necessary to minimize the chance that others will learn the truth, judge negatively, and reject the survivors. If the suicide is denied, the caregiver must work to eliminate this denial within the family group, regardless of whether or not the suicide is admitted publicly. To the extent that the caregiver helps mourners admit the reality of the suicide and not tolerate further victimization in the form of stigmatization by self or others, mourning will be facilitated.

As noted earlier, the psychological reactions of abandonment, guilt, and lowered self-worth contribute to the significant degree of shame usually experienced following the suicide of a loved one. They can also promote withdrawal from others. These reactions are strongly reinforced by social stigma and lack of support following this type of death. Suicide qualifies as what Lazare (1979) terms a *socially unspeakable loss*, or one that generates a conspiracy of silence and promotes social withdrawal because of ignorance of what to say and discomfort with the issue. This situation offers a prime example of a social factor promoting failure to mourn.

Range and Calhoun (1990) studied individuals bereaved through suicide, comparing them with mourners whose loved ones had died as a result of accident, homicide, or natural causes (either anticipated or unanticipated deaths). These investigators reported that mourners whose loved ones had died by suicide were expected to explain the nature of the death to others and that they lied about the cause of death. These mourners received less community support than did those bereaved through other types of death, even though all the mourners seemed to share a common core of bereavement experience and appreciated the same types of treatment from others.

Unfortunately, such stigmatization often results in everything from obituaries being omitted to insurance payments being invalidated. It will be beneficial for the caregiver to predict the possibility of negative social reactions, but it should be made clear that any negative reactions stem from problems in those doing the reacting, not in the survivors. In addition, people may wonder why the survivors' love was not enough to stop the victim from killing himself. In this case, the caregiver must help survivors avoid accepting responsibility for the actions of the deceased and "buying into" shame or guilt and must find ways to enable them to reestablish connections with others.

Often, the mourning experience may be complicated by the involvement of legal and insurance systems called upon in the investigation of the suicide. The unpleasant experiences associated with this process exacerbate survivor shame and interfere with mourning by strengthening negative grief responses, heightening already existing anger at the deceased for leaving such turmoil, and forcing mourners to deal with shame for the actions of the deceased—shame from which they frequently have difficulty separating themselves. The caregiver can predict the probable discomfort associated with any medical, legal, and insurance investigations; remain available during these processes to support mourners; and help them differentiate themselves from the deceased's actions.

Stigmatization becomes quite problematic when it deprives mourners of necessary support or interferes with the receipt or experience of appropriate social and religious rituals required for healthy confirmation of the death and mourning. Too often, obituaries and wakes are foregone. Although in the past certain religious groups denied funeral rites to those who committed suicide, this trend is changing, and recognition is growing of survivors' need for the psychological and social benefits of these rituals (Conley, 1986; Rando, 1984). Sometimes mourners themselves refuse to engage in these rituals to avoid dealing publicly with the death or admitting its cause. Others decline such rituals in an effort to punish the deceased. For whatever reason, the lack of appropriate funeral rituals after suicide predisposes these mourners to complications, just as it does other mourners, and may serve to increase stigmatization. The caregiver should help survivors see that their discomfort with the mode of death—and the guilt, shame, and stigma it brings—must not be allowed to disenfranchise them or interfere with their reaping the psychological benefits of such rituals. Postdeath activities following suicide should be kept as much as possible like those following a death of any other kind.

Treatment Modalities in Suicide

Individual, couples, family, and group work have all been suggested as useful treatment modalities for working with individuals whose loved ones have committed suicide. However, it is consistently noted that group work is especially helpful—even as an adjunct—because it provides benefits other modalities lack.

Arguments for the utility of support groups devoted to suicide survivors have been well made by Appel and Wrobleski (1987) and Billow (1987). These arguments essentially focus on the benefits of mutual aid groups in general and the specific benefits to the survivors of suicide. The latter include not only the enfranchisement of these usually disenfranchised mourners, but also therapeutic attention and assistance focusing on a number of specific issues.

1. The fact that the loved one chose death, to abandon the mourner, and not to let the mourner help, which results in the relatively greater need for the suicide survivor to come to an understanding of why the choice was made and/or to learn to live with not having the answer—or an acceptable answer—to questions

2. The need to understand the nature of the crisis that engulfed the loved one and that the person "resolved" through suicide

3. Voyeuristic publicity and speculation as to the cause of the suicide, the latter often resulting in the family's indictment as others search for a single explanation of what is undeniably a multidetermined phenomenon

4. Suicidal behavior and dynamics and the need to reconceptualize the event from the deceased's perspective in order to reframe events to make the suicide seem less meaningless

5. Intensified feelings (e.g., guilt, shame); specifically related issues (e.g., unacceptable feelings of anger at the deceased and/or murderous impulses toward others thought to be in some way responsible); and the need for self-forgiveness, relinquishment of the passive victim role, and ultimately a renewed reason for living

Although a bereavement support group may embrace suicide survivors who meet their criteria, they may not be able to offer all that is needed. It will be important that any group chosen be able to address the specific needs of suicide survivors. For example, The Compassionate Friends offers support for parental bereavement and welcomes parents whose children have committed suicide. However, the unique issues posed by suicide may not be adequately addressed in a generic group of bereaved parents. For this type of mourning, a self-help or support group formed specifically for suicide survivors is perhaps most useful. Safe Place, run by the international suicide prevention group The Samaritans, is one such specialized group; other regional or local groups provide similar services. These and other resources can be identified by contacting local suicide prevention centers or the American Association of Suicidology (2459 South Ash Street, Denver, Colorado 80222). Participation in a focused group need not preclude additional participation in a group like The Compassionate Friends or a heterogeneous bereavement support group sponsored by, for example, a church or synagogue.

Caregiver Issues in Suicide

It is important to note that the mental health profession in general has had historical difficulty treating mourners whose loved ones have committed suicide. The reasons for this are complex but certainly include the obvious fact that for many caregivers a completed suicide confronts both personal and professional limits (Dunne, 1987). Such attitudes demand that caregivers working with suicide survivors look at themselves carefully in a number of ways. The following specific recommendations are adapted from Dunne's excellent work.

1. Caregivers must examine their attitudes about suicide and acknowledge their limitations in dealing with the issue.

2. Caregivers must guard against countertransference responses such as blaming the victim (i.e., the mourner) and colluding in scapegoating others (especially the deceased's therapist).

3. Caregivers must avoid subtly stigmatizing the mourner by blaming the family for the perceived mental health problems of the deceased.

4. Caregivers who have survived suicide in their own lives, either of significant others or of their patients or clients, must avoid projecting their own guilt or anger onto the mourner.

5. Caregivers must be knowledgeable about the typical grief and mourning processes after suicide in order to avoid labeling normal responses as pathological.

6. Caregivers must be respectful of the mourner's grief despite the fact that at times this may place limits on the process of uncovering unconscious material.

Additional discussion of caregiver issues in treatment is provided in chapter 14.

HOMICIDE

Depending on the source of the statistic, when lifetime risk is analyzed, 1 out of every 133 to 153 persons will be the victim of a homicide (U. S. Department of Justice, 1985). Given this mind-boggling statistical probability, it seems strange that there is a relative dearth of clinical and empirical literature on the topic of homicide survivors. A number of well-known and highly respected books on grief and mourning, offering in-depth discussion of responses to a wide variety of losses, scarcely mention homicide.

Those who have addressed homicide and its consequences for survivors mostly work in the areas of post-traumatic stress and victimization. Together with selected authors from the field of thanatology, they have contributed to the following resources, to which the reader is referred for more comprehensive information about homicide and the treatment of its effects: Amick-McMullan, Kilpatrick, Veronen, and Smith (1989); Bard and Sangrey (1986); Burgess (1975); Danto, Bruhns, and Kutscher (1982); Figley (1985b, 1986); Getzel and Masters (1984); Goldenberg and Goldenberg (1982); Janoff-Bulman (1985); Lord (1987); Masters, Friedman, and Getzel (1988); Michalowski (1976); Ochberg (1988a); Ochberg and Fojtik (1984); Peterson and Seligman (1983); Rando (1988); Redmond, (1989); Rinear (1985, 1988); Rynearson (1984, 1987a, 1988); Schmidt (1986); and van der Kolk (1987b).

Homicide deaths often inherently contain a number of elements that contribute to their high-risk status. As described in the following discussion, these elements are amenable to specific treatments delineated for anger, guilt, and disenfranchised death (chapter 10). Treatments recommended for sudden, unexpected death and traumatic death (chapter 12) are also relevant. As for other deaths, the caregiver should (a) provide appropriate psychoeducational information to help the mourner prepare for and understand the dynamics of this type of loss and (b) explain and legitimize any confusing or frightening reactions that may develop (e.g., intrusive images, disorganized thinking, increased vulnerability).

A Social Perspective on Homicide

Without question, murder terrifies most sane human beings. If this assertion requires any documentation, one need only turn to Michalowski's (1976) excellent article on the social meanings of violent death. Noting that there are differential responses to various forms of violent death, he proposes that "It is the manner of dying, and not the death itself, that determines the social meaning of any death" (p. 83). However, different social reactions exist even among the diverse types of violent death.

In comparing and contrasting social reactions to murders and fatal traffic accidents, Michalowski notes that the odds of dying in a traffic accident are three times those for homicide and that the average cost of a single traffic fatality is 23 times that of a single criminal homicide. Nonetheless, public opinion and action focus more on murder than on traffic fatalities. Michalowski identifies five dimensions that combine to make one form of violent death more salient than another.

1. *Inevitability.* Homicide is not perceived as an accident, whereas many traffic fatalities are. The causal relationship between a human act and a resulting death is much more obvious and direct in the case of murder than it is in traffic fatalities. Although traffic fatalities may be caused by human behavior, this may be obscured by the complex causal sequence of such events. It is assumed that traffic fatalities result from an inevitable concurrence of circumstances beyond human control (although in fact they may not). This is not assumed for homicide.

2. *Controllability.* Notwithstanding the valid arguments of MADD to the contrary, traffic fatalities are often presumed to arise from fateful occurrences not controllable through the rational manipulation of human behavior. Thus, they are less the object of strong demands for control than homicide, which is perceived as controllable in that it arises from the willful acts of individuals. Ironically, many individuals actively oppose measures that would control traffic fatalities (e.g., mandatory seat belt laws), saying that they violate individual freedoms.

3. *Intent.* The intent ascribed to a wrong determines the social response to the harm producer. In most traffic fatalities—even vehicular homicide, in which clear negligence is present—no direct and specific intent to cause harm exists; accidents are seldom premeditated. In contrast, homicide by definition involves

intent. As such, it becomes legitimate and purposeful to direct much more stringent social controls against those who commit murder, despite the fact that in both cases the victim is equally dead.

4. *Deviance.* A traffic fatality is perceived as less of a social problem than a murder because the context in which it occurs is defined as being more normal. In contrast, murder is illegal and considered abnormal. Interestingly, hostilities leading to murder (e.g., hostile verbal exchanges) are perceived as an abnormal form of deviance despite the fact that they are not necessarily illegal, whereas the antecedents of traffic fatalities (e.g., negligent driving) are not perceived as an abnormal form of deviance, yet usually they are illegal.

5. *Social utility.* The motor vehicle is critically necessary to our society and is perceived as a positive and important element in achieving other socially defined goals. Therefore, it and its consequences are tolerated. Conversely, inasmuch as we desire social and domestic tranquility, our society views social hostility—the antecedent of murder—as making no utilitarian contribution. As Michalowski notes, "This further directs social control efforts away from the traffic fatality and towards homicide, even when the undesirable violent consequences of the former may exceed the latter" (p. 91).

This analysis of the differential social response to traffic fatalities and homicide clearly suggests that, despite the fact that other deaths happen more frequently and incur greater cost, the event of murder so horrifies human beings that it assumes prominence in their effort for control and their search for deterrence and punishment. The intensity of the terror evoked by homicide presages the intensity of the bereavement that takes place after it occurs.

Conceptualizations of Bereavement After Homicide

The bereavement witnessed after homicide has been described as a form of post-traumatic stress disorder (PTSD; see Masters et al., 1988; Redmond, 1989; Rinear, 1988; Rynearson, 1984, 1987a, 1988). After personally counseling hundreds of families coping with the homicide of a loved one, Redmond (1989) put into perspective the confluence of bereavement and post-traumatic stress routinely observed after homicide, noting its longevity and its normalcy for these mourners:

Homicide survivors may present symptomatic behaviors characteristic of PTSD up to five years following the murder of a loved one. *This becomes a normal range of functioning for this distinct population.* All homicide survivors with whom I have worked were assessed at intake with some characteristics of PTSD. Survivors present with a history of nightmares, flash- backs, fear of strangers, emotional withdrawal, eating and sleeping disturbances, constant intrusion of thought of the murder, case-related associations, irritability, angry outbursts, and avoidance of reminders. (p. 52, emphasis added)

Not unlike parental loss of a child and many cases of suicide, the loss of a loved one via homicide routinely generates a bereavement response that, as compared with other types of bereavement, renders a significantly pathological appearance. It is critically important that caregivers be aware of this fact, not only to maintain appropriate expectations and be able to normalize reactions for survivors, but also to employ the most effective treatment techniques.

In this case, mourners will need treatment for both PTSD and compli- cated mourning. The caregiver typically must work through aspects of PTSD before therapeutic access can be gained to many of the aspects of mourning. Strong support for blending approaches to clinical intervention following homicide is given by Amick-McMullan et al. (1989), who caution against dichotomous classification of homicidal bereavements. These investigators assert that thinking of survivors as suffering from either PTSD or grief reactions is an oversimplification, with the problem arising that "Either label, PTSD or grief, underestimates the complexity of what appears to be a fairly consistent, very debilitating pattern of posthomicide reactions." (p. 24)

Additional dimensions of a conceptual framework for responses to unnatural death (i.e., accident, suicide, and homicide) have been postu- lated by Rynearson (1987a). These three forms of unnatural death form a hierarchy in the ascending order noted. Because homicide best embodies the dynamics of the reactions to these types of deaths, Rynearson's postu- lations, briefly noted at the beginning of this chapter, are addressed in detail here, although they are also relevant to death by accident or suicide. Rynearson offers four propositions to explain adjustment to unnatural death.

1. The adjustment to unnatural death involves a variable combina- tion of violence, violation, and volition. Violence is defined as "an unanticipated, lethal, injurious act" (Rynearson, 1987a, p. 82). Violation is defined as "an unprovoked, transgressive, exploitative act" (p. 83). Volition is defined as "an act of willful, intentional killing (homicide and suicide) or as an irresponsible negligence leading to death (accidental death is usually a product of human error)" (p. 86). Thus, accident involves intense violence, moderate violation, and weak volition when it results from human negli- gence or recklessness and involves absent volition when it results

from a random occurrence. Suicide involves intense violence, absent violation, and intense volition on the part of the deceased. Finally, homicide involves intense violence, intense violation, and intense volition on the part of the murderer.

2. The adjustment to an unnatural death is a complex state that dynamically controls in a self-regulatory manner the ratio of acceptance and denial of these dissonant variables of violence, violation, and volition. Each variable is associated with a compensatory psychological response: Violence with post-traumatic stress; violation with victimization; and volition with compulsive inquiry to establish the locus of responsibility and the purpose of the death, if the death was intended.

3. The adjustment to an unnatural death is positively correlated with the degree of identification with the victim. It is rare that the actual death is witnessed. However, through the mechanism of identification, the demand is common for paradoxical recapitulation and adjustment to violence, violation, and volition for the survivor rather than for the victim.

4. The adjustment to an unnatural death must include the sociocultural consequences of transgressive violence, violation, and volition. Sociocultural support tends to evaporate in unnatural death and leave the survivor isolated and blamed.

For these reasons, a caregiver can expect to observe more intense and more prolonged reactions and will witness a "greater incidence of symptoms of post-traumatic stress, victimization, and compulsive inquiry in subjects adjusting to unnatural versus natural dying" (Rynearson, 1987a, p. 90). Therefore, as with others who have been victimized, it is important to structure treatment to result in the empowerment of the homicide survivor.

Amick-McMullan et al. (1989) offer a multidimensional symptom formulation model based on Mowrer's (1960) two-factor learning theory to explain homicide bereavement reactions and the general agreement found across studies with respect to survivors' symptoms in the cognitive, affective, physiological, and behavioral dimensions. These investigators note that the model offers promise in explaining the acquisition and maintenance of intrusive cognitions, aversive emotional responses, physiological hyperarousal, and phobic avoidance, and that it has been successfully applied to both sexual assault victims (Holmes & St. Lawrence, 1983; Kilpatrick, Veronen, & Resick, 1982) and combat veterans (Keane, Zimering, & Caddell, 1985). Amick-McMullan et al. summarize their paradigm as follows:

Being told of the murder of a loved one is a profoundly traumatic, threatening experience which is likely to elicit powerful unconditioned (unlearned) stress responses such as physiological hyperarousal, intense fear, rage, sorrow, and very aversive homicide-related thoughts . . . classical conditioning occurs as previously neutral stimuli (e.g., a telephone ringing, a police officer at the door) become associated with the traumatic event. . . . Mowrer's Factor One describes this classical conditioning paradigm, through which a great variety of previously benign stimuli such as news reports, criminal justice officials, and even one's own home become cues for very aversive responses. . . . The abundance of such homicide cues and the repetitive pattern of their occurrence helps to account for the chronic nature of survivor reactions (Masters et al., 1988).

Once classical conditioning has occurred, an individual naturally seeks to avoid those stimuli that elicit traumatic responses. . . . Mowrer's Factor Two postulates that such avoidance behavior actually maintains the strength of the classically conditioned traumatic responses by preventing opportunities for extinction of the responses. . . . A secondary danger of such avoidance behavior is that survivors are likely to isolate themselves from much needed sources of support during their periods of crisis. It is not unusual for survivors to find themselves avoiding helping professionals and even family members and friends who have become reminders of the homicide or of their lost loved ones. (pp. 25–26)

Following their comprehensive study of the clinical and empirical literature related to the reactions of family survivors of homicide victims, Amick-McMullan et al. (1989) concluded that mourning differs from that following other bereavements in the depth of horror, rage, and vengefulness; the persistence of anxiety and phobic reactions; and the impediments to the adjustment process posed by involvement with the criminal justice system. These dimensions contribute to other conclusions drawn from their study of the literature.

1. As concerns the cognitive dimension, studies are unanimous in reporting the existence of intrusive, repetitive thoughts and/or nightmares.

2. Consensus among studies also emerges along the affective dimension, with survivors displaying intense, overwhelming levels of affect typically labeled as variations of rage, terror, numbness, and depression.

3. Studies addressing the physiological dimension also show considerable agreement regarding survivor symptomatology,

with frequent identification of disturbances in sleep and appetite, increased heart rate, headaches, gastrointestinal upset, and increased startle responses.

4. Behavioral changes noted in the studies include phobic avoidance of homicide-related stimuli and increased self-protective behavior, changing roles in the family and relationship disruption, and a tendency to try to hunt for the killer.

In addition, their own empirical study provides convincing evidence of the high level of general psychiatric distress among homicide survivors and the striking relationship between psychological adjustment and satisfaction with how the criminal justice system handles the case.

Factors Complicating Mourning After Homicide

The factors placing homicide survivors at high risk for complicated mourning include those associated with the particular circumstances of homicide deaths and the reactions they stimulate: suddenness and lack of anticipation; violence, trauma, and horror; preventability of the death and its unnecessary nature; anger, guilt, self-blame, and shattered assumptions; and, in many cases, randomness. In addition, various external agents, systems, and situations secondarily victimize survivors.

Suddenness and lack of anticipation

The suddenness and lack of anticipation of most homicides sets the survivor up for the unanticipated mourning syndrome and its pathological concomitants. As well, these factors provoke the problem of incomprehensibility of the event. The mourner has a strong need to understand the death and the reasons for it and to put it in some perspective; however, the abruptness of the loss and the violation of expectations it brings cause a shattering of the assumptive world, making it difficult for the mourner to make sense of the death. This confusion is exacerbated by the association of suddenness with violence.

It is important to realize that the suddenness of the death leaves the mourner in psychological and systemic distress for a significant time. There are long-lasting physical repercussions, as well as more anger and guilt in this type of bereavement, with an internalized emotional response described as an "anger-in" or intrapunitive response causing prolonged physical stress (Sanders, 1982–1983). Like a rubber band stretched to its limit, the mourner's nervous system is so reactive that it appears to increase the intensity of the experience of other grief reactions. A stretched-to-the-limit physiological system cannot help but contribute to the development of symptoms of increased arousal found in PTSD or post-traumatic stress symptoms observed in homicide survivors. According to the DSM-III-R (American Psychiatric Association, 1987), chief among these symptoms are difficulty falling or staying asleep, irritability or outbursts of anger, difficulty concentrating, hypervigilance, an exaggerated startle response, and physiologic reactivity upon exposure to events that symbolize or resemble an aspect of the traumatic event.

Violence, trauma, and horror

Homicide always involves violence, trauma, and horror. As such, it engenders feelings of vulnerability, helplessness, and threat, as well as extreme feelings of being out of control. All of these emotions prompt in the mourner enormous efforts to find a reason for and meaning in the death, determine who is to blame and assign responsibility, mete out punishment, and regain a sense of personal control and of order in the universe. The more brutal the murder, the greater the anger, fear, violation, and sense of powerlessness. Bodily mutilation appears to result in stronger identification with the deceased and in the survivor's losing more control of his personal life and environment (Redmond, 1989). The caregiver must recognize and respond to the crucial importance of the mourner's compulsive inquiry into the events surrounding the death, the need to assign blame and responsibility, and the search for meaning. Each of these responses is intricately related to the need to restore control, predictability, and a sense of justice and order in the world.

Strong and pervasive fear is typical after homicide. Unremitting for a long time—if not forever—fear generates a heightened anticipation and protective avoidance of violence. Survivors are hypervigilant, specifically dreading anticipated violence to self or others. Apprehension, feelings of vulnerability to further psychological or physical assaults, and profound insecurity in the world combine to cause phobic reactions and compulsive self-protective behaviors. According to Rynearson (1984):

> Compulsive behaviors of self-protection were so intense during the first year of bereavement that the subjects' usual range of territorial and affiliative behaviors was constricted; unfamiliar surroundings were circumvented, home became a protected fortress, strangers were avoided, and there was a compulsive need for the proximity and tangible assurance of the safety of the remaining family members. (p. 1453)

Life after the homicide of a loved one involves numerous practical and concrete changes developing out of the survivors' fear. Such changes are not easy to incorporate into one's sense of self or one's assumptive world. They may be abstract (e.g., paralyzing fear) or concrete (e.g., keeping a gun to protect one's family despite having a terror of guns). Often, they are quite distressing. Behavioral and social interventions are frequently mandated to help mourners be able to negotiate the world again.

Homicide, with its severe violence and volition, constitutes a traumatic stressor and hence predisposes toward post-traumatic stress reactions, as previously mentioned. Homicide is viewed as "an aversive stimulus that mobilizes so much painful affect that psychological adaptive mechanisms are overwhelmed, initiating the alternating responses of hyperreactivity and hyporeactivity" (Rynearson, 1988, p. 217). Coinciding with this situation is the clinical reaction of victimization, in which physical assault or threat of it is accompanied by PTSD "plus a residual attitude of resignation and/or rage. Victims commonly experience humiliation, isolation, worthlessness, compensatory hatred, and obsessions of vengeance" (Rynearson, 1988, p. 217).

Not uncommonly, death imagery becomes intense and frightening in survivors who did not witness the trauma directly or view the body. Because of personal attachment and identification, survivors are compelled to work through an internalized fantasy of grotesque dying that not only increases their own fears, but also complicates mourning by presenting the task of assimilating the violence and transgression implicit in this type of death (Rynearson, 1984, 1988).

As with accidents, disasters, and war, if the mourner was absent at the time of the death, he may experience similar concerns about not being with the loved one and wonder about what the last moments were like (e.g., whether or how much the loved one suffered, experienced fear, or called out for the mourner). Also like these other deaths, the mourner's fantasies may be even worse than the reality. Intrusive, repetitive images of the murder, fashioned from witness or police reports and often focused on the victim's terror and helplessness, are frequently mixed with fantasized scenarios. They can interfere with cognitive processing and with ongoing daily life as they emerge as recurrent obsessive thoughts, unbidden recollections, conscious fantasies, or dreams. Rinear (1985) has identified three types of dreams in her work with parents of murdered children: (a) wish-fulfillment dreams, in which the deceased is seen as alive and well; (b) dreams associated with the desire to undo the murder, in which the mourner attempts to warn the victim of the impending danger or to intervene to protect that person but is in some way thwarted; and (c) dreams focused on some particularly painful aspect of the event, in which the mourner relives the occurrence (e.g., identification of the body).

Caregivers must be mindful of and prepared to work with the intentional repression that many homicide survivors undertake. Misinterpreting repression as resistance or trying to break through it inappropriately suggests that the caregiver incompletely understands the normalcy of the phenomenon and its defensive purposes in this situation.

Other issues are directly attributable to the violence, trauma, and horror of homicide: anger, guilt, self-blame, and shattered assumptions. These will be discussed after the issue of preventability has been considered.

Preventability

Preventability is an issue not exclusive to homicide, although it certainly is underscored there: The mourner's perception of the death as preventable is a high-risk factor for complicated mourning no matter the circumstance. If the death is construed to have been preventable, this means it did not have to happen except for the carelessness, negligence, or maliciousness of another. Thus, anger is a central effect of the perception of preventability. In addition, if carelessness or negligence is presumed to have caused the death, the mourner is likely to obsess about "if onlys" (e.g., if only she had left work earlier, the death wouldn't have happened). If maliciousness is present, issues of intentionality become pertinent and complicate mourning by increasing victimization and confronting the mourner with issues associated with aggression, destructiveness, and vulnerability in contemporary society. As noted previously, there is a need to assign blame and responsibility and mete out punishment. Searching for reasons and causes; attempting to rectify the moral order of the universe in terms of responsibility, blame, and punishment; and striving to regain control and meaning all complicate the mourner's adjustment to the loss. Trying to figure out why the death happened when it was preventable becomes a preoccupation, even a major obsession, for many mourners. The fact that not everything was done that might have been done to avoid the death causes the same type of distress as other types of unfinished business and prompts many of the same reactions. Attempting to get a cognitive handle on the death is a difficult task because closure is missing, and there is no comfort, as in other types of death, that everything that could have been done was done. Other problems inherent in the death (e.g., suddenness and trauma) can be expected to compound the situation. Treatment for mourners who perceive the loved one's death as preventable necessarily encompasses therapeutic work to help the mourner deal with violation of the assumptive world (see chapter 9) as well as anger (see chapter 10).

Anger, guilt, self-blame, and shattered assumptions

In the case of homicide, the death would not have taken place but for the conscious intent of the perpetrator, who arbitrarily decided to end the life of the loved one. No matter what rationale the murderer may have had, to the mourner the death is an unreasonable and senseless event. In such cases, no death is acceptable, no death is timely, no death is anticipated, no death is unpreventable, and no death surround is comforting. The problems each of these negative factors brings individually to any death situation are compounded in homicide.

The outrage and indignation at the ultimate arrogance of someone who assumes the right to exterminate another living being amount to blinding fury. Accentuating this is the incredible rage at the violence of the killing and at the helplessness to which it gives rise. The fear and psychosocial and behavioral responses the mourner experiences to it are maddening—he feels victimized without respite due to his identification with the deceased and his own personal reactions. His world has been forever changed by the perpetrator, and he finds the intransigence of the undesirable alteration infuriating.

The normal anger experienced after the death of a loved one is unbounded following homicide, and the intensity of anger and thoughts of retaliation often amaze and frighten the survivor. Prior to the death, the mourner may have associated the notion of revenge with evil, violent individuals—individuals quite unlike the type the mourner always has considered himself. Yet elaborate fantasies for revenge and contemplations of ways to torture, castrate, degrade, and agonize the murderer—to make the murderer suffer more than the loved one suffered and the mourner is suffering—can dominate the life of the mourner, who may or may not be able to understand these as natural reactions to such a situation. Such retaliatory thinking is an effort to assume control in the situation, restore a sense of justice in the world, and confine violence to the realm of imagination by providing the outlet of violent imagery as a restraint against transformation into actual violent behavior. The anger and associated desire for revenge are part of the critical survival struggle to assert vitality. By attacking the victimizer, the survivor escapes the realm of inner deadness caused by the victimization (Lifton, 1979). In this way, such emotion and the images embodying it "can also be a way of holding onto a psychic lifeline when surrounded by images of death" (p. 176).

Survivors may be concerned that they are no better off than the murderer as they experience rage and entertain murderous impulses. Some may worry that such thoughts mean they might be unsafe around their own families, and this concern can lead to shame, fear, emotional withdrawal, deep depression, and fears of going crazy (Redmond, 1989). Also, overwhelming internal conflict exists with one's own sense of values, beliefs, and justice. The normal fear seen in acute grief as the mourner confronts unfamiliar and/or uncharacteristic reactions reaches its zenith here. The caregiver must normalize and legitimize these feelings. One way to do this is to convey some of the retaliatory thoughts other survivors have and to place these into a proper psychological perspective. If such feelings are not normalized and legitimized, mourners can turn their rage inward and/or become obsessed with the notion that they are as evil as the perpetrator.

Mourners will need to acknowledge, explore, and appropriately express their rage, as well as their violent imagery, and then decide how to channel and transform their anger to avoid becoming destructive to themselves or others. Although fantasizing about acting out one's rage is normal, actually acting it out in transgressive violent behavior must be prevented. Displacement of anger, often onto those most proximate—even those trying quite diligently to help—must be guarded against because it may only serve to alienate the mourner from needed support, thus causing further problems. Efforts at retribution via the criminal justice system are quite common and, providing the promise of justice is realized, offer one avenue whereby punishment may be secured. Sometimes the focus on retribution can become a psychological defense to obscure and avoid the painful affects associated with acceptance of the death and mourning of the loss, further complicating mourning.

In the majority of situations, anger coexists with feelings of guilt and self-blame. Although these emotions are common initially to some extent after all losses, homicide can increase these emotions if the mourner feels there was something he should have done (e.g., provided his son with a larger allowance so he would not have been working at the gas station where he was robbed and murdered) or should not have done (e.g., prevented his daughter from dating the boyfriend who ultimately murdered her). Given that the death was completely preventable, because it was not prevented the mourner may feel that blame must be placed somewhere. This is especially true when the perpetrator is known by the mourner. In situations where the murderer is a member of the family, as is the case in 15 percent of homicides (Federal Bureau of Investigation, 1990), mourners are doubly victimized: They identify not only with the victim, but also with the murderer. Feelings of rage and desire for retribution coexist, and the dual identification is so confusing that the loss becomes most difficult to work through and assimilate (Rynearson, 1984, 1988).

Masters et al. (1988) report on their work between 1979 and 1984 with 1,182 families of homicide victims at the Victim Services Agency of New York City. They comment how they were "unprepared for the violence, severity, and prolonged duration of the symptoms which the families had to endure" (p. 113). Dispelling a myth, they point out that "the psychological reactions to the murder of poor, working-class, and middle-class clients did not differ significantly. Clients of widely differing ethnic, economic and social background shared common emotions, defensive patterns, and processes of working through their pain" (p. 113).

These observers also comment on a number of the specific psychological reactions they perceived. Along with post-traumatic stress reactions, repeated emotional firestorms, despair, and psychic numbing, they note that rage and guilt are the two emotional reactions most frequently reported. Rage is directed at the perpetrator, society, and other family members for failing to protect the victim. Guilt becomes directed at the self for not warning or protecting the victim, not foreseeing the tragedy, and not intervening more or sooner.

Masters et al. reveal how these reactions can serve as defensive responses as well as reflect realistic responses to the loss. Writing that caregivers must be aware that "multiple concerns, conscious and unconscious, underlie the manifest content of a survivor's statements" (p. 118), they point out that conscious feelings of guilt may serve to defend the survivor from unconscious feelings of vulnerability. This corroborates information previously addressed and predicts that caregiver efforts to convince a survivor that he is not at fault may be resisted fiercely out of that person's need to preserve a sense of security and self-esteem. In addition, guilt may have a basis in reality in that surviving relatives may have unconsciously incited or encouraged dangerous behavior by the victim. In this regard, the survivors with whom Masters et al. worked had to become aware of the problems in their relationship that the deceased may have acted out at the time of the murder (e.g., courting danger at a bar or walking late at night in a dangerous area). In addition, they also had to recognize that in most cases the familial conflicts being acted out were common maturational problems that unfortunately happened to end catastrophically. Caregivers need to be aware that survivors often magnify their role from one of contributing to the victim's behavior to that of being the primary cause of the victim's death.

As Masters et al. additionally stress, conscious rage and blame often serve as defensive displacement of guilt, with the survivor's directing such feelings toward others because the perception that he may have contributed to the victim's behavior is enormously painful. Guilt also can serve as defensive displacement of anger against others, especially close family members. To avoid the loss of another loved one, the survivor may avoid expressing anger toward that person for failure to protect the victim or for having encouraged the victim to behave dangerously, instead directing rage toward the self. Thus, anger at others turned inward becomes guilt.

In conclusion, the authors note the dual significance of guilt and rage in work with homicide survivors:

> Guilt and rage, the conscious feeling of which the survivor is usually aware, can constitute both a direct and realistic reaction to actuality and simultaneously complex defensive unconscious maneuvers aimed at avoiding conscious awareness of unbearable pain, anger, guilt, and fear. (Masters et al., 1988, p. 120)

Further concern about the adaptive importance of self-blame and the need of the caregiver to respect its utility has been articulated by Janoff-Bulman (1985). In discussing the shattered assumptions and psychosocial stressors of victims, Janoff-Bulman notes that, in addition to using certain other coping mechanisms, mourners attempt to rebuild via attributions of behavioral self-blame the three assumptions violated by the experience of victimization (i.e., personal invulnerability, sense of the world as meaningful, and perception of self as positive). At this point, it is important to reiterate that, with the invalidation of the assumptive world, the mourner experiences excruciating distress and loss of comfort and coping beliefs, with ensuing anger, disillusionment, and despair. Mourning is significantly complicated as a result.

Randomness

In accepting personal blame and in feeling guilty for the murder, mourners may seek to avoid the terror associated with utter randomness. As noted earlier, truly random events are appalling because they signify that one can never be secure in the protection of self or others. Although self-blame is a high price, it is one unconsciously paid to maintain a sense that the world is not arbitrary and unpredictable and to minimize fear. It also bolsters the illusion that if certain elements are identified and then controlled or avoided, the individual will be able to forestall trauma. (Such thinking is not unlike the rationale and dynamics underlying the phenomenon of blaming the victim.)

Secondary victimization

Throughout the literature on survival after the homicide of a loved one, the point is made that the responses or lack thereof of those upon whom the survivor counts for support frequently revictimize that person. Such *secondary victimization,* also known as *second injury* or *second wound* (Ochberg, 1988b), additionally violates the survivor's assumptive world. The National Organization for Victim Assistance (cited in Rinear, 1988) has identified four common reactions to survivors of violent crimes: isolation, blame, stigmatization, and injustice. These reactions, which arise from others' needs to defend themselves against the fear of violence and homicide, embody secondary victimization. It often has been asserted that such victimization is in many ways worse than the murder itself because it occurs at the hands of those whom survivors expect will help them contend with the loss and protect their rights.

Parties guilty of such abuse include family and friends; the law enforcement and criminal justice systems; the media; and emergency, medical, and mental health professionals. Thus, on the social level, one can observe tactics similar to the mourner's assumption of self-blame and responsibility, with such behaviors offering others the illusion that the death was preventable and that elements can be identified that, if avoided, will assure that such a trauma could never happen to them or their loved ones. By blaming the victim and the survivors for the murder, those attributing blame explain the event to counteract feelings of fear and anxiety arising from their own sense of vulnerability and the perception of randomness. They comfort themselves with the illusion that they are exempt from a similar type of victimization and feel protected by convincing themselves that they would never be such persons, nor do such things, as did the victim and the survivors.

The price for others' peace of mind is the survivors' stigmatization and alienation, which exacerbate existing feelings of vulnerability, lack of control, injustice, anger, loss, frustration, despair, impotence, guilt, sadness, insecurity, loneliness, and shame. Even if some of these attributions of blame are valid (e.g., the victim or survivors were involved in illegal activities), survivors' feelings of loss are not eliminated. The death of a loved one will bring pain and grief despite social approval of the demise or social devaluation of the victim. Family members of those killed in criminal activities mourn as do the families of innocent bystanders killed by that criminal. In instances where the victim courted danger to the dismay or disapproval of the survivors, this knowledge brings no comfort, only more difficulties in mourning:

> Those who have opposed parental or spousal wishes do not deserve to be murdered! The survivor must subsequently endure not only the loss of the loved one, but the death of personal hopes, dreams, and unfulfilled expectations that perhaps someday the son, daughter or spouse would have functioned in a more productive lifestyle. The survivor experiences a greater sense of personal failure when there is ambivalence in the relationship, and the process of bereavement becomes more exaggerated and complicated. (Redmond, 1989, p. 38)

The absence of social support that occurs in response to the anxiety-provoking nature of homicide and the revulsion stimulated by its violence, terror, and horror are profoundly negative influences on the survivor's mourning. In these circumstances, disenfranchisement amplifies the feelings of rage, pain, violation, and secondary loss already so prevalent. Mourning is made infinitely more complicated. The very nature of the death further victimizes those left behind to mourn it.

Many people believe that the law enforcement and criminal justice systems exist to protect the interests of the victim and survivors. However, the reality is that other interests are being protected as well (i.e., the accused's, the state's). Procedures to protect these interests may conflict with or take precedence over mourners' interests and needs. Already victimized by the murder of the loved one, survivors can be stunned to discover that victimization does not necessarily stop with apprehension of the perpetrator, if that even occurs. Thrust into a new world, with new demands and rules, homicide survivors can find another nightmare beginning with the pursuit of justice. Redmond (1989) quotes one mother's frustration in trying to negotiate the system:

> I could deal with the murderer, I knew he had to be sick to do such a terrible thing to my daughter, what I have had the hardest time accepting is the way the system has treated us. There's MORE frustration and pain in dealing with the system, than with the murderer. There's one closed door after another. Everyone tells you what you can't do: *can't* come into the courtroom, *can't* show any emotion in the courtroom, *can't* get a trial date set, *can't* get a first degree murder charge. My worst victimization was by our criminal justice system. I needed to be in that courtroom, I needed to see the pictures of her body, and understand how she had fought him off. They wouldn't recognize my ability to make those decisions for myself. (p. 40)

Mourning is always complicated by repetitive and protracted interactions with the criminal justice system. These continue to provoke acute grief reactions in survivors, with each proceeding opening wounds that are not allowed to heal. Violations and victimization persist and are created anew. The family is torn by the conflicting desire to see justice done and to avoid the pain of the experience. Continual drains on survivors' personal, economic, social, and physical resources are determined by how they feel they must respond to this type of death. In cases where the matter takes years to come to trial and exhaust all appeals, the survivors' mourning continues to be complicated by supplemental victimization and a torturous lack of closure. When the perpetrator receives what survivors consider to be an inappropriate sentence, they feel additionally victimized and have their assumptive worlds further assaulted. Frequently, they articulate the notion that the perpetrator gave their loved one and themselves a life sentence but received comparably little punishment. Their belief in justice is eroded, and they must contend with the feeling that the life of their loved one appears to have mattered little to society.

It is abundantly clear that survivors must intentionally and consciously suppress certain aspects of their mourning until the conclusion of legal maneuvers. Emotional energy is simply unavailable to deal with both criminal proceedings and mourning processes. Because legal processes may take up to 7 years to complete (Redmond, 1989), the duration of this suppression and its consequences can be substantial. As in other situations in which a necessary process is not undertaken, lack of full mourning is often quite stressful and unhealthy. Typically—and unfortunately— survivors are additionally victimized by the negative sequelae of such suppression: psychological or physical illness, family dysfunction, substance abuse, and work-related problems, among other difficulties. Even after sentencing, mourners continue to be confronted by the trauma and frequently feel compelled to monitor the perpetrator's incarceration to ensure that subsequent appeals, early release, or parole do not cut it short. If and when the perpetrator is released or escapes, mourners live in fear of his retaliation on them, or, in some cases, their retaliation on him. Even if they are not overly concerned about their own potential for violence, the potential for encountering the murderer face to face can cause them to limit their activities, adding further insult to injury.

In situations where the perpetrator remains at large, the survivors live with many additional stresses. There is continual anxiety and the fear that anyone could be the killer and that the murderer could return and kill other loved ones. Sometimes this fear can lead survivors to paranoia that causes them to turn on other family members in their attempt to identify the murderer. Survivors experience exacerbated emotional responses stemming from the absence of a target for their rage; their lack of closure; their anger at the law enforcement system; and their internalized lethal violence and transgression, unbuffered by the solving of the murder and the apprehension and punishment of the murderer (Rynearson, 1984, 1988). Usually these feelings coincide with continued efforts directed toward the criminal's apprehension and punishment.

Plainly, caregivers must appreciate the significant impact of the legal process on mourning and must offer treatment that can withstand that impact. They must be prepared to offer information on how legal proceedings can delay and complicate mourning and help mourners weigh the costs and benefits to determine whether or not to pursue legal action. If mourners choose to take legal action, caregivers must assist them while minimizing their inevitable distress. Therefore, it is important that caregivers be aware of the various aspects of the legal process in order to be a useful resource to mourners. Caregivers must not misinterpret delays in mourning due to involvement with the legal system as resistance. They also should avoid focusing exclusively on abstractions and be prepared to deal with the practical realities that assume significance (e.g., economic constraints that interfere with hiring a private investigator or traveling to attend a trial).

The media are well known for intrusion into the pain of the bereaved (e.g., pushing a microphone in the face of an anguished survivor who has just learned of a loved one's death) and for presenting repeated painful stimuli that intensify survivors' horror and feelings of loss of control and invasion of privacy (e.g., repeatedly telecasting the discovery of the loved one's body or traumatic details of the death). In all fairness, it must be recognized that many conscientious media professionals, while advocating the public's right to know, do strive to respect the rights of the bereaved. I myself have participated in numerous educational events over the last several years in which the topic has been how the media can inform without further victimizing. Although productive for the media, sensationalism is most destructive to mourners. Intimate details of their lives and their mourning become public, and their loved one's privacy no longer exists. Mourners, like everyone else, are not necessarily assertive in times of trauma; they may not realize they can refuse interviews or request the use of alternate file footage on television.

Finally, systems of health care—emergency workers, medical staff, and mental health professionals—can ameliorate or exacerbate the experience for mourners. Too often, the needs of survivors are overlooked in the crisis (e.g., with notification accomplished poorly, insufficient time given for mourners to spend with the body, and questions ignored). Later on, despite good intentions, survivors are misunderstood, pathologized, and mistreated due to a lack of understanding of the needs and type of mourning generated by homicide.

It appears that in those instances where there is less secondary victimization, survivors have less complicated mourning reactions, given other factors (Redmond, 1989). The caregiver must therefore recognize the impact of secondary victimization and gear interventions to provide appropriate proactive information to help the mourner understand and deal with—if not avoid—these problems.

Treatment Modalities in Homicide

As for those who have survived the suicide or traumatic death of a loved one, homicide survivors can profit from a mutual support or self-help group because of the unique therapeutic benefits such groups offers. It is fairly common for mourners to engage in individual treatment and attend a group simultaneously. Unless contraindicated or deemed unnecessary for some idiosyncratic reason, I routinely suggest group attendance for all homicide survivors. The same rationale as for suicide survivors applies with regard to the need for a specific versus a generic group focus. For caregivers interested in running a group for homicide survivors, there is no better reference than Redmond's (1989) *Surviving: When Someone You Love Was Murdered.* This book, written specifically for those providing group therapy, is also most helpful for caregivers working with homicide survivors in other modalities.

Caregiver Issues in Homicide

As noted earlier, homicide and one's powerlessness in the face of it generate significant feelings of anxiety and vulnerability. Therefore, the treatment of the homicide survivor is quite demanding not only because of the complexity of interventions for the numerous risk factors involved, but also because of the enormous stress it places on the caregiver. Certainly, the general issues faced by caregivers, discussed in chapter 14, are heightened in this scenario. The horror of the act and the awareness on some level that the victim could just as easily have been the caregiver's own loved one fuel discomfort, as do the intensity and duration of the reactions with which these mourners present.

It is not uncommon for homicide survivors to describe how they have endured indignities, psychological assaults, insults, pain, and, not infrequently, aggression in their attempts to seek treatment. Unfortunately, much secondary victimization is perpetrated upon these individuals by caregivers otherwise committed to helping those in distress. Victimization is sometimes blatant, sometimes subtle. Nevertheless, it remains a sad commentary on how fear can bring out the worst in us. The issue for those concerned and courageous enough to treat these mourners is how to achieve enough self-protection to enable one to be therapeutic to the mourner without becoming so protected as to be untouched by the tragedy. This is a very thin line to walk—one best traversed in the company of peers, confidants, or supervisors who can steady the caregiver if the need arises.

CHAPTER 12

Risks and Therapeutic Implications Associated With Sudden and Unexpected, Multiple, and Traumatic Death

In addition to risks associated with individual, relationship, and system factors (detailed in chapter 10) and risks associated with mode of death (discussed in chapter 11), certain additional traumatic characteristics of the death can pose problems for the mourner. Among these important characteristics are the degree to which the death is sudden and unexpected, the number of deaths with which the mourner is confronted simultaneously, and the degree and quality of trauma. This chapter discusses these risks and describes appropriate therapeutic interventions for each type. As for other chapters, the treatment suggestions presented here are in addition to the philosophical perspectives on treatment and the generic treatment guidelines presented in chapter 8 and the specific interventions for the six "R" processes of mourning detailed in chapter 9. Other difficult issues arise when the death is of a child and when the death is associated with AIDS. These last two circumstances will be addressed in chapter 13.

SUDDEN, UNEXPECTED DEATH

If I were restricted to asking a mourner only one question in my evaluation, that question would have to be, To what extent, if any, had you expected the death of your loved one? More than any other single piece of data, the answer to this question helps the caregiver know what to expect from the mourner and decide what specific intervention strategies and techniques offer the highest probability for efficacy.

Suddenness is a nonspecific variable that can be found in all types of death. Without a doubt, it is one of the two risk factors contributing most to complicated mourning (the other being a markedly angry, ambivalent, or dependent premorbid relationship with the deceased). It is an inherent aspect of most acute natural deaths; accidental, disaster, and war deaths; suicides; and homicides. Suddenness and a lack of anticipation also tend to occur concurrently on a frequent basis with certain other factors contributing to complicated mourning by constituting a traumatic death (i.e., violence, mutilation, and destruction; randomness and/or preventability; multiple death; and the mourner's personal encounter with the death; Rando, in press-a). Because sudden deaths account for the greatest percentage of deaths of those under age 37 (National Safety Council, 1991), they are also highly associated with the deaths of children and adolescents. Many of the complications associated with these types of deaths derive from their sudden and unexpected nature.

Sudden, unexpected death has been found to be a generic determining factor for at least three of the complicated mourning syndromes, although it certainly may play a part in the others as well. According to Raphael (1983), sudden death—specifically, the kind for which someone is blamed—is a frequent precipitant of distorted mourning of the extremely angry type. In addition, Raphael reports that sudden death of all kinds is commonly associated with chronic mourning. The third type of complicated mourning associated with sudden death is the syndrome specifically identified as following from it—the unanticipated mourning syndrome (Parkes & Weiss, 1983).

Briefly, in the unanticipated mourning syndrome, the death so severely disrupts the mourner's life that uncomplicated recovery or accommodation to the loss can no longer be expected and functioning is seriously impaired. The world is experienced as being totally out of control—the mourner does not know it anymore. She is unable to grasp the full implications of the loss: It is inexplicable, unbelievable, and incomprehensible. Although intellectually the mourner knows her loved one has died, she cannot accept this fact emotionally. The mourner's coping abilities are assaulted, and her adaptive capacities are completely overwhelmed. She suffers from extreme bewilderment, anxiety, insecurity, self-reproach, depression, and despair—all of which significantly handicap her on a daily basis. The mourner perceives the world as a frightening place and fears that at any time she or someone else she loves may die. This causes profound insecurity and anxiety, to which the mourner may respond with avoidance and social withdrawal. Acute grief symptomatology persists much longer than usual, and the mourner remains in physiological and emotional shock for an extended period of time. (For additional information about the unanticipated mourning syndrome and its treatment, see chapter 4.)

Caregivers must understand that many of these responses occur early in bereavement in the majority of mourners whose loved ones die suddenly. It is only when some or all of the typical responses to sudden, unexpected death persist too long and solidify, thus interfering with the "R" processes of mourning, that reactions become pathological. Prior to this, even in the presence of the exact same behaviors, responses must be viewed as normal under the circumstances.

Issues Complicating Mourning After Sudden, Unexpected Death

A number of issues inherent in sudden, unexpected death combine to make it a high-risk factor for complicated mourning. Basically, these issues revolve around the fact that the unexpected loss itself constitutes a personal trauma for the individual. The shock effects of the death (Raphael, 1983) can be so stressful as to overwhelm the ego, which becomes taken up trying to master the helplessness and other flooding affects (e.g., shock, horror, anxiety, vulnerability). In this sense, trauma exists regardless of whether the death occurs under what could be termed explicitly objective traumatic circumstances (e.g., mutilating accident or violent suicide). In other words, suddenness and lack of anticipation adversely influence the mourner's internal world and coping abilities, thus constituting the trauma. When these elements are accompanied by external traumatic circumstances, the impact on the mourner is increased, as is the risk for complications.

The following issues particularly complicate mourning after sudden, unexpected death.

1. The capacity to cope is diminished: A sudden, unexpected death is such an assault on the mourner that her adaptive and coping abilities become dysfunctional. In brief, she experiences both increased distress and decreased capacities to cope.

2. The assumptive world is violently shattered: Without time to incorporate the change, the mourner's assumptive world is abruptly destroyed. Control, predictability, and security are lost, and the assumptions, expectations, and beliefs upon which the mourner has based her life are violated.

3. The loss does not make sense: Because of the stunning impact of the destruction of the assumptive world and the shock to the mourner's psyche, the mourner cannot understand or absorb what has happened. Very simply, she cannot grasp the implications of what has occurred, and the crucial first "R" process of mourning is compromised.

4. There is no chance to say good-bye and finish unfinished business with the deceased: Lack of closure in the relationship leaves the mourner feeling robbed, anguished, depressed, anxious, despairing, guilty, enraged, frustrated, and hurt. The mourner may be predisposed to seek closure by acting out.

5. Symptoms of acute grief and physical and emotional shock persist for a prolonged period of time: Persistent symptoms often demoralize the mourner and make it more difficult for her to cope with mourning processes. These mourning processes are themselves complicated and protracted by the mourner's symptoms.

6. The mourner obsessively reconstructs events in retrospect: Reconstruction of events is the mourner's attempt after the fact to provide herself some control and predictability, to gain a perception of logical progression, and to regain a sense of anticipation. Although such reconstruction can help the mourner grasp the event, it can be harmful if she holds herself responsible for not perceiving cues prior to the death that actually were imperceptible or nonexistent. Problems with guilt can ensue, as can difficulties if the mourner's focus on the past and her attempts to grasp and make sense out of it interfere with current functioning or persist too long.

7. The mourner experiences a profound loss of security and confidence in the world, which affects all areas of her life: A death without warning and the shattering of the mourner's assumptive world can make her chronically afraid that another unexpected loss will befall her. This can make the mourner hesitant to reinvest in others or take risks and can contribute to her becoming rigid, compulsive, frightened, or overprotective in her attempts to defend herself or other loved ones from another sudden trauma. Such behavior in turn can compromise her relationships with others.

8. The loss cuts across experiences in the relationship and tends to highlight what was happening at the time of the death: This propensity can cause mourners to overfocus on negative aspects of the relationship that may have been occurring at the time of the death, without placing them in the context of the entire relationship. This out-of-balance picture can cause the mourner to be inordinately guilty.

9. The death tends to leave the mourner with relatively more intense emotional reactions: Heightened emotional reactions often—although not exclusively—include greater anger, guilt,

helplessness, death anxiety, vulnerability, insecurity, need to understand and (where appropriate) affix blame and responsibility, confusion and disorganization, obsession with the deceased, and search for meaning.

10. A sudden, unexpected death is often followed by a number of major secondary losses because of the consequences of the lack of anticipation (e.g., loss of home because of lack of financial planning).

11. The death can provoke a post-traumatic stress response: Implicit traumatic aspects of sudden death can add an overlay of post-traumatic symptoms that intensify the mourning experience and frequently require partial or total working through before mourning can be addressed. (See the section in this chapter on traumatic death for more about treatment of post-traumatic stress symptomatology.)

Parkes and Weiss (1983) conjecture that, because this type of death seems so disconnected to anything that precedes it, the mourner's ability to understand and explain it is compromised. If this is true, it may account for some of the severity of complications witnessed after this type of loss. As noted previously, impairments in the earlier "R" processes of mourning interfere with successful completion of subsequent ones. Because sudden, unexpected death appears to jeopardize what essentially is the basic foundation of the "R" processes of mourning (i.e., recognition of the loss), it is not surprising that significant disturbances can arise in the other aspects of mourning.

In addition, the extended duration of acute grief symptomatology, which coincides with similarly extended emotional and physiological shock (Sanders, 1982–1983), leaves the mourner poorly equipped to deal with the issues and conflicts associated with this type of death. These issues and conflicts concern not only lack of opportunity to finish unfinished business and violation of the mourner's assumptive world but also the typical concerns present in mourning any loss.

Sudden, Unexpected Death in the Context of Terminal Illness or Recovery

One important issue that has received virtually no attention in the literature, with the exception of the work subsequently noted, involves the mourner's idiosyncratic interpretation of sudden, unexpected death. As noted in Rando (1987b), two scenarios may be especially problematic in this regard. In the first, a sudden death—often but not always caused by acute natural causes—occurs to someone who has been chronically or terminally ill and for whom the family had expected a different kind of death (e.g., the cancer patient dies suddenly from a heart attack instead of slipping into the coma the family had been told to expect). In the second, death occurs after hopes have been raised by the loved one's unexpected recovery.

In the first scenario, because the family is prepared only for a certain kind of a death at a certain time, their assumptions and expectations are violated. In reality, therefore, they are unprepared. As such, they often require the same types of support and intervention as do other mourners experiencing a sudden, unexpected death. Unfortunately, society may erroneously believe that the family was prepared, and necessary support may not be forthcoming. The following case example makes this idea plain:

> A. J. was an elderly male whose physical abilities had been declining for several years. Upon what proved to be his final admission to the hospital, he was diagnosed as having a debilitating neurological disease that was expected to be terminal within six months. His family was attempting to cope with this news and making plans to bring A. J. home to die when they were notified that an undiagnosed aneurysm had burst and A. J. had died. To the family, this was a completely unexpected and unacceptable death. They responded with many of the same reactions witnessed in families of accident victims. Not only was the death untimely in terms of what the physician had told them, but they also felt robbed of the opportunity to take A. J. home, participate in his care, finish unfinished business, say good-bye, and engage in many other important processes of anticipatory grief.
>
> In contrast to the family, friends perceived this as a death that was expected. They had known of the continuing decline of A. J. over the previous several years and had assumed that the death was a natural consequence of this. Their expectation was that the family knew that A. J. would die soon and that the family had been prepared for the death. They failed to appreciate that it was the "wrong" death occurring at the "wrong" time. Unfortunately, because others' viewpoints were totally different from that of the family, the family never received appropriate support. Friends never realized the type of loss nor its impact. Additionally, those friends had unrealistic expectations of the family's bereavement and recovery, since they were based on an incorrect assessment of what the family had experienced. (Rando, 1988, pp. 103–104)

This kind of death not only violates expectations and thereby causes increased emotional distress, it also exacerbates the normal responses to loss; increases self-blame; frustrates the facilitation of what has been termed an *appropriate death* (Weisman, 1972a; Weisman & Hackett, 1961); promotes feelings of failure, depression, guilt, frustration, loss of meaning, and being robbed; exacerbates problems related to intensified involvement during the illness; overburdens depleted mourners with systemic shock and other negative sequelae of sudden, unexpected death; and in some instances counterpoises shock and relief (Rando, 1987b).

In the second scenario, the family has resigned itself to the death of a loved one who is seriously ill or in an acute crisis. However, the individual begins to recover, and in response the family change their expectations. Then, in an abrupt reversal of the recovery process, the individual dies from some acute cause. As in the previous situation, others may mistakenly believe that the family was prepared for the death. They fail to realize that during the ensuing time since initial resignation, marked as it has been by a change in the loved one's condition, the family's expectations changed as well. They no longer anticipated the death. In fact, in some regards the family now experience the death as a worse insult because of their revived hopes, their having reinvested in the loved one, their being subjected to the loss when they are unprepared, and their feeling that it is so much more cruel and unfair for them to have to be unprepared for the death after initially having been prepared. The following case example illustrates this scenario:

> Eileen was a fifty-three-year-old woman with a history of cardiovascular problems. Following three serious heart attacks, a stroke, the development of three heart blockages and an aneurysm, it was determined that she required open heart bypass surgery. Her family was prepared for the very worst. To their joy, Eileen survived the painful surgery. She was recuperating in perfect fashion when, ten days following her surgery, she unexpectedly experienced massive gastro-intestinal bleeding. This so destabilized her blood pressure that she developed a ventricular arrhythmia and suffered a myocardial infarction that killed her. The family was in total shock. Because of her positive recuperation they had dared to raise their hopes again about her survival, after having worked diligently at keeping such hopes moderate and realistic before and during the operation. They were particularly outraged and bitter that these hopes had been resurrected only to be dashed by her death, leaving them with "so much farther to fall" when she died suddenly. Their expectations had been that the danger had passed and, consequently, when Eileen died, her family responded to it as a sudden, unanticipated death. Also, the family felt exceptionally angry that Eileen had had to endure the pain of the operation only to die so soon thereafter. It seemed senseless and cruel.

Friends of Eileen's family appeared not to recognize that there had been a dramatic shift in hopes and expectations during the ten days following the operation when Eileen had been improving. All they had known was how seriously ill she had been and that the operation was risky. From their perspective, the death was expected, and they responded as they would have if Eileen had died during the operation itself. This failure to take into account the changes that ten days of positive recuperation had made in the hopes and expectations of the family left the family without adequate support and understanding by their friends. Everyone responded as if it were an expected death for which the family had prepared, and they expected the family to act accordingly. (Rando, 1988, pp. 104–105)

In the case of sudden, unexpected death during the context of terminal illness or recovery, the loss may be experienced as more of a shock than if it had occurred unexpectedly in the normal course of life. This may result in more intensified bereavement responses, increased problems making sense out of the death, and additional complications resulting from mourners' reflections about previous decisions or actions during the illness and recovery (Rando, 1987b). In both scenarios, risk is associated with not only the suddenness of the death but also the following problems.

1. Requisite support may be lacking because of society's misinterpretation of the position of the family and erroneous responses in light of it, pressure from unrealistic and inappropriate expectations, and problems resulting from nonexistent or misapplied treatment interventions. All of these, in turn, increase mourners' anger and guilt.

2. The manner and timing of the death provoke anger and a heightened sense of injustice. This type of emotional response is especially prevalent when the loved one initially was in crisis and then dies after the commencement of recovery. When the individual had to undergo pain in order to recover (e.g., surgery), the death seems particularly tragic and unfair because all that pain came to naught.

3. Families may be depleted at the time the death occurs. As such, they may be unable to grapple successfully with their emotional responses or to clarify that society's interpretation of their preparedness for the death and their insufficient response in light of it is incorrect.

4. Mourners may be particularly vulnerable to self-blame and consequent guilt and anger for the perceptions, interpretations, decisions, and actions occurring during the illness or the recovery

phase (e.g., they had started to decrease their visits because they perceived the crisis to have passed).

5. Unmet and violated expectations inherent in the death not only result in additional secondary losses, but often shatter the mourner's assumptive world and generate additional emotional responses that must be dealt with in the treatment experience. Such responses especially include increased anger, depression, and disillusionment.

6. Intensified grief and mourning reactions are aggravated by the distinct issues in each scenario.

In conclusion, whether a death is considered sudden or anticipated is not determined by the objective length of time mourners knew the loved one was dying, but rather by its subjective timing for them, given their particular states of mind, expectations, and circumstances.

Treatment Concerns

The mourner who has experienced the sudden, unexpected death of a loved one is like a stunned and dazed person attempting to make sense out of a foreign language in a strange world while being overwhelmed with intense emotion and excruciating pain. The great helplessness experienced by the mourner therefore necessitates treatment strategies that enhance a sense of control.

If reactions persist in the form of the unanticipated mourning syndrome, specific interventions for this syndrome are in order. Even if the mourner works through these initial reactions, it is still possible for him to develop another sort of complicated mourning that would require treatment. If the individual develops inhibited mourning, for example, the dynamics causing the inhibited mourning must be addressed and worked through, along with any unresolved aspects of the unanticipated mourning syndrome that may remain. (See chapter 4 for discussion of treatment for various complicated mourning syndromes.)

Interventions recommended for the first "R" process of mourning (i.e., recognize the loss) will be especially helpful in treating the mourner's initial reactions. The caregiver also must understand that sudden death often exacerbates whatever was going on at the time of death and blows it out of proportion to the rest of the relationship. For this reason, the mourner may need assistance in appropriately engaging in the "R" process of recollecting and reexperiencing the deceased and the relationship to achieve a more balanced image of the relationship and to deal with guilt. The heightened anger and guilt often common after sudden deaths should be treated as suggested in chapter 10. Extra time and effort also may be required to help the mourner work through the fourth "R" process (relinquishing the old attachments to the deceased and the old assumptive world) and the fifth "R" process (readjusting to move adaptively into the new world without forgetting the old), especially as it involves revision of the assumptive world. Assisting the mourner in achieving closure on any unfinished business remaining with the deceased decreases the mourner's need to act it out. (See chapter 9 for specific guidelines for intervening in the six "R" processes of mourning.)

Given that the shock of a sudden, unexpected loss may make it difficult for the mourner to achieve cognitive mastery of the situation, work should focus on helping the mourner actualize the loss, as discussed in chapters 8 and 9. To assist in this, the caregiver should avoid euphemisms (e.g., use the word *dead,* not *passed away*) and repeatedly use the deceased's name, not his role (e.g., *Jack,* not *your brother*). Also to actualize the loss, the caregiver must support the mourner's repeated review and retrospective reconstruction of events. At this stage, the caregiver should avoid limiting the repetition of information or becoming unduly concerned about the onset of chronic mourning patterns. The mourner will need to repeat extensively all aspects of the death and what led up to it in order to accommodate the loved one's demise. However, nonfunctional, inappropriate assumption of guilt and responsibility during the repetitions should be gently addressed, keeping in mind the caveats noted in chapter 10 about not stripping guilt away prematurely and handling it therapeutically as a defense or resistance when it serves a functional purpose.

Because coping capacity is diminished, it will be especially important for the caregiver to help the mourner achieve structure and a sense of control. For example, the caregiver must provide a cognitive set that will facilitate appropriate expectations for and orientation to treatment. In addition, the caregiver must help establish a treatment pace that the mourner can meet, break down the mourning processes and their tasks into the smallest possible components, and encourage the use of such mnemonic devices as lists and schedules.

If the mourner experiences high death anxiety regarding self and other loved ones, the caregiver should help give this feeling words and put it into proper perspective. In doing so, it is important to encourage the mourner to channel his increased awareness about potential loss and his heightened insecurity and vulnerability into positive responses (e.g., increased sensitivity, reordered priorities, minimization of unfinished business, augmented appreciation for life). Other interventions for anxiety are suggested later in this chapter in the discussion of traumatic death.

If the trauma of sudden, unexpected death generates post-traumatic reactions, work must be undertaken to keep these reactions from causing or exacerbating complications in mourning (e.g., intrusive thoughts or images, emotional numbing, hyperarousal). Given the fact that this type of death exerts a significantly negative physiological impact on the mourner, the caregiver also must encourage proper rest, nutrition, exercise, and so forth, along with a medical consultation if warranted.

Finally, it is important to realize that a relatively longer time period and more intense reactions are the norm in the case of sudden, unexpected deaths. The caregiver must be especially aware of the 6-month phenomenon (Rando, 1988), in which approximately 6 to 9 months after the death the mourner experiences an upsurge in grief and erroneously believes himself to be back where he was initially.

MULTIPLE DEATH

The term *multiple death* may refer either to the loss of two or more loved ones in the same event or to the experience of a number of losses occurring sequentially within a relatively short period of time. Each of these circumstances has been demonstrated to give rise to bereavement overload (Kastenbaum, 1969), one of the psychological reasons for failure to mourn (Lazare, 1979). The reason it is important to distinguish between these two types of multiple death is that when deaths occur concurrently, the mourner is faced with relatively more difficult choices than when one loss precedes another, no matter how brief the interval between them. In effect, the mourner must prioritize the losses when they take place at the same time. Unwillingness to assign priority can contribute to a survivor's refusal or inability to mourn. Examples of such concurrent losses include the deaths of several family members in a common accident, deaths resulting when a community is devastated by a natural disaster, or losses occurring when families lose loved ones to murder-suicide.

Although the loss of a number of beloved individuals in rapid succession can create many problems in mourning (e.g., AIDS takes the lives of four close friends within a period of weeks), this discussion will concern only situations in which all of the loved ones die in a common experience. Because concurrent losses are, generally, relatively more difficult for the mourner to handle than are sequential losses, focusing the discussion in this way will better illuminate important treatment concerns. Treatment implications for the sequential type of multiple loss can be readily extrapolated from this discussion.

As noted previously, simultaneous multiple deaths are by definition traumatic. They essentially confront the mourner with the high-risk factor of concurrent crisis when it comes to mourning each individual loved one. Mourning for that loved one is compromised by the concurrent crisis of the ongoing, stalled, or delayed mourning for the other loved ones. If the mourner were to sustain post-traumatic stress or have unfinished business from a prior loss that interfered with current mourning, the caregiver usually would attend to those factors first. However, with multiple deaths, a vicious cycle exists: The death of person A cannot be worked on in the fashion ideally desired because of the emotional press and unfinished business of the deaths of persons B and C; each of these deaths, in turn, cannot be worked through because of incomplete mourning and stress associated with the death of person A.

Dilemmas in Mourning Multiple Deaths

The mourner who has lost several loved ones simultaneously faces a number of dilemmas, each of which requires working through. These dilemmas occur in the following specific areas.

Approach to mourning

When more than one death occurs, the question of how to approach mourning is raised. Should mourning take place sequentially? Should one person be mourned totally before another one is mourned? Is leaving mourning for some loved ones incomplete for an extended period of time unhealthy? Should each loved one be mourned a little and then the focus changed to another loved one? If so, does this make for a less continuous experience than normally sustained in mourning? Should the mourner move from person to person without a plan? If the mourner chooses to focus on one or some of the deceased and put mourning for the others "on hold," will mourning automatically become complicated?

Prioritization

As noted earlier, perhaps the most difficulty in mourning multiple deaths is caused by questions associated with prioritization. Who should be mourned first? If the mourner chooses one person, what does that say about the others? Are they less important? Does choosing mean that once the first person is mourned, that loved one will be "done with"? How can one avoid showing favoritism? Will it be fair if the survivor is emotionally depleted from having mourned others by the time she gets to the last loved one? Is one person being betrayed because he is taken to be mourned first? Is another being betrayed because she is taken last? If the mourner is concentrating on one loved one at a given time, does that mean that the other loved ones are less important?

Differentiation

In the case of multiple deaths, the pain is undifferentiated. It may be that much common history is shared, as is the case for siblings in the same family. How can the mourner differentiate among the loved ones in order to mourn each of them? Will overlap in the form of common history contaminate some of the review processes of mourning by reducing the work to be accomplished for those mourned later?

Loss of support

Often, when multiple deaths occur, the people to whom the mourner would ordinarily go for support are gone. To whom does the survivor go to for support when it is the survivor's usual support system that is mourned? What can offer security?

Conflict

Multiple deaths frequently provoke a great deal of conflict. What does the mourner do when one of the deceased loved ones is blamed (e.g., fire, accident, murder-suicide)? What happens if the mourner holds one of the deceased responsible for not preventing the deaths of the others? How does the survivor mourn a conflicted relationship—difficult enough under normal circumstances—and at the same time mourn an unconflicted one? Where should the mourner put her energies? Will one death contaminate the others in some way and contribute to inhibition of mourning?

Overwhelming nature of the situation

When a number of loved ones die—usually in sudden and tragic circumstances that exacerbate trauma and complicate mourning—how does the survivor begin to mourn? Can the mourner give herself permission to feel all the emotion and pain that come with the deaths of several loved ones? Will the deluge of pain and sorrow cause her to become dysfunctional? Should the mourner even try to take on all this pain, or will she become burned out in the attempt?

Compromise of the six "R" processes

Multiple deaths specifically affect the "R" processes of mourning in a number of ways. How can the mourner face the pain involved in recognizing so many losses? How can she deal with so many secondary losses? How can she recollect and reexperience each deceased and relationship when competing demands for response exist? How many old attachments can be relinquished at or around the same time? How much of the assumptive world can be violated before it collapses entirely? How many new relationships with deceased loved ones can be developed at or around the same time? How much of the mourner's identity can be changed before the mourner becomes a stranger to herself? How many of the "R" processes can be completed for one deceased loved one before problems arise because they have not been completed for others?

Survivor guilt

In many cases, the mourner may experience survivor guilt because she has been spared death in the same circumstance that took the lives of her loved ones. Even if she did not live through the actual event, she may feel guilty for her continued existence. How does the mourner deal with the feeling that she should be dead like the others? How does this feeling interact with her relief that she did not die? What does one do with the sense that one's continued existence has been purchased at the cost of another's? In what fashions will the mourner's feeling of being undeserving to survive affect the rest of her life?

Treatment Concerns

In general, the prevailing thought is that when an individual loses a number of loved ones, that person should mourn first the loss of the person with whom he has had the least conflicted relationship, then work up to mourning the person with whom he has sustained the most conflicted relationship. It is presumed that this will be an easier progression for the mourner, providing mastery experiences before he comes to the more difficult scenarios.

However, the caregiver should recognize that there are no universally correct answers: What is therapeutic for one mourner may not be so for another. The caregiver will have to process carefully the meanings and reasons for each mourner's decisions. For one, it may be appropriate to mourn family members in sequence; another may find it necessary to oscillate among loved ones. Some may want to deal with the least conflicted relationship first; others may choose the most conflicted. Because no data exist on what is healthiest, it is more important that appropriate issues and questions be considered, processed, and worked through to the mourner's satisfaction than it is for the caregiver to agree with the mourner's decisions. Of course, if the mourner makes an unhealthy decision on a less arbitrary issue (e.g., never thinking about the deceased), the caregiver will need to confront the mourner with the evidence for why this is held to be unhealthy.

Another important point is that decisions made, or made by default, regarding the dilemmas previously discussed do not have to be permanent or mutually exclusive. For instance, a mourner may decide that he wants to work on mourning the loss of his brother and plan to work later on the loss of his sister, only to find that he keeps bringing his sister into the picture. The caregiver can point this out and inquire about what it means but should not expect the mourner to adhere rigidly to the original plan unless there is some specific therapeutic reason to do so.

Typically, it will be important for the caregiver to adjust expectations about the intensity of reactions, pacing, and duration of treatment for these types of mourners. Greater intensity, a slower pace, and longer treatment durations will be the norm. The feeling of not knowing where to begin is typical and must be responded to with great empathy. Indeed, all that may be possible for some time is discussion about ways to approach the various ways to approach mourning. The caregiver may see a mourner in treatment for an extended period of time, feeling that little is happening and wondering why the mourner continues to return. If this were the case with another mourner, the caregiver might be inclined to confront the lack of progress earlier and more vigorously. Although it is appropriate to comment that some interference seems to be keeping the mourner from moving forward in treatment, stronger confrontation should be avoided. In most cases, the mourner is moving as rapidly as he can despite the fact that his progress may seem minuscule. Treatment must consistently reflect the perspective and interventions appropriate to this individual as a traumatized person, as discussed in the next section.

It must be realized that before the survivor will be able to tackle the overwhelming task of mourning multiple deaths, trust must be established in the therapeutic relationship. The mourner will need a great deal of trust to rely on the caregiver to support him in relinquishing his defenses and facing his enormous pain. As with traumatized mourners in general, the caregiver cannot expect the mourner to confront this type of overwhelming trauma without feeling safe, protected, and enabled by the therapeutic relationship.

Multiple deaths may leave the individual so overwhelmed that self-direction is missing. Thus, self-direction is an important therapeutic goal. Until some of this can be regained, the caregiver may need to be relatively more directive than usual.

In cases where multiple deaths have decimated the mourner's support system, the mourner will need to be connected to other sources and systems of support. In these situations, family members left behind are typically more burdened than after an individual death. For this reason, the caregiver must be particularly alert and responsive to family systems issues, in terms of need for both assistance and interventions to limit breakdowns in communication and other dysfunction.

Perhaps the most critical treatment problem is the psychic numbing that multiple deaths can engender as a result of a high level of pain, loss of the support system, and demands and conflicts occasioned by simultaneous multiple mourning. Psychic numbing is a diminished or absent capacity to feel, an insulation from the self and the world. It may be partial or complete, temporary or permanent. A number of multiple death scenarios (e.g., major accidents or disasters) contain elements that produce post-traumatic stress responses, which also contribute to psychic numbing. If numbing is part of a post-traumatic stress response, traumatic elements will have to be worked through as suggested in the next section before the more traditional work of mourning can commence. Even if the caregiver perceives psychic numbing to be less an element of an overall post-traumatic stress response than an idiosyncratic defense, this response must be worked through before mourning can begin.

Another treatment issue concerns the fact that conflicts causing complicated mourning for one individual may generalize to others. This means that for any given deceased loved one, an increased chance of complicated mourning exists not only because of the difficulties and conflicts inherent in mourning multiple deaths, but also because of the contiguity of mourning. The caregiver can help the mourner separate the individual deaths (i.e., identifying, differentiating, and labeling the particular issues specific to each death), caution against the resulting defenses and resistances in mourning one death's becoming inappropriately generalized to others, and keep the mourner appropriately focused.

Because of questions about prioritizing mourning, it is especially important that the caregiver provide appropriate information about normal ambivalence, imperfection, and guilt in human relationships. The caregiver should also help the mourner move away from dichotomous thinking and toward more relativistic thinking. Being able to tolerate shades of gray instead of insisting that circumstances be either all black or all white is necessary in confronting the inherent dilemmas and conflicts in mourning multiple losses.

Any survivor guilt will require attention relatively early in treatment if it is of the type that prohibits or sabotages the mourner's treatment or adaptation to the losses (see chapter 10). In addition, intervention strategies enabling confrontation of pain and directed toward bereavement overload should be incorporated into treatment (see suggestions in chapter 9 for intervening in the second "R" process, reacting to the separation).

Finally, because of the difficulty inherent in this type of treatment, it will be most helpful for the caregiver to secure ongoing supervision and to become familiar with readings on related topics (e.g., post-traumatic stress disorder and disaster).

TRAUMATIC DEATH

Stemming from the Greek word for wound, *trauma* in *Webster's Ninth New Collegiate Dictionary* is defined as a disordered psychic or behavioral state resulting from mental or emotional stress or physical injury. It is also defined as an agent, force, or mechanism that causes trauma. Elements of personal and/or objective trauma are present in virtually all high-risk deaths and are common to many of the specific factors complicating mourning. For this reason, and because traumatic death is becoming increasingly prevalent, it is examined here in depth.

Risk Factors Associated With Traumatic Death

Although virtually any death may be perceived by the mourner as personally traumatic because of the internal subjective experience involved (e.g., feeling helpless, perceiving the deceased's death as untimely) circumstances that are objectively traumatic are associated with five factors known to increase complications for mourners. Specifically, factors that make a particular death circumstance traumatic include (a) suddenness and lack of anticipation; (b) violence, mutilation, and destruction; (c) preventability and/or randomness; (d) multiple death; and (e) the mourner's personal encounter with death, where there is either a significant threat to personal survival or a massive and/or shocking confrontation with the death and mutilation of others (Rando, in press-a).

All of these variables have been addressed previously except violence, mutilation, and destruction. These are among the most significant factors complicating traumatic death and differentiating it from other types of sudden, unexpected death. These factors arouse massive feelings of horror, shock, helplessness, vulnerability, and threat. The more the violence, destruction, or brutality, the greater the mourner's anxiety, fear, violation, powerlessness, and, ultimately, anger, guilt, self-blame, and shattered assumptions.

Psychodynamically, violent and mutilating deaths are more difficult to mourn because the mourner's previous aggressive fantasies and wishes regarding the deceased inevitably stir guilt. Volkan (1972, 1981) empirically demonstrates that mourning is often complicated when the death is violent (e.g., suicide) or mutilating (e.g., accident). He believes that complications arise because the mourner—naturally angered at being left by the loved one and damaged narcissistically by the inherent rejection—is forced to recognize the violence. In such a situation, bereavement is compromised because the mourner feels more than the usual guilt. In addition, it appears that violence associated with the event stimulates generalized aggression on the part of the survivor. Thus, aroused hostility can cause conflict within the conscience and can lead to feelings of guilt or shame for aggressive thoughts and emotions (Horowitz, 1986a).

Violence, mutilation, and destruction fulfill the most primitive destructive fantasies and reawaken the most basic death anxiety and fears of annihilation, leaving those affected called upon to master these additional stresses (Raphael, 1983). Mutilation particularly distresses survivors by conjuring up images of the suffering victims presumably experienced. Violence therefore calls forth not only guilt but also anxiety and fear.

The violence and mutilation involved in traumatic deaths also frequently force the mourner to confront the general destructiveness of humankind and/or nature. They breach the mourner's sense of personal invulnerability and violate her assumptive world. The result is that the mourner can no longer be as before—innocent of death and possessed of an unbroken continuity of intrapsychic and psychosocial life. Responses to this reality will define the mourner's post-traumatic reactions in both the short and long term:

> This confrontation with the destructiveness of man and
> nature may be defended against with defenses that are
> adaptive, so that it may be encompassed as only one facet
> of human behavior, but one that must be accepted as part of

the self. There may be grief here too for the loss of innocence that makes one no longer able to deny this component of man and self. Or, the defenses that are adopted may lead to denial; splitting projection; seeing destructiveness only as part of others; or to internalization with depression, self-destructive life-style, or even suicide; or the acting out of rage, violence, and destruction because impulses can no longer be controlled. These patterns have all been described for the war veteran, but they are also found in those whose encounter with personal disaster is the battle field of accident, injury, illness, assault, or bereavement. (Raphael, 1983, pp. 350–351)

Sequelae of Traumatic Death

Trauma can produce a number of sequelae in the mourner, most notably post-traumatic stress reactions, the stress response syndrome (Horowitz, 1986a), anxiety, helplessness and powerlessness, survivor guilt, personality disturbances, and a violated assumptive world.

Post-traumatic stress reactions

Traumatic deaths typically, although not inevitably, tend to produce post-traumatic responses in the mourner. Hereafter, the generic term *post-traumatic stress* will be used to refer to (a) full-blown post-traumatic stress disorder (PTSD), (b) post-traumatic reactions that do not meet the criteria for full-blown PTSD, (c) post-traumatic decline (Titchener, 1986), and (d) personality syndromes identified to occur after traumatic stress (e.g., Krystal, 1984; Ochberg, 1988b; Spitzer, 1990; Titchener, 1986). Briefly, the mourner is at particularly high risk for developing post-traumatic stress if, while being involved in the same traumatic event that took the life of the loved one, she has feared for her own life (i.e., the trauma involved a serious threat of death), felt helpless and powerless (i.e., the event was beyond individual control), and had no forewarning (i.e., the event was shocking and unanticipated).

The DSM-III-R describes the type of stressor producing full-blown PTSD as "a psychologically distressing event that is outside the range of usual human experience . . . [and that] would be markedly distressing to almost anyone, and is usually experienced with intense fear, terror, and helplessness" (American Psychiatric Association, 1987, p. 247). Examples provided are of four types: (a) serious threat to one's life or physical integrity; (b) serious threat or harm to one's loved ones; (c) sudden destruction of one's home or community; and (d) seeing another person who has recently been, or is being, seriously injured or killed as the result of an accident or physical violence. Thus, deaths caused by accidents, disasters, war, suicide, and homicide, as well as the death of a child, readily qualify as traumatic stressors. These deaths, more so than others, tend to embody the five risk factors mentioned earlier as being related to traumatic death.

The association of PTSD with complicated mourning has been observed in chapter 5. Suffice it to say that the three categories of PTSD symptoms (i.e., reexperience of the traumatic event, avoidance of stimuli associated with the traumatic event or numbing of general responsiveness, and increased physiological arousal) are consistent with symptomatology commonly witnessed in complicated mourning. In fact, remarkable similarities between uncomplicated acute grief and PTSD are frequently observed. The reason acute grief cannot legitimately be called a type of PTSD is that, in many cases, the death is not outside of the range of usual human experience. Other than this, the criteria for PTSD and acute grief are identical.

For some traumatized individuals, reactions will be minimal or relatively short-lived due to personal factors or a lower degree of exposure. However, for many others post-traumatic reactions can become entrenched and evolve into full-blown PTSD. According to Raphael (1986), factors influencing severe reactions to trauma include (a) the shock effects of sudden, unexpected trauma, which leave the ego no time to protect itself; (b) the severity of the threat to life; (c) the degree to which the individual feels helpless and powerless in the face of the trauma; and (d) the intensity, degree, proximity, and duration of exposure to shocking stimuli, violence, death, destruction, mutilation, and grotesque imagery. Preexisting vulnerability from earlier psychological wounding or trauma plays a part as well.

Specific risk factors for PTSD have been identified in an especially valuable investigation of an explosion and industrial fire in a paint factory (Weisæth, 1984, cited in Raphael, 1986). PTSD was found to be associated with the following: (a) survivors' initial reactions, with severity of PTSD in the acute (1 week) and subacute (7 months) phases being associated with a greater likelihood of the presence and severity of the disorder 4 years later; (b) some background variables (adaptational problems in childhood and adulthood, previous psychiatric impairment, high psychosomatic reactivity, and character pathology); (c) gender, with women being at greater risk; and (d) intensity of original exposure, intensity of ongoing stress relating to the catastrophe, and current life stressors.

Notwithstanding this study's finding that individuals with previous psychiatric impairment experienced more intense post-traumatic responses, it must not be assumed that a person who has developed a mental disorder after a traumatic event is a person who was more impaired at the time of exposure (Horowitz, 1985). Psychological trauma can produce post-traumatic symptomatology in almost anyone, regardless of premorbid characteristics. Certainly, individual variables will influence how the person perceives and interprets the trauma, copes with resultant symptomatology, and eventually integrates the experience. However, the caregiver should avoid presupposing psychopathology unless there is clear evidence that such problems preexisted and have influenced post-traumatic reactions over and above the normal response consequent to trauma.

Fear or inability to acknowledge the impact of the trauma, the multiplicity of symptoms and the defenses erected against them, the temporal distance symptoms often have from the original trauma, and the memory disturbances interfering with recall can make PTSD difficult to recognize. Scurfield (1985) observes that the axiom "diagnosis follows treatment" may be more characteristic of PTSD than any other disorder.

Stress response syndrome

As conceptualized by Horowitz (1986a), in the stress response syndrome the individual reacts to a stressful event with an initial response of outcry, which is followed by denial and numbing and intrusion phases. Briefly, the denial and numbing phase typically is seen in reaction to the initial realization that a traumatic event has occurred. After this initial phase, the mourner is confronted with intrusive repetitions of traumatic memory, thought, feeling, or behavior. These phases then alternate repeatedly until cognitive completion is achieved. (For in-depth examination of the theoretical basis for the stress response cycle and its treatment implications, the reader is referred to chapters 3 and 7, respectively.)

As relates to traumatic death, intrusion and denial are normal, expectable processes that involve reliving and reexperiencing the trauma and, inversely, attempting to shut out all memories, reminders, and stimulus cues of the terror. As such, the process is a way of modulating emotional reactions to a serious event by containing them within tolerable, paced doses. Intrusive repetitions reflect the mourner's tendency to review cognitions and experience affects repeatedly in order to integrate the traumatic event into the inner model of reality (i.e., assumptive world). The controls of the denial phase are aimed at avoiding the pain evoked by these intrusive thoughts and feelings, as well as any cues that might stimulate them. Only when the mourner is able to integrate the traumatic event cognitively and emotionally and can develop appropriate adaptational responses will the stress response be resolved and the press for cognitive completion with affective release be relieved, thus terminating the distress.

Horowitz (1985) specifically applies the notion of the stress response cycle to disaster and personally traumatic events in the following way:

> Disasters and personally traumatic events set in motion a
> cycle of reaction that is aimed at restoring an equilibrium
> between schemata of the self in the self-surrounding world
> [i.e., the assumptive world] and new realities. This involves
> a process of grieving for losses and injuries and a process of

developing new modes of adaptation. There is a preparation of new plans for the future which include considering the possibility of a repetition of the stressful event. When these processes have accomplished these purposes, the person can be said to have completed his reaction to the disaster. On the way toward such completion there may be states of mind which have seemingly opposite qualities: extremes of response ranging from intensive thoughts and feelings about the disaster and its implications to unrealistic avoidance of, and numbing to, its themes. (p. 161)

In many ways, this completion process is similar to the "R" processes of mourning.

Horowitz (1986a) has identified nine themes in the content of deliberately contemplated ideas, warded-off ideas, or intrusive ideas. They include the following: fear of repetition, fear of merger with victims, shame and rage over vulnerability, rage at the source, rage at those exempted, fear of loss of control of aggressive impulses, guilt or shame over aggressive impulses, guilt or shame over surviving, and sadness over losses. These themes are quite common in uncomplicated, as well as complicated, mourning. Any one of them can merge the current stress event with previous conflicts over prior stress events. Unfortunately, this can lead to diagnostic problems in determining precisely how much present symptomatology is due to the recent life event and how much accrues to earlier events.

According to Horowitz (1986a), post-traumatic stress reactions involve increased arousal accompanying the dual and opposite response states and their associated phenomena. Specifically, in the intrusive state, images, nightmares, and dreams can come to mind unbidden, accompanied by anxiety, palpitations, and tremors; in the denial state, avoidance can become generalized to attempts to repress all memories and avoid all reminders of the trauma (e.g., people, noises, places, smells, sights). These phenomena distress the survivor to a varying degree, depending upon factors such as past experience, defenses, and degree of exposure to death. Generally, however, the sleep disturbances, anxiety, irritability, general distress, and wish to be finished and free of the experience make for difficulties in interpersonal relationships, work functioning, capacity for pleasure, physical health, and psychological well-being.

Anxiety

Anxiety has been defined as "the apprehension cued off by a threat to some value that the individual holds essential to his existence as a personality" (May, 1977, p. 205). The threat may be to physical existence, as in the threat of death, or it may be to psychological existence, as in the threat of meaninglessness or loss of one's identity. The danger stimulating the threat may be either external or internal. Resulting anxiety consists of a psychological side and a somatic and behavioral side (i.e., motor tension, autonomic hyperactivity, apprehensive expectation, and vigilance and scanning). Anxiety differs from fear in that the apprehension, tension, or uneasiness occurs in the absence of a specific danger.

In practically all cases, the caregiver can expect some amount of anxiety in mourning—whether uncomplicated or complicated—merely because the loss of a loved one and the processes of mourning that ensue inherently contain a number of the dynamics known to stimulate this emotion (see Rando, 1988). In addition, anxiety is a cardinal component of post-traumatic stress reactions, being by definition always present to some degree.

Anxiety in the individual whose loved one has died under traumatic circumstances has innumerable possible causes. This is true regardless of what circumstances give rise to the reactions and whether or not the mourner was present to witness the death. It would be impossible to list all the forms anxiety can take after traumatic death. However, some of the more common ones are as follows.

1. Death anxiety

2. Annihilation anxiety

3. Separation anxiety

4. Existential anxiety

5. Anxiety arising from the unknown, unfamiliar, and uncertain

6. Anxiety arising from helplessness, vulnerability, and insecurity during and after the trauma

7. Anxiety arising from unexpressed and/or unacceptable feelings, thoughts, behaviors, and impulses during and/or after the trauma or from internal conflicts the mourner sustains concerning them

8. Anxiety caused by heightened emotional and physiological arousal

9. Anxiety relating to flooding of the psyche with stimuli that disorganize ego functions and create intrapsychic and external disorganization

10. Anxiety caused by the experience of the intrusion phase of the post-traumatic stress response, which raises feelings that one has lost control and may be losing one's mind

11. Anxiety arising from the violation of the assumptive world caused by the trauma and victimization of the mourner, as well as by the fact that the mourner is now so different than before the trauma

12. Anxiety stimulated by defenses used to cope with the trauma

13. Anxiety stemming from survivor guilt

Numerous aspects posing certain idiosyncratic threats to the individual also may generate anxiety (e.g., the loved one died from drowning, and the mourner has always had a terrifying fear of this type of death). No matter what the causes of anxiety, it is incumbent upon the caregiver to identify, differentiate, label, and address each one in treatment.

Helplessness and powerlessness

A central feature of trauma appears to be the helplessness and powerlessness it engenders. Realizing that one cannot escape at the point of traumatic impact, that one's control and power are useless, and that one is unable to undo what has happened or recover what has been lost assaults one's sense of competence. In other words, the individual confronts his own ineffectiveness, a trait generally despised by society. Fear escalates along with feelings of helplessness, which in turn can lead to additional fear. In addition, childhood feelings of powerlessness and inadequacy can be resurrected.

Frustration, anger, and heightened arousal tend to occur during the traumatic event, but it is helplessness that predominates during that victimizing experience. The quality, intensity, and experience of that helplessness profoundly affects the person and is a main factor in the traumatic imprinting of the impact (Raphael, 1986). For many, helplessness may be not only the most distressing and threatening aspect of the trauma, but also the most difficult to integrate and the most traumatic to the individual's stimulus barrier (Raphael, 1981). Later on, reactions to helplessness will directly affect survivor guilt and anger, interpersonal relationships, attempts at mastery by activity and undoing, and the formulation of meaning and a new identity.

Typically, feelings of shame—irrational though they may be—associated with feelings of helplessness assault the person either at the time of crisis or afterward. Thus, a major goal in the treatment of all post-traumatic responses, as well as in the treatment of victimization in general, will be the empowerment of the survivor after the trauma and throughout the remainder of the individual's life. It is the subsequent gaining of mastery that will mitigate to a degree the deleterious effects of helplessness and powerlessness in the face of the trauma (Raphael, 1986).

Survivor guilt

In traumatic experiences, questions may arise as to how survival was achieved: Was it purchased at the expense of others? Were one's actions consistent with one's self-image, responsibilities, and expectations? Negative answers contribute to shame and survivor guilt. Even if the mourner is blameless, the issue of surviving while others have died is a major one. It colors the survivor's post-traumatic reactions and, unfortunately, too often exerts a negative impact on the rest of the survivor's adaptation in life. (See chapter 10 for additional commentary about guilt in general.)

Personality disturbances

Trauma and victimization can cause a disruption in the normal flow of life and development. Such disruption may result from the traumatic experience itself, its sequelae (e.g., post-traumatic stress symptomatology), defenses and behaviors used to cope with traumatic memories or symptoms resulting from the event, or secondary losses or victimization. The elements and degree of fixity, rupture, or inability to proceed in life depend on the time, duration, extent, and meaning of the trauma and/or victimization for the individual, as well as on any secondary victimization that occurs (Danieli, 1985, 1988).

Profound personality change can emanate from trauma, especially as regards affect, personal relationships, and sense of self. For instance, PTSD robs the person of the ability to anticipate and symbolize, fantasize, and sublimate as ways of anticipating and modifying emotion (van der Kolk, 1987a). Deprivations of these psychological mechanisms, involved in coping with everyday stress, contribute to an inability to tolerate affect. This can in turn impair the individual's ability to mourn and work through ordinary conflicts, limiting capacity to accumulate restitutive and gratifying experiences (van der Kolk, 1987a).

Krystal (1984) has described the disaster syndrome, which includes such elements as loss of capacity to use community supports, chronic recurrent depression with feelings of despair, psychosomatic symptoms, emotional anesthesia and a blocked ability to react affectively, and alexithymia. The person sustains a robot-like existence devoid of fantasy and empathy for others, often accompanied by alcoholism, drug dependence, or chronic physical illness.

Another reaction related to trauma, post-traumatic decline, has been identified by Titchener (1986). This chronic syndrome develops secondary to unrecognized conflict over aggressive impulses created by the traumatic experience. The defenses elicited by the conflict are of such magnitude that the survivor's life becomes severely constricted, if not deadened. She becomes "a shadow person moving about but hardly participating in the social system, striving only for the space and sustenance required for a shadow's survival" (Titchener, 1986, p. 8). Hypochondriasis, social withdrawal, isolation, mistrust, and preoccupation with the physical self ensue, with the survivor's becoming imbued with hopelessness, anger, and feelings of incompetence. The person becomes an invalid and invalidated. The personality is devastated, and the survivor is removed from meaningful participation in family, society, work, and all forms of gratification.

It should be noted that the impact of trauma on affect is not solely blunting or deadening. Frequently, because trauma survivors respond with hyperarousal to emotional or sensory stimuli, many have difficulty controlling anxious and aggressive feelings, with the warding off of anxiety and aggression becoming a focal issue (van der Kolk, 1987a).

Problems modulating the intensity of affect are cited as the reason so many trauma survivors self-medicate with drugs and alcohol (Lacoursiere et al., 1980). It is important not to overlook the defensive purpose of covering grief with anger, then medicating anger with alcohol. Unfortunately, this "cure" only aggravates the problem by exacerbating both depression and anxiety.

Other sequelae of victimization (Ochberg, 1988a, 1988b) and of extreme stress (Spitzer, 1990), including chronic personality and psychosocial changes consequent to traumatization, have been delineated in chapter 10.

Violated assumptive world

The violation of one's assumptive world, involving the shattering of global and/or specific assumptions, is a major aspect of mourning. In trauma, there is an automatic violation of assumptions. Coping with victimization is a process that involves rebuilding the assumptive world and incorporating into one's identity one's experiences as a victim. To the extent that old assumptions have been held with extreme confidence and have not been challenged previously, they are more likely to be utterly shattered, with devastating results (Janoff-Bulman, 1985). Consequently, the nature and strength of the mourner's prior assumptions will to some degree determine the extent of the particular secondary losses sustained and will influence the success with which the mourner copes with the trauma. Taylor (1983) reports that cognitive adaptation to threatening events (i.e., the adjustment process) centers on (a) a search for meaning in the experience, (b) an attempt to gain mastery over the event in particular and over one's life more generally, and (c) an effort to restore self-esteem through self-enhancing evaluations. According to Taylor, successful adjustment depends in large part on the ability to sustain and modify illusions that buffer against present and future threats. Specific coping strategies include redefining the event, finding meaning, changing behaviors, seeking social support, and assuming behavioral self-blame (Janoff-Bulman, 1985).

Major Catastrophes Versus Personal Disasters

Certainly, widely varying parameters exist for what constitutes trauma among different individuals. Although much of the research cited in the present discussion focuses on major catastrophes and disasters (e.g., the bombing of Hiroshima, concentration camp internment, combat experience, floods, airplane crashes), far more frequently individuals are called upon to contend with a personal disaster experience (Raphael, 1981).

Although a personal disaster usually is less dramatic than a larger scale event, it engenders the same types of issues, and treatment implications can be extrapolated from one category to the other. In each, the person's reactions, defenses, behaviors, and coping mechanisms are contingent upon personal history and the idiosyncratic factors involved in the experience in and after a particular event. Raphael (1981) has identified five key similarities between personal disaster and more widespread catastrophe: shock and denial, distress, helplessness, death and destruction, and images of the trauma. She also notes that both types of trauma involve psychological defense processes, the need for cognitive completion with affective release, and mitigating behaviors. Raphael has concluded that personal disasters are particularly traumatic when they entail experiences that are undesirable; involved with exit (a person's leaving); associated with loss, high distress, and a high level of change; not preventable or controllable; and unanticipated.

Three Conditions Associated With Post-Traumatic Reactions

The three main conditions giving rise to post-traumatic reactions in mourning are (a) personal encounter with death, where there is a significant threat to one's own survival; (b) massive, shocking, and sudden confrontation with the death and mutilation of others; and (c) confrontation with the traumatic and/or mutilating death of a loved one. Each of these conditions is addressed in the following discussion, which relies heavily upon the extraordinary synthesizing work of Beverley Raphael and the groundbreaking theoretical contributions of Mardi Horowitz. The reactions described are those most characteristic of each condition; however, they may be found in whole or part in the other conditions as well.

Personal encounter with death

In a personal encounter with death, the individual experiences helplessness, anxiety, heightened arousal, fear, terror, a sense of abandonment, increased vulnerability, and the yearning for relief and rescue. The traumatic stimulus of such an event can overwhelm the ego and cause post-traumatic stress reactions. The degree of threat to life is a crucial factor, with experience of a "near miss" and/or more direct exposure to the threat of death resulting in more intense emotional reactions. One such scenario would be a mugging in which the loved one is mortally stabbed. The mourner feels she is next but is then rescued by the police. Alternatively, an automobile accident might fatally injure the loved one but leave the mourner with only superficial wounds.

Following a serious threat to one's life, the need often exists to relive and reexperience the event, as well as to defend against it by avoiding it or shutting it out. As Freud (1920/1955a) suggests, the need to relive the event is an effort to gain mastery of the trauma through the repetition compulsion. Within the context of the stress response syndrome (Horo-witz, 1986a), the alternation of denial and intrusive states in the effort to achieve completion of the event is also pertinent.

Risk is increased if the mourner already has sustained some past psychological vulnerability, has been injured herself and requires energy for survival, has experienced multiple deaths of loved ones during the traumatic experience, or has sustained other losses that cause concur-rent stress (e.g., loss of home and personal possessions in a fire or re-location to a different community after a flood). Notably, these factors exacerbate mourning under all conditions of traumatic death, not just this one.

Massive, shocking, and sudden confrontation with the death and mutilation of others

In the case of massive, shocking, and sudden confrontation with the death and mutilation of others, the mourner loses a loved one in circum-stances that expose him to intense terror, sudden helplessness, and fright-ening perceptions. Examples of such scenarios include automobile and airplane crashes, natural disasters, or war. These types of events frequently give rise to post-traumatic stress.

In all of these circumstances, survivors must contend with a variety of stimuli stemming from severe injuries to other human beings. For instance, the mourner may have had body parts hurled into his face after an airplane crash, smelled burned flesh after an explosion during an earth-quake, or heard the screams of comrades wounded in battle. Witnessing the magnitude and destructiveness of death in these circumstances causes enormous disturbance and distress. The images of death become embla-zoned in the mourner's mind and have a powerful impact.

Links between mourning and these types of events were made early on by such clinicians as Lindemann (1944), who wrote of grief following the Cocoanut Grove nightclub fire in Boston, and Anderson (1949), who commented on his patients' reactions to the horrors of World War II. Other early observers also have commented on wartime neuroses (e.g., Kardiner, 1941; Lidz, 1946; Teicher, 1953). Yet other literature has centered on responses to three additional situations: Chowdoff (1975), Dimsdale (1974, 1980), Eitinger (1980), Eitinger and Askevold (1968), Hocking (1965), Krystal (1968, 1978), and Krystal and Niederland (1971) wrote of the reac-tions of those who had been confined in concentration camps during the Holocaust. Lifton (1964, 1976) and Janis (1951) focused on survivors of the atomic bombs dropped on Hiroshima and Nagasaki. And Church (1974); K. Erickson (1976a, 1976b, 1979); Gleser, Green, and Winget (1981); Lifton and Olson (1976a, 1976b); Rangell (1976); Titchener and Kapp (1976); and Titchener, Kapp, and Winget (1976) investigated those who lived through the Buffalo Creek flood.

Raphael (1986) notes that, as is the case with personal threat of death, the individual's distressing encounter with the deaths of others—the sights, smells, sounds, and especially mutilation and death of children— produce reactive phenomena that require integration. There will be intrusive memories, images, and nightmares. Situations and stimulus cues may trigger memories and may bring back the emotional intensity of the original experience, even when it is thought to be forgotten. As noted earlier, these intrusions usually alternate with defensive avoidance, repression, and general numbing, which in the stress response syndrome serve to distance the mourner from intrusive images and feelings (Horowitz, 1986a).

Confrontation with the traumatic and/or mutilating death of a loved one

Examples of a confrontation with the traumatic and/or mutilating death of a loved one would include a woman's returning home to find the blue, bloated body of her husband hanged in their garage after his successful suicide attempt; a father's having to identify the burned and mutilated body of his kidnapped daughter; or a man's coming to consciousness after a car accident to find the decapitated body of his sister lying on top of his in the wreckage.

In these types of situations, the individual is not necessarily fearful for her own life at the moment of confrontation with the death stimuli. Thus, although circumstances confront the mourner with her own mortality in a general way, these scenarios do not fit into the category of a personal encounter with death. Because they typically involve only one death (or a few at most), neither can these scenarios be classified as massive, shocking, and sudden confrontations with the death and mutilation of others. However, the same issues apply here as do in the former two scenarios. There is helplessness, terror, fear, anxiety, heightened arousal, increased vulnerability, threat, and shock. The stress response syndrome (Horowitz, 1986a) is stimulated.

Many of the common post-traumatic responses in this situation already have been considered in the examination of unique issues and dynamics associated with accident, suicide, and homicide (see chapter 11). Indeed, all of the elements of post-traumatic stress are manifested in some way in both acute uncomplicated grief and complicated mourning.

Characteristic Themes of Trauma Survivors

Lifton (1976, 1979) describes the trauma survivor as one who has come into contact with death in some bodily or psychic fashion and has remained alive. He identifies five characteristic themes in survivors that may be extrapolated to traumatized mourners in most circumstances of loss involving personal confrontation with death or confrontation with the traumatic and/or mutilating deaths of others: death imprint, death guilt, psychic numbing, conflicts over nurturing and contagion, and formulation of meaning or significance. Each of these five themes, discussed at length in Lifton's (1979) *The Broken Connection,* can be seen to a varying extent in mourning generated by any of the three conditions associated with post-traumatic reactions.

Death imprint

The death imprint involves the radical intrusion of an image/feeling of threat or end to life that calls forth prior imagery of actual death or death equivalents. It may develop suddenly, as in war or traumatic accident, or it may come on more gradually over time, as in rescue work. The degree of unacceptability of death contained in the image—its prematurity, grotesqueness, and absurdity—is a pivotal factor in the development of the death imprint.

Because the imagery involved is sudden, extreme, protracted, or associated with the terror of premature, unacceptable dying, assimilating the death imprint is impossible. Consequently, a high degree of anxiety often accompanies it. Despite differing degrees of individual vulnerability to death imagery, if the threat or trauma is sufficiently great, it can produce a traumatic syndrome (including a death imprint) in anyone. The survivor can become so bound to the image that he becomes enthralled with death and under a "death spell." His subsequent life can become dominated by the compelling and indelible death imprint, and identification with death and the dead can produce within the survivor a veritable picture of death in life.

The survivor retains the indelible image, clinging to the death imprint as he continues to struggle to master and assimilate the threat and as larger questions of personal meaning are raised by the death encounter. Associated with the image is a special form of knowledge and potential for inner growth—the sense of having "been there" and returned. The reality of the death encounter undermines the magical sense of invulnerability by means of its terrible lesson that death is real and inescapable. This knowledge vies with a sense of relief at no longer having to maintain the illusion of invulnerability.

The extent of grief and loss will affect the outcome and degree of the survivor's anxiety. In severe traumatic experience, grief and loss tend to be too overwhelming in their suddenness and relationship to unacceptable death and death equivalents to be resolved. Many of the symptoms in the traumatic syndrome have to do precisely with impaired mourning. The survivor is unable to reconstruct shattered personal forms in ways that reassert vitality and integrity. Lifton (1979) concludes:

> Thus the death imprint in traumatic syndrome simultaneously
> includes actual death anxiety (the fear of dying) and anxiety

associated with death equivalents (especially having to do with disintegration of the self). *This powerful coming together of these two levels of threat may well be the most characteristic feature of image-response in the traumatic syndrome.* (p. 170, emphasis added)

Death guilt

Death guilt, also known as survivor guilt, imbues the death imprint with much of its power and indelibility. The limited capacity to respond to the threat and self-blame for that inadequate response fuel this emotion. In other words, actual survival stimulates guilt. In addition, what one did to survive can present problems that must be faced in the aftermath of many traumas. Concerns relating to competitive aggression to ensure the survival of self and family—especially when survival has involved the killing of another—are not uncommon, despite an intellectual understanding of the basic human instinct for self-preservation (Raphael, 1986). Sacrifice for survival, atonement through guilt and behavior, and a sense of obligation are high prices frequently paid by those who survive and must live with the fact that others died.

Severe psychic consequences also ensue as a result of inactivation in threatening situations. Under traumatic circumstances, and especially in a massive immersion of death, physical and psychic action are virtually eliminated:

> One can neither physically help victims nor resist victimizers; one cannot even psychically afford experiencing equivalent feelings of compassion or rage. . . . One feels responsible for what one has not done, for what one has not felt, and above all for the gap between that physical and psychic inactivation and what one felt called upon . . . to do and feel. (Lifton, 1979, p. 171)

Inactivation is captured within the image of the trauma itself. Because the image has never been adequately enacted, it keeps recurring in dreams and in waking life: In the repetition, there is the attempt to replay the situation—to rewrite the scene retrospectively to permit more acceptable action "whether by preventing others from dying, taking bolder action of any kind, experiencing strong compassion and pity, or perhaps suffering or dying in place of the other or others" (Lifton, 1979, p. 171). Through this, the survivor hopes to be relieved of the burden of self-blame. However, the relief is less dependent upon rewriting the scenario than on the survivor's capacity to grasp and accept the nature of inactivation under such circumstances.

Death guilt implies a number of questions and statements that reveal a gradual escalation of the survivor's feelings of responsibility. These are as follows: (a) Why did I survive while he died? (b) Why did I survive while letting him die? (c) I killed him, and (d) If I had died instead, he would have lived. Feelings of responsibility associated with these questions and statements result from the sense that a resumption of vitality is wrong in the face of failure to prevent the dead from dying (i.e., after being inactive in the face of death and threat).

In essence, death guilt stems from the sense that, until some enactment is achieved, the survivor has no right to be alive. The traumatic syndrome, then, involves the state of being haunted by images that can be neither enacted nor relinquished. Suffering is associated with being stuck in this state:

> Hence the indelible image is always associated with guilt, and in its most intense form takes the shape of an image of ultimate horror: a single image (often containing brutalized children or dying people whom the survivor loved) that condenses the totality of the destruction and trauma and evokes particularly intense feelings of pity and self-condemnation in the survivor. To the extent that one remains stuck in such images, guilt is static, there is a degree of continuing psychological incapacity, and traumatic syndrome can turn into traumatic neurosis. (Lifton, 1979, p. 172)

In addition, any feelings of relief or joy that coexist with discomfort at having survived can contribute to supplemental guilt.

Caregivers often misconstrue the functions and meanings of the experience and expression of survivor guilt as resistance or negative therapeutic reactions. As a result, caregivers tend to become intolerant of the survivor's apparently stubborn suffering, which often disrupts treatment. Danieli (1988) has identified a number of central meanings and functions of guilt following trauma as they relate to Holocaust survivors and their offspring. These are applicable to other survivors of trauma and victimization. According to Danieli, survivor guilt may be any of the following.

1. A defense against intolerable existential helplessness: This involves an unconscious attempt to deny or undo passive helplessness in the face of trauma by presupposing the presence of choice and the power, ability, and possibility to exercise it (e.g., one could have done the right thing but chose wrong).

2. A way of working through delayed mourning and bereavement for loss of loved ones: This provides a means of survival in a chaotic world in which all love objects have been lost and there is no one left with whom to mourn. Because the survivor fears that successful mourning means letting go and committing the deceased to oblivion, guilt serves a commemorative function and is a vehicle of loyalty to the dead.

3. A way of counteracting psychological aloneness and reestablishing and maintaining a sense of belonging and familial, social, and cultural continuity

4. A reaffirmation of morality and of the world as a just and compassionate place

The caregiver's full understanding and acceptance of the meanings and functions of survivor guilt are mandatory in order to help the individual constructively transcend it.

Psychic numbing

Psychic numbing is at the heart of the traumatic syndrome. The decision to effect a psychic closing off is neither voluntary nor conscious under conditions of acute trauma. It is essentially a reversible form of symbolic death as a defense to avoid a permanent physical or psychic death. In order to dissociate itself from grotesque death, the mind becomes deadened, and feeling is severed from knowledge and awareness of what is happening:

> To say that emotion is lost while cognition is retained is more or less true, but does not really capture what the mind is experiencing. What is more basic is the self's being severed from its own history, from its grounding in such psychic forms as compassion for others, communal involvement, and other ultimate values. That is what is meant by the mind's being severed from its own forms. And that severance, in turn, results in the failed enactment and guilt. . . . This kind of process was described even before Freud by Janet under the concept of dissociation. It includes not only stasis in the sense of inactivation, but also disintegration in the sense of a coming apart of crucial components of the self. To be sure, that disintegration, like the stasis, is partial and to a considerable degree temporary—in fact, is in the service of preventing more total and lasting forms of disintegration. *But we can say that this dissociative disintegration characterizes the psychic numbing of the traumatic syndrome, and is at the heart of that experience.* (Lifton, 1979, p. 175, emphasis added)

Initially, psychic numbing may help the survivor by protecting her from being overwhelmed by massive confrontation with death and mutilation, helplessness, emotional pain, and severe death anxiety and guilt. It is common at the time of trauma and afterwards. However, it loses its adaptive quality when it persists chronically, with the person closing out all feeling. It also serves to undermine the most fundamental psychic processes because it renders the individual unable to proceed with psychic action and causes a suspension of the formative-symbolizing process, leaving her in a state of severe desymbolization. This is why Lifton perceives psychic numbing as the essential mechanism of mental disorder.

Conflicts over nurturing and contagion

As he struggles toward, and in some ways against, reexperiencing himself as a vital human being with human relationships, the survivor experiences conflicts over nurturing and contagion. He feels weak and needy, resenting the help offered as a reminder of his weakness. The mourner perceives any assistance as counterfeit, not only because of its association with weakness, but as a consequence of his feelings about the unreliability of dependency in human relationships after the trauma shatters his human web. Consequently, he remains on guard against false promises of protection, vitality, or even modest assistance and evidences what Lifton (1979) calls a suspicion of the counterfeit, which eventually can coincide with a fear of contagion that may develop from his own death experience:

> One fends off not only new threats of annihilation but gestures of love or help. Part of this resistance to human relationships has to do with a sense of being tainted by death, of carrying what might be called the psychic stigma of the annihilated . . . if one is treated so cruelly [i.e., by the trauma], one tends to internalize that sense of being worthless. (p. 176)

The survivor feels himself to have become part of the entire constellation of annihilation and destruction, and to be identified with and to live in the realm of death and destruction. To the survivor's concern about contagion is added the reality of others' fear of the survivor's death taint. He can become for them a stimulus that activates their own latent anxieties concerning death and death equivalents.

Related to the struggle around nurturing and contagion is what Lifton (1979) calls the "insufficiently appreciated survivor emotion . . . of perpetual anger and frequent rage" (p. 176). The survivor often appears to require this anger and rage, and frequently its violence, as an animating alternative to the sense of inner deadness and living in the realm of the annihilated. Thus, anger becomes a way to assert vitality in the face of images of death—a way of holding onto a psychic lifeline. Generally, anger has to do with the struggle to put forward life by attacking the other rather than the self. In addition, it appears the survivor is more comfortable dealing with anger than with guilt or other forms of severe anxiety.

Formulation of meaning or significance

The trauma survivor's overall task is ultimately to formulate meaning or significance in the trauma in order that the remainder of life not be devoid of these qualities. According to Lifton (1979), this means "establishing the lifeline on a new basis" (pp. 176–177) or, to use the terminology of the present text, revising the assumptive world.

Indeed, a recent psychoanalytic study of trauma concludes that trauma actually is caused by the shattering of the central organizing fantasies of self in relation to others (Ulman & Brothers, 1988). These fantasies form the organizing core of self-experience. Post-traumatic stress symptoms of numbing and reexperiencing are seen as resulting from the shattering of these fantasies and as an attempt to restore them. On the basis of this numbing and reexperiencing, Ulman and Brothers argue that PTSD actually should be classified as a dissociative disorder rather than as an anxiety disorder. Regardless of classification, impact on the assumptive world and the need to address personal constructs within it prove crucial for the survivor.

Although this process is rarely recognized as crucial in the formulation of meaning and significance after traumatic experience, the survivor must struggle to achieve resurgent modes of symbolic immortality that lend re-animation, purpose, and meaning. As Lifton (1979) points out, if she does not, she risks the continuation of the traumatic syndrome:

> Some Hiroshima survivors, for instance, could reanimate their lives around peace-movement activities, which offered a sense of immediate activity in like-minded groups and ultimate significance within which their otherwise inassimilable experience could be understood. If the world could receive a valuable message from Hiroshima, that is, and they could be the agents and disseminators of that message, then what happened to them could be said to have a larger purpose. The same principle applied to Nazi death-camp survivors in their struggle to establish and participate in the State of Israel. More typical is the quest for vitality around direct biological continuity—the tendency of many survivors to reassert family ties and reproduce, and thereby assert biological and bio-social modes of symbolic immortality.
>
> Without this kind of formulation the survivor remains plagued by unresolved conflicts in the other areas mentioned —by death anxiety, death guilt, psychic numbing, and immobilizing anger and suspicion of the counterfeit. Numbing in particular, the desymbolizing center of the traumatic syndrome, is likely to persist. For to overcome that numbing, new psychic formations that assert vitality and one's right to it must evolve. (p. 177)

In traumas involving victimization or violence committed by another person (e.g., war, homicide, torture, hostage taking), the survivor is forced to contend with emotions aroused by the fact that violence was intentionally perpetrated by another person. The mourner must make meaning of this in terms of other people and relationships, as well as her assumptive world. This not only brings emotional reactions, but also has social and philosophical reverberations. (For more discussion on the roles of intent and agency, see the discussion of homicide in chapter 11.)

Lifton proclaims that actions akin to the "R" process of relinquishing the old attachments to the deceased and the old assumptive world are required after traumatic situations, whether or not they have resulted in deaths. Using Lindemann's (1944) concept of emancipation from bondage to the deceased, Lifton writes that there must be a parallel emancipation of the survivor from the bondage of her own inner deadness. This requires not total severance but the creation of imagery that "maintains fidelity to the end or to one's experience of inner deadness, fidelity in the sense of remembering what the experience entailed and including its excruciating truths in the sense of self that is being recreated" (Lifton, 1979, p. 177).

What the survivor does with guilt and self-condemnation will be crucial to bereavement outcomes. Ideally, she will proceed through a three-stage process of confrontation, reordering, and renewal. Without guilt-associated struggles concerning fidelity to the dead, the experience of deadness, and one's role as a witness to the trauma, Lifton believes no renewal or formulation of meaning or significance is feasible. Questions of the degree to which the survivor remains bound to the death encounter also are important. Too great a degree of fidelity will result in the mourner's allowing herself no psychic movement in relation to the experience. The degree to which she can engage in appropriate blaming and scapegoating and can look forward as well as backward in time in order to assert the continuity of life will influence the formulation of the meaning of the traumatic experience within the context of her life.

Treatment Concerns

No matter what the specific circumstance, traumatic death can leave the individual with an overlay of post-traumatic symptomatology (which may or may not have solidified into full-blown PTSD) that overrides mourning or an integration of post-traumatic elements within mourning. In the former condition, the symptomatology is like a blanket covering the mourning and first requires full-scale intervention for post-traumatic stress in order to get to the mourning underneath. Where PTSD is a major part of the experience, there is more likely to be interrupted treatment because of the fear that treatment will overwhelm the fragile barrier protecting the patient from traumatic memories. In the latter condition, the post-traumatic elements are interspersed with mourning. Here, intervention requires incorporation of selected techniques for working through post-traumatic symptomatology into the overall mourning interventions. In many cases, the intervention into both realms occurs simultaneously, although if post-traumatic elements are obscuring or interfering sufficiently they will require address first in order to access the mourning.

Treatment of post-traumatic stress overlying mourning

Many specific approaches have been developed to treat established PTSD. These approaches include behavioral intervention (e.g., Keane, Fairbank, Caddell, Zimering, & Bender, 1985), psychoanalytically oriented intervention (e.g., Horowitz, 1986a; Lindy, 1986), and eclectic methods (e.g., Danieli, 1985, 1988; Herman, 1990; Raphael, 1986; Scurfield, 1985). A review of these various approaches to PTSD indicates that general goals in the treatment of post-traumatic stress are to empower the individual and to liberate him from the traumatic effects of victimization. Issues of grief and mourning are consistently mentioned as inherent aspects of healthy adaptation to traumatic stress. In addition, examination of the goals and strategies for the treatment of post-traumatic stress reveals its similarity to the "R" processes of mourning. In general, the caregiver attempts to help the individual do the following.

1. Bring into consciousness the traumatic experience, repeatedly reviewing, reconstructing, reexperiencing, and abreacting the experience until it is robbed of its potency

2. Identify, dose, express, work through, and master the affects of the traumatic encounter (e.g., helplessness, shock, horror, terror, anxiety, anger, guilt)

3. Integrate memories, affects, thoughts, images, behaviors, and somatic sensations of the traumatic experience (including reclaiming, owning, and reintegrating any that have been split off) and recognize that, because detoxifying one part of the trauma does not mean detoxifying others, each part of the trauma must be addressed

4. Mourn relevant physical and psychosocial losses

5. Discourage maladaptive processes and address therapeutically the defenses and behaviors used to cope with the trauma itself and with the mechanisms employed to deal with it

6. Focus on the acquisition and development of new skills and behaviors and/or the retrieval of overwhelmed ones in order to promote healthy living in the world after the trauma; recognize that the targets for intervention should not only relate to existing post-traumatic symptomatology but also promote adaptation and ongoing development

7. Counter the helplessness and powerlessness with experiences, interactions, activities, and actions supporting mastery, a sense of personal worth and value, connectedness to others, coping ability, and release of feelings in small doses; as appropriate, support giving testimony, participating in rituals, working for change in or to help others with similar traumatic experiences, and avoiding further victimizing or helplessness-producing experiences

8. Develop a perspective on what happened, by whom, to whom, why, and what one was and was not able to do and control within the situation; recognize and come to terms with the helplessness and shock of trauma and set these in the past by gaining an understanding and emotional distance from them; ultimately accept the reality that events happened the way they did

9. Accept full responsibility for one's behaviors as is appropriate and ultimately relinquish any inappropriate assumption of responsibility and guilt after identifying, working through, and constructively transcending the meanings and functions of survivor guilt

10. Create meaning out of the traumatic experience

11. Integrate into the assumptive world all of the negative and positive aspects of the trauma and the meaning of the experience; place such aspects in psychic continuity within the totality of one's past, present, and future; make the requisite cognitive adaptations to promote adjustment reflecting an acquisition of meaning in the event, mastery over the trauma and life in general, and restoration of self-esteem (Taylor, 1983)

12. Form a new identity that reflects one's survival of the traumatic experience and integrates the extraordinary into one's life

13. Reinvest in love, work, and play; reconnect with others and resume the continued flow of life and developmental growth halted by the traumatic victimization, its sequelae, and consequent reactions and defenses

These treatment goals are reached through four specific processes. First, there is the establishment of a trusting relationship. Second, there is a provision of psychoeducational and normative information about post-traumatic stress and loss, grief, and mourning. Third, interventions are focused not only on the cardinal symptoms of post-traumatic stress, but also on (a) defenses erected against the symptoms (e.g., distancing and distortion), (b) behaviors used to control the symptoms (e.g., acting out, self-medication through drug abuse), and (c) skills required to implement alternative responses to the symptoms and promote healthy post-traumatic existence (e.g., assertiveness, problem solving). Fourth, the caregiver helps the mourner recollect and integrate traumatic memories into a new identity, along with which the survivor adapts to, reconnects to, and reinvests in a revised assumptive and external world. Throughout, the caregiver helps the mourner manage stress and acquire skills, and facilitates mourning processes. As appropriate, any of the suggestions for treatment of mourning complicated by post-traumatic stress, delineated in the next section, may be incorporated in intervention for post-traumatic stress overlying mourning.

Treatment of mourning complicated by post-traumatic stress

In addition to the treatment suggestions just described for post-traumatic stress overlying mourning, treatment of mourning complicated by post-traumatic stress involves specific interventions depending upon which stress elements are found. The following areas of concern are particularly relevant.

The therapeutic relationship.   There appear to be two groups of individuals who survive the loss of a loved one under traumatic circumstances: those who do not want to talk about it and those who do. Interestingly, these responses reflect the two states of mind the survivor works through to achieve cognitive completion following exposure to trauma (i.e., denial and numbing, and intrusion; Horowitz, 1986a) and the two defensive tendencies by which the mourner handles information about the death of a loved one. The first of these is the inhibitory tendency, which by repression, avoidance, postponement, and so forth limits the perception of disturbing stimuli in the new world without the deceased. The second is the facilitative or reality-testing tendency, which enhances perception and thought about disturbing stimuli (Parkes, 1987). The survivor of a traumatic experience resulting in the death of a loved one is predisposed to these responses with regard to both trauma and loss: The trauma engages these responses via the stress response syndrome, and the loss engages them via the two tendencies of information handling.

In those instances where the mourner is willing to share feelings, thoughts, and memories, the establishment of a trusting relationship with the caregiver proceeds in a fairly typical fashion, with the usual therapeutic attempts to create a positive alliance. However, individuals traumatized by specific circumstances of the death or by the relationship they now must mourn often require additional endeavors. Such persons are frequently difficult to engage in treatment because they sustain a fear of attachment, which reawakens fear of abandonment, and a reluctance to recall the trauma (van der Kolk, 1987a).

For example, let us consider two different traumatized mourners coming for treatment of complicated mourning. One mourner is a victim of her father's chronic sexual abuse. The primary treatment issues concern mourning her father's anticipated death from cancer. For this mourner, traumatization is secondary to the relationship with the deceased. Another mourner has survived a devastating earthquake that destroyed his community, took the life of his spouse, and exposed him to the massive death and mutilation of others. His traumatization is secondary to the traumatic event.

It can be anticipated that both of these traumatized individuals will require special efforts in the establishment of a trusting relationship, without which little progress in treatment can be made. Specifically, the incest survivor, as a traumatized mourner, must deal with the incestuous experiences with her father in her mourning of him. In the treatment of incest survivors in general, it is imperative that the caregiver form an alliance with the survivor around the principle of safety (Herman, 1990). This involves providing the locus of control to the survivor, with the caregiver serving as consultant and ally. Care and control of the body, creation of a safe living environment, and assistance in learning self-soothing and control of self-harm through biobehavioral, cognitive/verbal, interpersonal, and social strategies round out the caregiver's interventions in the development of a relationship of safety and trust (Herman, 1990). As a traumatized individual who has been victimized by the one who was to care for her, the incest survivor understandably requires patience and perseverance from her caregiver. Although she is terrified of attachment because of her fear of repeated betrayal, she desperately wants that attachment, as well as protection and rescue. The attachment will take time to develop, and much painstaking work will be required. Failure to wait until basic safety is established prior to reliving the trauma may revictimize the survivor. The caregiver also will need to be "safe" in the treatment of incest because he or she will bear witness to the atrocity; experience intense emotional reactions; and confront wishes to deny, rescue, blame, or punish (Herman, 1990). (See chapter 14 for more on caregiver issues.)

In the situation of the traumatized disaster survivor, the issues around trust and the disinclination to discuss the traumatic experience lie not in characterological concerns about betrayal, insecurity, and victimization. Rather, the survivor has developed a sensitivity to individuals unfamiliar with the particular meaning of the trauma who might serve to stimulate unwanted traumatic memories without a constructive context for healing. The survivor devises many ways to keep such persons outside of his *trauma membrane* (Lindy, 1985). Like the outer surface of an injured cell, the trauma membrane guards the inner reparative process of the individual or group. As such, it protects the individual or group from foreign matter that might disturb its healing, permitting entrance only to those selectively viewed as promoting recovery. Usually, fellow survivors—those who truly know the absurd reality of the traumatic event or have shared its experience—have a special place of closeness (Lindy, 1986).

The caregiver may be invited within the trauma membrane if there is successful negotiation of issues around trust. In analyzing psychotherapy with survivors of the Beverly Hills Supper Club fire, Lindy, Green, Grace, and Titchener (1983) found that a number of responses helped consolidate the treatment alliance: First, the survivor felt the caregiver to be sensitive to the unique circumstances of the traumatic event and trusted the caregiver with feelings about the experience. Second, the caregiver was genuinely moved by the narration of the survivor's experience in the traumatic event and communicated this to the survivor. Third, there was successful negotiation of the threat of affect overload, with the caregiver communicating an expectant but noncoercive attitude regarding the traumatic material. Finally, somewhere between the beginning of the second and the end of the fourth session the survivor described a relatively neutral event in the external world, which was manifestly unrelated to the trauma and which caused the survivor to reveal an intense currently experienced affect. This affect (e.g., rage; guilt; or shame colored by anxiety, hypervigilance, or agitation) was identified by the caregiver and linked to aspects of the trauma as yet not worked through. This latter type of linking intervention appeared to mark the consolidation of the working alliance and the beginning of the working through phase of treatment. It appears that such actions on the part of the caregiver could be equally beneficial in achieving a positive working alliance with other traumatized mourners.

Another issue that may play a part in this scenario—and one that may have some parallel with the incest survivor's concerns about trusting the caregiver—is Lifton's (1979) concept of suspicion of the counterfeit, which stems from conflicts the survivor now sustains with nurturance as a consequence of traumatic victimization. The caregiver who wishes to work through this suspicion must demonstrate trustworthiness and a lack of anxiety in attitudes toward and interactions with the survivor, always proving reliable and consistently following through. The therapeutic alliance also will be enhanced if the caregiver continually treats the survivor with the utmost respect and gives her maximum control, conveys the appropriateness of atypical responses to atypical conditions, and avoids pathologizing her reactions.

In both of these cases, the caregiver-survivor unit provides the security and strength needed for the survivor to risk examining memories of the trauma and its associated affects and thoughts. The purpose of the unit is to enable the survivor to confront dosed amounts of the trauma. Essentially, the unit comes to serve as a temporary cohesive self, which is capable of managing doses of trauma greater than those the survivor alone could tolerate (Lindy, 1986). Throughout the work, as the survivor journeys back to reclaim the denied and unintegrated traumatic memories and feelings, which have been kept separate from yet intrude daily into the rest of life, the caregiver helps maintain an emotional balance between numbness and being overwhelmed. The caregiver must keep this balance in mind, especially when the mourner exhibits negative transference reactions, suspicion of the counterfeit, and projected anger. The caregiver will require support and knowledge of how to deal with his or her own counter-transference feelings (see chapter 14).

Normalizing information. As noted previously, education is exceptionally important, especially about trauma and its consequences. The appropriate normalization of feelings, thoughts, impulses, behaviors, and experiences that cause anxiety or fear of losing one's mind is enormously helpful in creating the type of climate required for self-disclosure. General information about loss, grief, and mourning also must be provided.

With regard to education about post-traumatic reactions, the following points, adapted from Scurfield (1985), are among the most important to bring to the awareness of the survivor, both initially and throughout treatment.

1. Trauma is such a catastrophic experience that it can produce post-traumatic symptomatology in almost anyone, regardless of prior background.

2. Some psychological aftershocks during or after the trauma are normal and expected. These may include, among others, intrusive imagery, numbing, rage, and grief.

3. Some survivors continue to have significant post-traumatic symptomatology years or even decades following the trauma, usually when effective counseling assistance has not been provided.

4. It is not unusual to fear loss of control of emotions (e.g., crying or rage) sometime following a trauma. Such loss of control does not mean that the survivor is going crazy, only that there are some important things to work though about the trauma and its impact.

5. Symptomatology usually gets worse before it gets better. This trend is only temporary, and the caregiver will stay with the survivor throughout the process.

6. Post-traumatic stress reactions are definitely responsive to treatment.

7. Because there are a number of experiences in life in general—positive as well as negative—that one never completely forgets, some symptomatology may not go away completely or forever. Treatment will help identify the connections that may arise between current issues and experiences and past memories and feelings. If traumatic memories revive in the future, the survivor usually will be able to discern these connections, even though the events initially appear unrelated.

8. If post-traumatic stress symptomatology cannot be extinguished, at the very least it can be controlled and its severity or frequency limited. The survivor will gain understanding of past, present, and future occurrences and learn what can be done about them.

9. Although it may be difficult to believe, the survivor may find some benefits in the traumatic experience and in the willingness to face and work through the experience (e.g., recognition that she must be very strong).

In work with incest survivors, Herman (1988) adds the following suggestions: Regardless of any behavior on the survivor's part, the fact that she had an incest experience means that she was not properly cared for. The survivor must be assured that she is not to blame for the incest. In addition, difficulties in establishing trusting relationships and the survivor's own lack of entitlement to self-care must be explained as consequences of the abuse. Finally, post-traumatic stress symptoms and defensive strategies emanating from the trauma should be identified.

Denial and numbing reactions. Called the most normal and the most prevalent of defenses (Menninger, 1954), denial and general emotional numbing are found in virtually all forms of complicated mourning and post-traumatic stress. Clearly, denial and numbing have adaptive functions in coping with loss and trauma. Despite some thanatological misunderstanding of their purposes stemming from misinterpretation of Kübler-Ross's (1969) work with dying individuals, their necessity is unquestioned.

Discrete numbing reactions during the course of therapy serve to (a) promote withdrawal from or numb anxiety associated with therapeutic issues or the relationship with the caregiver, (b) avoid recall of the trauma, (c) avoid integration of material learned in therapy, (d) maintain safety in treatment, and (e) defend against shame (Courtois, 1988). They occur outside of therapy for similar reasons.

As Horowitz (1986a) clarifies, the numbness present during the denial phase is more than an absence of emotions. Rather, it is a sense of being "benumbed" or surrounded by a layer of emotional insulation that blunts or deadens emotions. Initially, numbing is of great value in helping the mourner avoid painful memories, thoughts, and feelings about the trauma. As an aspect of dissociation—which consistently appears as a response to trauma—numbing contributes to disturbance in the normal integration of thoughts, feelings, and memories into consciousness and helps to separate them from normal awareness. Over time, however, it interferes with the requisite processing of the experience and prevents essential assimilation of the trauma and appraisal of its implications, thus impeding adaptation and accommodation.

Numbing reactions have varying impacts upon the individual's consciousness and involve lesser to greater degrees of disruption of and separation from awareness. They may be as fleeting and as faint as an eye blink or as dramatic and persistent as a prolonged trance-like state. Pathological intensification of denial experiences can lead to maladaptive avoidances, such as withdrawal, drug or alcohol abuse, counterphobic frenzy, or fugue states (Horowitz, 1986a).

Horowitz (1986a) makes a number of suggestions to reduce defensive overcontrol, as noted in Table 7.1. Among these are to interpret defenses and attitudes that make controls necessary (in order to reduce the controls); encourage abreaction and description, the latter through association and use of images; and encourage catharsis, explore emotional aspects of relationships and experiences of self during the event, and encourage relationships to counteract numbness.

Additional techniques can help the mourner confront affect and experience emotional expression and catharsis. These may include the following.

1. Gestalt therapeutic exercises (e.g., empty chair, role-play and role-reversal, body awareness)

2. Creation of a therapeutic bereavement ritual (see chapter 7)

3. Psychodrama (e.g., mirror technique, use of auxiliary egos, waking dream)

4. Writing (e.g., letters, journals, poetry, sentence completion)

5. Art (e.g., drawing, painting, sculpting, photography)

6. Movement (e.g., interpretive dance, pantomime)

7. Music (e.g., composing, listening)

8. Construction (e.g., building objects or structures)

The following strategies for addressing numbing symptoms have been adapted from Courtois (1988).

1. Explain and depathologize numbing dissociative reactions.

2. During numbing episodes in therapy, ask the mourner where he is and how he feels while observing which topics, memories, or emotions precipitate the numbing (e.g., rage) and what functions they serve (e.g., rage can be controlled if split off). Process this information with the mourner to enable him to experience consciously the warded-off material in manageable doses. Simple techniques for accessing dissociated material include writing about it, dialoguing with the split-off part of the self, and drawing the experience.

3. Although on occasion it may be useful to encourage the mourner to accept the dissociation as a means to protect himself, gradually help him stay in the present with the formerly split-off material. Stress the safety and security of the therapeutic setting as a context within which to face the traumatic memories and point out that he is not alone, as he may have been during the trauma.

4. Separate the present experience from the past trauma (i.e., differentiate "here and now" from "then").

5. Ground or bring the mourner back to the present.

6. As necessary, use hypnosis to help bring material to consciousness.

7. Once the dissociative reaction has been identified, help the mourner monitor it, especially when it involves prolonged periods of disrupted awareness (e.g., trance).

8. Assist the mourner in identifying cues indicating when he may seriously dissociate or enter a trance and help him master techniques to ground himself during such episodes. (This will be especially important if the mourner is operating machinery or a motor vehicle.)

Other techniques for confronting denial and numbing may be found among those noted in subsequent sections on recall of the trauma and anxiety associated with traumatic memories.

Because smashing through defenses can retraumatize the mourner, denial and numbing must be addressed gradually. Certainly contact with warded-off emotions, cognitions, and memories may bring great emotional reaction. However, the main goal is to gain access to this material in order to be able to integrate it, not merely to experience an emotional outburst. It must be recognized that the long-range goal is not to reduce controls, but to reduce the need for controls by helping the person complete the cycle of ideational and emotional response to the stress event (i.e., work through the traumatic memories, feelings, and thoughts so that the trauma can be assimilated and accommodated; Horowitz, 1986a).

Before introducing techniques to penetrate denial and numbing, the caregiver must ensure that a strong alliance with the mourner exists and that he has a sense of safety. The least threatening and intense techniques should be used first, with the caregiver continually monitoring the mourner to avoid emotional flooding or decompensation in those so inclined. Courtois (1988) has urged caution and pointed out that, rather paradoxically, the trauma survivor's reactions may be muted or masked, particularly if he is feeling overwhelmed. The caregiver must allow sufficient time to assess reactions and work through material before introducing additional cathartic techniques.

As denial and numbing are lessened, the caregiver must help the individual dose exposure to the unfrozen memories and reexperience of the trauma. Before some people can tolerate contemplating any aspect of the trauma, they first must become comfortable passively relinquishing denial or numbing for periods of time. Only when they can drop this blanket of protection can they proceed actively to withstand and/or examine the traumatic elements.

Intrusive and repetitive reactions. Intrusive repetitions can involve thoughts and images of the event (ranging from nightmares to recurrent obsessive thoughts), feelings related to the original event (with or without conscious awareness of their origins), behavioral reenactments of portions of the experience (ranging from compulsive verbalizations of the story of the trauma, to recurrent expression in artistic productions, to patterning of interpersonal relationships), and physiological responses to stress. The man who cannot rid himself of the sight of his son in the morgue, the woman who has flashbacks to the scene of a fatal accident, the Vietnam veteran who has unrelenting dreams of the firefight, and the incest survivor who dissociates when recalling the relationship with the deceased abuser are all individuals whose traumatic memories require assimilation and accommodation.

Intrusive and repetitive reactions—often the symptoms that propel the individual to seek assistance through therapy—constitute dissociative reactions through which repressed and split-off memories, thoughts, feelings, behaviors, and physiological reactions return to awareness. Although for some survivors such involuntary repetitions persist without change or respite, they need not be static replicas of the original experience. Successive revisions can indicate a progressive mastery of the experience.

Symptoms can be stimulated by any trigger in the survivor's life or in the lives of others. Even media reports or hearing from a friend about a similar trauma can generate overwhelming recall. The return of repressed affective, cognitive, behavioral, and/or somatic memories can extend into both sleep and waking life and be extremely painful and disruptive.

As Horowitz (1986a) notes in his discussion of the stress response syndrome, intrusive-repetitive states reflect the mind's repeated attempts to process and integrate with the individual's assumptive world new information concerning the stress event and its implications. The ultimate establishment of new schemata (i.e., revision of the assumptive world) is accomplished via repeated examination and processing of information about the trauma (i.e., memories, thoughts, and feelings about it, as well as its behavioral and/or physiological reenactments). This repeated processing, interspersed with periods of denial and numbing that facilitate necessary restabilization after contact with painful content, is necessary in order to work through and complete the adaptation to stress. However, as is true for denial, sometimes there can be "too much of a good thing." The intrusive-repetitive phases can become overwhelming and not only disrupt the accommodation of the trauma, but also contribute to the development of flooded and impulsive states, despair, impaired world and social functions, and compulsive reenactments (Horowitz, 1986a).

When contending with a mourner's intrusive-repetitive states, Horowitz (1986a) advises the caregiver to bear in mind a number of points. First, the victim remains vulnerable to entering a distraught state of mind, even in states of safety and months after the event. This latter point is important because, although the victim may expect to be upset subsequent to the trauma, she often is unprepared for the distress that may occur following a period of restored good functioning. (This phenomenon is not unlike the 6-month phenomenon, witnessed after sudden, unexpected death; Rando, 1988). She may interpret the change as a serious loss of control or an indication that she is losing her mind. For this reason, it is helpful to provide information about the normal phases that occur in the stress response syndrome and especially to note that intrusive ideas and emotions frequently reemerge after a period of denial and numbing.

In addition, distraught, intrusive states such as searing grief, remorse, terror, or diffuse rage are attenuated and less likely if the victim is surrounded by supportive companions. However, the more the person has been traumatized, the longer the phases of response will be, with considerable revision required in both the internal and external worlds following major loss.

Sleep disruption is a common component of post-traumatic stress responses, and the victim may come to associate states of relaxation and sleep with panic or unpleasant imagery if either has occurred during these times. Such an association is common because this is when one's guard is lowered and distractions are minimal. Therefore, sleep patterns may need to be restructured: The mourner may need to leave room lights on, sleep with a pet or another person, or have a companion stay awake and watch while the mourner sleeps.

The person who has been traumatized may sustain cognitive impairments of which she is unaware. She may feel more effective, alert, or responsive than is actually the case and may be more reactive to even minimal amounts of alcohol or drugs. Despite protestations otherwise, the trauma survivor may have to be prohibited from driving or performing other potentially hazardous tasks. Any such prohibitions must be undertaken in a tactful fashion to avoid installation of incompetent self-concepts.

Finally, immediately after the trauma, the survivor will be requested to relive the experience and retell it repeatedly. Later, she will want to repeat the story, but others may discourage this or offer their own tales. This can leave the individual with a great need to repeat the traumatic experience and to communicate her conceptual and emotional responses to it. For this reason, at later stages, empathic listening is quite useful. Over time, the survivor's attention can be brought gradually to the present—ultimately, it can be directed toward future concerns.

In evaluating intrusive repetitions, Horowitz (1986a) asserts that the caregiver must inquire specifically about intrusive experiences because the mourner often has difficulty describing them on her own. Labeling intrusions as an expected part of the stress response can normalize them and reassure the individual that she is not losing her mind. When she describes the intrusion, the caregiver can encourage her to develop the meaning of the event. Nonspecific questions like, Can you tell me more about that? Is there anything else? and, What was it like for you? can elicit more information. The caregiver listens carefully to the mourner expound upon the topic, remaining alert for any blocks in her thinking or feeling that might interfere with acceptance of or closure on the event (e.g., if a mourner feels she may have caused an accident, she may block her thinking about it in order to avoid experiencing guilt).

When the caregiver discovers a block to working through reactions, he or she may help the mourner by looking at the differences between realistic and fantastic appraisal (Horowitz, 1986a). For example, the caregiver can help the mourner understand that the connection between the mourner's wish that his sister would get out of his life and the sister's fatal accident is based on fantasy and can indicate that the mourner did not cause the accident and is not to blame. For the traumatized mourner, the presence of someone who is not overwhelmed by the trauma and who is able to contemplate events logically is typically reassuring, especially during an intrusive-repetitive phase.

In a significant number of those suffering from post-traumatic reactions, the walling off of memories and the warding off of unresolved psychological trauma become a central focus in life, creating constricted involvement with surroundings and causing superficial or nonexistent love relationships (van der Kolk & Kadish, 1987). Hence, the goal of bringing trauma into consciousness and putting it into perspective is not only to secure symptom reduction for the traumatized mourner, but also to eliminate further secondary losses as a consequence of the mourner's reactions.

Horowitz (1986a) suggests a number of specific supportive interventions for use when the individual is experiencing the relative undercontrol inherent in intrusive-repetitive states. These interventions include, among others, supplying structure, reducing demands, and facilitating rest; working through and reorganizing stress-related material, defusing triggers, and teaching dosing; and providing support and suppressing distress with selective use of medication and behavioral intervention. (For a full listing of suggested treatments, see Table 7.1.) The chief aims of these interventions are to (a) supplement the individual's weakened controls over the tendency to repetition; (b) reduce the intensity of intrusive ideas, feelings, memories, and behavioral and physiological reenactments; and (c) diminish emotional and ideational triggers to repeated representations.

Courtois (1988) has also discussed strategies for intervention with intrusive symptoms (especially jarring, recurrent flashbacks; nightmares; intrusive images; and body sensations), suggesting that the caregiver develop a repertoire of containment messages and techniques to limit the exposure of the trauma survivor to sources of information that stimulate recall. Guided imagery and/or hypnotic instructions can be used:

> Close the door to the memories and lock it. Keep the key
> so you can unlock the door when you are again ready to

do so. . . . Imagine yourself putting the thoughts and memories out of your mind. Put them in a safe place as you focus on something pleasant right now. Focus on being in the safety and security of this room. (Courtois, 1988, p. 299)

Courtois has offered other treatment suggestions for dealing with trauma flashbacks. Adapted for working with the traumatized mourner, they include the following: First, teach the mourner that flashbacks are normal and that she is not losing her mind and predict that, following temporary intensification during treatment, flashbacks will likely become less frequent and intense, although some flashbacks may present periodically throughout life. Second, stress that, although the mourner may not have control over when flashbacks occur, she does have some control over what happens when they do. Help the mourner control rather than avoid panic associated with flashbacks. Change the goal from eliminating all flashbacks—which is often impossible—to reducing anxiety and improving coping with their occurrence. (In this regard, the goals for managing flashbacks and phobias are similar.) Third, given that the issue of control is paramount and that the mourner needs to know she has a way out of the situation at all times, encourage her to take whatever actions are necessary to feel safe. By receiving encouragement over time to experience increased doses of anxiety, the mourner can manage them and reengage in anxiety-provoking behavior (Sprei & Courtois, 1988; Sprei & Goodwin, 1983). Fourth, teach the mourner techniques to use when a flashback occurs. Such techniques include (a) identifying and verbalizing when she is having a flashback, (b) describing what she is experiencing in the present as the caregiver tells her she is safe and not actually in the situation being experienced, (c) reorienting or grounding herself in the present by focusing on the here-and-now and the safety of the immediate environment, (d) recognizing that the flashback is in her mind and that she is not actually having the experience, (e) using relaxation techniques to control and break her anxiety, and (f) identifying triggers to the flashback and avoiding or modifying them. Caregivers or concerned partners may also appropriately touch or hold the traumatized mourner, offering reassurances that she is safe and in the present.

In discussing treatment for individuals with multiple personality disorder, Putnam (1989) advocates the use of *screen techniques* to view, relive, and describe a traumatic event while obtaining sufficient distance from it. Such techniques can be adapted for survivors of all types of traumatic death. The mourner is asked to visualize a screen—similar to a movie or television screen—and to project onto it the events or experiences that need to be explored. In watching from a psychological distance and with a sense of detachment, the mourner can slow down, speed up, reverse, or freeze images as needed. The screen can be split or subdivided to view more than one event at a time. The mourner can zoom in on details or zoom back and pan for a larger perspective. This repertoire of camera techniques greatly facilitates recovery of memories by permitting the mourner to see more than would be possible from a single perspective. It also gives her enormous control over the proceedings because she can modify or switch off the events on the screen when she has the need.

Additional techniques for intrusive repetitions may be found among those noted in the subsequent sections on recall of the trauma and anxiety associated with traumatic memories.

Recall of the trauma. Two main difficulties exist in the recollection and integration of traumatic memories. First, problems occur in the retrieval of traumatic memories due to dissociation and post-traumatic amnesia. Second, anxiety associated with the memories is so intense that the individual avoids contemplating them and thereby never has them available to work with. This section suggests ways to facilitate recall; the following section focuses on ways to deal with anxiety.

An intrinsic part of the treatment of traumatic aspects of a death is recall of the trauma. Recall is necessary in order to work through the trauma and integrate it with the rest of the individual's life. This process is known by various names in the traumatic stress literature (e.g., retrieval of memories, uncovering, recollection, reconstruction of the trauma, recovery of the affect-laden traumatic memories, reclaiming disavowed affect, return of the repressed, reexperience of the trauma, regression back to the trauma). However it is designated, this process entails bringing the images, thoughts, feelings, and memories elicited by the trauma into the present in order to make them available for the working through that never occurred during or after the trauma. Lindy (1986) describes the process of working through in this context:

> Within limits, we assume that the psychic organism is capable in its own time of breaking down the impact of traumatic stressors and their associated affect states into manageable amounts that permit gradual intrapsychic processing. We identify this process as the working through of trauma. This task requires (1) the recovery of affect-laden memory traces; (2) the attribution of meaning to these memory traces; and (3) the reestablishment of psychic continuity with the past. (p. 198)

The approach to the working through process also has been articulated by Lindy (1986):

> Therapy is an effort to remove the blocks to an essentially spontaneous healing process. In order to do this, [the caregiver] must be invited to the boundary of the trauma

membrane, be permitted entry, and maintain that as healing space, dosing or titrating traumatic memory and its process-ing. (pp. 200–201)

The reader will note how this process parallels precisely the goal of inter-vention in complicated mourning, which is to remove the complications of mourning so that uncomplicated mourning processes can proceed.

Although Lindy (1986) has defined the tasks of the working through phase of post-traumatic stress in terms of psychoanalytic psychotherapy, these tasks can fit other types of treatment as well. Before undertaking treatment, the caregiver first interprets and reestablishes for the mourner the link between currently experienced derivative reminders of the trauma and the traumatic memories and affects. This is necessary because, with time, these reminders have become disguised and the mourner has begun to attribute them to causes other than the original trauma. Adapted to re-late to the traumatized mourner, Lindy's subsequent therapeutic steps are as follows.

1. Assist the mourner in organizing into manageable doses the currently experienced pathological reflections of segments of specific traumatic experiences (i.e., exposure to traumatic memories, thoughts, images, and feelings).

2. Clarify the mourner's defenses (e.g., splitting, disavowal) and underlying affect states (e.g., helplessness, rage, guilt, shame) in the context of the absurd (i.e., the trauma).

3. Enable the caregiver-mourner unit to serve as a temporary cohesive self capable of managing doses of trauma greater than those the mourner could tolerate alone, thus permitting the mourner to address the traumatization.

4. Work with the mourner to dissect and process each memory trace, identifying and feeling each fear and emotion and addressing the affect and meaning of the losses in the trauma.

Lindy (1986) contends that these tasks accomplish the following goals:

The patient himself begins to experience mastery as he works with new reminders of his trauma. He gains confidence in his capacity to maintain ongoing cohesion in the presence of such threats. *Grief now spontaneously surfaces, and the opportunity to work through delayed bereavement connected with the catastrophe becomes central. Mourning is now ready to occur.*

As a result of the working through of trauma and the acti-vation of mourning, the patient has reclaimed his disavowed affect, given meaning to the absurd catastrophe, and regained

> psychic continuity between past, present, and future. . . . As trauma and grief are reclaimed by the psychic organism as a whole, the specific meaning of the catastrophe becomes clear as it relates both to the earlier psychogenetic conflicts of the individual and to the capacity to invest the future with energy and ambition. (p. 202, emphasis added)

Again, the reader will observe a similarity to interventions in mourning, which are mentioned by Lindy as an inherent part of the process of working through post-traumatic stress. He asserts that psychological recovery from the impact of catastrophic events almost always entails the working through of both trauma and loss. The mourning to which Lindy refers is mourning over the losses of the trauma, which may or may not involve the death of a loved one. In most cases, when such a death has occurred within a traumatic experience, mourning can be addressed successfully only after overlying post-traumatic stress elements have been worked through.

In bringing memories, feelings, thoughts, and images about the traumatic event to conscious awareness, the mourner will experience a temporary increase in feelings of grief, existential despair, guilt, anxiety, and so forth. These feelings must be worked through. In essence, the individual may feel worse for a while before he feels better, yet this is necessary and unavoidable. Both caregiver and mourner need to be prepared for acute distress prior to relief.

As discussed previously, it is imperative that no recall or reconstruction of the trauma be attempted until a sense of safety has been established and a strong therapeutic alliance has been forged. The caregiver who does not first take the time to create this alliance revictimizes the individual. In addition, if the traumatized mourner cannot feel safe with the caregiver, it is doubtful that he will be able to tolerate the painful thoughts and feelings that accompany recollection of traumatic memories. In brief, the caregiver who believes that treatment can proceed immediately to trauma reconstruction without first building an effective therapeutic alliance is doomed to fail.

In many situations, the time needed to form a therapeutic alliance and uncover repressed material can be lengthy, although short-term models are available (e.g., Horowitz, 1986a; Lindy et al., 1983). As noted previously, whether or not treatment for mourning is long or short term depends upon what the goals are in terms of the six "R" processes. If the goals are to assist the mourner throughout most of these processes, caregivers who eschew anything beyond brief treatment should think twice before seeing traumatized mourners. If the goals are primarily to address post-traumatic symptomatology and some of the underlying dynamic issues, then more structured short-term therapies for stress response syndromes or complicated mourning are valid options.

The locus of control in uncovering memories should always remain with the individual in terms of timing, pacing, and dosing. Nevertheless, the caregiver must ensure that recollection is a mastery experience for the trauma survivor, not a reenactment of the trauma. Therefore, the caregiver must know how to help the mourner dose his experiences, contain his recollections and associated thoughts and feelings, and pace himself as necessary in order to avoid being overwhelmed.

Trauma may be stimulated and dissociated material accessed in a number of ways. However, it must be remembered that, contrary to what may be portrayed in the popular media, uncovering typically proceeds in small steps that must themselves often be processed before further progress is made. The use of techniques mentioned for multiple death and intrusive-repetitive reactions (noted previously in this chapter), for confronting pain and bereavement overload (delineated in chapter 9), and for anxiety (noted in the following section) will help reduce, desensitize, manage, or extinguish the unwanted or aversive symptoms that interfere with memory retrieval.

In addition to the important processes of caregiver identification and interpretation of themes and patterns manifested in therapy, other useful techniques to facilitate recollection include the following.

1. Asking the mourner to give a detailed chronology of the traumatic events, including the mourner's accompanying thoughts, feelings, behaviors, impulses, and bodily awareness, as well as those of pertinent others

2. Asking the mourner to detail this chronology in a journal and to keep a daily diary

3. Asking the mourner to keep a record of dreams and associations while in treatment

4. Asking the mourner to read, view, or listen to appropriate material on related subjects

5. Asking the mourner to attend a group for individuals who have undergone similar experiences

6. Asking the mourner to express the experience nonverbally (e.g., through art, music, dance, drama, pantomime)

7. Using Gestalt therapy techniques

8. Using screen techniques (Putnam, 1989) for reviewing trauma and permitting previously repressed aspects to be made conscious

9. Using guided imagery and metaphor

10. Using projective techniques (e.g., Rorschach, sentence completion, Thematic Apperception Test, create-a-story)

11. Using free association to specific triggering stimuli or to traumatic memories, images, feelings, and thoughts

12. Using affect bridge techniques or age regression (Putnam, 1989)

13. Using hypnosis

14. Using narcotherapy procedures

15. Using in vivo techniques

16. Directing work toward surrounding material to encroach on less retrievable memories bit by bit; directing work toward the last memory first, working backwards in time to trace memory and affect in parallel fashion and slowly assembling a coherent whole from abreactive fragments

Given that pathologies of memory are characteristic features of most post-traumatic stress reactions, it is not surprising that nonverbal methods must be employed to access some individuals' memories, thoughts, and affects. Greenberg and van der Kolk (1987) describe retrieval and integration of one patient's memories through the use of painting. They note the potential benefits of such treatment as follows:

> Special cognitive resources outside the verbal realm can be reawakened and utilized, first to uncover and recall traumatic events, and then to transform the meaning of the trauma with resulting psychological growth. Images, scenes, bodily sensations, and emotions related to the trauma can be retrieved. This reversal of dissociation affords the patient an opportunity to recall significant autobiographical episodes and integrate the trauma into his or her personal history. In this process, the patient can transcend the trauma and cease the compulsion to repeat and reenact it. (pp. 194–195)

Finally, it should be recognized that complete recall of the trauma or aspects that intrude on the survivor's memory may be impossible. Sometimes this post-traumatic amnesia comes from the individual's having been of preverbal capacity at the time of the trauma or from a mismatch between cognitive capacities at the time the event was experienced and encoded and at the time of recall. Amnesia also may result from situations of terror in which experiences are not processed in symbolic/linguistic forms, but are encoded in sensorimotor or iconic forms (e.g., organized as visceral sensations, fight-flight reactions, or horrific images). In the last case, memories cannot easily be translated into the symbolic language necessary for linguistic retrieval and are only reactivated by affective, auditory, or visual cues similar to those present when the trauma originally occurred (Greenberg & van der Kolk, 1987). In any circumstance, the traumatic experience and its consequence of leaving the victim in a state of unspeakable terror do not fit into the person's existing conceptual schemata. The victim is overwhelmed, and necessary accommodation and assimilation are precluded. The caregiver's goal is to prevent the mourner's subsequent recovery and adjustment from being jeopardized by retrieving as much as possible so that it can be integrated, as well as by helping the victim to understand and learn to live with the fact that some material may not be retrieved.

Anxiety associated with traumatic memories. Just as there are many sources of anxiety after a traumatic death, so are there many interventions. It is beyond the scope of this work to review all of the individual and collective interventions proposed for treatment of this discomforting and prevalent affect. Discussion is therefore limited to interventions most often cited in work with both post-traumatic stress and complicated mourning. The ones noted here are in addition to those for intrusive and repetitive reactions (discussed previously in this chapter) and for dealing with the confrontation of pain and bereavement overload (discussed in chapter 9).

One of the most important interventions to help a traumatized mourner —indeed, any mourner—is to break down anxiety into its component parts (i.e., specific fears and concerns) so they can be identified, labeled, differentiated, traced, problem-solved, and worked through individually. As is true for the treatment of complicated mourning in general, it is always easier to cope with well-defined, explicit fears than to grapple with global, diffuse, and undifferentiated anxiety.

Another remedy for many sources of anxiety is provision of information and normalization of the experience. Offering education and validation minimizes the uncertainty with which individuals must contend. Doing so promotes the legitimization and normalization of feelings, thoughts, and impulses that may have been unacceptable and conducive to anxiety and the assorted defense mechanisms mobilized to handle it. In other words, information and normalization provide a sense of control and allow the mourner's experiences to be less of a threat. Where threat is diminished, anxiety is lowered.

Compulsive inquiry is typical in cases of traumatic death. Mourners have been known to devote enormous time, effort, and expense to secure information about the event in order to cope and achieve even minimal closure. It must be remembered that mourners who lack sufficient explanation of the death tend to have more complicated mourning, marked by anxiety and insecurity (see chapter 9). As an adaptive coping behavior, information seeking is helpful on several accounts and, in appropriate amounts, should be facilitated. It gives the mourner the ability to take some control—a critical issue because the mourner is powerless and helpless in the face of the traumatic event and is unable to undo the death of the loved one. Information seeking also works against the passivity of victimization. As subsequently noted, Flannery (1987) has developed a stress management program specifically to override learned helplessness secondary to trauma.

Certain cognitive techniques have been identified as being particularly helpful in the amelioration of anxiety. They include specialized techniques found under the rubric of cognitive restructuring, such as thought stopping, cognitive reprocessing (or cognitive reconceptualization), reattribution, logical analysis, decatastrophizing, evaluation of belief, reframing, hypnosis, metaphor, and guided imagery.

Other approaches to intervention in anxiety include assertiveness training, physical exercise, relaxation exercises (e.g., breathing exercises, progressive relaxation, safe place imagery, yoga), problem solving, social networking and support, and pharmacotherapy.

In PTSD and to a lesser extent in the more moderate forms of post-traumatic stress, extinction of anxiety does not occur over time despite the frequent reliving of traumatic memories. In fact, in cases of chronic PTSD, there appears to be increasing disturbance. It is believed that extinction does not occur because the individual is not exposed to all elements of the traumatic memory and because those that are extinguished become reconditioned by the unexposed components (Keane, Fairbank et al., 1985). Keane and colleagues note that exposure to the entire memory of the trauma would promote extinction and foster adaptive recovery, but that this tends to be precluded by (a) the individual's aversion to the memories, (b) reinforcement for competing emotions and behaviors, and (c) the necessity for specifically aroused states—similar to those accompanying the trauma—to promote recollection of the trauma (i.e., affective state dependent storage of memories).

In their work with Vietnam veterans suffering from PTSD, Keane and colleagues employ implosive therapy (i.e., emotional flooding) to eliminate avoidance of the memory and, through exposure to an extinction procedure, to reduce anxiety associated with the traumatic events, related stimuli, and disturbing cognitions. Their purpose is not to change the nature of the trauma but to decrease the individual's response to memories of it via the two treatment phases of relaxation training followed by repeated imaginal presentation of the traumatic scenes. Ultimately, the individual is exposed to all elements of the memories. Although after successful treatment the traumatic events still remain traumatic in nature and are still likely to be recalled with sorrow, avoidance of memories and associated levels of anxiety are markedly reduced, and symptom reduction and improved psychological functioning are achieved.

This technique could easily be adapted for traumatized mourners. However, Courtois (1988) has suggested that the technique might be countertherapeutic for incest survivors because it may recreate conditions of the trauma, especially lack of control and feelings of powerlessness. She urges that implosive therapy be considered only as a last resort and underscores the necessity of further research to determine its usefulness for this population. Similar cautions may or may not be necessary for other trauma victims. The caregiver will need to determine this based on the conditions of the original traumatic event, as well as the characteristics of the individual mourner and her current physiological and psychosocial situation.

Implosive therapy is but one approach to reducing severe anxiety interfering with the requisite processing of traumatic memories. Other techniques are noted in the subsequent section on specific treatment packages.

Reintegrating, rebuilding, and reconnecting. The goal of intervention in post-traumatic stress is to recover traumatic memories, affects, thoughts, and images and to reintegrate them into the totality of who the person has been, is, and will be in the future. This entails the development of a new identity that incorporates and integrates the mourner's sense of self and life before, during, and after the victimization. Psychic continuity must be achieved in order to avoid the creation of a reality focused too heavily on the victimization and to restore normal development and the capacity for investment in love, work, and play.

This process inherently involves rebuilding the assumptive world to accommodate the actual experience of the trauma, the perspective the survivor has developed toward it, and the existential fact that something of this sort could occur. The reader is urged to review chapters 8 and 9 from the perspective of traumatization and victimization. Discussion of the mourner's violated assumptive world, presented earlier in this chapter as one of the sequelae of traumatic death, is also pertinent.

With specific regard to recovery from trauma, Figley (1985a) has noted that victims become survivors by answering to their satisfaction five fundamental questions that help them place their experiences in perspective and ultimately eliminate trauma and subsequent stress: What happened? Why did it happen? Why did I act as I did then? Why did I act as I have since then? and, What if it [the catastrophe] happens again? By gradually recapitulating and reconstructing the trauma, mourners create a new world that incorporates the trauma, its post-traumatic stress, and the sequelae of both.

Scurfield (1985) has asserted, as is the case for bereavement work, that it is essential for the traumatized individual to integrate both positive and negative aspects of the trauma with notions of what one was before, during, and after the traumatic experience, accepting full personal responsibility for one's own actions and understanding what was beyond one's own control. There may be a special need for clarification and atonement of guilt (see chapter 10).

Finally, the survivor must redirect toward the living any major identifications with the dead. If connections with others have been disrupted by the effects of the trauma (e.g., post-traumatic decline, psychic numbing, survivor guilt, preoccupation with intrusive-repetitive symptoms), reconnection must take place. Heathy reconnection decreases isolation, shame, and stigma. It increases self-esteem, trust, and security. For many, social action and/or a "survivor mission" help transcend the trauma by giving to others and making something meaningful come from a meaningless event.

Specific treatment packages for post-traumatic stress

A number of specific treatment packages have been proposed to help individuals with post-traumatic stress. As is the case for the treatment of anxiety in general, most include some form of the following techniques: assertiveness training, physical exercise, relaxation (e.g., breathing exercises, progressive relaxation, safe place imagery, yoga), problem solving, and social networking and support. Stress management and coping skills training techniques are also typical.

Three particularly well-designed treatment packages for trauma have been proposed, each of which can be modified for use with a variety of trauma survivors, including traumatized mourners. The first treatment package, offered by Veronen and Kilpatrick (1983), is designed for rape victims. Its goal is the management, not elimination, of anxiety. Veronen and Kilpatrick use stress inoculation training, which emphasizes the analysis of cognition and internal dialogues and images and encourages the active participation of the survivor. The six cognitive-behavioral coping skills employed are muscle relaxation, breath control, role-playing, covert modeling (i.e., imaginal role-playing), thought stopping, and guided self-dialogue.

Flannery (1987) has designed a package to address the sense of helplessness and numbing that often can generalize following exposure to traumatic events. He essentially teaches the stress management strategies of stress-resistant persons to those who have been traumatized in order to improve the latter group's coping strategies. Skills shift the victims' psychology from learned helplessness to mastery through the enhancement of personal control, task involvement, certain healthful life-style choices, and use of social supports. Four specific areas of intervention for stress management are identified: (a) reduction of dietary stimulants (refined white sugar, caffeine, and nicotine), (b) strenuous aerobic exercise, (c) relaxation exercises, and (d) stress inoculation to master adaptive coping strategies. The stress inoculation process emphasizes direct behavioral action to reduce somatic stress; specific skills to solve specific problems; and delineation of cognitive strategies to inhibit negative thinking, keep the problem in proper perspective, and provide self-praise for reasonable mastery.

Finally, Keane, Fairbank et al. (1985) have designed a stress management package to help Vietnam veterans cope with current symptomatology and teach specific skills for dealing with the social, behavioral, and cognitive deficits typically found in PTSD. The goal is not to achieve symptom reduction by removing stressors from everyday life, but rather to teach veterans how to control emotional reactions to those stressors and choose more appropriate behavioral responses to them. The program addresses four areas: First, relaxation training is specifically applicable to sleep disturbances and nightmares, intrusive thoughts, and increased irritability and anger. Second, cognitive restructuring is particularly useful in intervening with increased irritability and anger, interpersonal difficulties involving feelings of detachment and withdrawal from others, and guilt. Third, problem solving is especially effective for dealing with the reexperience of trauma in intrusive thoughts, nightmares, and flashbacks; interpersonal difficulties; and exaggerated startle response. In problem solving, suggested alternatives to PTSD symptomatology include escaping or avoiding the situation, deep muscle relaxation/pleasant imagery, and cognitive restructuring. Anger control is the final program component.

CHAPTER 13

Risks and Therapeutic Implications Associated With Death of a Child and AIDS-Related Death

In addition to risks associated with individual, relationship, and system factors (chapter 10); mode of death (chapter 11); and traumatic circumstances of the death (chapter 12), death of a child and AIDS-related death confront the individual with special risks. This chapter outlines these risks and discusses treatment concerns important for each type of death. As is the case for other high-risk factors and circumstances, the treatment suggestions presented here are in addition to the philosophical perspectives on treatment and the generic treatment guidelines offered in chapter 8 and the interventions for the six "R" processes of mourning proposed in chapter 9.

DEATH OF A CHILD

Consistently, the loss of a child is identified as a high-risk variable in the development of complicated mourning. Research findings document that, when compared to other types of bereavement, parental mourning is particularly intense, complicated, and long-lasting, with major and unparalleled symptom fluctuations occurring over time (Rando, 1986g). This section offers a description of typical parental reactions to the death of a child and outlines some of the reasons this type of death is so difficult to accommodate. The parent-child relationship addressed in this section is the "ideal" one. To the extent that any particular relationship departs from this ideal, one can expect to see corresponding variations in the parental bereavement discussed here. Variations from this bereavement also will be found when circumstances differ from the traditional family structure (i.e., single parents, remarried parents, loss of an only child) and must be reflected in modified expectations and treatment interventions. For a comprehensive resource on the topic of parental bereavement, the reader is referred to *Parental Loss of a Child* (Rando, 1986g). Other helpful resources include Donnelly (1982), Klass (1988), Leon (1986), Limbo and Wheeler (1986), Littlefield and Rushton (1986), Miles (1984), Rando (1983, 1985a, 1991), Rubin (1984–1985), Sanders (1979–1980), and Videka-Sherman (1982).

Age of the Child

In general, the age of the child is irrelevant in this type of death. Many similar feelings and issues are present for bereaved parents whether the child is 2 days old, 2 years old, or 72 years old. These issues center around the loss of the person who was in a child role with those adults. Regardless of the child's age, parents have lost their hopes, dreams, expectations, fantasies, and wishes for that child. They have lost parts of themselves, each other, their family, and their future. Their assumptive worlds have been violated.

Although the age of the child is generally irrelevant, age does define some of the specific issues to be addressed in parental bereavement. This is the case because age identifies the developmental issues present in the parent-child relationship at the time of the death, and these issues affect parents' grief and mourning. For instance, when a child who has been actively involved in adolescent rebellion and conflict with his parents dies, his death may be relatively more difficult to accommodate because of the normal ambivalence in the parent-child relationship during that tumultuous stage. This does not mean it is necessarily harder or easier to lose a child of one age as opposed to another; the pain is merely different (Macon, 1979).

There is a curious social phenomenon of denying the significance and number of losses inherent in the death of a child at one or the other end of the age spectrum (i.e., when the death is a miscarriage, ectopic pregnancy, stillbirth, loss in multiple pregnancy, or infant death, or when the death is of an adult child). When a pregnancy or infant is lost, parents are reminded that they can have other children and told they are lucky they did not have more time to become attached. Often, the fact that emotional bonding occurs well in advance of birth is totally overlooked. Usually, such bonding takes place more quickly for mothers, who are able to feel the child develop within them, but it also transpires for many fathers. Both parents typically bring with them into the situation long-held dreams, hopes, beliefs, expectations, assumptions, feelings, thoughts, and meanings about themselves as the parents they ultimately will be and about the children they ultimately will have. In addition, they begin to invest specifically during the actual pregnancy in the image of the child-to-be, the family that will be created, and their own abilities to carry out the parental role. All of these constitute major secondary losses that must be mourned no matter what the age of the child. Even in death before birth, parents lose much. To say that a miscarriage is only the loss of blood and tissue overlooks all of these other profound losses.

When an already-born infant dies, the family typically experience a deep psychological wound, as the little person to whom they were oriented to providing care is ripped away. Profound reactions and consequences exist in this case (Rando, 1984, 1986g, 1988). However, others outside the family may not have had the opportunity to develop a bond with the child or to have experienced her as an individual. They mistakenly may believe that the loss is minimal because the life was so brief. They fail to appreciate that the family has had a bond with this child since pregnancy and before. Although the actual life to be mourned may have been short, the needs, feelings, thoughts, behavior and interaction patterns, hopes, wishes, fantasies, dreams, assumptions, expectations, beliefs, and meanings associated with the child are enormous, and her fleeting existence and the memories of it are often excruciatingly painful. Usually, the loss is negated and the family's mourning becomes disenfranchised (Doka, 1989).

Correspondingly, after the death of an adult child who has his own family, parents tend to be overlooked. The primary attention, control, and decision-making responsibilities are given to that child's spouse and children. Numerous issues compromise parental bereavement in this case. Such issues especially concern the relationship parents have with an adult child as opposed to a younger one, psychosocial circumstances at the time of the death, incredulity that the child has died after having survived more dangerous times, difficulty in witnessing the child's responsibilities left unattended, and resentment over the unfairness of the child's inability to reap the fruits of his labors (Rando, 1986b, 1988). These issues contribute to five special bereavement problems in parents who lose adult children: (a) compromise of successful accommodation of the loss, (b) exclusion from the concern of others, (c) existence of multiple factors contributing to complicated grief and mourning, (d) significant lack of control, and (e) presence of numerous and difficult secondary losses (Rando, 1986b, 1988). Unfortunately, this unique population of bereaved mourners can be expected to increase dramatically as compared to other groups. Longer life spans mean greater numbers of parents alive to witness the deaths of their adult children.

Psychological Relationship Between Parent and Child

The unique psychological relationship between parent and child contributes to the appearance that bereaved parents' mourning is atypical, abnormal, or pathological when in fact it is typical for the circumstance. The very aspects of the relationship between parent and child that define its intimacy and uniqueness are the same factors that intensify bereavement following the death. These factors can be grouped into the following four categories.

Feelings, hopes, and meanings projected onto the child

Although an individual brings her own needs, feelings, thoughts, behavior and interaction patterns, hopes, wishes, fantasies, dreams, assumptions, expectations, beliefs, and meanings to every relationship, in no other relationship are so many of these projected onto the other as in the parent-child relationship. This is because the parent begins the process of projection onto a fantasized child-to-be long before the birth of the child. Although projection takes place in relationships with an already-born individual, it is somewhat attenuated by the fact that the individual already has a formed personality with its own characteristics. He may or may not tolerate the projections placed upon him. Because with the exception of temperamental and biological predispositions a child is a tabula rasa, it is easier for parents to make such projections.

Although all relationships are multiply determined (i.e., influenced by a number of conscious and unconscious factors and conflicts), none is as multiply determined as the parent-child relationship. This is true for reasons in addition to parental projection. First, the child is an extension of the parents. Therefore, feelings about the child are a mixture of feelings about the parents and their significant others, as well as about the individual child. Second, because the child is a product of one's self and one's partner, feelings inherently contain emotion about the self and the other. These feelings can run the gamut from delight to disgust. Finally, feelings about the child can come from the past, present, or future. In terms of the past, the child may symbolize an extension of what has been, resurrect and/or resolve previous sibling or parent-child conflicts, and be a link with ancestors. In terms of the present, the child may signify something special to the parents, such as purpose, meaning, or worth; serve as a hope for resolution of a conflict; stand as a replacement (e.g., someone to need and love the parents or to compensate for the parents' own deprived childhood); be a source and object of love; serve as proof of worth, status, or competence; provide the opportunity to rectify past mistakes; and serve as a chance for growth and engagement with life. In terms of the future, the child may represent a new beginning or the promise of things to come, embody parental hopes and dreams, and constitute the parents' continuity and immortality. Therefore, each child has specific, idiosyncratic meanings to each of his parents.

There are no unselfish reasons for having a child. Even having a child solely to create a new life with one's beloved spouse or to serve humankind are purposes that represent the wishes and needs of the parents. Consequently, a number of parental hopes and needs always are represented in each child. However, whatever a child represents to his parents, he is also a unique individual. The parents' relationship to the child will be determined by the distinctly original person he is—his personality, characteristics, abilities, and roles—as well as the meanings, hopes, and needs his parents have placed upon him.

A child is not only an extension of the parents biologically; he is also an extension of them psychologically. Freud (1914/1957d) points out that parental love for a child is actually the parents' own long-abandoned childish narcissism born again. Unwittingly, parents are in love with themselves as children. This accounts for parental investment in the child, with its attendant overestimation, positive bias, and determination that the child will have things better than his parents did. It also means that the child is expected to fill the unmet dreams and wishes of his parents, meet their needs, and provide them with security in the face of mortality. This attitude feeds the parents' drive to provide the child with more than they had. However, it can be unhealthy if it causes the child to feel compelled to perform tasks the parents never completed, fulfill wishes they could never gratify, or heighten parental self-esteem in ways they themselves could not do.

Inherently assumed and socially assigned responsibilities

More inherently assumed and socially assigned responsibilities exist in the parent-child relationship than in any other relationship. Unfortunately, most of them are totally unrealistic. Parents are expected to be all loving and all good, totally selfless, and all concerned, motivated solely by the child and her welfare. Most parents take their parental role more seriously than their other roles. For example, many more jokes are made about spouses and in-laws than about children. Although the parental role is typically undertaken with greater solemnity and commitment than others, it is also subject to more inappropriate expectations. Little or no allowance is given for the normal ambivalence, frustration, anger, and need for limit setting that exists in all relationships.

Parents are burdened by unachievable ideals, yet they internalize these unrealistic expectations and therefore measure themselves against impossible standards. Even in situations unrelated to the death of a child, parents are haunted with guilt whenever these expectations—unrealistic though they may be—are unmet. They continue to believe that they should be able to love, nurture, and protect the child unequivocally in all situations.

Guilt is a normal consequence after any loss when there is a failure of the mourner to meet self-expectations (see chapter 10). Hence, when a child dies, the parents are predisposed to extreme guilt because of the unrealistic expectations that have not been met as a result of the death. These failures pertain to both parental responsibilities and parental roles.

Incorporation of roles into parental identity

In most normal circumstances, as the child becomes an integral part of the parents' lives—an extension of them who internalizes their feelings, thoughts, behaviors, and attitudes—the parents begin to define themselves by their parental roles. Into their identities they incorporate the roles of protector, provider, problem solver, and adviser. They become accustomed to being in control of what happens to and for the child. They get used to being able to "fix" things so they will work out to the child's advantage (e.g., the broken bicycle is repaired, the hurt feelings after a friend's rejection are soothed). These daily successes in caring for the child serve to define the parents' sense of self, role, and identity, thus cementing the parent-child relationship. The close identification between parents and child often breeds a type of empathy in which parents are able to feel what the child feels and understand him in ways that do not require words. In many ways, the child may perceive parents as being omnipotent—and parents themselves may feel this way despite having insight into their own limitations (Benedek, 1970). In brief, the identity of the adult who has a child centers in large part around providing and doing for that child. These functions become basic elements of adulthood.

Closeness and intensity of the relationship

The parent-child relationship is the closest and most intense life can generate, not only physically, but psychologically and socially as well. In other relationships, the adult has an attachment to another—he is separate from but connected to that other person. With a child, that child has sprung from the adult—she is part of and in many ways the same as the adult. Therefore, a different type of mourning after the child dies is mandated because the process involves dealing both with the loss of the specific child and with the loss of parts of oneself, given that parental attachment consists of both love for the child and self-love. This internal dimension was articulated by one woman who was both a widow and a bereaved parent: "When you lose your spouse, it is like losing a limb; when you lose your child, it is like losing a lung." The centrality of the injury appears to stem from the nature of the attachment.

Factors Exacerbating Mourning for a Child

Aspects of the parent-child relationship that define its intimacy and uniqueness are the same as those that intensify bereavement following the death of the child. Bereaved parents encounter 10 specific dilemmas as a consequence of the loss of a child (Rando, 1991). These are associated with the following areas.

Loss of the parenthood function

When a child dies, there is a failure to sustain the basic function of parenthood (i.e., to preserve some dimension of the self, the family, and the social group; Jackson, 1977). Parents are supposed to protect and provide for the child so one day that child can bury the parents. This expectation is unfulfilled.

Loss of parts of the self

As compared with other deaths, more losses of parts of the self occur when a child dies. This is the result of the numerous specific investments placed in the child as a consequence of the needs, feelings, thoughts, behavior and interaction patterns, hopes, wishes, fantasies, dreams, assumptions, expectations, beliefs, and meanings projected onto him and due to the fact that parental attachment consists of self-love as well as love for the child.

Secondary losses

Multiple secondary losses occur as a consequence of the death. In addition to the loss of this particular individual and all of the roles he played and what he signified, parents lose the dreams and hopes they invested in that child and all of the other specific investments in and projections made on him. They also lose a very special source of love—someone who needs, depends upon, admires, and appreciates them in a unique and gratifying way.

Assault on parental identity

The death of a child monumentally assaults parental identity. Parents often report feeling mutilated not only from the loss of the child as an extension of the self or the self in relation to the child, but also from the ripping asunder of the adult identity centered on providing and caring for the child. Because of the death, parents are robbed of their ability to carry out the important functional role of parent. This causes an oppressive sense of failure, the loss of power and ability, a deep sense of violation, an extreme decrease in self-esteem, and an overwhelmingly confused identity. In turn, these assaults lead to additional secondary losses that derive from the diminished sense of self. Specifically, these include disillusionment, emptiness, and insecurity. There is a need for a profound identity shift and the mourning and relinquishment of former beliefs and assumptions about the self and one's parental capabilities.

Loss of a sense of immortality

Children are their parents' future and embody their parents' symbolic immortality. Death may claim parents physically; however, it cannot claim the parts of the parents perpetuated in the child (e.g., through the continuation of parental thoughts, values, attitudes, and beliefs instilled in the child) or negate the numerous ways the child chooses to commemorate the parents after their deaths. As long as the parents have a surviving child, death will not put an end to their influence in the world. The death of the child destroys this influence.

Violation of the assumptive world

The unnaturalness of the child's predeceasing his parents is a stumbling block underestimated by professionals and laypersons alike. The death of the child constitutes a major violation of the parental assumptive world and is incomprehensible because it shatters the very laws of nature in which the young grow up to replace the old. (This is precisely why many consider it the worst violation of the assumptive world possible for any mourner.) The orderliness of the universe is undermined (Gorer, 1965). Survivor guilt becomes a tremendous burden.

Loss of family subsystems

With the death of the child comes the loss of the family as it has been known. This comes from the irretrievable loss of the presence and role-fulfilling behaviors and functions of the child, as well as from the loss of parts of each parent's self (i.e., the special interactive part of the parent that was in a unique relationship with the child). The subsystems in the family made up of the unique relationships between each parent and the child are now gone. Even if other surviving children must be parented, the parental role associated with the deceased child must be mourned and relinquished.

Related high-risk variables

The National Center for Health Statistics (1990) reports that the leading cause of death category for children from 1 through 14 years is accidents and adverse effects. The same category is the leading cause of death for adolescents and young adults ages 15 through 24, with suicides and homicides being the two other major causes. Therefore, loss of a child often occurs in circumstances in which the death is sudden, traumatic, and preventable. This means that bereaved parents must contend simultaneously with a number of high-risk variables in their mourning. All of these variables contribute to a greater sense of helplessness and threat, prompting enormous efforts to find a reason for and meaning in the death, determine who is to blame, assign responsibility, mete out punishment, and regain a sense of control, predictability, order, and justice in the universe.

Where the death of the child results from genetic or unexplained medical illness, the parents' biological role predisposes them to assume even greater guilt and responsibility. Logic, reason, and scientific understanding often fare poorly against parents' beliefs that they are responsible for the death. As one bereaved father put it, "My daughter died from cancer. Her genes allowed her to develop cancer. I gave her her genes.

Therefore, I killed my daughter." Parents hold themselves responsible for not producing a healthy child who could survive longer and often feel deficient and worthless as a result. When answers about the cause of death are not immediately forthcoming, parents often will search all the way back to the earliest prenatal experiences in their attempt to identify a reason: "Perhaps it was because I took aspirin when I was pregnant that she developed the illness that took her life at age 11."

Loss of a future caretaker

Although parents do not frequently admit to this notion, the loss of a child can portend the loss of a future caretaker. If parents currently are (or had in the future anticipated) being cared for by their child emotionally, physically, financially, or socially, the death of that child can leave them with the enormous difficulties of parental bereavement and at high risk in the areas formerly supported (or to have been supported) by the child.

Intensified responses

Although bereaved parents typically experience intensified responses in all aspects of uncomplicated grief and mourning, a number of specific reactions are particularly intense because of the dynamics involved in loss of a child. The following reactions can potentially complicate mourning.

1. Guilt is especially intense due to inappropriate and unrealistic parental expectations, falling short of one's self-image, the assault on parental identity, surviving one's child, and feelings that one contributed to the death or could have prevented it but did not.

2. Anger is intensified because of what the loss of a child means in terms of the parental role, the secondary losses that ensue, and the fact that it is unnatural for a child to predecease a parent.

3. Pain of separation is heightened because of the incomparable closeness of the relationship with the child.

4. Yearning and searching are fueled by the dynamics of the loss, which demand that the parent find and recover the lost child.

5. The search for meaning is accelerated due to the unnaturalness of the death, parental sense of guilt and failure, and the assault on the assumptive world caused by the nonsensical nature of the loss.

6. Despair is magnified by the meaninglessness and unnaturalness of the loss, failure to fulfill an important adult role, conflict between present helplessness and prior parental control, assault on parental identity, loss of a sense of immortality, and monumental violations of the assumptive world.

7. Problems with social support and unrealistic expectations are aggravated by others' reluctance to validate and respond to this type of death because it represents their worst fears. These fears result in avoidance of bereaved parents, who suffer from the inappropriate belief that the loss is similar to other bereavements, and from the lack of necessary support.

8. Upsurges of acute grief (i.e., STUG reactions) are greater and more numerous than for other types of bereavement. These STUG reactions reflect the parental tendency to demarcate life in terms of specific events experienced by the child. Thus, parents become painfully aware of things that would have occurred had the child lived (e.g., when the child would have graduated from high school or been married). Sometimes this tendency is called "growing up with the loss."

Issues in the Marital Dyad

Coinciding with the difficulty bereaved parents sustain intrapsychically in mourning the death of a child are a number of common marital complications. Although in past stress situations one spouse could turn to the other for support, in this circumstance the other spouse's struggle with the death of the child can effectively remove the partner's most important therapeutic resource. Whereas previously the couple may have been able to pull together and work toward solving a particular problem, now their closeness can lead to blame and anger. The situation can also interfere with seeking available respites from pain because seeing a beloved other in torment can generate guilt for desiring respites and may foster a sense of incompetence for being unable to alter the situation.

Although the parents struggle over the death of the same child, each partner actually has sustained a different loss and has a unique mourning experience. Frequently, spouses labor under the misconception that they have suffered the same loss because the same child died. Nevertheless, each had a unique relationship with the child, and this is what is mourned by that parent. The unique relationship influences what that parent misses and when it is missed (e.g., a mother may miss her child's coming home from school and sharing details of the school day, whereas a father may miss the play time he spent with the child after he returned from work at the end of the day). Although parents may pay lip service to the fact that no one mourns exactly like anyone else, this reality is often forgotten when it comes to their own situation. Spouses also mourn differently because of the influence of the various factors affecting mourning (see Table 2.1).

Sex-role conditioning is a major factor contributing to differences between mourning spouses. Often what is required in mourning (e.g., review of the relationship, emotional expression, sharing of memories, being vulnerable, asking for and receiving support, appropriate regression) is incompatible with traditional male upbringing and runs counter to the training to act, do, produce, and problem-solve.

Normal asynchronicity of grief and mourning between two individuals means that bereaved parents are seldom at the same place at the same time because of their roles in the family, normal fluctuations in grief, and differences in how they respond to areas of grief work within the six "R" processes of mourning. Such disparities are especially apparent in (a) experiencing and expressing feelings and thoughts, (b) reminiscing, (c) responding to work and daily activities, (d) relating to objects that trigger memories, (e) searching for meaning, (f) dealing with the support of others, (g) coping with the sexual relationship, (h) responding to surviving children, (i) reacting to socializing and resumption of life, and (j) experiencing particular problem areas in mourning (Rando, 1988). Data suggest that incongruence between spouses dramatically increases from 2 through 4 years after the death of a child. After the fifth year, it declines only slightly (Fish, 1986). Significant problems develop if one spouse assumes that another's nonidentical response means that the other did not love the child enough or is not sufficiently concerned about the spouse.

A major problem following the death of the child concerns communication impairments between spouses. Day-to-day problems frequently are not confronted due to one or both partners' preoccupation with the death, lack of strength, desire to protect the other spouse, and attempts to avert a mutual downward spiral. This lack of communication can cause an accumulation of stress and resentment that may explode inappropriately at another time. Unanswerable questions (e.g., Why did this happen?) and irrational demands (e.g., Take away the pain) and/or rational but unrealistic demands placed upon a spouse (e.g., Do my job, too) can breed stress.

Another major area of stress following the death of a child is the sexual relationship. A classic and quite frequent problem is the inhibition of sexual response and intimacy in one or both of the bereaved parents. There may be fears of having and losing other children or feelings of guilt over any pleasure that derives from sexual intimacy. Often the relationship is compromised because of vegetative symptoms of depression associated with grief. Although the intimacy of sexual contact may be what one may need in distress, it may be precisely what another cannot endure at that time. Because sexual intimacy and orgasm can put a spouse in touch with feelings at a deep level, they may be avoided for fear of tapping into painful emotions (i.e., if one lets down barriers to feel closeness to another, one may then make contact with undesired pain). In most cases, both bereaved parents are hurting and attempting to minimize their own pain. Difficulties ensue when their needs for sexual intimacy are discrepant. This discrepancy can pose an area of misunderstanding and constitute a major secondary loss. It is not at all unusual for the sexual relationship to be compromised by lack of interest, depression, avoidance, or other grief-related responses for 2 or more years following the death of a child.

Caregivers must recognize that it is a significant error to assume that the male is always the one who is more interested in sexual relations. Fathers, as well as mothers, can sustain significant lack of interest and dysfunction in this area of the marital relationship. In addition, it should not be assumed that sexual problems are inevitable. For some couples, sex is the sole area in which there can be some satisfactory relating, one that can provide a brief respite from the pain and serve to reconnect them to something associated with life while they contend with death.

The changes in parents occasioned by the death of a child will necessarily lead to a changed marital relationship. Each must recognize that any major loss changes people, both for the better and for the worse. Consequently, the relationship will be altered because the people composing it are altered. It is important for each spouse to recognize these changes and work to accommodate and integrate them positively into the relationship. In this effort, the couple must avoid continual use of coping mechanisms that direct attention away from the mourning processes and/or the marriage or that seriously compromise the relationship (e.g., overuse of alcohol and drugs, overwork, overinvestment in other areas of life, and extramarital affairs).

Sometimes one spouse can remind another of the deceased child. This is not usually recognized as a problem; however, to some individuals this situation can be quite distressing. Looking at one's spouse—or another family member—and seeing the deceased child's eyes or smile is comforting for some bereaved parents but excruciatingly painful for others.

Issues in the Family System

When other dependent children are present after the loss of a child, parents are put in a difficult situation. They must not only struggle with their own intense grief and mourning, they must fulfill the precise role with surviving children that they are struggling to relinquish with the deceased (i.e., the role of parent). In no other loss is there such an intense demand for continued, specific behavior in the same role that one is mourning with regard to the deceased. For example, if a person loses his spouse, unless he is a bigamist there is no other wife for whom he is expected to act as husband. A person who loses a sibling or friend may still be expected to function in relationship to other siblings or friends; even so, these roles inherently involve far fewer and much less intense role-specific demands and responsibilities. However, a bereaved parent is still expected to care for and parent surviving dependent children. Thus, bereaved parents are in the unique position of having to accomplish the enormously difficult psychological task of simultaneously surrendering and maintaining the same role.

Often problems occur when parents attempt to care for remaining children. Bereaved parents perceive all too well the parenting deficiencies that develop secondary to intense grief and mourning. This awareness can exacerbate their frustration and sense of loss of control, competence, and identity. If bereaved parents feel they are giving inadequate care to surviving children due to their preoccupation with the deceased child or to other problems secondary to mourning, even more agony is added to their failure-frustration cycle. Often, the overwhelming stress of mourning for the deceased child leaves parents with little to give to anyone else. In addition, the normal tendency in grief to displace hostility onto others in close proximity may result in anger toward surviving children. This can make parents feel even more guilty.

It is not uncommon for a bereaved parent to experience some resentment that other children continue to live or to feel that they have not mourned enough or have adjusted too quickly to the death of their sibling. Frequently, this resentment stems from a lack of understanding of a child's mourning. Often, the responses of a bereaved child erroneously suggest to the parent that the child either does not comprehend or is unaffected by the sibling's death. However, typically the child's response only reflects the differences in a child's ability to cope with mourning. (See Rando, 1984 and 1988, for further discussion of mourning in children.)

Often bereaved parents fear that their relationships with their surviving children are less intense than they were before the loss or believe that they have lost their ability to love or do not love enough. This common response to loss, in which one may be temporarily unable to invest in others to the same extent as before, often derives from the bereaved parents' concern that another child could be lost, too, or from the emotion-deadening effect of overwhelming grief. Usually, as mourning progresses, parents reclaim their former intensity of feelings for surviving children.

Bereaved parents frequently idealize the deceased child as they focus upon and desire to reunite with her. In the process of concentrating on all of the deceased child's good points and overlooking many of her negative ones, bereaved parents may make comparisons with their surviving children. Unfortunately, they often fail to recognize that living children with problems compare poorly with a sanctified deceased one, especially if parents focus on qualities in the deceased child for which they now long (e.g., attentiveness, sensitivity). This focus upon and longing for the deceased child can make parents feel guilty unless they can realize that they would similarly mourn, idealize, and attend to the special qualities of their surviving children were they to be lost.

An additional issue is that, to bereaved parents, surviving children can serve as reminders of the deceased child if they look or behave like the lost sibling or use her personal effects. This can be either comforting or distressing. Either way, it may influence the parents' reaction to the surviving siblings.

Because parents fear losing surviving children, too, overprotection is not uncommon, even though its effects are negative. Often such behavior robs surviving children of the normal experiences of life, usually desperately needed following the abnormal event of losing a sibling. Further problems can ensue when overprotection denies them needed opportunities for psychological, social, and physical development or when it increases fears and anxieties that interfere with normal growth. Reactions such as hostility, resentment, insecurity, counterphobic behavior, and estrangement from parents can result from overprotection. If children are not allowed age-appropriate responsibilities and experiences, and if they are prevented from developing normally, there can be serious repercussions for both children and parents, despite good intentions. The irony is that, in their attempts to hold on, many bereaved parents actually push their surviving children away. When this occurs, bereaved parents experience additional secondary losses and increased stress.

Parents—often but not exclusively fathers—may try to protect other family members. Although anyone can strive to rescue other family members, the parental role predisposes bereaved parents to this type of behavior. This can lead to ignoring one's own needs in an effort to meet the needs of others or to creating distractions in order to divert attention away from the grief of others. Sometimes attempts to protect are not undertaken solely for the benefit of others but serve as a way of escaping one's own pain. No matter what the purpose, it is unrealistic to think anyone can be rescued from the pain of the loss of a loved one, and attempts to do so only interfere with necessary mourning.

Clinical evidence suggests that extended family members—especially the parents' own parents—and close friends can frequently add to distress, although just as frequently they may assist in its amelioration, with some bereaved parents feeling they could not survive without such support. When such individuals fail to acknowledge the bereaved parents' pain sufficiently, do not help enough, are too egocentric, resent the parents' receiving attention (especially if they themselves did not receive such attention if they had a child die), or place inappropriate expectations on the bereaved parents, problems can arise. The situation can complicate mourning by causing major secondary losses, violating parents' expectations, robbing them of needed support, and generating much concurrent stress.

Social Issues

Until fairly recently, there has been a relative paucity of information about parental bereavement in the thanatological literature. However, in the 1980s, the topic drew more attention. It became clear that, among mourners, bereaved parents are the most stigmatized and that they suffer enormously because their loss represents the worst fears of others. This strange and callous social response actually harms bereaved parents, who often report feeling like social lepers (Rando, 1984, 1986g, 1988). Although society appears to value the parent-child relationship above all others, it frequently fails to help bereaved parents. In English there is no word even to describe a parent who has lost a child, as exists for one who loses parents *(orphan)* or a spouse *(widow/widower)*. Combined with wildly inappropriate social expectations held about parental grief and mourning, the already complicated mourning of bereaved parents thus becomes intensified and even more difficult.

The rejection and social disenfranchisement of bereaved parents is often internalized as further evidence of their deficiency or lack of value. This internalization usually occurs despite an intellectual recognition that others in society are probably responding to their own anxiety. It is especially harmful when the intensity of bereavement causes parents to feel that they are going crazy and when they lack the validation they could get from others, if not about the pain of their grief, at least about ongoing reality. In the absence of others with whom to check out perceptions and communicate, individuals become disorganized and develop serious impairments in reality testing. Social reactions to the death of a child frequently place bereaved parents in this situation. This robs them of needed support and exacerbates the already high levels of stress and anxiety under which they must operate. In brief, the social reactions to bereaved parents are not only unhelpful, they are actually hurtful.

Parental Bereavement: An Exception to General Conceptualizations of Mourning

Three conclusions can be derived regarding parental bereavement (Rando, 1986f, 1991). The following discussion illuminates these conclusions.

Failure of general conceptualizations to describe parental bereavement

Parental bereavement fails to be explained adequately by general conceptualizations held for grief and mourning, and actually is compromised therein. As noted previously, most conceptualizations of grief and mourning come from the study of white middle-class women whose husbands had died expectedly from cancer or suddenly and unexpectedly in automobile accidents or from heart attacks. However, different role relationships give rise to different bereavement experiences, which in turn mandate different treatment interventions. Therefore, what is experienced and needed in the loss of a spouse is necessarily distinct from what is found in the loss of an aged parent—or in the loss of a child.

In the case of a child's death, parental mourning is compromised because what is required in successful mourning is made difficult or even impossible by the consequences of the severing of the parent-child bond. If analyzed according to the six "R" processes of mourning, it is clear that bereaved parents have a number of built-in obstacles.

Bereaved parents have difficulty *recognizing the loss* because:

1. It violates their basic function and defies the laws of nature.

2. It multiply victimizes them and savagely assaults their sense of self and their abilities.

3. If other children survive, continuing in the parental role makes it easier to deny that the child has died (i.e., no dramatically changed function confirms the loss).

4. Social negation of the loss often exists.

5. With the loss of pregnancies and the deaths of young infants and adult children residing outside of the parental home, no dramatic absence is apparent to signal the loss and confirm its reality. Without unmet expectations to see and interact with the child, parents can have difficulty internalizing the fact that the death has really occurred and learning that the loved one is truly gone.

Bereaved parents have difficulty *reacting to the separation* because:

1. This type of loss results in intensified pain of a longer duration.

2. Interferences often exist with the ability to identify, differentiate, and express psychological reactions to the loss (e.g., the intensity of the pain precludes the ability to differentiate, the social role of the parent interferes with identification and expression of negative feelings toward the child).

3. More secondary losses take place in this type of bereavement, especially those relating to the self.

4. The experience of pain is subverted by the lack of social support, the loss of the spouse as the most therapeutic resource, and inappropriate social expectations.

Recollecting and reexperiencing the deceased and the relationship is made more difficult for bereaved parents because:

1. If the child is unborn or an infant, there is little or nothing concrete to review or remember realistically.

2. Negative feelings are not socially accepted in parents, and the mourning of negative aspects of the relationship is thus complicated or made impossible.

Bereaved parents have difficulty *relinquishing the old attachments to the deceased and the old assumptive world* because:

1. Attachments to the deceased child also include attachments to the self, making it difficult to distinguish what belongs to the child and to the parent, and to detach from the child. In addition, problems occur in relinquishing some aspects of the self in the deceased child while retaining others in surviving children.

2. Given the unique nature of the parental role, the parent-child relationship is less amenable than any other to relinquishment of attachments.

3. Relinquishing attachments to the old assumptive world mandates a complete revision of the most fundamental assumptions underpinning one's adult identity (i.e., those concerned with being a parent and fulfilling parental responsibilities and roles).

4. Revision of the assumptive world usually demands some reassignment of roles to indicate the loss and to confirm the change, yet with surviving children the bereaved parent continues to operate in the old world with the same roles and expectations.

5. In the loss of a pregnancy, infant, or adult child who lives outside of the home, no dramatic absence signals that the death has occurred and demands relinquishment of attachments.

6. Identification is more problematic because of the role of parent to child and because of inherent difficulty in identifying with a young child when the mourner is an adult.

Bereaved parents are compromised in their ability to *readjust to move adaptively into the new world without forgetting the old* because:

1. The number and severity of violations of the assumptive world often leave bereaved parents stunned, incredulous, and with a mutilated identity. This leads to profound negative psychological reactions and impairments in revision of the assumptive world and formation of a new identity.

2. Developing a new relationship with the deceased may be difficult because the parental relationship demands role behaviors that are not as amenable to healthy translation on an intrapsychic plane as other relationships. In other words, a parental relationship with a child usually involves "doing for" versus "being done for" or "being done with," as is the case with one's own parent or a peer. Thus, it is more difficult to retain internally the role "to mother" than "to be mothered" because mothering requires more interactive participation. The younger the child (i.e., the more hands-on caretaking required by the relationship), the more difficult it is to develop a new intrapsychic relationship, in contrast to the

myriad possibilities available for maintaining an intrapsychic relationship with a much older child, peer, or parent.

3. As a method of maintaining a connection with the deceased, identification may be problematic for parents of young children if the behaviors with which they would identify would be inappropriate to adult functioning and/or incongruous with other roles.

4. The consequences of social disenfranchisement interfere with any adaptive movement into the new world and the adoption of required new ways of being.

5. When much of the world remains the same, as is the case when other dependent children are present, it is difficult to form a new identity and/or adopt new ways of being in the world because one still functions in the same parental role, demanding the same behaviors, skills, and responsibilities. Moving adaptively into a new world is problematic because so much of it is the same as the old.

Bereaved parents have more difficulty *reinvesting* because:

1. Reinvesting in a similar relationship—one of many ways of reinvesting—is more feasible when the relationship is with a spouse, peer, or parent than when the relationship is with a child because more opportunities exist for reinvestment in the former types of relationship. For example, it typically is easier to find a new mate or parent figure than to have another child. There also is often more social support for the former type of reinvestment.

2. Although many parents are often inappropriately urged to have a new child as a way of dealing with the pain of the older child's death, others are treated in the opposite fashion. Great social concern exists about bereaved parents' having subsequent children to replace the child who was lost. Bereaved parents may experience a lack of support from others, who may question their motivation and timing in having a subsequent child. In both scenarios, bereaved parents may experience social pressure that jeopardizes this "R" process. (See Pollock, 1970, for a discussion of the important difference between succession and replacement.)

Vulnerability to complicated mourning and diagnosis of pathology

Three compelling sets of data delineate precisely why bereaved parents are vulnerable to complicated mourning and to erroneous diagnosis of pathology. First, bereaved parents inherently have the greatest number of factors known to promote failure to mourn in any individual, as identified by Lazare (1979). Specifically, bereaved parents must typically contend with five out of the six psychological issues Lazare contends interfere with mourning: guilt, loss of an extension of the self, reawakening of an old loss, multiple loss, and idiosyncratic resistances to mourning. Of the five social reasons Lazare identifies as contributing to failure to mourn, bereaved parents usually must deal with four (especially, although not exclusively, if the child who dies is an infant or an adult): social negation of the loss, socially unspeakable loss, social isolation and/or geographic distance from social support, and assumption of the role of the strong one.

Second, the death of a child involves the greatest number of factors known to affect any individual's bereavement, as identified in Table 2.1. Personal factors aside, the following represent the most salient of the potentially negative situational influences on parental mourning.

1. The unique nature and meaning of the loss sustained and the relationship severed

2. Qualities of the relationship lost (psychological character, strength, and security of the attachment)

3. Roles the deceased occupied in the mourner's family or social system (number of roles, functions served, their centrality and importance)

4. Characteristics of the deceased

5. Amount of unfinished business between the mourner and the deceased

6. Mourner's perception of the deceased's fulfillment in life

7. Number, type, and quality of secondary losses

8. Nature of any ongoing relationship with the deceased

9. Presence of concurrent stresses or crises

10. Timeliness

11. Mourner's perception of preventability

12. Mourner's social support system and the recognition, validation, acceptance, and assistance provided by its members

Third, a number of characteristics and determinants associated with typical parental bereavement are the same as those generally associated with particular syndromes of complicated mourning. Characteristics aligned with the conflicted mourning syndrome are not usually associated with parental loss in general, although in specific cases they certainly could be. However, significant overlap does exist with regard to absent mourning, delayed mourning, inhibited mourning, distorted mourning of either the extremely angry or guilty type, unanticipated mourning, and chronic mourning (see chapter 4).

Need for a new model of parental mourning and new criteria for pathology

It appears clear that the inherent aspects of the loss of a child are the same aspects that in any other situation of mourning predispose a mourner to complications in bereavement. Therefore, it is no wonder bereaved parents traditionally have been diagnosed as evidencing pathological mourning. Clinical and empirical data mandate a new model of parental mourning and new criteria for identification of pathology in bereaved parents. The traditional criteria for pathology are inapplicable here: The simple fact is that what is considered abnormal or pathological in other losses is typical after the death of a child in the sense that it is experienced by the majority of bereaved parents. Failure to delineate a new, more appropriate model of mourning and to determine what constitutes pathology within this group has resulted in the development of inappropriate and unrealistic expectations for bereaved parents, who cannot and must not be expected to have the same bereavement experiences as other mourners.

Treatment Concerns

Regardless of which treatment approaches a caregiver chooses, interventions must be designed to address each of the issues specific to this type of bereavement. Concerns relating to preventability and violation of the assumptive world will no doubt be a central focus. As appropriate, the caregiver will also need to address other high-risk factors in the situation. Factors likely to be associated with death of a child include concurrent stress, anger, guilt, and disenfranchised grief (see chapter 10). The unique issues posed by the mode of death and degree to which the death is sudden and unexpected or traumatic will also need to be taken into account (see chapters 11 and 12).

For an in-depth examination of treatment needs and intervention strategies for bereaved parents, the reader is referred to Rando (1984, 1985a, 1986b, 1986c, 1986g). The information presented in these sources concerns (a) clarifying expectations for parental grief and mourning, (b) adjusting the parental role, (c) adjusting the marital relationship, (d) teaching coping skills, and (e) helping parents understand the grief and mourning needs of surviving children. The following discussion summarizes recommendations made in these sources.

In constructing treatment, the caregiver will need to take into account the unique issues involved in this type of loss and adjust treatment plans and expectations accordingly. It will be especially important to help parents work through the specific complications of each of the "R" processes of mourning and to identify, explore, and work through issues related to the unique psychological relationship between parent and child.

In this context, the caregiver must provide parents with psychoeducational and normative information to help them appropriately frame and understand their experiences, comprehend specifically what has been lost, and know how to dose their exposure to the pain. It will be necessary to work with parents to anticipate and deal with misdiagnoses of pathology (made personally and by friends, loved ones, and professionals) and to address the need for expectations and criteria different from those for traditional conceptualizations of mourning. The caregiver must also legitimize specific issues for parents mourning miscarriage, ectopic pregnancy, stillbirth, loss in multiple pregnancy, infant, or adult child death.

Providing parents with proper information about the fluctuations and discrepancies of parental bereavement—and their reactions to them—will be helpful. The caregiver must also work with parents to adjust expectations about parental roles and responsibilities, and assist in the major revisions of the assumptive world usually necessary after the loss of a child. Facilitating communication and helping parents deal therapeutically with the grief and mourning of surviving children will be critical, as will enabling them to understand the process of family reorganization that takes place after the death of a child.

In terms of the marital relationship, the caregiver must help parents recognize the differences between and within themselves and to readjust their relationship to accommodate these. Intervention should assist parents in using coping mechanisms that do not direct attention away from their relationship or the healthy address of mourning. It will be important to specify that each parent is mourning a different loss, even though the same child died, and to stress that parents must take care not to misinterpret the differences between them. Caregivers must help parents find ways of working through their different needs with regard to the sexual relationship, communication processes, and ways of relating to the aspects of grief work and mourning. It may be helpful to enlist a commitment from parents to keeping communication lines open and recognizing the need for solitary time. Any interventions undertaken must reflect the need to maintain the integrity of the marital relationship in order to sustain each individual partner as well as surviving family members.

Finally, given that the spouse may be unable to provide much support following the loss of a child, the caregiver must help parents express their needs to others and identify a range of sources of support. He or she also may wish to refer parents to the nearest chapter of The Compassionate Friends or to another self-help support group for their particular loss (e.g., suicide, stillbirth).

AIDS-RELATED DEATH

Even in the field of clinical thanatology, in which terminal illness, stress, loss, grief, pain, suffering, and death are routinely confronted, AIDS-related bereavement is perceived as a scourge. Doka (1989) conceptualizes the situation quite well when he calls AIDS "the Great Disenfranchiser." AIDS is the archetypal dread disease because it contains all the worst elements of the great pandemics (e.g., the bubonic plague), which devastated entire communities, and the shameful stigmas (e.g., cancer and leprosy), associated with an insidious and painful process of individual death.

This section examines the experience of individuals left behind following the death of a loved one from AIDS-related illness. Like persons with AIDS (known herein as PWAs), members of this group are at significant risk for complicated mourning because of certain factors associated with this type of death—specifically, overly lengthy illness, the mourner's perception of the death as preventable, and the mourner's perceived lack of social support. All three of these factors are known to complicate mourning. For more information about AIDS-related bereavement, the reader is referred to the following resources: Anderson, Gurdin, and Thomas (1989); Andriote (1986, 1987); Burnell and Burnell (1989); Colburn and Malena (1988); Dean, Hall, and Martin (1988); Doka (1989); Frierson, Lippmann, and Johnson (1987); Fuller, Geis, and Rush (1988, 1989); Geis, Fuller, and Rush (1986); Giacquinta (1989); Gonsiorek (1982); Klein and Fletcher (1986); Martelli (1987); Martin (1988); Morin and Batchelor (1984); S. E. Nichols (1986); Nichols and Ostrow (1984); E. Rosen (1989); Shilts (1987); Siegel and Hoefer (1981); Walker (1987); and Worden (1991).

Demographics of the Disease

PWAs are a diverse group, and, even as this is written, the demographics of AIDS are changing. PWAs are of every color, ethnic group, social strata, occupation, and religious persuasion. They are of every age and sexual orientation. They contract the disease through homosexual activity, heterosexual activity, intravenous drug use, contaminated blood transfusions, accidental needle-sticks, and prenatal infection. Despite all these differences, they share the fact that they die and are mourned.

Recent statistics by the World Health Organization (WHO) indicate that, between April 1991 and January 1992, 1 million people contracted the Human Immunodeficiency Virus (HIV), 90 percent of them through heterosexual intercourse (Nellis, 1992). This brings the total number infected worldwide to 10 to 12 million individuals and supports projections that, by the year 2000, infections will at best triple and at worst quadruple, resulting in a total of 30 to 40 million people having contracted the infection. The WHO predicts that during the 1990s HIV-related disease will be among the leading causes, if not the leading cause, of death for adults aged 20 to 40 in North America, Western Europe, and Southern Asia.

The rates of infection for women are rising dramatically. At the WHO's third annual World AIDS Day, held in 1990, the theme reflected the increasing concern for women and AIDS. The WHO predicts that AIDS among women around the world will increase dramatically over the next 10 years and that three-fourths of HIV infections will result from heterosexual contact, reflecting an increase from 60 percent now to as high as 80 percent worldwide by the year 2000 ("Women and AIDS," 1990). United States Surgeon General Antonia Novello addressed the first National Conference on HIV and Women in December 1990 and noted that, worldwide, by the year 2000 the number of AIDS cases in women will begin to equal the number of cases in men. She also predicted that in the next several decades the heterosexual mode of transmission will become the primary means of spreading HIV infection in most industrialized countries (Freiberg, 1991). The increase in HIV-positive women can be expected to lead to an upsurge in the number of infants who contract the virus prenatally.

Minority groups reporting increasing percentages of members with HIV infections and AIDS include the elderly and young African American women. As noted in *Hospice* ("AIDS Update," 1990), a *Journal of Gerontology: Medical Sciences* prediction is that by 1992 there will be 10,000 victims of AIDS over 60, and *The Wall Street Journal* has reported that young African American women are dying of HIV infection at a rate nine times higher than Caucasian women the same age.

Without question, the rates for children and infants are climbing, and in a growing number of cases multiple family members have HIV infection or AIDS. In some locations, HIV and AIDS have become a major cause of death for young children. For instance, in New York State in 1988, the disease was the leading cause of death among Hispanic children ages 1 to 4 and the second leading cause of death among African American children of the same age. Deaths from the disease exceeded deaths from unintentional injuries among Hispanic children and from all other infectious diseases among both groups (Centers for Disease Control, 1991).

As of today, in this country the gay community has been disproportionately faced with grief and mourning associated with HIV, and most of the available information on the psychosocial outcomes of such losses comes from this group. Estimates of the percentage of PWAs who are homosexual males have ranged in the past from two-thirds (Giacquinta, 1989) to three-quarters (Andriote, 1987) of the cases. Recent statistics from the Centers for Disease Control (1991) for the years 1981 through 1990 suggest that 59.1 percent of deaths from AIDS have occurred among homosexual or bisexual men, whereas 21 percent have occurred among women and heterosexual men who had been intravenous drug users. Although heterosexual transmission of the disease is rapidly changing this picture— and it is imperative that we expand our mindsets, our educational pro- grams, and our treatments to populations other than gay men and intra- venous drug users—we still cannot overlook the current prevalence of the infection in the groups hardest hit by the disease. For the foreseeable future, the loved ones of members of these groups are statistically most likely to be affected by loss.

The fact that the current majority of those infected are male homo- sexuals and intravenous drug users compounds the stigma associated with the disease. It also belies the critically important fact that transmission of the disease to other groups is escalating dramatically. The rates for non- sexually transmitted cases (e.g., from tainted blood transfusions, needle sticks, prenatal infection, dental procedures) continue to rise. Indeed, in the United States one of the groups in which the HIV infection is growing fastest appears to be white middle class and upper middle class college students (Fulton, personal communication, February 6, 1991).

In brief, society as a whole, as well as the PWA and her loved ones, must confront the fact that AIDS is not exclusively a disease of male homo- sexuals or intravenous drug users. This means that resources, support, and research must be undertaken with these newly expanding popula- tions in order to know how best to assist them in confronting the illness and its associated losses.

Unique Issues in Mourning AIDS-Related Deaths

Mourning the loss of a loved one from an AIDS-related illness is in many ways the same as mourning any other loss through terminal illness. Thus, information on the experiences, stresses, demands, dilemmas, and issues that generally arise in bereavement following a terminal illness must be considered. Failure to place AIDS-related issues into this broader context will result in an unrealistically narrow focus and a consequent lack of the perspective needed to provide the most effective assistance. The reader is therefore encouraged to review the discussion in chapter 11 on terminal illness as one form of natural death.

Despite its similarity to bereavement following other terminal illnesses, mourning associated with an AIDS-related death incorporates greater than usual rage, fear, shame, and unresolved grief (E. Rosen, 1989). In addition, clinical research has revealed that the emotional havoc and deva- station in families of PWAs far surpasses that experienced in other life tragedies (Giacquinta, 1989). These findings should not be surprising, given the constellation of factors that circumscribe mourning in this situa- tion. The following discussion examines the ways in which mourning a loss related to AIDS differs from mourning other types of losses.

Stigmatization and disenfranchisement

The two issues that most adversely affect the receipt of necessary social support for mourners of AIDS-related deaths are stigmatization and disenfranchisement. Both of these malignant processes contribute to the high-risk factor of a perceived lack of social support (see chapter 10). They can occur during and after the experience of the illness, which legitimately can be viewed as a type of traumatic stress.

Personal confrontations with negative social responses can complicate mourning considerably, and AIDS is viewed quite negatively by many. Whereas those who have acquired the disease through routes of transmission unrelated to homosexuality or drug use are perceived to be innocent victims, both homosexuals and intravenous drug users are perceived as being responsible for their own fate (E. Rosen, 1989). As reported by Lattin (1986), some have even defined the disease as a plague by God to punish sinners. Fuller and colleagues (1989) quote the philosopher Anthony Quinton, who captures the essence of this mindset: "There is surely no doubt that if AIDS were caused by some absolutely morally neutral activity, like eating cod's roe or drinking goat's milk, most people would feel differently about it" (p. 38). Because AIDS is not perceived to be morally neutral, many PWAs and their loved ones have difficulty admitting to having the disease or mourning one who has died from it, choosing instead to keep their losses hidden. When these losses are revealed, they can bring additional distress to those already overburdened.

Of four themes found in the first year of a field research investigation of families dealing with AIDS (Giacquinta, 1989), two pertain directly to social stigmatization and disenfranchisement. The first of these themes concerns the fact that many families are cut off from social support as a consequence of (a) distancing imposed by relatives unwilling to have contact with the PWA, (b) the family's own self-imposed retreat and desire not to divulge anything to others, or (c) a combination of both. The second theme in many of these families is difficulty with, or an absence of, intrafamilial communication, often based on fear, protection, and anger. The socially unspeakable nature of AIDS-related matters means stifling communication with others outside of the family unit; it also means that immediate family members may refrain from sharing thoughts, emotions, and concerns among themselves. Therefore, the potential for nurturance and support from either quarter is compromised.

Discrimination may take the form of acts of either omission or commission. Those mourning the death of a loved one from AIDS-related illness have been asked to relocate, been taunted and harassed, and made the subject of gossip and aggression. These and other experiences of discrimination are powerful reasons why survivors may keep from identifying themselves or seeking help from their peers. Although shielding the truth robs survivors of experiences and supports that could be therapeutic, survivors often feel they must do so to avoid adding fuel to an already intense fire.

Confrontation with alternative life-styles

On a global level, Fuller and colleagues (1989) note how AIDS has forced society to acknowledge the presence of diverse sexual life-styles and has made, even more than before, the gay and lesbian populations targets of fear, hatred, and disgust. On a more specific plane, for many families the AIDS diagnosis occurs simultaneously with the crisis of learning or confirming their loved one's homosexuality, bisexuality, sexual promiscuity, or intravenous drug use. For others, it may cap off intense family conflict about these life-styles and possibly even break a long period of estrangement.

It is not unusual for families to have denied or rejected the PWA's life-style for many years prior to the illness. Notice of a loved one's nontraditional choices may result in extraordinary stress, replete with agonizing and conflicted emotions and accompanied by numerous and unremitting physical and psychosocial losses. All of these problems only serve to exacerbate and complicate mourners' reactions during the illness and after the death.

Problems obtaining health care

Because of prevailing attitudes and fears about AIDS, the PWA may not receive the same type of health care available to patients with other diagnoses. Many health care facilities and professionals are unwilling to treat PWAs (Colburn & Malena, 1988) and, if they do, may exhibit avoidant behavior and denial, offering inferior care (Tsoukas, 1988). Thus, hysteria about AIDS leaves PWAs and their loved ones with the additional burden posed by the reduced number of health care workers willing to treat PWAs and the psychological consequences of being stigmatized, discriminated against, and victimized during a traumatic time.

This sort of discrimination ultimately has a profound effect on survivors' postdeath mourning. Recognizing that social reactions have affected the life and death of their loved one and having been helpless to change this situation, mourners may experience unparalleled feelings of rage, frustration, injustice, powerlessness, and victimization. These feelings can turn to bitterness, despair, depression, and guilt. The reality that the loved one simply wasn't "good enough" to get proper health care can be exasperating. Further awareness of insufficient social, political, and economic support to wage the battle against AIDS can fuel all of these feelings.

Guilt and anger

As noted previously, stigma associated with AIDS-related illness complicates receipt of social support during and after the illness. It also can initiate defensive and protective behaviors that may affect survivors adversely and later be expressed in the form of guilt and concerns about betrayal of the PWA. For example, one young man with AIDS came home to die in a rural part of the country. Because his parents feared the neighbors would observe his return and inform the landlord, who would have evicted them, their son was forced to make trips to the doctor covered with a blanket on the floor of the parents' car. This deception was most distressing for the parents to contemplate after the death of their child. Frequently, mourners lie about the actual cause of the loved one's death and then suffer the emotional toll of fear of discovery, guilt, and anger that a lie was necessary.

Guilt on the part of the mourner may be exacerbated if she perceives herself to have been responsible for infecting her loved one. This perception, difficult enough when the route of transmission is sexual relations or shared needles, engenders even more complications when the infection is transmitted prenatally. As for other types of death, complications in mourning arise because the mourner construes herself as having been responsible for the death or having had the power to prevent it but having failed to do so.

Guilt associated with significant family conflict over the deceased's life-style and any ambivalence or hostility felt toward the deceased may create additional problems. Guilt also may develop if fear of contagion has prompted the mourner to engage in now seemingly unwarranted actions or omissions (e.g., avoiding the loved one during the last stages of illness). Such problems compound the guilt already known to be associated with any terminal illness (Rando, 1986e, 1986h).

Anger is commonly exacerbated following the loss of a loved one from an AIDS-related illness. Unfortunately, the kind of nonjudgmental acceptance of others required to process anger is often absent in an AIDS-related death. Anger at the PWA for engaging in risk behaviors that contributed to the death is not unusual and must be confronted by a majority of mourners as they struggle to make sense out of the tragedy. For example, a parent might feel furious with his daughter for having had intercourse with an infected partner or anger at God that an expression of love between two people brought about the death.

Anger directed toward the deceased, also common, may be a form of blaming the victim. This response frequently occurs in other types of stigmatized deaths, although not usually in other types of terminal illness. If others blame the loved one for her life-style choices, the mourner will likely become reticent to discuss any similar feelings of blame he may have and any regrets he may have over them. This situation does nothing but victimize the mourner further by compounding his anger and decreasing his ability to trust those in whom he confides.

Anger also may be directed toward others, especially when the PWA has been infected through the error of another (e.g., transfusion or dental procedure). Depending upon the specific circumstances, anger can extend to those who may have caused the infection (e.g., the medical personnel who gave the contaminated transfusion) or to those who contributed to it (e.g., the peer group that years previously supported intravenous drug use). Mourners may even feel angry with God for the additional burdens posed by this type of death. Also common is anger toward those who blame the deceased for her own death or who seem insensitive to the loss.

Often, mourners' anger is heightened by the sense of unfairness and injustice in this type of illness, especially because it affects many individuals who never wanted to hurt anyone but merely wanted to be allowed to live their own lives in peace. In many cases, these individuals contracted the disease as a consequence of intimacy, for which no one should have to die. If the loved one became infected through no action of her own but is grouped with homosexuals and intravenous drug users and stigmatized as a result, mourners can be expected to experience additional emotional reactions that complicate their bereavement. These aspects can intensify anger and helplessness and can shatter forever a number of assumptions by which mourners have lived.

Views of AIDS as punishment or retribution

Negative reactions from others or the absence of needed support can appear to give credence to beliefs the mourner may hold that the illness and death are a form of punishment or retribution. Concerns in this area, typically found after deaths from other terminal illnesses, are heightened when AIDS-related illnesses are involved because the disease is associated with behaviors that are morally condemned by some. Indeed, the life-styles of many individuals with the disease have been denounced by their biological families as well as by their former churches. The fact that AIDS-related illnesses can be especially extreme compounds the problem.

Even if survivors merely wonder whether the disease is a form of punishment, such questioning means that they must struggle not only with the death itself but also with the additional burden of the loved one's having been "bad" in some fashion. Such doubt further complicates the relationship with the loved one during the illness as well as after the death.

Illness-related complications

The length of an illness has been identified as a significant variable influencing coping both before and after the death, with death from an overly lengthy illness being one of the identified high-risk factors for complicated mourning (see chapter 11). Illnesses that persist for too long, or during which family and friends fail to engage in appropriate amounts and types of anticipatory grief, tend to be associated with intensified grief and complicated mourning (Rando, 1983, 1986e).

The fluctuating course of the illnesses to which the PWA is prey can leave the individual's family and friends with the expectation that the person will survive this crisis just as he has survived so many in the past (Rando, 1983). The myriad secondary illnesses and acute crises that HIV infection can spawn thus may result in a death for which family and friends are unprepared—one that can seriously complicate their mourning. In addition, the difficulty of dealing with AIDS-related illnesses can leave survivors so depleted at the time of death that their ability to adjust is severely compromised (Rando, 1983). (See chapter 12 for more on sudden, unexpected death in the context of terminal illness.)

Worden (1991) has identified two other illness-related issues that adversely affect AIDS bereavement: (a) protracted illness and disfigurement and (b) neurological complications. The former often result in abandonment of the PWA or traumatization of those who stay connected, whereas the latter deteriorations of mental functioning (often mimicking impairments in Alzheimer's disease) can bring about social and/or psychological death for the PWA long before actual physiological death and can subject loved ones to the stresses and dilemmas inherent in such situations.

Reactions of Specific Survivor Groups

Parents, siblings, and lovers of the PWA each experience specific problems in mourning, as the following discussion details. Because homosexual men have been affected longer by AIDS than any other group, most of the available information concerns them. Thus, the following discussion primarily concerns this population. Presently, we just do not have enough data to provide definitive information on the experience of the other groups who are increasingly being affected by the disease. Until such information is available, the caregiver can certainly extrapolate from these observations to fit the particular circumstance in which he or she is involved.

Parents of the PWA

Because at present the majority of PWAs are young male homosexuals, a high probability exists that those mourning AIDS-related deaths will be parents. As noted previously in this chapter, the parent-child relationship exponentially increases the potential for complications in bereavement. Death of a child typically produces grief and mourning that appear pathological when compared with the bereavement responses of those who have had a different relationship with the loved one. Thus, when attempting to comprehend bereavement under these circumstances, caregivers also must take into account the dynamics of parental loss of a child.

Reports exist of parental reactions during a gay adult child's AIDS-related illness of severe depression, suicidal behavior, and full-blown psychosis requiring psychiatric hospitalization (Morin & Batchelor, 1984;

Nichols & Ostrow, 1984). Reports such as these about parental reactions help to demonstrate further that parents who have lost a child to AIDS-related illness may experience significant disturbance in their mourning.

Factors exacerbating parental mourning.   Parental mourning is exacerbated in the case of AIDS-related illness by the frequent need to maintain secrecy and by any shame and guilt internalized by the family about the PWA's life-style. Disenfranchisement by or conscious estrangement from extended family members can further deplete parents' needed psychosocial resources. The fact that the PWA is often young and looking forward to life makes the death untimely; the fact that the disease is often preventable intensifies reactions, complicates mourning, and makes the death even more difficult to bear.

As noted earlier, if parents have not recognized homosexuality, bisexuality, sexual promiscuity, or intravenous drug use, their reactions to news of it can make coping both before and after the death even more difficult. The concurrent crises of the death and recognition of life-style differences can produce a form of bereavement overload (Kastenbaum, 1969).

If the PWA is forced to return home for care, potential stresses may be magnified. The developmental reversal of active caretaking for the adult child, now infantilized, may produce a range of responses in parents. Some relish the opportunity to assume parental role behaviors again. Some feel saddened and need to mourn the reversal. Some are resentful of the interference and demands at this time of their lives. Some want to help but cannot, either for pragmatic reasons or due to the need for psychological defense and/or social protection. Some truly want to feel and act one way (e.g., grant the adult child full autonomy) yet cannot achieve this goal despite their best intentions and efforts. Some refuse to be involved at all. And some feel a combination of these reactions at different times during the course of the illness.

Despite the very real difficulties faced by parents providing care, some benefits may accrue. For the PWA, the AIDS diagnosis heightens the need for attachment and security, and parents can provide emotional and tangible support. Those persons who have a family to sustain them, especially in the face of social disenfranchisement, cope much better. The benefits known to occur in any terminal illness where the family engages appropriately in the loved one's care (Rando, 1986e) also can come to parents of PWAs. Most parents need to feel that they have done all that they could for their child. In providing support and care, they can make explicit their feelings and can work through any previous conflicts or feelings of guilt or responsibility. Thus, in situations where there has been a breach between one or both of the parents and the PWA prior to the illness, caring for the child may offer experiences of reparative value (Weiss, 1988).

In the increasingly common situation in which one or both parents and one or more young children in the family are HIV positive, the dynamics of parental loss of a child become intertwined with loss of spouse and self, presenting parents with unparalleled losses and stresses. Mourners and their caregivers often become overwhelmed as they witness the death of the family in bits and pieces. Further work is necessary to generate guidelines for treatment in such cases.

Differences between mothers' and fathers' responses. Differences between mothers' and fathers' responses to a child during the terminal portion of an AIDS-related illness are another potential source of complications in mourning. Burnell and Burnell (1989) have observed that the parents of homosexual sons with AIDS exhibit a wide discrepancy in feelings and attitudes. Specifically, they note that mothers tend to be "overprotective, attentive, and forgiving, having no difficulty accepting their sons' life-styles. They readily offer their love and support. As one mother stated, 'No matter what, he is my son. I'll be there until he does not need me anymore'" (p. 89).

Burnell and Burnell observe that fathers have far more difficulty overcoming the shame and stigma of the disease, becoming in some cases so immobilized that they have trouble even talking to their sons. These observers feel that this fact is not surprising, given the likelihood that the relationship between fathers and sons had probably been virtually nonexistent or fraught with tension, animosity, and resentment for many years. Thus, both fathers and sons find it difficult to forgive the hurt and rejection and to reach a comfortable level of intimacy at the time of death. In contrast, stepfathers and adoptive fathers appear to have little difficulty providing needed support and are better able to overcome their feelings of shame and hurt. (One can only speculate about the concerns biological fathers might have about the significance of their genetic contribution to their sons' homosexuality.)

Burnell and Burnell point out that sometimes mothers become angry at fathers for withholding support from them and their sons. Mothers may volunteer for AIDS causes or join parent support groups in their attempts to cope with their mourning, whereas fathers tend to shy away from active participation, instead demonstrating their support by offering money to AIDS groups and verbally encouraging their sons to beat the illness.

Conflict between biological and chosen family. Conflict also may occur when the PWA's biological family must contend with his chosen family. Although this situation may occur in any family when an adult child marries, in the instance of the PWA, frequently the chosen family is of a life-style unacceptable to the biological family. Both families may fight for the PWA's loyalty, attention, and the right to care for him and ultimately to authorize postdeath rituals. Where peaceful coexistence can be negotiated, the chosen loved ones tend to cope better with the loss. The biological family may or may not cope better, depending upon their ability to accept the chosen ones.

Numerous instances exist where the two families share concern for each other out of the common bond of love for the PWA and the desire to remain connected to ones to whom he had been connected. All too often after the death, however, the lack of legal status of chosen family members puts them at the mercy of the biological family. Unless the PWA has specified otherwise (e.g., arranged for a durable power of attorney), the biological family has all legal rights and social sanctions. This can rob the chosen family of the rituals, good-byes, finances, and tangible artifacts of the relationship, leaving them disenfranchised. It should be noted that biological families do not have a monopoly on contentiousness. The chosen family can also be quite critical of the biological family, although because they usually are not in a position of power, the chosen family does not tend to have the same type of impact as the biological family.

Conflict between the biological and chosen families is amplified by the fact that it occurs at the precise time when, as a concurrent stressor, it complicates mourning for the deceased PWA. In some cases, the PWA can make his reconciliation with the biological family only if he rejects chosen others and repudiates his "sinful" or "sick" past. When this is the case, the chosen family are left with the additional losses of rejection by and isolation from the PWA, ambivalence about the outcome of the love relationship, and assaults upon their sense of worth (Fuller et al., 1989).

To the extent that either the biological family or the chosen loved ones are not acting out of love and desire to do what the PWA would want but out of their own political motives, the situation has little chance of settlement. If the chosen family becomes the scapegoat for the biological family's anger or the recipient of blame for the PWA's life-style decisions and their fatal impact, the possibilities for agreement dwindle, whereas those for exacerbated mourning increase.

Each family—biological and chosen—must mourn the individual they have lost. Frequently, the child the parents knew and loved was heterosexual and/or drug free. Parents must create the rituals to help them mourn the person they have lost. If, to them, the PWA was a heterosexual Catholic altar boy, that is the person they must relinquish. By the same token, the chosen family will need to give up the atheistic gay activist whom they have loved. Unfortunately, the altar boy and the activist are the same man, and compromise comes hard to those who have only one last chance to be with and say good-bye to their loved one.

Siblings of the PWA

Siblings—as well as certain other relatives—often are significantly affected by a loved one's death from an AIDS-related illness. However, little mention is given to this group in the literature, and it may well be that they are the disenfranchised of the disenfranchised. This assertion is consistent with what generally has been observed regarding adult mourning for the death of an adult sibling (Rando, 1988). Despite passive social devaluation of the sibling relationship and expectations to the contrary, adult siblings can sustain substantial difficulties as they mourn the death of a brother or sister. Factors contributing to such difficulties include the following.

1. Unrecognized special characteristics of the sibling relationship

2. Unrealized meaning of the loss—specifically, (a) the loss of one who shared a unique, long-term history with the mourner and had been a constant in that person's life; (b) concerns raised about the mourner's own potential death; and (c) lack of social recognition

3. Specific complications of mourning an adult sibling: ambivalence, unrealistic expectations about family relationships, a lack of control or participation in the illness and/or rituals after the death, and problems accepting the death if there is no acute absence to signal it

4. Changes occurring in family relationships as a consequence of the death

The reader is referred to Rando (1988) for a complete discussion of this traditionally overlooked experience. At this juncture, it is important to recognize that brothers and sisters of the PWA can, and often do, suffer great distress at the illness and death of a sibling and, by virtue of the aforementioned realities, are predisposed to complications in mourning.

Lovers of the PWA

Lovers of PWAs—whether heterosexual, bisexual, or homosexual—experience bereavement similar to that experienced by spouses whose mates have succumbed to any other long-term chronic illness. However, they also must deal with the potential for infection with the HIV virus, discrimination, and disenfranchisement, as well as with a variety of other complicating psychological, social, medical, financial, and political issues. Because gay male lovers of the PWA have all of these complicating issues to contend with and more, and because presently more is known about them than others, they will be the focus of this discussion. Certainly, however, much of the information presented here can be extrapolated to other groups.

Gay lovers of PWAs typically experience very intense and painful mourning, often accompanied by survivor guilt and feelings that they are somehow to blame for the death. It has been noted that they frequently develop a feeling of worthlessness, somatic complaints, or panic attacks with overwhelming anxiety and terror (Moffat, 1986). And, as the following discussion makes clear, they are confronted with a number of other distinctive issues and stresses that further complicate their mourning. In outlining some of these issues, Klein and Fletcher (1986) assert the following:

> Those who have lost someone to the ravages of AIDS experience multifaceted repercussions. . . . Partners must confront . . . discrimination, their own fears relating to AIDS, and possible legal and financial problems. . . . The AIDS crisis complicated their lives and unquestionably added a new dimension to their grief. They felt stigmatized and were fearful either of being carriers or of having contracted the disease. They lost numerous friends and co-workers, were evicted from their homes, were rejected by friends and families, and felt unsafe and confused. (p. 24)

In general, the unique problems faced by this group center on fears of contagion, social isolation and disenfranchisement, psychological and spiritual issues, and bereavement overload.

Fears of contagion. A number of negative outcomes result from the possibility that the mourner is himself infected with the HIV virus, not the least of which is that the gay community may isolate him in the desire to protect itself. Certainly, a great deal of support for the majority of gay PWAs comes from segments of the gay community organized to fill that specific need (Tavares & Lopez, 1984). However, it is a myth that because the gay community are a persecuted minority, they universally reach out to those who have suffered this disenfranchising loss. Survivors can be abandoned by members of their own community as well as by the heterosexual community. Often recognition that support is unavailable is particularly painful, especially at a time when the need for support, nurturance, acceptance, and a sense of worth is so great. For many PWAs and their lovers, contagion-prompted isolation from particular members of their chosen families before and after an AIDS-related death is doubly devastating because they already may be estranged from their biological families.

Social isolation and disenfranchisement. As for other disenfranchised mourners, the processes of mourning are compromised for the lovers of PWAs. In addition to general problems associated with disenfranchisement (see chapter 10) and the specific practical problems posed by lack of legal status, financial benefits, and sympathetic bereavement leave policies, the fear of AIDS has a tremendous impact on the mourner's reentry into the social environment and ability to meet new partners (Klein & Fletcher, 1986).

In particular, the mourner may suffer from the lack of intimate contact because of his exposure to AIDS. He may fear that no one will ever want to have sex with him again and that he will never find another relationship. He stigmatizes himself, feeling he is marked for exclusion from future relationships, and grieves for himself as well as for his deceased lover (Andriote, 1987). If there is anger at his lover for having exposed him to the disease and then having left him, this may be followed by guilt and self-blame for such feelings and may make the mourner more difficult to work with than the PWA himself.

When, due to others' fears of contagion, the lover is socially isolated, his feelings of being unworthy and unlovable are deepened. Unfortunately, such isolation takes place at precisely the time his need for attachment, love, and touch is sharpened. Often the mourner is denied even the comfort of nonsexual physical contact, something those who have lost loved ones to other terminal illnesses generally do not forego.

If intimate physical contact is still possible, the consolation it can bring may be tainted by fear of fatal consequences. In brief, the mourner is denied the ability to express freely the powerful human need of sex and grieves not only for his dead loved ones, his dying friends, and himself, but for a way of life that is gone and may never come again (Klein & Fletcher, 1986). For the older gay man, fears of acquiring or transmitting a terminal illness are added to the already traumatic search for a fitting companion in a youth-oriented culture.

If the lover's own social support system is inadequate, as it all too frequently is, he may be left with no one with whom to share his grief and may appear chronically depressed (Gonsiorek, 1982). The consequences of such social disenfranchisement are severe: Feelings of anger may take longer to dissipate and resolve when no other person shares the experience, and the perceived lack of social support may engender complicated mourning. If the mourner is rejected by his own family, he may experience even more difficulty (Siegel & Hoefer, 1981). Social isolation leaves the mourner feeling alone and unable to express the regrets, guilt, hopelessness, and helplessness that need to be addressed.

The mourner also may at times be subjected to embarrassment, shame, and possible exposure during investigation and handling of the death by the biological family, police, or medical officials (Burnell & Burnell, 1989). If he is forced to relocate because of community reaction, the mourning processes of adjusting to the environment without the deceased and learning from the absence that the loved one is truly dead may be compromised. Secondary losses increase.

Finally, the rituals of mourning do not generally address the needs of the gay community. Many of those closest to the PWA will not be in the position of making decisions for that person during the illness and after the death. This lack of authority often forces them to endure hypocrisies, lies, and postdeath rituals they know do not reflect the wishes or life of the deceased. In addition, the biological families of PWAs may regard the grief of lovers as inappropriate and may reject their participation in the mourning rituals that do take place (Nichols, 1986).

Psychological and spiritual issues. Certain psychological issues confronting the lover during the PWA's illness also may color postdeath bereavement. These include the possibility of the PWA's reconciliation with his family and rejection of the lover or denunciation of himself, the homosexual life, and, by implication, the mourner (Fuller et al., 1989). In reaction, the lover is shocked and additionally bereaved.

The survivor also may assume that he is being punished for his lifestyle or has been bad in some regard. Unfortunately, like the PWA, the lover may be disenfranchised by his own traditional religious beliefs, and the pathways to spiritual reconciliation may be blocked. Indeed, it has been observed that religion may be the most devastating tool by which gay men exposed to AIDS are stigmatized (Geis et al., 1986).

During the PWA's illness, the lover's normal feelings of grief are entangled with a web of guilt and doubt: guilt for being gay and for having loved another man and doubt about the worth and validity of that love (Andriote, 1987). Already vulnerable, the mourner may internalize messages of hatred, fear, and alienation from much of the world around him and consequently may minimize, invalidate, or reject his relationship with the PWA or even actually abandon him. Clearly, these are not issues with which mourners dealing with loss of loved ones from other terminal illnesses must contend. When, for example, would a woman whose husband is dying of cancer have to minimize their relationship or feel guilty after his death for having loved him? When would she be forced to consider that their relationship might have been sinful?

Being potentially if not already infected, the survivor must also contend with his own reactions of anxiety, hopelessness, and helplessness about this fatal disease (Colburn & Malena, 1988). Significant stress from living with the HIV infection and anxiety-provoking uncertainty about future health are present in those who have HIV. For those with AIDS, all of the issues pertinent for a terminally ill patient obtain (Rando, 1984). Increased depression and suicide risk in the person who has lost a lover to AIDS may coincide with the individual's consideration of his own risk and mortality. Substance abuse, which can be significant in this population, often increases. Anger at the deceased loved one for transmitting the disease can be problematic because of the ambivalence it generates. If there are no therapeutic outlets, anger may be turned in on the self. Guilt if a person perceives himself responsible for infecting the deceased or for having participated in and/or condoned activities resulting in transmission (e.g., intravenous drug use) can significantly complicate mourning.

Finally, given warnings from the medical establishment to live as if infected if one has had intimate relations with a PWA, the mourner may feel it makes more sense and poses less risk to keep alive the former relationship with the deceased than to reinvest in another relationship. If memories of the former relationship are the closest the mourner gets to a loving relationship, chronic mourning may be established (Colburn & Malena, 1988). In brief, the "triple whammy" in these losses is that the lover must contend simultaneously with complicated mourning over the lost loved one, fear for the survival of the self, and grief over secondary losses he may have to face during that survival.

Bereavement overload in the gay community. A significant issue for the gay community is multiple loss or bereavement overload (Kastenbaum, 1969). Two empirical studies have examined the psychological consequences of chronic and intermittent AIDS-related bereavement among gay men in New York City (Dean et al., 1988; Martin, 1988). Martin (1988) found a direct relationship between the number of bereavements (i.e., deaths of lovers or close friends) and symptoms of traumatic stress response, demoralization, sleep problems, sedative use, recreational drug use, and use of psychological services because of AIDS-related concerns. He concludes that, because symptoms of distress increase directly with the number of bereavements, gay men are not adapting psychologically to repeated experiences of AIDS-related loss.

Although the families of PWAs undergo severe distress over the illness and death of their loved one, their experience tends to occur only once. By contrast, for lovers and others in the gay community, the experience is continual:

> When friends and associates die, not only in large numbers
> but in year after succeeding year, without a sufficient interval
> of time to resolve the grief from one death or set of deaths
> before the next occurs, the grief reaction may be compounded
> and contribute to a sense of impending doom and chronic
> mourning. Not only are gay men losing those with whom
> they have shared strong emotional ties, but they are also
> losing acquaintances, role models, and co-workers at a very
> fast rate. The community life which they so recently created,
> or moved to the city to take part in, has undergone extreme
> and rapid changes as men have adapted to losses and brace
> themselves to experience more. (Dean et al., 1988, pp. 54–55)

Those who are the most chronically bereaved tend to be (a) more active in organizations devoted to AIDS and in taking care of other men and (b) at higher risk for AIDS and its related illnesses. Caregivers must be aware of these facts in order to appreciate the complex clinical problems they face when treating such individuals (Dean et al., 1988). Because immunologic deficits have been demonstrated to follow bereavement (Stein, Schleifer, & Keller, 1981; Zisook, 1987), it may be especially important to relieve bereavement distress in gay men, who are at higher risk of infection. Because subtle neurological and medical disorders are associated with the HIV infection (Martin, 1988), caregivers must carefully differentiate symptoms related to bereavement or stress from those related to the virus. This complex task will become increasingly necessary as more AIDS-related bereavement reactions are seen in men who are themselves becoming ill with AIDS. (See Winiarski, 1991, for more on psychotherapy with persons who are HIV positive.)

Treatment Concerns

AIDS-related mourning inherently encompasses a number of the high-risk factors previously addressed in this book and will require treatment that integrates them as targets. Treatment must encompass the philosophical perspectives on treatment and the generic treatment guidelines provided in chapter 8, as well as incorporate the specific strategies outlined in chapter 9 for intervening in the six "R" processes of mourning. Specifically, the caregiver must recognize that AIDS-related bereavement poses particular problems with the following "R" processes and subprocesses.

1. Acknowledging the death and experiencing the pain (e.g., if access to and participation in appropriate postdeath rituals are denied or bereavement overload becomes too severe)

2. Reacting to the separation (e.g., because there is much pain but often little social support and because bereavement overload inhibits addressing psychological reactions to the loss and processing secondary losses)

3. Recollecting and reexperiencing the deceased and the relationship (e.g., secondary to guilt and consequent to a lack of social support and bereavement overload)

4. Relinquishing the old attachments to the old assumptive world (e.g., in cases where the mourner experiences multiple loss of loved ones from AIDS, the violation of the assumptive world and the destruction of the psychosocial one may be so wide ranging and/or complete that the mourner refuses to let go of anything else, even if outdated)

5. Revising the assumptive world (e.g., because of significant assaults on assumptions and prior beliefs), adopting new ways of being in the world (e.g., given that the world is greatly changed by negative social reactions and the deaths of so many people), and forming a new identity (e.g., because of difficulties in revising the assumptive world and adopting new ways of being)

6. Reinvesting (e.g., if ostracism from the community has resulted from concerns about contagion and has interfered with the reestablishment of new intimate relationships)

Another critical target for intervention is socially disenfranchised grief. Treatment suggestions for disenfranchised grief, discussed in chapter 10, specifically involve the validation of the loss and the promotion of appropriate mourning. Also provided in this chapter are guidelines for intervening with mourners experiencing a number of other problems commonly associated with AIDS-related deaths: prior and concurrent losses or stresses; anger, ambivalence, and guilt; and a general lack of social support. Treatment suggestions helpful for mourning a death following a long-term illness, noted in chapter 11, may be incorporated as the situation warrants. Because the medical course of HIV infection is unpredictable, acute crises are common. As a result, it is quite possible for the mourner to experience a sudden, unexpected loss in the context of terminal illness relating to AIDS. Treatment therefore should take this problem into account, along with the problem of multiple loss. Both of these issues are discussed in chapter 12. Finally, because the victims of AIDS-related illness are often relatively young and have surviving parents, interventions for the loss of a child, delineated earlier in this chapter, may be useful.

The caregiver also must work to accomplish the following specific goals.

1. Help the mourner identify and work through feelings about the way AIDS is contracted. This means working with the mourner's guilt and associated distress if she is the one who passed the virus on to the deceased. It also means addressing any issues of victimization relating to the transmission (e.g., in the case of a blood transfusion that was intended to help, not hurt, the loved one) and fighting against misinformation and discrimination brought about by the stereotype that AIDS is a disease of homosexuals and intravenous drug users.

2. Empower the mourner following any victimization of the loved one or self (e.g., insufficient medical attention, housing and employment discrimination).

3. Provide family treatment and training in communication skills in light of the devastation wreaked in families of PWAs.

4. Without necessarily agreeing with or condemning their actions, appreciate the perspectives of both biological and chosen families.

5. Therapeutically reframe and work through any assumption of guilt, low self-esteem, and sense of worthlessness associated with having had a relationship with a PWA.

6. Pay particular attention to the individual whose mourning is complicated by guilt arising from omissions or commissions secondary to her inability to accept or approve the PWA's life-style choices.

7. Teach assertiveness and communication skills to enable the mourner to contend with any social blame and denigration of the PWA.

8. Help the mourner who fears or knows she is infected with the HIV virus to realize whatever potential is available for continued meaningful and rewarding existence and relationships, including those that are sexual in nature. Intervene to help the mourner cope with the fear or reality of having a chronic, fatal illness (see Rando, 1984).

9. Work with the mourner to address concerns about AIDS as punishment for moral transgressions, helping her find a way to incorporate a viewpoint on this issue in her revised assumptive world.

10. If the mourner wishes, help her find some meaning and/or comfort in activities to make a difference to other PWAs and their loved ones.

11. Identify and legitimize the stress caused by the medical and social aspects of AIDS-related illnesses. Help the mourner understand that dealing with a loved one's terminal illness can be very depleting and work to promote appropriate anticipatory grief (see Rando, 1986c, 1988).

12. Respond to the need to differentiate the organic symptoms of HIV infection from those related to bereavement or stress.

13. If the mourner is a gay male who had denigrated the relationship with the PWA or had been rejected by the PWA, address any issues of low self-esteem and guilt that may be exacerbated by introjected homophobic attitudes.

14. Work with parents to address issues accompanying the loss of a grown child or associated with prenatal transmission of the HIV virus. If both parent and child have the virus, help the parent cope with any parenting limitations she may have due to her own illness. Enable as much as possible a positive parent-child relationship.

CHAPTER 14

Caregiver Concerns in the Treatment of Complicated Mourning

A number of authors have explored, explained, and warned about the common dangers of the personal and professional stresses inherent in the care of the ill, the dying, and the bereaved (e.g., Fulton, 1979; Harper, 1977; Kalish, 1981; Maslach & Jackson, 1979; Mitchell & Bray, 1990; Paradis, 1987; Rando, 1984; Raphael, 1980b; Vachon, 1987a; Wolfelt, 1991; Worden, 1982). The general consensus of such writers is that work in these areas is inherently intimate; powerful in eliciting the caregiver's own feelings, thoughts, memories, and fantasies about loss; and commanding in its life-and-death nature. In brief, this kind of work demands a deep emotional response from the caregiver. Both giving and withholding this type of emotional response can severely tax the caregiver.

Caregivers face a number of difficult professional issues even when bereavement is uncomplicated. When mourning is complicated, these issues are intensified and new ones arise. It is well known that the failure to attend to such matters can result in caregivers' distress in all dimensions: psychological, spiritual, behavioral, social, physical, occupational, and economic. In general, as discussed in Rando (1984), caregivers are advised to practice continual active grieving for those they lose through illness, death, or termination of treatment and to implement personal and organizational stress management strategies designed for work in this field.

The reader is referred directly to the resources already cited for in-depth analyses of and strategies for intervening in caregiver stress. The content of this excellent body of work is assumed as prerequisite to the information presented here and will not be repeated. What this chapter will do is outline briefly the caregiver stresses particular to work with complicated mourning and suggest some ways to mitigate them. Discussion will focus first on two preliminary concerns: caregiver characteristics necessary to provide treatment of complicated mourning and therapeutic errors to which caregivers are prone when working with this population.

CAREGIVER CHARACTERISTICS

Before undertaking work in complicated mourning, it is of course essential that the caregiver have the skills to provide treatment in general and to facilitate uncomplicated grief and mourning. Beyond that, a number of more specialized qualities are important.

With regard to the treatment of post-traumatic stress reactions, which often accompany complicated mourning, Scurfield (1985) notes that extraordinary events and the reactions to them require extraordinary efforts in treatment by both the client and the caregiver. Specifically, Scurfield has identified three essential caregiver qualities: (a) a willingness and sensitivity to probe quite directly into the various aspects of the traumatic experience (i.e., loss); (b) the ability to face honestly one's own reactions and those of the survivor to such probes; and (c) the sensitivity to navigate the murky boundaries between uncovering that which the survivor has been trying, often desperately, to avoid and full integration of the traumatic experience within the survivor's current existence.

Other characteristics of the successful caregiver relate to the following four areas: professional knowledge and skills, personality, success in confronting one's own prior losses, and ability to care for oneself as a caregiver.

Professional Knowledge and Skills

Incorrect or insufficient information can adversely affect both uncomplicated and complicated situations. Specifically, this may concern (a) the experiences, processes, implications, and causes of grief and mourning; (b) important clinical aspects thereof (especially as regards psychosocial and secondary loss, the importance of the assumptive world and of cognitive processes, psychiatric complications, the use of medication, the two criteria for determining appropriateness of continued connection with the deceased, and high-risk factors and their impact); and (c) required treatment perspectives, strategies, and techniques. Without the proper information, the caregiver runs the risk of committing a number of serious errors. He or she may misdiagnose certain reactions as pathological, be ignorant of what therapeutic interventions to use and why, or misapply the basic information that underpins therapeutic strategies and techniques. It therefore is imperative that the caregiver have a command of information about and the skills necessary for prediction, identification, classification, assessment, and treatment of uncomplicated and complicated mourning, as well as a clear understanding of the overlap and differences between the two. In particular, the caregiver must answer the following questions.

1. Is this person truly evidencing complicated mourning?

2. Is the type or style of treatment I provide for complicated mourning suited to this particular individual?

3. Are there contraindications for treating this situation as I usually would treat someone in a situation like this?

4. Do concomitants of the complicated mourning exist that require additional types of (or agents for) intervention?

5. Can I provide access to the complete array of treatment required by the mourner (e.g., referral to a psychiatrist for prescription of medication)?

Caregiver Personality

The caregiver's personality must be able to withstand the demands of work in complicated mourning. If the caregiver's personality is not suited to the work, not only is success undermined, but both the mourner and caregiver can suffer iatrogenic effects of the treatment process. Some of the questions to be posed by the caregiver are as follows.

1. What personal attributes and qualities are necessary to treat complicated mourning?

2. Is there any chance I am a codependent caregiver?

3. Am I personally and professionally able to work with an individual who has been through this type of loss (e.g., murder of a child)

4. Am I personally and professionally able to work with this particular mourner (e.g., one who exhibits a specific personality disorder or type of complicated mourning response, such as extreme anger)?

Success in Confronting One's Own Prior Losses

Just as the mourner is compromised in coping with a current loss if a prior loss is unfinished or has left sequelae impeding future accommodation of losses, so, too, can the caregiver's work be adversely affected by the status or consequences of previous and poorly accommodated losses. The conscientious caregiver must be aware of any continuing impact of prior losses and know how to account for or manage them in the best interests of healthy and professional occupational functioning. The caregiver must ask the following questions.

1. Where am I with my own losses and my mourning over them?

2. Is there unfinished business or any other indication that suggests it is inappropriate for me to be doing this work with this person now?

3. Am I able to differentiate my own issues and needs from the mourner's?

4. Do I have the ability to set appropriate limits with this particular mourner, given my own prior loss history?

Ability to Care for Oneself as a Caregiver

As noted in the resources cited at the beginning of this chapter, the inability to care sufficiently for oneself as a caregiver compromises the care of the mourner. It is the responsibility of each caregiver to monitor and attend to the personal and professional expectations and stresses that arise in this type of treatment. Specific stress management strategies are mentioned later in this chapter. The following questions are pertinent.

1. What are my expectations and limitations for myself in this work? Are they appropriate?

2. What are the most stressful aspects of work with complicated mourning?

3. What am I doing to help myself cope with the stressful aspects of my work?

4. What are my personal warning signs indicating I am being stressed?

5. How do I come to appropriate closure, nurture, and replenish myself in work with complicated mourning?

COMMON THERAPEUTIC ERRORS

Even if the caregiver possesses the necessary characteristics for treating complicated mourning, he or she may unwittingly commit a number of therapeutic errors. These errors, frequently made in good faith, are most often the result of incorrect or insufficient information about complicated mourning, although they also may be the result of the caregiver's own response to emotions elicited in the specific treatment situation. Some of the most problematic acts of omission are as follows.

1. Failing to conduct a comprehensive and in-depth assessment at the beginning of treatment, assess for fluctuations and changes in mourning throughout treatment, and design treatment to respond specifically to the mourner's idiosyncratic needs

2. Failing to incorporate into treatment psychosocial and secondary losses, appreciation of the assumptive world and cognitive processes in mourning, understanding of psychiatric implications, use of

medication when warranted, use of the two criteria for determining appropriateness of continued connection with the deceased, specific interventions tailored to pertinent high-risk factors, and recognition of the normalcy of STUG reactions, among others

3. Failing to comprehend, be sensitive to, and properly treat the mourner's resistances in undertaking the requisite processes of mourning and/or underlying concerns or issues beneath apparent reactions (e.g., guilt covering helplessness or serving as self-punishment), as well as neglecting to convey an appreciation of the mourner's need for these resistances

4. Failing to take the mourner beyond the passive processes of grief to the active processes of mourning (i.e., incomplete processing of the six "R" processes of mourning)

5. Focusing too much on the generic aspects of grief and mourning and too little on the other specific issues relating to the mourner's idiosyncratic situation (i.e., the general and high-risk factors circumscribing the mourner and the loss)

6. Failing to integrate the treatment of complicated mourning with psychotherapeutic and/or medical treatment mandated for any mental or physical disorders that may coincide with or develop subsequent to complicated mourning

7. Failing to proceed past an issue to ascertain where and how it has interfered with the successful completion of the "R" processes of mourning and to intervene at the appropriate time to enable the completion

Some of the most potentially dangerous acts of commission are as follows.

1. Pushing the mourner too fast

2. Pushing the mourner to sever all connection with the deceased without assisting in the appropriate establishment of a new relationship

3. Colluding with the mourner to avoid the requisite "R" processes of mourning (e.g., overlooking an inappropriate attachment to the deceased because it is too stressful to confront the mourner with more loss)

4. Becoming involved, due to guilt and/or unresolved reactions to the particular death being mourned, to the degree that the mourner's proper treatment and successful mourning are compromised (Levinson, 1972), or allowing one's own personal or professional issues to interfere with intervention to promote the "R" processes of mourning

5. Becoming caught up in specialized techniques to treat complicated mourning or focusing on complications to the extent that a sense of the mourner as a person is lost

6. Befriending the mourner in response to the victimization; becoming a surrogate griever (Fulton, 1979), surrogate sufferer (R. Nichols, 1983), codependent bereavement caregiver (Wolfelt, 1990a, 1990b, 1991), or rescuer; or in some other fashion failing to balance the roles of compassion, empathy, sensitivity, and objectivity

7. In an effort to depathologize bereavement, focusing on the uncomplicated or "normal" aspects and overlooking the complicated ones

Proper information about uncomplicated and complicated grief and mourning can help the caregiver avoid these therapeutic errors. However, equally important is an awareness of the particular stressors involved in such treatment.

CAREGIVER STRESSORS

In the treatment of complicated mourning, three main types of caregiver stressors exist: mourner-related stressors, death-related stressors, and stressors related to the difficulty of treating complicated mourning. For the purpose of this discussion, mourner-related and death-related stressors are considered separately. It should be pointed out, however, that in reality the distinction between these two types is not so clear and that interaction between them often occurs.

Mourner-Related Stressors

Mourner-related stressors involve the symptoms or syndromes of complicated mourning manifested by the mourner (see chapter 4) and factors associated with the individual, premorbid relationship, and social system (see chapter 10). For the most part, mourner-related stressors typically prompt less overwhelming responses in the caregiver than do death-related stressors. A notable exception concerns stress associated with a scenario in which the mourner's premorbid relationship involved abuse or victimization by the deceased. In this case, the caregiver may experience a negative reaction to the mourner's trauma within the relationship similar to that experienced when the death to which the mourner must accommodate is in some way traumatic. Thus, if abuse and victimization have been present, the caregiver may experience any of the reactions subsequently described as being related to exposure to traumatic death. In addition, he or she might engage in blaming the victim to achieve distance from the frightening notion that such capricious victimization can take place.

Even though they may cause less difficulty than death-related stressors, mourner-related stressors often engender frustration in the caregiver—and the subsequent tendency to push the mourner too fast in treatment or insufficiently work through the resistance first. Such frustration is quite common in the caregiver whose therapeutic efforts are thwarted or stalled by the mourner's anger, ambivalence, guilt, dependency, or codependency. Mourners who are dependent or codependent may be especially grating on some caregivers. If their fears, insecurities, and anxieties are not understood, these mourners may be perceived as immature or gutless, prompting the caregiver's misdirected advice that they grow up or take more risks without addressing first their underlying concerns.

The mourner's responses can prompt not only frustration in the caregiver, but also fear if rage or aggression are part of the picture. Dealing with a mourner's anger can cause enormous stress for the caregiver, especially when concerns exist about the mourner's acting out the aggression or otherwise having inadequate impulse control. In addition, the mourner may displace anger onto the caregiver because the caregiver is unable to bring the loved one back and/or because the treatment process is causing the mourner more pain. In such cases, the caregiver may become a target for hostility or aggression.

Contending with the mourner's guilt can also be problematic. Adherence to seemingly irrational guilt or lack of ability to perceive its functional purpose can be exasperating for the caregiver. In an effort to achieve progress or to "rescue" the mourner from guilt, the caregiver may try to minimize it, rationalize it away, or strip the mourner of it. Unless accompanied by the mourner's working through and relinquishment of guilt, any of these actions can traumatize a mourner by depriving him of the defense and exposing him to material with which he is not prepared to contend. Alternatively, such actions may contribute to increased defensiveness or even flight from treatment. Guilt also can stimulate the caregiver's countertransference reactions based on personal concerns and/or unfinished business in his or her own life.

Often the extensive preparatory work and the working through of resistances to permit the mourner to face unacceptable affects—especially anger, ambivalence, and dependency—and the repetition required in the processing of a sudden, unexpected death can be frustrating, if not irritating, to the caregiver, who may want to move along in the treatment. The caregiver may be tempted to hurry treatment if the mourner fails to move through resistances, resolve conflicts, or work through the "R" processes of mourning as quickly as the caregiver would like. In this event, a control struggle often follows, with both parties losing. Control struggles of this sort also are typical when the mourner displays symptoms or syndromes of complicated mourning of the absent, delayed, or inhibited types. In these situations, the caregiver can err by overemphasizing promotion of expression without first working through the mourner's resistances. The same is true with mourners who express ambivalence, guilt, dependency, or codependency.

Caregivers must recognize that treatment of complicated mourning often takes much time, preparation, patience, repetition, and working through. If the caregiver is not suited for this, he or she should not work in this area. Even if one is suited, the work can be stressful on occasion because of these requirements.

Specific mourner liabilities such as prior and concurrent losses or stresses and problems in mental or physical health can cause problems for the caregiver if they create limitations. To the extent that the mourner has a poor prior loss history, too much concurrent stress, or fragile mental health, the caregiver must modify expectations, treatment, and goals. In addition, the mourner with perceived insufficient social support can place many extra demands on the caregiver, or the caregiver may assume responsibility for providing the missing support even in the absence of demands.

Those whose mourning is absent, delayed, or inhibited often can be persuasively articulate about not needing to emote or deal with mourning at all. Those whose mourning is chronic may be quite convincing about their inability to stop. Such assertions can lead to stress for the caregiver if they challenge therapeutic beliefs and cause cognitive dissonance. Those whose mourning is distorted, either by extreme anger or guilt, can alienate their caregivers. In addition, the conflicted, unanticipated, and chronic mourning syndromes embody characteristics that often cause impatience and provoke in the caregiver an "All-right-already-let's-end-this" type of attitude. Problems in intervening in conflicted mourning can result if the caregiver mistakenly assumes the mourner should be relieved by the death and builds that expectation into treatment.

Death-Related Stressors

Death-related stressors pertain to the characteristics of the specific death to which the caregiver is exposed. Specifically, these stressors are associated with the mode of death (see chapter 11); the degree to which the death was anticipated, the number of deaths involved, and the extent of trauma (see chapter 12); and whether the loss was of a child or related to AIDS (see chapter 13).

Negative emotional reactions to these types of stressors may stem from the caregiver's exposure to specific aspects of these losses. For example, the caregiver working with a mourner who has experienced a sudden, unexpected death may find that his or her own fears of being separated suddenly from loved ones interfere with the development of a strong therapeutic alliance. Just as likely to provoke the caregiver's negative response is the mourner's own heightened level of distress at such a loss. For instance, a mourner's volatile anger in response to the murder of a loved one might make it difficult for the caregiver to provide necessary support. Regardless of their origins, such caregiver reactions can be dysfunctional if they exert a negative personal impact upon the caregiver or if they contribute to the mourner's distress by interfering in treatment.

Problems caused by death-related stressors

Sudden, traumatic, violent, mutilating, preventable, senseless, horrifying, and often random deaths are overrepresented in complicated mourning as compared to uncomplicated mourning. To the degree that the particular death embodies these or other high-risk characteristics, the caregiver can be expected to experience additional problems and anxieties. The critically important nonspecific therapist variables of genuineness, empathy, and support may become especially strained under such circumstances: Genuineness and empathy create vulnerability in the caregiver, which in turn compromises the ability to lend therapeutic support.

High-risk deaths often generate in the caregiver, as well as in the mourner, high anxiety and threat, increased vulnerability, heightened insecurity, intensified feelings of helplessness, and a strong sense of loss of control. This is one reason why individuals mourning such deaths, especially homicide or the death of a child, traditionally have been overlooked. The anxiety provoked by such losses—as well as reactions of grief, rage, terror, and so forth in both mourner and caregiver—has simply been too overwhelming.

In addition, these types of losses tend to leave the mourner searching intensely to find some meaning in the death, assign blame and mete out punishment, and regain a sense of control. This process can be agonizing for the caregiver, whose confrontation with the fact that victimization happens to innocent people can increase a personal sense of vulnerability. Observing that an individual's assumptive world can be so viciously shattered without warning can be terrifying and can prompt the caregiver to search for meaning and existential sustenance that may be difficult to find. As is true for the mourner, the recognition of the injustice in these types of deaths can leave the caregiver cynical and hardened.

For the caregiver who has problems contending with anger, coping with the rage shown by many of these mourners may be difficult, especially after suicide, homicide, or loss of a child. If the stress becomes too great, the caregiver may begin to avoid the mourner in certain ways. This can contribute to guilt in the caregiver, which then can prompt further avoidance, in a vicious cycle. If the caregiver feels sympathy instead of appropriate empathy for the mourner, countertherapeutic responses ultimately can result.

Caregiver responses to traumatic death

Treating those whose loved ones have died a traumatic death can be especially difficult for the caregiver. To the extent that the caregiver is exposed to the details of traumatic death or to his or her own traumatic experiences secondary to the mourner's emotional reactions, traumatic material, and fears, the caregiver becomes vulnerable to the stress response syndrome (Horowitz, 1986a).

Although this concept is not new, McCann and Pearlman (1990b) have suggested a new framework to explain the psychological effects experienced by those working with victims of trauma. Within the context of a constructivist self-development theory, these observers interpret caregivers' reactions to mourners' trauma as vicarious traumatization. They see such traumatization as being related to the graphic and painful material presented by traumatized individuals and to the caregiver's unique cognitive schemas, beliefs, expectations, and assumptions (i.e., assumptive world). As they point out, persons who work with victims may experience profoundly disruptive and painful psychological effects that can persist for months or years, if not forever. Working with trauma survivors also can disrupt the caregiver's assumptive world and precipitate major conflicts, fears, and disorganization in the areas of dependency/trust, safety, power, independence, esteem, intimacy, and frame of reference. Usually, the alternating tendencies either to reexperience the mourner's painful images and emotions or to avoid various components of the mourner's traumatic memories are transient. However, these tendencies and certain traumatic memories can become permanently incorporated into the caregiver's own memory system. This is particularly true when the content is personally salient and relates closely to the caregiver's psychological needs and life experience or when the caregiver has insufficient opportunity to talk about and process the experience of the traumatic event. In brief, the caregiver can experience post-traumatic stress reactions, including intrusive thoughts or images and painful emotional reactions.

It is for such reasons that the need has been identified to provide safety in treatment not only for the victimized individual, but also for the caregiver (Herman, 1990). Safety is necessary because the caregiver is a witness to atrocity who is exposed to experiences that can raise intense emotional reactions such as terror, grief, rage, and excitement. These reactions can evoke in the caregiver wishes to deny, rescue, blame, and punish.

Coping with atrocity has been further addressed by Haley (1974), who notes that, in situations where the individual reports atrocities, as is the case in work with Vietnam veterans, the caregiver must "be with" and tolerate the existential reality of the individual's overt or covert self-image as a murderer. In addition to dealing with issues intrinsic to post-traumatic stress, the caregiver must confront his or her own sadistic feelings and envision the possibility that under certain situations of extreme stress and in an atmosphere of encouragement, he or she also might murder. Another difficult issue in such work concerns the fact that the caregiver must not deny the reality of the individual's perception of guilt about actual participation in atrocious acts, but must align himself or herself with a part of the patient's ego that views such actions as alien while simultaneously exploring the factors involved when the individual's usual sense of morality gave way. The establishment of such an alliance is a difficult but critical component of the treatment process.

Haley (1974) notes that the caregiver also must manage countertransference reactions that arise from work with those lacking a clear feeling of guilt (e.g., those who have severe character disorders or who do not openly express their guilt). Countertransference with these individuals stresses the caregiver's tolerance to its limit. However, Haley asserts that "the therapist's countertransference and real, natural response to the realities of the patient's experience must be continually monitored and confronted for a therapeutic relationship to be established" (p. 196).

Additional emotional demands on the caregiver working with traumatized persons are outlined by Putnam (1989), who discusses the treatment of individuals with multiple personality disorder (MPD). In this situation, a number of countertransference difficulties are encountered. These are of particular concern to mourners who have been victimized by an abuser, have significant dissociated traumatic material that requires integration, or in fact have MPD. First, if the victim has acted to become a victimizer, this can activate within the caregiver strong feelings of anxiety, rage, and revulsion, along with an existential fear of death. These emotions may be accompanied by equally strong feelings of concern, sympathy, and helplessness. Second, empathic reactions elicited by the mourner's description of the abuse can be powerful. These reactions may coexist with sadistic, punitive, or voyeuristic impulses that are activated by the explicit details of physical or sexual abuse. Such impulses can be most disturbing for the caregiver to acknowledge. Third, observation of the mourner's recall of traumatic material can be enormously stressful to the caregiver not only because of the revelation of the original trauma, but also because of the depth of the individual's pain during abreaction. Finally, the desire and fantasy of reparenting these abused individuals can set up the caregiver for inappropriate responses that can damage the treatment and its ultimate goals.

In situations where the death has received, or continues to receive, media attention, the caregiver may be seduced from the tasks at hand by feelings of self-importance. Sometimes pressured by publicity surrounding the event, the caregiver may push the mourner too fast or too far to satisfy curiosity—either personal or that of others—about the details of a particular traumatic experience. In addition, the caregiver who specializes in complicated mourning, especially in complicated mourning associated with trauma, may become vulnerable to overstepping therapeutic limits by believing that he or she is the only one who can help. Such beliefs are certain to eventuate in caregiver burn-out.

Stressors Associated With Treatment Difficulty

As noted, the sheer difficulty in providing treatment for complicated mourning can itself be a major source of stress for the caregiver. Clearly,

complicated mourning challenges the caregiver with tasks more difficult than those present in an uncomplicated mourning scenario. Specific
mourner liabilities (e.g., prior or concurrent losses or stresses and mental
or physical disorders; mourner problems with anger, ambivalence, guilt,
dependency, or codependency; perceived lack of social support) can place
inordinate demands on the caregiver and the treatment process. Likewise,
dealing with the myriad problems associated with a high-risk death can tax
the caregiver's abilities. For instance, the repetition necessary in processing
a traumatic death might prove difficult for the caregiver to manage.

Because each situation is different, it is impossible to specify all of the
treatment difficulties that could potentially cause the caregiver stress.
However, the following list briefly specifies a few of the problems most
commonly experienced as stressful.

1. In many cases, grief and mourning reactions are greater and
   persist longer in complicated mourning than in uncomplicated
   mourning.

2. Horrific, gruesome, senseless, or preventable losses—all associated
   with complicated mourning—will likely intensify, prolong, and
   complicate treatment at the same time they make the caregiver
   want to avoid the mourner or the issues involved. They also may
   bring personal stress that can compromise one's treatment efficacy.

3. Complicated mourning is associated relatively more often than
   uncomplicated mourning with suicide potential—both intentioned
   and subintentioned—and acting-out potential (e.g., revenge after
   a homicide).

4. The time it takes to work through some of these issues (e.g., unrealistic feelings of guilt after the death of a child) can be difficult
   for the caregiver to endure while witnessing the suffering that
   occurs in the interim. Although the caregiver knows no one can
   take away the mourner's pain and that it is part of the healing
   process, the mourner's suffering often appears unnecessary.

5. Cases of complicated mourning involving prior or concurrent
   losses or stresses, or mental and physical illness, necessarily
   require more complex intervention and altered expectations and
   goals. In addition, they often require collaboration with other
   professionals or the involvement of support system resources.

6. Treatment of complicated mourning is often distressing to the caregiver because of the frequent need to promote the mourner's painful confrontation with the loss and/or trauma. Forcing the mourner
   to endure pain after already having been through so much can be
   especially difficult.

7. Working with chronic mourners can be particularly stressful, discouraging, and frustrating for caregivers because this population is known to be especially recalcitrant.

8. Countertransference feelings of anger, resentment, and rejection can develop in the caregiver when the mourner begins to make progress and rely on others besides the caregiver (e.g., family, friends, support group).

STRATEGIES FOR REDUCING CAREGIVER STRESS

The resources cited at the beginning of this chapter for contending with stress in general and for working with the bereaved in particular offer numerous suggestions for reducing caregiver stress. The reader is referred to these resources for specific guidance. However, in applying any of the suggestions these resources contain, it will be particularly important to identify the sources of stress and discern which are generic in treating any complicated mourning, which are inherent in the specific work at hand, and which are personally idiosyncratic. It will be necessary to recognize one's personal vulnerabilities in the work and build in ways to deal with them by limiting the number or type of cases. For example, the caregiver who has issues with infant death may wish to avoid treating parents who have lost a child to Sudden Infant Death Syndrome.

The caregiver especially needs to process, both alone and with others, the reactions elicited by this type of work and to understand that one must acknowledge, express, and work through painful experiences if one is to prevent or ameliorate some of the potentially damaging effects of this work. As Herman (1990) notes, the caregiver requires ongoing support. Just as no mourner can recover alone, no caregiver can do this work alone. Therefore, the caregiver must tap into potential sources of support within the professional network to avoid professional isolation.

As specifically regards the healthy transformation of vicarious traumatization, McCann and Pearlman (1990b) advocate a series of strategies. In addition to other strategies relevant to work with uncomplicated mourning, they suggest that support groups be focused around (a) normalizing the reactions caregivers experience in the course of this type of work, (b) applying constructivist self-development theory to understand caregivers' specific reactions, and (c) providing a safe environment where caregivers feel free to share and work through painful or disruptive reactions. They also note that any countertransference reactions must not be presumed inevitably to reflect caregivers' own unresolved issues, despite the fact that caregivers' psychic conflicts and unresolved victimizations in early childhood certainly can contribute to vicarious traumatization. Caregivers must understand how the assumptive world is specifically disrupted through the course of work with traumatized individuals and how this shapes their responses, assessing which need areas are particularly personally salient. If caregivers learn more about their own particular psychological needs, they will be more effective in processing traumatic material and limiting its impact on the assumptive world and functioning.

Finally, in discussing coping strategies, McCann and Pearlman encourage caregivers to find a way to challenge the dark sides of humanity observed in this work. They underscore the need to develop the essential components of optimism and hopefulness in the face of tragedy by acknowledging and confirming the many positive experiences and effects work with traumatized individuals can have. These include (a) drawing personal meaning from knowing one is involved in an important social problem and making a contribution to ameliorate some of the destructive impact of violence on human beings; (b) having enhanced awareness of the social and political conditions that lead to violence, which can lead the caregiver to greater social activism; (c) developing heightened sensitivity and enhanced empathy for victims' suffering, which may result in a deeper sense of connection with others; (d) increasing feelings of self-esteem from helping trauma victims regain a sense of wholeness and meaning; (e) developing a deep sense of hopefulness about the capacity of human beings to endure, overcome, and even transform their traumatic experience; and (f) achieving a more realistic view of the world through the integration of the dark sides of humanity with healing images.

The reader should be very clear on one most significant point: Just as mourners have a choice about how ultimately to respond to their loss, so also do caregivers who work with these mourners. In each case, mourner and caregiver can let the situation overcome them or determine that something positive will come out of it. Thus, all of the sources of caregiver stress noted here could become sources of positive consequences. For instance, the traumatic nature of a death can just as easily depress one caregiver as it can intensify the determination in another to live life as meaningfully as possible.

This notion of exercising individual choice does not imply that the stress of working with complicated mourning is insignificant. There could be few, if any, more difficult positions to be in as a caregiver. Even those who strive diligently to make the stressful elements of this work more manageable or conducive to positive outcomes can be affected adversely at times. However, by choosing how to manage stress, one can minimize its deleterious effects and maximize its benefits for the ultimate good of the mourner as well as oneself.

APPENDIX

Grief and Mourning Status Interview and Inventory (GAMSII)

PART I: DEMOGRAPHIC INFORMATION

Name _____ Sex _____

Date of birth _____ Age _____

Address _____

_____

Where mourner calls home _____

Residence history _____

_____

_____

Note. The GAMSII is a clinical instrument based on Dr. Therese A. Rando's professional experience. Permission is granted for caregivers to reproduce the GAMSII for clinical use only, with the following acknowledgment: From *Treatment of Complicated Mourning* by T. A. Rando, 1993, Champaign, IL: Research Press. Copyright 1993 by T. A. Rando. Reprinted by permission.

Readers are urged to see chapter 6 in this volume for important background on use of the GAMSII and for a listing of other critical areas to explore in assessment.

Social/cultural/ethnic/religious background _____

_____

_____

Marital status _____   Year of current marriage _____

Dates, durations, and outcomes of previous marriages _____

_____

_____

Highest level of formal education _____

Military history _____

_____

Occupation _____

Occupational/work history _____

_____

_____

Income level and degree of financial security _____

_____

Religion and extent of practice _____

Number of pregnancies _____

Number of live births _____

Number of live-birth children who died _____

Names, sexes, and circumstances _____

_____

_____

Number and dates of abortions _____

_____

Number and dates of miscarriages _____

_____

Number, dates, sexes, gestational ages, and postdeath rituals for stillbirths

_____

_____

Surviving children (names, sexes, ages, occupations, family status, health, locations)

_____

_____

_____

_____

_____

_____

Family-of-origin members (names, sexes, ages, occupations, family status, health, locations)

_____

_____

_____

_____

_____

_____

Close relatives, friends, and other supports (names, sexes, ages, occupations, family status, health, locations)

_____

_____

_____

_____

_____

_____

_____

_____

Prior losses (physical and psychosocial)

_____

_____

_____

_____

_____

_____

_____

_____

Date of identified current loss(es) _____

_____

_____

_____

PART II: COMPREHENSIVE EVALUATION OF HISTORY, MENTAL STATUS, AND SELECTED PREMORBID PERSONALITY CHARACTERISTICS

The caregiver must obtain the following information according to the standard practices of the discipline to which he or she belongs.

Comprehensive Psychosocial/Medical History

- Presenting problem
- History of presenting problem
- Past personal history and current psychological functioning

> Psychosocial history and current functioning
> Occupational history and current functioning
> Past psychiatric history and current status
> Substance use history and current status
> Medical history and current status
> Financial history and current status

- Family history (psychosocial, psychiatric, medical, financial) and current status
- Concurrent stresses or crises

Mental Status Examination

In the modified mental status examination suggested here, the following areas must be evaluated.

- Appearance
- Behavior and psychomotor activity
- Speech and language
- Mood and affect
- Thought process and content
- Perceptual disturbances
- Sensorium functions
- Insight and judgment
- Symptoms of depression

- Symptoms of anxiety and post-traumatic stress disorder (PTSD)
- Suicide and homicide risk

Selected Premorbid Personality Characteristics

- Ego functioning and strength
- Coping and defense mechanisms, styles, and abilities (specifically when dealing with stress, anxiety, threat, and feelings)
- Frustration tolerance
- Personality dynamics and conflicts
- Characterological scripts
- Sense of self, self-concept, and self-esteem
- Internal versus external locus of control and processing
- Cognitive style and biases
- Problem-solving skills
- Maturity
- Assumptive world components
- Sense of personal meaning and fulfillment in life
- Philosophy of life and values
- Spirituality
- Communication style
- Relationship patterns
- Characteristic ways of managing psychosocial transitions
- Specific strengths, skills, and assets
- Specific vulnerabilities and liabilities

DIAGNOSTIC/CLINICAL IMPRESSIONS
BASED ON DATA FROM PARTS I AND II

_____

_____

_____

_____

_____

_____

_____

_____

_____

_____

_____

_____

_____

_____

_____

_____

_____

_____

_____

PART III: STRUCTURED INTERVIEW SCHEDULE

Topic Area A: Circumstances of the death; events that led up to and followed it

A–1. Tell me about the death and what led up to it.

a. If _____'s death followed an illness, please answer the following:

   (1) What was _____'s experience during his/her illness?

   (2) What was your experience during _____'s illness?

   (3) What was the length and course of the illness?

   (4) What, if any, was the nature of your participation in _____'s care during the illness?

   (5) Did you ever discuss _____'s dying with him/her? If so, what was this like?

   (6) What, if anything, was the nature of your anticipatory grief during _____'s illness?

   (7) What were the hardest parts for you in _____'s illness?

   (8) Do you have any unfinished business or unresolved conflicts about anything that happened or didn't happen during _____'s illness? If so, please explain.

   (9) What would you change, if anything, if you could about the illness experience for you? For _____?

   (10) Were you prepared when _____ died?

   (11) How could things have been better for you during _____'s illness? At his/her death?

   (12) What, if anything, do you feel good about regarding your interaction with _____ during his/her illness? Guilty about? Regretful about?

A–2. What happened immediately after the death and in the few days thereafter?

a. What kind of funeral activities or rituals took place?

   (1) How were they for you?

   (2) What kind of impact have they had on you?

Topic Area B: Nature and meaning of what has been lost

B–1. Tell me about _____.

    a. Help me to know him/her as a person.

    b. What was he/she like?

B–2. What type of relationship did the two of you have?

    a. How did you get along?

    b. How did your relationship start and what course did it take?

B–3. You've told me a great deal about what was positive in the relationship. Could you tell me a little about the aspects that were not so positive?

B–4. Exactly what did _____ and the relationship with him/her mean to you and give to you in your life?

    a. In what ways (positive and negative) did _____ help you or cause you to be the person that you are/were?

B–5. Specifically, what have you lost in your life physically or symbolically with _____'s death?

    a. What has/have been the impact(s) on you of this/these secondary loss(es)?

B–6. Do you have any unfinished business with _____? Anything you would have wanted to say or do that would have made you more comfortable with ending the relationship but that you never said or did and therefore lack closure on?

    a. What do you think you need to do to finish this business?

Topic Area C: Mourner's reactions to the death and coping attempts

C–1. Please describe for me the type, quality, extent, and intensity of all the various reactions you have had since _____'s death.

    a. What specific kinds of responses did you find yourself having and what particular kinds of behaviors did you witness in yourself?

    b. Did you have any reactions and/or behaviors that were unexpected or that frightened you? If so, what were they?

   c. Have you experienced any changes in your self-esteem, self-image, or sense of self? If so, what?

C–2. Tell me what you have done to cope with _____'s death.

   a. How do you cope on an everyday basis?

   b. Over the long haul?

   c. Do you have what you personally require to cope with this loss? If not, why do you think that you do not?

   d. If and when you feel pain over this loss, how do you deal with/defend against/protect yourself from it?

C–3. Please complete this sentence: "I feel that I am coping/have coped with this death . . ."

   a. Rate your coping on a scale of 1 (worst possible coping) to 10 (best possible coping).

C–4. How would you complete these sentences?

   a. "The things that I do/did that help/helped me the most are/were . . ."

   b. "If I have/had problems related to this loss, they seem/seemed to be in the areas of . . ."

   c. "The most difficult parts of this for me are/have been . . ."

   d. "My most major concerns in all of this are . . ."

   e. "What I have specifically done to try and help myself is . . ."

Topic Area D: Reactions of others in the mourner's world and perceived degree of support

D–1. How have others reacted to _____'s death?

D–2. How have they reacted to your reactions?

   a. How have their reactions affected you?

D–3. Have your relationships with others changed since _____'s death?

   a. If so, with whom, how, and why?

   b. How do you feel about these changes?

   c. Have these changes caused you any specific problems?

D–4. What types of support have you received from others to help you cope with _____'s death?

    a. Who gave it and what did they do?

    b. What was helpful? Not helpful?

    c. Do you have some person(s) you can confide in? If so, who?

D–5. Were there any types of support or recognition you required but did not receive or any specific persons from whom you needed support or recognition but did not receive it?

    a. Why do you think this happened?

D–6. How did the support or recognition you did and did not receive affect you and your grief and mourning?

D–7. What needs for support or recognition remain unmet?

    a. From whom in particular?

Topic Area E: Changes in the mourner and the mourner's life since the death

E–1. Please describe what has happened to you in the time since _____ died. For example, what changes (either gains or losses; internal or external; physical or psychosocial; psychological, behavioral, social, physical, spiritual, occupational, or financial), if any, have occurred to you, in you, and in your life since _____'s death?

E–2. Do you feel changed by this death?

    a. If so, in what ways are you different (positively and negatively)?

    b. In what ways are you the same as before?

    c. What percentage of your old self are you back to?

    d. Do you feel, think, or act any differently than before? If so, how?

    e. What is the current impact, if any, of grief and mourning on your ability to function normally (psychologically, behaviorally, socially, physically, spiritually, occupationally, financially)?

    f. Have you blocked off any corners of the world since the death?

g. Have you experienced any changes in habits, activities, pleasures?

h. Have any new problems developed since _____'s death?

E-3. If this death has affected the way you look at and live life, how has it done so?

a. How has the death affected your assumptive world (i.e., your assumptions, expectations, and beliefs about and view of the world), religion, or philosophy of life?

E-4. What, if anything, have you learned (positively or negatively) from this loss?

Topic Area F: Mourner's relationship to the deceased and stimuli associated with the deceased

F-1. How would you describe _____'s role, if any, in your life at this time? In other words, do you have an ongoing sense of connection to _____ or does _____ play an active part in your ongoing life?

a. Do you think about _____?

b. Talk to _____?

c. Have you found yourself acting, thinking, or feeling in any ways _____ used to act, think, or feel? If so, how?

d. How do you relate to _____ at this time, if you do?

e. What types of things do you do to keep _____ "alive" to yourself and others or to maintain a sense of connection with _____?

f. What, if anything, do you do to memorialize _____?

g. What is it like for you to have this type of relationship or sense of connection with _____?

h. How do you feel about the ways in which you relate to, maintain a sense of connection to, or keep _____ "alive"?

i. What is the meaning in your life today of your current relationship with _____?

j. What about you today is influenced (positively or negatively) by your current relationship with _____?

k. What is your current image of yourself with regard to _____ (e.g., dependent child, adult)?

1. Was there anything in _____ that you would choose to develop in yourself? If so, what?

F–2. Many times after a person loses a loved one, he or she has some experiences in which there is a sense of the presence of the loved one. Sometimes the mourner takes these experiences as a "sign" or as some form of communication from the loved one. Sometimes there are vivid dreams, or the mourner has an experience of seeing the image of the deceased or hearing that person's voice. Sometimes mourners are reluctant to talk about this because they think it makes them sound crazy, even though they are not. I know that this happens with many mourners, and I am wondering if anything like this has ever happened to you. Have you ever had any of these types of experiences or anything like them?

   a. What was it like for you to have this happen?

   b. How did you respond?

   c. What was the nature of the experience for you? Did you view it as positive (as comforting or something that made you feel good) or was it more negative (something frightening that you would not want to have happen again)?

F–3. How are you choosing to deal with _____'s room? Clothing? Other possessions?

   a. What is this like for you?

   b. Have you saved any special items?

      (1) What do you do with it/them?

      (2) Where do you keep it/them?

      (3) What made you choose it/them?

      (4) What does/do it/they represent to you?

      (5) How does/do it/they make you feel when you encounter it/them?

F–4. At this point, how is it for you when you come across things that remind you of _____ or bring back memories of him/her? For example, how may you react when you see pictures of him/her, suddenly remember a special time you shared, or go to an event and wish he/she would be there with you, such as a wedding or holiday gathering?

a. How do you tend to handle these things?

b. Are there some things that are more difficult than others?

c. What kind of reactions, if any, do you have?

d. What types of memories tend to come back to you?

e. What characteristics do your memories have and what types of reactions do they precipitate in you?

f. Do you talk about your memories to anyone? If so, who?

g. Is it comfortable or uncomfortable to remember _____? Under what conditions?

F–5. Have you noticed any responses on your part around the anniversary of the death, during other occasions, or under other circumstances (i.e., STUG reactions)?

a. If so, what are they like?

b. How intense are they?

c. How do you cope with them?

F–6. How do you think _____ would want you to respond in your grief and mourning over him/her?

a. What would he/she want of you as you live without him/her?

b. Did you and _____ ever discuss how he/she wanted you to go on? If so, what was said?

c. Even if you two never discussed this topic, what do you think _____ would expect you to do?

d. Is there anything from your relationship with _____ that guides you in your going on without him/her? If so, what?

Topic Area G: History, status, and influence of prior loss experiences, including mourner's methods of coping

G–1. What other difficult physical or psychosocial losses have you experienced in your life?

G–2. What types of things did you do to cope with each loss?

a. How effective were you in coping?

b. In what ways did the loss affect you then?

    c. How does the loss affect you now, if it still does?

    d. Did you learn anything in particular from the loss?

    e. Was that loss different for you from this one? If so, in what ways?

Topic Area H: Mourner's self-assessment of healthy accommodation of the loss now and in the future

H-1. Compared to how you coped with and functioned in life in general prior to the death, how do you think you are doing now?

    a. Rate your previous and present general coping on a scale of 1 (worst possible coping) to 10 (best possible coping).

H-2. How do you think you are coping/have coped with this specific loss?

    a. Rate your coping on a scale of 1 (worst possible coping) to 10 (best possible coping).

H-3. To what extent, if any, has the loss been integrated into your life?

H-4. How do you view the future?

H-5. How do you think you will ultimately do in your grief and mourning, and in learning to live without _____?

    a. Rate how you think you will ultimately do on a scale of 1 (worst possible outcome) to 10 (best possible outcome).

H-6. What remains for you to do or change in your grief and mourning and in your life to reach the point where you will be doing the best you can in coping with this loss and living without _____?

H-7. Have you made a decision to "make it"?

H-8. In what areas is/will it be the hardest to rebuild your life and/or to reinvest in it?

    a. The easiest?

H-9. How do you, if you do, make sense out of this loss and its having occurred in your life?

H–10. In retrospect thus far, is there anything you would do differently in your grief and mourning?

Topic Area I: Mourner's degree of realistic comprehension of and expectations for grief and mourning

I–1. What do you think is necessary to cope with or survive a loss like this?

I–2. In your estimation, what is normal to experience after this kind of death?

I–3. In what ways do you think you have been a healthy and successful mourner?

   a. In what ways do you think you have been unhealthy or unsuccessful?

I–4. How do you anticipate the rest of your mourning will go?

I–5. What will indicate to you when you have achieved the best possible accommodation of this loss or are coping the very best you ever will be able to with _____'s death?

Topic Area J: Open topic

J–1. Are there any areas pertinent to your grief and mourning that we have not examined?

J–2. Are there any topics we have discussed that you feel we should consider further?

J–3. What do you feel is the most important piece of information about your grief and mourning?

DIAGNOSTIC/CLINICAL IMPRESSIONS
BASED ON DATA FROM PART III

_____

_____

_____

_____

_____

_____

_____

_____

_____

_____

_____

_____

_____

_____

_____

_____

_____

_____

_____

_____

_____

SUMMARY: DIAGNOSTIC/CLINICAL IMPRESSIONS BASED ON SYNTHESIS OF PARTS I, II, and III

_____

_____

_____

_____

_____

_____

_____

_____

_____

_____

_____

_____

_____

_____

_____

_____

_____

_____

REFERENCES

Abraham, K. (1949a). Notes on the psycho-analytical investigation and treatment of manic depressive insanity and allied conditions. In K. Abraham, *Selected papers on psycho-analysis*. London: Hogarth. (Original work published 1911)

Abraham, K. (1949b). A short study of the development of the libido; viewed in the light of mental disorders. In K. Abraham, *Selected papers on psycho-analysis*. London: Hogarth. (Original work published 1924)

Abrahms, J. (1981). Depression versus normal grief following the death of a significant other. In G. Emery, S. Hollon, & R. Bedrosian (Eds.), *New directions in cognitive therapy*. New York: Guilford.

Aguilera, D. (1990). *Crisis intervention: Theory and methodology*. St. Louis: C. V. Mosby.

AIDS update. (1990). *Hospice, 1*(3), 5.

Akiskal, H., & McKinney, W. (1973). Depressive disorders: Towards a unified hypothesis. *Science, 182,* 20–29.

Akiskal, H., & McKinney, W. (1975). Overview of recent research in depression. *Archives of General Psychiatry, 32,* 285–305.

Alarcon, R. (1984). Single case study: Personality disorder as a pathogenic factor in bereavement. *Journal of Nervous and Mental Disease, 172,* 45–47.

American Psychiatric Association. (1987). *Diagnostic and statistical manual of mental disorders* (3rd ed. rev.). Washington, DC: Author.

Amick-McMullan, A., Kilpatrick, D., Veronen, L., & Smith, S. (1989). Family survivors of homicide victims: Theoretical perspectives and an exploratory study. *Journal of Traumatic Stress, 2,* 21–35.

Anable, W. (1978). Homicidal threat as grief work. *Psychiatric Opinion, 15,* 43–46.

Anderson, C. (1949). Aspects of pathological grief and mourning. *The International Journal of Psycho-Analysis, 30,* 48–55.

Anderson, G., Gurdin, P., & Thomas, A. (1989). Dual disenfranchisement: Foster parenting children with AIDS. In K. Doka (Ed.), *Disenfranchised grief: Recognizing hidden sorrow*. Lexington, MA: Lexington.

Andrews, G., Tennant, C., Hewson, D., & Vaillant, G. (1978). Life event stress, social support, coping style, and risk of psychological impairment. *Journal of Nervous and Mental Disease, 166,* 307–316.

Andriote, J. M. (1986, September 19–25). The survivors: How do you grieve the loss of a forbidden love? *City Paper* (Washington's Free Weekly), *6*(38).

Andriote, J. M. (1987, April). *The special needs of AIDS survivors.* Paper presented at the annual meeting of the Massachusetts Psychological Association, Cambridge, MA.

Anthony, E., & Koupernik, C. (Eds.). (1973). *The child in his family: The impact of disease and death* (Vol. 2). New York: Wiley.

Appel, Y., & Wrobleski, A. (1987). Self-help and support groups: Mutual aid for survivors. In E. Dunne, J. McIntosh, & K. Dunne-Maxim (Eds.), *Suicide and its aftermath: Understanding and counseling the survivors.* New York: Norton.

Arieti, S., & Bemporad, J. (1978). *Severe and mild depression.* New York: Basic.

Arkin, A. (1973). The use of medications in the management of the dying patient and in the bereaved. In I. Goldberg, S. Malitz, & A. H. Kutscher (Eds.), *Psychopharmacologic agents for the terminally ill and bereaved.* New York: Columbia University Press.

Attig, T. (1986, April). *Grief, love and separation.* Paper presented at the eighth annual conference of the Forum for Death Education and Counseling, Atlanta.

Averill, J. (1968). Grief: Its nature and significance. *Psychological Bulletin, 70,* 721–748.

Averill, J., & Wisocki, P. (1981). Some observations on behavioral approaches to the treatment of grief among the elderly. In H. J. Sobel (Ed.), *Behavior therapy in terminal care: A humanistic approach.* Cambridge, MA: Ballinger.

Bahr, H. M., & Harvey, C. D. (1979). Correlates of loneliness among widows bereaved in a mining disaster. *Psychological Reports, 44,* 367–385.

Bahr, H. M., & Harvey, C. D. (1980). Correlates of morale among the newly widowed. *Journal of Social Psychology, 110,* 219–233.

Baker, H., & Brewerton, D. (1981). Rheumatoid arthritis: A psychiatric assessment. *British Medical Journal, 282,* 2014.

Bankoff, E. (1981). *The informal social network and adaptation to widowhood.* Unpublished doctoral dissertation, University of Chicago.

Bankoff, E. (1983a). Aged parents and their widowed daughters: A support relationship. *Journal of Gerontology, 38,* 226–230.

Bankoff, E. (1983b). Social support and adaptation to widowhood. *Journal of Marriage and the Family, 45,* 827–839.

Bard, M., & Sangrey, D. (1986). *The crime victim's book* (2nd ed.). New York: Brunner/Mazel.

Barnacle, C. (1949). Grief reactions and their treatment. *Diseases of the Nervous System, 10,* 173–176.

Barnes, D. (1987). Previous losses: Forgotten but not resolved. In M. A. Morgan (Ed.), *Bereavement: Helping the survivors* (Proceedings of the 1987 King's College Conference). London, Ontario: King's College.

Barrett, C. (1978). Effectiveness of widows' groups in facilitating change. *Journal of Counsulting and Clinical Psychology, 46*, 20–31.

Barrett, T., & Scott, T. (1986, May). *Suicide versus other bereavement recovery patterns.* Paper presented at the joint meeting of the American Association of Suicidology and the International Association for Suicide Prevention, San Francisco.

Barry, M. (1973). The prolonged grief reaction. *Mayo Clinic Proceedings, 48*, 329–335.

Barry, M. (1981). Therapeutic experience with patients referred for "prolonged grief reaction": Some second thoughts. *Mayo Clinic Proceedings, 56*, 744–748.

Barton, D. (1977a). The family of the dying person. In D. Barton (Ed.), *Dying and death: A clinical guide for caregivers.* Baltimore: Williams & Wilkins.

Barton, D. (1977b). The process of grief. In D. Barton (Ed.), *Dying and death: A clinical guide for caregivers.* Baltimore: Williams & Wilkins.

Beattie, M. (1987). *Codependent no more.* New York: Harper & Row.

Belitsky, R., & Jacobs, S. (1986). Bereavement, attachment theory, and mental disorders. *Psychiatric Annals, 16*, 276–280.

Bendiksen, R., & Fulton, R. (1975). Death and the child: An anterospective test of the childhood bereavement and later behavior disorder hypothesis. *Omega, 6*, 45–59.

Benedek, T. (1970). The family as a psychologic field. In J. Anthony & T. Benedek (Eds.), *Parenthood: Its psychology and psychopathology.* Boston: Little, Brown.

Bergler, E. (1948). Psychopathology and duration of mourning in neurotics. *Journal of Clinical Psychopathology, 9*, 478–482.

Berlinsky, E., & Biller, H. (1982). *Parental death and psychological development.* Lexington, MA: Lexington.

Bibring, E. (1954). Psychoanalysis and the dynamic psychotherapies. *Journal of the American Psychoanalytic Association, 2*, 745–770.

Billow, C. (1987). A multiple family support group for survivors of suicide. In E. Dunne, J. McIntosh, & K. Dunne-Maxim (Eds.), *Suicide and its aftermath: Understanding and counseling the survivors.* New York: Norton.

Birtchnell, J. (1975). Psychiatric breakdown following recent parent death. *British Journal of Medical Psychology, 48*, 379–390.

Birtchnell, J. (1981). In search of correspondence between age at psychiatric breakdown and parental age of death—"Anniversary reactions." *British Journal of Medical Psychology, 54*, 111–120.

Black, C. (1987). *It will never happen to me.* New York: Ballantine.

Blanchard, C., Blanchard, E., & Becker, J. (1976). The young widow: Depressive symptomatology throughout the grief process. *Psychiatry, 39*, 394–399.

Blankfield, A. (1982–1983). Grief and alcohol. *American Journal of Drug & Alcohol Abuse, 9*, 435–446.

Blankfield, A. (1989). Grief, alcohol dependence and women. *Drug and Alcohol Dependence, 24*(1), 45–49.

Blauner, R. (1966). Death and social structure. *Psychiatry, 29,* 378–394.

Bloom-Feshbach, J., & Bloom-Feshbach, S. (Eds.). (1987). *The psychology of separation and loss.* San Francisco: Jossey-Bass.

Bolton, I. (1986). Death of a child by suicide. In T. A. Rando (Ed.), *Parental loss of a child.* Champaign, IL: Research Press.

Bolton, I., & Mitchell, C. (1983). *My son . . . My son . . . A guide to healing after a suicide in the family.* (Available from Bolton Press, 1325 Belmore Way N. E., Atlanta, GA 30338)

Bornstein, P., Clayton, P., Halikas, J., Maurice, W., & Robins, E. (1973). The depression of widowhood after 13 months. *British Journal of Psychiatry, 122,* 561–566.

Bowen, M. (1976). Family reaction to death. In P. Guerin (Ed.), *Family therapy: Theory and practice.* New York: Gardner.

Bowlby, J. (1960). Grief and mourning in infancy and early childhood. *The Psychoanalytic Study of the Child, 15,* 9–52.

Bowlby, J. (1961a). Childhood mourning and its implications for psychiatry. *The American Journal of Psychiatry, 118,* 481–498.

Bowlby, J. (1961b). Processes of mourning. *The International Journal of Psycho-Analysis, 42,* 317–340.

Bowlby, J. (1963). Pathological mourning and childhood mourning. *Journal of the American Psychoanalytic Association, 11,* 500–541.

Bowlby, J. (1969). *Attachment and loss: Vol. 1. Attachment.* New York: Basic.

Bowlby, J. (1973). *Attachment and loss: Vol. 2. Separation: Anxiety and anger.* New York: Basic.

Bowlby, J. (1980). *Attachment and Loss: Vol. 3. Loss: Sadness and depression.* New York: Basic.

Bowlby, J. (1982). Attachment and loss: Retrospect and prospect. *American Journal of Orthopsychiatry, 52,* 664–678.

Bowlby, J. (1988). *A secure base: Parent-child attachment and healthy human development.* New York: Basic.

Brabant, S. (1989–1990). Old pain or new pain: A social psychological approach to recurrent grief. *Omega, 20,* 273–279.

Bradshaw, J. (1988a). *Bradshaw on: The family: A revolutionary way of self-discovery.* Deerfield Beach, FL: Health Communications.

Bradshaw, J. (1988b). *Healing the shame that binds you.* Deerfield Beach, FL: Health Communications.

Brasted, W., & Callahan, E. (1984). A behavioral analysis of the grief process. *Behavior Therapy, 15,* 529–543.

Brenner, C. (1976). *Psychoanalytic technique and psychic conflict.* New York: International Universities Press.

Breuer, J., & Freud, S. (1955). Case 5: Fraulein Elisabeth von R. In J. Strachey (Ed. and Trans.), *The standard edition of the complete psychological works of Sigmund Freud* (Vol. 2). London: Hogarth. (Original work published 1893)

Briscoe, C., & Smith, J. (1975). Depression in bereavement and divorce. *Archives of General Psychiatry, 32,* 439–443.

Brom, D., Kleber, R., & Defares, P. (1989). Brief psychotherapy for post traumatic stress disorders. *Journal of Consulting and Clinical Psychology, 57,* 607–612.

Brown, G. (1982). Early loss and depression. In C. M. Parkes & J. Stevenson-Hinde (Eds.), *The place of attachment in human behavior.* New York: Basic.

Brown, G., & Harris, T. (1978). *The social origins of depression.* London: Tavistock.

Brown, J., & Stoudemire, G. (1983). Normal and pathological grief. *Journal of the American Medical Association, 250,* 378–382.

Bruce, M., Kim, K., Leaf, P., & Jacobs, S. (1990). Depressive episodes and dysphoria resulting from conjugal bereavement in a prospective community sample. *American Journal of Psychiatry, 147,* 608–611.

Bugen, L. (1979). Human grief: A model for prediction and intervention. In L. Bugen (Ed.), *Death and dying: Therapy, research, practice.* Dubuque, IA: William C. Brown.

Bunney, W., Goodwin, F., & Murphy, D. (1972). The "switch process" in manic-depressive illness: Part 3. Theoretical implications. *Archives of General Psychiatry, 27,* 312–319.

Burch, B. (1988). Melanie Klein's work: An adaptation in practice. *Clinical Social Work Journal, 16*(2), 125–142.

Burgess, A. (1975). Family reaction to homicide. *American Journal of Orthopsychiatry, 45,* 391–398.

Burnell, G., & Burnell, A. (1989). *Clinical management of bereavement: A handbook for healthcare professionals.* New York: Human Sciences.

Cain, A. (Ed.). (1972). *Survivors of suicide.* Springfield, IL: Charles C Thomas.

Calhoun, L. G., Selby, J. W., & Selby, L. E. (1982). The psychological aftermath of suicide: An analysis of current evidence. *Clinical Psychology Review, 2,* 409–420.

Cameron, J., & Parkes, C. M. (1983). Terminal care: Evaluation of effects on surviving family of care before and after bereavement. *Postgraduate Medical Journal, 59,* 73–78.

Campbell, J., Swank, P., & Vincent, K. (1991). The role of hardiness in the resolution of grief. *Omega, 23,* 53–65.

Cannon, W. (1927). *Bodily changes in pain, hunger, fear and rage* (2nd ed.). New York: Appleton-Century-Crofts.

Caplan, G. (1964). *Principles of preventive psychiatry.* New York: Basic.

Capstick, N., & Seldrup, J. (1973). Phenomenological aspects of obsessional patients treated with clomipramine. *British Journal of Psychiatry, 122,* 719–720.

Carey, R. (1977). The widowed: A year later. *Journal of Counseling Psychology,* 24, 125–131.

Cassel, E. (1982). The nature of suffering and the goals of medicine. *The New England Journal of Medicine, 306,* 639–645.

Cassem, N. (1975). Bereavement as indispensable for growth. In B. Schoenberg, I. Gerber, A. Wiener, A. H. Kutscher, D. Peretz, & A. C. Carr (Eds.), *Bereavement: Its psychosocial aspects.* New York: Columbia University Press.

Cattell, R., Eber, H., & Tatsuoka, M. (1970). *Handbook for the 16 Personality Factor Questionnaire.* Champaign, IL: Institute for Personality and Ability Testing.

Centers for Disease Control. (1991). *Morbidity and Mortality Weekly Report, 40*(3).

Cermak, T. (1986). *Diagnosing and treating co-dependence.* Minneapolis: The Johnson Institute.

Chenoweth, R., Tonge, J., & Armstrong, J. (1980). Suicide in Brisbane— A retrospective psychosocial study. *Australian and New Zealand Journal of Psychiatry, 14,* 37–45.

Chodoff, P. (1975). Psychiatric aspects of the Nazi persecution. In S. Arieti (Ed.), *American handbook of psychiatry* (Vol. 6., 2nd ed.). New York: Basic.

Church, J. (1974). The Buffalo Creek disaster: Extent and range of emotional problems and/or behavioral problems. *Omega, 5,* 61–63.

Clark, A. (1982). Grief and Gestalt therapy. *The Gestalt Journal, 5,* 49–63.

Clayton, P. (1974). Mortality and morbidity in the first years of widowhood. *Archives of General Psychiatry, 30,* 747–750.

Clayton, P. (1979). The sequelae and nonsequelae of conjugal bereavement. *American Journal of Psychiatry, 136,* 1530–1534.

Clayton, P. (1982). Bereavement. In E. Paykel (Ed.), *Handbook of affective disorders.* New York: Guilford.

Clayton, P., & Darvish, H. (1979). Course of depressive symptoms following the stress of bereavement. In J. Barrett (Ed.), *Stress and mental disorder.* New York: Raven.

Clayton, P., Desmarais, L., & Winokur, G. (1968). A study of normal bereavement. *American Journal of Psychiatry, 125,* 64–74.

Clayton, P., Halikas, J., & Maurice, W. (1971). The bereavement of the widowed. *Diseases of the Nervous System, 32,* 597–604.

Clayton, P., Halikas, J., & Maurice, W. (1972). The depression of widowhood. *British Journal of Psychiatry, 120,* 71–78.

Clayton, P., Herjanic, M., Murphy, G., & Woodruff, R. (1974). Mourning and depression: Their similarities and differences. *Canadian Psychiatric Association Journal, 19,* 309–312.

Colburn, K., & Malena, D. (1988). Bereavement issues for survivors of persons with AIDS: Coping with society's pressures. *The American Journal of Hospice Care, 5*(5), 20–24.

Coleman, S. (1975). *Death as a social agent in addict families.* Paper presented at the annual convention of the American Psychological Association, Chicago.

Coleman, S. (1980). Incomplete mourning and addict family transactions: A theory for understanding heroin abuse. In D. Lettieri (Ed.), *Theories on drug abuse* (National Institute on Drug Abuse, Research Monograph 30, DHHS Publication No. ADM 80–967). Washington, DC: U. S. Government Printing Office.

Coleman, S. (1991). Intergenerational patterns of traumatic loss: Death and despair in addict families. In F. Walsh & M. McGoldrick (Eds.), *Living beyond loss: Death in the family.* New York: Norton.

Coleman, S., & Stanton, M. (1978). The role of death in the addict family. *Journal of Marital and Family Counseling, 4,* 79–91.

Conley, B. (1986). *Handling the holidays: C.O.P.E.* (Available from Human Services Press, PO Box 2423, Springfield, IL 62705)

Corr, C., & McNeil, J. (Eds.). (1986). *Adolescence and death.* New York: Springer.

Courtois, C. (1988). *Healing the incest wound: Adult survivors in therapy.* New York: Norton.

Danieli, Y. (1985). The treatment and prevention of long-term effects and intergenerational transmission of victimization: A lesson from holocaust survivors and their children. In C. Figley (Ed.), *Trauma and its wake: The study and treatment of post-traumatic stress disorder.* New York: Brunner/Mazel.

Danieli, Y. (1988). Treating survivors and children of survivors of the Nazi holocaust. In F. Ochberg (Ed.), *Post-traumatic therapy and victims of violence.* New York: Brunner/Mazel.

Danto, B., Bruhns, J., & Kutscher, A. H. (Eds.). (1982). *The human side of homicide.* New York: Columbia University Press.

d'Aquili, E., Laughlin, C., & McManus, J. (Eds.). (1979). *The spectrum of ritual: A biogenetic structural analysis.* New York: Columbia University Press.

Davanloo, H. (1978). *Basic principles and techniques in short-term dynamic psychotherapy.* New York: Spectrum.

Davidowitz, M., & Myrick, R. (1984). Responding to the bereaved: An analysis of "helping" statements. *Research Record, 1,* 35–42.

Davis, H., & Franklin, R. (1970). "Continuing grief" as a method of psychotherapy following EST. *Diseases of the Nervous System, 31,* 626–630.

Day, G. (1951). The psychosomatic approach to pulmonary tuberculosis. *Lancet, i,* 1025–1028.

Dean, L., Hall, W., & Martin, J. (1988). Chronic and intermittent AIDS-related bereavement in a panel of homosexual men in New York City. *Journal of Palliative Care, 4,* 54–57.

Demi, A. S. (1984). Social adjustment of widows after a sudden death: Suicide and non-suicide survivors compared. *Death Education, 8* (Suppl.), 91–111.

Dennehy, C. (1966). Childhood bereavement and psychiatric illness. *British Journal of Psychiatry, 112,* 1049–1069.

Deutsch, H. (1937). Absence of grief. *Psychoanalytic Quarterly, 6,* 12–22.

DeVaul, R., & Zisook, S. (1976). Unresolved grief: Clinical considerations. *Postgraduate Medicine, 59,* 267–271.

DeVaul, R., Zisook, S., & Faschingbauer, T. (1979). Clinical aspects of grief and bereavement. *Primary Care, 6,* 391–402.

Dimsdale, J. (1974). The coping behavior of Nazi concentration camp survivors. *American Journal of Psychiatry, 131,* 792–797.

Dimsdale, J. (Ed.). (1980). *Survivors, victims and perpetrators: Essays on the Nazi holocaust.* New York: Hemisphere.

Dixson, M., & Clearwater, H. (1991). Accidents. In D. Levitan (Ed.), *Horrendous death, health, and well-being.* New York: Hemisphere.

Dohrenwend, B., & Dohrenwend, B. (1974). *Stressful life events: Their nature and effects.* New York: Wiley.

Doka, K. (Ed.). (1989). *Disenfranchised grief: Recognizing hidden sorrow.* Lexington, MA: Lexington.

Donnelly, K. (1982). *Recovering from the loss of a child.* New York: Macmillan.

Dopson, C. (1979). Unresolved grief presenting as chronic lymphedema of the hand. *American Journal of Psychiatry, 136,* 1333–1334.

Dorpat, T. (1973). Suicide, loss, and mourning. *Life-Threatening Behavior, 3*(3), 213–224.

Drucker, P. (1969). *The age of discontinuity.* New York: Harper & Row.

Dunne, E. (1987). Special needs of suicide survivors in therapy. In E. Dunne, J. L. McIntosh, & K. Dunne-Maxim (Eds.), *Suicide and its aftermath: Understanding and counseling the survivors.* New York: Norton.

Dunne, E., McIntosh, J. L., & Dunne-Maxim, K. (Eds.). (1987). *Suicide and its aftermath: Understanding and counseling the survivors.* New York: Norton.

Eggert, D. (1983). *Eysenck-Persönlichkeits-Inventar* [Eysenck Personality Inventory]. Göttingen, West Germany: Hogrefe.

Eitinger, L. (1980). The concentration camp syndrome and its late sequelae. In J. Dimsdale (Ed.), *Survivors, victims and perpetrators: Essays on the Nazi holocaust.* New York: Hemisphere.

Eitinger, L., & Askevold, F. (1968). Psychiatric aspects. In A. Strom (Ed.), *Concentration camp survivors.* New York: Humanities.

Engel, G. (1961). Is grief a disease? A challenge for medical research. *Psychosomatic Medicine, 23,* 18–22.

Engel, G. (1962a). Anxiety and depression-withdrawal: The primary affects of unpleasure. *The International Journal of Psycho-Analysis, 43,* 87–89.

Engel, G. (1962b). *Psychological development in health and disease.* Philidelphia: Saunders.

Engel, G. (1964). Grief and grieving. *American Journal of Nursing, 64*(9), 93–98.

Engel, G. (1967). Psychoanalytic theory of somatic disorder. *Journal of the American Psychoanalytic Association, 15,* 344–365.

Engel, G. (1968). A life setting conducive to illness: The giving-up, given-up complex. *Archives of Internal Medicine, 69,* 293–300.

Erickson, E. (1963). *Childhood and society* (2nd ed.). New York: Norton.

Erickson, K. (1976a). *Everything in its path: Destruction of community in the Buffalo Creek flood.* New York: Simon & Schuster.

Erickson, K. (1976b). Loss of communality at Buffalo Creek. *American Journal of Psychiatry, 133,* 302–304.

Erickson, K. (1979). *In the wake of the flood.* London: Allen & Unwin.

Evans, D., Jeckel, L., & Slott, N. (1982). Erotomania: A variant of pathological mourning. *Bulletin of the Menninger Clinic, 46*(6), 507–520.

Eysenck, H. (1967). Single-trial conditioning, neurosis and the Napalkov phenomenon. *Behaviour Research and Therapy, 5,* 63–65.

Eysenck, H. (1968). A theory of the incubation of anxiety/fear responses. *Behaviour Research and Therapy, 6,* 309–321.

Eysenck, H., & Eysenck, S. (1964). *Manual of the Eysenck Personality Inventory.* London: University of London Press.

Faravelli, C., & Pallanti, S. (1989). Recent life events and panic disorder. *American Journal of Psychiatry, 146,* 622–626.

Faschingbauer, T., Zisook, S., & DeVaul, R. (1987). The Texas Revised Inventory of Grief. In S. Zisook (Ed.), *Biopsychosocial aspects of bereavement.* Washington, DC: American Psychiatric Press.

FBI reports: Violent crimes up 10%. (1991, April 29). *Providence Journal,* pp. A1, A6.

Federal Bureau of Investigation. (1990). *Uniform crime reports for the United States.* Washington, DC: U. S. Department of Justice.

Feifel, H. (1971). The meaning of death in American society: Implications for education. In B. Green & D. Irish (Eds.), *Death education: Preparation for living.* Cambridge, MA: Schenkman.

Fenichel, O. (1945). *The psychoanalytic theory of neurosis.* New York: Norton.

Ferguson, T. (1973). Decision-making and tranquilizers in widowhood. In I. Goldberg, S. Malitz, & A. H. Kutscher (Eds.), *Psychopharmacologic agents for the terminally ill and bereaved.* New York: Columbia University Press.

Figley, C. (1985a). From victim to survivor: Social responsibility in the wake of catastrophe. In C. Figley (Ed.), *Trauma and its wake: The study and treatment of post-traumatic stress disorder.* New York: Brunner/Mazel.

Figley, C. (Ed.). (1985b). *Trauma and its wake: The study and treatment of post-traumatic stress disorder.* New York: Brunner/Mazel.

Figley, C. (1986). *Trauma and its wake: Vol. 2. Traumatic stress theory, research, and intervention.* New York: Brunner/Mazel.

Figley, C., & McCubbin, H. (Eds.). (1983). *Stress and the family: Vol. 2. Coping with catastrophe.* New York: Brunner/Mazel.

Finlay-Jones, R. (1981). Showing that life events are a cause of depression—A review. *Australian and New Zealand Journal of Psychiatry, 15,* 229–238.

Fish, W. (1986). Differences of grief intensity in bereaved parents. In T. A. Rando (Ed.), *Parental loss of a child.* Champaign, IL: Research Press.

Flannery, R. (1987). From victim to survivor: A stress management approach in the treatment of learned helplessness. In B. van der Kolk (Ed.), *Psychological trauma.* Washington, DC: American Psychiatric Press.

Flesch, R. (1977). Mental health and bereavement by accident or suicide: A preliminary report. In B. Danto & A. H. Kutscher (Eds.), *Suicide and bereavement.* New York: MSS Information Corporation.

Forrest, G., Standish, E., & Baum, J. (1982). Support after perinatal death: A study of support and counselling after perinatal bereavement. *British Medical Journal, 285,* 1475–1479.

Freiberg, P. (1991, February). Women and AIDS: The crisis mounts. *The APA Monitor,* p. 30.

Freud, S. (1955a). Beyond the pleasure principle. In J. Strachey (Ed. and Trans.), *The standard edition of the complete psychological works of Sigmund Freud* (Vol. 18). London: Hogarth. (Original work published 1920)

Freud, S. (1955b). Notes upon a case of obsessional neurosis. In J. Strachey (Ed. and Trans.), *The standard edition of the complete psychological works of Sigmund Freud* (Vol. 10). London: Hogarth. (Original work published 1909)

Freud, S. (1955c). Totem and taboo. In J. Strachey (Ed. and Trans.), *The standard edition of the complete psychological works of Sigmund Freud* (Vol. 13). London: Hogarth. (Original work published 1913)

Freud, S. (1957a). Contributions to a discussion on suicide. In J. Strachey (Ed. and Trans.), *The standard edition of the complete psychological works of Sigmund Freud* (Vol. 11). London: Hogarth. (Original work published 1910)

Freud, S. (1957b). Five lectures on psycho-analysis. In J. Strachey (Ed. and Trans.), *The standard edition of the complete psychological works of Sigmund Freud* (Vol. 11). London: Hogarth. (Original work published 1910)

Freud, S. (1957c). Mourning and melancholia. In J. Strachey (Ed. and Trans.), *The standard edition of the complete psychological works of Sigmund Freud* (Vol. 14). London: Hogarth. (Original work published 1917)

Freud, S. (1957d). On narcissism: An introduction. In J. Strachey (Ed. and Trans.), *The standard edition of the complete psychological works of Sigmund Freud* (Vol. 14). London: Hogarth. (Original work published 1914)

Freud, S. (1957e). Thoughts for the times on war and death. In E. Jones (Ed.), *Collected papers of Sigmund Freud* (Vol. 14). London: Hogarth. (Original work published 1915)

Freud, S. (1957f). On transience. In J. Strachey (Ed. and Trans.), *The standard edition of the complete psychological works of Sigmund Freud* (Vol. 14). London: Hogarth. (Original work published 1916)

Freud, S. (1959a). Creative writers and day-dreaming. In J. Strachey (Ed. and Trans.), *The standard edition of the complete psychological works of Sigmund Freud* (Vol. 9). London: Hogarth. (Original work published 1908)

Freud, S. (1959b). Inhibitions, symptoms, and anxiety. In J. Strachey (Ed. and Trans.), *The standard edition of the complete psychological works of Sigmund Freud* (Vol. 20). London: Hogarth. (Original work published 1926)

Freud, S. (1960). Letter to Binswanger (Letter 239). In E. L. Freud (Ed.), *Letters of Sigmund Freud*. New York: Basic. (Original work published 1929)

Freud, S. (1961). The ego and the id. In J. Strachey (Ed. and Trans.), *The standard edition of the complete psychological works of Sigmund Freud* (Vol. 19). London: Hogarth. (Original work published 1923)

Freud, S. (1964). New introductory lectures on psycho-analysis. In J. Strachey (Ed. and Trans.), *The standard edition of the complete psychological works of Sigmund Freud* (Vol. 22). London: Hogarth. (Original work published 1933)

Freud, S. (1966a). Draft G: Melancholia (Extracts from the Fliess papers). In J. Strachey (Ed. and Trans.), *The standard edition of the complete psychological works of Sigmund Freud* (Vol. 1). London: Hogarth. (Original work published 1895)

Freud, S. (1966b). Draft N (Extracts from the Fliess papers). In J. Strachey (Ed. and Trans.), *The standard edition of the complete psychological works of Sigmund Freud* (Vol. 1). London: Hogarth. (Original work published 1897)

Frierson, R. L., Lippmann, S. B., & Johnson, J. (1987). AIDS: Psychological stresses on the family. *Psychosomatics, 28*(2), 65–68.

Fromm, E. (1941). *Escape from freedom*. New York: Rinehart.

Fromm-Reichmann, F. (1950). *Principles of intensive psychotherapy*. Chicago: The University of Chicago Press.

Frost, N., & Clayton, P. (1977). Bereavement and psychiatric hospitalization. *Archives of General Psychiatry, 34*, 1172–1175.

Fuller, R., Geis, S., & Rush, J. (1988). Lovers of AIDS victims: A minority group experience. *Death Studies, 12*, 1–7.

Fuller, R., Geis, S., & Rush, J. (1989). Lovers and significant others. In K. Doka (Ed.), *Disenfranchised grief: Recognizing hidden sorrow*. Lexington, MA: Lexington.

Fulton, R. (1970). Death, grief and social recuperation. *Omega, 1*, 23–28.

Fulton, R. (1976). The traditional funeral and contemporary society. In V. Pine, A. H. Kutscher, D. Peretz, R. Slater, R. DeBellis, R. Volk, & D. Cherico (Eds.), *Acute grief and the funeral*. Springfield, IL: Charles C Thomas.

Fulton, R. (1979). Anticipatory grief, stress, and the surrogate griever. In J. Taché, H. Selye, & S. Day (Eds.), *Cancer, stress, and death*. New York: Plenum.

Fulton, R., & Fulton, J. A. (1971). A psychosocial aspect of terminal care: Anticipatory grief. *Omega, 2*, 91–100.

Fulton, R., & Gottesman, D. J. (1980). Anticipatory grief: A psychosocial concept reconsidered. *British Journal of Psychiatry, 137*, 45–54.

Furman, E. (1974). *A child's parent dies: Studies in childhood bereavement*. New Haven: Yale University Press.

Furman, R. (1973). A child's capacity for mourning. In E. Anthony & C. Koupernik (Eds.), *The child in his family: The impact of disease and death* (Vol 2.). New York: Wiley.

Gallagher, D., Breckenridge, J., Thompson, L., & Peterson, J. (1983). Effects of bereavement on indicators of mental health in elderly widows and widowers. *Journal of Gerontology, 38,* 565–571.

Gallagher, D., Dessonville, C., Breckenridge, J., Thompson, L., & Amaral, P. (1982). Similarities and differences between normal grief and depression in older adults. *Essence, 5,* 127–140.

Garfield, C. (Ed.). (1978). *Psychosocial care of the dying patient.* New York: McGraw-Hill.

Gauthier, J., & Marshall, W. (1977). Grief: A cognitive-behavioral analysis. *Cognitive Therapy and Research, 1,* 39–44.

Gauthier, J., & Pye, C. (1979). Graduated self-exposure in the management of grief. *Behaviour Analysis and Modification, 3*(3), 202–208.

Geis, S., Fuller, R., & Rush, J. (1986). Lovers of AIDS victims: Psychosocial stresses and counseling needs. *Death Studies, 10,* 43–53.

Gerber, I., Wiener, A., Battin, D., & Arkin, A. (1975). Brief therapy to the aged bereaved. In B. Schoenberg, I. Gerber, A. Wiener, A. H. Kutscher, D. Peretz, & A. C. Carr (Eds.), *Bereavement: Its psychosocial aspects.* New York: Columbia University Press.

Getzel, G., & Masters, R. (1984). Serving families who survive homicide victims. *Social Casework, 65,* 138–144.

Giacquinta, B. (1989). Researching the effects of AIDS on families. *The American Journal of Hospice Care, 6,* 31–36.

Glaser, B. G., & Strauss, A. L. (1965). *Awareness of dying.* Chicago: Aldine.

Gleser, G., Green, B., & Winget, C. (1981). *Prolonged psychosocial effects of disaster: A study of Buffalo Creek.* New York: Academic.

Glick, I. O., Weiss, R. S., & Parkes, C. M. (1974). *The first year of bereavement.* New York: Wiley.

Goalder, J. (1985). Morbid grief reaction: A social systems perspective. *Professional Psychology: Research and Practice, 16,* 833–842.

Goin, M. K., Burgoyne, R. E., & Goin, J. M. (1979). Timeless attachment to a dead relative. *American Journal of Psychiatry, 136,* 988–989.

Goldberg, D. (1972). *The detection of psychiatric illness by questionnaire* (Maudsley Mimeograph No. 21). London: Oxford University Press.

Goldberg, I., Kutscher, A. H., & Malitz, S. (Eds.). (1986). *Pain, anxiety, and grief: Pharmacotherapeutic care of the dying patient and the bereaved.* New York: Columbia University Press.

Goldberg, I., Malitz, S., & Kutscher, A. H. (Eds.). (1973). *Psychopharmacologic agents for the terminally ill and bereaved.* New York: Columbia University Press.

Goldenberg, H., & Goldenberg, I. (1982). Homicide and the family. In B. Danto, J. Bruhns, & A. H. Kutscher (Eds.), *The human side of homicide.* New York: Columbia University Press.

Goldstein, K. (1939). *The organism. A holistic approach to biology.* New York: American Book.

Gonda, T. (1989). Death, dying, and bereavement. In H. I. Kaplan & B. J. Sadock (Eds.), *Comprehensive textbook of psychiatry* (Vol. 2, 5th ed.). Baltimore: Williams & Wilkins.

Gonsiorek, J. C. (1982). The use of diagnostic concepts in working with gay and lesbian populations. *Journal of Homosexuality, 6*(3), 9-20.

Gorer, G. (1965). *Death, grief, and mourning.* Garden City, NJ: Doubleday.

Gorkin, M. (1984). Narcissistic personality disorder and pathological mourning. *Contemporary Psychoanalysis, 20,* 400–420.

Gove, W. (1973). Sex, marital status, and mortality. *American Journal of Sociology, 79,* 45–67.

Granville-Grossman, K. (1966). Early bereavement and schizophrenia. *British Journal of Psychiatry, 112,* 1027–1034.

Greenberg, M., & van der Kolk, B. (1987). Retrieval and integration of traumatic memories with the "painting cure." In B. van der Kolk (Ed.), *Psychological trauma.* Washington, DC: American Psychiatric Press.

Gregory, I. (1966). Retrospective data concerning childhood loss of a parent. *Archives of General Psychiatry, 15,* 354–361.

Hackett, T. (1974). Recognizing and treating abnormal grief. *Hospital Physician, 1,* 49–50, 56.

Haley, S. (1974). When the patient reports atrocities. *Archives of General Psychiatry, 30,* 191–196.

Harkulich, J., & Calamita, B. (1989). Grief and Alzheimer's disease clients. *The Forum* (Newsletter of the Association for Death Education and Counseling), *13*(1), 4–5.

Harper, B. (1977). *Death: The coping mechanism of the health professional.* Greenville, SC: Southeastern University Press.

Hartz, G. (1986). Adult grief and its interface with mood disorder: Proposal of a new diagnosis of complicated bereavement. *Comprehensive Psychiatry, 27,* 60–64.

Hathaway, S., & McKinley, J. (1951). *The Minnesota Multiphasic Personality Inventory manual.* New York: Psychological Corporation.

Hauser, M. (1987). Special aspects of grief after suicide. In E. Dunne, J. L. McIntosh, & K. Dunne-Maxim (Eds.), *Suicide and its aftermath: Understanding and counseling the survivors.* New York: Norton.

Herman, J. (1981). *Father-daughter incest.* Cambridge, MA: Harvard University Press.

Herman, J. (1988). Father-daughter incest. In F. Ochberg (Ed.), *Post-traumatic therapy and victims of violence.* New York: Brunner/Mazel.

Herman, J. (1990, May-June). *The treatment of trauma: Incest as a paradigm.* Paper presented at a course on psychological trauma cosponsored by the Harvard Medical School and the Massachusetts Mental Health Center, Cambridge, MA.

Heyman, D., & Gianturco, D. (1973). Long-term adaptation by the elderly to bereavement. *Journal of Gerontology, 28,* 359–362.

Hilgard, J. (1969). Depressive and psychotic states as anniversaries to sibling death in childhood. *International Psychiatry Clinics, 6,* 197–211.

Hilgard, J., & Newman, M. (1959). Anniversaries in mental illness. *Psychiatry, 22,* 113–121.

Hilgard, J., & Newman, M. (1963). Parental loss by death in childhood as an etiological factor among schizophrenic and alcoholic patients compared with a non-patient community sample. *Journal of Nervous and Mental Disease, 134,* 108.

Hocker, W. (1989). President's perspective. *The Director, 60*(7), 5, 8.

Hocking, F. (1965). Human reactions to extreme environmental stress. *Medical Journal of Australia, 2,* 477–482.

Hodgkinson, P. (1982). Abnormal grief—The problem of therapy. *British Journal of Medical Psychology, 55,* 29–34.

Hodgkinson, P. (1989). Technological disaster—Survival and bereavement. *Social Science Medicine, 29,* 351–356.

Hogshead, H. (1976). The art of delivering bad news. *Journal of the Florida Medical Association, 63,* 807.

Hollins, S. (1989). Grief and people with mental retardation. *The Forum* (Newsletter of the Association for Death Education and Counseling), *13*(1), 3, 7.

Hollister, L. (1973). Psychotherapeutic drugs in the dying and bereaved. In I. Goldberg, S. Malitz, & A. H. Kutscher (Eds.), *Psychopharmacologic agents for the terminally ill and bereaved.* New York: Columbia University Press.

Holmes, M., & St. Lawrence, J. (1983). Treatment of rape-induced trauma: Proposed behavioral conceptualization and review of the literature. *Clinical Psychology Review, 3,* 417–433.

Horowitz, M. J. (1973). Phase oriented treatment of stress response syndromes. *American Journal of Psychotherapy, 27,* 506–515.

Horowitz, M. J. (1976). Diagnosis and treatment of stress response syndromes. In H. Parad, H. Resnik, & L. Parad (Eds.), *Emergency and disaster management.* Bowie, MD: Charles.

Horowitz, M. J. (1979). *States of mind.* New York: Plenum.

Horowitz, M. J. (1985). Disasters and psychological responses to stress. *Psychiatric Annals, 15,* 161–167.

Horowitz, M. J. (1986a). *Stress response syndromes* (2nd ed.). Northvale, NJ: Jason Aronson.

Horowitz, M. J. (1986b). Stress-response syndromes: A review of posttraumatic and adjustment disorders. *Hospital and Community Psychiatry, 37,* 241–249.

Horowitz, M. J., & Kaltreider, N. (1979). Brief therapy of the stress response syndrome. *The Psychiatric Clinics of North America, 2*, 365–377.

Horowitz, M. J., & Kaltreider, N. (1980). Brief therapy of stress response syndromes. In T. Karasu & L. Bellak (Eds.), *Specialized techniques in individual psychotherapy*. New York: Brunner/Mazel.

Horowitz, M. J., Marmar, C., Krupnick, J., Wilner, N., Kaltreider, N., & Wallerstein, R. (1984). *Personality styles and brief psychotherapy*. New York: Basic.

Horowitz, M. J., Marmar, C., Weiss, D., DeWitt, K., & Rosenbaum, R. (1984). Brief psychotherapy of bereavement reactions: The relationship of process to outcome. *Archives of General Psychiatry, 41*, 438–448.

Horowitz, M. J., Marmar, C., Weiss, D., Kaltreider, N., & Wilner, N. (1986). Comprehensive analysis of change after brief dynamic psychotherapy. *American Journal of Psychiatry, 143*, 582–589.

Horowitz, M. J., Weiss, D., Kaltreider, N., Krupnick, J., Marmar, C., Wilner, N., & DeWitt, K. (1984). Reactions to the death of a parent: Results from patients and field subjects. *Journal of Nervous and Mental Disease, 172*, 383–392.

Horowitz, M. J., Wilner, N., Kaltreider, N., & Alvarez, W. (1980). Signs and symptoms of posttraumatic stress disorder. *Archives of General Psychiatry, 37*, 85–92.

Horowitz, M. J., Wilner, N., Marmar, C., & Krupnick, J. (1980). Pathological grief and the activation of latent self-images. *American Journal of Psychiatry, 137*, 1157–1162.

Hughes, C., & Fleming, D. (1991). Grief casualties on skid row. *Omega, 23*, 109–118.

Hunter, E. (1983). Captivity: The family in waiting. In C. Figley & H. McCubbin (Eds.), *Stress and the family: Vol. 2. Coping with catastrophe*. New York: Brunner/Mazel.

Huston, P. (1971). Neglected approach to cause and treatment of psychotic depression. *Archives of General Psychiatry, 24*, 505–508.

Huttunen, M., & Niskanen, P. (1979). Parental loss of father and psychiatric disorders. *Archives of General Psychiatry, 35*, 429–431.

Imber-Black, E., Roberts, J., & Whiting, R. (Eds.). (1988). *Rituals in families and family therapy*. New York: Norton.

Irion, P. (1966). *The funeral—Vestige or value?* Nashville, TN: Parthenon.

Irion, P. (1988). The value of mourning customs. *The Director, 58*(7), 36–38.

Irwin, M., Daniels, M., Bloom, E., Smith, T., & Weiner, H. (1987). Life events, depressive symptoms, and immune function. *American Journal of Psychiatry, 144*, 437–441.

Jackson, E. (1957). *Understanding grief*. Nashville, TN: Abingdon.

Jackson, E. (1977). Comments in section on "The Parents." In N. Linzer (Ed.), *Understanding bereavement and grief*. New York: Yeshiva University Press.

Jackson, E. (1983). *Coping with the crises in your life* (2nd ed.). Northvale, NJ: Jason Aronson.

Jacobs, S. (1987). Bereavement and anxiety disorders. In E. Chigier (Ed.), *Grief and bereavement in contemporary society* (Vol. 1). London: Freund.

Jacobs, S., & Douglas, L. (1979). Grief: A mediating process between a loss and illness. *Comprehensive Psychiatry, 20,* 165–176.

Jacobs, S., Hansen, F., Berkman, L., Kasl, S., & Ostfeld, A. (1989). Depressions of bereavement. *Comprehensive Psychiatry, 30,* 218–224.

Jacobs, S., Hansen, F., Kasl, S., Ostfeld, A., Berkman, L., & Kim, K. (1990). Anxiety disorders during acute bereavement: Risk and risk factors. *Journal of Clinical Psychiatry, 51,* 269–274.

Jacobs, S., & Kim, K. (1989, May). *Pathological grief, depression, and anxiety disorders.* Paper presented at the International Symposium on Pathologic Bereavement, Seattle.

Jacobs, S., & Kim, K. (1990). Psychiatric complications of bereavement. *Psychiatric Annals, 20,* 314–317.

Jacobs, S., & Lieberman, P. (1987). Bereavement and depression. In O. Cameron (Ed.), *Presentations of depression.* New York: Wiley.

Jacobs, S., Nelson, J., & Zisook, S. (1987). Treating depressions of bereavement with antidepressants: A pilot study. *The Psychiatric Clinics of North America, 10,* 501–510.

Jacobs, S., & Ostfeld, A. (1977). An epidemiological review of the mortality of bereavement. *Psychosomatic Medicine, 39,* 344–357.

Janis, I. (1951). *Air war and emotional stress: Psychological studies of bombing and civilian defense.* Westport, CT: Greenwood.

Janoff-Bulman, R. (1985). The aftermath of victimization: Rebuilding shattered assumptions. In C. Figley (Ed.), *Trauma and its wake: The study and treatment of post-traumatic stress disorder.* New York: Brunner/Mazel.

Janoff-Bulman, R., & Frieze, I. (Eds.). (1983). Reactions to victimization [Special issue]. *Journal of Social Issues, 39*(2).

Jennings, L., & France, R. (1979). Management of grief in the hypochondriac. *Journal of Family Practice, 8,* 957–960.

Johnson, P., & Rosenblatt, P. (1981). Grief following childhood loss of a parent. *American Journal of Psychotherapy, 35,* 419–425.

Kalish, R. A. (1970). The onset of the dying process. *Omega, 1,* 57–69.

Kalish, R. A. (1981). *Death, grief, and caring relationships.* Pacific Grove, CA: Brooks/Cole.

Kanas, N., Kaltreider, N., & Horowitz, M. J. (1977). Response to catastrophe: A case study. *Diseases of the Nervous System, 37,* 625–627.

Karasu, T. (1989). Psychoanalysis and psychoanaltyic psychotherapy. In H. I. Kaplan & B. J. Sadock (Eds.), *Comprehensive textbook of psychiatry* (Vol. 2, 5th ed.). Baltimore: Williams & Wilkins.

Kardiner, A. (1941). *The traumatic neuroses of war.* New York: Hoeber.

Kastenbaum, R. (1969). Death and bereavement in later life. In A. H. Kutscher (Ed.), *Death and bereavement*. Springfield, IL: Charles C Thomas.

Kaufman, G. (1980). *Shame: The power of caring*. Cambridge, MA: Schenckman.

Keane, T. (1990, May-June). *Cognitive and behavioral treatments of post traumatic stress disorder*. Paper presented at a course on psychological trauma co-sponsored by the Harvard Medical School and the Massachusetts Mental Health Center, Cambridge, MA.

Keane, T., Fairbank, J., Caddell, J., Zimering, R., & Bender, M. (1985). A behavioral approach to assessing and treating post-traumatic stress disorder in Vietnam veterans. In C. Figley (Ed.), *Trauma and its wake: The study and treatment of post-traumatic stress disorder*. New York: Brunner/Mazel.

Keane, T., Zimering, R., & Caddell, J. (1985). A behavioral formulation of post-traumatic stress disorder in Vietnam veterans. *Behavior Therapy, 8,* 9–12.

Kellner, R. (1975). The clinical pharmacology of anxiety. In M. Marshall (Ed.), *Clinical psychopharmacology 1975*. Northvale, NJ: Jason Aronson.

Kellner, R., Rada, R., & Winslow, W. (1986). Psychopharmacologic treatment of bereavement. In I. Goldberg, A. H. Kutscher, & S. Malitz (Eds.), *Pain, anxiety, and grief: Pharmacotherapeutic care of the dying patient and the bereaved*. New York: Columbia University Press.

Kelly, G. (1955). *The psychology of personal constructs* (Vols. 1 & 2). New York: Norton.

Kierkegaard, S. (1944). *The concept of dread* (W. Lowrie, Trans.). Princeton, NJ: Princeton University Press. (Original work published 1844)

Kilpatrick, D., Veronen, L., & Resick, P. (1982). Psychological sequelae to rape: Assessment and treatment strategies. In D. Doleys, R. Meredith, & A. Ciminero (Eds.), *Behavioral medicine: Assessment and treatment strategies*. New York: Plenum.

Kissen, D. (1958). *Emotional factors in pulmonary tuberculosis*. London: Tavistock.

Klass, D. (1988). *Parental grief: Solace and resolution*. New York: Springer.

Kleber, R., & Brom, D. (1987). Psychotherapy and pathological grief controlled outcome study. *The Israel Journal of Psychiatry and Related Sciences, 24,* 99–109.

Klein, M. (1935). A contribution to the psychogenesis of manic-depressive states. *The International Journal of Psycho-Analysis, 16,* 145–174.

Klein, M. (1940). Mourning and its relation to manic-depressive states. *The International Journal of Psycho-Analysis, 21,* 125–153.

Klein, S., & Fletcher, W. (1986). Gay grief: An examination of its uniqueness brought to light by the AIDS crisis. *Journal of Psychosocial Oncology, 4,* 15–25.

Klerman, G., & Izen, J. (1977). The effects of bereavement and grief on physical health and general well-being. *Advances in Psychosomatic Medicine, 9,* 63–104.

Kluft, R. (Ed.). (1990). *Incest-related syndromes of adult psychopathology.* Washington, DC: American Psychiatric Press.

Kollar, N. (Ed.). (1983). *The Forum* (Newsletter of the Association for Death Education and Counseling) [Special issue], *6*(7).

Kollar, N. (1989). Rituals and the disenfranchised griever. In K. Doka (Ed.), *Disenfranchised grief: Recognizing hidden sorrow.* Lexington, MA: Lexington.

Kosten, T., Jacobs, S., & Mason, J. (1984). The dexamethasone suppression test during bereavement. *Journal of Nervous and Mental Disease, 172,* 359–360.

Krause, N. (1986). Life stress as a correlate of depression among older adults. *Psychiatry Research, 18,* 227–237.

Krupnick, J. (1980). Brief psychotherapy with victims of violent crimes. *Victimology, 5,* 347–354.

Krupnick, J., & Horowitz, M. J. (1985). Brief psychotherapy with vulnerable patients: An outcome assessment. *Psychiatry, 48,* 223–233.

Krupnick, J., & Soloman, F. (1987). Death of a parent or sibling during childhood. In J. Bloom-Feshbach & S. Bloom-Feshbach (Eds.), *The psychology of separation and loss.* San Francisco: Jossey-Bass.

Krupp, G. (1972). Maladaptive reactions to the death of a family member. *Social Casework, 53,* 425–434.

Krystal, H. (Ed.). (1968). *Massive psychic trauma.* New York: International Universities Press.

Krystal, H. (1978). Trauma and affects. *The Psychoanalytic Study of the Child, 33,* 81–116.

Krystal, H. (1984). Psychoanalytic views on human emotional damages. In B. van der Kolk (Ed.), *Post-traumatic stress disorder: Psychological and biological sequelae.* Washington, DC: American Psychiatric Press.

Krystal, H., & Niederland, W. (Eds.). (1971). *Psychic traumatization: Aftereffects in individuals and communities.* Boston: Little, Brown.

Kübler-Ross, E. (1969). *On death and dying.* New York: Macmillan.

Kübler-Ross, E. (1973). On the case for psychopharmacologic agents for the dying patient and the bereaved. In I. Goldberg, S. Malitz, & A. H. Kutscher (Eds.), *Psychopharmacologic agents for the terminally ill and bereaved.* New York: Columbia University Press.

Lacoursiere, R., Godfrey, K., & Rubey, L. (1980). Traumatic neurosis in the etiology of alcoholism. *American Journal of Psychiatry, 137,* 966–968.

LaGrand, L. (1986). *Coping with separation and loss as a young adult: Theoretical and practical realities.* Springfield, IL: Charles C Thomas.

Lattin, D. (1986, January 18). AIDS: A sign of God's wrath, Baptist leader claims. *Rocky Mountain News,* p. 119.

Laughlin, C., & d'Aquili, E. (1979). Ritual and stress. In E. d'Aquili, C. Laughlin, & J. McManus (Eds.), *The spectrum of ritual: A biogenetic structural analysis.* New York: Columbia University Press.

Lavin, C. (1989). Disenfranchised grief and the developmentally disabled. In K. Doka (Ed.), *Disenfranchised grief: Recognizing hidden sorrow.* Lexington, MA: Lexington.

Lazare, A. (1979). Unresolved grief. In A. Lazare (Ed.), *Outpatient psychiatry: Diagnosis and treatment.* Baltimore: Williams & Wilkins.

Lehman, D., Ellard, J., & Wortman, C. (1986). Social support for the bereaved: Recipients' and providers' perspectives on what is helpful. *Journal of Consulting and Clinical Psychology, 54,* 438–446.

Lehman, D., Wortman, C., & Williams, A. (1987). Long-term effects of losing a spouse or child in a motor vehicle crash. *Journal of Personality and Social Psychology, 57,* 218–231.

Lehrman, S. (1956). Reactions to untimely death. *Psychiatric Quarterly, 30,* 564–578.

Leon, I. (1986). Psychodynamics of perinatal loss. *Psychiatry, 49,* 312–324.

Levav, I. (1982). Mortality and psychopathology following the death of an adult child: An epidemiological review. *The Israel Journal of Psychiatry and Related Sciences, 19,* 23–38.

Levenson, H. (1973). Multidimensional locus of control in psychiatric patients. *Journal of Consulting and Clinical Psychology, 41,* 397–404.

Levinson, P. (1972). On sudden death. *Psychiatry, 35,* 160–173.

Levitan, H. (1985). Onset of asthma during intense mourning. *Psychosomatics, 26,* 939–941.

Lewis, H. (1971). *Shame and guilt in neurosis.* New York: International Universities Press.

Lidz, T. (1946). Nightmares and the combat neuroses. *Psychiatry, 9,* 37–49.

Lieberman, M. (1986). Social supports—The consequences of psychologizing: A commentary. *Journal of Consulting and Clinical Psychology, 54,* 461–465.

Lieberman, M., & Videka-Sherman, L. (1986). The impact of self-help groups on the mental health of widows and widowers. *American Journal of Orthopsychiatry, 56,* 435–449.

Lieberman, P., & Jacobs, S. (1987). Bereavement and its complications in medical patients: A guide for consultation liaison psychiatrists. *International Journal of Psychiatry in Medicine, 17*(1), 23–39.

Lieberman, S. (1978). Nineteen cases of morbid grief. *British Journal of Psychiatry, 132,* 159–163.

Lifton, R. (1964). On death and death symbolism: The Hiroshima disaster. *Psychiatry, 27,* 191–210.

Lifton, R. (1976). *Death in life: Survivors of Hiroshima.* New York: Touchstone.

Lifton, R. (1979). *The broken connection.* New York: Simon & Schuster.

Lifton, R., & Olson, E. (1976a). Death imprint in Buffalo Creek. In H. Parad, H. Resnik, & L. Parad (Eds.), *Emergency and disaster management: A mental health sourcebook.* Bowie, MD: Charles.

Lifton, R., & Olson, E. (1976b). The human meaning of total disaster: The Buffalo Creek experience. *Psychiatry, 39,* 1–18.

Limbo, R., & Wheeler, S. (1986). *When a baby dies: A handbook for healing and helping.* LaCrosse, WI: LaCrosse Lutheran Hospital, Resolve Through Sharing.

Lindemann, E. (1944). Symptomatology and management of acute grief. *American Journal of Psychiatry, 101,* 141–148.

Lindemann, E. (1979). *Beyond grief: Studies in crisis intervention* (Elizabeth Lindemann, Ed.). Northvale, NJ: Jason Aronson.

Lindemann, E., & Greer, I. (1953). A study of grief: Emotional responses to suicide. *Pastoral Psychology, 4,* 9–13.

Linder, R. (1955). *The fifty-minute hour.* New York: Holt, Rinehart & Winston.

Lindy, J. (1985). The trauma membrane and other clinical concepts derived from psychotherapeutic work with survivors of natural disasters. *Psychiatric Annals, 15,* 153–160.

Lindy, J. (1986). An outline for the psychoanalytic psychotherapy of post-traumatic stress disorder. In C. Figley (Ed.), *Trauma and its wake: Vol. 2. Traumatic stress theory, research, and intervention.* New York: Brunner/Mazel.

Lindy, J., Green, B., Grace, M., & Titchener, J. (1983). Psychotherapy with survivors of the Beverly Hills Supper Club fire. *American Journal of Psychotherapy, 37,* 593–610.

Littlefield, C., & Rushton, J. (1986). When a child dies: The sociobiology of bereavement. *Journal of Personality and Social Psychology, 51,* 797–802.

Livingston, M. (1971). Working through in analytic group psychotherapy in relation to masochism as a refusal to mourn. *International Journal of Group Psychotherapy, 21,* 339–344.

Lopata, H. Z. (1979). *Women as widows: Support systems.* New York: Elsevier North Holland.

Lord, J. (1987). *No time for goodbyes: Coping with sorrow, anger and injustice after a tragic death.* Ventura, CA: Pathfinder.

Lowenthal, M. F., & Haven, C. (1968). Interaction and adaptation: Intimacy as a critical variable. *American Sociological Review, 33,* 20–30.

Lund, D. (Ed.). (1989). *Older bereaved spouses: Research with practical applications.* New York: Hemisphere.

Lund, D., Diamond, M., Caserta, M., Johnson, R., Poulton, J., & Connelly, J. (1985–1986). Identifying elderly with coping difficulties after two years of bereavement. *Omega, 16,* 213–224.

Lundin, T. (1984a). Long-term outcome of bereavement. *British Journal of Psychiatry, 145,* 424–428.

Lundin, T. (1984b). Morbidity following sudden and unexpected bereavement. *British Journal of Psychiatry, 144,* 84–88.

Lynn, E., & Racy, J. (1969). The resolution of pathological grief after electroconvulsive therapy. *Journal of Nervous and Mental Disease, 148,* 165–169.

MacElveen-Hoehn, P. (1987, June). *Sexual response to death.* Paper presented at the meeting of the International Work Group on Death, Dying and Bereavement, London.

Macon, L. (1979). Help for bereaved parents. *Social Casework, 60,* 558–565.

Maddison, D. (1968). The relevance of conjugal bereavement for preventive psychiatry. *British Journal of Medical Psychology, 41,* 223–233.

Maddison, D., & Raphael, B. (1972). Normal bereavement as an illness requiring care: Psychopharmacological approaches. *Journal of Thanatology, 2,* 785–798.

Maddison, D., & Raphael, B. (1973). Normal bereavement as an illness requiring care: Psychopharmacological approaches. In I. Goldberg, S. Malitz, & A. H. Kutscher (Eds.), *Psychopharmacologic agents for the terminally ill and bereaved.* New York: Columbia University Press.

Maddison, D., & Viola, A. (1968). The health of widows in the year following bereavement. *Journal of Psychosomatic Research, 12,* 297–306.

Maddison, D., & Walker, W. (1967). Factors affecting the outcome of conjugal bereavement. *British Journal of Psychiatry, 113,* 1057–1067.

Madow, L. (1988). *Guilt: How to recognize and cope with it.* Northvale, NJ: Jason Aronson.

Malan, D. (1963). *A study of brief psychotherapy.* London: Tavistock.

Malan, D. (1976). *Toward the validation of dynamic psychotherapy.* New York: Plenum.

Mancini, M. (1986). Creating and therapeutically utilizing anticipatory grief in survivors of sudden death. In T. A. Rando (Ed.), *Parental loss of a child.* Champaign, IL: Research Press.

Mandelbaum, D. (1959). Social uses of funeral rites. In H. Feifel (Ed.), *The meaning of death.* New York: McGraw-Hill.

Mann, J. (1973). *Time-limited psychotherapy.* Cambridge, MA: Harvard University Press.

Marcus, E. (1979). *Gestalt therapy and beyond.* Cupertino, CA: META.

Marks, I., Hodgson, R., & Rachman, S. (1974). Treatment of chronic obsessive-compulsive neurosis by in-vivo exposure. *British Journal of Psychiatry, 127,* 349–364.

Marmar, C., Horowitz, M. J., Weiss, D., Wilner, N., & Kaltreider, N. (1988). A controlled trial of brief psychotherapy and mutual-help group treatment of conjugal bereavement. *American Journal of Psychiatry, 145,* 203–209.

Marris, P. (1958). *Widows and their families.* London, England: Routledge & Kegan Paul.

Martelli, L. J. (1987). *When someone you know has AIDS.* New York: Crown.

Martin, J. (1988). Psychological consequences of AIDS-related bereavement among gay men. *Journal of Consulting and Clinical Psychology, 56,* 856–862.

Martinson, I., Davies, B., & McClowry, S. (1991). Parental depression following the death of a child. *Death Studies, 15,* 259–267.

Maslach, C., & Jackson, S. (1979, May). Burned-out cops and their families. *Psychology Today,* p. 59.

Maslow, A. (1962). *Toward a psychology of being.* Princeton, NJ: Van Nostrand.

Masters, R., Friedman, L., & Getzel, G. (1988). Helping families of homicide victims: A multidimensional approach. *Journal of Traumatic Stress, 1,* 109–125.

Mawson, D., Marks, I., Ramm, L., & Stern, R. (1981). Guided mourning for morbid grief: A controlled study. *British Journal of Psychiatry, 138,* 185–193.

May, R. (1977). *The meaning of anxiety* (rev. ed.). New York: Norton.

McCann, I., & Pearlman, L. (1990a). Psychological trauma and the adult survivor: Theory, therapy, and transformation. New York: Brunner/Mazel.

McCann, I., & Pearlman, L. (1990b). Vicarious traumatization: A framework for understanding the psychological effects of working with victims. *Journal of Traumatic Stress, 3,* 131–149.

McIntosh, J. L., & Wrobleski, A. (1988). Grief reactions among suicide survivors: An exploratory comparison of relationships. *Death Studies, 12,* 21–39.

Melges, F., & DeMaso, D. (1980). Grief-resolution therapy: Reliving, revising, and revisiting. *American Journal of Psychotherapy, 34,* 51–61.

Melson, S., & Rynearson, E. (1982). Unresolved bereavement: Medical reenactment of a loved one's terminal illness. *Postgraduate Medicine, 72,* 172–179.

Menninger, K. (1954). Regulatory devices of the ego under major stress. *The International Journal of Psycho-Analysis, 35,* 412–420.

Merlis, S. (1972). Antianxiety agents in the management of the bereaved. *Journal of Thanatology, 2,* 723–726.

Meyerson, A. (1944). Prolonged cases of grief reactions treated by electric shock. *The New England Journal of Medicine, 230,* 255–256.

Michalowski, R. (1976). The social meanings of violent deaths. *Omega, 7,* 83–93.

Miles, M. (1984). Helping adults mourn the death of a child. In H. Wass & C. Corr (Eds.), *Childhood and death.* Washington, DC: Hemisphere.

Milgram, N. (1982). Wartime bereavment. In C. D. Spielberger & I. G. Sarason, *Stress and anxiety* (Vol. 8). Washington, DC: Hemisphere.

Mitchell, J., & Bray, G. (1990). *Emergency services stress: Guidelines for preserving the health and careers of emergency services personnel.* Englewood Cliffs, NJ: Brady.

Moffat, B. (1986). *When someone you love has AIDS.* New York: Penguin.

Moore, B., & Fine, B. (1990). *Psychoanalytic terms and concepts.* New Haven, CT: American Psychoanalytic Association and Yale University Press.

Moore, S., & Myerhoff, B. (Eds.). (1977). *Secular ritual.* Amsterdam: Van Gorcum.

Moos, R. H., & Tsu, V. D. (1977). The crisis of physical illness: An overview. In R. H. Moos (Ed.), *Coping with physical illness.* New York: Plenum.

Morillo, E., & Gardner, L. (1979). Bereavement as an antecedent factor in thyrotoxicosis of childhood: Four case studies with survey of possible metabolic pathways. *Psychosomatic Medicine, 41,* 545–556.

Morin, S. F., & Batchelor, W. F. (1984). Responding to the psychological crisis of AIDS. *Public Health Reports, 99*(1), 4–10.

Moss, M., & Moss, S. (1984–1985). Some aspects of the elderly widow(er)'s persistent tie with the deceased spouse. *Omega, 15,* 195–206.

Mowrer, O. H. (1960). *Learning theory and behavior.* New York: Wiley.

Murphy, G., Armstrong, J., Hermele, S., Fischer, J., & Clendenin, W. (1979). Suicide and alcoholism. *Archives of General Psychiatry, 36,* 65–69.

Murphy, G., & Robins, E. (1967). Social factors in suicide. *Journal of the American Medical Association, 199,* 81–86.

Murrell, S., & Himmelfarb, S. (1989). Effects of attachment bereavement and pre-event conditions on subsequent depressive symptoms in older adults. *Psychology and Aging, 4,* 166–172.

Muskin, P., & Rifkin, A. (1986). Tricyclic antidepressants in the treatment of depression in conjugal bereavement: A controlled study. In I. Goldberg, A. H. Kutscher, & S. Malitz (Eds.), *Pain, anxiety, and grief: Pharmacotherapeutic care of the dying patient and the bereaved.* New York: Columbia University Press.

Napalkov, A. (1963). Information process of the brain. In N. Weiner & J. Schade (Eds.), *Progress in brain research: Nerve, brain and memory models.* Amsterdam: Elsevier.

National Center for Health Statistics. (1990). *Prevention profile: Health, United States (1989).* Hyattsville, MD: Public Health Service.

National Safety Council. (1991). *Accident facts—1991 edition.* Chicago: Author.

National Victim Center. (1991). *America speaks out: Citizens' attitudes about victims' rights and violence* (Executive Summary). Fort Worth, TX: Author.

Nellis, C. (1992, February 13). One million more AIDS victims: Report blames heterosexuals. *The Providence Journal-Bulletin,* pp. A-1, A-3.

Ness, D., & Pfeffer, C. (1990). Sequelae of bereavement resulting from suicide. *American Journal of Psychiatry, 147,* 279–285.

Nichols, R. (1983). Professionals and the funeral: Do we help or hinder? *The Forum* (Newsletter of the Association for Death Education and Counseling) 6(7), 6–7.

Nichols, S. E. (1986). Psychotherapy and AIDS. In T. S. Stein & C. S. Cohen (Eds.), *Contemporary perspectives on psychotherapy with lesbians and gay men.* New York: Plenum.

Nichols, S. E., & Ostrow, D. G. (1984). (Eds.). *Psychiatric implications of Acquired Immune Deficiency Syndrome.* Washington, DC: American Psychiatric Press.

Nightingale, A. (1989). Unresolved grief presenting with features of a negative therapeutic reaction. *British Journal of Psychiatry, 155,* 862–864.

Ochberg, F. (Ed.). (1988a). *Post-traumatic therapy and victims of violence.* New York: Brunner/Mazel.

Ochberg, F. (1988b). Post-traumatic therapy and victims of violence. In F. Ochberg (Ed.), *Post-traumatic therapy and victims of violence.* New York: Brunner/Mazel.

Ochberg, F., & Fojtik, K. (1984). A comprehensive mental health clinical service program for victims: Clinical issues and therapeutic strategies. *American Journal of Social Psychiatry, 4,* 12–23.

Opp, L., & Samson, A. (1987, October). *A taxonomy of guilt for combat veterans.* Paper presented at the third annual meeting of the Society for Traumatic Stress Studies, Baltimore.

Osterweis, M., Solomon, F., & Green, M. (Eds.). (1984). *Bereavement: Reactions, consequences, and care.* Washington, DC: National Academy Press.

Palgi, P. (1973). The socio-cultural expressions and implications of death, mourning and bereavement arising out of the war situation in Israel. *The Israel Journal of Psychiatry and Related Disciplines, 11,* 301–329.

Papadatou, D., & Papadatos, C. (Eds.). (1991). *Children and death.* New York: Hemisphere.

Paradis, L. (Ed.). (1987). Stress and burnout among providers caring for the terminally ill and their families [Special issue]. *The Hospice Journal, 3*(2 & 3).

Parkes, C. M. (1964). Effects of bereavement on physical and mental health—A study of the medical records of widows. *British Medical Journal, 2,* 274–279.

Parkes, C. M. (1965). Bereavement and mental illness. *British Journal of Medical Psychology, 38,* 1–26.

Parkes, C. M. (1970). The first year of bereavement. *Psychiatry, 33,* 444–467.

Parkes, C. M. (1972). *Bereavement: Studies of grief in adult life.* New York: International Universities Press.

Parkes, C. M. (1975). Determinants of outcome following bereavement. *Omega, 6,* 303–323.

Parkes, C. M. (1979). Psychological aspects. In C. Saunders (Ed.), *The management of terminal disease.* London: Edward Arnold.

Parkes, C. M. (1980). Bereavement counseling: Does it work? *British Medical Journal, 281,* 3–6.

Parkes, C. M. (1981). Evaluation of a bereavement service. *Journal of Preventive Psychiatry, 1,* 179–188.

Parkes, C. M. (1985). Bereavement. *British Journal of Psychiatry, 146,* 11–17.

Parkes, C. M. (1987). *Bereavement: Studies of grief in adult life* (2nd ed.). Madison, CT: International Universities Press.

Parkes, C. M. (1987–1988). Research: Bereavement. *Omega, 18,* 365–377.

Parkes, C. M. (1988). Bereavement as a psychosocial transition: Processes of adaptation to change. *Journal of Social Issues, 44*(3), 53–65.

Parkes, C.M., & Brown, R. (1972). Health after bereavement: A controlled study of young Boston windows and widowers. *Psychosomatic Medicine, 34*, 449–461.

Parkes, C.M., & Stevenson-Hinde, J. (Eds.). (1982). *The place of attachment in human behavior.* New York: Basic.

Parkes, C.M., & Weiss, R.S. (1983). *Recovery from bereavement.* New York: Basic.

Paterson, G. (Ed.). (1986). *Children and death: Proceedings of the 1985 King's College Conference "Helping Children Cope with Death."* London, Ontario: King's College.

Pattison, E.M. (1969). Help in the dying process. *Voices: The Art and Science of Psychotherapy, 5,* 6–14.

Pattison, E.M. (Ed.). (1977). *The experience of dying.* Englewood Cliffs, NJ: Prentice-Hall.

Pattison, E.M. (1978). The living-dying process. In C.A. Garfield (Ed.), *Psychosocial care of the dying patient.* New York: McGraw-Hill.

Paul, N., & Grosser, G. (1965). Operational mourning and its role in conjoint family therapy. *Community Mental Health Journal, 1,* 339–345.

Paul, N., & Paul, B. (1982). Death and changes in sexual behavior. In F. Walsh (Ed.), *Normal family processes.* New York: Guilford.

Paulley, J. (1983). Pathological mourning: A key factor in the psychopatho-genesis of autoimmune disorders: A special contribution. *Psychotherapy and Psychosomatics, 40*(1–4), 181–190.

Paulley, J., & Hughes, J. (1960). Giant cell arteritis or arteritis of the aged. *British Medicine Journal, ii,* 1562–1567.

Paykel, E., Myers, J., Dienelt, M., Klerman, G., Lindenthal, J., & Pepper, M. (1969). Life events and depression: A controlled study. *Archives of General Psychiatry, 21,* 753–760.

Pearson, L. (Ed.). (1969). *Death and dying: Current issues in the treatment of the dying person.* Cleveland: The Press of Case Western Reserve University.

Pedder, J. (1982). Failure to mourn, and melancholia. *British Journal of Psychiatry, 141,* 329–337.

Pennebaker, J.W., & Beall, S. (1986). Confronting a traumatic event: Toward an understanding of inhibition and disease. *Journal of Abnormal Psychology, 95,* 274–281.

Pennebaker, J.W., Kiecolt-Glaser, J., & Glaser, R. (1988). Disclosure of traumas and immune function: Health implications for psychotherapy. *Journal of Consulting and Clinical Psychology, 56,* 239–245.

Pennebaker, J.W., & O'Heeron, R.C. (1984). Confiding in others and illness rate among spouses of suicide and accidental-death victims. *Journal of Abnormal Psychology, 93,* 473–476.

Perls, F. (1947). *Ego, hunger, and aggression.* New York: Vintage.

Perls, F., Hefferline, R., & Goodman, P. (1951). *Gestalt therapy: Excitement and growth in the human personality.* New York: Delta.

Peterson, C., & Seligman, M. (1983). Learned helplessness and victimization. *Journal of Social Issues, 39*(2), 103–116.

Piers, G., & Singer, M. (1953). *Shame and guilt.* New York: Norton.

Pihlblad, C. T., & Adams, D. L. (1972). Widowhood, social participation, and life satisfaction. *Aging and Human Development, 3,* 323–330.

Polak, P., Egan, D., Vandenbergh, R., & Williams, W. (1975). Prevention in mental health: A controlled study. *American Journal of Psychiatry, 132,* 146–149.

Pollock, G. (1961). Mourning and adaption. *The International Journal of Psycho-Analysis, 42,* 341–361.

Pollock, G. (1970). Anniversary reactions, trauma, and mourning. *Psychoanalytic Quarterly, 39,* 347–371.

Putnam, F. (1989). *Diagnosis and treatment of multiple personality disorder.* New York: Guilford.

Radloff, L. (1975). Sex differences in depression: The effects of occupation and marital status. *Sex Roles, 1,* 249–265.

Rado, S. (1925). The economic principle in psychoanalytic technique. *The International Journal of Psycho-Analysis, 6,* 35–44.

Rahe, R. (1979). Life change events and mental illness: An overview. *Journal of Human Stress, 5,* 2–10.

Ramsay, R. (1976). A case study in bereavement therapy. In H. Eysenck (Ed.), *Case studies in behavior therapy.* London: Routledge & Kegan Paul.

Ramsay, R. (1977). Behavioural approaches to bereavement. *Behaviour Research and Therapy, 15,* 131–135.

Ramsay, R. (1979). Bereavement: A behavioral treatment of pathological grief. In P. Sjöden, S. Bates, & W. Dockins (Eds.), *Trends in behavior therapy.* New York: Academic.

Ramsay, R., & Happée, J. (1977). The stress of bereavement: Components and treatment. In C. D. Spielberger & I. G. Sarason (Eds.), *Stress and anxiety* (Vol. 4). Washington, DC: Hemisphere.

Rando, T. A. (1983). An investigation of grief and adaptation in parents whose children have died from cancer. *Journal of Pediatric Psychology, 8,* 3–20.

Rando, T. A. (1984). *Grief, dying, and death: Clinical interventions for caregivers.* Champaign, IL: Research Press.

Rando, T. A. (1985a). Bereaved parents: Particular difficulties, unique factors, and treatment issues. *Social Work, 30,* 19–23.

Rando, T. A. (1985b). Creating therapeutic rituals in the psychotherapy of the bereaved. *Psychotherapy, 22,* 236–240.

Rando, T. A. (1986a). A comprehensive analysis of anticipatory grief: Perspectives, processes, promises, and problems. In T. A. Rando (Ed.), *Loss and anticipatory grief.* Lexington, MA: Lexington.

Rando, T. A. (1986b). Death of the adult child. In T. A. Rando (Ed.), *Parental loss of a child.* Champaign, IL: Research Press.

Rando, T. A. (1986c). Individual and couples treatment following the death of a child. In T. A. Rando (Ed.), *Parental loss of a child*. Champaign, IL: Research Press.

Rando, T. A. (1986d). Introduction. In T. A. Rando (Ed)., *Parental loss of a child*. Champaign, IL: Research Press.

Rando, T. A. (Ed.). (1986e). *Loss and anticipatory grief*. Lexington, MA: Lexington.

Rando, T. A. (1986f). Parental bereavement: An exception to the general conceptualizations of mourning. In T. A. Rando (Ed.), *Parental loss of a child*. Champaign, IL: Research Press.

Rando, T. A. (Ed.). (1986g). *Parental loss of a child*. Champaign, IL: Research Press.

Rando, T. A., (1986h). Understanding and facilitating anticipatory grief in the loved ones of the dying. In T. A. Rando (Ed.), *Loss and anticipatory grief*. Lexington, MA: Lexington.

Rando, T. A. (1987a). Death and dying are not and should not be taboo topics. In A. H. Kutscher, A. C. Carr, & L. Kutscher (Eds.), *Principles of thanatology*. New York: Columbia University Press.

Rando, T. A. (1987b). The unrecognized impact of sudden death in terminal illness and in positively progressing convalescence. *The Israel Journal of Psychiatry and Related Sciences, 24*, 125–135.

Rando, T. A. (1988). *Grieving: How to go on living when someone you love dies*. Lexington, MA: Lexington.

Rando, T. A. (1991). Parental adjustment to the loss of a child. In D. Papadatou & C. Papadatos (Eds.), *Children and death*. Washington, DC: Hemisphere.

Rando, T. A. (in press-a). Complications in mourning traumatic death. In I. Corless, B. Germino, & M. Pittman-Lindeman (Eds.), *Death, dying, and bereavement*. Boston: Jones and Bartlett.

Rando, T. A. (in press-b). The increasing prevalence of complicated mourning: The onslaught is just beginning. *Omega*.

Range, L., & Calhoun, L. (1990). Responses following suicide and other types of death: The perspective of the bereaved. *Omega, 21*, 311–320.

Rangell, L. (1976). Discussion of the Buffalo Creek disaster: The course of psychic trauma. *American Journal of Psychiatry, 133*, 313–316.

Raphael, B. (1975). The management of pathological grief. *Australian and New Zealand Journal of Psychiatry, 9*, 173–180.

Raphael, B. (1977). Preventive intervention with the recently bereaved. *Archives of General Psychiatry, 34*, 1450–1454.

Raphael, B. (1978). Mourning and the prevention of melancholia. *British Journal of Medical Psychology, 51*, 303–310.

Raphael, B. (1980a). Primary prevention: Fact or fiction. *Australian and New Zealand Journal of Psychiatry, 14*, 163–174.

Raphael, B. (1980b). A psychiatric model for bereavement counseling. In B. Schoenberg (Ed.), *Bereavement counseling: A multidisciplinary handbook*. Westport, CT: Greenwood.

Raphael, B. (1981). Personal disaster. *Austrialian and New Zealand Journal of Psychiatry, 15,* 183–198.

Raphael, B. (1983). *The anatomy of bereavement.* New York: Basic.

Raphael, B. (1986). *When disaster strikes: How individuals and communities cope with catastrophe.* New York: Basic.

Raphael, B., & Maddison, D. (1976). The care of bereaved adults. In O. Hill (Ed.), *Modern trends in psychosomatic medicine.* London: Butterworth.

Raphael, B., & Middleton, W. (1987). Current state of research in the field of bereavement. *The Israel Journal of Psychiatry and Related Sciences, 24,* 5–32.

Raphael, B., Middleton, W., Dunne, M., Martinek, N., & Smith, S. (1990). *Normal and pathological grief: The need for diagnostic criteria.* Manuscript submitted for publication.

Redmond, L. (1989). *Surviving: When someone you love was murdered.* Clearwater, FL: Psychological Consultation and Education Services.

Reeves, N., & Boersma, F. (1989–1990). The therapeutic use of ritual in maladaptive grieving. *Omega, 20,* 281–291.

Resnik, H. (1969). Psychological resynthesis: A clinical approach to the survivors of a death by suicide. In E. S. Shneidman & M. Ortega (Eds.), *Aspects of depression.* Boston, MA: Little, Brown.

Rickarby, G. (1977). Four cases of mania associated with bereavement. *Journal of Nervous and Mental Disease, 165,* 255–262.

Rinear, E. (1985). *Parental response patterns to the death of a child by homicide.* Unpublished doctoral dissertation, Temple University, Philadelphia.

Rinear, E. (1988). Psychosocial aspects of parental response patterns to the death of a child by homicide. *Journal of Traumatic Stress, 1,* 305–322.

Robinson, M. (1981). Informing the family of sudden death. *American Family Physician, 23,* 115–118.

Robinson, M. (1982). Telephone notification of relatives of emergency and critical care patients. *Annals of Emergency Medicine, 11,* 616–618.

Robinson, P., & Fleming, S. (1988, June). *Depressotypic cognitive patterns in conjugal bereavement and major depression.* Paper presented at the annual meeting of the Canadian Psychological Association, Montreal.

Robinson, P., & Fleming, S. (1989). Differentiating grief and depression. *The Hospice Journal, 5,* 77–88.

Rogers, J., Sheldon, A., Barwick, C., Letofsky, K., & Lancee, W. (1982). Help for families of suicide: Survivors' support program. *Canadian Journal of Psychiatry, 27,* 444–449.

Rosen, E. (1989). Hospice work with AIDS-related disenfranchised grief. In K. Doka (Ed.), *Disenfranchised grief: Recognizing hidden sorrow.* Lexington, MA: Lexington.

Rosen, H. (1986). *Unspoken grief: Coping with childhood sibling loss.* Lexington, MA: Lexington.

Rosenblatt, P. (1983). *Bitter, bitter tears: Nineteenth-century diarists and twentieth-century grief theories*. Minneapolis: University of Minnesota Press.

Rosenblatt, P., Jackson, D., & Walsh, R. (1972). Coping with anger and aggression in mourning. *Omega, 3,* 271–284.

Rosenblatt, P., Spoentgen, P., Karis, T., Dahl, C., Kaiser, T., & Elde, C. (1991). Difficulties in supporting the bereaved. *Omega, 23,* 119–128.

Rosenzweig, S., & Bray, D. (1943). Sibling deaths in the anamneses of schizophrenic patients. *Archives of Neurology and Psychiatry, 9,* 71–74.

Rubin, S. (1982). Persisting effects of loss: A model of mourning. In C. Spielberger & I. Sarason (Eds.), *Stress and anxiety* (Vol. 8, N. Milgram, Guest Ed.). Washington, DC: Hemisphere.

Rubin, S. (1984–1985). Maternal attachment and child death: On adjustment, relationship, and resolution. *Omega, 15,* 347–352.

Rubin, S. (1985). The resolution of bereavement: A clinical focus on the relationship to the deceased. *Psychotherapy, 22,* 231–235.

Rudestam, K. E. (1977a). The impact of suicide among the young. *Essence, 1,* 221–224.

Rudestam, K. E. (1977b). Physical and psychological responses to suicide in the family. *Journal of Consulting and Clinical Psychology, 45,* 162–170.

Rudestam, K. E. (1987). Public perceptions of suicide survivors. In E. Dunne, J. L. McIntosh, & K. Dunne-Maxim (Eds.), *Suicide and its aftermath: Understanding and counseling the survivors.* New York: Norton.

Rudestam, K. E., & Imbroll, D. (1983). Societal reactions to a child's death by suicide. *Journal of Consulting and Clinical Psychology, 51,* 461–462.

Rynearson, E. (1981). Suicide internalized: An existential sequestrum. *American Journal of Psychiatry, 138,* 84–87.

Rynearson, E. (1984). Bereavement after homicide: A descriptive study. *American Journal of Psychiatry, 141,* 1452–1454.

Rynearson, E. (1987a). Psychological adjustment to unnatural dying. In S. Zisook (Ed.), *Biopsychosocial aspects of bereavement.* Washington, DC: American Psychiatric Press.

Rynearson, E. (1987b). Psychotherapy of pathologic grief: Revisions and limitations. *The Psychiatric Clinics of North America, 10,* 487–499.

Rynearson, E. (1988). The homicide of a child. In F. Ochberg (Ed.), *Post-traumatic therapy and victims of violence.* New York: Brunner/Mazel.

Rynearson, E. (1990). Pathologic grief: The queen's croquet ground. *Psychiatric Annals, 20,* 295–303.

Sable, P. (1989). Attachment, anxiety, and loss of a husband. *American Journal of Orthopsychiatry, 59,* 550–556.

Sadock, B. J. (1989). Group psychotherapy, combined individual and group therapy, and psychodrama. In H. I. Kaplan & B. J. Sadock (Eds.), *Comprehensive textbook of psychiatry* (Vol. 2., 5th ed.). Baltimore: Williams & Wilkins.

Sanders, C. (1979). The use of the MMPI in assessing bereavement outcome. In C. S. Newmark (Ed.), *MMPI: Clinical and research trends.* New York: Praeger.

Sanders, C. (1979–1980). A comparison of adult bereavement in the death of a spouse, child, and parent. *Omega, 10,* 303–322.

Sanders, C. (1982–1983). Effects of sudden vs. chronic illness death in bereavement outcome. *Omega, 13,* 227–241.

Sanders, C. (1986). Accidental death of a child. In T. A. Rando (Ed.), *Parental loss of a child.* Champaign, IL: Research Press.

Sanders, C. (1989). *Grief: The mourning after.* New York: Wiley.

Sanders, C., Mauger, P., & Strong, P. (1977). *A manual for the Grief Experience Inventory.* Palo Alto, CA: Consulting Psychologists Press.

Sanua, V. (1977, August). *Coping with war bereavement in the United States and Israel.* Paper presented at the convention of the World Federation for Mental Health, Vancouver.

Saunders, C. M. S. (1975). Terminal care. In K. D. Bagshawe (Ed.), *Medical oncology: Medical aspects of malignant disease.* Oxford, England: Blackwell Scientific.

Schafer, R. (1968). *Aspects of internalization.* New York: International Universities Press.

Scheff, T. (1977). The distancing of emotion in ritual. *Current Anthropology, 18,* 483–490.

Schmale, A. (1958). Relationship of separation and depression in disease: A report of a hospitalized medical population. *Psychosomatic Medicine, 20,* 259–277.

Schmidt, J. (1986). Murder of a child. In T. A. Rando (Ed.), *Parental loss of a child.* Champaign, IL: Research Press.

Schneider, J. (1980). Clinically significant differences between grief, pathological grief and depression. *Patient Counseling and Health Education, 3,* 161–169.

Schoenberg, B., Carr, A. C., Peretz, D., & Kutscher, A. H. (Eds.). (1970). *Loss and grief: Psychological management in medical practice.* New York: Columbia University Press.

Schowalter, J., Patterson, P., Tallmer, M., Kutscher, A. H., Gullo, S., & Peretz, D. (Eds.). (1983). *The child and death.* New York: Columbia University Press.

Schultz, C. (1980, May–June). Sudden death crisis: Prehospital and in the emergency department. *Journal of Emergency Nursing,* 46–50.

Schuyler, D. (1973). Counseling suicide survivors: Issues and answers. *Omega, 4,* 313–321.

Scott, C. (1964). Mania and mourning. *The International Journal of Psycho-Analysis, 45,* 373–379.

Scurfield, R. (1985). Post-trauma stress assessment and treatment: Overview and formulati   . In C. Figley (Ed.), *Trauma and its wake: The study and treatment of post-traumatic stress disorder.* New York: Brunner/Mazel.

Segal, J. (1986). *Winning life's toughest battles: Roots of human resilience*. New York: Ballantine/Ivy.

Seitz, F. (1971). Behavior modification techniques for treating depression. *Psychotherapy, 8*, 181–184.

Seligman, M. (1975). *Helplessness: On depression, development, and death*. San Francisco: Freeman.

Shand, A. (1920). *The foundations of character* (2nd ed.). London: Macmillan.

Shanfield, S. (1987). The prediction of outcome in bereavement. In S. Zisook (Ed.), *Biopsychosocial aspects of bereavement*. Washington, DC: American Psychiatric Press.

Shanfield, S., & Swain, B. (1984). Death of adult children in traffic accidents. *Journal of Nervous and Mental Disease, 172*, 533–538.

Sheldon, A., Cochrane, J., Vachon, M., Lyall, W., Rogers, J., & Freeman, S. (1981). A psychosocial analysis of risk of psychological impairment following bereavement. *Journal of Nervous and Mental Disease, 169*, 253–255.

Sheperd, D. M., & Barraclough, B. M. (1974). The aftermath of suicide. *British Medical Journal, 2*, 600–603.

Sheperd, D. M., & Barraclough, B. M. (1976). The aftermath of parental suicide for children. *British Journal of Psychiatry, 129*, 267–276.

Sheskin, A., & Wallace, S. E. (1976). Differing bereavements: Suicide, natural and accidental deaths. *Omega, 7*, 229–242.

Shilts, R. (1987). *And the band played on: Politics, people, and the AIDS epidemic*. New York: St. Martin's.

Shneidman, E. S. (1963). Orientations toward death: A vital aspect of the study of lives. In R. White (Ed.), *The study of lives*. New York: Atherton.

Shneidman, E. S. (1969). Suicide, lethality, and the psychological autopsy. In E. S. Shneidman & M. Ortega (Eds.), *Aspects of depression*. Boston, MA: Little, Brown.

Shneidman, E. S. (1972). Foreword. In A. Cain (Ed.), *Survivors of suicide*. Springfield, IL: Charles C Thomas.

Shneidman, E. S. (1973). *Deaths of man*. New York: Quadrangle/The New York Times.

Shneidman, E. S. (1978). Some aspects of psychotherapy with dying persons. In C. A. Garfield (Ed.), *Psychosocial care of the dying patient*. New York: McGraw-Hill.

Shneidman, E. S. (1981). Postvention: The care of the bereaved. *Suicide and Life-Threatening Behavior, 2*(4), 349–359.

Shuchter, S. R., & Zisook, S. (1986). Treatment of spousal bereavement: A multidimensional approach. *Psychiatric Annals, 16*, 295–305.

Shuchter, S. R., & Zisook, S. (1987). The therapeutic tasks of grief. In S. Zisook (Ed.), *Biopsychosocial aspects of bereavement*. Washington, DC: American Psychiatric Press.

Shuchter, S. R., & Zisook, S. (1988). Widowhood: The continuing relationship with the dead spouse. *Bulletin of the Menninger Clinic, 52*(3), 269–279.

Shuchter, S. R., & Zisook, S. (1990). Hovering over the bereaved. *Psychiatric Annals, 20,* 327–333.

Shuchter, S. R., Zisook, S., Kirkorowicz, C., & Risch, C. (1986). The dexamethasone suppression test in acute grief. *American Journal of Psychiatry, 143,* 879–881.

Siegel, K., & Weinstein, L. (1983). Anticipatory grief reconsidered. *Journal of Psychosocial Oncology, 1,* 61–73.

Siegel, R. L., & Hoefer, D. D. (1981). Bereavement counseling for gay individuals. *American Journal of Psychotherapy, 35,* 517–525.

Sifneos, P. (1972). *Short-term psychotherapy and emotional crisis.* Cambridge, MA: Harvard University Press.

Sifneos, P. (1979). *Short-term dynamic psychotherapy: Evaluation and technique.* New York: Plenum.

Siggins, L. (1966). Mourning: A critical survey of the literature. *The International Journal of Psycho-Analysis, 47,* 14–25.

Simpson, M. (1979). *Dying, death, and grief: A critical bibliography.* Pittsburgh: University of Pittsburgh Press.

Simpson, M. (1987). *Dying, death, and grief: A critical bibliography.* Pittsburgh: University of Pittsburgh Press.

Singh, B., & Raphael, B. (1981). Postdisaster morbidity of the bereaved: A possible role for preventive psychiatry? *Journal of Nervous and Mental Disease, 169,* 203–212.

Skolnick, V. (1979). The addictions as pathological mourning: An attempt at restitution of early losses. *American Journal of Psychotherapy, 33,* 281–290.

Slaby, A. (1989). Other psychiatric emergencies. In H. I. Kaplan & B. J. Sadock (Eds.), *Comprehensive textbook of psychiatry* (Vol. 2, 5th ed.). Baltimore: Williams & Wilkins.

Smith, E. (1985a). *The body in psychotherapy.* Jefferson, NC: McFarland.

Smith, E. (1985b). A Gestalt therapist's perspective on grief. In E. Stern (Ed.), The grieving patient [Special issue]. *The Psychotherapy Patient, 2*(1), 65–78.

Smith, J. (1971). Identificatory styles in depression and grief. *The International Journal of Psycho-Analysis, 52,* 259–266.

Smith, J. (1975). On the work of mourning. In B. Schoenberg, I. Gerber, A. Wiener, A. H. Kutscher, D. Peretz, & A. C. Carr (Eds.), *Bereavement: Its psychosocial aspects.* New York: Columbia University Press.

Snow, C., & Willard, D. (1990). *I'm dying to take care of you; Nurses and co-dependence: Breaking the cycles.* Redmond, WA: Professional Counselor Books.

Snowdon, J., Solomons, R., & Druce, H. (1978). Feigned bereavement: Twelve cases. *British Journal of Psychiatry, 133,* 15–19.

Sobel, H. J., & Worden, J. W. (1982). *Helping cancer patients cope: A problem-solving intervention program for health care professionals.* New York: BMA Audio Cassette Publications.

Soreff, M. (1979). Sudden death in the emergency department: A comprehensive approach for families, emergency medical technicians, and emergency department staff. *Critical Care Medicine, 7,* 321–323.

Spielberger, C., & Sarason, I. (Eds.). (1991). *Stress and anxiety in modern life* (Vol. 12). Washington, DC: Hemisphere.

Spitzer, R. (1990, May-June). *Problems and promises in the classification of post traumatic psychopathology.* Paper presented at a course on psychological trauma cosponsored by the Harvard Medical School and the Massachusetts Mental Health Center, Cambridge, MA.

Spitzer, R., Williams, J., & Gibbon, M. (1985). *Structured clinical interview for DSM-III.* New York: New York State Psychiatric Institute, Biometrics Research Department.

Sprei, J., & Courtois, C. (1988). The treatment of women's sexual dysfunctions arising from sexual assault. In J. Field & R. Brown (Eds.), *Advances in the understanding and treatment of sexual problems: Compendium for the individual and marital therapist.* New York: Spectrum.

Sprei, J., & Goodwin, R. (1983). The group treatment of sexual assault survivors. *The Journal for Specialists in Group Work, 8,* 39–46.

Stamm, J., & Drapkin, A. (1966). The successful treatment of a severe case of bronchial asthma: A manifestation of an abnormal mourning reaction and traumatic neurosis. *Journal of Nervous and Mental Disease, 142,* 180–189.

Steele, C. (1974). Obese adolescent girls: Some diagnostic and treatment considerations. *Adolescence, 9*(33), 81–96.

Stein, M., Schleifer, S., & Keller, S. (1981). Hypothalamic influences on immune responses. In R. Ader (Ed.), *Psychoneuroimmunology.* New York: Academic.

Stengel, E. (1939). Studies on the psychopathology of compulsive wandering. *British Journal of Medical Psychology, 18,* 250–254.

Stengel, E. (1941). On the aetiology of the fugue states. *Journal of Mental Sciences, 87,* 572–599.

Stengel, E. (1943). Further studies on pathological wandering. *Journal of Mental Sciences, 89,* 224–241.

Stroebe, M., & Stroebe, W. (1983). Who suffers more? Sex differences in health risks of the widowed. *Psychological Bulletin, 93,* 279–301.

Stroebe, W., & Stroebe, M. (1987). *Bereavement and health: The psychological and physical consequences of partner loss.* Cambridge, England: Cambridge University Press.

Stroebe, W., Stroebe, M., & Domittner, G. (1985). *The impact of recent bereavement on the mental and physical health of young widows and widowers.* Tübingen, West Germany: The Psychological Institute of Tübingen University.

Swigar, M., Bowers, M., & Fleck, S. (1976). Grieving and unplanned pregnancy. *Psychiatry, 39,* 72–80.

Tait, R., & Silver, R. (1989). Coming to terms with major negative life events. In J. Uleman & J. Bargh (Eds.), *Unintended thought: The limits of awareness, intention, and control.* New York: Guilford.

Tavares, R., & Lopez, D. (1984). Response of the gay community to Acquired Immune Deficiency Syndrome. In S. E. Nichols & D. G. Ostrow (Eds.), *Psychiatric implications of Acquired Immune Deficiency Syndrome.* Washington, DC: American Psychiatric Press.

Taylor, S. (1983). Adjustment to threatening events: A theory of cognitive adaptation. *American Psychologist, 38,* 1161–1173.

Taylor, S., Wood, J., & Lichtman, R. (1983). It could be worse: Selective evaluation as a response to victimization. *Journal of Social Issues, 39*(2), 19–40.

Teicher, J. (1953). "Combat fatigue" or "death anxiety neurosis." *Journal of Nervous and Mental Disease, 117,* 232–242.

Terr, L. (1979). Children of Chowchilla: A study of psychic trauma. *The Psychoanalytic Study of the Child, 34,* 547–623.

Thompson, L., Breckenridge, J., Gallagher, D., & Peterson, J. (1984). Effects of bereavement on self-perceptions of physical health in elderly widows and widowers. *Journal of Gerontology, 39,* 309–314.

Titchener, J. (1986). Post-traumatic decline: A consequence of unresolved destructive drives. In C. Figley (Ed.), *Trauma and its wake: Vol. 2: Traumatic stress theory, research, and intervention.* New York: Brunner/Mazel.

Titchener, J., & Kapp, F. (1976). Disaster at Buffalo Creek: Family and character change. *American Journal of Psychiatry, 133,* 295–299.

Titchener, J., Kapp, F., & Winget, C. (1976). The Buffalo Creek syndrome: Symptoms and character change after a major disaster. In H. Parad, H. Resnik, & L. Parad (Eds.), *Emergency and disaster management: A mental health sourcebook.* Bowie, MD: Charles.

Toffler, A. (1970). *Future shock.* New York: Random House.

Tooley, K. (1978). The remembrance of things past. *American Journal of Orthopsychiatry, 48,* 174–182.

Tsoukas, C. (1988). The dying leper syndrome. *Journal of Palliative Care, 4,* 13–14.

Turner, T. (1977). Transformation, hierarchy and transcendence: A reformulation of van Gennep's model of the structure of *rites de passage.* In S. Moore & B. Myerhoff (Eds.), *Secular ritual.* Amsterdam: Van Gorcum.

Ulman, R., & Brothers, D. (1988). *The shattered self: A psychoanalytic study of trauma.* Hillsdale, NJ: Analytic.

U. S. Department of Justice. (1985). *The risk of violent crime* (Bureau of Justice Statistics Special Report NCJ–97119). Washington, DC: Author.

Vachon, M. (1976). Grief and bereavement following the death of a spouse. *Canadian Psychiatric Association Journal, 21,* 35–44.

Vachon, M. (1987a). *Occupational stress in the care of the critically ill, the dying, and the bereaved.* Washington, DC: Hemisphere.

Vachon, M. (1987b). Unresolved grief in persons with cancer referred for psychotherapy. *The Psychiatric Clinics of North America, 10,* 467–486.

Vachon, M., Lyall, W., Rogers, J., Freedman-Letofsky, K., & Freeman, S. (1980). A controlled study of self-help intervention for widows. *American Journal of Psychiatry, 137,* 1380–1384.

Vachon, M., Sheldon, A., Lancee, W., Lyall, W., Rogers, J., & Freeman, S. (1982). Correlates of enduring distress patterns following bereavement: Social network, life situation, and personality. *Psychological Medicine, 12,* 783–788.

van Bommel, H. (1987). *Choices: For people who have a terminal illness, their families, and their caregivers.* Toronto: NC Press.

VandenBos, G., & Bryant, B. (Eds.). (1987). *Cataclysms, crises, and catastrophes: Psychology in action.* Washington, DC: American Psychological Association.

van der Hart, O. (1983). *Rituals in psychotherapy: Transition and continuity.* New York: Irvington.

van der Hart, O. (1988a). *Coping with loss: The therapeutic use of leave-taking rituals.* New York: Irvington.

van der Hart, O. (1988b). Myths and rituals: Their use in psychotherapy. In O. van der Hart (Ed.), *Coping with loss: The therapeutic use of leave-taking rituals.* New York: Irvington.

van der Hart, O. (1988c). Symbols in leave-taking rituals. In O. van der Hart (Ed.), *Coping with loss: The therapeutic use of leave-taking rituals.* New York: Irvington.

van der Hart, O. (1988d). Transition rituals. In O. van der Hart (Ed.), *Coping with loss: The therapeutic use of leave-taking rituals.* New York: Irvington.

van der Hart, O., & Ebbers, J. (1981). Rites of separation in strategic psychotherapy. *Psychotherapy, 18,* 188–194.

van der Hart, O., & Goossens, F. (1987). Leave-taking rituals in mourning therapy. *The Israel Journal of Psychiatry and Related Sciences, 24,* 87–98.

van der Kolk, B. (1984). *Post-traumatic stress disorder: Psychological and biological sequelae.* Washington, DC: American Psychiatric Press.

van der Kolk, B. (1987a). The psychological consequences of overwhelming life experiences. In B. van der Kolk (Ed.), *Psychological trauma.* Washington, DC: American Psychiatric Press.

van der Kolk, B. (Ed.). (1987b). *Psychological trauma.* Washington, DC: American Psychiatric Press.

van der Kolk, B., & Kadish, W. (1987). Amnesia, dissociation, and the return of the repressed. In B. van der Kolk (Ed.), *Psychological trauma.* Washington, DC: American Psychiatric Press.

van der Wal, J. (1989–1990). The aftermath of suicide: A review of empirical evidence. *Omega, 20,* 149–171.

van Gennep, A. (1960). *The rites of passage.* Chicago: University of Chicago Press.

van Rooijen, L. (1979). Widow's bereavement: Stress and depression after 1½ years. In I. Sarason & C. Spielberger (Eds.), *Stress and anxiety* (Vol. 6). Washington, DC: Hemisphere.

Veronen, L., & Kilpatrick, D. (1983). Stress management for rape victims. In D. Meichenbaum & M. Jaremko (Eds.), *Stress reduction and prevention.* New York: Plenum.

Videka-Sherman, L. (1982). Coping with the death of a child: A study over time. *American Journal of Orthopsychiatry, 52,* 688–698.

Videka-Sherman, L., & Lieberman, M. (1985). The effects of self-help and psychotherapy intervention on child loss: The limits of recovery. *American Journal of Orthopsychiatry, 55,* 70–82.

Volkan, V. (1970). Typical findings in pathological grief. *Psychiatric Quarterly, 44,* 231–250.

Volkan, V. (1971). A study of a patient's re-grief work through dreams, psychological tests, and psychoanalysis. *Psychiatric Quarterly, 45,* 255–273.

Volkan, V. (1972). The linking objects of pathological mourners. *Archives of General Psychiatry, 27,* 215–221.

Volkan, V. (1975). "Re-grief" therapy. In B. Schoenberg, I. Gerber, A. Wiener, A. H. Kutscher, D. Peretz, & A. C. Carr (Eds.), *Bereavement: Its psychosocial aspects.* New York: Columbia University Press.

Volkan, V. (1981). *Linking objects and linking phenomena: A study of the forms, symptoms, metapsychology, and therapy of complicated mourning.* New York: International Universities Press.

Volkan, V. (1985). Psychotherapy of complicated mourning. In V. Volkan (Ed.), *Depressive states and their treatment.* Northvale, NJ: Jason Aronson.

Volkan, V. (1987). Severe reactions to bereavement and special professional care. In A. H. Kutscher, A. C. Carr, & L. Kutscher (Eds.), *Principles of thanatology.* New York: Columbia University Press.

Volkan, V., Cillufo, A., & Sarvay, T. (1975). Re-grief therapy and the function of the linking objects as a key to stimulate emotionality. In P. T. Olsen (Ed.), *Emotional flooding.* New York: Human Services Press.

Volkan, V., & Josephthal, D. (1979). The treatment of established pathological mourners. In T. B. Karasu & L. Bellak (Eds.), *Specialized techniques and psychotherapy.* Northvale, NJ: Jason Aronson.

Volkan, V., & Showalter, C. (1968). Known object loss, disturbance in reality testing, and "re-grief work" as a method of brief psychotherapy. *Psychiatric Quarterly, 42,* 358–374.

Volkart, E. (1957). Bereavement and mental health. In A. Leighton, J. Clausen, & R. Wilson (Eds.), *Explorations in social psychiatry.* New York: Basic.

Wahl, C. (1970). The differential diagnosis of normal and neurotic grief following bereavement. *Psychosomatics, 11*(2), 104–106.

Walker, K., McBride, A., & Vachon, M. (1977). Social support networks and the crisis of bereavement. *Social Science Medicine, 11,* 35–41.

Walker, L. (1987, June 21). What comforts AIDS families. *The New York Times Magazine*, 16–22, 63, 78.

Walls, N., & Meyers, A. (1985). Outcome in group treatments for bereavement: Experimental results and recommendations for clinical practice. *International Journal of Mental Health, 13*, 126–147.

Warnes, H. (1985). Alexithymia and the grieving process. *Psychiatric Journal of the University of Ottawa, 10*, 41–44.

Warren, M. (1972). Some psychological sequelae of parental suicide in surviving children. In A. Cain (Ed.), *Survivors of suicide.* Springfield, IL: Charles C Thomas.

Wass, H., & Corr, C. (Eds.). (1984). *Childhood and death.* Washington, DC: Hemisphere.

Watt, N., & Nicholi, A. (1979). Early death of a parent as an etiological factor in schizophrenia. *American Journal of Orthopsychiatry, 49*, 465–473.

Wegscheider-Cruse, S. (1989). *The miracle of recovery: Healing for addicts, adult children, and co-dependents.* Deerfield Beach, FL: Health Communications.

Wegscheider-Cruse, S., & Cruse, J. (1990). *Understanding co-dependency.* Deerfield Beach, FL: Health Communications.

Weisman, A. D. (1972a). *On dying and denying: A psychiatric study of terminality.* New York: Behavioral Publications.

Weisman, A. D. (1972b). Psychosocial considerations in terminal care. In B. Schoenberg, A. C. Carr, D. Peretz, & A. H. Kutscher (Eds.), *Psychosocial aspects of terminal care.* New York: Columbia University Press.

Weisman, A. D. (1973). Coping with untimely death. *Psychiatry, 36*, 366–378.

Weisman, A. D. (1975). Thanatology. In A. M. Freedman, H. I. Kaplan, & B. J. Sadock (Eds.), *Comprehensive textbook of psychiatry* (Vol. 2, 2nd ed.). Baltimore: Williams & Wilkins.

Weisman, A. D. (1977). The psychiatrist and the inexorable. In H. Feifel (Ed.), *New meanings of death.* New York: McGraw-Hill.

Weisman, A. D., & Hackett, T. (1961). Predilection to death. *Psychosomatic Medicine, 23*, 231–255.

Weisman, A. D., & Hackett, T. (1967). Denial as a social act. In S. Levin & R. Kahana (Eds.), *Psychodynamic studies on aging: Creativity, reminiscing, and dying.* New York: International Universities Press.

Weisman, A. D., & Worden, J. W. (1975). Psychosocial analysis of cancer deaths. *Omega, 6*, 61–75.

Weiss, R. S. (1988). The experience of AIDS: Hypotheses based on pilot study interviews. *Journal of Palliative Care, 4*, 15–25.

Welu, T. (1975). Pathological bereavement: A plan for its prevention. In B. Schoenberg, I. Gerber, A. Wiener, A. H. Kutscher, D. Peretz, & A. C. Carr (Eds.), *Bereavement: Its psychosocial aspects.* New York: Columbia University Press.

Whitfield, C. (1987). *Healing the child within: Discovery and recovery for adult children of dysfunctional families.* Deerfield Beach, FL: Health Communications.

Whitfield, C. (1990). *A gift to myself: A personal workbook and guide to healing my child within*. Deerfield Beach, FL: Health Communications.

Whitman-Raymond, R. (1988). Pathological gambling as a defense against loss. *Journal of Gambling Behavior, 4*, 99–109.

Wholey, D. (1988). *Becoming your own parent: The solution for adult children of alcoholic and other dysfunctional families*. New York: Doubleday.

Wiener, A. (1973). The use of psychopharmacologic agents in the management of the bereaved. In I. Goldberg, S. Malitz, & A.H. Kutscher (Eds.), *Psychopharmacologic agents for the terminally ill and bereaved*. New York: Columbia University Press.

Williams, W., Lee, J., & Polak, R. (1976). Crisis intervention: Effects of crisis intervention on family survivors of sudden death situations. *Community Mental Health Journal, 12*, 128–136.

Williams, W., & Polak, P. (1979). Follow-up research in primary prevention: A model of adjustment in acute grief. *Journal of Clinical Psychology, 35*, 35–45.

Williams, W., Polak, P., & Vollman, R. (1972). Crisis intervention in acute grief. *Omega, 3*, 67–70.

Wilson, J. (Ed.). (1989). *Trauma, transformation, and healing: An integrative approach to theory, research, and post-traumatic therapy*. New York: Brunner/Mazel.

Windholz, M., Marmar, C., & Horowitz, M.J. (1985). A review of the research on conjugal bereavement: Impact on health and efficacy of intervention. *Comprehensive Psychiatry, 26*, 433–447.

Windholz, M., Weiss, D., & Horowitz, M.J. (1985). An empirical study of the natural history of time-limited psychotherapy stress response syndromes. *Psychotherapy, 22*, 547–554.

Winiarski, M. (1991). *AIDS-related psychotherapy*. New York: Pergamon.

Winnicott, D. (1965). *The maturational processes and the facilitating environment*. New York: International Universities Press.

Woititz, J. (1983). *Adult children of alcoholics*. Deerfield Beach, FL: Health Communications.

Woititz, J. (1985). *Struggle for intimacy*. Deerfield Beach, FL: Health Communications.

Woititz, J., & Garner, A. (1990). *Lifeskills for adult children*. Deerfield Beach, FL: Health Communications.

Wolfelt, A. (1990a). Toward an understanding of the codependent bereavement caregiver (Part 1). *Thanatos, 15*(1), 20–22.

Wolfelt, A. (1990b). Toward an understanding of the codependent bereavement caregiver (Part 2). *Thanatos, 15*(2), 26–29.

Wolfelt, A. (1991). Exploring the topic of codependency in bereavement caregiving. *The Forum* (Newsletter of the Association for Death Education and Counseling) 15(6), 6–7.

Women and AIDS. (1990, November 30). *USA Today*, p. 1-D.

Wong, N. (1989). Classical psychoanalysis. In H. I. Kaplan & B. J. Sadock (Eds.), *Comprehensive textbook of psychiatry* (Vol. 1, 5th ed.). Baltimore: Williams & Wilkins.

Wong, P., & Weiner, B. (1981). When people ask "why" questions, and the heuristics of attributional search. *Journal of Personality and Social Psychology, 40,* 650–663.

Woodfield, R., & Viney, L. (1984–1985). A personal construct approach to the conjugally bereaved woman. *Omega, 15,* 1–13.

Worden, J. W. (1982). *Grief counseling and grief therapy: A handbook for the mental health practitioner.* New York: Springer.

Worden, J. W. (1991). Grieving a loss from AIDS. *The Hospice Journal, 7,* 143–150.

Wortman, C., & Silver, R. (1987). Coping with irrevocable loss. In G. VandenBos & B. Bryant (Eds.), *Cataclysms, crises, and catastrophes: Psychology in action.* Washington, DC: American Psychological Association.

Wortman, C., & Silver, R. (1989). The myths of coping with loss. *Journal of Consulting and Clinical Psychology, 57,* 349–357.

Wretmark, G. (1959). A study in grief reactions. *Acta Psychiatrica Scandinavica, 136* (Suppl.), 292–299.

Wrobleski, A., & McIntosh, J. L. (1987). Problems of suicide survivors: A survey report. *International Journal of Psychiatry and Related Sciences, 24*(1–2), 137–142.

Zisook, S. (1987). Unresolved grief. In S. Zisook (Ed.), *Biopsychosocial aspects of bereavement.* Washington, DC: American Psychiatric Press.

Zisook, S. (1989, May). *Widowhood during old age.* Paper presented at the annual meeting of the American Psychiatric Association, San Francisco.

Zisook, S., & DeVaul, R. (1976–1977). Grief-related facsimile illness. *International Journal of Psychiatry in Medicine, 7*(4), 329–336.

Zisook, S., & DeVaul, R. (1983). Grief, unresolved grief, and depression. *Psychosomatics, 24*(3), 247–256.

Zisook, S., & DeVaul, R. (1984). Measuring acute grief. *Psychiatric Medicine, 2*(2), 169–176.

Zisook, S., DeVaul, R., & Click, M. (1982). Measuring symptoms of grief and bereavement. *American Journal of Psychiatry, 139,* 1590–1593.

Zisook, S., & Lyons, L. (1988). Grief and relationship to the deceased. *International Journal of Family Psychiatry, 9*(2), 135–146.

Zisook, S., & Lyons, L. (1988–1989). Bereavement and unresolved grief in psychiatric outpatients. *Omega, 20,* 43–58.

Zisook, S., & Shuchter, S. R. (1985). Time course of spousal bereavement. *General Hospital Psychiatry, 7*(2), 95–100.

Zisook, S., & Shuchter, S. R. (1986). The first four years of widowhood. *Psychiatric Annals, 16,* 288–294.

Zisook, S., & Shuchter, S. R. (1991). Depression through the first year after the death of a spouse. *American Journal of Psychiatry, 148,* 1346–1352.

Zisook, S., Shuchter, S. R., & Lyons, L. (1987). Adjustment to widowhood. In S. Zisook (Ed.), *Biopsychosocial aspects of bereavement.* Washington, DC: American Psychiatric Press.

Zisook, S., Shuchter, S. R., & Mulvihill, M. (1990). Alcohol, cigarette, and medication use during the first year of widowhood. *Psychiatric Annals, 20,* 318–326.

Zisook, S., Shuchter, S. R., & Schuckit, M. (1985). Factors in the persistence of unresolved grief among psychiatric outpatients. *Psychosomatics, 26,* 497–503.

AUTHOR INDEX

SUBJECT INDEX

ABOUT THE AUTHOR

Therese A. Rando, Ph.D., is a clinical psychologist in private practice in Warwick, Rhode Island. She is the clinical director of Therese A. Rando Associates, Ltd., a multidisciplinary team providing psychotherapy, training, and consultation in the area of mental health, specializing in loss and grief, traumatic stress, and psychosocial care of the chronically and terminally ill. She is the founder and executive director of the Institute for the Study and Treatment of Loss, established in 1991 to provide advanced instruction and supervision to professionals working with the dying and bereaved. Since 1970, she has consulted, conducted research, provided therapy, written, and lectured internationally in areas related to loss, grief, and death.

Dr. Rando holds a doctoral degree in clinical psychology from the University of Rhode Island and has received advanced training in psychotherapy and in medical consultation-liaison psychiatry at Case Western Reserve University Medical School and University Hospitals of Cleveland. A former consultant to the United States Department of Health and Human Services' Hospice Education Program for Nurses, Dr. Rando was the recipient of the Association for Death Education and Counseling's 1987 Outstanding Contribution to the Study of Death, Dying, and Bereavement Award and a 1990 grantee of its lifetime certification as Certified Death Educator.

Dr. Rando is presently the media resource expert in dying, death, and loss for the American Psychological Association and in this capacity is a frequent commentator on national news and talk shows. She has published over 45 articles and chapters pertaining to the clinical aspects of thanatology. Among her book publications are *Grief, Dying, and Death: Clinical Interventions for Caregivers* and *Parental Loss of a Child* (both Research Press titles), *How to Go On Living When Someone You Love Dies* (Bantam), and *Loss and Anticipatory Grief* (Lexington).

751